CONFLICT OF LAWS

Second Edition

John O'Brien, MA, LLB, LLM, Barrister
Lecturer in Law, University of Hertfordshire

Cavendish
Publishing
Limited

London • Sydney

First published in 1999 by Cavendish Publishing Limited, The Glass House, Wharton Street, London WC1X 9PX, United Kingdom.

Telephone: +44 (0) 171 278 8000   Facsimile: +44 (0) 171 278 8080

E-mail: info@cavendishpublishing.com

Visit our Home Page on http://www.cavendishpublishing.com

O'Brien, John
Conflict of laws – 2nd ed
1. European Community 2. Conflict of laws – European Union countries
I. Title II. Smith, Raymond
340.9

ISBN 1 85941 285 8

Printed and bound in Great Britain

To the memory of Dr Monika Mösslang

PREFACE

The first edition of *Smith's Conflict of Laws* was published in 1994. Raymond Smith (who, unfortunately, I did not know personally) lectured at the University of Hull from 1964 until his death in 1995; for a time, he served as Head of the Law School within the University. He is remembered by his former colleagues as a conscientious and dedicated law teacher who did much to promote the study of private international law within that university.

Writing in 1993, Mr Smith observed that the subject of the conflict of laws had witnessed a silent revolution, as established common law rules had been set aside in favour of statutory codes, which themselves had been enacted to give effect both to international conventions and the requirements of European Community law. There can be little doubt that, since that date, the general movement towards codification has increased, not least with the enactment of the Private International Law (Miscellaneous Provisions) Act 1995.

In the preface to the first edition, the author noted that the purpose of the book was 'to introduce the subject of the conflict of laws to those who are new to it and to reintroduce it to those who have not kept up with the changes the last few years have brought'. That remains the principal objective of the present edition, although an attempt has been made to expand the treatment of leading cases and to provide more detailed references to relevant articles.

The present edition has been the subject of some restructuring, and a decision has been taken to divide the work into three distinct parts. Part I embraces the general principles of the subject. Part II is devoted to the increasingly important topics of jurisdiction and the recognition of judgments. Part III is devoted to those specific areas that tend to generate litigation and, indeed, often form the basis of undergraduate courses in private international law. For those who are familiar with the first edition, the following are the principal changes:

(1) material contained in Chapters 7 and 8 has been moved to Part I of the present edition, so that matters of general principle are dealt with at the outset;

(2) in consequence, Part I now contains distinct chapters devoted to: domicile (Chapter 3); substance and procedure (Chapter 6); proof of foreign law (Chapter 8); and the exclusion of foreign law (Chapter 9);

(3) in Part II, an attempt has been made to expand the treatment of both jurisdiction and recognition of judgments, so as to include distinct chapters on both the common law rules and also on the scheme introduced under the Brussels Convention;

(4) in Part III, the topics included reflect the general scheme of the first edition, but a decision has been taken to include distinct chapters on both the law of contract and the law of tort. The latter chapter has been substantially rewritten to take account of the impact of the Private International Law (Miscellaneous Provisions) Act 1995. It has been decided to deal with family law in three chapters, rather than in a single chapter as in the first edition.

In respect of the subject itself, there can be little doubt that recent developments provide ample justification for a new edition. While the pace of legislative change may have slowed, the courts have been more than active. The House of Lords has considered: the Brussels Convention (*Sarrio SA v Kuwait Investment Authority* [1999] 1 AC 32); the Modified Convention (*Kleinwort Benson Ltd v Glasgow City Council* [1997] 3 WLR 923); and at least one important Hague Convention (*Re H (Minors) (Abduction: Acquiescence)* [1998] AC 72); the House did all this before finding time to examine the principles relating to both the doctrine of *forum non conveniens* (*Connelly v RTZ Corporation plc* [1998] AC 854) and those pertaining to anti-suit injunctions (*Airbus Industrie GIE v Patel* [1999] 1 AC 119). Some of these same areas have engaged the attention of the Court of Appeal (*Jarrett v Barclays Bank plc* [1999] QB 1; *Jordan Grand Prix Ltd v Baltic Insurance Group* [1998] 1 WLR 1049). At first instance, important judgments have been delivered in both the Queen's Bench Division (*Hough v P & O Containers Ltd* [1998] 3 WLR 851) and the Chancery Division (*Mecklermedia Corporation v DC Congress GmbH* [1998] Ch 40) while judges of the Family Division have continued to grapple with the difficult problems posed by parents, children and foreign jurisdictions. One feature that should not pass without comment is that the increasing emphasis on questions of jurisdiction has contributed to a growing volume of cases proceeding to the Court of Appeal and the House of Lords. In the 1920s and 1930s, the normal dispute in private international law concerned the ascertainment of property rights; such a case would start and normally conclude with a ruling at first instance in the Chancery Division. Today, a typical case in private international law involves consideration of an international convention, and normally gives rise to a problem of jurisdiction; such litigation frequently proceeds beyond the judgment at first instance, if only because going abroad is often more expensive and less attractive than going on appeal. All in all, a steady flow of case law in recent years has justified the production of a new edition.

Several friends, colleagues and practitioners have helped in the production of this edition. Some have offered encouragement; others have answered my questions. A number have given me the benefit of their practical experience, while others have indicated the detailed background to a reported case. I am indebted to Peter Marsh, Mary Percival, Catherine Rendell and Harjit Singh. However, I alone am responsible for the errors, omissions and infelicities that remain.

I have attempted to state the law at 31 December 1998, although it has proved possible to take account of certain later developments when correcting proofs.

Finally, I should like to thank Jo Reddy and the editorial staff at Cavendish Publishing for their patience, good humour and efficiency in organising the production of this edition.

John O'Brien
London
April 1999

CONTENTS

Contents

PART II

Contents

Contents

TABLE OF CASES

Table of Cases

TABLE OF STATUTES

TABLE OF OTHER LEGISLATION

GLOSSARY

Although the influence of continental thinking has not been significant in modern English law, conflict lawyers use some Latin terms which have been adopted or derived from continental jurists.

lex actus ....the law governing a transaction, for example, the applicable law of the contract.

lex causae ....the law which the court has determined as the governing law of an issue.

lex domicilii ....the law of a person's domicile.

lex fori ....the law of the court dealing with the issue. Where an English court decides to apply its own law regardless of the conflict issue, it applies English law as the *lex fori*; where, however, it determines on the application of English law as a result of operating its choice of law rules, it applies English law as the *lex causae*.

lex loci ....abbreviated form of *lex loci actus, delicti, celebrationis,* as indicated by the particular context.

lex loci actus ....the law of the place where an act was done.

lex loci celebrationis ....the law of the place where a marriage was celebrated.

lex loci contractus ....the law of the place where a contract was made.

lex loci delicti ....the law of the place where the wrongful act (tort) was committed.

lex loci delicti commissi ....the law of the place where a tort is committed.

lex loci solutionis ....the law of the place where the contract is to be performed.

lex patriae ....the law of the nationality.

lex propria causae ....the proper law (see below).

lex propria delicti ....the proper law of the tort (see below).

renvoi ....the reference of an issue, by the conflict rules of the foreign law to which the forum's conflict rules first refer the issue, to the law of the forum or the law of a third country.

lex situs ....the law of the place where a thing, particularly but not exclusively a piece of land, is situated.

situs ....the location of the property in question.

locus regit actum ....the law of the place governs the deed. An old maxim that finds its modern expression in the *lex loci* rules listed above.

mobilia sequuntur personam ......movables follow the person. In modern law, this is shown by the rule that succession to movables is governed by the personal law of the deceased.

Some other terms which are in general use among conflict lawyers should also be noted:

applicable law....................sometimes used generally to mean the governing law, this term is used specifically to mean the *lex causae* in the conventions governing contracts and trusts.

choice of jurisdiction...............the selection, often by the parties to a contract, of the national court before which any dispute is to be heard.

choice of law...........................the process or the result of discovering the law to apply to the cause.

country......................................any area or law district which has its own legal system, for example, Scotland, Ontario, New York.

governing law.........................the *lex causae*.

jurisdiction selection...............the process of choice of law by reference to the law of a country as a whole, theoretically without regard to the content of that law.

proper law..............................the law which has the closest connection with the issues under consideration, usually on the basis of preponderant groupings.

rule selection...........................the process of choice of law by reference to the specific rules of the competing legal systems.

State...................................normally used in this book to indicate the international unit only. Sometimes, where the State has a unitary legal system, the terms State and country can be used interchangeably – for example, France, Italy, Japan – in other cases, they cannot – for example, the United Kingdom, United States of America, Australia.

PART I

CHAPTER 1

INTRODUCTION

INTERNATIONAL LAW

The world is divided into States; the State is the basic political unit of the 20th century.[1] Problems may arise between one State and another State or between the citizens of one State and the legal system of another State. The law governing such disputes is at sometimes referred to as international law. The expression 'international law' is itself divided into public international law[2] and private international law[3] (conflict of laws, as it is sometimes known).

Public international law is principally concerned with the relations between States, and the sources of public international law are normally said to have been set out in Art 38(1) of the Statute of the International Court of Justice 1945.[4] A typical problem in public international law would be an examination of the circumstances in which State A was entitled to employ force against State B. A less extreme example might be the question as to whether the fisherman of State A were entitled to fish off the coast of State B. Public international law is generally thought to have developed in Western Europe in the 16th and 17th centuries as the autonomous secular State became the basic political unit. International law or the law of nations,[5] as it was then described, developed in order to provide basic rules adequate to regulate relations between nations. We are not concerned with public international law but with private international law or the conflict of laws, as it is sometimes described. In the most general terms, private international law is that body of law which comes into operation whenever a municipal court is faced with a claim that contains a foreign element. The expression 'private international law' is thought to have been first employed by Joseph Story[6] and is commonly

---

1   The State is the basic political unit since the 17th century as post Reformation Europe began to divide into nation States.

2   The expression, public international law, is the 20th century equivalent of the 19th century expression, the law of nations. The expression, public international law is generally thought to have been first employed by Jeremy Bentham (1748–1832), in his *Introduction to the Principles of Morals and Legislation* (1780).

3   The expression, private international law, is generally thought to have first been employed by Joseph Story (1779–1845).

4   Reproducing, in almost identical terms, the provisions of the Statute of the Permanent Court of International Justice 1920, Art 38.

5   The expression, the law of nations, or *droit des gens*, is traceable back to the Roman concept of *ius gentium*.

6   Joseph Story (1779–1845); see *Commentaries on the Conflict of Laws* (1834). The term, private international law, was also favoured by John Westlake (1842–1913) – see *A Treatise on Private International Law* (1890) – but not by AV Dicey (1835–1922) – see *The Conflict of Laws* (1896).

adopted in most civil law countries. It is the expression favoured within the European Union[7] and by those international organisations[8] of which the UK[9] is a member. It is the expression presently used by the legislature.[10] However, at the end of the 19th century, the influential jurist AV Dicey[11] chose the title 'conflict of laws' for his treatise upon the subject. The expression, conflict of laws, has tended to be used in common law countries; the title itself is misleading in that the entire object of the subject is to promote harmony rather than conflict between the different legal systems of the world. Likewise, the title, private international law, is open to criticism in that it can lead to confusion with public international law and does not properly reflect the fact that the subject embraces the difficulties that arise when one State includes more than one jurisdiction.[12] Both titles are employed today in the UK and each is acceptable.[13]

In considering the relationship between public international law and private international law a number of points need to be made:

(a) in theory there is a single system of public international law so that, in respect of a similar point, the answer provided should broadly be the same in respect of litigation in the House of Lords or the US Supreme Court;

(b) difficult questions can arise as to whether public international law is part of UK law (that is, municipal law). The answer to this question depends on whether the state has a monist or dualist tradition. In principle, in the UK, the courts consider customary international law to be part of domestic law, while treaty obligations do not form part of UK law unless followed by implementing legislation;[14]

(c) there is no doubt that private international law is part of English law. Each developed legal system has its own rules of private international law so that, while private international law is part of municipal law, its content will vary from State to State[15] and from jurisdiction to jurisdiction;[16]

---

7   The majority of whose countries have a civil law tradition.

8   See, eg, the work of the Hague Conference on Private International Law, whose first meeting was held in 1893.

9   The UK has participated in the Hague Conferences since 1925.

10   See the Private International Law (Miscellaneous Provisions) Act 1995.

11   Perhaps better known today as an influential writer on constitutional law; a jurist whose writings are frequently adopted by the courts (see *Council of Civil Service Unions v Minister for the Civil Service* [1985] AC 374).

12   As is the case in the United States and the UK.

13   As evidenced by Parliament adopting the title the Private International Law (Miscellaneous Provisions) Act 1995.

14   See *R v Keyn (The Franconia)* (1876) 2 Ex D 63; *West Rand Central Gold Mining Co v R* [1905] 2 KB 391.

15   Eg, between France and Spain.

16   As between England and Wales, Scotland and Northern Ireland.

(d) for private international law, a foreign system of law means one prevailing in a territory other than that in which the court functions. For a court in London, the law of Scotland or Northern Ireland represents foreign law, being the product of a different legal district. Likewise, in the USA, both California and Texas represent distinct legal districts;

(e) for the public international lawyer, the UK is a single State and a member of the United Nations.[17] Further, it matters little in public international law[18] whether the State is unitary (as in the UK) or federal (as in the USA). Attention is principally devoted to the question of whether the State exists on the international plane; the form of the State is a matter for the constitutional lawyer.

THE CONFLICT OF LAWS

This book is concerned with the problems which arise when one legal system has to deal with the legal rules of another in matters of private rights. More particularly, because the ultimate test of the recognition of foreign law is what the courts do about it, the book is concerned with how a court sitting in one country treats a case in private litigation, in which the parties, the events or the circumstances demonstrate connections with one or more legal systems foreign to the court. The issue can arise in multifarious ways. An ordinary, apparently purely domestic, case may be found to have a significant connection with a foreign legal system. A case with obvious contacts with one country may happen to be litigated in another because the plaintiff finds some advantage in bringing an action there or the defendant cannot be made subject to the jurisdiction of the country with which the case is, legally, most closely connected. A case may be so genuinely international that it would be a foreign case in any court.

This book is about the English conflict of laws in the sense that it looks specifically at English law's response to situations where another jurisdiction's rules arguably ought to apply in a case before an English court. Just as the conflict of laws exists because there are differences in systems of municipal law, so there are differences in the approaches that legal systems take to solving problems in the conflict of laws. The English conflict of laws[19] is, thus, as distinctive as any other area of English law. Even among societies with a common legal tradition, differences in domestic law are mirrored in different

---

17 An original signatory to the United Nations Charter 1945 but only a single State within the body of 185 constituent States of the United Nations.

18 Save, of course, in respect of capacity to conduct diplomatic relations and to enter into treaties.

19 Originally, a system of law developing from the end of the 18th century and comprising little in the way of statutory sources.

approaches to conflict adjudication. As between societies with very different legal traditions, the differences both in domestic law and in conflict law are more marked. Thus, while the *raison d'être* of the conflict of laws is the difference in municipal legal systems, the solution of conflict problems is, itself, reflective of those differences.

There are several possible responses which a court can make when faced with a case having foreign contacts. First, and most primitively, it can treat the case as a purely domestic one and apply its own law to its resolution regardless of the foreign element. There are more and less sophisticated versions of this approach. The less sophisticated version merely turns a blind eye to the foreign aspects of the case and treats it in all respects as a domestic one, even to the extent of applying local technical rules which can have no possible relevance to the foreign aspects of the case. The more sophisticated version would recognise that there are special aspects to the case, which make the application of technical rules of domestic regulation inappropriate and would, therefore, not apply them, but would make no further concessions to the foreign dimensions of the litigation. The injustice that such an approach can produce is easily demonstrated. A plaintiff who has no ground of complaint by any law connected with the defendant's actions can create a right for himself by selecting a forum which applies a law which gives him one. The process of forum shopping will be considered later[20] but an illustration of it now will make the point. In *Machado v Fontes*,[21] the English court allowed the plaintiff's claim for libel to proceed, although the document complained of was written in Portuguese and published solely in Brazil, whose law provided no civil remedy in such cases.

Secondly, a court could take the view that its processes are inappropriate for a case with foreign contacts and refuse to adjudicate upon it. There are more and less sophisticated versions of this approach as well. The less sophisticated version would simply have the court close its doors to the alien case on the assumption that there was a foreign court somewhere where the case could find a home. This 'sorting office' concept of conflict resolution is false because it presupposes that every dispute has a natural home to go where the local courts can dispose of it by the application of domestic law. In reality, of course, the more significant conflict problems will transcend national boundaries, will be truly multi-contact and will have no 'natural home' in any legal system anywhere in the world. The more sophisticated version would recognise this truth but would seek to ensure that national courts took jurisdiction only where they were, in their own eyes, the

---

20 See below.
21 [1897] 2 QB 231; 66 LJKB 542. An interlocutory appeal in the Court of Appeal which must now be regarded as wrongly decided following the judgment in *Boys v Chaplin* [1971] AC 356; [1969] 2 All ER 1085; 3 WLR 322.

appropriate forum or, at least, not an inappropriate one. The doctrines of *forum conveniens* and *forum non conveniens* have received much attention in recent years and constitute a retreat from the traditional open forum policy of English courts.[22]

The remaining possibility, and the one with which this book is concerned, is that the court recognises that cases with foreign contacts cannot simply be turned away, and that they are special in the sense that they pose particular problems which demand serious treatment. The basic principle of justice – that like cases should be treated alike and different cases differently – precludes the unreflective application of domestic law to a case which is manifestly not domestic. To what extent these differences should be recognised and how far a court should go in the accommodation of foreign interests is a subject of considerable contention.

THE RATIONALE

Why should the forum not simply apply its own law to the determination of the case before it, without regard to the foreign connections it might have, and have done with it? After all, it will dispose of most cases, even those with international connections where the foreign legal contact is not pleaded or proved, by the application of its own domestic rules, so why make exceptions? There are several answers to this question, at various levels of philosophical generality and practical convenience. However, a review of the case law in England in the last 100 years indicates that the subject is grounded in either a desire to do justice between the parties or considerations of comity. It is sensible to examine each of these justifications in turn.

Starting from a mundane proposition, it would be clearly intolerable if a married couple on holiday abroad found that neither their marriage nor their property rights were recognised, as the former had been celebrated and the latter acquired in circumstances which would not have produced these effects according to the domestic law of the country visited.[23]

If the uncritical application of the court's own law, the *lex fori*, cannot be justified, as it clearly cannot, then a reason which is not purely pragmatic ought to be available, not only to justify the departure from the *lex fori*, for that is inevitable, but to indicate how that ought to be done – but here we have the

---

22 The law on this matter was reviewed in detail by Lord Goff in *Spiliada Maritime Corporation v Cansulex Ltd* [1987] AC 460; [1986] 3 All ER 843; 3 WLR 972.

23 An example being *Re Bonacina, Le Brasseur v Bonacina* [1912] 2 Ch 394, CA, in which the court was required to determine whether a contract concluded in Italy could be enforced in England notwithstanding the absence of consideration; see, now, the Contracts (Applicable Law) Act 1990.

failure of theory. The attempts, which have been made to justify departure, are not very convincing, largely because they start from the wrong place. There is no theoretical basis for preferring the *lex domicilii*, or the law of the habitual residence, to the *lex patriae* as the determinant of personal status, though there are a number of practical ones. Equally, there are no theoretical reasons for a particular choice of law rules, save that some are seen as better fitted than others for the task at hand.

As we shall see later, there are only a limited number of possible connections which a jurisdiction selecting approach can utilise in identifying the *lex causae*, and the choice among them depends on their practical use in getting to the legal system which appears to be the most suitable for the particular issue in hand.

For the moment, then, it can be said that English law engages in the conflict process because it would be unjust to treat an international case as a domestic one and apply to it the rules of domestic law, in disregard of other legal systems which are clearly connected to the case and may have a proper interest in its solution. It would be wrong to treat parties, who have acted under one legal system, as if they had acted under another and to make their rights and status depend on the accident of the forum.

A second justification for the existence of private international law is said to be the doctrine of comity.[24] In general, the term 'comity' can be interpreted as 'courtesy' and the doctrine was relied upon both by both Huber (1636–94)[25] and Joseph Story (1779–1845).[26] There are many references to the doctrine in the case law; however, comity pertains to the relations between sovereigns[27] and is not appropriate as a justification where a judge is determining the private rights of parties. The doctrine would leave the application of foreign

---

24 References to the doctrine of comity can be found in a number of decided cases; see, in particular, *Igra v Igra* [1951] P 404; *Travers v Holley* [1953] P 246; *Garthwaite v Garthwaite* [1964] P 356. In recent years, the doctrine has been alluded to in cases involving aspects of forum shopping: see *Amin Rasheed Shipping Corporation v Kuwait Insurance Co* [1984] AC 50; *Spiliada Maritime Corporation v Cansulex Ltd* [1987] AC 460; *Societe Nationale Industrielle Aerospatiale v Lee Kui Jak* [1987] AC 871.

25 Ulrich Huber (1636–94), in *De Conflictu Legum* (1689), stressed that municipal law, is in principle, territorial and that, if it is applied beyond that territory, then it is done by virtue of the courtesy of others.

26 Joseph Story (1779–1845), in his *Commentaries on the Conflict of Laws* (1834), viewed comity as a device to promote mutual interest and avoid inconvenience. Story, who sat in the US Supreme Court for 34 years, would have been familiar with the role courtesy had played in the formulation of the law on sovereign immunity by Marshall CJ, in *The Schooner Exchange v McFaddon* (1812) 7 Cranch 116.

27 As Marshall CJ had indicated, in *The Schooner Exchange v McFaddon* (1812) 7 Cranch 116, where the learned judge said: 'This perfect equality and absolute independence of sovereigns, and this common interest impelling them to mutual intercourse ... have given rise to a class of cases in which every sovereign is understood to waive the exercise of a part of that complete exclusive territorial jurisdiction ...'

law as a matter completely at the discretion of the court[28] rather than as part of a desire to do justice in a particular case. Moreover, the doctrine of comity would not explain why English courts apply foreign law even when a state of war exists.[29]

Private international law is, thus, that part of domestic law that arises when an issue comes before an English court affecting some fact, event or transaction so clearly connected with a foreign system of law that justice requires recourse to that system. The nature of private international law was clearly expressed by Lord Parker, in *Dynamit Actien Gesellschaft v Rio Tinto Co Ltd*, where the learned judge observed:

> Every legal decision of our own courts consists of the application of our own law to the facts of the case as ascertained by appropriate evidence. One of these facts may be the state of some foreign law, but it is not the foreign law but our own law to which effect is given ... As has often been said private international law is really a branch of municipal law and obviously there can be no branch of municipal law in which the general policy of such law can be properly ignored.[30]

As is implied in the statement of Lord Parker, it is the need to do justice between the parties rather than considerations of comity that necessitates recourse to foreign law. On the assumption that private international law is part of domestic law and that, in certain circumstances, justice will require recourse to foreign law, the question arises as to whether any limits exist. For example, should an English court recognise a contract for the supply of heroin even if it is lawful by the *lex loci solutionis*? Should an English court recognise and enforce a contract to promote sexual immorality or an agreement to damage or injure another individual? The general response is that there will be circumstances where the public policy of the *lex fori* prevents the recognition and enforcement of foreign law. This matter is dealt with in detail later, but it is important to note at this point that there will be circumstances[31] in which public policy in England does prevent the recognition and

---

28 For this reason, it was subject to criticism by AV Dicey (1835–1922), in *The Conflict of Laws* (1896). Such a doctrine would have been at variance with Dicey's broadly Austinian outlook and, in any event, could not stand with his theory of vested rights.

29 Note the consideration shown to German law by Uthwatt J, in *Re Cohn* [1945] 1 Ch 5, and the careful efforts of the judge to properly classify foreign law; see, also, Morris (1945) 61 LQR 340.

30 *Dynamit Actien Gesellschaft v Rio Tinto Co Ltd* [1918] AC 260 (Lord Parker was speaking in the context of a case that concerned a contractual dispute with a German company arising during World War I).

31 Such as contracts infringing the laws of a friendly country: *Regazzoni v KC Sethia (1944) Ltd* [1958] AC 301; or where problems of contracts in restraint of trade have arisen, as in *Rousillon v Rousillon* (1880) 14 Ch D 351.

enforcement of foreign law[32] and it is important to pay regard to the precise facts of any particular case when considering whether a head of public policy has been invoked.[33]

It would be comfortable to suggest that the object of private international law was to produce uniformity; to ensure that wherever a case was brought the same result would follow. Certainly, such an aspiration has been influential in the development of conflict rules. But, although the subject is often called private international law, it remains centred on domestic legal systems,[34] whose differences prevent uniform results. It may be harsh that a right under one system is not accepted under another or that a remedy, available in one system, is not available or, if available, is worth less under another, or that there are limping marriages where the parties are regarded as married by one system of law but not by another. But, without uniformity in domestic systems, such results are inevitable. The task of the conflict of laws is to minimise such discrepancies.[35]

THE HISTORY

Every legal subject has its own history and a study of that history normally provides some guidance both to the structure of the topic and to the degree of evolution of its basic principles. It is probably the case that no legal rule can be properly understood without some knowledge of its individual history. For example, in the English law of contract, the relatively late attempts by the courts and the legislature to protect the consumer[36] do indeed owe something to the 19th century doctrine of freedom of contract.[37] Likewise, the feudal concept of the estate in land in real property law serves to influence the content of the modern legislation relating to registered conveyancing.[38] It

---

32 *Scott v Attorney General* (1886) 11 PD 128, where there was a refusal to recognise an incapacity created under a foreign law; although, on this point, see, also, *R v Brentwood Superintendent Registrar of Marriages ex p Arias* [1968] 2 QB 956 and the Family Law Act 1986, s 50.

33 See, eg, *Oppenheimer v Cattermole* [1976] AC 249; *Vervaeke v Smith* [1983] AC 145.

34 As indicated earlier, there is little that is truly international in a case giving rise to problems in English and Scottish Law; both jurisdictions being within the UK.

35 A task made easier by the increasing number of international conventions seeking to harmonise or to create uniform rules. A considerable volume of recent legislation being enacted is simply to give effect to international obligations. For a recent example, see *Re H (Minors) (Abduction Acquiesence)* [1997] 2 WLR 653, where the House of Lords was required to interpret the Hague Convention on the Civil Aspects of International Child Abduction 1980.

36 As examples of the relatively late attempt to introduce specific statutory protection in the case of consumer contracts, see the Supply of Goods (Implied Terms) Act 1973 and the Unfair Contract Terms Act 1977.

37 The classic statement being that of Jessel MR, in the case of *Printing and Numerical Registering Company v Sampson* (1875) 19 Eq 462.

38 Only a person who holds a legal estate in land is capable of being recognised as the registered proprietor under the terms of the Land Registration Act 1925.

therefore follows that private international law, as part of domestic law, has been influenced by its own particular history.

In reviewing the history of the subject, there are two aspects that need to be kept distinct, namely, the questions, how rules of private international law began to develop outside the UK, and at what point English courts became aware of and adopted distinct rules of private international law? It is proposed to take each question in turn.

Historians generally assert[39] that little guidance can be obtained on the development of either public or private international law by an examination of the written sources dating from the period of the Roman Empire. For public international law to develop, there would need to be a number of distinct sovereign entities and this cannot properly be claimed to exist until the development of city-States in post 14th century Italy.

For private international law to evolve, it would be necessary to identify a number of conflicting territorial laws. By the time of the close of the Roman Republic, it was possible to note the development of a number of pre-urban communities. At this time, a distinction could be discerned between citizenship and domicile and it was possible for an individual to have links with more than one place. He might be born in A, subject to manumission in B and choose to live in C. In cases of conflict, Savigny[40] held that the individual was subject to the system of law that pertained where he was a citizen.

After the fall of the Empire, tribes settled in land where Roman law had previously prevailed and individuals became subject to personal or tribal laws. It is generally accepted that this system of personal laws lasted from the 6th century to the 10th century.[41] From the 10th century, the system of personal laws began to give way to a system based upon territory. At the end of the 10th century, it was possible to discern differences between developments on either side of the Alps. North of the Alps, the development of the feudal system[42] led to a system of local laws, whereby the individual was subject to the rulings of his local lord; any external legal system was not recognised within the fiefdom. Such a state of legal development could exist only in a static agricultural economy.

---

39 The account that appears below has been influenced by Yntema, 'The historic bases of private international law' (1953) 2 AJCL 297.

40 The history of this development being traced by Friedrich Carl von Savigny (1779–1861). The final volume of his *System des Heutigen Romischen Rechts* (1849) is translated into English as *Private International Law, A Treatise on the Conflict of Laws and the Limits of their Operation in Respect of Place and Time* (1869) (trans William Guthrie).

41 See Cheshire and North, *Private International Law* (12th edn, 1992), p 16, where the learned author admits that, in the absence of records, it is difficult to be emphatic about how the rules operated.

42 On the subject of feudalism generally, see Bloch, *La Société Feodale* (1940), translated as *Feudal Society* (1961), and Ganshof, *Feudalism* (1952).

South of the Alps, it is possible to identify two developments that would, in time, lead to the development of public and private international law. In Northern Italy, it became possible to recognise urban communities with their own local laws that entered into trade with other municipalities. The development of trading communities in Milan, Padua and Florence raised the question as to which law should regulate commerce. The social and economic changes in Northern Italy in the years following the end of the 10th century were accompanied by changes in the pattern of study. The universities of Northern Italy had, in the 11th century, witnessed a revival of interest in the study of Roman law[43] by a group who were to become known as the Glossators.

By the end of the 13th century, a group of scholars (sometimes known as the Post Glossators or Bartolists) endeavoured to apply Roman law, as interpreted by the Glossators, to the legal problems of their own day. In particular, they endeavoured to find a theoretical framework that could reconcile the conflicting laws between the various municipal communities.

The Post Glossators[44] developed the statuist theory. By this, the jurists of Bologna and other universities in Northern Italy would interpret local laws or statutes to determine whether they were in substance real or personal. A real statute applied only within the territory but a personal statute might bind beyond the territory. Problems arose as to how a statute was to be interpreted. Bartolus[45] addressed himself to three questions, namely, the effect of a statute on a non-subject,[46] the extra-territorial effect of such a statute and the method of interpretation. According to Bartolus, the nature of a statute was contingent on its interpretation and, thus, it was possible, by the process of construction, to determine the object and, thus, the territorial scope of the local law.

The statute theory, which originated in 14th century Italy, was taken up in 16th century France, where it was thought to have some relevance to the particular political circumstances then prevailing. Although France constituted a single State, the division of the country into provinces each with its own particular system of laws,[47] gave rise to difficulties as the volume of commercial trade increased.

According to Westlake, not only did French writers adopt the statuist theory but, also, they[48] endeavoured to apply it to the entire range of legal

---

43 The earliest group being centred at Bologna under Irenius (c 1055–1130) and his successors Bulgarus, Martinus and Accursius (1184–1263). The main emphasis of the study was to write commentaries or glosses upon Justinian's *Digest*. This study began in the universities of Northern Italy (Ravenna, Verona and Bologna) but would spread to France (Montpellier, Arles).

44 The best known being Bartolus (1314–57) and his pupil Baldus (1327–1400).

45 See Beale, *Bartolus on the Conflict of Laws* (1914); Woolf, *Bartolus of Sassoferrato* (1913); Ehrenzweig (1963) 12 AJCL 384.

46 Eg, the visiting merchant.

47 Known as *coutumes*.

48 The most important being Du Moulin (1501–66); Gui Coquille (1523–1603); D'Argentre (1519–90).

relations. Du Moulin drew a distinction between rights arising under a statute and rights arising *ex contractu*, where the choice of the parties as to the relevant law would prevail over the authority of a statute. However, it is clear that all subsequent developments in the subject were influenced by the doctrine of sovereignty. Jean Bodin's analysis of the sovereignty,[49] appearing at the end of the 16th century, would lead Grotius[50] to outline the basic principles of public international law[51] and would lead others to state the implications for private international law.

Just as the trading interests of the Netherlands may have influenced the approach of Grotius in matters of public international law,[52] so the separatism of the seven provinces and the doctrine of sovereignty influenced the writings of Ulric Huber.[53] In *De Conflictu Legum*,[54] he endeavoured to reconcile the doctrine of sovereignty with the conflict of laws, in the form of three broad principles that can be expressed as follows:

(a) that the laws of each State have absolute force but only within its territory;

(b) that all persons whether permanently or temporarily within the territory are bound by the laws of the State; and

(c) by reasons of comity, the laws of another State which have been applied within its frontiers maintain their force everywhere, so long as no prejudice results to the subjects of the sovereign by whom recognition is sought.

The expression of these views by Huber was certainly consistent with the positivist trend of international law and the needs of inter-State commerce. Nothing could be more disruptive to the demands of increasing commerce than that legal acts valid in State A, should be viewed as a nullity in State B. In broad terms, people are bound by the laws of the territory in which they act and such transactions will not vary in their legal effects in other jurisdictions. Huber views private international law not as an extension of Roman law but as a distinct legal regime founded upon the twin doctrines of comity and vested rights. Huber's work remained influential because it was adopted by Joseph Story in his *Commentaries on the Conflict of Laws*, which appeared in 1834. Story, endorsed Huber's theory of comity and his textbook remained the cardinal legal source in Anglo-American law until the first edition of Dicey appeared in 1896.

---

49 *Les Six Livres de la République* (1576).
50 Grotius (1583–1645).
51 *De Jure Belli ac Pacis* (1625).
52 Grotius was a diplomat and in his work he did favour the freedom of the high seas; an opinion in line with the interests of the Dutch East India Company.
53 Ulric Huber (1636–94).
54 Being the second volume of *Praelectiones Juris Civilis* (3rd edn, 1711).

Following the death of Huber, some jurists, such as Bouhier (1673–1746) began to consider the related question of the possible extra-territorial effect of legislation. However, by the middle of the 18th century, it is possible to note the emergence of the subject in England. The early case law clearly owes little to continental writers, and all the evidence points to English judges seeking to find practical solutions to unfamiliar problems.[55]

The most influential writer after Huber was Savigny. In broad terms, Savigny was a member of the German Historical School and was much concerned with legal reform. He held the view that legal reform could only be based on historical research and proper analysis and that the nature of any system of law was a reflection of the spirit of the people who produced it.[56] The statute theory[57] and the principles propounded by Huber were subject to criticism by Savigny.[58] He argued that the important task was to determine, for each legal relation, the proper law which its nature demanded. Thus, the proper task of the subject was to determine the appropriate local law, but this would involve classifying the problem, which might be: (a) determining where a judicial act had been done; (b) ascertaining where a particular thing is situated; or (c) choosing the domicile of a person affected by a particular legal relation. The attempt to distinguish between those matters in which *locus regit actum* and those matters in which the will of the parties is effective to determine the law had been advanced earlier by Du Moulin.[59] The difficulty with such an approach is that particular facts may constitute a breach of contract in one jurisdiction but only a tort in another. Secondly, as the relevant part of Savigny's work on the conflict of laws was not translated into English until 1869, it would never be in a position to challenge Story, whose work was, by that time familiar to and accepted as authoritative by English lawyers. The fact that so much of Savigny's work drew upon Roman law, made it alien to the pragmatic common law tradition. By the middle of the 19th century, the English courts were already begining to develop their own rules of private international law founded upon precedent rather than on any general theoretical scheme. It is to those developments we must now turn.

---

55 See *Scrimshire v Scrimshire* (1752) 2 Hagg Con 395.

56 Carl von Savigny (1779–1861) served as Prussian Minister of Legislation and was part of the early 19th century Prussian attempts to reform German institutions in the light of the triumphs of the armies of Napoleon. Savigny's views were outlined in *Vom Beruf unserer Zeit für Gesetzbung und Rechtwissenschaft* (*On the Vocation of our Age for Legislation and Jurisprudence*); *Das Recht des Besitzes* (1803) (translated as *The Law of Possession* (1848)).

57 Savigny had written *A History of Roman Law in the Middle Ages*, which appeared in six volumes between 1815 and 1831.

58 Savigny's views are set out in his *System des Heutigen Romischen Rechts* (1849) in the final volume. The eight volumes were translated into English as *System of Modern Roman law*, by William Guthrie in 1869, although, prior to that date, they had been cited by counsel in the case of *Liverpool, Brazil and River Plate Navigation Company v Benham, The Halley* (1868) LR 2 PC 193.

59 See Yntema (1953) 2 AJCL 297, pp 310–12.

English law was slow to develop a concept of private international law or the conflict of laws. As the economy began to develop from the purely agricultural to the trading and commercial, the earliest recorded cases appear to have concerned problems relating to the recognition of foreign judgments;[60] the subject was considered so marginal that it was not even mentioned by Blackstone.[61] The evidence indicates an increased emphasis in the second half of the 18th century, as the volume of trade increased, and Lord Mansfield[62] began to apply his fertile and capacious mind towards developing a distinct corpus of commercial law. The earliest leading cases in the subject date from the second half of the 18th century.[63]

Some writers assert that it is not until the middle of the 19th century that the subject begins to establish a recognisable form. The development of an industrial and trading economy, increased travel, the growth of railways and the varied forms of financial instruments available all contributed to the evolution of the subject. An equally important domestic development was the enactment of the Matrimonial Causes Act 1857,[64] which ensured that family law would develop within the common law courts.[65] As Englishmen went abroad to administer the Empire or to establish trading ventures, the courts were confronted with problems of domicile,[66] foreign marriages[67] and legitimation. At the same time, domestic tribunals were confronted with problems arising in other jurisdictions.[68] In this task, the courts might call

---

60 *Wier's Case* (1607) 1 Rolle Ab 530.

61 W Blackstone (1723–80), *Commentaries on the Laws of England* (1765–70). Blackstone devoted little attention to other subjects that would be considered central today, eg, the law of evidence.

62 William Murray, Lord Mansfield (1705–93) became Lord Chief Justice in 1756 and was the dominant English judge between Lord Hardwicke (died 1764) and Lord Eldon (Lord Chancellor from 1801).

63 Examples of late 18th century case law would be: *Scrimshire v Scrimshire* (1752) 2 Hagg Con 395 (validity of a foreign marriage); *Robinson v Bland* (1760) 2 Burr 1077 (enforceability of a contract made in France); *Mostyn v Fabrigas* (1774) 1 Cowp 161 (liability in the law of tort) *Holman v Johnson* (1775) 1 Cowp 341 (the circumstances in which an English court will recognise a foreign law).

64 In effect, the legislation would transfer jurisdiction in matrimonial causes from Church to State. It provided for the establishment of a Court for Divorce and Matrimonial Causes, with jurisdiction over matrimonial causes and with power to grant civil divorces. The measure was opposed clause by clause by WE Gladstone. The new court became part of the Probate, Divorce and Admiralty Division in 1875 and was reconstituted as the Family Division of the High Court in 1972.

65 The Matrimonial Causes Act 1857 would be followed by the Matrimonial Causes Acts 1923 and 1937; for more detailed consideration, see below, Chapter 18.

66 See *Bell v Kennedy* (1868) LR 1 Sc & Div 307; 6 Macq 69; *Udny v Udny* (1869) LR 1 Sc & Div 441 (where an officer in the Life Guards went abroad to avoid his creditors).

67 *Scrimshire v Scrimshire* (1752) 2 Hagg Con 395; *Brook v Brook* (1861) 9 HL 193.

68 As railways permitted large numbers of people to travel, problems would arise as to which foreign judgments to enforce.

upon the works of deceased foreign authors[69] but, because of the slow start to legal education in the universities, it was not until AV Dicey[70] published the first edition of the *Conflict of Laws*, in 1896, that English judges began to consider local texts.

In the period until 1945, the contours of the subject remained little affected by legislation;[71] the principles emerged on a case by case basis and the main focus of judicial decisions tended to be on choice of law problems rather than questions of jurisdiction.[72] This broad outline continued into the post-War period and, indeed, until the early 1960s. Since that date, the structure has changed beyond recognition, as the subject has come to be dominated by statutory enactments. This legislation is partly the result of international conventions[73] and partly as a result of the decision of the UK to enter the European Community on 1 January 1973. The consequence[74] is that private international law is now dominated by a mass of statutory material designed to give effect to international obligations. A second important aspect is that for a number of complex reasons, to be examined later, questions of jurisdiction are now more important and occupy much more of the court time than problems of choice of law. However, it is now necessary to say a little about the broad structure of the subject.

THE CONTENT

Introduction

In the most general terms, private international law is concerned with the following problems:

---

69 There seems little doubt that, in the 19th century, Joseph Story (1779–1845) was the favoured textbook author, deriving from his *Commentaries on the Conflict of Laws* (1st edn, 1834).

70 AV Dicey (1835–1922); Dicey had already published his *Law of the Constitution* in 1885. See on Dicey: Cosgrove, *The Rule of Law: Albert Venn Dicey* (1981); Hood Phillips, O [1985] PL 587.

71 As indicated by the various cases in the Chancery Division in the 1920s and 1930s concerned with choice of law problems; see *Re Berchtold* [1923] 1 Ch 192; *Re Annesley* [1926] Ch 692.

72 Not surprising in view of the reluctance of the courts in the inter-war years to admit any doctrine of *forum non conveniens* and the emphasis on an open door policy.

73 An example would be the Hague Convention on the Forms of Testamentary Dispositions (1961), given effect to in the Wills Act 1963.

74 At a risk of over simplification, such conventions can be divided into: (a) those deriving from the Hague Conferences on Private International Law and seeking to harmonise the rules of the conflict of laws; (b) those deriving from membership of the European Community such as the Brussels Convention on Jurisdiction and Judgments in Civil and Commercial Matters 1968 or the Rome Convention on the Law Applicable to Contractual Obligations 1980; and (c) those that seek to introduce uniform domestic rules such as the Carriage of Goods by Sea Act 1971.

(a) do the courts of a country (or law district) possess jurisdiction over the particular parties and the cause of action? That is, the jurisdiction question;

(b) what is the correct legal classification of the question that requires decision? That is, the classification of the cause of action. An example would be whether the claim was based upon a breach of contract, the infringement of a copyright or the commission of a tort;

(c) what is the legal system that governs the matter? The answer to this question normally requires the determination of the appropriate connecting factor (sometimes referred to as the choice of law question);

(d) how and to what extent is foreign law to be applied? Sometimes referred to as the substance/procedure distinction; and

(e) what rules exist for the recognition of foreign judgments and arbitral awards?

As has been indicated by other writers,[75] it is sensible for a court to follow the first four steps in some form of logical order; however, an examination of the case law indicates that this logical order is often departed from. In England, much will depend on the court in which the problem arises. If the question arises in the Chancery Division of the High Court,[76] then the first concern of the judge will be to answer the precise questions posed by the parties in the originating summons.

At this stage, it is necessary to say a little about each of the above concepts, although detailed consideration will be postponed until later.

Jurisdiction

Jurisdiction is a central concept in both public and private international law. Jurisdiction may be regarded as an aspect of State sovereignty.[77] The government of any State is traditionally thought to contain three branches: the legislative, the executive and the judicial.[78] Two distinctions can therefore be drawn:

---

75 A view advanced by Cheshire, in his *Private International Law* (1st edn, 1935) and endorsed by the learned authors of the present edition (see Cheshire and North, *Private International Law* (12th edn, 1992), p 43).

76 As is often the case with disputes giving rise to problems in private international law; see, eg, *Re O'Keefe* [1940] Ch 124; *Re Cohn* [1945] 1 Ch 5.

77 The doctrine of sovereignty can be traced back to Jean Bodin and the analysis contained in his *Six Livres de la République* (1576).

78 The doctrine dating back to John Locke and his *Second Treatise on Civil Government* (1690) but, today, particularly associated with Baron de Montesquieu (1689–1759) and his work *De l'Esprit des Lois* (1748).

(a) jurisdiction may be legislative (or prescriptive) in the sense that it concerns the capacity to make laws within a territory. Jurisdiction may be executive in the sense that the executive branch may enforce laws within its territory. Judicial jurisdiction concerns the power of the courts of a legal system[79] to try and determine cases, particularly those involving a foreign element. It is judicial jurisdiction that will be our principal concern;

(b) in respect of judicial jurisdiction, a legal dispute may be broadly of a civil or criminal nature. As indicated above, States tend to be jealous of the circumstances in which other States may exercise criminal jurisdiction. In consequence, public international law recognises a number of principles under which the courts of a particular State may exercise criminal jurisdiction. Although complete agreement does not yet exist, the following principles are recognised by a large number of States:

- the territorial principle;[80]
- the active nationality principle;[81]
- the passive personality principle;[82]
- the protective principle;[83] and
- the universality principle.[84]

It has been traditional for textbooks on public international law to deal with the principles governing the allocation of criminal jurisdiction. The role of private international law has been to indicate how the courts of country A may deal with civil cases that give rise to problems of a foreign element.

In respect of civil matters, States tend to make less wide claims as to jurisdiction since civil actions tend to attract less publicity and, thus, are less likely to excite public opinion in other States. However, this does require rules that are capable of dealing with the manner in which proceedings can be brought and also with such questions as: 'can the plaintiff invoke the assistance of the court?'; 'has the court authority over the defendant?'; 'has the court the power to determine the issue?'; and 'must the court exercise the power or may it decline to do so?' These rules will, generally, have been

---

79 The State being able to accommodate more than one legal system/law district within its territory. As in the UK, where there are three jurisdictions (England and Wales, Scotland and Northern Ireland).

80 *MacLeod v AG for New South Wales* [1891] AC 455 – 'all crime is local', '*extra territorium jus dicenti impune non paretur*', per Lord Halsbury LC; see, also, *Compania Naviera Vascongado v SS Cristina* [1938] AC 485.

81 Offences Against the Person Act 1861, ss 9, 57; Official Secrets Act 1911, s 10.

82 *The Lotus* (1927) PCIJ, Series A, No 10; and see, also, legislation in the United States in recent years, such as the Diplomatic Security and Anti Terrorism Act 1986.

83 See *Joyce v DPP* [1946] AC 347; applied also by the Supreme Court of Israel in *Eichmann v AG* (1962) 36 ILR 277.

84 *In re Piracy Jure Gentium* [1934] AC 586.

formulated with the domestic case in mind and it will be necessary to consider how far the same facilities and obstacles should apply to cases that are not entirely domestic. For example, a country may have very lax rules over personal jurisdiction and may, as does English law, allow jurisdiction to be invoked in an ordinary action for breach of an obligation by the mere service of process on the defendant or on his agent in England.[85] If a defendant may be made subject to a jurisdiction simply by being there, with no requirement of any other connection with the country and possibly with no assets there, it may be found that plaintiffs, who also have no connection with the country, are bringing actions there simply because of the ease of process. Now the practice of 'forum shopping', as it is known, is not necessarily objectionable, but it may be. Thus, every domestic system must decide how far its rules should be amended, if at all, to restrict the availability of its processes. Similarly, a court system has to decide whether or not its processes should be open to all or restricted in some way with regard to identity of those who can invoke it and of those against whom it can be invoked. English law does not restrict plaintiffs on personal grounds, save for those who have been declared vexatious litigants or who are 'alien enemies',[86] but it does restrict those against whom actions can be brought in the recognition, for example, of diplomatic immunities[87] and international conventions.[88]

Another issue here relates to the types of actions which may be brought. Should a court permit a case to be brought before it where the plaintiff seeks to enforce an exotic right unknown to the domestic law? Should a defence be allowed only if it would be allowable in a domestic case? Are there some types of cases which, though perfectly acceptable in domestic litigation, should not be entertained if they involve foreigners or foreign property? How far should the court go in asserting its own national policy? Let us take a few examples from English law. An English court would not, for over 100 years, allow an action based on a tort committed abroad to be litigated here, unless the wrong complained of would have constituted a tort by domestic English law.[89] English courts will not generally entertain actions involving rights to

---

85 As will be seen below, the traditional attitude at common law was that civil jurisdiction tended to be grounded on the ability to serve a writ on the defendant within the jurisdiction, even if that presence were only fleeting: see *Maharanee of Baroda v Wildenstein* [1972] 2 QB 283; 2 All ER 689; 2 WLR 1077.

86 *Netz v Chuter Ede* [1946] Ch 224; *R v Bottril ex p Keuchenmeister* [1947] KB 41.

87 The basic law being contained in the Vienna Convention on Diplomatic Relations 1961, the relevant parts being given effect to in the Diplomatic Privileges Act 1964.

88 The most important being the Brussels Convention on Jurisdiction and the Enforcement of Judgments in Civil and Commercial Matters 1968, given effect in the UK by the Civil Jurisdiction and Judgments Act 1982, which came into force on 1 January 1987.

89 The so called rule in *Phillips v Eyre* (1870) LR 6 QB 1, as extended in *Machado v Fontes* [1897] 2 QB 231 and reviewed in *Boys v Chaplin* [1971] AC 356; but, see now, Private International Law (Miscellaneous Provisions) Act 1995, Pt III, ss 9–16.

foreign immovable property.[90] While it is obvious that an English court will not allow a claim which fundamentally offends English morality,[91] it is not so clear when an English court should apply other aspects of domestic policy to exclude claims founded upon foreign law.[92]

Classification

Legal systems work on the basis of categories. It is necessary for many purposes to put an issue into a particular box. In many instances, the categorisation will be so obvious as to be automatic. A buyer's claim against the seller that the thing he bought does not work as it is supposed to, is so obviously a contractual issue that any court or lawyer dealing with it would not even advert to the classification process before turning to the law of contract to seek the solution. But, if the malfunction causes injury or damages property, or if the complainant is not the buyer of the product but the user of it, either the initial classification has to be amended in some way or the situation is seen as something else entirely – a tort, perhaps, or the subject of a statutory action.

To take other examples: whether the worker injured in the course of his employment sues his employer in tort or brings an action on the implied terms of his contract of employment (that the employer will take reasonable care to provide him with a safe system of work) may be no more than a conventional practice which has little to do with the nature of the relationship and much to do with traditional views of the proper scope of the conceptual categories of the domestic legal system. Is the deserted wife's claim to an interest in the matrimonial home a matrimonial right against the husband or a property right against the entire world, or both of these?[93]

In the conflict of laws, it is necessary to review the domestic categories to assess their suitability for dealing with foreign ideas and institutions. To take a simple example, every society has a concept of marriage[94] for its own

---

90 *British South Africa Company v Companhia de Mocambique* [1893] AC 602; *Deschamps v Miller* [1908] 1 Ch 856; *Hesperides Hotels Ltd v Aegean Turkish Holidays Ltd* [1979] AC 508. See, also, Merrills (1979) 28 ICLQ 523; Carter (1978) 49 BYIL 286. Note, also, the provisions of the Civil Jurisdiction and Judgments Act 1982, s 30 and *Pearce v Ove Arup Partnership Ltd* (1999) *The Times*, 11 February, the Court of Appeal reversing in part [1997] Ch 293.

91 *Kaufman v Gerson* [1904] 1 KB 591, CA

92 *Government of India v Taylor* [1955] AC 491.

93 A matter much discussed in the flood of cases that run from *Errington v Errington* [1952] 1 KB 290, through to *National Provincial Bank v Ainsworth* [1965] AC 1175, and which culminates in *William and Glyn's Bank v Boland* [1981] AC 487. See, now, *Abbey National Building Society v Cann* [1991] AC 56.

94 The traditional definition of marriage in England is that of Lord Penzance in *Hyde v Hyde* (1866) LR 1 P & D 130, p 133, namely, 'the voluntary union for life of one man and one woman to the exclusion of all others'. See, also, *Corbett v Corbett (orse Ashley)* [1970] 2 All ER 33; [1971] P 83.

domestic purposes. That concept may be very technical and specific including, for example, rules about the age at which parties can marry, listing the prohibited degrees of marriage, providing detailed regulations for the conduct of marriage ceremonies and the like.[95] Now, it is obvious that different societies are going to have different attitudes to these questions and, unless it is intended to exclude foreign marriages altogether, some accommodation must be found for foreign ways of doing things. At the same time, however, a domestic system will not want to give up all controls and will be reluctant to take a completely laissez faire attitude and simply say 'whatever goes for marriage in Ruritania will be accepted here'.[96] Between restricting marriages entirely to the domestic concept and the 'anything goes' policy, there is a position which will preserve the fundamental interests of the recognising system and yet show proper respect for foreign institutions. There is a need for answers to questions such as: 'will a monogamous society accept a foreign institution of polygamy[97] and for what purposes?'; 'is there an age below which it would be intolerable to accept that a party can be allowed to enter into marriage?';[98] 'is a foreign prohibition on marriage between people of different races, castes or religions to be accepted?'

The extension of the domestic categories, which every system of conflict adjudication demands, requires a solution of these fundamental issues (political in the sense of involving policy decisions) and the concept which emerges from the process will be determinative of many matters. To take a simple example, if one society, being monogamous itself, insists on framing its concept of marriage for conflict purposes to exclude polygamy,[99] then it is defining as outside its recognition all polygamous relationships, whatever hardship such a characterisation will inflict on the polygamously married.

One final example here of the classification issue in both domestic and conflict law and the matter can be left for further consideration later. Suppose a long standing cohabitational relationship between a man and a woman is terminated by disagreement. What, if any, are the rights of the parties? The first question one would have to ask is, are the parties married? If they are, then we can point to the law, English or foreign, to govern the termination of their status and to assess their mutual rights and obligations if they cannot agree on the allocation of what may have been, up to their parting, common resources. If they are not married, and assuming they had not made a formal

---

95 Marriage Act 1949; Marriage (Prohibited Degrees of Relationship) Act 1986.

96 See *Brook v Brook* (1861) 9 HL Cas 193, the case establishing the distinction between formalities of marriage and matters regarded as the essentials of marriage.

97 See the Matrimonial Proceedings (Polygamous Marriages) Act 1972, s 1; now re-enacted as the Matrimonial Causes Act 1973, s 47.

98 See *Mohammed v Knott* [1969] 1 QB 1, where the girl was 13 years old, but, the marriage was valid by the law of Nigeria.

99 As formulated by Lord Penzance in *Hyde v Hyde* (1866) LR 1 P & D 130.

contract, we must seek the law governing the precise identification of property rights or seek to find some overall contractual relationship. The task is the same, the manner of doing it, both in domestic and conflict law, is different.

Choice of law

Once an English court has decided that it has jurisdiction and, by its process of classification, has decided what the issue is about, it comes to the main purpose of the private international law, that is, to determine what significance is to be attributed to the foreign aspects of the case. Of course, it is not every foreign contact which introduces a relevant element to the situation or transaction. One would hardly suppose that a visiting Frenchman buying a tube ticket in London, could argue that French law should have a role to play in that contract,[100] or that a USA citizen could expect that his liability for, or right to recover in, an accident which occurs in England between himself and an Englishman, should be determined by the law of some State in the USA. However, which contacts have a relevance and which have not is not always apparent and, were our Frenchman to marry in England, or the USA citizen to die in England, owning property in England, the case might appear to be, and would be, different. In practice, of course, a foreign contact will only be raised in English litigation if it is relevant on the basis of existing conflict rules, or if it has a colourable case to be considered so, to warrant the trouble and expense of setting it up. However, some areas of law are not clearly settled and the choice of law rules are open to argument.[101]

It is for English law to determine which contacts are relevant and which are not and we will examine some of the choice of law rules later.

As will be seen, English courts have sought to deal with choice of law by a series of automatic rules following the classification. For example, there is a rule that the formal validity of a marriage which has been celebrated abroad be determined by the law of the country in which the marriage was celebrated.[102] So, if a petitioner comes before the English court seeking a decree declaring her foreign marriage void on the ground of informality, the

---

100 A contract made in England and intended to be performed in full in England; see the Contracts (Applicable Law) Act 1990, giving effect to the Rome Convention on the Law Applicable to Contractual Obligations 1980.

101 As will be seen below in Chapter 17, considerable problems arose in respect of the case of a tort committed abroad; see, now, the Private International Law (Miscellaneous Provisions) Act 1995, Pt III (ss 9–15).

102 One of the oldest rules of the private international law; see *Scrimshire v Scrimshire* (1752) 2 Hagg Con 395; *Dalrymple v Dalrymple* (1811) 2 Hagg Con 54; *Berthiaume v Dastous* [1930] AC 79.

court would, if it had jurisdiction[103] and agreed that the matter was one of formal validity, refer to the law of the place where the marriage was celebrated to discover whether or not the formalities required there had been observed. Of course, there is no actual contact with the foreign legal system; no messengers are sent there to make the inquiry. What happens is that the petitioner asserts and seeks to prove by expert witnesses that the foreign rule[104] that she alleges was not complied with. If the English court is satisfied that the foreign formalities were not observed, and that their non-observance made the marriage a nullity by that law, the English court will grant relief.

In some cases, it will not be possible to refer the case to a system of law in quite such a mechanical way, either because the issue is not susceptible to a simple formulation, or because the English court has no set rule to apply. For example, whether an act, which is alleged to constitute a breach of contract, has the effect of discharging the other party from his obligation, is not an issue which is susceptible to a simple location test. In some areas, the case law indicates that the task of classification and choice of law is straightforward,[105] while, in others, it has to be recognised that English Law had some difficulty in establishing a satisfactory rule.[106]

There are two sorts of dispute about choice of laws rules: in some situations, the English courts are still developing the rule to apply, so that what stands for the present may be amended or replaced and arguments can be raised at a high level of generality about the appropriate weighting to be given to the foreign contact.[107] In others, the courts have established firm rules or been provided with them by legislation, in which case, the arguments take a different line and relate either to the manner in which any discretion that the rule allows should be exercised, or whether the case actually falls within the ambit of the rule.[108]

Choice of law rules may take a variety of forms. A single localising rule, for example, that the formal validity of a marriage is governed by the law of the place of celebration, represents the simplest model. Slightly more complex,

---

103 See, now, the Domicile and Matrimonial Proceedings Act 1973, s 5, Sched 1; Family Law Act 1986, s 55.

104 Both the nature of the foreign rule and the fact of its non-compliance need to be proved by evidence.

105 Such as in family law, where the cases can normally be categorised as raising problems of formality, capacity and validity.

106 The obvious example being the law of tort, where, in the period from 1870, difficulties arose in applying the double actionability rule, as indicated by the differing judicial opinions expressed in *Boys v Chaplin* [1971] AC 356; see, now, the Private International Law (Miscellaneous Provisions) Act 1995.

107 The normal pattern is for the courts to have formulated a particular rule in the case law and then for legislation to be introduced to confirm or reject the rule that has been developed. See, eg, the Private International Law (Micellaneous Provisions) Act 1995, s 10, abolishing the rule in *Philips v Eyre* (1870) LR 6 QB 1.

108 As is now the case under the Contracts (Applicable Law) Act 1990.

are the rules which are multi-reference, in which a number of alternatives are presented, any one of which will do (the most dramatic example of this type of rule is the test for the formal validity of wills, where no fewer than seven legal systems may be relevant).[109]

While it should not be assumed that factual locating rules are always applicable in a straightforward fashion, there are some rules, for example, those involving references to a personal law which go beyond a factual test, and require evaluations to be made.[110] Finally, there are rules which require a wide judgmental input, for example, the cases under the Rome Convention 1980,[111] where the court is required to determine the system of law with which the contract is most closely connected.[112]

Application of law

English courts never apply foreign law as such; what they seek to do is to formulate their judgments in the light of the content of a foreign legal system. When conflict lawyers speak of 'a foreign law governing' or 'applying foreign law' they are simply employing a convenient shorthand for the more precise formulation that 'the court, having received evidence about the content of the rules of a foreign legal system has formulated its judgment in a way which takes account of those facts'. Foreign law is always a question of fact[113] and English judges do not have knowledge of foreign law.

Even where the relevant foreign law has been established to the satisfaction of the court there is still room for intervention by the forum. Public policy or the forum's morality[114] may intervene to prevent the application of the foreign law or the forum may regard it as not applicable. One clear example of this is the distinction between substance and procedure. Every forum governs its own procedure, that is, decides on its own process. The manner of bringing actions, the mode of proof, the order of business at trial, and the like, are obviously matters which the forum needs to control. It would be intolerable if an English court, when dealing with a Ruritanian case, was expected to abandon its proof by cross-examined witnesses in favour of

---

109 See the Wills Act 1963, giving effect to the Hague Convention on the Formal Validity of Wills (Cmnd 1729: 1961).

110 See, particularly, the cases on domicile at common law where inferences often have to be drawn from the conduct of the deceased: *Ramsey v Liverpool Royal Infirmary* [1930] AC 588.

111 Given effect to by the Contracts (Applicable Law) Act 1990.

112 The Rome Convention on the Law Applicable to Contractual Obligations 1980 opened for signature in Rome on 19 June 1980. It was signed by the UK on 7 December 1981 and given effect to by the Contracts (Applicable Law) Act 1990.

113 As a question of fact it requires to be demonstrated on evidence.

114 *Robinson v Bland* (1760) 2 Burr 1077 (contract of gaming valid in France but void in England).

some exotic method of proof used by Ruritanian courts. English courts are not going to return to trial by battle if that happens to be the mode of proof in some other country whose law happens to impinge on a trial going on in England. So, an English court never applies foreign procedural law. It is not, however, always easy to distinguish substance from procedure.[115]

The difficulty of distinguishing a matter of procedure from a matter of substance was candidly acknowledged by Scarman J in *Re Fuld's Estate (No 3)*, where the learned judge posed the question:[116]

> When is a question one of substantive law? When is a question merely one of evidence or procedure? I attempt no general answer to these questions; for an answer can only be made after an analysis of the specific questions calling for a decision, its legal background and factual content.

As will be seen below, considerable difficulties have arisen in trying to differentiate between rules of procedure and matters of substance. However, once it has been decided which rule of law is to apply to the determination of the case, English remedies, English damages and English methods of enforcement will apply.

Foreign judgments

There will be situations in which parties to foreign proceedings may want the effect of any judgment to be recognised[117] in England. A successful plaintiff before a foreign court may wish to have his judgment recognised in England so that he can enforce it against the defendant's assets in England. A successful defendant abroad may want the foreign judgment recognised in England to stop the plaintiff commencing another action. A person whose marriage has been dissolved by a foreign court may want to rely on that decree in order to be able to remarry in England.[118] A conflicts system has to establish rules to determine how and in what circumstances foreign judgments and other legal acts[119] will be recognised and enforced. These matters will be dealt with at the appropriate place.

---

115 This difficulty is illustrated by *Leroux v Brown* (1852) 12 CB 801; 138 ER 119, where a requirement in the Statute of Frauds 1677, s 4, was regarded as procedural and thus served to deprive the plaintiff of a remedy.

116 *Re Fuld's Estate (No 3)* [1968] P 675, p 695.

117 As will be indicated below, there are a number of regimes now in operation in relation to the recognition and enforcement of foreign judgments, namely: (a) common law; (b) the Administration of Justice Act 1920; (c) the Foreign Judgments (Reciprocal Enforcement) Act 1933; and (d) the provisions of the Civil Jurisdiction and Judgments Act 1982, implementing the Brussels Convention on Jurisdiction and Enforcement of Judgments in Civil and Commercial Matters 1968.

118 See *Adams v Adams* [1970] 3 All ER 572; [1971] P 188.

119 See *Luther v Sagor* [1921] 1 KB 456 (Roche J); 3 KB 532, CA.

Proof of foreign law

Foreign Law is a matter of fact before English courts and has to be proved by appropriate evidence like any other fact in dispute. It is, however, a special sort of fact and the evidence can only be presented by witnesses who possess the requisite degree of expertise in foreign law. This evidence will be partly evidence of fact and partly evidence of opinion. These experts, like any others, will be subjected to the processes of examination-in-chief and cross-examination, and any authorities on which they rely are open to the scrutiny of the court. Generally, the witnesses will be judges or practitoners in the legal system which is being considered, but this is not mandatory.[120] The nature of foreign law and the manner of proving it will be dealt with in detail at a later stage. However, at this juncture, it should be noted that for the purposes of English private international law, both Northern Ireland and Scotland are separate jurisdictions, so that their laws have to be proved before an English court in the same manner as the law of Italy, France or the USA. In cases where the House of Lords is sitting as the ultimate appellate tribunal on Scottish or Northern Ireland appeals,[121] it does take judicial notice of the law of the relevant jurisdiction.

Jurisdiction selection and rule selection

The English conflict of laws operates on the basis of jurisdiction selection – that is, its choice of law rules are directed at identifying the legal system from which will come the dispositive rule for the case in hand. So, for example, we say that the applicable law of this contract is French or the law to govern the essential validity of the marriage is Japanese. Theoretically, but only theoretically, the choice is made in ignorance of the actual rule that the system indicated would provide. You can select the relevant jurisdiction, but you do not know which legal rule it is going to specify.

The reality is rather different, of course. A party in English proceedings who wants to bring in foreign law has to plead and prove it. Very few litigants embark on the costly process of litigation with the Micawberish expectation that something of advantage will turn up. For them, the selection of a foreign legal system is incidental to the rule which assists their case. If I argue that French law is the legal system most closely connected to to the contract, I do so not for the metaphysics but because there is a rule of French law, say,

---

120 See the Civil Evidence Act 1972, s 4 (1).

121 No doubt aided by the fact, that at any time, two of the Law Lords will have been drawn from Scotland. Indeed, it is not unusual for the Law Lords to comprise a senior judicial figure drawn from Northern Ireland.

excusing the non-performance of the obligation, which is not available to me in any other legal system connected to the contract. If I want Japanese law applied to my marriage, it is because that law, rather than any other connected law, contains a rule which produces the result I want. A party will not call an expert witness on foreign law unless he broadly thinks that the content of that law is likely to be favourable to his case. All this is obvious enough, and all those involved in the process know, or ought to know, what is happening. When the court decides upon the choice of law, it does so in the knowledge of the consequence of its choice for the disposition of the case. It would be very naive to believe that this knowledge never influences the choice of the governing legal system.

This way of doing things is neither inevitable nor always efficient. Instead of searching for the jurisdiction (meaning here the entire legal system) to govern the case, the court should concentrate its attention on the matter in dispute and, then, select the rule which seems the most appropriate to determine the issue.

The practice of mechanically selecting a jurisdiction and then applying its laws regardless of the material content, has been the subject of extensive literature in the USA[122] but has received only limited attention in England. Such writers argue that a court should not mechanically select a jurisdiction, but should examine the material content of its laws and select the rule that appears most productive of justice in the individual case. The danger with such an approach is that it may give undue emphasis to the *lex fori* and may undermine that degree of certainty required by private citizens and foreign corporations. Moreover, many of the conflict problems in the USA are the result of different State laws; such laws may differ in detail while belonging to the same common law family. But, an English court may be obliged to consider the law of a separate State whose legal system has little connection with a common law jurisdiction. Just as in the 19th century, English private international law remained uninfluenced by the theories of European jurists[123] and there is little evidence that contemporary judges have paid much attention to academic disputes in the USA.[124]

---

122 Probably originating with Cavers, (1933) 47 HLR 173. Other contributors are: Currie (1963) 63 Col Law Rev 1233; Ehrenweig, *Treatise on the Conflict of Laws* (1962); Leflar, *American Conflicts Law* (4th edn, 1986). But, not all contributors endorse this approach; see Juenger (1984) 32 AJCL 1; Rosenberg (1981) 81 Col Law Rev 946; Baxter (1987) 36 ICLQ 92; Posnak (1988) 36 AJCL 681.

123 Although Brett QC (later, Lord Esher MR) did, in *The Haley* (1868) LR 2 PC 193, refer to the writings of Savigny at p 195. In general, in the 19th century, the most commonly cited author was Joseph Story.

124 Although, some discussion of these approaches can be found in the judgments of the House of Lords in *Boys v Chaplin* [1971] AC 356, particularly in the speech of Lord Wilberforce.

True and false conflicts

A true conflict occurs where a choice has to be made between the different laws of two or more legal systems which are potentially applicable to the case in hand and which would produce different overall results. If all the connected legal systems have the same rule on the matter in question, then, although the conflict exercise may still be gone through, nothing will turn on it. But, the choice of law rules which any country adopts may have the effect of creating a problem which has no real existence in the laws of any country. Suppose the question before the English court is the validity of a marriage which took place abroad of a couple who immediately thereafter made their matrimonial home in England. Suppose that the issue is not raised as a matrimonial cause (the couple are perfectly happy in their marriage) but arises in a succession case, where money has been paid over on the assumption which is now being contested, that the marriage is valid. The conflict rules of English law could point to one of the parties' premarital domicilary laws to discover that the couple were related to each other in a manner which, by that law, but not by English law, prevented marriage between them. If the English court stops, as it characteristically does, at the domestic law of the chosen system, it must hold the marriage to be void. Had it gone on to examine the conflict rules of the chosen system, it might have discovered that the prohibition would not actually have been applicable on the facts of this case, as the conflict rules of the chosen system would have referred say, to the law of the matrimonial home – English law – where the marriage is valid. The story cannot logically be left at the point I have abandoned it and there may be no satisfactory way out of this particular dilemma. The point is that the rules a system has for resolving conflicts may actually create them.

A good example of a false conflict is indicated by the New York case of *Babcock v Jackson*,[125] where the relevant facts were as follows: a New York couple took a friend, another New Yorker, with them on a weekend trip to Canada. While in the province of Ontario, an accident occurred, in which the friend was injured, due to the negligence of the driver. On their return to New York, the friend sued the driver for compensation. The court found for the plaintiff.

At first impression, this might be thought to be an ordinary case in the law of tort. Indeed, it may be thought the litigation was not a particularly friendly thing to do until it is remembered that the suit would effectively be against the driver's insurer rather than the driver himself. At this time, the conflict law of

---

125 (1963) 12 NY 2d 473; (1963) 2 LR 286. The case led the courts in New York to abandon the *lex loci delicti* in favour of an approach closer to the proper law of the tort. See, also, *McElroy v McAllister* 1949 SC 110; Morris (1951) 64 HLR 888.

New York was still wedded to the *lex loci delicti*, the law of the place of the commission of the tort, for the resolution of tort cases, and the *lex loci* was Ontario. The law of Ontario contained a special provision known as as a 'guest statute' which barred actions by gratutious passengers against their host drivers for personal injuries caused by negligence. Whatever the merits of such a provision in general, and most of the common law world has managed to get by without one, it is not immediately apparent why it should apply in this case at all. Certainly, the accident happened in Ontario, but there was nothing Ontarian about it; it could just as easily have occurred during the long drive up New York State or on the return journey. Most people would think that the New York law, whatever its content, would be the appropriate law from which to discover the dispositive law for this particular case.

Ontarian law came into play simply because the conflict rules of New York made the governing law the *lex loci delicti*. Had the New York court persisted with its habitual rule, the plaintiff would have lost her case. In the event, the court changed its choice of law rule to one which enabled the court to apply the most closely connected law and to assess the purpose of the Ontarian law to discover that there was no Ontarian interest which the plaintiff's success in the New York court would have infringed.

For the present, the point needs to be made that the mechanical choice of law rules, whatever their advantages in terms of certainty and predictability and their benefits in avoiding litigation, can create unsatisfactory results. The various thoeretical approaches canvassed in the USA will be returned to in due course.

THE CHANGING NATURE OF THE SUBJECT

Private international law is part of English law[126] and, as such, evolves in response to economic, social and political developments. In the period since 1945, English law has become more and more statute based[127] and, since 1973, English law has been required to recognise the principle of the supremacy of the European Union.[128]

As indicated earlier, English conflicts law began to be developed on a case by case basis[129] in the 18th century; it was not until 1858 that an Englishman

---

126 See, on this, *Dynamit Actien-Gesellschaft v Rio Tinto Co Ltd* [1918] AC 292, in particular, the judgment of Lord Parker of Waddington.

127 Something in the region of 3,000 pages of primary legislation is added to the statute book each year, an increase of about six times the level of 1914.

128 The principle of the supremacy of European law was established in the early years of membership; see *Costa v ENEL* [1964] ECR 585 (Case 6/64); *Van Gend en Loos v Nederlandse Administratie der Belastingen* [1963] ECR 1 (Case 26/62).

129 *Scrimshire v Scrimshire* (1752) 2 Hagg Con 395 (marriage); *Robinson v Bland* (1760) 2 Burr 1077 (the recognition of contracts); *Mostyn v Fabrigas* (1774) 1 Cowp 161 (tort); *Holman v Johnson* (1775) 1 Cowp 341 (foreign laws).

sought to reduce the corpus of the case law to a coherent body of principle. Until 1945, the cases coming before the courts tended to concentrate on choice of law problems.[130] All this has changed in the past 30 years. Today, there is a much greater emphasis on problems of jurisdiction and cases on jurisdiction provide a substantial part of the relevant case law in any given year;[131] much of the relevant law is contained in primary legislation designed to implement international agreements. There are at least four reasons for these developments.

First, the Law Commission[132] has, from its inception, displayed a close interest in the problems of private international law and its reports have provided the basis for significant legislative reforms.[133] Secondly, the UK has participated to a greater degree than before in the Hague Conferences on Private International Law and has ratified a number of international conventions. In accordance with the principle, such treaties require incorporation[134] before they can be given effect to in an English court. A relative flood of legislation has ensued. Examples of these would be the Hague Conventions on the Forms of Testamentary Dispositions 1961;[135] Adoption 1965;[136] Taking Evidence Abroad 1970;[137] Recognition of Divorces and Legal Separations 1970[138] and International Child Abduction 1980.[139] Whilst this is an impressive list, there are a number of Hague Conventions which the UK has chosen not to ratify.

---

130 *Re Berchtold* [1923] 1 Ch 192; *Re Annesley* [1926] Ch 692; *Re Ross* [1930] 1 Ch 377; *Re O'Keefe* [1940] Ch 124.

131 This is partly a consequence of English courts moving away from the doctrine of the open forum and the development of doctrines such as *forum non conveniens*.

132 The Law Commission was established under the Law Commission Act 1965. From the outset, the Law Commission was active in the field of family law – thus prompting proposals in the sphere of private international law.

133 Foreign Limitation Periods Act 1984, based upon the Law Commission Working Paper No 75 (1980) and the Law Commission Report No 114 (1982). See, also, Private International Law (Miscellaneous Provisions) Act 1995, deriving from a number of Law Commission reports.

134 The principle that an unincorporated treaty cannot be the source of legal rights and duties within domestic law was clearly established by the 19th century; see *The Parlement Belge* (1879) 4 PD 129; on appeal (1880) 5 PD 197. The long standing rule was confirmed in *Maclaine Watson and Co Ltd v The International Tin Council* [1990] 2 AC 418.

135 Implemented by the Wills Act 1963.

136 Implemented by the Adoption Act 1976.

137 Implemented by the Evidence (Proceedings in Other Jurisdictions) Act 1975.

138 Implemented by the Recognition of Divorces and Legal Separations Act 1971; see, now, the Family Law Act 1986, Pt II, ss 44–54.

139 Implemented by the Child Abduction and Custody Act 1985.

A third reason for the increase in domestic legislation is that the UK is a Member State of the European Union and has, thus, been obliged to participate in a number of initiatives designed to harmonise the rules of private international law not only in the areas of jurisdiction and enforcement of judgments[140] but, also, in the area of choice of law.[141] A fourth factor is that the UK is a signatory to an number of international conventions designed to facilitate commercial arbitrations.[142] The cumulative effect of these developments is that while, in the 1920s and 1930s, a case involving a point of private international law usually turned on reconciling past precedents, a case today in the High Court is much more likely to entail consideration of statutory materials and treaty obligations.

At the same time, reference should also be made to those international conventions designed not to harmonise rules within private international law, but to eliminate differences by the introduction of uniform domestic rules in respect of particular matters.[143] The cumulative effect of these changes, is that a case in private international law in the UK is most likely, today, to turn on a point of jurisdiction, or to involve consideration of a statute that, itself, has only been enacted to give effect to an international convention that seeks either to harmonise domestic law or to introduce a uniform system of law.[144]

---

140 Civil Jurisdiction and Judgments Act 1982 (as subsequently amended), giving effect to the Brussels Convention on Jurisdiction and the Enforcement of Judgments in Civil and Commercial Matters 1968, itself giving extended effect to the Treaty of Rome 1957, Art 220.

141 Contracts (Applicable Law) Act 1990, giving effect to the Rome Convention on the Law Applicable to Contractual Obligations 1980.

142 Protocal on Arbitration Clauses 1923; Geneva Convention on the Execution of Foreign Arbitral Awards 1927, implemented by the Arbitration Act 1950, Pt II; New York Convention on the Recognition and Enforcement of Foreign Arbitral Awards 1958, implemented by the Arbitration Act 1975. For the present law, see the Arbitration Act 1996.

143 Eg, the Carriage of Goods by Sea Act 1924 (implementing the 1921 Hague Rules relating to bills of lading) or the Carriage of Goods by Sea Act 1971 (implementing the Brussels Protocol of 1968, known as the Hague-Visby Rules). See, also, the Carriage by Air Act 1932 (giving effect to the Warsaw Convention on the Unification of Certain Rules Relating to International Air Carriage 1929), now replaced by the Carriage by Air Act 1961; see *Fothergill v Monarch Airlines* [1981] AC 251, as to the interpretation of international conventions.

144 Recent examples in the House of Lords would be *Sidhu v British Airways plc* [1997] 2 WLR 26; or *Re H (Minors: Abduction Acquiesence)* [1997] 2 WLR 653.

CHAPTER 2

THE POSSIBILITIES FOR CHOICE OF LAW

INTRODUCTION

Assuming that a legal system, faced with a case which it recognises has contacts with laws other than its own, is prepared to accommodate the foreign aspects of the case, how can it proceed? It has to find some way to link the facts to the foreign legal system but there are only a limited number of connections which can be made. The choice of law process involves the attribution of significance to the foreign contacts – turning factual contacts into legally relevant ones. This is done by choice of law rules, which embody factual connections; for example, the law of the place where the marriage was celebrated – the *lex loci celebrationis* – governs the formal validity of a marriage. We will examine some of the connections later but they only provide the means of choice, they cannot determine that choice directly; for example, if a Frenchman buys goods from an Englishman in England for delivery on the spot, there is little, if any, obvious significance in the French connection; whereas, if the Frenchman marries an Englishwoman in England, the potential significance of the French contract appears much greater. Why should this be so? The connections are in each case the same, so the difference between their apparent significance must depend on the nature of the transactions to which they relate. To decide what weight to accord to a particular connection depends, then, on two elements: the issue which is raised and the connection which is offered. Suppose the French buyer, dissatisfied with the goods, claims that the seller was in breach of contract by French law. One might rule out the objection on the grounds that the contract was made in England or that the controlling law must be English, as it would be impossible for the English seller to know about the personal laws of his casual customers and intolerable that identical contracts should be valid or not, or performed or not, according to diverse legal systems which could not be known in advance and which would produce different results. Could the same be said if the contract in England took place between two Frenchmen?

In the case of the marriage, should the French element play a part in any assessment of the validity of the marriage, and would it matter if a defect in the marriage – in the eyes of the French law – related to the form of its celebration or the capacity of one or other of the parties to enter it? Again, might the intention of the parties to make their matrimonial home in England or in France or somewhere else be significant?

These are relatively soft cases; take a harder one. A contract is made in New York between a French company and an English company, whereby the

English company is to manufacture goods which are to be delivered to the French company's branch in the USA. The contract is written in English and the goods are to be paid for in US dollars. There are several different contacts here with three different legal systems and more could be added. The choice of law process needs to provide answers to the various disputes which might arise out of the contract. These include, for example, a claim that the contract is formally invalid, that the contract price has not been paid, that the goods are defective or that they were delivered late as a result of industrial action by New York stevedores.

Before we look at the choice of law rules in some of the substantive areas, a brief examination of the available connections which can be used for this purpose will be made. These are sometimes called 'connecting factors'; they have no independent significance from the choice of law rules which incorporate them. Whilst it is possible to say that a party's capacity to marry is governed by the personal law, and then to qualify this statement by the assertion that, for most purposes of the English conflict of laws, the personal law is the law of domicile,[1] in all other cases, there is no formal distinction between the formulation of the rule and the connection. The formal validity of a marriage is governed by the *lex loci celebrationis* – the law of the place where the marriage is celebrated.[2] The connecting factor is clearly the place of the celebration but it is an integral part of the rule itself. I do not mean by this that there is no element of choice; there are always alternatives.

The possible connections will now be explored. It needs to be noted, however, that, while the connections are limited in number, they can be taken in various combinations.

THE PERSONAL LAW

One way of dealing with conflict problems is to recognise that everybody comes from somewhere and to seek to discover the 'home law' on the assumption that, like language, people carry their law around with them when they travel. Thus, we could say 'here is a Frenchman' and deal with his problems by reference to French law. There are two obvious problems with this approach. What do we mean by a 'Frenchman' and what happens when the legal issue involves another who cannot be characterised in the same way? To address the first of these: the attribution of a personal law can be done in

---

1   *Brook v Brook* (1858) 3 Sm & G 481; (1861) 9 HL Cas 193; *Sottomayor v De Barros* (1877) 3 PD 1; *Re Paine, Griffith v Waterhouse* [1940] Ch 46; *R v Brentwood Superintendent Registrar of Marriages ex p Arias* [1968] 2 QB 956.

2   *Scrimshire v Scrimshire* (1752) 2 Hag Con 395; *Middleton v Janverin* (1802) 2 Hag Con 437; *Dalyrmple v Dalyrmple* (1811) 2 Hag Con 54; *Berthiaume v Dastous* [1930] AC 79, PC.

several ways by reference to the national, domestic or religious law of the person.

The national law

While some systems of conflict law rely heavily on nationality,[3] the problems with it are obvious; there are persons of dual nationality and those who are stateless. Further, every legal system constitutes a distinct entity for the purpose of conflict of laws, irrespective of whether or not it constitutes a separate State as stipulated by public international law. So, in this context, one cannot speak of British law or of American law, because each of these international States comprises more than one legal system. For the UK, there are three major legal systems, those of England and Wales, Scotland and Northern Ireland, each with important differences despite their many common features. Any attempt to apply the national law to a person from a federal or composite State requires localising rules to identify the smaller unit[4] and, thus, to a considerable extent undermines the test. Although the problems of using the *lex patriae*, the law of the nationality, in a unitary State such as Italy are much reduced,[5] there remains the major difficulty, that whatever organic relationship is perceived between the citizen and the State as to which historical and cultural matters play a significant part, it by no means follows that the law of the nationality reflects the society in which the particular individual lives. People who settle abroad often do not change their nationalities,[6] with the consequence that the application of the *lex patriae* may well result in determining their legal status by a law which they have had no connection for many years – if at all. An example of the difficulties that can arise is *Re O'Keefe*.[7] The facts of the case were as follows: a woman of British nationality died intestate and domiciled in Italy leaving moveable property alone. The law applicable was Italian law, but Italian law referred the matter

---

3   The concept of nationality as a connecting factor was popular in Europe and partly follows upon the Code Napoleon 1804 (see, also, Austria (1811) and Holland (1829)). The employment of nationality was also an attempt by emerging national States to establish a distinct identity: see the Italian Civil Code 1865, Art 6. This was particularly important in Italy, where the emphasis was on building a nation State and asserting independence from foreign rule.

4   See, eg, Civil Jurisdiction and Judgments Act 1982, s 16, Sched 4; a matter discussed in *Kleinwort Benson Ltd v Glasgow City Council* [1997] 3 WLR 923.

5   The law on nationality in the UK is now set out in the British Nationality Act 1981, together with the British Nationality (Falkland Islands) Act 1983; British Nationality (Hong Kong) Act 1985; British Nationality (Hong Kong) Act 1990. The previous law was contained in the British Nationality Act 1948. In constitutional terms, the UK is, thus, a unitary State with three jurisdictions and, after the year 2000, will contain provision for devolved power.

6   An example of someone changing his nationality when working abroad is provided by *Re Flynn (Deceased)* [1968] 1 WLR 103 (Megarry J).

7   [1940] Ch 124; 1 All ER 216.

to the *lex nationalis*. The deceased had been born in India and and her domicile of origin was Southern Ireland, but she had only been there once. Since her birth, Ireland had become a separate State and had ceased to regard persons in her position as citizens. The question for the court was whether the estate should be distributed according to English law, the law of British India or the law of Eire.

Crossman J[8] concluded that to give effect to Italian law the only part of the British Empire that the deceased could be said to belong was Ireland and thus her estate was to be distributed in accordance with Irish law.

English law flirted with the possibility of using nationality as a connecting factor, but rejected it in favour of domicile[9] and a more recent reconsideration has come to the same conclusion.[10] Those who advocate nationality rather than domicile argue that it leads to a greater degree of certainty.[11] However, the problem is that it is not enough for a connecting factor to link an individual with the UK; the conflict of laws proceeds upon the basis that the individual can be linked with a law district within the State. It is for this reason that the UK, the USA, Australia and Canada have avoided nationality as a connecting factor. Some legal systems are however, wedded to nationality as a connecting factor, so that in order to arrive at international agreement, English law has had to accept the concept as one of a package of multi-reference connections in a limited number of situations. So, for example, nationality is one of the tests for the formal validity of wills[12] and one of the connections for the recognition of overseas divorces, annulments and legal separations.[13]

The domestic law

Here the concept is one of a relationship with a particular legal system by being in the country itself. In each case, it will be necessary to examine the evidence to determine whether the relationship exists. There are obviously many different degrees of connection and these will be explored.

---

8   Judge of the Chancery Division (1934–1941), but better known today as the father of the politician, RHS Crossman (1907–74).

9   See Lord Westbury, distinguishing nationality and domicile in *Udny v Udny* (1869) LR 1 Sc & Div 441.

10 Law Commission Report No 168 (1987); Scottish Law Commission Report No 107 (1987), following upon Law Commission Working Paper No 88 (1985) and Scottish Law Commission Consultative Memorandum No 63 (1985).

11 See, for an interesting discussion, Beckett (1939) 55 LQR 270, written while the author was serving as the Second Legal Adviser in the Foreign Office.

12 See the Wills Act 1963, s 1, giving effect to the Hague Convention on the Forms of Testamentary Disposition 1961.

13 See the Family Law Act 1986, s 46, the legislation replacing and extending the Recognition of Divorces and Legal Separations Act 1971.

Presence

This is, obviously, the weakest connection, as it involves no more than a temporary location in the country without any family, work, and political or emotional commitment to the place. For this reason, it cannot possibly suffice, of itself, as the determinant of the personal law. That is not to say, of course, that mere presence is not significant in the conflict of laws and we shall consider later some of the localising rules which depend, or at least operate upon, the mere presence of the parties within a particular jurisdiction, as, for example, the rule that the formal validity of marriage is refereeable to the law of the place of celebration (*lex loci celebrationis*),[14] however transient the parties' relationship with that place may be. However, those rules do not purport to be making a personal link, they are only making a factual link. Also, it should be noted that, at common law,[15] the mere presence of the defendant in England is sufficient to enable a process to be served on him and, thus, to make the individual subject to the jurisdiction of the English court.[16]

Residence

Residence connotes more than mere presence, in that it carries with it a notion of time.[17] Of itself, however, it does not convey any particular duration, so it would not be a misuse of English to say that someone was resident in a hotel for one night.[18] A period of residence,[19] however short, does suggest that someone was living in a particular place and it is this idea of living there which makes the concept of residence a potential candidate for the personal law. The main weakness of nationality lies in the fact that there is no necessary connection between the State of which one is a national, and the country in which one lives.[20] This defect is entirely overcome by the concept of residence, provided that a satisfactory degree of attachment can be established. How may this be done? There are two basic solutions here: duration and intention. Where a person has lived for a long time in the same place, it would not be

---

14 *Scrimshire v Scrimshire* (1752) 2 Hag Con; *Berthiaume v Dastous* [1930] AC 79, PC.

15 By 'at common law', one means the rules that were in operation prior to the date of the coming into effect of the Civil Jurisdiction and Judgments Act 1982 (ie, 1 January 1987).

16 *Watkins v North American Land and Timber Co Ltd* (1904) 20 TLR 534; *Colt Industries Inc v Sarlie* [1966] 1 All ER 673; 1 WLR 440; *Maharanee of Baroda v Wildenstein* [1972] 2 QB 283; 2 All ER 689.

17 Particularly important in taxation cases; on which, see *Levene v IRC* [1928] AC 217; *IRC v Lysaght* [1928] AC 234; *Reed v Clark* [1986] Ch 1.

18 *Colt Industires Inc v Sarlie* [1966] 1 WLR 440.

19 Any consideration of the concept of residence in modern law must begin with the House of Lords judgment in *R v London Borough of Barnet ex p Shah* [1983] 2 AC 309; 1 All ER 226.

20 As in *Re O'Keefe* [1940] Ch 124; 1 All ER 216.

unreasonable to characterise that place as his home and to regard the law of that place as his personal law. However, suppose that the long period of residence has not been a voluntary one but has been imposed by forces beyond the control of the individual[21] or, contrariwise, that a desired residence has been interrupted by factors beyond the individual's control. Would we still wish, in the one case, to impose a penal law on the basis of the protracted, though undesired, residence and, in the other case, to deny the desired connection on the basis of lack of duration? The expatriate working abroad because there is unemployment at home, the soldier or diplomat on a long tour of duty, the prisoner incarcerated in a foreign gaol, the invalid seeking[22] a better climate, the fugitive from political or racial persecution or, most dramatically, the long term political hostage may all have a long period of residence, but we may be reluctant to draw the inference from it that they have their home in the alien country and, by the same token, have lost all connection with their former homes.

Intention cannot by itself determine residence as there are those who, while living in one country, desire above all else to be living in another and those who, without any desire to be in any particular country, passionately wish to leave the place where they currently live. We can add here the person who, although perfectly happy where he is, has no intention of remaining in the country of his current residence when his immediate purpose, say, his fixed term contract or his course of study, is completed.[23] If such people were asked where they intended to go when they left, they might reply: 'Home'.

If we interpret intention as we do in other areas of law, not simply in terms of desire or aspiration but in terms of realistic purpose or the objective of bringing about a result, we have a basis for marrying intention and residence into a coherent concept of 'home' which would satisfy the requirements of a test for the personal law. What has still to be determined, however, is the necessary quality of intention and residence which will suffice. 'Residence',[24] 'ordinary residence'[25] and 'habitual residence'[26] are all tests which English law applies to conflict problems. Currently, it is the concept of habitual residence which is the most significant in English conflict of laws, though not for deciding the personal law – that is a matter for domicile, as we shall see later – so it is worth exploring it in more detail.

---

21 As in *Re Martin* [1900] P 211.

22 See *Hoskins v Mathews* (1856) 8 De GM & G 13.

23 Or, indeed, where a husband defers to his wife, as in *IRC v Bullock* [1976] 1 WLR 1178.

24 *Emanuel v Symon* [1908] 1 KB 302.

25 Domestic Proceedings and Magistrates' Courts Act 1978, Pt I. This is particularly important as a connecting factor in taxation – see *Levene v IRC* [1928] AC 217.

26 Wills Act 1963, s 1; Domicile and Matrimonial Proceedings Act 1973, s 5.

Habitual residence

Habitual residence first appeared in the English conflict of laws as a result of international efforts to obtain some limited agreement on choice of law rules. It arrived as a compromise between those States which insisted on the *lex patriae* as the test of the personal law and those countries which, like England, relied on domicile for that purpose – not, it should be noted, that the countries adopting domicile had a unified concept to offer. The compromise did not lead to replacement of the national law or of the domiciliary law by habitual residence, it was agreed merely as an alternative rule of reference. So, for example, the formal validity of a will may be tested by the law of the nationality, the law of the domicile or the law of the habitual residence.[27] An English court will recognise an overseas divorce if one of the parties to the marriage was habitually resident in the country where the divorce was obtained.[28] Further, an English court will assume jurisdiction in matrimonial causes if either of the parties to the marriage has been habitually resident in England for 12 months immediately preceding the presentation of the petition.[29] The first thing to notice about the English concept of habitual residence is that the concentration is upon the quality of the residence rather than its duration, so that a future petitioner to the English court for matrimonial relief will satisfy the jurisdictional requirement of one year's habitual residence even if he or she has been in the country for only one year, provided that the quality of the residence is sufficient. Clearly, one has to start somewhere and habitual residence for one year presupposes that the necessary quality to make the residence habitual could exist from day one. What is this necessary quality? The matter has been discussed in a number of cases.[30] An interesting example is afforded by the first instance case of *Cruse v Chittum*, where the relevant fact were as follows: an Englishman petitioned for a declaration in the Family Division of the High Court that his marriage had been validly dissolved. The answer to this question depended on whether the wife had been habitually resident in Mississippi when a divorce decree had been granted by a court of that State.

In granting a declaration, Lane J drew a distinction between 'ordinary residence' and 'habitual residence',[31] indicating that for the latter to be found the residence must be actual, bona fide and enduring. It is clear from the

---

27 Wills Act 1963, s 1.
28 Family Law Act 1986, s 46.
29 Domicile and Matrimonial Proceedings Act 1973, s 5.
30 *Cruse v Chittum* [1974] 4 Fam Law 152; 2 All ER 940; *R v London Borough of Barnet ex p Shah* [1983] 2 AC 309; 1 All ER 226; *Kapur v Kapur* [1985] Fam Law 22; [1984] FLR 920.
31 The Recognition of Divorces and Legal Separations Act 1971, s 3, required the spouse to have been habitually resident at the time of the initiation of the proceedings.

unreserved judgment that Lane J considered that 'ordinary residence' could be established on less demanding criteria.

However, there have been a number of cases since 1974 where habitual residence has been equated with ordinary residence. The modern liberal approach flows from the House of Lords judgment in *R v London Borough of Barnet ex p Shah*. The facts of the case were as follows: the applicant was endeavouring to show that he was ordinarily resident in a particular local government area in order to receive a mandatory student grant under the provisions of the Education Act 1962.

In giving judgment, the House of Lords considered that the concept of ordinary residence connoted residence that was voluntary and for a settled purpose and might be defined as 'a man's abode in a particular place or country in which he has adopted voluntarily and for settled purposes, as part of the regular order of his life for the time being'.[32] Prior to the judgment in *Shah*, there was a tendency to view the concepts as a hierarchy commencing with 'presence' and 'residence' and then proceeding to 'ordinary residence' with 'habitual residence' being subject to more stringent criteria. Since 1983, there has been a tendency not to draw a distinction between 'ordinary residence' and 'habitual residence'[33] The willingness to equate 'habitual residence' with 'ordinary residence' was demonstrated by the case of *Kapur v Kapur*,[34] where the facts were as follows: an Indian domicilary, resident in London for educational purposes,[35] petitioned for a decree of divorce in the Family Division. The jurisdiction of the court depended on whether he was habitually resident in England.[36]

In deciding that he was habitually resident, Bush J observed:

> In my view, there is no real distinction to be drawn between 'ordinary' and 'habitual residence'. It may be that in some circumstances a man may be habitually resident without being ordinarily resident, but I cannot at the moment conceive of such a situation.

Thus, in the last decade, there has been an increasing attempt to minimise the difference between 'ordinary residence' and 'habitual residence' and it is quite clear that 'habitual residence' is less demanding in terms of *animus* than the more technical concept of domicile.[37] It is arguable that, since the concept of habitual residence has been introduced into domestic law to give effect to

---

32 *R v London Borough of Barne ex p Shah* [1983] 2 AC 309.

33 In *V v B (A Minor) (Abduction)* [1991] 1 FLR 266, where habitual residence under the terms of the Hague Convention on the Civil Aspects of International Child Abduction (1980) was to be equated with ordinary residence.

34 [1985] Fam Law 22; [1984] FLR 920.

35 He hoped to sit the Bar Finals Examination.

36 Domicile and Matrimonial Proceedings Act 1973, s 5(2)(a).

37 On this point, the observations of Lane J, in *Cruse v Chittum* [1974] 2 All ER 940, remain good law.

international conventions, it is consistent with the normal canons of treaty interpretation that the concept should be given a non-technical meaning.[38]

It would seem that habitual residence can arise even if the purpose of the residence is limited in duration, for example, to attend a course of education.[39] It could also apply to the expatriate worker, who might be regarded as habitually resident in the country of his employment.

The concept of habitual residence is not without its difficulties – it is possible, for example, to be habitually resident in more than one place.[40] What happens when at the operative time the person has abandoned his habitual residence but has not yet acquired another? Nevertheless, the concept is a very useful one and many take the view that its freedom from over definition and over refinement makes it a better test for the personal law than the current test used by English law – domicile.[41]

Domicile

Some argue that domicile is a concept whose time has passed. In the 19th century, when[42] English courts were trying to decide[43] between nationality and domicile, the concept of domicile, which then obtained, was much more like the concept of habitual residence than the highly technical concept which pertains today. In the event, domicile won the day and the English courts spent nearly 80 years refining the concept. The concept of domicile, which had initially meant little more than permanent home,[44] took on an increasingly legalistic dimension,[45] with all sorts of unfortunate consequences which remain with us today. Having regard to the traditional importance of the topic, it will be dealt with in Chapter 3.

---

38 On the interpretation of legislation passed to give effect to international treaty obligations, see *Sidhu v British Airways plc* [1997] 2 WLR 26; *Re H (Minors) (Abduction: Acquiesence)* [1997] 2 WLR 653. In both cases, stress is placed on the need to ensure that international obligations are interpreted in a consistent and non-technical manner.

39 As in *R v London Borough of Barnet ex p Shah* [1983] 2 AC 309.

40 In the context of taxation and the concept of ordinary residence this had been recognised for some considerable time; *IRC v Lysaght* [1928] AC 234; *Hopkins v Hopkins* [1951] P 116.

41 Although this was not the view of the Law Comission; see the Law Commission Working Paper No 87 (1984).

42 The important 19th century cases are *Whicker v Hume* (1858) 7 HLC 124; *Moorhouse v Lord* (1863) 10 HLC 272; *Bell v Kennedy* (1868) LR 1 Sc & Div 307; *Udny v Udny* (1869) LR 1 Sc & Div 441.

43 See the judgment of Scarman J (as he then was), tracing the development of the law, in *Re Fuld's Estate (No 3)* [1968] P 675; [1965] 3 All ER 776.

44 *Whicker v Hume* (1858] 7 HLC 124.

45 The law on domicile developed in the years 1850–1900, during the years when many Englishmen went abroad to administer the Empire.

At present, it is sufficient to note that there are three varieties of domicile known to English law; the domicile of choice, the domicile of origin and the domicile of dependence. The three varieties work together to provide an overall and all embracing concept of the personal law.

The religious law

Many societies incorporate a religious tradition into the rules of their domestic legal systems;[46] this is merely one, albeit a major one, of the cultural influences which go to make domestic legal systems distinct and, thus, create a need for the conflict of laws in the first place. For example, the marriage laws of England are founded on the Christian tradition.[47]

This does not mean there has to be a religious element in the marriage but it does mean that those wishing to marry in England can do so only on the basis of broad compliance with the Christian model. Further, no marriage taking place in England can be polygamous.[48] Obviously, there will be mismatches between the dictates of religion and those of the civil law, thus, for example, a civil ceremony of marriage will not be recognised for religious purposes among the Roman Catholic, Muslim or Jewish communities in Britain, any more than an English divorce will be accepted by those communities as terminating a marriage between their members. There is no institutional framework in English law for the accommodation of religious groupings as such; they must conduct their activities within the legal system which is common to all.

Other societies take a different view and their legal systems may recognise directly, or incorporate, personal religious law – characteristically, in the areas of marriage, family and succession rights. Where a society does make specific provision for the cultural religious laws of a particular group,[49] that has to be recognised, whichever of the other personal laws has been adopted by the conflict system of another country. So, English law, though wedded to the concept of domicile, must recognise that the decision that a person is domiciled in, say, Sri Lanka, will not supply a complete answer to the question of his personal law and that it will be necessary to probe further to discover the religious group to which he belongs.

---

46 For the definition of religion in English law, see *Re The South Place Ethical Society* [1980] 3 All ER 918; 1 WLR 1565 (Dillon J), drawing upon *R v Registrar General ex p Segerdal* [1970] QB 697; 3 All ER 886. Religion extends beyond Christianity, see *Strauss v Goldsmid* (1837) 8 Sim 614.

47 The classic definition of marriage in English law being that of Lord Penzance (Sir James Wilde, as he then was) in *Hyde v Hyde* (1866) LR 1 P&D 130, which includes the expression 'marriage as understood in Christendom'.

48 *Chetti v Chetti* [1909] P 67; 25 TLR 146; *Maher v Maher* [1951] P 342; 2 All ER 37.

49 This would be in those States where the position of a particular religion is entrenched within a written constitution.

Could the personal religious law be used as the general determinant of the personal law for all purposes? The answer must be negative. Not only are there those without a religious grouping and those whose religion is not accorded any special status in the society to which they indubitably belong but, also, religious codes do not cover in precise form every aspect of life in a modern complex society. While a faith may well have moral prescriptions about, for example, keeping promises or basic duties of honesty, it is unlikely to give more than a moral guide on breaches of contract or duties of disclosure. In any case, it is not clear how far one can realistically speak about universal Jewry or Christianity or a pan-Islamic law.[50] Few societies are fundamentalist in this way; most have put a gloss upon the basic religious dictats in tune with their own needs and aspirations as societies.

The religious law will be significant for the purposes of the English conflict of laws only when the English test for the personal law – domicile – attaches the individual to a country which has, as part of its internal law, special regimes for particular religious groupings. In such cases, account will have to be taken of these special rules in order to determine the status of the individual. So, for example, if the question is whether or not X has capacity to marry polygamously, reference to the law of his domicile may involve a further reference to the rules relating to the particular religious group to which he belongs. This applies, of course, only to the extent that the *lex domicilii* itself recognises such groups for this purpose.

Conclusion

Although the attribution of a personal law may appear to be a more real and general association than, say, locating a tort or finding where a will was made, it is worth emphasising that the quest for the personal law in the English conflict of laws is always a means to an end and not an end in itself. This is obvious enough, but the purpose of the inquiry may well influence its results and not improperly so. Cases on domicile, in particular, can be influenced in this way for, although there is a basic single conceptual approach, there may well be a greater desire to find a particular domicile to validate a will or a marriage than to make the individual subject to UK taxation.[51]

---

50 Such an approach would create difficulties in seeking progress in international co-operation. It would be at variance with the general tendency in Western societies to differentiate between Church and State, and it would pose problems in those countries where neutrality between denominations is a basic constitutional provision.

51 In accordance with the traditional principle that the judiciary are not minded to give a liberal construction to taxing statutes. The constitutional justification being that the imposition of a tax must have a clear statutory basis and that the Inland Revenue are always free to secure the reversal of an unhelpful precedent by legislation in a new Finance Act.

The possibilities of connecting a person with a territorial system of law, by means of applying a personal law to him, is a very old idea and one which has considerable merit. It is not without its difficulties in cases of dispute and, whatever test is adopted, there are bound to be artificialities.

It must be noted that, lacking international agreement on the law to be identified as the personal law, it is possible for different systems to treat the same case in very different ways, which makes a consistent attitude to the issue raised impossible to attain. To take an example which is not too far fetched: Simon is a Nigerian national who has lived in England for many years and who regards England as his home. For the last two years he has been working for an English employer in Malaysia and expects to continue in his job there for several more years. He has no family in England but has a house in London and he comes to England for some of his leaves.

On these facts, a court applying a conflict system which used nationality, would find that Simon's personal law was Nigerian, one using the concept of domicile that it was English, and one using the concept of habitual residence that it was Malaysian. If these three legal systems all applied, the personal law to the issue of succession to the property of a person dying intestate (suppose Simon has just died) then all would depend on the court before which any dispute regarding Simon's property arose – likely to be the country where the bulk of it was situated. There is no way out of this dilemma, saving the unification of all countries'conflict systems, a prospect which is very distant.[52]

The response of English law is straightforward – we use our own test, currently domicile, we interpret it in our own way[53] and we stand by the results so obtained regardless of any other country's attitude. If the application of English law's test of domicile results in the finding that X is domiciled in Maryland, then that is conclusive and it matters not that a court in Maryland would find X domiciled elsewhere or, indeed, that it would use an entirely different test for the personal law.

There are two major departures from the English concept of domicile applied by English law. For the recognition of foreign divorces, annulments and legal separations, a domiciliary connection may be established either in the English sense or in the sense of domicile used in family law matters in the

---

52 The most far reaching attempt to harmonise choice of law rules being the EC (Rome) Convention on the Law Applicable to Contractual Obligations 1980, as implemented by the Contracts (Applicable Law) Act 1990.

53 In respect of domicile at common law, see *Re Annesley* [1926] Ch 692, where Russell J observed: 'the question whether a person is or is not domiciled in a foreign country is to be determined in accordance with the requirements of English law as to domicile, irrespective of the question whether the person in question has or has not acquired a domicile in the foreign country in the eyes of that country.'

country concerned.[54] More importantly, for the purpose of jurisdictional links under the Brussels and Lugano Conventions, a special concept of domicile, one much nearer to the idea of habitual residence, has been introduced into English law.[55]

It should be noted that both Australia[56] and Canada have introduced a concept of domicile which applies in matrimonial cases and enables a person to be domiciled in the composite State, whereas, for other purposes, domicile in a particular province or State is required.

It can hardly be assumed that the personal law can be applied in all situations. It cannot be that personal liability to others depends entirely on one's own law – for what of the personal law of the other party? Similarly, it would not be expected that liability upon a contract was entirely a matter for the personal law or, for example, that whether a transfer of property had the effect of securing the transferee against all the world should depend on the personal law of one of the parties to that transfer.

There are some matters, however, which seem to be ideally suited to the governance of the personal law. Questions of personal status – whether one has the power to marry or make a will or enter into a contract would seem fit matters to refer to it. For while these issues also affect those with whom one deals, they relate essentially to the individual himself.

Different societies place differing emphasis on the issue of status; generally speaking, the common law world is less status conscious in this context than the civil law world. Common lawyers tend to be more transaction oriented than their civilian colleagues. As we shall see, English law confines the personal law within fairly narrow grounds; within those grounds, however, it is given full scope.

THE LAW OF THE PLACE

Introduction

Like the personal law, the law of the place provides a fairly straightforward test and one which, unlike the personal law, can be applied automatically. The

---

54 Family Law Act 1986, s 46(5), which states: 'For the purposes of this section, a party to a marriage shall be treated as domiciled in a country if he was domiciled in that country either according to the law of that country in family matters or according to the law of the part of the United Kingdom in which the question of recognition arises.'

55 Civil Jurisdiction and Judgments Act 1982, ss 41–46, as amended by the Civil Jurisdiction and Judgments Act 1991, Sched 2, paras 16–21.

56 In Australia, the Family Law Act 1975 and Australian Divorce Act 1982; in Canada, the Divorce Act 1968.

law of the place where something was done or something happened also seems perfectly sensible. Two parties come together and make an agreement or perhaps, more violently, collide; there is one obvious common factor – they are both in the same place. Why should not the law of the place be used to deal with any dispute that may arise between them? Things are, as may be supposed, not quite so simple. First, it is not possible to encapsulate a complex legal relation into a simple factual issue in every case; one would not, for example, regard it as sensible to refer the whole of a contractual dispute solely to the law of the place where the agreement happened to be signed. Secondly, the place where an act was done may be entirely incidental if not fortuitous. For example, after protracted negotiations taking many months, an international contract is signed in a particular country with all due formality. It may be that the place of signing was chosen for reasons of convenience, ease of travel, or because it is picturesque and not for any reason concerned with the substance of the agreement. Accidents, by their very nature, are unplanned and, while the place of the accident may be the only common factor, it does not follow that the law of the place has any real connection with the parties[57] or the occurrence. Thirdly, the law of the place may not involve a simple factual inquiry but may give rise to a difficult legal analysis. Suppose that the plaintiff has been injured by a dangerous product that was made in country A, bought in country B, used in country C, and which gave rise to injuries, the effect of which was felt in country D. Suppose that the product liability laws of the four countries differ materially. Now, quite apart from the artificiality of attempting to see this problem as a single event, there is the problem of deciding the legal significance of each of the acts in the various countries of action.

However, the old maxim, *locus regit actum* – the law of the place governs the deed – has, despite the difficulties mentioned above, some real merit and has informed the English conflict of laws to a significant extent. It is sensible now to consider some examples of the operation of the principle.

Lex loci celebrationis

One of the more established rules of the English conflict of laws is that the formal validity of a marriage is determined by the law of the place where the marriage was celebrated.[58] Indeed, until the judgment in *Brook v Brook*,[59] the whole question of the validity of a marriage was referred to that law on the

---

57 As was the case with the servicemen in *Boys v Chaplin* [1971] AC 356.

58 *Scrimshire v Scrimshire* (1752) 2 Hag Con 395.

59 (1861) 9 HLC 193, in which the House of Lords drew a distinction between matters of formality, governed by the *lex loci celebrationis*, and matters of capacity (or essential validity), governed by the law of the domicile of the parties.

basis of the unity of Christendom. The remnant of this general rule[60] makes sense in that the majority of marriages take a deal of arrangement and the place of their celebration is unlikely to be casual or fortuitous.

All but the most primitive societies have formal requirements for marriage,[61] as the social consequences of the relationship, as well as the more mundane bookkeeping matters, require a degree of public involvement. So, those who choose to marry in country X are expected, both by country X and by the English conflict of laws, to follow the formal requirements of that law. In the vast majority of cases, this will produce no hardship for the parties concerned and, in most countries, the matter is so carefully regulated that there is little likelihood that the requirements are unknown to, or incapable of being observed by, the parties.

One area of potential difficulty is the religious marriage, which satisfies the needs of the faith but fails to satisfy the formal requirements of the local law. Such marriages are formally void in the eyes of the English conflict of laws, however much the parties to them consider themselves to be married. We looked earlier at the possibility of using the religious law to determine issues of personal status and the validity of religious marriages would be a prime area for that law. However, unless the country of the celebration of the marriage makes a special provision for religious marriages, in which case there is no problem anyway, their recognition by another country but not by the country where they were celebrated would create what is known as a limping marriage – one which is valid in one country but not in another. This situation, while it cannot be avoided altogether, is something which should be minimised as much as possible.

Lex loci contractus

The law of the place where a contract is made may, more obviously than the place where a marriage is celebrated, be casual or fortuitous. I have already alluded to the disadvantages and artificialities of applying that law as the general law to govern international contracts. In so far as the country where the contract is made has formal requirements for contracts of that type,[62] for example, that they should be in writing,[63] there is no great objection to

---

60 Ie, that matters of formal validity of marriage are governed by the *lex loci celebrationis*; see on this *Berthiaume v Dastous* [1930] AC 79.

61 In England, see the Marriage Act 1949; Marriage Acts Amendment Act 1958; Marriage Act 1983; Marriage (Prohibited Degrees of Relationship) Act 1986; Marriage (Registration of Buildings Act) 1990; Marriage Act 1994.

62 In England, see the Statute of Frauds 1677; Law Reform (Enforcement of Contracts) Act 1954, s 1; but, now, see the Law of Property (Miscellaneous Provisions) Act 1989, s 2. For a discussion of the modern law, see Bentley and Coughlin (1990) 10 LS 325.

63 *Leroux v Brown* (1852) 12 CB 801.

expecting that requirement to be carried out, though the chance inadvertent mistake is greater than in the case of marriages because of the lack of public participation.

More difficult is the problem that arises when the law of the place of contracting takes a view not merely about the form of the contract but about the substance of the obligation itself. It might declare that certain types of contract may not be made at all or might seek to include mandatory terms in any contract made within its territory, irrespective of the place of performance of the contract or of any other connections – these problems will be considered later.

Lex loci solutionis

The law of the place where a contract is to be performed has had an important position in the English conflict of laws.

Like the other localising rules, it seemed an obvious choice to make.[64] The performance of a contract is, obviously, the whole point of the contractual relationship and its completion the final act of that relationship. Unlike the *lex loci celebrationis* and the *lex loci contractus*, however, the influence of the *lex loci solutionis* has not centred on formalities – though, if the place of performance imposed formal requirements on the act of performance, there would be a strong case for compliance with them. The *lex loci solutionis* has been used by English courts as a major connection in the search for the governing law of the contract as a whole in those cases where the parties have failed to select a law to govern their dealings.

The major weakness of the *lex loci solutionis* as a localising rule is that it does not necesarily identify a single system of law. An international contract may have several places where acts of performance have to be performed and it may not always be possible to single out one place and, hence, one legal system, as more important than the rest.

Like all localising rules, it is open to the possibility that the connections it makes have only limited relevance to the wider relations between the parties. So, while the place of performance of a contract is unlikely to be casual or fortuitous, the legal system of that place may have no interest in, or any other connection with, the contractual relations between the parties. The local law must have the final say on the legality of the acts done within its boundaries, though the effects of the illegality, rather than the facts of it, may well, as we shall see, fall to be determined by some other law.

---

64 After 1865, the English courts developed a number of tests to determine the proper law of a contract; this case law is dealt with later. However, following the coming into force of the Contracts (Applicable Law) Act 1990, this stream of case law is of limited value. See Mann, FA (1991) 107 LQR 353.

Lex loci delicti commissi

Of all the localising rules which conflict systems have developed, the law of the place of the commission of the tortious act has been the most troublesome.[65] This rule of reference widely used in continental Europe and, until 30 years ago, the basis for ascertaining the governing law in the various States of the USA is substantive in nature. Until recently, the *lex loci delicti commissi* formed part of the governing rule on the choice of law in tort in England.[66] The approach proceeds on the basis that tortious liability is the creation of the law where the tort was committed[67] and governs the plaintiff's ability to recover and the defendant's liability to pay compensation, wherever the case happens to be brought. The concept is one of 'vested rights', that is, the commission of the tort creates, according to the law of the place of its commission, a right of action which the injured party can implement wherever he wishes.[68] It does not matter, according to this theory, whether the personal law of the plaintiff would regard him as having such a right or, indeed, whether the parties come from the same foreign country, in which the right given by the local law is unknown. This model of tortious libility is very similar to the notion of criminality, with which the conflict of laws is not directly concerned, where liability is usually a purely territorial matter. In taking this line, the concept of tort is artificially narrowed. Of course, there are some torts which have a very close affinity to crimes, not surprising in view of their common origin, but there are many that have no such affinity. Deliberate and violent interferences with person or property create liability in both criminal law and the law of tort, but they represent only a tiny part of tortious litigation. More characteristic of the modern law of torts are the accident cases where the issue of fault is not about guilt but about liability to pay compensation. Quite apart from the problem, already alluded to, of fixing the *locus delicti* in a complex case, one can question the whole concept of a crude localising rule. The place where the accident occurs is always fortuitous and

---

65   This was a subject that attracted little attention prior to 1945; the sixth edition of Dicey's *Conflict of Laws* (1949) contained no more than 11 pages (pp 799–807) on the subject but contained about 175 pages on the law of contract (pp 579–758). The increase in interest in the subject of the choice of law in tort is without doubt due to many factors, among the most significant being: (a) the increasing importance of civil aviation; (b) the increase in the popularity of holidays abroad; (c) improved methods of distribution of goods by multi-national enterprises that trade in a number of jurisdictions; and (d) the development of terrestrial and satellite television.

66   The so called rule as to double actionability, deriving from *Phillips v Eyre* (1870) 6 QB 1 and extended in *Machado v Fontes* [1897] 2 QB 231, was confirmed in *Boys v Chaplin* [1971] AC 356. The common law rule was abolished by the Private International Law (Miscellaneous Provisions) Act 1995, s 10, and a new statutory scheme was introduced. For details, see Chapter 17.

67   Although this is difficult to reconcile with *Machado v Fontes* [1897] 2 QB 231.

68   A view espoused by Dicey, and by Holmes J in *Slater v Mexican National Railway* 194 US 120 (1904), p 124.

the application of the local law may appear capricious. In the well known Scottish case of *M'Elroy v M'Allister*,[69] the facts were as follows: the pursuer was the widow of a Scotsman who had been killed in England as a result of a negligent act for which his employer's were vicariously liable. The enterprise was Scottish, the workmen were Scotsmen and the only fact linking the case with England was that the accident happened south of the Scottish border.

The remedies of Scots law and and those of English law for wrongful death were not then identical and, because the Scottish court looked for the common element in the two systems, the widow recovered only for the funeral expenses. The particular rule of the Scottish conflict of laws does not concern us here; the point is that English law was relevant to the case solely because the accident occurred in England.

As no English persons or property were damaged, there was nothing to concern English law about the case and the intrusion of English law into this Scottish tragedy was purely the result of the rules of the conflict of laws.[70]

Where a set of relations pre-exists the particular tortious act, the concentration on the locus delicti becomes even less justifiable, its artificiality even more pronounced. Some of the leading cases which have so troubled English courts and which will be examined later are false problems, in the sense that they result from the rules of the conflict of laws themselves, rather than from any real dispute between legal systems. A crude localising rule in the case of tort, while it undoubtedly has a place in the resolution of some issues for which there is no alternative, will not suffice as a general dispositive rule for torts in the conflict of laws.

Lex situs

The *lex situs*, the law of the place where something is situated, has a long history in conflict adjudication. Unlike other examples of *locus regit actum*, the concept of *situs* may be entirely passive, in that it does not presuppose the doing of anything within the *situs*; it may come into play by reason of an act done elsewhere which has implications for the object that is within the situs. Characteristically, English law has resorted to the law of the *situs* to deal with cases involving property, as control of the property is in the hands of those who are empowered by the local law to deal with it.[71] Where property is land,

---

69 1949 SC 110.

70 See Morris (1949) 12 MLR 248; (1951) 64 Harv L Rev 881.

71 This is of particular importance in those legal systems where a detailed system of registration of title prevails; in England, this is governed by the Land Registration Act 1925 and the subsequent amending legislation. See the Land Registration Act 1966; Land Registration and Land Charges Act 1971; Land Registration Act 1986.

or some other immovable interest, it obviously follows that only the officials of the territorial system of law can effectively deal with it[72] English courts have recognised this in two ways. First, at common law, English courts will not generally accept jurisdiction in cases involving disputes about foreign immovable property. The so called 'Mozambique' rule derived from the judgment of the House of Lords in the case of *British South Africa Company v Companhia de Mocambique*,[73] where the facts were as follows: the plaintiff, a Portuguese company, brought an action for damages for trespass against the defendant, an English company, alleging that it had wrongfully taken possession of large tracts of land and mines in South Africa.

In reversing the Court of Appeal,[74] the House of Lords ruled that an English court had no jurisdiction to entertain an action founded on a disputed claim of title or possession to foreign land.[75]

In addition to the reluctance to entertain disputes about foreign land, English law generally defers to the law of the current *situs* when the dispute is about movable property.

The acquisition of property rights may be made in several ways. If we ignore finding, making and the other more uncommon ways, we will concentrate on those transactions which most people experience as the means of getting property, namely, sale and gift. Now the problem with these is that there are two dimensions – the relationship between the parties themselves and the relations between the new owner and the rest of the world. As between each other, the seller and the buyer or donor and recipient stand in a relationship determined by the nature of the transaction; so that a question such as 'Have I got what I paid for?' or 'Can I have my present back?' is referable to the law, whatever it is, which governs that particular transaction – the law of contract or the law of gift. The central issue here is not that between the parties themselves but the recognition by others of the owner's rights in the country where the goods happen to be. Clearly, a theft does not become a legitimate form of transfer simply because the thief takes the goods across a border but, if the new country fails to recognise the former owner's interest the result might be very much the same. In short, the attitude of the *lex situs* is crucial to the issue of property, at least while the goods remain in the *situs* and

---

72 As, indeed, is the case under the Land Registration Act 1925, where the Chief Land Registrar exercises considerable quasi-judicial functions subject to the right of appeal to the Chancery Division of the High Court (Land Registration Act 1925, ss 138, 142).

73 [1893] AC 602.

74 [1892] 2 QB 358 (Fry, Lopes LJJ, with Lord Esher MR dissenting).

75 *British South Africa Company v Companhia de Mocambique* [1893] AC 602; as explained in *St Pierre v South American Stores (Gath and Chaves) Ltd* [1936] 1 KB 382. See, also, *Hesperides Hotels Ltd v Aegean Turkish Holidays Ltd* [1979] AC 508. For the modern rule, see the Civil Jurisdiction and Judgments Act 1982, s 30. See, also, *Pearce v Ove Arup Partnership Ltd* [1997] Ch 293 (Lloyd J).

the conflict of law cannot ignore its significance.[76] Where the property is immovable, the significance of the *lex situs* is obvious.

Conclusion

The law of the place has a strong claim in certain areas to govern the form of the transaction. Whether it has claims beyond this depends on whether it is possible to subsume a complex issue into a single question referable to a single fact location. Unless this can be done without too much distortion the danger is that a complex, interconnected legal problem will be resolved by the resort to a single connection which is no better than any other. Moreover, it must be remembered that the fact/place links can be entirely fortuitous.

THE TRANSACTIONAL LAW

Instead of trying to encapsulate a complex legal issue into a single factual question, as the local laws and the various personal laws would have us do, why not try to make an analysis of the relationship as a whole and try to find the legal system which overall, appears to have the greatest connection with, or the greatest interest in, that relationship? So, in a contract, we could look at the personal laws of the parties, the laws of the places where the contract was made and where it was to be performed, the *lex situs* of any physical property which formed its subject matter and any other connections there might be. We could then decide, on balance, with which legal system the contract was predominantly connected and apply that law either to all the issues or at least to those which did not admit of a single fact contact. The same approach could be adopted with marriage, in this case reference being made to the pre-marital and, possibly, post-marital personal laws of the parties, the place of the celebration of the marriage and so on. Again, with torts and property transactions, we could collect together all the relevant information and make a judgment about the appropriate law to apply. Such an apparently simple idea does not come without its difficulties; the major ones being what connections are relevant and which are not, and how the weighting is to be carried out.[77]

---

76 Of particular significance in this context are those cases where the courts of Country A may be obliged to consider questions of title arising in respect of acts of expropriation by Country B. See *AM Luther v James Sagor and Co* [1921] 3 KB 532; *Princess Olga Paley v Weisz* [1929] 1 KB 718. This matter, which has become very important in the present century, is discussed in Chapter 9 under the recognition of foreign laws.

77 The judge would have to decide whether a connection was relevant and, if so, what weight it should be accorded.

What connections are relevant?

Suppose we are dealing with a road accident case in tort, what significance, if any is to be given to the personal laws of the parties? Suppose they come from the same country, which happens not to be the place of the accident. It might be argued here that, if there is no damage to persons or property of the country where the accident occurs,[78] there is no case for referring to the place of injury at all. Suppose, however, that they have different personal laws; what is to be made of this? One would hardly argue that a plaintiff who came from California was entitled to higher damages by reason of the fact that personal injury awards were higher in his home country. To be sure, his expectations might well be inflated by his personal law but what about the defendant who, let us suppose, comes from a country in which personal injury awards are low?

The same conflict of expectations is equally applicable to the issue of liability as well as to its consequences. The rights which one personal law gives may not be mirrored in others; an act which is tortious by one system may be innocent by another.

In more complex tort cases, for example, actions by employees against their employers or by passengers against their carriers, there may be a contractual dimension to add to the personal law and the law of the place.

If we take the example of a marriage, it is not fanciful to imagine four systems of law which might have an interest in the matter. The personal laws of the parties before the marriage, the law of the place where the marriage took place and the law of the new country where the couple set up home might all be seen as having claims for consideration if the validity of the marriage is questioned. Are all these claims equal or can some be ruled out either completely or depending on the particular issue raised? If we accept that the *lex loci celebrationis* has the right to say in matters of the formal validity of the marriage, is it to have the last word? Does it have any contribution to make to questions about the essential validity of the marriage or is it to be confined to matters of form only?

In cases of succession, we may need to consider the personal laws of the deceased and of the beneficiaries, the laws which might be relevant to any will, and the laws of the countries in which any parts of the estate are situated. Each of these laws may have an interest in particular parts of the whole but which is to have the dominant position when they are in conflict?

In commercial contracts, it might be thought that the personal laws of the human parties have little relevance but the law of the places of business of the corporate parties might well be pertinent. The law of the places where the

---

78 As was the case in *Boys v Chaplin* [1971] AC 356 and, indeed, arguably in *Babcock v Jackson* (1963) 12 NY 2d 473; 2 LR 286.

contract was made or was to be performed, the legal systems indicated by the language of the contract and its form, the location or legal connections of the subject matter of the contract and, above all, the system of law which the parties have indicated as their chosen governing laws[79] all have potential relevance as significant connections.

Every conflict situation involves connections with at least two legal systems; many with more. The relevance of particular connections to any case depends not only on the issue in dispute[80] but on the way the connections cluster around particular legal systems. The examples I have used have all included connections which have some claim to consideration, on some matters at least, in current English conflict law.

Do only factual connections count?

Suppose that one visitor to a country runs down another visitor as a result of careless driving.[81] Assume that they are the only people involved. We have, potentially, three systems of law to consider – the plaintiff's personal law, the defendant's personal law and the law of the place of the accident. If there are, in fact, only two systems of law involved because the plaintiff and the defendant have the same personal law, there is a strong case for ignoring the *lex loci delicti* and applying the rules of the common personal law to the dispute. If, however, the plaintiff and the defendant have different personal laws, there would seem to be no common element beyond the place of accident and the case for applying the *lex loci delicti* would be a strong one.[82]

Suppose, however, that, although the parties come from different countries, their personal laws have the same rules on the issue in dispute. Does this provide a case for the displacement of the *lex loci delicti* in favour of the application of either of the personal laws?[83]

---

79 For the position at common law, see *Vita Food Products Incorporated v Unus Shipping Co* [1939] AC 277.

80 In a civil case, the precise issues will be determined by an examination of the relevant pleadings. Many cases giving rise to problems in private international law are heard in the Chancery Division, in which case the judge will be required only to answer the questions posed in the Originating Summons.

81 In effect, the facts of one of the best known cases in the law of obligations, namely, *Boys v Chaplin* [1971] AC 356, where both the plaintiff and the defendant were normally resident in England but temporarily stationed in Malta when the accident took place. The problems that the judgment gives rise to are discussed in Chapter 17, on the law of tort.

82 See, now, the Private International Law (Miscellaneous Provisions) Act 1995, s 11.

83 See the provisions in the Private International Law (Miscellaneous Provisions) Act 1995, s 12, providing for the displacement of the *lex loci delicti*; this is discussed in Chapter 17.

The English conflict of laws has been built around the jurisdiction selecting rule.[84] The connection is made with the whole of the jurisdiction – French law, Nigerian law and the like – theoretically, without regard to the content of the legal system so identified, at least at the time of initial selection. On this basis, then, an English court would not concern itself with the common quality of the laws if the parties were from different countries. Indeed, in such a case, it would not take the issue beyond the preliminary stage – recognising that the parties were from different countries and different legal systems.

Likewise, the attempt to find the appropriate law to govern the contract in default of choice would be based on the factual rather than the legal connections. Suppose the contract is found to have 10 points of significant connection: three with one country, three with another and four with a third. On a simple point count, the law of the third legal system would be applied and its rule would provide the dispositive rule for the case. This would be so even if the other two legal systems were to have identical rules on the issue in question, as the court has no method to make this sort of evaluation.

How are the contacts to be weighed?

It is obvious from the previous example that the mere counting of contacts without regard to their individual significance would be a very crude way of establishing the seat of the relationship. A mere point count could have the majority of trivial contacts outweigh the smaller number of more significant ones. On the other hand, to predicate which contacts must always enjoy superiority would remove the flexibility from the system and return it to a localising rule of the simple factual type. So, for example, to make the law of the place of performance of the contract always superior to the law of the place of contracting, while in the majority of cases a sensible thing to do, would not always fit the bill. The problem here is an obvious one, the court, seeking to do justice in the individual case wants to retain the maximum discretion and the businessman wants a clear rule to enable him to predict which way the court is likely to go. Additionally, he may well be prepared to sacrifice a better result in favour of a quicker one.

Too rigid a weighting arrangement leads us back to the single fact/law connection of the localising rules, too much free law finding leads to unpredictable results and to needless and expensive litigation.

The Rome Convention on the Law Applicable to Contractual Obligations 1980 seeks to steer a way between these polarities by applying,[85] where the

---

84 An approach that has attracted criticism from scholars in the USA, but such criticism has had little recognition in England.

85 Rome Convention on the Law Applicable to Contractual Obligations 1980, given effect to in England by the Contracts (Applicable Law) Act 1990, in force from 1 April 1991.

parties have not chosen a law to govern their contract, the system of law which is most closely connected to the contract but establishes a series of rebuttable presumptions to establish what that is.

Yet surely the principle is sound? For every set of legal relations there may be assumed to be a system which stands out among the others as having the closest relationship to the dispute taken as a whole.

There are various ways of characterising the process of looking for the predominant connection – the search for the closest and most real connection, the grouping of contacts, the seat of the relationship and, in the English conflict of laws, the proper law, the *lex propria causae*. In the English conflict of laws, the proper law concept first appeared in the context of the law of contract[86] and was related to the issue of the parties autonomy – which will be considered in the next section. The complex interrelations to which a contract may give rise do not lend themselves to a single factual contact. More recently, there have been moves to apply similar techniques to the problems of tort cases[87] as a reaction to the artificiality of the *lex loci delicti*[88] and it could be argued, the complex issues of marriage provide another field for possible proper law approaches. In the case of marriage,[89] however, the personal law supplies much of the proper law requirement.

THE LAW CHOSEN BY THE PARTIES

At first sight it might seem odd that the parties should be allowed to select the legal regime which is to govern their legal postion and it would indeed be odd if one could choose the system of criminal law by which one's behaviour was to be judged, or the system of tort law[90] which would determine the liability one had to one's neighbour.

However, the parties can in many ways control the legal system which is to apply to them, and we will look briefly at some ways here.

Any concept of the personal law is voluntary in the sense that a person can change his residence, domicile, nationality or religion with varying degrees of difficulty. Similarly, a corporation can establish its place of business or

---

86 The doctrine of the proper law of the contract (which will be examined in Chapter 16) can probably be traced back to the judgment of the Privy Council in *P & O Steam Navigation Co v Shand* (1865) 3 Moo PC (NS) 272, when the court began to move away from the *lex loci contractus*.

87 See Morris (1951) 64 HLR 881.

88 Private International Law (Miscellaneous Provisions) Act 1995, ss 11, 12.

89 The law in relation to marriage having been established by the middle of the 19th century; see *Scrimshire v Scrimshire* (1752) 2 Hagg Con 395; *Brook v Brook* (1861) 9 HLC 193.

90 One definition of a tort being 'the breach of an obligation imposed by operation of law'.

manufacture where it chooses. In most cases, the prime factor in these matters will be personal or financial, rather than legal, though it should not be supposed that legal effects do not follow or are not sought. To take some well known examples: the tax exile who sets up home or business in a new country where the incidence of taxation is lower; the fugitive from justice who goes to a country which has no extradition treaty with the country which wants him; the shipowner who registers his vessel with a country which makes fewer demands on him than the older maritime nations.

Parties can, by changing the location of themselves or their transactions, effectively choose the law by which their acts are to be judged. For example, the eloping couples who went to Gretna Green to enjoy Scots law's freedom from the requirement of parental consent to marriage; the contracting parties who choose the place of formal entry into the contract in order to get the benefit of that country's rules on formal validity (or to avoid those of some other country); the party who comes to England for a year to get an English divorce – all are engaging in law choosing processes. In the examples given, they are choosing the law indirectly by altering the facts in a way that triggers the operation of the law.

Another way in which parties can indirectly select the law to govern is by choosing where to litigate. Different countries have different rules for the establishment of jurisdiction[91] and some are more rigorous than others. It may be that a litigant can find a number of courts[92] in different countries whose jurisdiction he can invoke. One of the factors influencing his choice will be the law with which these different courts will apply to his dispute. He will need to be well advised if he is to make a sensible choice. In a genuinely international case, the conflict of law rules of the court will need to be considered.

In cases where the courts apply their own domestic law to particular matters coming before them, irrespective of the foreign elements in the case (as, for example, in the granting of divorces or in the assessment of damages for personal injury) the choice of forum constitutes a direct choice of law to be applied. So, for example, the liberal divorce jurisdictions of Nevada and South Dakota made those States places of resort for those seeking a speedy divorce. Similarly, victims of the Bhopal disaster in India[93] and the Piper Alpha[94]

---

91 In England, at common law, temporary presence within the jurisdiction would be sufficient to confer jurisdiction; see, on this, *Carrick v Hancock* (1895) 12 TLR 59; *Colt Industries Inc v Sarlie* [1966] 1 WLR 440; *HRH Maharanee of Baroda v Wildenstein* [1972] 2 QB 283; 2 All ER 689.

92 As will be seen elsewhere, the problem of 'forum shopping' has occasioned a considerable volume of case law in England since the mid-1970s, as plaintiffs became aware of the different remedies in other jurisdictions. Advertising by foreign lawyers, large jury awards and the operation of contingency fee systems have no doubt contributed to this trend.

93 1984.

94 1988.

disaster in the North Sea sought to bring their claims before courts in the USA where personal injury and wrongful death awards are much higher, rather than before the Indian courts and the courts in Scotland.

In commercial contracts,[95] it is not unusual to have what is known as a choice of jurisdiction clause specifying the country in which any litigation or arbitration is to take place.

In those countries like England, where foreign law has to be pleaded and proved, the parties may agree not to take the foreign law point at all and to let the case be decided according to the forum's own law.[96]

So, given a knowledge of the law which a court will apply either to the substance of the dispute or to the assessment of damages, the plaintiff, or, by agreement, both parties, can select the forum which will apply the law, whether its own or that of another country.

The aspects of choice looked at so far do not represent choice of law in the strict sense, being either examples of factual arrangements which have legal consequences or examples of choices of jurisdiction where the legal consequences follow from the law which the court applies in its ordinary resolution of such cases including, where appropriate, its conflict rules. What about explicit choices of the governing law, of the kind 'the law to govern this thing shall be the law of X'?[97] Clearly, the scope for this is limited.

One party cannot usually stipulate a law in a manner which would adversely affect the other party to the litigation. There are, however, situations where such a stipulation would not have such an adverse effect and where it might seem appropriate to have regard to the wishes of the party. A testator cannot make his otherwise invalid will valid merely by saying so, for all testators, one assumes, have the intention of leaving a valid will and there is a public interest in wills to which a legal system gives effect in its rules on validity. At the same time, a valid will is intended to give effect to the wishes of the testator and that these wishes should be frustrated by a misunderstanding of what he wanted to achieve would benefit no one, although there would be a windfall to the residuary legatees or to those entitled on intestacy. Allowing the testator to specify the law by which his will is to be construed would seem both sensible and workable. The same benefit could be conferred on the maker of any unilateral document. Where the

---

95 At common law, the connection between express choice of jurisdiction and implied choice of law was quite marked: *qui elegit iudicium elegit ius*. See *Hamlyn and Co v Talisker Distillery* [1894] AC 202; *Spurrier v La Cloche* [1902] AC 466. However, even at common law, there were limits to this principle: see *Compagnie Tunisienne de Navigation SA v Compagnie d'Armement Maritime SA* [1971] AC 572.

96 In accordance with the traditional principle, in the civil law of evidence, that the parties to a suit are free to agree to modify the rules of evidence in appropriate cases.

97 For the position at common law, see *Vita Food Products Inc v Unus Shipping Co Ltd* [1939] AC 277; 1 All ER 513.

dealing is bilateral or multilateral, the agreement of both or all of those concerned should, likewise, be respected.

As we shall see, the English conflict of laws has got round to this limited freedom of stipulation by a somewhat roundabout route, led by the autonomy of the parties to a contract to choose or incorporate a law for the transaction, but it is worth exploring in other areas. Self-regulation is not a concept incompatible with law: such regulation must fall within the prescribed legal limits, of course, and these limits will be fixed according to the notion of the particular society concerned. But, it would be wrong to think that, because in default of other arrangement, the job has to be done by the law, that there must therefore be a public interest in the narrow control of the matter. Parties are, in any event, generally free to settle their legal disputes without resort to the courts or to lawyers and the basis on which they settle is not, generally, a matter of interest to anyone else.

The traditional English view has always been that parties should be encouraged to settle their disputes without litigation if at all possible. The view that litigation is but a necessary evil in civil society is reflected in the principle that the legal burden of proof is normally placed on the party who initiates civil or criminal proceedings.[98]

MORE SOPHISTICATED APPROACHES

All the connections that we have looked at so far lead to the identification of a legal system and only indirectly to a legal rules. That is, they are jurisdiction selecting, not rule selecting approaches. Critics of the traditional system point to its failures not merely in terms of unfortunate results, to which any system of law can give rise, but in terms of the methodology which creates artificial problems. The weakness of traditional jurisdiction selecting processes, even if the connections are *prima facie* sensible and the rules properly applied, is that they take no account of interests. The rules of a legal system are applied to the determination of the issue irrespective of the of the views of the system from which the rules come. On occasion, the foreign court which is trying to apply them may drag the rules out of context.

The case of *Babcock v Jackson*[99] provides a suitable object lesson for present purposes. The facts have already been given: they all related to New York, except that the place where the accident occurred was Ontario, which had a

---

98 As reflected in the expression, *'ei qui affirmat non ei qui negat incumbit probatio'*. See *Abrath v North Eastern Rly Co* (1883) 11 QBD 440; (1886) 11 AC 247; *Wakelin v London and South Western Rly* (1886) 12 AC 41; *Joseph Constantine Steamship Ltd v Imperial Smelting Corpn* [1942] AC 154.

99 (1963) 12 NY 2 D 473; 2 LR 286.

'guest statute' preventing a gratuitous passenger from recovering from a negligent driver. There is an obvious case for applying New York law and none, save for the conflict rules of New York, for applying the law of Ontario. Assume, however, that we have to take account of Ontarian law, either because we have been persuaded to do so by the defendant or because the conflict rules to be applied require it. It does not follow that Ontarian law should control the outcome. The laws of Ontario and those of New York are the same in all respects for this case save for the 'guest statute'. The question arises as to what that provision is intended to achieve.

The attribution of purpose to rules of law is notoriously difficult – it should not be, but it is. The reasons for this are manifold but include the following:

(a) the difference between the original and the ultimate effect (the notorious history of the Statute of Frauds 1677 furnishes a clear instance);

(b) the fact that legislation passed by an assembly may have been approved for all sorts of motives by those who voted for it, even directly contradictory ones;

(c) the fact that a judge made rule suitable for one case may produce a different effect in another;

(d) the possibility that there was no single purpose that the rule was designed to meet in the first place, and so on.

Nevertheless, we can look at the Ontarian law and try to decide its purpose. Two possibilities immediately emerge – that the law was intended to prevent ungrateful behaviour by guests or that it was designed to prevent collusive frauds against motor insurers. Taking the first of these: where one person does a favour for another it may be thought most ungrateful if he is then asked to pay compensation for the harm which he happens to do in the process. Most people in most circumstances would never consider bringing an action at all, but, where the loss to them was severe or where it was known that a third party, in this case, the driver's insurers, would actually bear the loss, attitudes might be different.

In any event, the issue here is not whether Ontario is wise in having such a provision; that is a matter for the Ontarians alone, as there is clearly nothing in the law itself which makes it repulsive to the civilised conscience and requiring its rejection on moral grounds – as would indeed be the case with a racially discriminatory law. But, what is the proper ambit of such law? how widely should it apply? Should it apply to all actions before Ontarian courts so that Ontarian courts can prevent their processes being used to further the claims of ingrates? Should it apply to Ontarians – that ungrateful Ontarians should not be allowed to benefit anywhere? Should it apply to all accidents in Ontario irrespective of where the parties come from and the degree of relationship with Ontario?

Only if the third question received an affirmative answer would there be any case at all for a court in New York to apply the Ontarian rule to deny the plaintiff her compensation. Turning to the second possibility, that the law of Ontario is intended to prevent collusive frauds against insurance companies, a similar sort of analysis may be made. All systems of law have an interest in preventing fraudulent claims, but the common way to deal with the problem is on an ad hoc basis, to disallow the particular claim when the fraud is discovered, rather than to disallow a whole class of actions on the basis that some of them may be fraudulent. The Statute of Frauds 1677,[100] provides an unhappy example of an attempt to deal with the problem of fraud by generic description rather than on an individual basis. Again, we are not concerned with the sense of such a law but with the ambit of its operation. That the Ontarian courts should not lend their processes to this sort of claim is intellible, also, perhaps, that no Ontarian should be allowed to make such a claim anywhere might be the aspiration, but neither of these apply to the case in hand. Looked at from another angle, the object of the law may be to protect the funds of insurers from false claims and, thus, to protect the general body of premium payers form the knock on costs of such claims. If such were the case, it seems unlikely that Ontarian law was concerned with claims against foreign insurers being conducted before foreign tribunals. No Ontarian insurer was involved in this litigation and no direct interest of the law of Ontario was at stake. It is not inconceivable that in such a case a court sitting in the *locus delicti* might hesitate to apply the local law to foreign litigants. Enough has been said to establish the artificiality of the New York court woodenly applying the law of Ontario simply on the basis of a simple factual connection. What is the solution?

Three possibilities present themselves: change the jurisdiction selecting rule to avoid the artificial contact having too much significance; weed out the inappropriate rules at the law application stage; adopt a methodology that goes directly to the possibly applicable rules.

(a) *Solution one* – adopting a better choice of law rule, while maintaining jurisdiction selecting approaches – would lead to the acceptance of the law of the transaction as the governing rule. This possibility was considered above and, in its simplest form, would involve the grouping of contacts.[101] On this basis, the law of New York would apply because all the contacts are with that law save for the purely fortuitous event of the accident occurring in Ontario.

---

100 The Statute of Frauds 1677, s 4, provides that a contract for the sale of land would be unenforceable unless there was a sufficient memorandum in writing. For later developments, see the Law Of Property Act 1925, s 40; Law of Property (Miscellaneous Provisions) Act 1989. For a discussion of the statute in the context of private international law, see the celebrated case of *Leroux v Brown* (1852) 12 CB 801.

101 To some extent, this was the policy at common law when seeking to infer a choice of law in cases of contractual dispute; see *R v International Trustee for the Protection of Bondholders AG* [1937] AC 500; *The Assunzione* [1954] P 150.

(b) *Solution two* – weeding out the inappropriate rule at the law application stage – needs a little more explanation. Every court deciding a case will apply its own procedure and will ensure that its decision is congruent with the general policy of the country in which it sits.[102] It will, thus, not apply foreign law that results in a decision objectionable to the forum; objectionable in a real sense, of course, not merely something that it does not like. The inherent power may be used to vet the rules of a foreign system in terms of their appropriateness to determine the outcome of the case in hand, so that the court in *Babcock v Jackson*[103] could, on the basis of the analysis set out, simply have declared the rule of Ontarian law, though *prima facie* applicable, inappropriate on the facts of the case itself and, there being no other difference between Ontarian and New York law in this case, have applied either law to enable the plaintiff to recover.

(c) *Solution three* – the court looks at legal rules, rather than at legal systems and engages in direct purposive analysis of competing dispositive rules – involves adopting an entirely different methodology: one based on rule selection instead of jurisdiction selection. There are several varieties of this approach which have produced a vigorous debate in the USA over the last 30 years.

With the single exception of *Chaplin v Boys*,[104] these ideas have had no significant influence on the development of the conflict of laws in England. As the major battleground has been in the law of torts,[105] which has now been placed on a statutory basis,[106] and as English conflict law for contracts is already on a statutory jurisdiction selecting basis,[107] there is even less scope for American influence to be felt in England. It is for that reason that it is not necessary to consider in this context those who advocate a rethinking of the choice of law process.[108]

---

102 As in respect of the rules pertaining to the exclusion of foreign law; for a robust statement of the need to be mindful of public policy, see *Dynamit AG v Rio Tinto Zinc Co* [1918] AC 260, p 292, *per* Lord Parker.

103 (1963) 12 NY 2 D 473; 2 LR 286.

104 [1971] AC 356; [1969] 2 All ER 1085. References to the various developments in the USA are set out in the speech of Lord Wilbeforce. Interestingly, Lord Wilberforce thought that some of the views then being canvassed in the USA could be traced back to the views of Professor Westlake (*A Treatise on Private International Law* (7th edn, 1925), p 81).

105 In the USA, precipitated by accidents on motor car journeys, aeroplanes or transcontinental trips, where the place of accident is likely to be fortuitous, as noted by Lord Hodson in *Boys v Chaplin* [1971] AC 356.

106 Private International Law (Miscellaneous Provisions) Act 1995, Pt III, ss 9–15, in force from 1 May 1996, in respect of acts or omissions arising after that date.

107 Contracts (Applicable Law) Act 1990.

108 Among the leading contributors to the debate are Ehrenzweig, *A Treatise on the Conflict of Laws* (1962); Currie, *Selected Essays on the Conflict of Laws* (1963); von Mehren and Trautman, *The Law of Multistate Problems: Cases and Materials on Conflict of Laws* (1965); Cavers, *The Choice of Law Process* (1965); Leflar, *American Conflicts Law* (4th edn, 1986).

CONCLUSIONS

As has been seen, there are only a limited number of possibilities open to a court trying a case with a foreign contact or, increasingly, to a legislature or conference seeking to establish a code for the choice of law in a particular area, and none of them are suitable for all cases. While the number is small, permutations are possible, so that a rule could offer either a set of alternatives. The formal validity of a will[109] can be determined by three varieties of the personal law, each within two time frames, or by the law of the place of acting or by the application of a number of connections, for example, the law to govern certain types of consumer contract under the Rome Convention 1980[110] is the law of the consumer's habitual residence (but only if certain factual contacts with the contract exist there).[111]

How the various forms of personal law are employed in different areas of law is a matter that will require to be considered in subsequent chapters. However, it is important first to pay a little more attention to the concept of domicile, having regard to its traditional importance within English private international law.

---

109 See, now, the Wills Act 1963, s 1, implementing the Hague Convention on the Forms of Dispositions 1961.
110 Rome Convention on the Law Applicable to Contractual Obligations 1980, as implemented by the Contracts (Applicable Law) Act 1990, s 2.
111 *Ibid*, Art 5(1)–(3).

CHAPTER 3

DOMICILE

THE NATURE OF DOMICILE

It has long been recognised that there are a large number of questions that need to be determined by the personal law of the individual. Examples would be questions relating to the essential validity of a marriage, a will of movable property or jurisdiction in cases of divorce and nullity.

In the 19th century, English courts struggled to determine whether the personal law indicating a connection between an individual and the place should be that of nationality or domicile. Many of the cases concerned Englishmen or Scotsmen who had left their place of birth and gone abroad in the service of Empire.[1] At a later date, questions would arise as to whether the individual retained sufficient connection with England or Scotland. Given that, in the 19th century, the English courts tended to regard their justice as superior to that in less happy lands, the English judges came to regard domicile rather than nationality as the important link between the individual and the place. The 19th century witnessed an important legal development; in common law countries, the personal law tended to become that of domicile, while, in continental/civil law countries, the personal law tended to be that of nationality. In any event, the purpose of domicile as a concept of law[2] was to connect the individual to some legal system for particular legal purposes. Originally, it would seem that English law considered domicile to be a concept that indicated a permanent home[3] but, as the century progressed the rules as to the acquisition and loss of domicile became increasingly complex and artificial. Every case involving a question of domicile required a detailed chronological survey of the life of the *propositus*.[4]

The complexity of the English concept of domicile would have given rise to difficulties in implementing the Brussels Convention on Jurisdiction and Judgments in Civil and Commercial Matters 1968. Under the terms of the Convention, the normal rule is that the defendant is to be sued in the State in which he is domiciled. Therefore, to enable English courts to accept

---

1   Or, as in the case of Colonel Udny in *Udny v Udny* (1869) LR 1 Sc & Div 441, had left Scotland to serve in the Guards and then travelled to France to escape creditors.

2   'An idea of law', *per* Lord Westbury in *Bell v Kennedy* (1868) LR 1 Sc & Div 307, p 320.

3   *Whicker v Hume* (1858) 7 HLC 124, p 160, *per* Lord Cranworth: 'By domicile we mean home, the permanent home.'

4   The emphasis on the chronological survey and on inferences drawn from the life of a deceased meant that it was sometimes very difficult to advise with confidence: see Beckett (1939) 55 LQR 270.

jurisdiction, the Civil Jurisdiction and Judgments Act 1982 provides a simplified code for questions of domicile arising in cases of jurisdiction.[5]

THE PRINCIPLES OF THE LAW OF DOMICILE

Domicile is a legal concept.[6] It is a connecting factor which links a person with a particular legal system. The concept has played a significant role within the English conflict of laws since the middle of the 19th century.[7]

A tentative definition of 'domicile' would be 'permanent home'.[8] For many persons, their domicile will be their permanent home. The law of domicile operates on a chronological basis;[9] a person will be ascribed a domicile of origin at the time of birth and it will be difficult to demonstrate that this has been displaced. It should be borne in mind that the law on domicile grew up in England in the second half of the 19th century, when many individuals owning property in England might be required to spend long periods out of the country either as part of the administration of Empire[10] or in organising commercial ventures overseas. Such individuals would be reluctant to abandon all connection with England. Thus, the basic idea of domicile was that of permanent home:

'By domicile we mean home, the permanent home,'[11] observed Lord Cranworth in *Whicker v Hume*. 'And if you do not understand your permanent home, I'm afraid that no illustration drawn from foreign writers or foreign languages will very much help you do it.'

The principle that domicile was a legal concept distinct from nationality or residence was established by the middle of the 19th century.[12] The case law[13]

---

5   Civil Jurisdiction and Judgments Act 1982, ss 41–45. For the meaning of domicile in this particular context, see Chapter 13.

6   'An idea of law', *per* Lord Westbury in *Bell v Kennedy* (1868) LR 1 Sc & Div 307, p 320.

7   The evolution of the law of domicile can be traced in the case law from the middle of the 19th century; see *Munro v Munro* (1840) 7 Cl & F 876.

8   *Wicker v Hume* (1858) 7 HLC 124, p 160, *per* Lord Cranworth.

9   All cases on domicile involve a detailed examination of the history of the individual in question – see *Winans v AG* [1904] AC 287; *Ramsay v London Royal Infirmary* [1930] AC 588.

10 In *Udny v Udny* (1869) LR 1 Sc & Div 441, Colonel Udny left Scotland to serve in the Guards and then went to France to avoid his creditors.

11 *Whicker v Hume* (1858) 7 HLC 124, p 16.

12 *Udny v Udny* (1869) LR 1 Sc & Div 441, where Lord Westbury discusses the distinction and draws upon the work of Joseph Story.

13 The leading cases are: *Aikman v Aikman* (1861) 3 Macq 854; *Moorhouse v Lord* (1863) 10 HLC 272; *Pitt v Pitt* (1864) 4 Macq 627; *Bell v Kennedy* (1868) LR 1 Sc & Div 307; *Udny v Udny* (1869) LR 1 Sc & Div 441; *Winans v AG* [1904] AC 287; *Huntly v Gaskell* [1906] AC 56; *Lord Advocate v Jaffrey* [1921] 1 AC 146; *Ross v Ross* [1930] AC 1; *Ramsay v Liverpool Royal Infirmary* [1930] AC 588; *Wahl v AG* (1932) 147 LT 382.

that developed from the middle of the 19th century now permits five propositions to be stated with some degree of confidence. These are:

(a) no person can be without a domicile;[14]

(b) a person cannot at the same time have more than one domicile (at least, no more than one for the same purpose);[15]

(c) an existing domicile is presumed to continue until it is proved that a new domicile has been acquired;[16]

(d) the question of where a person is domiciled is determined solely[17] in accordance with English law;[18] and

(e) the relevant standard of proof is the civil standard of proof.[19]

There are three forms of domicile:

(a) domicile of origin, which is the domicile attributed at the time of birth;

(b) domicile of choice, which is the domicile a competent person may acquire during his lifetime; and

(c) a domicile of dependency, which means that the domicile of the dependent person is dependent on the conduct of another.

It is necessary to examine each of these concepts in turn

THE DOMICILE OF CHOICE

General principles

Every person in the World who is over the age of 16,[20] and is not mentally incapable, is regarded by English law as able to acquire a domicile of choice by residing in a country with the present intention of making it his permanent home.[21] There are, thus, two requirements – the fact of residence (*factum*) and the intention to reside (*animus*).

---

14 *Bell v Kennedy* (1868) LR 1 Sc & Div 307; *Udny v Udny* (1869) LR 1 Sc & Div 441.

15 *Udny v Udny* (1869) LR 1 Sc & Div 441; *Garthwaite v Garthwaite* [1964] P 356; *IRC v Bullock* [1976] 1 WLR 1178; *Lawrence v Lawrence* [1985] Fam 106.

16 *Bell v Kennedy* (1868) LR 1 Sc & Div 307; *Winans v AG* [1904] AC 287; *Ramsay v Liverpool Royal Infirmary* [1930] AC 588; *Re Lloyd Evans* [1947] Ch 695; *Re Fuld's Estate (No 3)* [1968] P 675.

17 Subject to statutory exceptions: Family Law Act 1986, s 46(5).

18 *Hamilton v Dallas* (1875) 1 Ch D 257; *Re Annesley* [1926] Ch 692; *Lawrence v Lawrence* [1985] Fam 106.

19 *Re Fuld's Estate (No 3)* [1968] P 675; *Re Edwards, Edwards v Edwards* (1969) 113 SJ 108; *Buswell v IRC* [1974] 1 WLR 1631; see, also, *Re Flynn (Deceased)* [1968] 1 WLR 103, p 115.

20 Domicile and Matrimonial Proceedings Act 1973, s 3(1).

21 It is not enough to be undecided; see *Bell v Kennedy* (1868) 1 Sc & Div 307.

In most cases, it will be quite straightforward to decide where someone is domiciled but the considerable bulk of the case law in the area demonstrates that, where the issue is contested, there can be great scope for argument.[22]

There can be no question, unlike in the case of habitual residence, of a person having two operative domiciles simultaneously or, as we shall see, having none at all but these benefits may be bought at too high a price.

Long residence in a country will raise the inference[23] that a person intended to remain there and this inference may be so strong as to be almost impossible to rebut. By the same token, a short period of residence may make it difficult to assert that domicile has been established.

The abandonment of a domicile requires the same two elements, the physical removal from the country and the intention not to return to it – leaving *animus non revertendi*. There must be a coincidence on non-residence and intention not to reside. So, a long period of absence does not destroy a domicile of choice and may not do so even if there is indecision about a possible return.

An illustration is afforded by the case of *Re Lloyd Evans (Deceased)*,[24] where the facts were as follows: Lloyd Evans, whose parents were British subjects, was born in Wales in 1864 and went to Java in 1880. He stayed until 1917, marrying a Dutch woman. He returned briefly to England before settling in Brussels in 1922, buying a house there. With great reluctance he was persuaded to leave Belgium in 1940 when the Germans invaded. He came to England and died there in July 1944, still undecided whether to return to Belgium or emigrate to Australia.

Wynn Parry J, in holding that he remained domiciled in Belgium, ruled that those who asserted that the domicile of choice had been abandoned bore the *onus probandi* and that the intention to abandon and the act of abandoning must be unequivocal. Thus, although he has fled to England and died before he had decided whether to return to Belgium or emigrate to Australia, he was held to remain domiciled in Belgium.

In contrast, all the desire in the world to be somewhere else will not destroy a domicile unless it is accompanied by removal from the country. So, an intention to leave England coupled with a mere visit to the intended new home is not enough to destroy the existing domicile. This is illustrated by the case of the *IRC v The Duchess of Portland*,[25] where the facts were as follows: the

---

22 See the amusing judgment of Megarry J in *Re Flynn (Deceased)* [1968] 1 WLR 103, in which the learned judge was required to trace the life history of the celebrated film actor Errol Flynn.

23 But, not if the *propositus* disliked the country and its people and wished to humble and humiliate it; see the unusual case of *Winans v AG* [1904] AC 287; or if the deceased kept an open mind as to whether he would return home: *Ramsay v Liverpool Royal Infirmary* [1930] AC 588.

24 [1947] 1 Ch 695; 177 LT 585 (Wynn Parry J).

25 [1982] Ch 314; 1 All ER 784.

taxpayer had a Canadian domicile of origin. She married in 1948 and acquired an English domicile of dependency. She retained links with Quebec, visiting each year and keeping a house. It was agreed that, when her husband retired, they would both live in Quebec. The question arose as to whether she was domiciled in England for income tax purposes.

Nourse J overruled the special commissioners to hold that the taxpayer remained domiciled in England. On marriage, the taxpayer had acquired a domicile of dependency.

When the Domicile and Matrimonial Proceedings Act 1973 provided for the independent domicile of the married woman,[26] the taxpayer's domicile of dependency became a domicile of choice[27] and that domicile of choice was not lost by an intention to settle in Quebec on retirement. It is interesting to reflect that, in this particular case, if the taxpayer had married after 1 January 1974, then it is arguable that, lacking the intention to remain in England permanently, she would have retained her domicile in Quebec.[28]

As in habitual residence, there is a relationship between fact and intent but the requirement for domicile is more exacting. A brief examination of some of the leading cases will demonstrate the relationship. In the turn of the century case of *Winans v AG*,[29] the facts were as follows: William Winans was born in Baltimore in 1823 but, in 1859, he came to England and lived there all his life at various places until his death in 1896. He built railways in Russia and helped that country in the Crimean War (1853–56) by constructing gunboats. He retained plans for his properties in Baltimore. He disliked England and appeared to be without friends. The evidence indicated that his sole remaining ambition was to enable the USA to acquire world maritime supremacy at the expense of England. On his death in 1896, the question arose as to his place of domicile. If he was domiciled in England then legacy duty was payable.

In giving judgment for the House of Lords and reversing the Court of Appeal,[30] Lord Macnaghten emphasised that domicile of origin is more enduring than domicile of choice and that, on the evidence, it could not be said that Mr Winans had acquired a domicile of choice in England. His hatred

---

26 Domicile and Matrimonial Proceedings Act 1973, s 1(1).

27 *Ibid*, s 1(2).

28 See, also, *In bonis Raffenel* (1863) 3 Swe & Tr 49, where it was held that a widow did not lose her domicile in France after she decided to return to England, her domicile of origin, but died on the cross channel ferry at Calais.

29 [1904] AC 287 (Lords Macnaghten, Halsbury, Lindley, dissenting), reversing the Court of Appeal (Lord Collins MR, Sterling and Mathew LJJ). The Court of Appeal judgment is reported at 18 TLR 81.

30 It is not without interest that the appellants had the advantage of being represented by HH Asquith QC, before the House of Lords.

of Britain eventually convinced the House of Lords that, despite his long residence here, he lacked the intention to acquire a domicile in England. Since Mr Winans had not acquired a domicile in England he remained domiciled in Baltimore.

To reach this conclusion, it was necessary for the court to examine in detail the life of the deceased and to draw the appropriate inferences. The same chronological approach is deployed in all the decided cases.

That strong evidence is required to prove the abandonment of a domicile of origin, and that the domicile of origin is retained until a domicile of choice is acquired is illustrated by the House of Lords judgments in *Bell v Kennedy*[31] and *Ramsay v Liverpool Royal Infirmary*.[32] In both cases, the question arose as to where an individual was domiciled at the time of death; in the case of *Bell v Kennedy*,[33] the facts were as follows: Mr Bell was born in Jamaica of Scottish parents. Educated in Scotland he returned to Jamaica where he married. In 1837, he left Jamaica and went to live with his mother in law while deciding whether to live in Scotland, England or the South of France. When his wife died in September 1838, the question arose as to where he was domiciled. The House of Lords overruled the Court of Session and decided that he retained his domicile of origin in Jamaica.

The case illustrates that to acquire a domicile of choice it is necessary to produce unequivocal evidence of both the facts of residence and the intention to permanently reside. As Lord Westbury[34] observed, the *propositus* was resident in Scotland without the *animus manendi*, so he still retained his domicile of origin.[35]

That clear evidence is required to show that the domicile of origin has been exchanged for a domicile of choice is afforded by the later House of Lords case of *Ramsay v Liverpool Royal Infirmary*.[36] As in the earlier case of *Winans*,[37] the question for the House of Lords was the domicile of the deceased at the time of death. The facts of Ramsay were as follows: George Bowie was born in Scotland and worked for a time as a commercial traveller in Glasgow. He gave up work in 1882 and decided in 1892 to live in Liverpool, where his brother and sister were resident. He lived in Liverpool for 36 years until his death in 1927 at the age of 82. The holograph will[38] that he left at his

---

31 (1868) LR 1 Sc & Div 307; 6 Macq 69; as with the later case of *Udny v Udny* (1869) LR 1 Sc & Div 441, both concerned Scotsmen travelling abroad.

32 [1930] AC 588.

33 (1868) LR 1 Sc & Div 307.

34 *Bell v Kennedy* (1868) LR 1 Sc & Div 307 (Lords Westbury, Cairns, Cranworth, Chelmsford and Colonsay).

35 *Ibid, per* Lord Westbury.

36 [1930] AC 588.

37 *Winans v AG* [1904] AC 287.

38 The will was signed but the signature not attested: see the Wills Act 1837.

death would be valid under Scottish law but not under English law. It therefore became necessary to determine his domicile at the date of death. If the will was upheld, the residue of his estate would have been shared among four charities, of which the Liverpool Royal Infirmary was one; if invalid, the residue would pass to those entitled upon his intestacy.

A unanimous House of Lords,[39] in upholding the Court of Session, decided that, despite his long stay in England, George Bowie had not acquired a domicile of choice, as he would have moved from England if those members of his family with whom he was living had decided to move. So that, although the fact of long residence had been established, it could not be shown that there was an intention to acquire another domicile.[40] The rationale of the House of Lords in *Ramsay* had been expressed earlier in succinct form by Cooton LJ in *Re Marrett*,[41] where the learned judge observed:

> The law as I understand it is this, that the domicile of origin clings to a man unless he has acquired a domicile of choice by residence in another place with an intention of making it his permanent place of residence.

The cases of *Winans*[42] and *Ramsay*[43] illustrate that long residence by itself will not be sufficient to acquire a domicile of choice. Long residence may go some way to demonstrating the *factum* but it will still be necessary to show the *animus*.

In examining the questions of *animus*, one writer[44] has argued that the case law reveals four common evidentiary situations:

(a) an intention to reside for a definite period, for example, a year and then leave;

(b) an intention to reside in a territory until a definite purpose is achieved, for example, to leave when a particular project is completed;

(c) an intention to reside in a country for an indefinite period unless and until a particular event happens, for example, relative dies; and

(d) an intention to reside forever regardless of domestic or external events.

It is quite clear that the first two forms[45] are insufficient to acquire a domicile of choice. But, *Winans*[46] and *Ramsay*[47] represent examples of class (c) and

---

39 Lords Thankerton, Buckmaster, Dunedin, Macmillan.

40 Or, as expressed by Scarman J, in *Re Fuld's Estate (No 3)* [1968] P 675: 'What has to be proved is no mere inclination arising from a passing fancy or thrust upon a man by an external but temporary pressure, but an intention freely formed to reside in a territory indefinitely.'

41 (1887) 36 Ch D 400, CA.

42 *Winans v AG* [1904] AC 287 (period of 36 years).

43 *Ramsay v Liverpool Royal Infirmary* [1930] AC 588 (period of 35 years).

44 See articles by Pollack QC (1933) 50 SALJ 449; (1934) 51 SALJ 1.

45 *AG v Rowe* (1862) 1 H & C 31; *Quershi v Quershi* [1972] Fam 173.

46 *Winans v AG* [1904] AC 287.

47 *Ramsay v Liverpool Royal Infirmary* [1930] AC 588.

would appear to indicate that such a state of conditional *animus* is not sufficient. It might be argued that the cases are unsatisfactory as they place considerable emphasis on the desires of an individual rather than what he proposed to do. Thus, in *Bell*,[48] *Winans*[49] and *Ramsay*,[50] while it was possible to produce evidence of the fact of residence, the difficulty arose as to the inferences to be drawn as to intention. The fact that individual judges might draw different inferences is particularly well illustrated by *Winans*,[51] where Lord Lindley,[52] in dissenting, observed of Mr Winans:

> He had one and only one home, and that was in this country; and long before he died I am satisfied that he had given upon all serious idea of returning to his native country.

Certainly, both George Bowie and William Winans could properly be said to be habitually resident in England and that may be taken to show the superiority of that test for the personal law. In defence of the judgment in *Ramsay*,[53] it should be noted that the court may well have been motivated by a desire to save the will and there was no other way of achieving that.

That the emphasis is upon the *animus* rather than the duration of residence has the consequence that even a brief residence may be sufficient to acquire a domicile of choice. This can be illustrated by a case arising in West Virginia where the court was confronted with the problem of a very brief residence. The facts of *White v Tennant*[54] were unremarkable: a family were moving home. The man abandoned his home in State A and moved about half a mile to his new home in State B. Having put their belongings in the new house, the family returned to their old State as the new house was not ready to inhabit. When the man died during the night the court decided that he died domiciled in State B and not State A.

It should be remembered that each State in the USA represents a separate country for the purposes of the conflict of laws. In *White v Tennant*,[55] the evidence as to the *animus* was clear, unlike *Bell v Kennedy*,[56] where Mr Bell was unsure whether he wished to live in Scotland, England or the South of

---

48 *Bell v Kennedy* (1868) 1 Sc & Div 307.

49 *Winans v AG* [1904] AC 287.

50 *Ramsay v Liverpool Royal Infirmary* [1930] AC 588.

51 In *Winans*, a majority in the House of Lords set aside the judgment of a strong Court of Appeal (Lord Collins MR, Mathew and Stirling LJJ) which had itself upheld the judgment of the lower court (Kennedy and Phillimore JJ); see (1904) 83 LT 634; 85 LT 508.

52 There were few 19th century judges as familiar with continental legal thought in private international law than Nathaniel Lindley (1828–1921), who was an enthusiast for Savigny and as a young man had translated Thibaut's *System des Pandektenrechts* (1855).

53 *Ramsay v Liverpool Royal Infirmary* [1930] AC 588.

54 (1888) 31 W Va 790.

55 *Ibid*.

56 (1868) LR 1 Sc & Div 307.

France. The fact that a brief residence may be sufficient to establish a new domicile is important if domicile has to be established shortly after an individual has arrived in a new country in which he intends to live permanently. Suppose, for example, that a couple intend to marry and set up their home in a country whose law would regard that marriage as valid, whereas one or both of them have a pre-nuptial domicile which does not allow marriage between them because, say, they are within the prohibited degrees. If they are regarded as domiciled in the new country at the time of the marriage, the marriage will be regarded as valid by the English conflict of laws; if not, it will not.

Although the considerable volume of case law makes it unwise to assert too general a proposition and much must depend on inferences drawn from proven facts, a modern summary by Scarman J in *Re Fuld's Estate (No 3)*[57] is worthy of consideration. After reviewing the prior case law the learned judge advanced three propositions:

(a) the domicile of origin adheres – unless displaced by satisfactory evidence of the acquisition and continuance of the domicile of choice;

(b) domicile of choice is acquired only if it be affirmatively shown that the propositus is resident within a territory, subject to a distinctive legal system, with the intention formed independently of external pressures of residing there indefinitely; and

(c) it follows that, though a man has left the territory of his domicile of origin with the intention of never returning, though he be resident in a new territory, yet if his mind be not made up or evidence be lacking or unsatisfactory as to what is his state of mind, his domicile of origin adheres.[58]

Where residence is contingent, the intention to remain permanently will not be negatived on that basis that the individual would leave the country if a vague and unlikely event were to happen,[59] such as the making of an improbable fortune.[60] However, a husband's intention to return home to his country of origin if his wife predeceased him was enough to prevent the acquisition of a domicile in England.[61]

What happens when a person abandons one domicile without acquiring another? Courts in England and the USA have come up with different

---

57 [1968] P 675; [1965] 3 All ER 776 (a case containing an interesting review of the previous case law by Scarman J, as he then was).

58 *Re Fuld's Estate (No 3)* [1968] P 675; [1965] 3 All ER 776.

59 *Ibid*; broadly accepted by the Court of Appeal in *Buswell v IRC* [1974] 2 All ER 520; 1 WLR 1631.

60 *Doucet v Geohegan* (1878) 9 Ch D 441; 26 WR 825.

61 *IRC v Bullock* [1976] 3 All ER 353; 1 WLR 1178, CA (a man with a domicile of origin in Nova Scotia, Canada, lived in England with his wife and children).

solutions. Within the USA jurisdictions, the practice is to regard the abandoned domicile as continuing until a new domicile is acquired.[62] One can over exaggerate the evils of setting up a model of a refugee fleeing persecution in his own country who, before he finds a new home, will be regarded as having a personal law related to the country he has struggled to leave. The solution is artificial, although at the time of writing the Law Commission is recommending its adoption into English law. The English solution is to allow the old domicile to be abandoned but to fill the gap with a special construct – the revival of the domicile of origin. This will be dealt with below.

Particular cases

In most cases, the general principles can be applied sensibly to the facts in dispute. However, such principles do assume that the individual is free to choose his residence. Indeed, such a principle was expressly asserted in *Udny v Udny*.[63] However, difficult cases do arise where the freedom of the individual is subject to constraints. It is sensible to examine these categories in turn.

The terminally ill

In those cases where a person has been diagnosed as seriously or terminally ill and then travels to a foreign country to live out the remainder of his days, either to seek a better climate or to be close to relatives, it is open to argument that such a choice is not truly free and that it would be revolting to common sense and humanity to argue that there had been a change of domicile.[64]

In other cases, where an individual simply moves abroad in order to seek a more agreeable climate, then the normal principles will be applied. In each case, the distinction will be between the individual who is exercising a preference, in which case a domicile may be acquired, and those cases where the individual is acting under a necessity; in the latter case, the original domicile will not be lost. The distinction was alluded to in *Hoskins v Mathews*,[65] where the court held that an Englishman who spent eight months a year in Italy to improve his health had acquired a domicile of choice in Italy because he was exercising a preference.

---

62 *Re Jones's Estate* (1921) 192 Iowa 78; 182 NW 227 (Welshman flees to the USA to escape affiliation proceedings but decides to return to Wales after the death of his wife, but dies in the Lusitania; held by the Supreme Court of Iowa to have died domiciled in Iowa).

63 'There must be a residence freely chosen, and not prescribed or dictated by any external necessity such as the duties of office, the demands of creditors, or the relief of illness.' *Udny v Udny* (1869) 1 Sc & Div 441, p 458, *per* Lord Westbury.

64 The phrase being that of Lord Kingsdown in *Moorhouse v Lord* (1863) 10 Cas 272, p 292.

65 (1856) 8 De GM & G 13.

Prisoners

The essence of imprisonment is that the individual is deprived of his personal freedom to move from place to place. In these circumstances, the prisoner will continue to retain the domicile that he possessed before his imprisonment.[66]

Refugees

In such cases, much will depend on the circumstances under which refugee status has been sought. It is sometimes argued that, in such situations, there is a presumption against a change of domicile. In cases of wartime, where the individual has not abandoned the possibility of returning home, then no new domicile will be acquired[67] but, in cases where it is clearly impossible to return home and the refugee intends to stay in the new country, then a new domicile is acquired.[68]

Fugitives from justice

A fugitive from justice may acquire a domicile of choice if it is clear that he intends to establish links with his new country; it is open to argument as to whether the mere flight from[69] justice raises a presumption in favour of the acquisition of a fresh domicile. In certain instances, there may be value in examining whether the individual has remained in a particular country long after he could have returned home in safety.

Where there is evidence that England is being used as a staging post in circumstances where the fugitive may move again[70] to avoid extradition, then a domicile of choice is not acquired.

Invalids

Where a person in indifferent health seeks of his own free will to live abroad for the good of his health, then the exercise of such a preference will normally result in the acquisition of a new domicile, since no element of necessity arises.[71]

---

66 *Burton v Dolben* (1756) 2 Lee 312; *Burton v Fisher* (1828) Milw 183; *Re The Late Emperor Napoleon Bonaparte* (1853) 2 Rob Eccl 606.

67 *Re Lloyd Evans* [1947] Ch 695.

68 *May v May* [1943] 2 All ER 146 (Jewish refugees from Nazi Germany).

69 *Re Martin* [1900] Ch P 211 (where Lindley MR thought that the ability to return home safely was of crucial importance, although this was not an opinion shared by the other members of the court (Vaughan Williams, Rigby LJJ)).

70 *Puttick v AG* [1980] Fam 1; see Schiff [1979] PL 353. For a sequel, see *Astrid Proll v Entry Clearance Officer, Dusseldorf* (1988) 2 CMLR 387.

71 *Hoskins v Mathews* (1856) 8 De GM & G 13.

Diplomats, employees, military forces

The 19th century view[72] was that service and residence abroad by diplomats, employees and service personnel would not normally give rise to a change of domicile because the residence was linked to duties that were intended only to endure for a limited period of time. The recent view, however, is that it is a question of nature and decree and that a soldier on active service abroad may acquire a new domicile if there is evidence that he intends to settle there once he becomes free from his obligation to reside there.[73]

DOMICILE OF ORIGIN

General principles

Every child is accorded a domicile by English law. Of course, the gift is a notional one until a matter arises to make the issue life. This attributed domicile is indelible[74] and remains with the person throughout his life, even if for much of the time or, indeed, always, it is overlaid by another sort of domicile.

The domicile of a legitimate child is the domicile, of whatever sort, his father had at the time of the child's birth. An illegitimate child[75] or a posthumous child takes its domicile of origin from its mother's domicile at the time of its birth but this is somewhat artificial, as the issue of legitimate status may itself depend on domicile.[76] The domicile of origin acts as a fall back:[77] whenever there is no other domicile, it comes to fill the gap. It avoids assuming the continuance of an abandoned domicile. The position is best illustrated by an example.

Suppose, for example, that Mary is born at a time when her father is domiciled in Jamaica, her parents having come to England, intending to return home after making some money. Shortly after Mary's birth, they decide to settle in England. For all her childhood and early adult life, Mary knows

---

72 *AG v Rowe* (1862) 1 H & C 31; *Sharpe v Crispin* (1869) LR 1 P & D 611; *Re Mitchell ex p Cunningham* (1884) 13 QBD 418.

73 *Donaldson v Donaldson* [1949] P 363 (Ormerod J); *Stone v Stone* [1959] 1 All ER 194; [1958] 1 WLR 1287.

74 The tenacity of the domicile of origin is illustrated by cases such as *Aikman v Aikman* (1861) 3 Macq 854; *Moorhouse v Lord* (1863) 10 HLC 272; *Pitt v Pitt* (1864) 4 Macq 627; *Bell v Kennedy* (1868) LR 1 Sc & Div 307; *Huntly v Gaskell* [1906] AC 56.

75 See *Udny v Udny* (1869) LR 1 Sc & Div 441.

76 As in *Re Bischoffsheim* [1948] Ch 79 (Romer J) (where the child was legitimate under the law of the State of New York (the domicile of his parents), but not under English law because the marriage was void for affinity).

77 As in *Bell v Kennedy* (1868) LR 1 Sc & Div 307, 'the domicile of origin adheres until a new domicile is acquired' (*per* Lord Westbury).

only England. Later, she marries an Italian and goes to live in Italy and remains there for the duration of her marriage. On the death of her husband, she decides to return 'home' to England but, on the way, she is killed in a motor accident. Suppose she has not left a will, so that her property will pass to those who are entitled to it according to the intestacy laws of her domicile.

If we trace Mary's domicilary history, we will find that her domicile of origin is Jamaican. During her childhood, she will have domicile dependent on her father, which, on the facts, will be English, as her parents settled in England shortly after her birth. The facts suggest that she abandoned that English domicile when she set up her home with her new husband in Italy and acquired a domicile in her new country. When she left Italy after her husband's death she abandoned her Italian domicile but died before she could establish a new domicile of choice. In the absence of a domicile of choice, her domicile of origin revives to fill the gap. Her intestacy will, therefore, be governed by Jamaican law – the law of a country which she may never have visited.

One can think of even more unsatisfactory scenarios but the point is that although the domicile of origin ensures that everyone has one domicile, of some sort, at all times, the artificiality means that sometimes it is not worth having.

How though should Mary's case be resolved? Would Italian law have been a better solution, albeit that she had left Italy forever? It is not easy to see how one could apply English law for, while England may have been Mary's actual home for many years in the past and may have continued to be her spiritual home throughout her life, England had not been her actual home, perhaps, for decades. There seems no satisfactory solution to this problem, though it is clear that Jamaican law is by far the worst result possible.[78]

It is worth noting that the concept of habitual residence would lead to the same result. It would be necessary to continue an abandoned habitual residence until a new one was established in order to avoid a gap in the personal law which could not otherwise be filled.

The enduring nature of the domicile of origin

The evolving 19th century case law made it clear that the domicile of origin could only be replaced by a domicile of choice and that the onus of demonstrating that it had been displaced was a heavy one.[79] In broad terms,

---

78 If the Law Commission proposals are implemented, Mary would have Italian law applied to her intestacy (Law Commission Report No 168 (1987)).

79 *Winans v AG* [1904] AC 287, 'domicile of origin differs from domicile of choice in that its character is more enduring, its hold stronger, and less easily shaken off' (*per* Lord Macnaghten).

the domicile of origin is fixed at birth and, save in the case of adopted children, cannot be changed.[80] The reason for the strong emphasis on the adhesive quality of the domicile of origin was that the courts were anxious in the 19th century to ensure that Englishmen or Scotsmen venturing abroad did not forfeit their nexus with English law.[81] As has been indicated earlier, the domicile of origin prevailed in the leading cases of *Bell*,[82] *Winans*[83] and *Ramsay*.[84] At this point, it is appropriate to refer to the other leading 19th century case, that of *Udny v Udny*,[85] where the paramount position of the domicile of origin was stressed. The salient facts of *Udny* were as follows: Colonel Udny was born in Leghorn in 1779 (where his father held a consular post) with a Scottish domicile of origin. He joined the Guards in 1797 and acquired a property in London, where he lived with his family until 1844. He then left for France to avoid pressing creditors but did not acquire a domicile of choice. At a later date, he fathered a child and then married the mother. In proceedings before the Scottish courts, the question arose as to whether the child was legitimated *per subsequens matrimonium*. That question depended the domicile of Colonel Udny.

In giving judgment for the House of Lords, Lord Westbury drew attention to the particular nature of the domicile of origin, observing:

It is a settled principle of law that no man shall be without a domicile, and to secure this result the law attributes to every individual, as soon as he is born, the domicile of his father if he be legitimate ... this has been called the domicile of origin and is involuntary.

In considering the particular nature of the domicile of origin, Lord Westbury further noted:

... as the domicile of origin is the creature of law, and independent of the will of the party, it would be inconsistent with the principles, of which it is by law created and ascribed, to suppose that it is capable of being by the act of the party entirely obliterated and extinguished.

In these circumstances, the House of Lords held that, even if Colonel Udny had acquired a domicile of choice in England, he had abandoned it by departing for France and, at that point, his Scottish domicile of origin revived.

---

80 Children Act 1975, s 8, Sched 1; Adoption Act 1976, s 39(1)–(5).

81 There was an assumption that English law was superior to that in other lands; a view that endured into the 20th century: see *The Atlantic Star* [1974] AC 436.

82 *Bell v Kennedy* (1868) LR 1 Sc & Div 307.

83 *Winans v AG* [1904] AC 287.

84 *Ramsay v Liverpool Royal Infirmary* [1930] AC 588.

85 (1869) LR 1 Sc & Div 441.

Revival of the domicile of origin

One of the legacies of the important cases on domicile is that the domicile of origin will be attributed to the *propositus* if one cannot be certain that a domicile of choice has been acquired or equally if the domicile of choice, having been acquired, has been abandoned.[86] In the latter situation, following the principle that no man can be without a domicile, it is said that the domicile of origin revives. The combination of the enduring nature of the domicile of origin and the possibility of its revival does mean that in many cases the *propositus* will be deemed not to have lost his domicile of origin notwithstanding the fact that he may have had little recent contact with the country in question.[87] In these circumstances, it is hardly surprising that, in the leading case, the foreign wanderings of the central characters were not sufficient to deprive them of their domicile. Neither the absence of Colonel Udny from Scotland,[88] nor the travels of Mr Winans,[89] were sufficient to displace the domicile of origin; likewise, the indecision of Mr Bell[90] and the inertia of Mr Bowie both lead to the same result.[91]

In these circumstances, the observations of Balcombe LJ in *Cramer v Cramer*,[92] alluding to the difficult evidentiary burden of proving a change of domicil of origin to a domicile of choice are both sensible and consistent with the decided cases. The adhesive nature of the domicile of origin together with the difficulty of demonstrating the acquisition of a domicile of choice will tend to weigh the scales in favour of the domicile of origin. Indeed, if Megarry J is correct in *Re Flynn*[93] in asserting that a domicile can be lost by departing without an intention to return, then[94] the circumstances in which the domicile of origin revives may be on the increase. Those who criticise the revival of the domicile of origin point to the artificial nature of the exercise and to the fact that the propositus may be attributed a domicile with which he has little if any recent connection. Such critics argue that the position in the USA is to be preferred in that the doctrine of revival of the domicile of origin is rejected and instead the doctrine of persistence of the abandoned domicile is adopted. The operation of this doctrine is illustrated by the case of *Re Jones's Estate*,[95]

---

86 *Udny v Udny* (1869) LR 1 Sc & Div 441.
87 Mr Winans in *Winans v AG* [1904] AC 287.
88 *Udny v Udny* (1869) LR 1 Sc & Div 441.
89 *Winans v AG* [1904] AC 287.
90 *Bell v Kennedy* (1868) LR 1 Sc & Div 307.
91 *Ramsay v Liverpool Royal Infirmary* [1930] AC 588.
92 [1987] 1 FLR 116.
93 [1968] 1 WLR 103, p 113 (a classic judgment).
94 As distinct from the situation where there is positive evidence of an intention not to return; see *IRC v Duchess of Portland* [1982] Ch 314.
95 (1921) 192 Iowa 78; 182 NW 227.

where the facts were as follows: Evan Jones was born in Wales in 1850 with an English domicile of origin. In 1883, he left for the USA in order to escape affiliation proceedings. He settled in Iowa where he worked hard, acquired an American wife and considerable property. After the death of his wife, he decided to return to Wales to be with his sister. He left New York, not intending to return, but was drowned when German forces sank the Lusitania. He died intestate. According to English law, his property would pass to his brother and sister but, according to the law of Iowa, it would pass to his illegitimate daughter.

The Supreme Court of Iowa[96] determined that Mr Jones retained his domicile of choice in Iowa until he acquired a new one and therefore he was deemed to have died domiciled in Iowa. It might be argued that the USA position is just as artificial as that pertaining in England. As both doctrines grew up in the 19th century, it is sensible to pay regard to the social background. In England and Scotland, much of the movement of property owners was to acquire better prospects abroad or to serve the Empire; the assumption was that, later in life, the individual would return to live in England. In the USA, on the other hand, the normal pattern of travel was from State to State and normally westward as the Union expanded; the assumption was that the individual would settle in the State where he acquired property. Indeed, not only was the movement within the USA, but much of it was motivated by a desire to acquire land and settle, unlike in the UK, where the assumption was that the individual would return to England to live out the remainder of his days.

It is open to argument that the doctrine of persistence of the last domicile, while itself artificial, is more likely to lead to a decision that is founded upon recent conduct.

DOMICILE OF DEPENDENCE[97]

A dependent person was unable to acquire a domicile of choice by his own act; in general the domicile of such a person is the same as, and will change in accordance with the domicile of the person on whom he is dependent. At common law, there were three categories[98] of persons that were regarded as being subject to a domicile of dependence, namely:

---

96 *Re Jones's Estate* (1921) 192 Iowa 78; 182 NW 227.

97 Wade (1983) 32 ICLQ 1; Carter (1987) 36 ICLQ 713.

98 Not unlike the three categories that gave rise to problems of competence in the law of evidence and capacity to hold land in property law.

(a) married women;

(b) children; and

(c) the mentally disturbed.

At common law, the rationale was that such persons lacked the capacity to acquire a domicile of choice. The law on the subject was changed by the Domicile and Matrimonial Proceedings Act 1973 and these changes will be considered below.

Married women

Prior to 1 January 1974,[99] the rule was that a married woman acquired the domicile of her husband and her domicile would change with that of her husband. The rule was based on the common law principle of the unity of husband and wife;[100] the rule was supported by clear authority in the highest courts. In *Lord Advocate v Jaffrey*,[101] the facts were as follows: a husband and wife were domiciled in Scotland. The husband left to live in Queensland with the consent of his wife. He contracted a bigamous marriage in Queensland. The wife remained in Scotland where she died. Proceedings were brought in Scotland to determine the domicile of the wife. On appeal to the House of Lords, it was ruled that the wife was domiciled in Queensland, even though she had never visited there.

The rule that a wife acquired a domicile of dependence on marriage was so clearly established that only a decree of divorce, not an order of judicial separation, could bring it to an end. The point was illustrated by the Privy Council judgment in *AG for Alberta v Cook*,[102] where the facts were as follows: a wife acquired a decree of judicial separation where she lived; she then presented a petition for divorce. Her husband retained his domicile of origin in Ontario. On appeal to the Privy Council, it was held that the Alberta court had no jurisdiction to hear the divorce petition because jurisdiction was dependent on domicile and the woman remained domiciled in Ontario.

In giving judgment for the Privy Council, Lord Merrivale explained the rationale as being:

> ... the contention that a wife judicially separated from her husband is given choice of a new domicile is contrary to the general principle on which the unity of the domicile of the married pair depends.

---

99 The Domicile and Matrimonial Proceedings Act 1973 became effective on 1 January 1974.

100 Reflected also in the rules concerning the compellability of witnesses.

101 [1921] 1 AC 146.

102 [1926] AC 444.

In the changing world after 1945, such a doctrine was regarded as incompatible with changing views as to the equality of the sexes and was seen as rendering the wife subordinate to her husband. It could also cause problems where a wife sought matrimonial relief and the jurisdiction of the court was founded on domicile. In *Gray v Formosa*,[103] the doctrine was referred to by Lord Denning MR as constituting 'the last barbarous relic of a wife's servitude'[104] and other judicial comment was not uncritical. The dependent domicile of the wife was abolished by s 1(1) of the Domicile and Matrimonial Proceedings Act 1973, which provides:

> ... the domicile of a married woman as at any time after the coming into force of this section [1 January 1974] shall, instead of being the same as her husband's by virtue only of marriage, be ascertained by reference to the same factors as in the case of any other individual capable of having an independent domicile.

The legislation is not retrospective so that, if a problem arises in respect of the domicile of a woman married prior to 1 January 1974, then the common law rules will apply. A woman married prior to 1 January 1974 will continue with her domicile of dependence but as a domicile of choice (if it is not her domicile of origin) until she acquires a new domicile of choice.[105] The matter was raised in the case of *IRC v Duchess of Portland*,[106] where the taxpayer had a domicile of origin in Quebec but married her husband in 1948 and acquired a domicile of origin in England. She continued to make trips to Quebec and sought to argue that in 1974 she had acquired a domicile of choice in Quebec by virtue of a summer visit paid to the province. Nourse J rejected this argument, holding that the effect of s 1(2) was to confer a domicile of choice which could only be lost by ceasing to reside in England without any *animus revertendi*.

Children

The general rule at common law was that, upon birth, a legitimate child acquired the domicile of its father,[107] while an illegitimate child acquired the domicile of its mother.[108] As a dependent domicile, this would change with that of the parent, so that a legitimate child born to a father domiciled in Italy would acquire a domicile of origin and dependence in Italy but, if the father then acquired a domicile of choice in France, the child would then acquire a domicile of dependence in France. The operation of the rules is not without

---

103 [1963] P 259.
104 *Ibid*, p 267.
105 Domicile and Matrimonial Proceedings Act 1973 , s 1 (2).
106 [1982] Ch 314.
107 *Re Duleep Singh* (1890) 6 TLR 385; *Henderson v Henderson* [1967] P 77.
108 *Pottinger v Wrightman* (1817) 3 Mer 67.

difficulty because the question of whether a child is legitimate or not is itself referred to the *lex domicilii* so that, in such circumstance, it will be necessary to come to a conclusion on the validity of the marriage of the parents. In respect of particular cases concerning children, the position can be summarised as follows:

(a) after the mother of an illegitimate child has died, or both parents have, in the case of a legitimate child, the child will continue with the domicile of dependence until he is capable of acquiring an independent domicile;

(b) a child is capable of acquiring an independent domicile when reaching the age of 16 or if he marries under that age;[109]

(c) in cases of a legitimate child whose the parents are living apart and where the child has a home with the mother, then the child will acquire the domicile of the mother and, in such a circumstance, if he lives with the father he will acquire the domicile of the father;[110]

(d) in situations where the father dies, the domicile of the child will normally follow that of the mother, save in those situations where the mother leaves the child with a relative when moving to a new country;[111]

(e) in the case of an adopted child, such a child will treated as if he were the natural child of his adopted parents. Thus, from the date of adoption, if not earlier, he will have the domicile of his parents.[112]

Mental disorder

While direct authority is lacking, it is generally agreed that a person insane or otherwise subject to mental disorder[113] is unable to change his domicile because he lacks the legal capacity to form the requisite intention.[114] It would seem that a person who becomes incapable of managing his own affairs retains the domicile that he had prior to that date. Prior to the age of 16, the domicile of a mentally disordered child can be changed by the conduct of his father.[115] It has been suggested that the statutory powers of the Court of Protection should be extended to allow changes of domicile. The most recent proposal of the Law Commission is to allow the mentally disordered person to acquire a domicile in the country with which he is most clearly connected.

---

109 Domicile and Matrimonial Proceedings Act 1973, s 3.

110 *Ibid*, s 4.

111 *Re Beaumont* [1893] 3 Ch 490.

112 Children Act 1975, s 8; Adoption Act 1976, s 39.

113 Mental Health Act 1983 (replacing the Mental Health Act 1959 and the Mental Health (Amendment) Act 1982).

114 See, generally, *Bempde v Johnstone* (1796) 3 Ves 198; *Urquhart v Butterfield* (1887) 37 Ch Div 357.

115 *Sharpe v Crispin* (1869) LR 1 P & D 611.

THE NATURE OF CORPORATE PERSONALITY

Problems arise in respect of corporations as to:

(a) whether the corporation is present within the jurisdiction;

(b) the precise residence of the company;

(c) the domicile of the corporation; and

(d) the nationality of the corporation.

Clearly, much will depend on the context in which the problem arises but the case law does indicate that the two areas in which these questions are important are those of jurisdiction and liability to taxation.

Presence

Whether a corporation is present in England is a material consideration in determining whether or not proceedings can be served upon it. This matter will be considered later in the context of the jurisdiction of the English court.

Residence

Whether a company is resident in England or not is an important consideration under a number of taxation statutes, since liability to tax is often contingent on a finding that the company is resident in England. The broad rule is that a company will be resident where its centre of control exists, that is, where its seat and direction is located. This rule derives from the case of *Cesena Sulphur Co v Nicholson*,[116] which has itself been approved in numerous subsequent cases.[117] In *Cesena Sulphur Co*, the company had been incorporated under the Companies Act 1862, but conducted all its mining operations at Cesena in Italy. The evidence indicated that none of its products was sent to England. However, the memorandum of association provided that the board of directors should meet in London; the shareholders meetings took place in England. In addition, the dividends were declared in England. On such facts, the court found that the central acts of direction took place in England and, thus, the company was resident in England for the purposes of income tax. In the subsequent case of *De Beers Consolidated Mines Ltd v Howe*,[118] the company was incorporated in South Africa and the whole of its

---

116 (1876) 1 Ex D 428.

117 The leading authorities are: *Cesena Sulphur Co v Nicholson* (1876) 1 Ex D 428; *São Paulo (Brazilian) Rail Co v Carter* [1896] AC 31; *De Beers Consolidated Mines v Howe* [1906] AC 455; *Swedish Central Rail Co Ltd v Thompson* [1925] AC 495; *Eygptian Delta Land and Investment Co v Todd* [1929] AC 1.

118 [1906] AC 455.

revenue was earned there. However, the fact that the directors met in London and, indeed, some resided there was sufficient to hold the company to be resident in England. As Lord Loreburn LC observed: 'the real business is carried on where the central management and control actually abides.' The tenor of this and subsequent cases is to hold that a company resides where its real business is actually carried on, and the real business is carried on where the central control and management abide. This will be the case even if the actual control departs from the provisions of the memorandum and articles of association.[119] Problems will arise where a degree of central control is exercised in more than one country, in which case, it may be necessary to determine in which location substantial control is exercised.[120]

Domicile

While the residence of a company will be determined by where its central control exists, the domicile of a company will normally be the place of its incorporation. This may be important if a question arises as to whether the legal personality of a foreign corporation should be recognised.[121] The law of domicile[122] was designed to apply to individuals and was fully developed before the concept of the separate legal personality of a company was established in English law.[123] Indeed, since a company does not marry and have children, the concept of domicile is not an easy fit. However, it may be necessary to consider questions relating to the constitution of a company or whether it has been dissolved; such questions will be governed by the law of domicile which will be the law of the place of incorporation.[124]

Nationality

In peacetime, the nationality of the corporation is rarely relevant in the English conflict of laws. In general, English law[125] takes the view that the nationality of a company is the country of its incorporation. It is sensible to distinguish this common law approach from those in civil law countries where the nationality of the company will be determined by the real seat of the corporation. The concept of the real seat is a technical one but normally

---

119 *Unit Construction Co Ltd v Bullock (Inspector of Taxes)* [1960] AC 351.
120 *Eygptian Delta Land and Investment Co v Todd* [1929] AC 1.
121 *Henriques v Dutch West India Co* (1728) 2 Ld Raym 1532; 92 ER 494.
122 For matters arising under the Civil Jurisdiction and Judgments Acts 1982 and 1991, see below, Chapter 13.
123 *Salomon v Salomon and Co Ltd* [1897] AC 22.
124 *Gasque v IRC* [1940] 2 KB 80.
125 *Janson v Dreifontein Consolidated Mines Ltd* [1902] AC 484.

means where the board of directors meets and where the general meeting takes place and the administrative centre is located.

REFORM OF THE LAW OF DOMICILE[126]

The technicalities of the current law of domicile make it an unsuitable test for the personal law in modern times.[127] In contested cases the task of establishing the domicile can be an expensive and protracted business as there is nothing in the individual's life which cannot be grist to the judicial mill.

This is an area that has attracted the attention of the Law Commission who produced a Working Paper in 1985[128] and a report in 1987.[129] The Law Commission considered the case for replacing domicile with nationality, not a serious contender, and habitual residence, which was. Habitual residence was rejected because the connection was felt to be too weak for the task to be performed. There was concern, particularly from US business people working in England, that a less stringent test of connection would render them liable to UK taxation, and there was also concern that expatriate workers might lose their status connection with England and have it replaced by, for example, Saudi Arabian law. Thus, in the 1985 Working Paper, although the Law Commission considered the case for replacing domicile with a connecting factor such as nationality or habitual residence, it came down against so doing. The final proposals of the Law Commission were set out in the Report of 1987. In assessing the proposals, it is sensible to bear in mind that criticisms of the present law tend to be threefold, namely:

(a) that it is difficult to determine where an individual is domiciled;

(b) that any litigation depends on a long chronological survey and involves inferences drawn from a life that may be uncertain; and

(c) that either an individual is assigned a domicile with which he has little connection or the domicile of origin is deemed to have revived.

---

126 See Mann (1963) 12 ICLQ 1326; Fawcett (1986) 49 MLR 225; Fentiman (1986) 6 OJLS 353; Carter (1987) 36 ICLQ 713

127 Reforms were recommended in the Private International Law Committee's First Report (Cmnd 9068 1954) and its seventh report (Cmnd 1955, 1963). Domicile Bills introduced in 1958 and 1959 failed to make progress in Parliament due to fears that foreign businessmen would be subject to the full taxation regime of the UK.

128 Law Commission Working Paper No 88 (1985); Scottish Law Commission Consultative Memorandum No 63 (1985).

129 Law Commission Report No 168 (1987); Scottish Law Commission Report No 107 (1987).

In the event, the Law Commission decided upon a substantial reform of the law of domicile and the recommendations were set out in the Report of 1987.[130] In broad terms, the proposals were as follows:

(a) the proposals are based on the premise that mobility is greater in the modern world and this fact alone makes it desirable that it should be easier to acquire a new domicile;

(b) that the concept of domicile should continue and should not be replaced by nationality[131] or habitual residence[132] as a determinant of the personal law;

(c) that the broad principles of the law of domicile should be placed on a statutory basis, but such provisions should not operate retrospectively;

(d) that in all disputes about domicile the normal civil standard of proof on the balance of probabilities should apply;[133]

(e) the particular concept of the domicile of origin should be abolished so that the domicile taken at birth would have no special character;[134]

(f) the concept of the revival of the domicile of origin would be abolished and an adult domicile would continue until another one was acquired;[135]

(g) in respect of children (that is, anyone under 16), the child would be domiciled in the country with which he had the closest connection;

(h) where the child's parents are domiciled in the same country and he or she has a home with either or both of them, then it is presumed, unless the contrary is shown, that the child is most closely connected with that country;

(i) while the child's parents are not domiciled in the same country and the child has a home with one of them but not the other, then it is to be presumed, unless the contrary is demonstrated, that the child is most closely connected with the country in which the parent with whom he or she has a home is domiciled;[136]

(j) an adult who lacks the mental capacity to acquire a domicile should be domiciled in the country with which he is for the time being most closely connected.

The proposals of the Law Commission and the accompanying draft Bill were formally welcomed and the original indication was that legislation was to be

---

130 Law Commission Report No 168 (1987).
131 *Ibid*, paras 3.9–3.11.
132 *Ibid*, paras 3.5–3.8.
133 *Ibid*, para 5.9.
134 *Ibid*, paras 4.21–4.24, 5.23–5.26.
135 *Ibid*, paras 5.23–5.26.
136 *Ibid*, paras 4.12–4.20.

introduced.[137] Taken in the round, the proposals have much in common with reforms introduced in New Zealand[138] and Australia.[139] The proposals would sweep away most of the prior case law and the concepts of domicile of origin and domicile of dependency would disappear. An individual, on attaining the age of 16, would continue with the same domicile but could acquire a domicile in another country if: (a) he is present there; and (b) he intends to settle there for an indefinite period.

The initial enthusiasm of 1991 has given way to caution and, in 1996, the Government announced that it had no present intention to introduce legislation.[140] At present, therefore, the law of domicile continues to be based on the common law principles as modified by the Domicile and Matrimonial Proceedings Act 1973.

NATIONALITY AND HABITUAL RESIDENCE

The above two concepts have been advocated by some as alternatives to domicile as a method to determine the personal law. Some writers favour the replacement of domicile with nationality.

Nationality is now used to determine the personal law in a number of European jurisdictions. Partly, this is a legacy of the rise of nationalism in 19th century Europe and, partly, it is a consequence of the *Code Napoleon*.[141] Nationality[142] was attractive to emerging States anxious or insecure about their own national identity. In the UK, the conflict of laws began to develop in the second third of the 19th century and a high proportion of the early cases concerned the relationship between Scotland and England; in these circumstances, domicile or the permanent home was the appropriate connecting factor. Where the conflict is between two jurisdictions within a single State, then domicile has its attractions. Secondly, the rules relating to nationality were vague at common law and difficulties would have arisen in defining a distinct English nationality within the context of the UK; after the British Nationality Act 1948, the entire subject of nationality was the subject to a considerable degree of political controversy. It was not until clarification in the British Nationality Act 1981 that nationality law was sufficiently

---

137 HC Deb Vol 196 Col 177, 17 October 1991.

138 Domicile Act 1976.

139 *Ibid.*

140 See (1996) *Hansard*, 16 January; see, also, Vaines (1996) 146 NLJ 371.

141 Civil Code (France) (1804), Art 3(1); Austria (1811); Holland (1829); Italy (1865). The Italian jurist Pasquale Mancini (1817–88) is generally thought to have been influential in asserting that nationality rather than domicile should govern questions of status, capacity, family relations and succession.

142 See, generally, Nadelmann (1969) 17 AJCL 418.

contemporary[143] so as to provide a basis for the personal law. Those who advocate nationality argue that it is more certain than domicile, and that it can only be changed by the relevant authorities within a State. The problem is that there is no single UK law and the UK comprises three distinct jurisdictions. It is not surprising that federal or quasi-federal common law States are attracted to the concept of domicile[144] (for example, the USA, Australia and Canada). Since nationality indicates a connection with a State,[145] and domicile indicates a connection with a law district, any attempt in the UK to employ nationality would require legislation similar in content to that in Sched 4 of the Civil Jurisdiction and Judgments Act 1982. Those who oppose nationality as a connecting factor point to the problems posed by cases of multiple nationality, statelessness or, indeed, those difficulties that arise when one State disapproves of the citizenship laws of another State. Having regard to the recent Law Commission reports, it is highly unlikely that any change will be made in this direction.

The concept of 'habitual residence' is a particular favourite of the Hague Conference on Private International Law. The expression appears in a number of international conventions and, not surprisingly, has been adopted in implementing legislation. However, the expression is now widely used in domestic legislation. Difficulties have arisen as to its precise meaning; clearly there is distinction between 'residence' and 'habitual residence', but it is by no means clear that there is a distinction between 'habitual residence' and 'ordinary residence'. It would seem that the word 'habitual' refers to the quality and not the duration of residence. For Lane J in *Cruse v Chittum*[146] 'habitual residence' was 'a regular physical presence which must endure for some time' and was to be distinguished from 'residence' and 'ordinary residence'. Since then, however, the tendency has been to equate 'ordinary residence' and 'habitual residence'.[147]

The House of Lords have ruled that[148] the presence or absence of habitual residence is a question of fact to be determined by all the relevant circumstances. A considerable number of cases have come before the courts in

---

143 One of the particular problems in the UK being the relationship between citizenship and immigration control; as manifested in legislation culminating in the Immigration Act 1971.

144 Although composite States may, indeed, have a concept of domicile for the entire State; see the Divorce Act 1968 (Canada); Family Law Act 1975 (Australia); Domicile Act 1982 (Australia).

145 In strict terms, nationality is a concept of international law while citizenship is a concept of municipal law.

146 *Cruse v Chittum* [1974] 2 All ER 940.

147 *R v Barnet London Borough Council ex p Shah* [1983] 2 AC 309; 1 All ER 226; *Re J (A Minor) (Abduction: Custody Rights)* [1990] 2 AC 562; *V v B (A Minor) (Abduction)* [1991] 1 FLR 266.

148 *Re J (A Minor) (Abduction: Custody Rights)* [1990] 2 AC 562.

respect of the habitual residence of children under the Child Abduction and Custody Act 1985 where the courts have been anxious to ensure that interpretation is not inconsistent with that in other jurisdictions.[149]

The expression 'habitual residence' is now to be found in legislation relating to the recognition of foreign divorces,[150] the formal validity of wills,[151] jurisdiction in divorce[152] and nullity.[153]

---

149 See *Re H (Minors) (Abduction: Acquiesence)* [1997] 2 WLR 653, where the House of Lords pointed out the need for consistency in cases under the Hague Convention on Civil Aspects of International Child Abduction 1980.

150 Family Law Act 1986, s 46(1)(b).

151 Wills Act 1963, s 1.

152 Family Law Act 1996, s 19(2)(b).

153 Domicile and Matrimonial Proceedings Act 1973, s 5(3)(b).

CHAPTER 4

CLASSIFICATION[1]

INTRODUCTION

All legal systems work on the basis of categories in their common need to structure human relations into legally manageable units. However, this common need is not mirrored in common categories or, if the categories are common, their contents are not. When a purely domestic case comes before an English court, the judge will be concerned to ensure that matters are dealt with in logical order. In broad terms, he will be concerned to pose and answer the following:

(a) does the court have jurisdiction over the parties and the cause of action?

(b) has admissible evidence established the basic facts?

(c) can one classify the cause of action by allocating the relevant legal questions disclosed by the facts to the appropriate legal category. For example, is the case about the commission of a tort, the breach of a contract or the infringement of a copyright?

(d) having formulated the correct legal questions, the judge will then be concerned to apply the relevant law as dictated by statute and precedent.

A process similar to steps (a)–(d) is undertaken on a daily basis by judges concerned with domestic litigation. In respect of step (c), the judge will not employ the word 'classify', but, in formulating the precise legal questions this is in fact the task that he is performing.

The question that then arises concerns the extent to which the process of reasoning is different in a case involving a foreign element. It has been clear for over 100 years that the process of classification is important in private international law. However, beyond this broad agreement, there is little common ground.

Before turning to the precise steps in the process, the following preliminary observations need to be made. First, although the topic of classification has attracted considerable literature,[2] there is little agreement as to what is to be classified or how the process should proceed. Secondly,

---

1   On aspects of classification, see Beckett (1934) 15 BYIL 46; Falconbridge (1937) 53 LQR 235; Morris (1945) 61 LQR 340; Cavers (1950) 63 HLR 822; Morris (1951) 64 HLR 881; Inglis (1958) 74 LQR 493; Lipstein [1972] CLJ 67.

2   Noted by Bartin (1897) Clunet 225, partly following the *Matese Marriage* case (1889); *Anton v Bartola* (1891) Clunet 1171; but, noted, also, by Khan (1891) 30 Ihering's Jahrbucher 1.

although there are a considerable number of authorities in which a problem of classification arises, there is little indication that judges have been influenced by the literature. The decided cases indicate that judges proceed on a pragmatic common sense basis without undue reference to the literature or the task of classification. In a case involving a foreign element in an English court, the following process will be central to judicial reasoning:

(a) does the court possess jurisdiction over the parties and in respect of the cause of action?

(b) the judge will then be required to classify the cause of action (sometimes described as initial classification/preliminary classification or classification of the issues). For example, the case may concern the following:

   (1) which law is to apply to a tort committed abroad?

   (2) is a marriage celebrated abroad formally valid?

   (3) should an English court recognise a foreign divorce granted abroad?

   At this stage, the judge is being asked to allocate the relevant legal questions disclosed by the facts to the appropriate legal categories;

(c) the judge will then proceed to identify the appropriate choice of law rule by selecting the appropriate connecting factor on the basis of statute and precedent. For example, in (1), above, the judge will consult the provisions of the Private International Law (Miscellaneous Provisions) Act 1995; in (2), above, the judge will consider those precedents that determine that questions of formal validity are governed by the *lex loci celbrationis*; and in (3), above, the judge will be concerned to consult the Family Law Act 1986.

   Some writers have pointed out that, in certain situations, where a judge selects a connecting factor, then the tribunal may be required to define and interpret the connecting factor by reference to a law other than the internal law. In this sense, one can speak of classification of connecting factors;

(d) by selecting the correct connecting factor, the judge will be able to determine the appropriate *lex causae* and apply it to the facts of the case. In performing this task, the judge will have to select the appropriate rule within the *lex causae*. Some writers argue that this is a case of classification of a rule of law. In performing this task a distinction is drawn between classification of a rule of English law and classification of a rule of foreign law.

It will be apparent that the expression, classification, is used in a variety of contexts. It is proposed to examine each in turn before considering the examples contained in the case law.

CLASSIFICATION AS TO THE CAUSE OF ACTION

When the court has established the essential facts, it will be necessary to engage in the first stage of the process of classification. In a purely domestic case, a tribunal may ask itself the following questions:

(a) was a contract concluded?

(b) if so, was it subsequently breached?

In cases involving a foreign element, it will be similarly necessary to select the correct legal category.

There are a number of theories as to how classification of the cause of action should be undertaken and they will be dealt with below. However, there is little doubt that, in England, initial classification is on the basis of the *lex fori*.[3] In recent years, there have been a number of judicial *dicta* to the effect that, where a foreign element is in issue, then the task of classification should be undertaken in a liberal and sympathetic spirit.[4]

The process of classification of a cause of action may be illustrated by the case of *De Nicols v Curlier*,[5] where the facts were as follows: a Frenchman and Frenchwoman married in Paris without any express agreement as to family property so that, under French law, their property rights would be regulated by the rule of *communaute de biens*. Both parties came to England in 1863 and lived here until the death of the husband in 1897. The husband died domiciled in England, leaving a will that failed to recognise the wife's rights under the doctrine of community of property. The widow took proceedings in England to recover her share under the doctrine.

Under English private international law, such proprietary rights are governed by the matrimonial domicile of the parties, save in cases where there is a contract, express or implied, prior to the marriage. So, the point of classification was to determine whether the action of the widow was testamentary, in which case, it would be governed by English law, or whether the claim was contractual, in which case, the the suit would be governed by French law. In finding for the widow and overruling the Court of Appeal, the House of Lords found that the claim of the widow was based on an implied contract arising at the time of the marriage and unaffected by the subsequent change of domicile.[6]

---

3   See the Private International Law (Miscellaneous Provisions) Act 1995, s 9 (2), which reads: 'The characterisation for the purposes of private international law of issues arising in a claim as issues relating to tort or delict is a matter for the courts of the forum.'

4   *G & H Montagne GmbH v Irvani* [1990] 1 WLR 667.

5   [1900] AC 20, HL; [1898] 2 Ch 60, CA; 1 Ch 403 (Kekewich J).

6   The Court of Appeal had considered themselves bound by the previous House of Lords case of *Lashley v Hog* (1804) 4 Pat 581; an interesting feature of the case is that AV Dicey, QC appeared for one of the parties, but did not cite his own textbook to the court.

The willingness of the courts to adopt a liberal approach to classification is particularly noticeable in the area of property law. In cases of private international law, it has been the policy of the courts not to apply the distinction between real property and personal property that pertains in the domestic system, but to follow the practice in continental jurisdictions and differentiate between movable and immovable property. As Farwell LJ observed, in *Re Hoyles*:[7]

> The division into movable and immovable is only called into operation here when the English courts have to determine rights between domiciled Englishmen and persons domiciled in countries which do not adopt our division into real and personal property. In such cases, out of international comity and in order to arrive at a common basis on which to determine questions between the inhabitants of two countries living under different systems of jurisprudence, our courts recognise and act on a division otherwise unknown to our law into movable and immovable.

An example of such flexibility is afforded by the case of *Re Berchtold*,[8] where an individual dying intestate abroad but leaving property held on trust for sale in England was held to have left immovable property and, thus, not to be affected by the operation of the then equitable doctrine of conversion.[9]

CLASSIFICATION OF CONNECTING FACTORS

Problems may arise as to the correct definition and interpretation of connecting factors. In many cases, no difficulty arises.[10] If, for example, the appropriate connecting factor is the *lex loci celebrationis*,[11] then the judge simply has to identify the appropriate jurisdiction on the basis of the available evidence. In other situations, the problem will be more complex as, for example, when the judge is not only obliged to select a connecting factor but to define it by reference to foreign law. In the limited situations in which nationality is a connecting factor, the tribunal will be obliged to determine and interpret nationality by reference to foreign law.[12]

---

7 [1911] 1 Ch 179 (Farwell, Fletcher Moulton LJJ and Cozens Hardy MR).

8 [1923] 1 Ch 192 (Russell J).

9 But, see, now, the Trusts of Land and Appointment of Trustees Act 1996; Oakley [1996] Conv 401; Hopkins [1996] Conv 411; Pettit (1997) 113 LQR 207.

10 Unless, perhaps, it is a question of domicile at common law, in which case, the court is required to consider a mass of earlier case law. See Chapter 3.

11 In respect of questions concerning the formal validity of marriage, see *Scrimshire v Scrimshire* (1752) 2 Hag Con 395.

12 Within public international law, it is probably the case that it is for each State to determine its own rules of citizenship, but whether that nationality is recognised on the international plane may give rise to problems as to whether a genuine link exists between the individual and the State. See the *Nottebohm* case (*Liechtenstein v Guatemala* [1955] ICJ 4).

In respect of connecting factors, it is important to be aware of the law by which the connecting factor is to be defined. At common law, a person domiciled in England could acquire a domicile of choice in France without complying with the requirements previously required by French law for the acquisition of a French domicile.[13]

However, in some circumstances, the concept of domicile is to be defined by a foreign law. Under the terms of the European Convention on Jurisdiction and the Enforcement of Judgments in Civil and Commercial Matters 1968,[14] the question of whether an individual is domiciled in another Contracting State may be a question required to be determined by the law of that other Contracting State.

Another example arises under the Family Law Act 1986. Under the terms of s 46,[15] in considering questions as to whether an individual was domiciled in a particular jurisdiction for the purpose of the recognition of divorces, the court must regard him as so domiciled if he be domiciled in that country according to the law of that country.

Although some writers refer to classification of connecting factors, it is strongly arguable that the expression, classification, is not the correct term to apply to this aspect of the problem. What is in issue here is whether, having selected a connecting factor, that connecting factor should be defined under the terms of the *lex fori*[16] or by virtue of some other law.

CLASSIFICATION OF A RULE OF LAW

As indicated earlier, once the main category has been identified, the appropriate connecting factor has to be selected in order to determine the choice of law. At this stage, there is no doubt that a second process of classification requires to be undertaken.[17] The case law indicates that a distinction has to be drawn between classification of a rule of English law and classification of a rule of foreign law. However, the decided authorities do not

---

13 *Collier v Rivaz* (1841) 2 Curt 855; *Bremer v Freeman* (1857) 10 Moo PC 306; *Hamilton v Dallas* (1875) 1 Ch D 257; *Re Annesley* [1926] Ch 692. The problem was more pronounced in the years prior to 1927, when French law required a person seeking domicile to obtain the authorisation of the French Government.

14 The Brussels Convention on Jurisdiction and the Enforcement of Judgments in Civil and Commercial Matters 1968, Art 52(2) reads: 'If a party is not domiciled in the State whose courts are seized of the matter, then, in order to determine whether the party is domiciled in another Contracting State, the court shall apply the law of that State.'

15 See the Family Law Act 1986, s 46(1)–(5), replacing earlier provisions in the Recognition of Divorces and Legal Separations Act 1971.

16 As was, indeed, the case with questions of domicile at common law.

17 This would actually be the third instance if one includes classification of connecting factors, so that the sequence will be: (a) issues/cause of action; (b) connecting factors; and (c) rule of law.

exhibit a consistent approach and it is necessary to examine each aspect. It should be borne in mind that a single case may give rise to problems in respect of both English law and foreign law.

Classification of a rule of English law

That a task of classification of the rules of English law may be required is illustrated by the facts of the case of *Leroux v Brown*;[18] in short form, the facts were as follows: an oral agreement had been made in France, whereby the defendant agreed to employ the plaintiff for a period of more than one year. The contract was governed by French law and was valid under that law. The plaintiff sued the defendant in England for breach of contract. The defendant pleaded non-compliance with s 4 of the Statute of Frauds 1677.

The court was therefore required to consider the operative statutory provision. If it were classified as a procedural rule of the *lex fori*,[19] it would constitute a good defence; if it were classified as a substantive provision, then not being a rule of the *lex causae* it would be ineffective. Maule J considered the rule to be procedural and, thus, capable of constituting a good defence.[20] The court approached the matter without any proper reference as to whether the Statute of Frauds 1677 was simply a rule of internal law or whether it could be applied even in cases concerning a foreign element. No attempt was made in *Leroux*[21] to consider the policy behind the legislation.

The purpose of private international law is to give effect as far as possible to rights acquired under foreign legal systems. In *Leroux*, the contract was valid by French law; a judgment obtained in France could have been recognised and enforced in England. The willingness to classify rules as procedural has the effect of restricting foreign legal rights. Clearly, in *Leroux*, the classification of a rule of English law as one of procedure rather than substance had the effect of restricting the enforcement of rights valid under another legal system.

---

18 (1852) 12 CB 801 (Maule J).

19 For later criticism, see *Williams v Wheeler* (1860) 8 CBNS 299; *Gibson v Holland* (1865) LR 1 CP 1.

20 The relevant provisions of the Statute of Frauds 1677 in respect of land were re-enacted in the Law of Property Act 1925, s 40, which was itself replaced by the Law of Property (Miscellaneous Provisions) Act 1989. See Pettit [1989] Conv 431; Annand (1989) 105 LQR 553. The provisions of s 4 relating to other contracts and s 17 of the Statute of Frauds 1677 (which had become s 4 of the Sale of Goods Act 1893) were repealed by the Law Reform (Enforcement of Contracts) Act 1954. The long term effect of *Leroux v Brown* (1852) 12 CB 801 in the domestic law of contract was that non-compliance with s 4 of the Statute of Frauds 1677 rendered a contract unenforceable, not void *ab initio*.

21 *Leroux v Brown* (1852) 12 CB 801 (Maule J).

There have been a number of cases concerning property law where it has been necessary to determine the nature of a rule of English law. Thus, in *Re Priest*,[22] the court was required to determine whether the rule in respect of gifts to attesting witnesses was a matter of form or essential validity, while, in the subsequent case of *Re Cohn*,[23] Uthwatt J was required to determine whether s 184 of the Law of Property Act 1925 created a rule of substance or procedure.

Classification of a rule of foreign law

There will be a considerable number of situations in which a rule of foreign law arises and needs to be classified. It may be that the English court has arrived at the rule of foreign law by the process indicated earlier in the chapter or it simply may be the case that the rule of foreign law arose in the course of oral argument. The case law indicates that the subject of classification of foreign law is an important topic even if the phrase classification appears nowhere in the judgments. It is proposed to examine a number of situations in turn.

The requirement of parental consent

Examples of the classification of foreign law have arisen in cases concerning the obtaining of foreign consent to marry. In the 19th century, the French Civil Code contained more extensive requirements in respect of parental consent than English law; thus, there was a strong temptation for French citizens to marry in England and then return to France. One such case was *Simonin v Mallac*,[24] where the facts were as follows:

Two domiciled French persons married in London and returned to Paris next day. The wife subsequently petitioned an English court for a decree of nullity on grounds of the absence of parental consent. Although the parties had attained age of majority under Art 148 of the *Code Napoleon*, they had not complied with the requirements as to prior parental advice under Arts 152 and 152.

After considering the content of the operative articles of the French Civil Code, Cresswell J concluded that the rule requiring parental consent was one of formality and, thus, governed by the *lex loci contractus* rather than the *lex domicilii*. Since the requirements of the *lex loci contractus* had been satisfied then the marriage was valid. Thus, the judgment in *Simonin* depended on

---

22 [1944] Ch 58; discussed (1944) 60 LQR 114; (1945) 61 LQR 124; (1946) 62 LQR 172; (1946) 7 MLR 238.

23 [1945] 1 Ch 5; Morris (1945) 61 LQR 340.

24 (1860) 2 Sw & Tr 67.

classifying the operative provisions of the French Civil Code. In the context of parental consent, a more controversial example arose in the case of *Ogden v Ogden*,[25] where the facts were as follows: a domiciled Frenchman, aged 19, married a domiciled Englishwoman without obtaining the consent of his father as required by Art 148[26] of the French Civil Code. The husband, having returned to France, obtained a decree of nullity in a French court. The wife subsequently went through a ceremony of marriage in England with a domiciled Englishman. In the action before the courts, the Englishman petitioned for a decree of nullity on the ground that the respondent was still validly married.

Clearly, in such a case, a question arises as to the correct classification of Art 148 of the French Civil Code. Manifestly, the rule governed capacity but, if capacity to marry was classified as a matter of essential validity, then the marriage would be void under the *lex domicilii*. However, the Court of Appeal considered that the provision pertained to formality and, as such, the question fell to be determined by the *lex loci contractus*. Since the *lex loci contractus* was English law, the original marriage was valid and the later marriage bigamous. In *Ogden*, it was classification of the rule of foreign law that determined the eventual outcome.[27]

Bona vacantia

An interesting example of a foreign rule of law being classified arose in the case of *Re Maldonado's Estate*,[28] where the relevant facts were:[29] a widow died intestate and domiciled in Spain with no ascendant, descendant or collateral relatives. The English estate comprised securities of £26,000 deposited in a London Bank. The Republic of Spain brought proceedings in the High Court to obtain a grant of administration and to claim ownership of the monies.

The English choice of law rule held that intestate succession to movable property must be governed by Spanish law as the *lex domicilii*. The relevant provision of the Spanish Civil Code provided that 'the State shall inherit'.[30]

The problem that arose was whether the provision should be classified as the State taking as *ultimus heres* or by virtue of a *jus regale*. If the State were to

---

25 [1907] P 107 (Bargrave Deane J); affirmed [1908] P 46, CA (Gorrell Barnes P, Cozens Hardy MR and Kennedy LJ).

26 Art 148 then read: 'The son who has not attained the full age of 25 years, the daughter who has not attained the full age of 21 years, cannot contract marriage without the consent of their father and mother ...'

27 For the distinction between matters of formal validity and essential validity, see the discussion in Chapter 18.

28 [1954] P 223; [1953] 2 All ER 300, CA (Barnard J).

29 See the interesting article by Lipstein [1954] CLJ 22, to which the author is indebted.

30 Spanish Civil Code 1889, Art 956; see, also, the German Civil Code 1900, Art 466.

take by virtue of a *jus regale*, then ownerless movable property in England would pass to the crown as *bona vacantia*.[31] It was argued on behalf of the Crown[32] that there could be no succession where there was no personal *nexus* with the deceased. This argument was rejected by Barnard J and the Court of Appeal,[33] who ruled that, following the reception of expert evidence on Spanish law, it was for the *lex domicilii* to determine the correct classification of the provision contained in Art 956. Since Spanish law would classify the provision as relating to succession by *ultimus heres*, then those assets passed to the Spanish State. The Court of Appeal, in upholding the earlier ruling of Barnard J, agreed that the meaning and nature of the term 'successor' was to be determined by Spanish law. As Morris LJ observed, 'the substance of the matter is that by the law to which reference is made, the property in England is to pass to an heir, that heir being the State of Spain'. Although the expression does not appear anywhere in the judgments, this is an example of classification being undertaken in accordance with the *lex causae*.

Other instances

There is a large number of examples[34] of cases that have come before the English courts where the tribunal has been required to classify a particular rule of foreign law. In normal circumstances, the court should be assisted by expert evidence as to foreign law. An example of such classification arose in *Huntingdon v Attrill*,[35] where the Privy Council was required to determine whether the provisions of a New York statute were penal in nature, while, in the later case of *Re Cohn*,[36] Uthwatt J interpreted Art 20 of the German Civil Code as substantive in content. As will be seen later, the classification adopted will often determine the outcome of the case.

THEORIES AS TO CLASSIFICATION

It is strongly arguable that theories as to classification have had no influence on the development of private international law in England.[37] This is hardly

---

31 *Re Barnett's Trust* [1902] 1 Ch 847 (Kekewich J); *Re Musurus's Estate* [1936] 2 All ER 1666 (Merriman P).

32 By Ungoed Thomas QC, as he then was.

33 Evershed MR, Jenkins and Morris LJJ.

34 In chronological order: *Huntingdon v Attrill* [1893] AC 150; *Re Doetsch* [1896] 2 Ch 836; *Re Martin* [1900] P 211; *Re Wilks* [1935] Ch 645; *Re Priest* [1944] Ch 58; *Re Cohn* [1945] Ch 5; *Apt v Apt* [1948] P 83; *Re Kehr* [1952] Ch 26.

35 *Huntingdon v Attrill* [1893] AC 150.

36 [1945] Ch 5.

37 See Dicey and Morris, *Conflict of Laws* (12th edn, 1993).

surprising given the lack of agreement as to what it is that is to be classified. The recent litigation in the case of *Macmillan Inc v Bishopsgate Investment Trust plc (No 3)*[38] does indeed contain a limited discussion of the problem but the majority in the Court of Appeal were content to approach the case on the basis of identifying the correct choice of law rule in the context of the specific defence pleaded.[39]

Having regard to the limited references to the process of classification, it is hardly surprising that one cannot locate a case in which all of the various theories have been discussed. There are examples in the case law of classification by the *lex fori*[40] and, indeed, such a course has been recently adopted by the legislature.[41] As to classification by the *lex causae*, it is generally accepted that *Re Maldonado's Estate*[42] represents an example of the process and it is arguable that, in *Re Cohn*,[43] the court was seeking to attain the same objective.

The international lawyer, WE Beckett,[44] urged English courts to approach the task of classification in accordance with the principles of analytical jurisprudence and comparative law. The problem is that such an approach may make one wiser as to the differences between legal systems but it provides little guide as to how the task of classification is to be accomplished. Such an approach would be at variance with the pragmatic tradition of the common law and there is no evidence of it having been endorsed in any decided case. In any event, it might require parties to spend more time producing evidence of foreign law which would add to the expense of the litigation.[45]

The Canadian lawyer, JD Falconbridge, sought to draw a distinction between classification by the *lex fori* and classification by the *lex causae*.[46] This approach is sometimes referred to as the *via media*. According to Falconbridge, classification requires a two stage process. The first stage is a preliminary classification by the *lex fori,* in line with its own rules of private international

---

38 [1995] 1 WLR 978 (Millett J); [1996] 1 WLR 387.

39 See Forsyth (1998) 114 LQR 141 for a discussion as to whether the issues of classification should have been more fully explored in the case (the case itself turned on the issue as to whether lending banks could be regarded as *bona fide* purchasers for value, in respect of shares improperly offered as security by the late Robert Maxwell).

40 *Huber v Steiner* (1835) 2 Bing NC 202; *Simonin v Mallac* (1860) 2 Sw & Tr 67; *Ogden v Ogden* [1908] P 46.

41 Private International Law (Miscellaneous Provisions) Act 1995, s 9(2).

42 [1954] P 223; [1953] 2 All ER 300.

43 [1945] Ch 5.

44 Beckett (1934) 15 BYIL 46.

45 It bears repeating that, in the Chancery Division, the judge will be principally concerned to answer questions posed by the parties in the originating summons.

46 Falconbridge (1937) 53 LQR 235, p 537; (1952) 30 Can Bar Rev 103, p 264.

law; thereafter, the appropriate *leges causae* should be classified within their own particular context to determine whether they provide an acceptable resolution of the problem before the court. It is argued that an example of this approach is to be found in *Re Cohn*,[47] although the author was not cited to the court.

A fifth approach to classification is that advocated by Sir Otto Kahn Freund; sometimes alluded to as the 'enlightened *lex fori*'[48] the theory holds that it is unrealistic to expect an internationally agreed set of concepts. Instead, the *lex fori* should develop its own particular concepts for use in conflict cases and, in doing so, should pay regard to classification within other foreign legal systems. It is arguable that this approach is already adopted in England in property law, where the distinction between movable and immovable property is employed rather than the domestic distinction between real and personal property.[49] Another example would be in the law of contract, where the domestic requirement that an agreement should be supported by consideration has been modified in appropriate cases.[50]

---

47 [1945] Ch 5.

48 Kahn Freund, *General Principles of Private International Law* (1976).

49 *In re Hoyles* [1911] 1 Ch 179.

50 *Re Bonacina* [1912] 2 Ch 294; *G & H Montague GmbH v Irvani* [1990] 1 WLR 667, CA.

CHAPTER 5

THE INCIDENTAL QUESTION

WHAT IS AN INCIDENTAL QUESTION?

In any case in private international law, there will be a central question that can only be resolved by reference to a particular foreign law and there may be a difference of opinion as to the appropriate foreign law to resolve that central question. However, in the same case, there may be another question also requiring reference to foreign law that requires to be resolved before the central legal question can be satisfactorily determined. That other legal question is sometimes alluded to as 'the subsidiary question' or 'the preliminary question' but it is more often known to the many writers on the topic as 'the incidental question'.[1]

To illustrate the point, a case might arise in the law of tort in which it was important to determine the appropriate choice of law rule in respect of the tort but the facts also indicated that the victim was working under a contract which contained an exemption clause. Manifestly, questions would arise as to the validity of such a contract and the court would have to determine whether the foreign law that governed the contractual questions was the same as that which applied to the tort. One approach would, of course, simply be to identify the law applicable to the main question and then simply determine that such a *lex causae* governed any other subsidiary question.

Since the problem of the incidental question is concerned with the resolution of questions posed, it is clear that the subject is closely related to the subject of classification. However, it is regarded today as a separate question and the distinction for identifying it as such probably belongs to the German jurist Wilhelm Wengler[2] in the 1930s, notwithstanding the fact that the topic had been discussed in academic circles prior to that date.

Whether an incidental question arises must depend on how the court classifies the questions arising. Suppose an individual testator dies domiciled in Arcadia, leaving movables in England to his wife; the central question here is the succession to movable property and whether it is governed by the law of Arcadia as that of the law of the domicile of the deceased. However, as a matter of logic, there will be a preliminary question as to whether the

---

1 For the literature, see Robertson (1939) 55 LQR 565; Cormack (1941) S Cal L Rev 221; Gotlieb (1955) 33 Can Bar Rev 523; Lysk (1965) 43 Can Bar Rev 363; Webb (1965) 14 ICLQ 659; Schmidt (1968) 17 SSL 91; Hartley (1967) 16 ICLQ 680; Gotlieb (1977) 26 ICLQ 734.

2 (1934) 8 Rabel's Zeitschrift 148.

deceased was married to X and this question may in turn depend on whether X was validly divorced in Blueland from her first husband, Y. In such a case, the central question can only be properly approached by disposing of a number of preliminary questions.[3]

Just as a conflict issue can arise in what appears to be a purely domestic case, so an incidental question can arise in any form of litigation. In a purely domestic case, of course, the incidental question will be subject to the same law as the main issue, so, for example, in a wrongful death case we may have a claim for damages for bereavement[4] from a 'wife' and we may have to ask questions, some easy, some not so, about what that means: whether the right to claim extends to a divorced wife and, if not, whether a decree *nisi* or only a decree absolute will do; whether it extends to a wife living apart from her husband, whether or not under the terms of a judicial separation; whether a wife of a void but putative marriage has a claim; whether cohabitees can be treated as husband and wife for this purpose; and whether the several wives of a valid polygamous marriage are excluded, can claim jointly and share the fixed sum, or can claim separately. These are all issues which are incidental to the main claim, which is the defendant's liability for the death. Of course, each of these issues is capable of arising as the sole question if the defendant's negligence is admitted, no issue of contribution arises and all the other aspects of damage assessment are agreed. Some of these matters, like the validity of a marriage, could raise conflict issues and, if they did, it would be English conflict of laws, not the domestic law of tort, which would be looked to for the answer.

Similar issues can arise in litigation which is undoubtedly conflictual. Suppose the intestate succession is entirely governed by a foreign *lex successionis* and the intestacy rules of that system identify the surviving spouse as the main beneficiary. We may now import some of the issues which were raised in the wrongful death example about who is a wife and what that concept means, with the addition here that we have at least three laws which might have an interest in answering the question and, most importantly, might answer it in different ways.

Suppose the problem is the initial validity of the marriage, a question quite clearly capable of a separate issue from the succession issue, and which could stand alone in, for example, a petition for nullity.

Clearly, the starting point must be the *lex successionis*, for our conflict rules have allocated to that system the main issue – the identification of those entitled to succeed on intestacy. If the 'wife' is clearly included in the

---

3 This, of course, is no different to a domestic case where a judge will seek to pose the relevant legal questions in some form of chronological and logical order; the only difference being that each of the questions will be answered by reference to the same domestic law.

4 Fatal Accidents Act 1976, s 1A (added by the Administration of Justice Act 1982, s 3).

succession, whether or not her marriage to the deceased is valid, if, for example, the foreign law has expressly included long term cohabitees in its definition of surviving spouses, then the problem ceases to exist by definition. If, however, the intestacy rules of the *lex successionis* merely say 'surviving spouse', we are left with a problem. Obviously, the *lex successionis* will have an answer to the question, or at least will have a means of providing one, but other systems have interests too.

The *lex fori* has an interest to the extent that, if the same question arose on its own, or in a different context, a different solution to that provided by the *lex successionis* might be reached. This would be particularly significant where a different solution had already been reached, for example, a marriage legally identical to the one in question had been held to be void. Perhaps even the actual marriage in question had been declared void in nullity proceedings or found so in a different context.

The personal law of the 'wife' has an interest too. She has the status under that law and her *lex domicilii* may also have determined, directly or indirectly, the validity of the marriage.

Now, although we may have a majority view on the matter – say, English law would regard the marriage as void but the *lex successionis* and the personal law would regard it as valid – the majority vote method of conflict adjudication is neither sound in principle nor realistic in practice.

To return to our example cited at the very outset, the central question is whether any question about the validity of the marriage of X or the recognition of the divorce is to be answered by reference to the English or Arcadian rules of private international law.[5]

It is sometimes argued that for a genuine incidental question to arise then three conditions must be fulfilled:

(a) the main question must, by the rules of English private international law, be governed by the law of some foreign country;

(b) a preliminary question must arise involving foreign elements but which is capable of arising in its own right and for which there is a separate conflict rule;

(c) the English rule in private international law for governing the subsidiary question must result in a different outcome from the equivalent conflict rule of the country whose law governs the main question.

In those cases where the problem of the incidental question has been acknowledged, then English courts have generally applied the *lex causae* of the main issue.

---

5   See Morris, *The Conflict of Laws* (4th edn, 1993), p 424.

THE EXPERIENCE OF THE CASE LAW

There are two forms of case where the problem of an incidental question and the question as to which law should apply has arisen. The first is drawn from the area of family law where problems arise in cases of remarriage and the second is drawn from the law of succession. Clearly, each case will depend on how the court classifies the questions and whether a clear distinction is drawn between the principal question and the secondary, or incidental, question. It is proposed to examine each of the subject areas in turn.

Cases concerning remarriage

Problems have arisen in the case law where a person seeks to remarry and questions then arise as to:

(a) capacity to remarry; and

(b) the recognition of any foreign decree of divorce or decree of nullity.

Difficulties have arisen in determining which is the principal question and which is the incidental question. An example is afforded by the Canadian case of *Schwebel v Ungar*,[6] where the facts were as follows: a husband and wife, domiciled in Hungary, decided to emigrate to Israel and en route they acquired an extra judicial divorce (by *ghet*). The parties then proceeded to Israel, where the wife acquired a domicile. The wife then went through a ceremony of marriage in Toronto with a second husband who, at a later date, petitioned the courts of Ontario for a decree of nullity. The original divorce was recognised in Israel but not in Hungary or by the conflicts rule in Ontario.

The main question in the case was the question of the capacity of the wife to remarry and the question of recognition of the divorce was treated as the incidental question. The Supreme Court of Canada in upholding the Court of Appeal of Ontario held that the remarriage was valid because, by the law of the prenuptial domicile, the wife was regarded as single. The court referred the incidental question, the validity of the *ghet*, to the *lex causae* of the main question, namely, the law governing capacity to marry, thus accepting the recognition of the divorce by a subsequently acquired domiciliary law. Thus, the incidental question relating to the validity of the divorce was determined by the *lex causae* of the main question and not by the conflicts rule of the *lex fori*.

A like approach can be discerned in the case of *Padolechia v Padolechia*,[7] where the facts were as follows: H, an Italian national domiciled in Italy, married W in Italy in 1953 but later obtained a divorce in Mexico. The divorce

6   (1964) 48 DLR (2d) 644, Supreme Court of Canada.
7   [1968] P 314 ; [1967] 3 All ER 863 (Simon P).

was not recognised in Italy. H then went to live in Denmark and, while on a one day visit to England, went through a ceremony of marriage with X, who was domiciled in Denmark. At a later date, H petitioned for a decree of nullity, alleging that, at the time of the second ceremony, he was still married to his first wife. It was uncertain whether he had capacity under the law of Denmark.

Simon P, in applying the dual domicile test, held that, since H lacked capacity by his Italian domicile, then the subsequent marriage was void. In giving judgment, the learned judge approved the approach in *Schwebel v Ungar* and indicated that the incidental question as to the validity of the Mexican divorce should be referred to the *lex causae* of the main question. In both *Schwebel v Ungar* and *Padolechia v Padolechia*, the question of capacity to marry was treated as the primary question, while the problem of recognition of a foreign decree was treated as an incidental question. In both cases, the incidental question was determined by the *lex causae* of the main question rather than by the appropriate conflicts rule of the *lex fori*.

A different approach to the problem can be identified in *R v Brentwood Superintendent Registrar of Marriages ex p Arias*:[8] an Italian husband married a Swiss wife and later obtained a divorce form her in Switzerland where they were both domiciled. After the divorce the wife remarried. The husband wished to marry in England a Spanish woman who was domiciled in Switzerland. By Swiss law capacity to marry is governed by the law of the nationality and Italian law did not recognise the divorce. The Registrar refused to allow the ceremony to proceed.

On appeal to the Divisional Court,[9] the refusal of the Registrar was upheld. The main question, the capacity of H to remarry, was governed by the *lex domicilii*, while the incidental question was the recognition of the divorce. The divorce was capable of being recognised in England but it was referred also to Swiss law, where it was not sufficient to enable the husband to remarry. The case is an example of primacy being given to the issue of capacity to remarry and is an example of an incidental question being referred to the *lex causae*.

With legislative reform in the 1970s,[10] the approach of the courts began to change and the incidental question of the validity of the decree began to be treated as if it were the sole question and was not referred to the *lex causae* of the main question, the law governing capacity to marry. This is illustrated by the cases of *Perrini v Perrini*[11] and the subsequent case of *Lawrence v*

---

8   [1968] 2 QB 956.
9   Parker LCJ, Sachs LJ and Bridge J.
10 Recognition of Divorces and Legal Separations Act 1971.
11 [1979] Fam 106; 2 All ER 323.
12 [1985] Fam 106; 1 All ER 506.

Lawrence.[12] The cases indicate that much depends on how the judge arranges the questions; if what was thought to be an incidental question becomes the main question, then any problem disappears. In *Perrini v Perrini*,[13] the facts were as follows: H, domiciled and resident in Italy, married a woman from New Jersey while she was on holiday in Italy.The marriage was never consummated and the wife obtained a decree of nullity in New Jersey. The decree was not recognised in Italy, where H was regarded as validly married. At a later date, H married an Englishwoman in London. Thereafter, H acquired a domicile of choice in England. At a later date, the wife applied for a decree of nullity.

In refusing the decree, Baker P held that, as the New Jersey decree of nullity was recognised in England, then the wife was free to marry him in London, even though the decree of nullity was not recognised by his personal law.

The effect the judgment was to make recognition of the decree rather than capacity to remarry the principal question and this approach was followed in the subsequent case of *Lawrence v Lawrence*,[14] where the facts were: a husband and wife married in Brazil and lived there until 1970. In 1970, the wife obtained a divorce in Nevada, USA. The divorce was not recognised in Brazil. However, the next day, the wife married a second husband in Nevada. The couple then acquired a domicile of choice in England. At a later date, the second husband petitioned for a declaration as to the validity of the second marriage. A first problem arose in that, under the English choice of law rules, the wife did not have capacity under her Brazilian domicile. A second question arose because the Nevada decree was recognised in England.

The approach followed in *Perrini v Perrini* was adopted by Lincoln J, in holding the marriage to be valid. The learned judge regarded the principal issue as the recognition of the foreign decree and held that the marriage was valid by the law of the intended matrimonial home. The wife's lack of capacity under Brazilian law was regarded as a secondary question and not permitted to determine the outcome. The approach of the learned judge in upholding the marriage was supported by the Court of Appeal,[15] who gave a wide variety of reasons for so doing, but all appeared to accept that the issue of recognition should be accorded priority to that of capacity to remarry by the personal law.

Such cases are unlikely to arise in the future in exactly the same form because s 50 of the Family Law Act 1986 requires that, where a divorce is recognised, then any incapacity by the personal law is to be ignored.[16]

---

13 [1979] Fam 106.

14 [1985] Fam 106; 1 All ER 506.

15 Ackner, Cairns and Purchas LJJ.

16 Unlike the Recognition of Divorces and Legal Separations Act 1971, s 7, the provisions of s 50 apply to divorces and nullity decrees, be they domestic or foreign, and to remarriages, wherever celebrated.

Succession

In cases concerning succession, difficulties have arisen when the court is required to determine whether the person entitled under the *lex successionis* is in fact the lawful spouse or legitimate child of the deceased. In such cases,[17] the opinion in most Commonwealth jurisdictions is that the incidental question (the legitimacy of the child or the lawfulness of the marriage) should be governed by the *lex causae* of the main question.

An example is afforded by the case of *Re Johnson*,[18] where the facts were as follows: Mary Johnson, who was born in Malta, died domiciled in Baden, Germany. A question arose as to the distribution of her movable property, which was referred by the law of Baden to the law of her nationality. The court determined that the property was to be distributed according to the law of her domicile of origin.

Having reached the conclusion that Maltese law was the *lex successionis*, Farwell J then referred any question of the legitimation of the deceased *per subsequens matrimonium* to the law that governed the main question.

An example in similar form is afforded by the judgment of the High Court of Australia in *Haque v Haque*, a succession case on appeal from Western Australia, where the court applied the conflicts rule of the *lex successionis* and not that of the *lex fori* to determine the formal validity of a marriage celebrated in Western Australia.

DEPECAGE

Depecage,[19] a French abbatorial term for the process of chopping up or dismembering, suggests that separate parts of a conflict problem may be severed from the whole and referred to different systems of law. If the issues are referred to different systems of law, this is called '*depecage*' by the French and 'picking and choosing' by the Americans.[20]

The starting point, as with the incidental question, is what is seen as the problem as a whole. In some cases, *depecage* simply recognises existing conflict practices, for example, if the whole issue is seen to be the validity of a marriage, the existing conflict rules would draw a distinction between formal validity, which is referable to the *lex loci celebrationis*, and capacity or essential validity, which is referred to the personal law. Similarly, testate succession

---

17 *Re Johnson* [1903] 1 Ch 821; *Haque v Haque* (1962) 108 CLR 230.
18 [1903] 1 Ch 821.
19 From *depecer*, to cut up, to dismember.
20 Reese (1973) 73 Col L Rev 58.

may be referred to one law for the formal validity of the will and another for interpretation, while the essential validity of the dispositions is referable to the *lex domicilii* at death for movables and to the *lex situs* for immovables.

It can be seen from these examples that *depecage* is a real issue or an invented one depending on the way the question is posed. If we ask not 'is this marriage valid?' but 'is this marriage formally valid?', then there is no problem with *depecage*, as we have converted the complex issue into a single one. But, take, for example, a contract. We may accept that capacity and formal validity raise issues distinct from essential or material validity, but can different aspects of essential validity be hived off from the whole and referred to different systems of law? The Rome Convention on the Law Applicable to Contractual Obligations 1980 adopts this view,[21] as indeed does the Hague Convention on the Law Applicable to Trusts and on their Recognition 1986.[22]

Depecage can be seen either as a variant of the incidental question or as a matter of classification. Suppose H injured his wife, W, by careless driving in country X, to which neither of them belong. Their common domicile is in country Y, where there is a prohibition on interspousal suits. Suppose W sues H in the country of injury, X, which allows interspousal actions. Now, although the place of injury may be a perfectly reasonable place in which to litigate, it is likely, in the present case, that W is suing there in order to avoid the interspousal ban she would meet in the country of her, and her husband's, domicile.

What is a court of country X to do? It could, if it was free to, refuse jurisdiction, on the basis that country Y is the *forum conveniens*, but this would be a harsh decision, as the place of injury is not a contrived jurisdiction. If it classifies the ban on interspousal actions as tortious, then it chooses to apply its own rule rather than that of the domicile (assuming the *lex causae* of the tort action is the *lex loci delicti* and not, say, the *lex domicilii*). Equally, if it classifies the interspousal ban as procedural, it thereby rules out the possibility of applying any law other than its own.

It is possible, then, for the question 'can W recover from H?' (actually, his insurers) to be seen to be raising two questions:

(a) can W sue H? This first issue of interspousal immunity could be seen as a procedural matter for the *lex fori*, a status matter for the *lex domicilii*[23] or a tortious matter for the *lex causae* of the tort claim;

---

21 Rome Convention 1980, Arts 3(1), 4 (1).

22 Hague Convention 1986, Art 9.

23 As was, indeed, the case in *Haumschild v Continental Casualty Co* (1959) 7 Wis 2d 130, where the Supreme Court of Wiconsin held that a Wisconsin wife could recover damages from a Wisconsin husband in respect of a tort committed in California, notwithstanding the Californian rule of interspousal immunity.

(b) is H liable to W? This involves two questions: is H guilty of the negligence or other default which caused the injury (clearly a tortious matter)? And is he liable to her? Whatever reasons there may be for interspousal immunity, it can hardly be justified on the basis that W has no right not to be injured by H. This would argue for the separation of the issue from tort and its reference to the law governing status.

As conflict rules become codified, it may be expected that attention will increasingly turn towards the separation of issues, with the object of taking severable issues outside the scope of the codified rules. It may be expected that issues of *depecage* will become more common.

CHAPTER 6

SUBSTANCE AND PROCEDURE

THE DISTINCTION BETWEEN
SUBSTANCE AND PROCEDURE1

When an English court, applying its own conflict rules, has arrived at a foreign law and found it potentially applicable and not objectionable on policy grounds, the task of classification is not necessarily complete. Only rules of foreign law which are substantive[2] will be taken into account; those which are procedural will be disregarded, as it is well established that the *lex fori* exclusively governs procedure.[3] It is obvious that too broad a view of procedure, easier to take in the common law tradition[4] than in others, perhaps, could subvert the whole conflicts enterprise by exaggerating the role of the forum and the English courts need to be wary of this.

An examination of the case law indicates that there have have been difficulties in distinguishing between matters of procedure (governed by the *lex fori*) and matters of substantive law, which may be governed by foreign law. In principle, such questions cannot be divorced from the context in which they arise. As Scarman J observed:[5]

> When is a question one of substantive law? When is a question merely one of evidence or procedure? I attempt no general answer to these questions; for an answer can only be made after an analysis of the specific questions calling for a decision, its legal background and factual content.

In the vast majority of cases, the distinction between substance and procedure will be obvious. The order of process, the manner of the examination of witnesses and the proceedings generally are clearly matters of procedure, whereas rules which directly impose liability or provide a defence on the merits of the case are clearly substantive. The original tendency of judges in the 19th century had been to categorise as much as possible as procedural. As AV Dicey observed, 'English lawyers give the widest possible extension to the

---

1   Szasy (1966) 15 ICLQ 436; Spiro (1969) 18 ICLQ 949.
2   For a recent discussion of the difficulties the distinction can give rise to, see *Boys v Chaplin* [1971] AC 356
3   *British Linen Company v Drummond* (1830) 10 B & C 903; *Huber v Steiner* (1835) 2 Bing NC 202; *Boys v Chaplin* [1971] AC 356.
4   Where the emphasis on the practical rather than the theoretical has meant that much of the substantive law is based upon procedural requirements, eg, the entire nature of the law of tort.
5   *Re Fuld's Estate (No 3)* [1968] P 675, p 695.

meaning of the term 'procedure'.[6] However, it has become clear in recent years that to give a wide extension to procedural law would be to permit claims which do not exist in the *lex causae* or to eliminate rights which still pertain in another jurisdiction. As always the problems, which arise, are those rules which are in the middle, limitation rules, for example, which can be viewed either as extinguishing the right or as barring the remedy,[7] or with provisions which appear to be applicable to all cases.

An illustration is afforded by the case of *Leroux v Brown*,[8] where the facts were as follows: an oral agreement was made in France, whereby the defendant, resident in England, agreed to employ the plaintiff for a period longer than one year. The agreement was valid and enforceable by French law, the law by which it was to be governed. But, it would be unenforceable in England under the terms of the Statute of Frauds 1677.[9] An action brought in England to enforce the contract failed on the ground that the relevant rule was a rule of procedure binding on all litigants.

Maule J considered himself bound by the plain words of the Statute, 'no action shall lie'. This was a clear prohibition on allowing the action to continue in England, irrespective of the contract's total validity by French law. It is worth noting that, had the plaintiff obtained judgment from a French court, there was no basis for refusing to enforce that judgment in England.

If the Statute of Frauds established a procedural rule, then clearly Maule J was correct. If it was a substantive rule, there was no case for its application to defeat the plaintiff's claim, for the contract was neither made in, nor to be performed in, England. The decision has been much criticised and it does seem remarkably wooden. However, if the purpose of the statute was to avoid the occasion of fraud by making litigation depend on written evidence of the agreement (or an act of part performance), then it was clearly applicable to all litigation, including foreign contracts. Such a policy towards the discouragement of fraud, crude, harsh and counterproductive as it was, is a policy matter which is not confined to domestic contracts but would extend to all cases, even those involving foreign contracts, as constituting a procedural bar to action. It should not be supposed that procedural rules cannot embody policy considerations just like substantive rules. The decision that such a rule

---

6 Dicey, *Conflict of Laws* (1st edn, 1896), p 712.

7 Now declared to be substantive – Foreign Limitation Periods Act 1984.

8 (1852) 12 CN (NS) 801.

9 Which required that contracts not to be performed in one year had to be evidenced in writing. The Statute of Frauds 1677, s 4, was eventually repealed by the Law Reform (Enforcement of Contracts) Act 1954. The case of *Leroux v Brown* (1852) 12 CB 801 is not without its element of irony, since recent research has shown that the inspiration for the Statute of Frauds may have been drawn from French law and the Ordonnance sur la Reforme de la Justice 1566; see Rabel (1948) 63 LQR 174.

is procedural is defensible. In contrast, the provision under English law that a collective labour agreement should be conclusively presumed not to be legally enforceable, unless the agreement clearly states that it is,[10] was correctly classified as a rule of English substantive law not applicable to contracts governed by a foreign *lex causae*.[11]

Although a clear distinction between matters of substance and procedure requires some consideration of the context, attempts have been made to define the expression 'the law of procedure', the best known being that of Lush LJ in *Poyser v Minors*:[12]

> The mode of proceeding by which a legal right is enforced, as distinguished from the law which gives or defines the right, and which by means of the proceeding the court is to administer the machinery as distinct from its product.[13]

As private international law is part of English law and as it is trite law that the substantive law has been influenced by questions of procedure, it is also obvious that no logical or scientific distinction can be made between questions of procedure and questions of substance. The matter should be approached pragmatically and there is much force in the point made by WW Cook, where he stated that the line is drawn by asking, 'How far can the court of the forum go in applying the rules taken from the foreign system of law, without unduly hindering or inconveniencing itself?'[14]

It is now necessary to examine a number of particular areas where difficulties have arisen over whether a matter should be classified as substantive or procedural.

STATUTES OF LIMITATION

The experience at common law

Most countries have detailed rules as to the limitation of actions. In the United Kingdom, such legislation has existed for over 400 years and the public policy

---

10   *Monterosso Shipping Co Ltd v International Transport Workers' Federation* [1982] 3 All ER 841, where the Court of Appeal was required to classify the provisions of the Trade Union and Labour Relations Act 1974, s 18.

11   For the earlier treatment of such agreements, see *Ford Motor Company Ltd v Amalgamated Union of Engineering and Foundary Workers* [1969] 2 All ER 481; 1 WLR 339 (Lane J); Industrial Relations Act 1971, s 34 (1).

12   (1881) 7 QBD 329, p 333.

13   *Poyser v Minors* (1881) 7 QBD 329, p 333; see, also, *Re Shoesmith* [1938] 2 KB 637.

14   Cook, *Logical and Legal Bases of the Conflict of Laws* (2nd edn, 1942), p 166.

reasons for legislative restrictions hardly need to be stated.[15] Limitation rules may be in one of two forms: rules that bar the action of the plaintiff are procedural in nature and rules eliminating the legal rights of the plaintiff are viewed as substantive. Most English domestic rules fall within the former category.[16] The tendency of English courts was to categorise as much as possible as procedural and the approach to rules of limitation was no different; this contrasted with the attitude in civil law countries which was to interpret most limitation rules as substantive. By proceeding in this manner, English judges were able to apply the *lex fori* in situations where the foreign rule of limitation was regarded by the lex causae as substantive. This tendency may be traced back to the 19th century, when English judges were not slow to assert the superiority of English law. In respect of foreign statutes of limitation, the approach of English courts had been to categorise them as procedural; it was therefore open to a plaintiff to bring an action in England when it was out of time under the *lex causae*. Thus, from the turn of the century, the English approach was out of line with approach in Europe. An action permitted in the *lex causae* might be barred in England if the limitation period was shorter,[17] while an action barred in the *lex causae* might be brought in England if the limitation period was longer.[18]

The difference between the two approaches was illustrated by the case of *Black Clawson International v Papierwerke Waldhof-Aschaffenburg AG*,[19] where the facts were as follows: the plaintiffs, an English company, brought actions in England and Germany in respect of dishonoured bills of exchange, shortly before the six year limitation period in England was about to expire. The German limitation period was three years and, thus, the claim was struck out by the German trial court. The defendants then argued in the English proceedings that the foreign judgment was a judgment on merits and should be recognised in England for the purpose of s 8 of the Foreign Judgments (Reciprocal Enforcement) Act 1933.

The House of Lords ruled that this defence could not prevail,[20] since the relevant German law of limitation simply barred the remedy and was, thus,

---

15 See 32 Hen VIII c 2 (1540); Limitation Act 1623; Real Property Limitation Act 1833; the main legislation today is the Limitation Act 1980, which replaces the legislation commencing with the Limitation Act 1939 and culminating in the Limitation Amendment Act 1980. The Limitation Act 1980 came into force on 1 May 1981 (s 41(2)).

16 Examples in the Limitation Act 1980 of the latter category would be s 3 (conversion of goods) and s 17 (land), where title is extinguished.

17 *British Linen Company v Drummond* (1830) 10 B & C 903.

18 *Huber v Steiner* (1835) 2 Bing NC 202 (Tindall CJ) (action barred in France, but brought in England); *Harris v Quine* (1869) LR 4 QB 653 (Isle of Man Statute of Limitation held to be procedural only).

19 [1975] AC 591.

20 Though the English proceedings were stayed, pending an appeal to the Federal Supreme Court (*Bundesgerichtshof*).

procedural in nature and so not a decision on merits for the purpose of the Foreign Judgments (Reciprocal Enforcement) Act 1933.[21]

The judgment in the case prompted a reference of the rules on limitation to the Law Commission, which produced two reports recommending the abolition of the common law rules and the substitution of a new statutory framework.[22]

The other impetus for reform was that the UK, as a member of the European Community, intended to ratify the European Convention on the Law Applicable to Contractual Obligations 1980.[23] The Convention had shifted the boundaries between matters of procedure and matters of substance. Certain matters that English courts had treated as procedural in the past would now be determined by the law governing the contract (that is, as a matter of substantive law); among these would be the law governing the assessment of damages,[24] provisions as to presumptions and the burden of proof,[25] and questions relating to the limitations of actions.[26]

The objections to the prior law could be summarised as follows:

(a) the distinction between barring a remedy and extinguishing a right was unsustainable;

(b) a claim valid in country A might be barred in England if the limitation period were shorter;

(c) a claim barred in country A might be brought in England if the limitation period were longer;

(d) it was arguable that such discrepancies might accentuate the tendency towards forum shopping;

(e) such differing outcomes would be at variance with efforts within the European Community to harmonise rules on jurisdiction and choice of law.

For these reasons, Parliament accepted the recommendations of the Law Commission and enacted the Foreign Limitation Periods Act 1984.

---

21 See Jaffey (1975) 38 MLR 385; Carter (1975) 47 BYIL 381.
22 Law Commission Report No 114 (1982), drawing upon the Law Commission Working Paper No 75 (1980).
23 Incorporated into English law by the Contracts (Applicable Law) Act 1990, s 2.
24 Contracts (Applicable Law) Act 1990, s 2, Sched 1, Art 10(1)(c).
25 *Ibid*, s 2, Sched 1, Art 14(1).
26 *Ibid*, s 2, Sched 1, Art 10(1)(a).

The statutory regime[27]

The Foreign Limitation Periods Act 1984[28] gives effect to the prior recommendations of the Law Commission and brings English law broadly into line with European thinking on matters of limitation of actions. The legislation, which applies to both actions and arbitrations, adopts the fundamental principle that the limitation rules of the *lex causae* are to be applied in actions in England.[29] Indeed, to put the matter another way, the law governing the substantive issue will be the law that governs questions of limitation. This general principle is subject to a public policy exception.[30] English rules on limitation are not to apply unless English law is the *lex causae* or one of the two *leges causae*.[31] However, there are some restrictions on the application of foreign limitation rules. It is for English law to determine when a foreign limitation period stops running and proceedings have been commenced;[32] foreign rules as to whether the running of the period is to be suspended by reason of the absence of a party are to be ignored.[33] However, if the foreign law provides for a discretion on the running of the limitation period, then the English court is to exercise it in manner in which it is exercised in comparable cases by the court of that other country.[34]

The legislation preserves the English position that, in cases of delay, equitable remedies may be refused[35] but, in applying these rules to a case in relation to which the law of a country outside England is applicable, the court shall have regard to the provisions of the law that is so applicable.[36] The legislation further provides that, where a foreign court has given judgment on a matter involving limitation, such a judgment shall be treated as a judgment on the merits.[37]

---

27 See Carter (1985) 101 LQR 68.

28 Received royal assent on 24 May 1984.

29 Foreign Limitation Periods Act 1984, s 1(1)(a).

30 *Ibid*, s 2(1), (2); there is, of course, a public policy exclusion within the Rome Convention; see Contracts (Applicable Law) Act 1990, Sched 1, Art 16.

31 Foreign Limitation Periods Act 1984, s 1 (1)(b), (2).

32 *Ibid*, s 1 (3).

33 *Ibid*, s 2(3).

34 *Ibid*, s 1(4).

35 *Partridge v Partridge* [1894] 1 Ch 351, p 359.

36 Foreign Limitation Periods Act 1984, s 4(3).

37 *Ibid*, s 3; thus, reversing *Harris v Quine* (1869) LR 4 QB 653 and limiting the *ratio* of *Black Clawson International v Papierwerke Waldhof Aschaffenburg AG* [1975] AC 591.

THE LAW OF EVIDENCE

It is generally accepted that most questions within the law of evidence are procedural in nature.[38] What is required to be proved, who bears the burden of proof and what is the appropriate standard of proof are all procedural questions and, in principle, are governed by the *lex fori*. In most jurisdictions,[39] there is a close relationship between the law of evidence and the mode of trial, so that to depart from the *lex fori* would cause considerable practical problems for the courts of the forum. The matter was expressed by Lord Brougham[40] with characteristic bluntness, when he observed:

> Whether a witness is competent or not, whether a certain matter requires to be proved by writing or not, whether certain evidence proves a certain fact or not, that is to be determined by the law of the country where the question arises.

It is proposed now to examine a number of specific areas of the law of evidence.

The admissibility of evidence

Questions of admissibility of evidence are determined by the *lex fori*. In principle, evidence inadmissible by the *lex causae* might be admissible by virtue of the *lex fori*.[41] Difficulties can arise in contractual disputes as to whether to admit extrinsic evidence; there is a distinction between evidence admitted to interpret a document and evidence tendered to vary, modify, add or contradict the terms of a written contract. Past case law indicates that this is the principal cause of difficulty.[42] It would seem from the case law that a distinction should be drawn between facts that are relevant and need to be proved, and the evidence by which such facts are to be demonstrated. In general, the former is a matter for the governing law while the latter is a matter for the *lex fori*. An example of the distinction being drawn is afforded by the case of *St Pierre v South American Stores Ltd*,[43] where the facts were as follows:

---

38 *Bain v Whitehaven and Furness Rly* (1850) 3 HLC 1; *Mahadervan v Mahadervan* [1964] P 233; *Re Fuld's Estate (No 3)* [1968] P 675.

39 As was pointed out by James Thayer (1831–1902), the leading historian of the law of evidence, the Anglo-American law of evidence has been considerably influenced by the adversarial system of trial and by the resulting need to limit the evidence received by the jury; see *A Preliminary Treatise on Evidence at Common Law* (1898).

40 *Bain v Whitehaven and Furness Rly* (1850) 3 HLC 1

41 *Bristow v Sequeville* (1850) 5 Exch 275.

42 *The Gaetano and Maria* (1882) 7 PD 137; *St Pierre v South American Stores Ltd* [1936] 1 KB 382; *Korner v Witkowitzer* [1950] 2 KB 128; *Vitkovice v Korner* [1951] AC 869.

43 [1937] 1 All ER 206 (Branson J); 3 All ER 349, CA (Greer, Slesser and Mackinnon LJJ) There had been proceedings in respect of a previous lease reported at *De Beche v South American Stores Ltd and Chilean Stores Ltd* [1935] AC 148; there had been earlier proceedings in respect of jurisdiction, reported as *St Pierre v South American Stores (Gath and Chaves) Ltd* [1936] 1 KB 382.

the plaintiffs, who owned property in Chile, sued the defendants to recover arrears of rent under a lease of premises in Santiago. Amongst the issues arising in the litigation was a question as to the construction of a covenant to pay rent.

Branson J, after concluding that the agreement was governed by Chilean law, observed:

> I have no hesitation in holding that the proper law of the contract is Chilean law. It is my duty, therefore, in ascertaining the rights and duties of the parties under the contract, to apply the canons of construction which would be applied by a Chilean court, and to admit and consider such evidence as a Chilean court would admit and consider, in order to arrive at the intention of the parties.

The decision of the judge to admit evidence of prior correspondence and subsequent documentation was upheld by the Court of Appeal, even though such evidence would fall foul of the parol evidence rule under English law.[44]

Witnesses

Whether a witness is competent or compellable is a question to be determined by the *lex fori*,[45] although where compellability is contingent on ascertaining marital status then reference will have to be made to the *lex causae*.[46]

The burden of proof

The whole basis of the trial process in England depends upon one or other party bearing the *onus probandi*; in normal circumstances, it is the person who initiates the litigation. If the party that bears the *onus probandi* fails to discharge that onus to the appropriate standard, then the judge is obliged to decide the case against him and in favour of the other party, regardless of his own particular view of the matter. While no judge likes to decide a case on the onus of proof, there will be cases where the central facts cannot be established on the evidence and no other course is open to the judge.[47] The weight of authority holds that questions relating to the burden of proof are matters for

---

44 *Prenn v Simmonds* [1971] 1 WLR 1381; *Schuler AG v Wickman Machine Tool Sales* [1974] AC 235. In England, the emphasis is on the parties' manifested intentions, while Chilean law, in the Civil Code, appeared to focus on the actual intention of the parties (Art 1560).

45 *Bain v Whitehaven and Furness Rly* (1850) 3 HLC 1.

46 In criminal cases, the confused law on compellability was replaced by provisions in the Police and Criminal Evidence Act 1984, s 80.

47 *Rhesa Shipping Company SA v Edmunds* [1985] 1 WLR 948, *per* Lord Brandon.

the *lex fori*.[48] The one exception to this general proposition is contained in Art 14 (1) of the Rome Convention on the Law Applicable to Contractual Obligations 1980, which provides that the governing law under the Convention applies to the extent that it contains in the law of contract rules that determine the burden of proof.[49]

Presumptions

The expression, presumption, is used in three senses: presumptions of fact, irrebuttable presumptions of law and rebuttable presumptions of law. It is strongly arguable that presumptions of fact are no more than inferences drawn from facts.[50] Indeed, some have argued that the concept is simply a step in judicial reasoning and that to describe it as a presumption only serves to confuse. We need not concern ourselves with presumptions of fact.

In respect of contractual disputes, Art 14 of the Rome Convention[51] provides that presumptions of law (rebuttable or irrebuttable) shall be applied under the governing law of the contract. With regard to presumptions of law generally, there is authority for the proposition that an irrebuttable proposition of law constitutes a rule of substantive law.[52]

In respect of rebuttable presumptions of law, although there is only limited authority, the accepted view appears to be that presumptions of marriage,[53] legitimacy[54] and resulting trust are provisions of substantive law.

Evidence and other jurisdictions

English law makes provision to enable parties to obtain evidence abroad,[55] although such powers need to be exercised with appropriate sensitivity and discretion.

The UK is a signatory to the Hague Convention on the Taking of Evidence Abroad in Civil and Commercial Matters (1970); ratification was made possible after the enactment of the Evidence (Proceedings in Other Jurisdictions) Act

---

48 *Bain v Whitehaven and Furness Rly* (1850) 3 HLC 1; *The Roberta* (1937) 58 LR 159; *Re Fuld's Estate (No 3)* [1968] P 675.
49 Contracts (Applicable Law) Act 1990, s 2, Sched 1, Art 14(1).
50 Phipson, *Evidence*, 14th edn, para 5–02.
51 Rome Convention on the Law Applicable to Contractual Obligations (1980).
52 *Re Cohn* [1945] Ch 5 (concerning the presumption of survivorship arising under the provisions of the Law of Property Act 1925, s 184).
53 *Mahadervan v Mahadervan* [1964] P 233 (a presumption of formality arising under the law of Ceylon was regarded as a matter of substance).
54 Of less importance since the Family Law Reform Act 1969.
55 Supreme Court Act 1981, s 36; RSC Ord 39 r 1.

1975. The legislation permits a request for the obtaining of evidence by a court abroad[56] and provides that, if the request is in respect of civil proceedings,[57] then the High Court has power to make orders in respect of the examination of witnesses,[58] the production of documents[59] and the inspection of property.[60] The court has discretion whether or not to make an order; it will not assist a 'fishing expedition',[61] but the phrase, civil proceedings, is widely enough defined to permit an action by a government to obtain evidence in respect of suspected tax evasion.[62]

PARTIES

Questions may arise as to whether particular entities are the appropriate parties to a specific legal action. The first aspect concerns who is the appropriate plaintiff; the authorities indicate that a balance has to be struck between the principle that courts seek to give effect to the rights of an individual under foreign law and the equally important principle that municipal rules of procedure should, in general, be applied. The decided cases would seem to indicate that the former principle would apply in cases of receivership,[63] bankruptcy,[64] and the guardianship of the mentally ill.[65]

In normal circumstances, the identity of the plaintiff is not a problem but difficulties can arise when the plaintiff is not the original owner of a particular legal right but simply acquired it from some other person. Therefore, the area of assignment has given rise to a number of problems. Under the terms of s 136 of the Law of Property Act 1925, a statutory assignment is required to comply with certain formalities; if these formalities are complied with, then the assignee can sue the debtor in his own name without joining the original creditor.[66] If, however, the statutory formalities have not been complied with and there is simply an equitable assignment of a legal or equitable chose in action, then the assignee will be required to join the original creditor if he

---

56 Evidence (Proceedings in Other Jurisdictions) Act 1975, s 1.
57 *Ibid*, ss 1, 9.
58 *Ibid*, s 2(2)(a).
59 *Ibid*, s 2(2)(b).
60 *Ibid*, s 2(2)(c).
61 *Re State of Norway's Application (Nos 1 and 2)* [1990] 1 AC 723; Lipstein (1990) 39 ICLQ 120.
62 It will not be viewed as an indirect attempt to enforce a foreign revenue law.
63 *Schemmer v Property Resources Ltd* [1975] Ch 273.
64 *Macaulay v Guarantee Trust Co of New York* (1927) 44 TLR 99.
65 *Didisheim v London and Westminster Bank* [1900] 2 Ch 15.
66 *Re Westerton* [1919] 2 Ch 104.

seeks to enforce the proprietary right.[67] The question that arises is whether the rule that the assignee should join the assignor as co-plaintiff is a rule of substance or procedure. The authorities are divided on this point, with some cases holding that the rule is one of substance,[68] while other authorities tend toward the view that the rule is procedural.[69]

The second problem that arises in respect of the parties concerns the identity of the defendant. Under many systems of municipal law, there are restrictions on suing a particular defendant (D2) until another defendant (D1) has been proceeded against. An example of such restrictions arises in the different municipal laws relating to contracts of suretyship. Once again, the question arises as to whether the rules are procedural or substantive in nature. If the rule of the *lex causae* holds that D2 is under no liability until D1 has been sued, then this is a rule of substance and will be applied in England.[70] If however, the rule of the *lex causae* provides that D2 is liable but that D1 must be sued first, then this is a rule of procedure and will not be enforced in England.[71] Thus, in *Re Doetsch*, where an action was brought in England against the estate of the deceased partner in a Spanish firm, the defendants pleaded a rule of Spanish law – that the assets of the firm must first be exhausted; the defence was rejected as being procedural in nature.[72]

THE NATURE OF THE REMEDY

As a judgment given in any conflict case is a judgment of the forum, it follows that only those remedies which the forum has to offer are available to the successful litigant.

Just as he cannot expect, say, a mode of trial different from that which is used by the forum, so he cannot claim an exotic remedy. More than that, the remedy he obtains is the remedy which is appropriate for his case in the view of the forum, even if the remedy available in a court of the *lex causae* is known to English law. So, a successful litigant will not get an order for specific performance, though a court of the *lex causae* would give him one, if that

---

67   *Performing Right Society Ltd v London Theatre of Varieties Ltd* [1924] AC 1; *Holt v Heatherfield Trust Ltd* [1942] 2 KB 1; *Walter and Sullivan Ltd v J Murphy and Sons Ltd* [1955] 2 QB 584.

68   *Innes v Dunlop* (1800) 8 TR 595; *O'Callaghan v Thomond* (1810) 3 Taunt 82.

69   *Wolf v Oxholm* (1817) 6 M & S 92; *Jeffrey v M'Taggart* (1817) 6 M & S 126; *Barber v Mexican Land Company* (1899) 16 TLR 127.

70   *General Steam Navigation Co v Guillou* (1843) 11 M & W 877; *Bank of Australasia v Harding* (1850) 9 CB 661; *Bullock v Caird* (1875) LR 10 QB 276; *The Mary Moxham* (1876) 1 PD 107 *Re Doetsch* [1896] 2 Ch 896.

71   *General Steam Navigation Co v Guillou* (1843) 11 M & W 877; *Bullock v Caird* (1875) LR 10 QB 276; *Re Doetsch* [1896] 2 Ch 836.

72   *Re Doetsch* [1896] 2 Ch 896.

remedy is not available for his case under English law. By the same token, however, he could obtain an order for specific performance from an English court, even though the *lex causae* would provide him with damages only.

Equitable remedies are, of course, discretionary. So, even if specific performance or injunctive relief was, in general terms, available both by the *lex fori* and by the *lex causae*, it would be for the forum to apply its own principles and to refuse the relief, say, on the basis of the plaintiff's dirty hands, even if, by the *lex causae*, his hands were clean or not grubby enough to be taken into account.[73]

As will be seen below (see Chapter 19), matrimonial orders are entirely within the control of the forum, even when made on the basis of a foreign *lex causae*, and the petitioner cannot claim for their adaptation on the basis of what a court of the *lex causae* might do.

DAMAGES

Most commonly, in a conflict case, the litigant will be seeking damages for the breach of an obligation owed to him under the *lex causae*. The obligation, its breach and the consequent losses complained of will have to be established by the *lex causae* and that law's rules of remoteness of damage will determine whether losses are legally attributable to the breach. In considering this area, it is important to preserve a distinction between two concepts, namely, remoteness of damage and measure of damages.

Needless to say, given the pragmatic evolution of the common law, this distinction has not always been preserved in the case law.[74] Another difficulty in this area lies in the very limited number of decided cases in which these questions have been openly canvassed in the case law.

In English law, a distinction is drawn between two questions, namely, 'for what kind of damage is the plaintiff entitled to recover compensation?' and 'upon what principle must the damage be quantified in terms of money?'. The first question is referred to as a question relating to remoteness of damage and, in principle, this question includes the question of which items of loss the plaintiff is entitled to receive compensation for.

---

73 As has been remarked in other jurisdictions, 'Equity does not demand that its suitors have led blameless lives' and what prevents a claim is that which has 'an immediate and necessary relation to the equity sued for'; see *Loughran v Loughran* 292 US 216 (1934), p 229, *per* Brandeis J; *Dering v Earl of Winchelsea* (1787) 1 Cox Eq 318 ; 2 W & TLC 488, p 489, *per* Eyre CB.

74 In *NV Handel Maatschappij J Smits Import-Export v English Exporters Ltd* (1955) 2 LR 69, where McNair J candidly remarked on 'the greatest possible difficulty in appreciating the distinction between ... remoteness of damage and measure of damage'.

The second question is referred to as the question relating to measure of damages.

In broad terms, the question of remoteness of damage is a matter of substantive law to be governed by the *lex causae*, while the question as to measure of damages is a question of procedure to be governed by the *lex fori*.[75]

Remoteness of damage

In English law, questions as to the remoteness of damage are matters of substantive law and will be governed by the *lex causae*. If the *lex causae* is to determine the existence of a legal obligation, then it is only logical that it should also determine the extent of that obligation. In respect of contractual disputes, this is expressly provided for in Art 10(1)(c) of the Rome Convention, which provides that the consequences of a breach of contract should be determined by the the governing law.

The case law at common law did support the view that remoteness of damage was governed by the *lex causae*. An example is afforded by the case of *D'Almeida Araujo Lda v Becker and Co Ltd*,[76] where the facts were as follows: the plaintiffs, merchants in Portugal, contracted to sell 500 tons of palm oil to the defendants, a company based in London. The contract was governed by Portuguese law. To comply with the contract, the plaintiffs agreed to purchase the palm oil from a Portuguese dealer. The plaintiffs were forced to pay an indemnity under this contract when the defendants failed to honour the primary contract. In an action in England, the plaintiffs sought to recover the sum paid as an indemnity.

In giving judgment, Pilcher J identified the claim as one turning on remoteness of damage and observed:

> ... the question whether the plaintiffs are entitled to claim from the defendants depends on whether such damage is, or is not, too remote. In my view, the question here is one of remoteness and therefore falls to be determined in accordance with Portuguese law.

Subsequent case law has emphasised the importance of preserving the distinction between questions of remoteness of damage and questions of measure of damages.[77]

---

75 It is respectfully submitted that this is in line with the observations in *Boys v Chaplin* [1971] AC 356, although, having regard to the wide variety of views expressed in that case and the subsequent changes in the law, there is little purpose at this stage in dealing with the individual judgments. The case is dealt with in respect of choice of law in tort (see Chapter 17).

76 [1953] 2 QB 329.

77 *Boys v Chaplin* [1971] AC 356.

Although clear authority is lacking, it would be safe to assume that questions of economic loss in the law of tort are questions relating to remoteness of damage. Matters of substantive law are, thus, governed by the *lex causae*. Equally, claims for mental anguish in tort cases would also be regarded as matters of substantive law.

Measure of damages

The purpose of the concept of measure of damages is to quantify in money terms the sum to be paid by the defendant. It would seem that quantification is a matter for the *lex fori*. As Pilcher J observed in *D'Almeida Araujo Lda v Becker & Co Ltd*:[78]

> ... the quantification of damage, which according to the proper law is not too remote, should be governed by the *lex fori*.

This probably represents the state of the law and receives some support from the speeches in *Boys v Chaplin*;[79] the practical advantage of such a course is that the court of the forum may wish to consider whether the payment of damages should be made in a lump sum or in the form of periodical payments. In tort actions, at least in those actions where unliquidated damages are claimed, the damages awarded will be those which would apply in a purely domestic case, for which one can research the going rate for personal injuries of a similar type and start from there. It would clearly be unacceptable to value an individual's pain and suffering by reference to the going rate in the *lex causae*, even if the consequence of not doing so is the encouragement of forum shopping.[80]

However, in the case of contracts, the law relating to damages is now partly procedural and partly substantive and, under the Rome Convention, the law governing the substance of the agreement will also govern 'the consequences of the breach, including the assessment of damages in so far as it is governed by rules of law'.[81]

---

78 [1953] 2 QB 329, p 336.
79 [1971] AC 356.
80 It would seem that the size of the damages likely to be awarded is an important factor when an individual is considering which forum to litigate in; see the views expressed by Lord Denning MR in the Court of Appeal in *Castanho v Brown and Root UK Ltd* [1980] 3 All ER 72, p 76.
81 Contracts (Applicable Law) Act 1990, Sched 1, Art 10(1)(c).

nary provisions of s 1(3) of the Law Reform (Frustrated Contracts)
. This aspect of the judgment was upheld in both the Court of Appeal
House of Lords. In *Ozalid Group (Export) Ltd v African Continental Bank*
Donaldson J awarded (as a head of contractual damages) to the
s a sum to compensate for the interim loss caused by devaluation
e defendants failed to make payment on the due date.

lood of case law meant that the area was ripe for consideration by the
mmission and this was undertaken in two reports.[101] The broad
ons of the Law Commission can be expressed as follows:

the *Miliangos* rule was soundly based and application of it had
ted in a more satisfactory state of the law than that which had
ded it;[102]

e the general devlopment of the law could be left to case law, that
ul attention should be paid in contractual disputes to the form of
nent stipulated by the parties;

arties should be free to agree that payment should be in a particular
gn currency.

g *Miliangos*, a problem was identified in respect of the interest on
ts in foreign currency. Since the *Miliangos* judgment, interest on a
nt in foreign currency had been paid at the appropriate English
rate for judgment debts.[103] The Law Commission concluded that the
interest payments had not kept pace with the changes in the rules on
ts. If the foreign currency was stronger than sterling then a plaintiff
e overcompensated, but, if the foreign currency was weaker than
a plaintiff might suffer a loss.[104] The Law Commission proposed that
ts should be given the power, in the case of foreign currency
ts, to order at their discretion that a specified rate of interest other
t arising under the Judgments Act 1838 should be paid.[105] The
e of the recommendations in relation to interest on foreign currency
ts was given effect to by Part I (ss 1–4) of the Private International
scellaneous Provisions) Act 1995.

---

2 Lloyd's Rep 237.

Commission Working Paper No 80 (1981); Law Commission Report No 124

Commission Report No 124 (1983), para 3.8.

e Direction [1976] 1 All ER 669, as modified by [1977] 1 All ER 544.

vel of interest rates being a reflection of the strength of the currency.

Commission Report No 124 (1983), para 4.9.

JUDGMENTS IN A FOREIGN CURRENCY

The old rule at common law

It was a well established rule at common law that an English court could only
order the payment of a debt or damages in English currency.[82] The sum due
to the plaintiff in foreign currency had to be converted into sterling and the
appropriate exchange rate was that prevailing at the time when the cause of
action arose, for example, the time of the commission of the tort.[83] The rule
that damages were to be paid in sterling had been confirmed before 1914[84] at
a time of fixed exchange rates secured by gold and when sterling was
regarded as 'a stable curency which had no equal'.[85] On a practical level, the
reason was that it was thought that the sheriff could only execute a judgment
in sterling.

In the 1970s, the experience of two devaluations,[86] the increasing problem
of inflation during that decade and the movement towards floating exchange
rates all contributed to the willingness of the courts to re-examine their
approach. Thus, the rule that judgment had to be in sterling was subject to
gradual erosion in the early 1970s as sterling depreciated against some
European currencies.[87] The entire matter was therefore suitable to be
reviewed by the House of Lords. An opportunity arose when leave to appeal
was granted in *Miliangos* v *George Frank (Textiles) Ltd*,[88] where the plaintiff, a
Swiss company, agreed to sell yarn to the English defendants. The yarn was
delivered in 1971. The proper law of the contract was Swiss law and payment
was to be made in Swiss francs. The defendants did not pay. The plaintiffs
originally claimed the sterling equivalent of the sum in Swiss francs computed
at the date when payment should have been made. However, the pleadings
were amended in the light of intervening Court of Appeal judgments and the
plaintiff attempted to recover the sum due in Swiss francs.[89]

---

82 *Manners v Pearson & Sons* [1898] 1 Ch 581.

83 *Re United Railways of Havana and Regla Warehouses Ltd* [1961] AC 1007; [1960] 2 All ER 332.

84 *Manners v Pearson & Sons* [1898] 1 Ch 581.

85 *Schorsch Meir GmbH v Hennin* [1975] QB 416, p 424, *per* Lord Denning MR.

86 Sterling having been devalued in September 1949 and November 1967.

87 *Jugoslavenska Oceanska Plovida v Catle Investment Co Inc* [1974] QB 292 (arbitral award
    in a foreign currency); *Schorsch Meir GmbH v Hennin* [1975] QB 416 (judgment for debt
    in a foreign currency).

88 [1976] AC 443; see Mann (1976) 92 LQR 165.

89 The original payment was SFr415,000 (worth, at the time of payment, £42,000, but
    worth £60,000 at the time of the hearing beause of the depreciation of the pound
    against the Swiss franc). This problem also arose in *Multiservice Bookbinding Ltd v
    Marden* [1979] Ch 84.

JUDGMENTS IN A FOREIGN CURRENCY

The old rule at common law

It was a well established rule at common law that an English court could only order the payment of a debt or damages in English currency.[82] The sum due to the plaintiff in foreign currency had to be converted into sterling and the appropriate exchange rate was that prevailing at the time when the cause of action arose, for example, the time of the commission of the tort.[83] The rule that damages were to be paid in sterling had been confirmed before 1914[84] at a time of fixed exchange rates secured by gold and when sterling was regarded as 'a stable curency which had no equal'.[85] On a practical level, the reason was that it was thought that the sheriff could only execute a judgment in sterling.

In the 1970s, the experience of two devaluations,[86] the increasing problem of inflation during that decade and the movement towards floating exchange rates all contributed to the willingness of the courts to re-examine their approach. Thus, the rule that judgment had to be in sterling was subject to gradual erosion in the early 1970s as sterling depreciated against some European currencies.[87] The entire matter was therefore suitable to be reviewed by the House of Lords. An opportunity arose when leave to appeal was granted in *Miliangos v George Frank (Textiles) Ltd*,[88] where the plaintiff, a Swiss company, agreed to sell yarn to the English defendants. The yarn was delivered in 1971. The proper law of the contract was Swiss law and payment was to be made in Swiss francs. The defendants did not pay. The plaintiffs originally claimed the sterling equivalent of the sum in Swiss francs computed at the date when payment should have been made. However, the pleadings were amended in the light of intervening Court of Appeal judgments and the plaintiff attempted to recover the sum due in Swiss francs.[89]

---

82 *Manners v Pearson & Sons* [1898] 1 Ch 581.

83 *Re United Railways of Havana and Regla Warehouses Ltd* [1961] AC 1007; [1960] 2 All ER 332.

84 *Manners v Pearson & Sons* [1898] 1 Ch 581.

85 *Schorsch Meir GmbH v Hennin* [1975] QB 416, p 424, *per* Lord Denning MR.

86 Sterling having been devalued in September 1949 and November 1967.

87 *Jugoslavenska Oceanska Plovida v Catle Investment Co Inc* [1974] QB 292 (arbitral award in a foreign currency); *Schorsch Meir GmbH v Hennin* [1975] QB 416 (judgment for debt in a foreign currency).

88 [1976] AC 443; see Mann (1976) 92 LQR 165.

89 The original payment was SFr415,000 (worth, at the time of payment, £42,000, but worth £60,000 at the time of the hearing beause of the depreciation of the pound against the Swiss franc). This problem also arose in *Multiservice Bookbinding Ltd v Marden* [1979] Ch 84.

The House of Lords decided to set aside the rule in *Havana*[90] and, exercising their recently asserted freedom in respect of past judgments,[91] ruled that in appropriate cases, damages could be awarded in a foreign currency.[92] Since the House of Lords had confined itself to that particular case, the question naturally arose as to whether the *Miliangos* principle could be extended to other cases or whether it was restricted to claims for liquidated damages where the contract was subject to foreign law and provided for payment in foreign currency. While the basic justice of the principle was subject to general acceptance, there was room for dispute as to its scope.

The evolution of the *Miliangos* rule

In the years after 1976,[93] it became clear that attempts would be made to extend the *Miliangos* principle to other cases. A later judgment of the House of Lords in *Services Europe Atlantique Sud v Stockholms Rederiaktiebolag SVEA, The Folias*[94] indicated that the rule would extend to claims for unliquidated damages. The plaintiff, a French company, chartered a Swedish ship from the defendants for the carriage of cargo from the Mediterranean to Brazil; upon arrival, the cargo was found to be damaged. The plaintiff company compensated the receivers of the cargo by paying in Brazilian currrency; they did this by buying Brazilian cruzieros with French francs. The claim was submitted to arbitration and the defendants, while admitting liability, contended that the award should be in Brazilian currency. In the interim the Brazilian cruziero had fallen in value by nearly 50%.

In allowing the plaintiffs to claim damages in French francs, the House of Lords ruled that the *Miliangos* principle would extend to claims for unliquidated damages. The court further held that claims for damages in a foreign currency should be referred to the proper law of the contract and any specific contractual provision but that, in the absence of such provision, damages could be calculated in 'the currency in which the loss was felt by the plaintiff'. When looking at loss, the court will be required to survey the entire flow of events following from the breach of contract; in the present case, the loss was incurred when the plaintiffs were obliged to sell francs in order to acquire the foreign exchange to compensate the cargo owners. As in the *Miliangos* case, the depreciation of the Brazilian currency had been

---

90 *Re United Railways of the Havana and Regla Warehouses Ltd* [1961] AC 1007.

91 [1966] 1 WLR 395.

92 Although not Lord Simon of Glaisdale, who felt that such a change in the law should be left to Parliament.

93 See Mann (1976) 92 LQR 165; Bowles and Phillips (1976) 39 MLR 196; Bowles and Whelan (1979) 42 MLR 452; Knott (1980) 43 MLR 18.

94 [1979] AC 685.

considerable; to some extent these problems increased in the 1970s as different economies experienced different rates of inflation. One of the features of the case law in the 1970s is the willingness of the courts in England to re-examine old rules and to look at new solutions to protect an innocent party against the consequences of inflation and a fluctuating exchange rate.[95]

At the same time, the House of Lords extended the *Miliangos* rule to claims in tort; this advance was made in *The Despina R.*[96] The plaintiffs' ship, *The Despina R*, and the defendants' ship collided in Shanghai harbour. The plaintiffs' ship was repaired in Shanghai, Yokohama and Los Angeles. Consequently, the defendants were obliged to make payments for repair in Chinese yuan, Japanese yen and US dollars. The plaintiffs sought to recover damages for negligence in US dollars because that was the currency in which they conducted their business and that was the currency used for all bank accounts which related to the ship.

The House of Lords ruled that, in principle, damages in tort should, as in contract, be payable in the currency of the plaintiff's loss; this will normally be the currency in which the plaintiff conducts his ordinary business operations. In the present case, United States dollars had been used to acquire the foreign currency to pay the necessary repair bills. At the same time, the House of Lords cautioned against any hard and fast rules and pointed out that, in matters of foriegn currency, the plaintiff bears the *onus probandi* of demonstrating that the currency is either its own trading currency or the appropriate currency in all the circumstances of the case.

An example of the extension of the rule to an action in tort was illustrated by the case of *Hoffman v Sofaer*.[97] In *Hoffman*, an American businessman on holiday in England received negligent medical treatment. The resulting disability caused him to lose his position as company president. A claim was made for damages for pain and suffering and loss of amenity and a further claim was made for damages for loss of earnings. Talbot J ruled that the award for pain and suffering should be made in sterling because of the difficulties that would arise in respect of any other currency, but that the claim for loss of earnings should be made in dollars.

From the late 1970s, cases began to arise where the courts were asked to apply the *Miliangos* rule to different factual situations. The years after 1976 witnessed a number of cases in which application of the *Miliangos* rule proved problematic.[98] In *BP Exploration Co (Lybia) Ltd v Hunt (No 2)*,[99] Robert Goff J at first instance awarded the plaintiffs a sum in US dollars under the

---

95 As is demonstrated by the case law on personal injury awards in the 1970s.
96 [1979] AC 685.
97 [1982] 1 WLR 1350.
98 The rule itself being one of procedure not substance: see *The Despina R* [1979] AC 685, p 704.
99 [1979] 1 WLR 783 (*per* Robert Goff J in the High Court); [1983] 2 AC 283, HL.

restitutionary provisions of s 1(3) of the Law Reform (Frustrated Contracts) Act 1943. This aspect of the judgment was upheld in both the Court of Appeal and the House of Lords. In *Ozalid Group (Export) Ltd v African Continental Bank Ltd*,[100] Donaldson J awarded (as a head of contractual damages) to the plaintiffs a sum to compensate for the interim loss caused by devaluation when the defendants failed to make payment on the due date.

The flood of case law meant that the area was ripe for consideration by the Law Commission and this was undertaken in two reports.[101] The broad conclusions of the Law Commission can be expressed as follows:

(a) that the *Miliangos* rule was soundly based and application of it had resulted in a more satisfactory state of the law than that which had preceded it;[102]

(b) while the general devlopment of the law could be left to case law, that careful attention should be paid in contractual disputes to the form of payment stipulated by the parties;

(c) that parties should be free to agree that payment should be in a particular foreign currency.

Following *Miliangos*, a problem was identified in respect of the interest on judgments in foreign currency. Since the *Miliangos* judgment, interest on a judgment in foreign currency had been paid at the appropriate English statutory rate for judgment debts.[103] The Law Commission concluded that the rules on interest payments had not kept pace with the changes in the rules on judgments. If the foreign currency was stronger than sterling then a plaintiff might be overcompensated, but, if the foreign currency was weaker than sterling, a plaintiff might suffer a loss.[104] The Law Commission proposed that the courts should be given the power, in the case of foreign currency judgments, to order at their discretion that a specified rate of interest other than that arising under the Judgments Act 1838 should be paid.[105] The substance of the recommendations in relation to interest on foreign currency judgments was given effect to by Part I (ss 1–4) of the Private International Law (Miscellaneous Provisions) Act 1995.

---

100 [1979] 2 Lloyd's Rep 237.

101 Law Commission Working Paper No 80 (1981); Law Commission Report No 124 (1983).

102 Law Commission Report No 124 (1983), para 3.8.

103 *Practice Direction* [1976] 1 All ER 669, as modified by [1977] 1 All ER 544.

104 The level of interest rates being a reflection of the strength of the currency.

105 Law Commission Report No 124 (1983), para 4.9.

Part I of the Private International Law (Miscellaneous Provisions) Act 1995

The operative provisions which are not retrospective and only apply to England and Wales are contained in ss 1–4 of the legislation. The broad objective of the provisions is to treat sterling and foreign currency judgments on a similar basis.

Section 1, which operates by amending the Adminstration of Justice Act 1970, confers upon the court a discretion to order the interest rate that it thinks fit where a judgment in a foreign currency is given. Section 1 applies only to the High Court and, while it does not set out any criteria on which interest rates are to be set, the expression 'such rate as the court thinks fit' would appear to indicate the rate applicable to the currency in question as demonstrated by evidence.[106] The statutory power conferred on the High Court by s 1 is extended to the county court by s 2. In accordance with the recommendations of the Law Commission, provision is made in s 3 of the legislation to confer the same power on arbitrators.[107]

---

106 *Shell Tankers (UK) v Astro Comino Armadora SA* [1981] 2 Lloyd's Rep 40.
107 Law Commission Report No 124 (1983), para 4.7.

CHAPTER 7

RENVOI

INTRODUCTION

It is necessary to determine what exactly the meaning and scope of any reference to foreign law is to be. There are two situations:

(a) there are cases where all the significant connections are with the same foreign legal system, so that the court of that system would properly regard the case as a domestic one;

(b) a case may be truly international, so that it might be seen as involving the conflict of laws in any court in which litigation was brought.

In the first situation, there can be no objection to the English forum applying the domestic law of the system with which the case is wholly connected. Indeed, in cases like this, the English court may feel that it should refuse jurisdiction as *forum non conveniens*. Where the defendant is content to allow proceedings to continue in England or there are good reasons for English litigation, for example, that, after the issue arose, the defendant became domiciled in England, then the application of the foreign law is relatively straightforward and there is a chance then that the same law will be applied in England as would have been applied in the 'home' country. There are, however, other factors beside the choice of law which stand in the way of decisional uniformity.

Cases which are truly international and which would be seen as conflict cases in any forum present some difficulties. If the case has no obvious single legal 'home', then its governing law must be a matter of contention. As any conflicts system is part of a domestic legal system, it follows that different national courts might apply different choice of law rules to the same issue. The Rome Convention on the Law Applicable to Contractual Obligations 1980 is an attempt to standardise the approach of European Union States to contractual disputes. In non-standardised areas, individual legal systems will maintain their own particular approaches.

Suppose an English forum is faced with a question about the capacity to marry of a French national who is domiciled in Italy. It would refer to the Italian domiciliary law. An Italian court, dealing with the same case, would refer to the French national law. If Italian law and French law happen to differ on the particular capacity in dispute, the results would be different. Should it just be accepted as a fact of legal life that the result of a case will depend on the place of litigation and leave lawyers to take it on board when advising their clients – just an international dimension to a fact already known? Should it be left to international efforts to standardise the choice of law rules?[1] Should it be a matter for the forum to consider in its approach to the particular case?

What are the possibilities open to a court embarrassed by the realisation that a foreign forum would decide the same case differently; more than that, that the courts of the legal system which the English court has selected as the governing law for the case would take such a different view of the matter?

If the choice of law rule is judge made, the court may be able to change it. If a choice of law rule regularly produces unsatisfactory results and there is an obvious and preferable alternative, there is no reason not to go to it. In the example of capacity to marry, however, the case for the application of the personal law is overwhelming and, whatever the defects of the current law of domicile, there is no case for replacing it with that of nationality.

Changes in the choice of law rules, unless the result of international agreement, are unlikely to advance the consistency of decisions unless the former rules were out of step with the common practice elsewhere. In the formation of choice of law rules, a consideration of how other systems tackle the job can provide useful information. However, the search must always be for the system of law which most effectively encapsulates the legal relationship which is in question. That, in turn, depends on the view that the forum takes of the nature of the relationship; a view which depends on the legal culture of the forum.

English law has persisted with the concept of domicile as a connecting factor despite the many criticisms of its arcane legislation and the manifest inflexibility. Nationality as a possible alternative was abandoned in the 19th century and there is even less case for it now. Habitual residence presents a strong case to displace domicile and, perhaps, in time, it will, either directly or by the addition of greater flexibility to the traditional view of domicile. A decision to shift from domicile to habitual residence would not help in our marriage example. Unless the country of the habitual residence happened to be France, or a country which happened to have the same legal rules as French law, there would still be a discrepancy between the English courts and Italian court's solution of the problem. Such a coincidence would be purely fortuitous and not determined by the change in the connecting factor – the possibility of domicile and nationality coinciding is just as great

POSSIBLE APPROACHES TO *RENVOI*

Renvoi is a method or technique for resolving problems that inevitably arise out of the differences between the connecting factor used by English law and

---

1   There is a Hague Convention on Celebration and Recognition of the Validity of Marriages 1978, but it has gained little acceptance.

that of the law to which the English connecting factor refers. The case law indicates that this may arise in one of two forms, either:

(a) because English Law and the *lex causae*, say, German law, use the same connecting factor for the legal category, for example, domicile, but mean different things by it; or

(b) English law and the *lex causae*, say, Austrian law, use different connecting factors for the same legal problem, for example, domicile and nationality.

Many of the newly emerging European States chose nationality as a connecting factor in the 19th century, so that problems, as in (b), above, became increasingly common as the connecting factors of domicile and nationality came into contact.[2] It has to be acknowledged that *renvoi* is a subject that has attracted a considerable volume of academic literature, although none of the literature has been influential in the limited number of cases that have come before the courts in England.[3]

If we take the preliminary view that *renvoi* is a method for resolving problems encountered when the English connecting factor comes into contact with foreign law, we can identify three possible situations. Before doing so, in addition to the example cited above of the French national domiciled in Italy, we can consider the following case. Suppose an English court has to consider the case of X, an Englishman, who dies domiciled in Arcadia, and a question arises as to the beneficial distribution of his movable property.

Apply the internal law: the rejection of *renvoi*

In the example cited immediately above, English law would refer the question of the distribution of the movable property to the *lex domicilii* of the deceased; by the law of the domicile, one could mean simply the internal law of Arcadia. As Maugham J observed in *Re Askew*:

> When the English courts refer the matter to the law of Utopia as the *lex domicilii*, do they mean the whole of that law or do they mean the local or municipal law which in Utopia would apply to Utopian subjects.[4]

Therefore, one possibility is to apply the internal law of Arcadia minus its conflict rules, so that, in the example, the beneficial distribution of the movable property will be governed by the intestacy law of Arcadia in the same manner as any other like case coming before the courts of Arcadia. This approach has the virtue of simplicity but it fails to take account of the fact that

---

2   The first case involving *renvoi* in England is usually seen as *Collier v Rivaz* (1841) 2 Curt 855, involving a possible conflict with the requirements of Belgian law. Belgium had secured its independence from Holland as a separate State as recently as 1830–31.

3   See Abbott (1908) 24 LQR 133; Lorenzen (1910) 10 CLR 190; (1917) 27 YLJ 509; Schreiber (1917) 31 HLR 523; Dobrin (1934) 15 BYIL 36; Morris (1937) 18 BYIL 32; Griswold (1938) 51 HLR 1165.

4   *Re Askew* [1930] 2 Ch 259.

a court in Arcadia might consider that such a case raised a conflicts problem and should be referred to another law. There is some support for this approach[5] in 19th century case law.[6]

Partial or single *renvoi*

The second possible approach is to adopt the doctrine of partial or single *renvoi*.[7] The doctrine of partial *renvoi* involves a reference to the conflicts rules of the chosen system, which results in either transmission to another legal system or remission to the forum's law. So that, if we revert to the example concerning Arcadia, then the meaning of the law of Arcadia is the law of Arcadia, including its conflict rules but minus its conflict rules applying *renvoi*, if such exist. So, in relation to the case of the intestate dying domiciled in Arcadia, if the relevant Arcadian conflicts rule referred to English law as the law of the nationality,[8] then, if the English court 'accepts' the remission and decides the case in accordance with English law, this would be an example or partial or single *renvoi*.[9]

The operation of single *renvoi* can involve the reference of the issue to a third system (that is, transmission). This was the case in the original example of the Italian domiciled French national where Italian conflict law would refer to the *lex patriae* – French law. This is an example of transmission. Now, an English court could go along with this if it wished,[10] though the consequences of doing so, while it would produce consistency between the decision of the English court and the Italian court in this case, would not produce any overall consistency, as we would just be substituting one system of conflict law for another. The criticism that, if English law wants to use nationality, it should do so itself, and not through the medium of Italian law, is pertinent. While the practical objections have great force, there is a logical objection which has at least equal weight – why stop there? If the process itself has any logical basis, that logic cannot artificially terminate the inquiry at first reference. Why not see what the French conflict rules have to say about the question of capacity to marry? Suppose French conflict law would look to the law of the habitual residence and suppose that law to be German. Should we then look to

---

5   This approach is followed in Italian law.

6   *Bremer v Freeman* (1857) 10 Moo PCC; *Hamilton v Dallas* (1875) 1 Ch D 257.

7   This has been referred to as partial, single simple or continental *renvoi*.

8   As indicated elsewhere, this causes difficulties in the UK where it is not possible to identify an English nationality; this will always be a problem where the nationality refers to a State that has more than one law district; see *Re O'Keefe* [1940] Ch 124.

9   The doctrine of partial or single *renvoi* is adopted by German, Belgian and French law.

10   *R v Brentwood Superintendent Registrar of Marriages ex p Arias* [1968] 2 QB 956, represents an example of single *renvoi* in the context of capacity to marry but such a result is unlikely to arise in the future, having regard to the Recognition of Divorces and Legal Separations Act 1971, s 7 and the Family Law Act 1986, s 50.

German conflict law and see what a German court would do if it had been seized of the case?

Given both different choice of law rules and different connecting factors and also different interpretations of common connecting factors, it would be possible to construct a scenario where references went on and on with no logical stopping place, or sooner or later became caught up in a reciprocal or circular motion which would have no end beyond the patience of the forum.

Total *renvoi*

The third possible approach is that of total *renvoi*.[11] Modifying the problem indicated above, suppose an English court is faced with the problem of the capacity to marry of an English national domiciled in Italy; the total *renvoi* doctrine requires an English court to follow what an Italian court would do if its reference to English law was met by a reference back to Italian law. So that Italian law, for the purposes of the first example, or Arcadian law, in the second example, is taken as all the relevant law of Italy or Arcadia, including its conflicts rules and *renvoi*, if it is included. In the case of the capacity of the Englishman to marry, the doctrine of total *renvoi* would involve three steps:

(a) the English court determines the *lex causae* in the usual way. In the example of the Englishman domiciled in Italy, the English court applying the dual domicile test would refer his marital capacity to Italian law, his *lex domicilii*;

(b) the English court then applies the conflict rules of the *lex causae*. In the example, it would find that an Italian court dealing with the matter would refer to English law as the *lex patriae*;

(c) as English conflicts law refers to Italian law, we are back where we started. To avoid any further toing and froing, the English court looks to Italian law to see whether an Italian court would accept or reject the remission. If an Italian court would accept the reference back, the English court would apply Italian domestic law to the question of marital capacity. If, as is the case, an Italian court would not accept the remission, the English court would apply English domestic law to the substantive issue.

Although some writers regard *Collier v Rivaz*[12] as a judgment consistent with the doctrine of total *renvoi*, the consensus of opinion is that is was not until the judgment of Russell J in *Re Annesley*[13] that the doctrine can be said to have been recognised in English law. In *Re Annesley* the facts were as follows: an Englishwoman left a will; according to English law, she died domiciled in

---

11 Sometimes alluded to as the foreign court theory or English *renvoi* or double *renvoi*.

12 (1841) 2 Curt 855.

13 [1926] 1 Ch 692.

France but, according to French law, she had not acquired a French domicile because of a failure to comply with registration formalities. The testamentary dispositions were valid by English law but invalid by French law because she had failed to leave two thirds of the property to her children.

In proceedings in the Chancery Division to determine the domicile of the deceased and the validity of the testamentary dispositions, Russell J came to the conclusion that French law should apply, although the reasoning in the judgment is not as clear as it might be. As that was the case, the relevant dispositions were invalid. The reasoning of the judge proceeded as follows.

(a) the domicile of the deceased is to be determined in accordance with English law and, by that law, the deceased died domiciled in France;

(b) but, French law would refer questions of validity to the *lex patriae*;

(c) the rules of English private international law would refer the matter to French law;

(d) the French legal system accepts the doctrine of single *renvoi*. The French judge would accept the remission and decide the matter in accordance with French municipal law. Thus, the English court should decide as the French court would decide.

Russell J clearly had reservations about the process because he concluded his judgment with a plea for a more direct method:

> Speaking for myself, I should like to reach the same conclusion by a much more direct route, along which no question of *renvoi* need be encountered at all. When the law of England requires that the personal estate of a British subject, who dies domiciled, according to the requirements of English law, in a foreign country, shall be administered in accordance with the law of that country, why should this not mean in accordance with the law which that country would apply, not to the *propositus*, but to its own nationals legally domiciled there? In other words, when we say that French law applies to the administration of the personal estate of an Englishman who dies domiciled in France, we mean that French municipal law which France applies in the case of Frenchmen. This appears to me a simple and rational solution which avoids altogether the endless oscillation which otherwise results from the law of the country of the nationality invoking the law of the country of domicile, while the law of the country of domicile in turn invokes the law of the country of the nationality.[14]

The extract cited indicates that Russell J had misgivings about the process that had formed the basis of his judgment. However, the matter was considered again in another first instance case of *Re Ross*,[15] where the facts were as follows: an Englishwoman died domiciled in Italy, leaving a will of movable

---

14 [1926] 1 Ch 708, pp 708–09 (Russell J).

15 [1930] 1 Ch 376 (Luxmore J).

property in England and Italy and immovable property in Italy. By English law, succession to the property was governed by Italian law as the *lex domicilii*. The will was partly invalid by Italian law. The Italian choice of law rule, being founded on nationality, referred to English law for both forms of property.

Luxmore J, after hearing expert evidence on the likely attitude of an Italian court, concluded that such a court would reject *renvoi* and simply apply English law. In reviewing the evolution of the case law, Luxmore J concluded that 'the law of the country of the domicile is the law as it would be decided by the courts of that country in reference to the facts of the particular case to be considered'. The judge rejected the claim of those who questioned the validity of the will under Italian law; he assumed that the notional Italian judge would have referred to the law of the nationality and rejected the remission made to him by English law.

While subsequent cases at first instance are not without difficulties,[16] it would seem that the English courts, in so far as they adopt a doctrine of *renvoi*, favour the foreign court theory and proceed upon the basis of detailed consideration of expert evidence of foreign law. Clearly, such a course is expensive and it is not without interest that the five leading cases in this area are only at first instance.

THE APPLICATION OF THE DOCTRINE OF *RENVOI*

One practical limitation of the doctrine of *renvoi* is that it normally involves calling detailed expert evidence as to the state of foreign law; normally, parties will seek to avoid such a course. *Renvoi* has been employed in cases concerning the formal validity of wills,[17] but is now excluded in respect of the formal validity of wills by s 6(1) of the Wills Act 1963. This legislation implements the Hague Convention on the Conflicts of Law Relating to the Form of Testamentary Dispositions 1961. The wide terms of the legislation permitting formal validity render any advantages from the doctrine otiose.

The doctrine of *renvoi* has been used to legitimate an adulterine child,[18] which would not have been possible under English law at the time. As

---

16 *Re Askew* [1930] 2 Ch 259, Maugham J appeared to favour the rational solution indicated by Russell J; in *Re the Duke of Wellington* [1947] Ch 506, Wynne Parry J confessed to finding difficulty in determining the attitude of the Spanish courts to *renvoi*; see, also, *Re Fuld's Estate (No 3)* [1968] P 675 (Scarman J).

17 *Collier v Rivaz* (1841) 2 Curt 855; *Re Fuld's Estate (No 3)* [1968] P 675; see, now, Wills Act 1963.

18 *Re Askew* [1930] 2 Ch 259; but the case is of little relevance today, having regard to the changes in this area of law in the Legitimacy Act 1959; see, now, Legitimacy Act 1976.

indicated above, the doctrine has been applied to the essential validity of wills in respect of movables[19] and immovables,[20] and to intestate succession to movables.[21] *Re O'Keefe (Deceased)*,[22] on an issue of intestate succession to movables, *renvoi* took the English court, via reference to the Italian *lex domicilii*, to the law of the south of Ireland, with which the deceased had no connection and which had no separate existence for most of her life. However, this is a compelling argument against the use of nationality as a connecting factor, not against *renvoi* as such.

In the sphere of family law, there is some authority for the view that *renvoi* applies to formal validity of marriage[23] and it has, in the past, been employed in questions of capacity to marry, although subsequent changes make this a precedent of limited value.[24]

The doctrine of *renvoi* is not applied in the area of commercial law; a stipulation that a contract is to be governed by the law of Arcadia is normally taken as a reference to the internal law of Arcadia. The doctrine of *renvoi* did not apply to contractual disputes at common law[25] and it is now specifically excluded by statute.[26] In like terms, the doctrine did not apply to the law of tort at common law[27] and is now specifically excluded by statute.[28]

THE ADVANTAGES AND DISADVANTAGES OF *RENVOI*

Not surprisingly, the doctrine of *renvoi* has its advocates and opponents. Its advocates argue that, by resorting to foreign choice of law rules, the court avoids a foreign internal law that has no connection with the *propositus*. Secondly, it is argued that it promotes the reasonable expectation of the parties. It might be argued that this was the case in *Re Annesley*[29] but it is difficult to imagine how the same could have been said of the result in *Re O'Keefe*.[30] Thirdly, it is argued that *renvoi* produces a degree of uniformity of

---

19 *Re Trufort* (1887) 36 Ch D 600; *Re Annesley* [1926] Ch 692; *Re Ross* [1930] 1 Ch 377.

20 *Re Ross* [1930] 1 Ch 377.

21 *Re O'Keefe (Deceased)* [1940] Ch 124.

22 *Ibid*.

23 *Taczanowska v Taczanowski* [1957] P 301.

24 *R v Brentwood Superintendent of Marriages ex p Arias* [1968] 2 QB 956. The decision now has to be read in the light of the Recognition of Divorces and Legal Separations Act 1971 and the Family Law Act 1986, s 50.

25 *Re United Rlys of Havana Ltd* [1960] Ch 52; *Amin Rasheed Shipping Corporation v Kuwait Insurance Co* [1984] AC 50.

26 Contracts (Applicable Law) Act 1990, Sched 1, Art 15.

27 *McElroy v McAllister* 1949 SC 100.

28 Private International Law (Miscellaneous Provisions) Act 1995, s 9(5).

29 [1926] Ch 692 (Russell J).

30 [1940] Ch 124 (Crossman J).

decision, in terms of the governing law at least, in cases where the English choice of law rules put a premium on this, that is, where the *lex situs* is applied on the basis of effectiveness. In such cases, not to conform the decision to that which a court of the *situs* would produce defeats the purpose of the original reference. Suppose the English court is faced with a case involving intestate succession and some of the immovable estate is situated in Italy. If the reference to Italian law, as the *lex situs*, is confined to the domestic law of Italy, the result will be that the deceased's immovables will be distributed as would those of his Italian neighbours. However, such a course of succession would not be ordered by an Italian court, as Italian conflicts law would refer the matter to the deceased's *lex patriae*. If the deceased would be regarded as having British nationality and would be linked with English law by an Italian court, then an Italian court would refer to English law and find that English conflict law would refer the matter back to Italian law. Italian law would not accept the reference back, so an English court adopting total *renvoi* would emulate that approach, apply English law and, thereby, achieve a legally consistent result.

Against this, it must be observed that, in a world in which different connecting factors are used, then such a degree of uniformity is probably unattainable. Moreover, it is arguable that such a degree of uniformity is not achieved by the single *renvoi* doctrine; if both country A and country B adopt connecting factors of domicile and nationality respectively and then both adopt the partial *renvoi* doctrine, then the result will differ according to where the case is litigated. In respect of the total *renvoi* technique, while, in principle, it should produce uniformity of decisions, it can, in practice, be applied only by one country because, if the *lex causae* were also to apply it, then there would be no way out of the revolving door. The experience since 1945 is that uniformity of decision making is more likely to be achieved by the implementing of internationally agreed conventions.

Advocates of the doctrine of *renvoi* argue that the technique can be manipulated to avoid applying an inappropriate foreign rule; however, the same object can be achieved by the development of appropriate public policy rules. Indeed, in the earliest case of *Colier v Rivaz*,[31] it is arguable that the learned judge was more concerned with the public policy of seeking to uphold testamentary dispositions than to formulate any precise theory of *renvoi*.[32]

Those who oppose the doctrine of *renvoi* argue that a study of the cases indicates that the English court concludes by subordinating its own choice of

---

31 (1841) 2 Curt 855 (although seen as the *fons et origo* of the doctrine, a reading of the judgment indicates that Sir Herbert Jenner did not employ the word *renvoi* and devoted very little attention to the actual process).

32 Which may explain why some writers have claimed it as an authority for partial *renvoi*, while some argued that it is consistent with the foreign court theory.

law rules to those of another country. Against this, however, it can be argued that this would not happen in those cases where the foreign rule offended some particular rule of public policy. Secondly, its opponents argue that the application of the doctrine requires that the courts receive detailed evidence of foreign law and that the judge is required to familiarise himself with (a) the foreign internal law; (b) the relevant foreign choice of law rules; and (c) the policy, if any, of the foreign law towards the doctrine of single *renvoi*. The difficulty of the task is indicated by the terms of the judgment of Wynne Parry J in *Re The Duke of Wellington*,[33] where the learned judge found he was being asked to decide on the approach of Spanish law to *renvoi* without the benefit of any clear prior ruling from the Supreme Court of Spain. However, this objection fails to take into account the fact that English judges have to consider the contents of foreign law in many cases arising under the conflicts of laws. Moreover, since entry into the European Community, English judges are more familiar with the general approach of legal systems in Western Europe. In any event, as foreign law is a question of fact, it is always open to the judge to indicate to the parties those areas in which he feels expert evidence is required. In *Collier v Rivaz*,[34] the learned judge was able to receive evidence of three witnesses as to Belgian law. Having regard to the increase in the development of law as an academic discipline since 1841, it cannot be said that the obtaining of evidence of foreign law represents a practical obstacle.

Thirdly, the opponents of *renvoi* argue that, having regard to the fact that nationality is the connecting factor most commonly employed in the civil law world, the English court puts itself in a position of being unduly influenced by nationality when there is no concept of English nationality having regard to the status of the UK. Such opponents point to cases such as *Re O'Keefe*[35] but it is arguable that this is an argument against the use of nationality as a connecting factor, not against *renvoi* as such.

It has also been suggested that *renvoi* can defeat the expectations of the parties; so it can. However, there is no more reason to suppose that a British national domiciled in Italy, who dies intestate, decided against making a will because he was happy with the domestic Italian intestacy rules than that he believed that his intestacy would be governed by his national law. It is not without interest that a considerable number of the English cases on *renvoi* have concluded at first instance; while parties may choose not to appeal for a number of reasons, it must be the case that, in a proportion of the cases, the

---

33 [1947] Ch 506.
34 (1841) 2 Curt 855.
35 [1940] Ch 124.

parties felt that the process of judicial reasoning was consonant with justice in that particular case.[36]

---

36 This may be connected to the fact that many of the cases are by originating summons in the Chancery Division, thus enabling the parties to reach agreement in advance of the hearing as to the precise legal questions that the judge will be required to answer. With the correct questions formulated in advance and with the judge reserving judgment, there is less likelihood of important precedents not being cited to the court.

CHAPTER 8

THE PROOF OF FOREIGN LAW

THE NATURE OF FOREIGN LAW

In many cases arising in the conflict of laws, an English court will be required to ascertain and take account of foreign law.[1] English law is subject to the doctrine of judicial notice[2] as, indeed, is the law of the European Union.[3] Foreign law is not subject to the doctrine of judicial notice, but is regarded as a question of fact. In broad terms, 'foreign law' is the law of any country other than England.[4] There are only a limited number of situations in which judicial notice can be taken of foreign law.[5] In general, foreign law is a question of fact and, like any fact, must be proved by admissible evidence. The party that asserts that foreign law is different from English law bears the onus of proof.[6] Unless such foreign law is demonstrated on evidence, then the court may assume that it is the same as English law.[7]

Public international law or the law of nations does not come within the class of 'foreign law'. Since the middle of the 18th century, rules of customary international law[8] are considered as part of English law. The other principal source of public international law comprises treaty obligations and it is well established that treaties are not a source of legal obligations unless followed by implementing legislation.[9]

---

1   See Fentiman (1992) 108 LQR 142.

2   Meaning that evidence does not have to be produced.

3   In respect of domestic legislation at common law and in respect of public Acts prior to 1850. By virtue of the Interpretation Act 1978, ss 3, 22(1), Sched 2, para 2, in respect of public Acts passed after 1851, the European Communities Act 1972, s 3(2), provides for judicial notice in respect of European Union law.

4   Rules of public international law are not foreign law; see *R v Keyn (The Franconia)* (1876) 2 QBD 90; *West Rand Central Gold Mining Co v R* [1905] 2 KB 391; *Chung Chi Cheung v R* [1939] AC 160.

5   The exceptions to the general rule are: (a) the common law of Northern Ireland; (b) Scots law in civil cases, of which judicial notice may be taken by the House of Lords in its appellate capacity; and (c) the law in relation to maintenance orders in the UK, by virtue of the Maintenance Orders Act 1950, s 22(2).

6   *The King of Spain v Machado* (1827) 4 Russ 225, p 239; *Ascherberg Hopwood and Crew v Casa Musicale Sonzogno* [1971] 1 WLR 173; 1 All ER 577; 3 All ER 38.

7   But, see *R v Brixton Governor ex p Coldough* [1961] 1 All ER 606.

8   *Dolder v Huntingfield* (1805) 11 Ves 283; *Empreror of Austria v Day and Kossuth* (1861) 30 LJ Ch 690; *R v Keyn (The Franconia)* (1876) 2 QBD 90; *West Rand Gold Mining Co v R* [1905] 2 KB 391.

9   *The Parlement Belge* (1879) 4 PD 129; (1880) 5 PD 197; *Maclaine Watson v The Department of Trade* [1990] 2 AC 418.

HOW FOREIGN LAW IS PROVED

In general, foreign law will be proved by expert witnesses; the court will need to receive 'appropriate evidence from appropriately qualified witnesses'. In many situations, this may be done on affidavit and by agreement but, where the issue is contested, then the witness will be subject to cross-examination.[10]

Foreign law must be proved to the satisfaction not of the jury but the judge.[11] The operative provisions are now contained in the Supreme Court Act 1981, which reads as follows:

> Where ... it is necessary to ascertain the law of any other country which is applicable to the facts of the case, any question as to the effect of the evidence given with respect to that law shall, instead of being submitted to the jury, be decided by the judge alone.

In principle, each case involving a point of foreign law would require separate and distinct proof since as foreign law was a question of fact, it could not be subject to the doctrine of precedent.[12] However, s 4 of the Civil Evidence Act 1972 makes the process less onerous by providing that, where any question of foreign law has been determined[13] in civil or criminal proceedings in the High Court, Crown Court or certain other courts[14] and in appeals therefrom[15] or before the Judicial Committee of the Privy Council,[16] any finding made or decision given in such proceedings,[17] if reported in citable form,[18] is admissible in later civil proceedings as evidence of the foreign law.[19] These provisions remain unaffected by the recently enacted Civil Evidence Act 1995.

---

10 In theory, the witness is always subject to cross-examination but, if the evidence is not in dispute, the other party may not seek to cross-examine; in the law of evidence, failure to cross-examine will normally constitute acceptance of the evidence.

11 The present provision is the Supreme Court Act 1981, s 69(5), replacing the Supreme Court of Judicature (Consolidation) Act 1925, s 102 and the Administration of Justice Act 1920, s 15. The legislation also applies to criminal trials: *R v Hammer* [1923] 2 KB 786.

12 And the rule of foreign law might have changed since it had been last adopted in England. This is a problem in public international law, where different views have been expressed on the role of the doctrine of precedent.

13 Civil Evidence Act 1972, s 4(2).

14 *Ibid*, s 4(4)(a).

15 *Ibid*, s 4(4)(b).

16 *Ibid*, s 4(4)(c).

17 *Ibid*, s 4(2)(a).

18 *Ibid*, s 4(5).

19 Subject to compliance with the Civil Evidence Act 1972, s 4(3).

WHO CAN TESTIFY AS TO FOREIGN LAW?

In principle, the witness must be an expert in the particular system of foreign law.[20] Although evidence of the relevant legislative enactments should be given, the witness will be required to express an opinion on questions of interpretation. At common law, such opinion evidence could only be given by an expert and such expertise had to derive from practical experience within that particular system. Thus, in *Bristow v Sequeville*,[21] evidence as to the law in force at Cologne could not be given by a Prussian consular official in London who had studied in Leipzig and had acquired familiarity with the *Code Napoleon*. Baron Alderson appeared to rule that actual practical experience before the courts of a particular jurisdiction was essential; the learned judge observed:

> If a man who has studied law in Saxony and never practised in Prussia is a competent witness to prove the law of Prussia, why may not a Frenchman, who has read books relating to Chinese law, prove what the law of China is?

Although it was probably true that, until the end of the 19th century, the courts were minded to demand that the witness had actual practical experience,[22] there are some signs of flexibility as the century progressed. In the case of *Re The Goods of Dhost Aly Khan*,[23] a diplomat based in the Persian Embassy in London was allowed to give evidence as to the law of Persia after it was demonstrated that there were no professional lawyers in Persia and that diplomatic staff were trained in the relevant law.

The modern flexible approach probably dates from the turn of the century[24] and is illustrated by *Brailey v Rhodesia Consolidated Ltd*,[25] where the Reader in Roman Dutch Law at the Council of Legal Education in London[26] was permitted to give evidence as to Rhodesian law, even though he had not practised in that jurisdiction.

---

20 The rationale being that the courts only permit the opinion evidence of an expert when a degree of expertise is necessary to permit the tribunal of fact to reach a correct conclusion.

21 (1850) 5 Exch 275. At this time, the 19th century expansion in law teaching within the universities had yet to take place.

22 Problems do arise in respect of the expert witness who draws upon literature (ie, the work of others of which he has no first hand knowledge); the relationship between this and the rule against hearsay was not settled until recently; see *R v Abadom* [1983] 1 All ER 364; 1 WLR 126. It may be this consideration that led to the demand for actual practical experience.

23 (1880) 6 PD 6.

24 An interesting question arises as to whether a change in attitude can be detected at the turn of the century, as legal education within the Universities began to expand and various teachers of law became well known public figures, eg, AV Dicey (1835–1922); FW Maitland (1850–1906); F Pollock (1845–1937); and W Anson (1834–1914).

25 [1910] 2 Ch 95.

26 RW Lee.

The common law emphasis upon practical experience sometimes resulted in evidence being received from a person who had acquired a working knowledge of foreign law through his administrative duties. In *Cooper King v Cooper King*,[27] the court was content to accept evidence as to the marriage law of Hong Kong from an ex-Governor.

As the question was whether the witness was competent to express an opinion, the case law indicates that the court would be influenced by (a) the precise matter on which the opinion was required;[28] and (b) whether a foreign lawyer was available.[29]

Indeed, in some situations, the court has considered practical experience within the jurisdiction to be more important than formal qualifications. This experience has been found to exist in a businessman,[30] a diplomat[31] and a former Governor General.[32]

Against this background, it can be seen that the provisions of the Civil Evidence Act 1972[33] simply give effect to the position at common law. The operative provisions provide:

> ... in civil proceedings, a person who is suitably qualified to do on account of his knowledge or experience is competent to give expert evidence as to the law of any country or territory outside the United Kingdom, or of any part of the United Kingdom, other than England and Wales, irrespective of whether he has acted or is entitled to act as a legal practitioner there.[34]

THE ROLE OF THE COURT IN RESPECT OF FOREIGN LAW

As indicated above, expert evidence will normally be given on affidavit; as with any oral testimony, the expert witness may be subject to cross-examination. The court may inspect texts relied on by the witness but should not consult texts not relied upon by the witness or by counsel.[35] If the expert

---

27 [1900] P 65.

28 The *Sussex Peerage* case (1844) 11 Cl & Fin 85 (Roman Catholic bishop allowed to testify as to the matrimonial law of Rome).

29 *Wilson v Wilson* [1903] P 157 (English barrister allowed to give evidence as to the marriage laws in Malta). *Re Whitelegg's Goods* (1899) P 267 (English solicitor allowed to give evidence as to the law in Chile without practical experience within the jurisdiction).

30 *Ajami v Customs Controller* [1954] 1 WLR 1405 (evidence from a banker allowed).

31 *Re the Goods of Dhost Aly Khan* (1880) 6 PD 6 (evidence from diplomat accepted).

32 *Cooper King v Cooper King* [1900] P 65 (evidence of former Governor of Hong Kong accepted).

33 Civil Evidence Act 1972, s 4 (1).

34 *Practice Direction (Foreign Law Affidavit)* [1972] 3 All ER 912; 1 WLR 1433; the Civil Evidence Act 1972, is based upon the Law Reform Committee Report, *Evidence of Opinion and Expert Evidence* (1970).

testimony is uncontradicted, then, in principle, the court should be reluctant to reject it unless it is manifestly absurd. If a conflict exists as to the evidence of foreign law, then the court will have no option[36] but to weigh the evidence and produce its own interpretation of the state of the foreign law.[37]

As foreign law is a question of fact, then, normally, an appellate court will be slow to interfere but, because such facts are based not on the perception of witnesses but on the evaluation and interpretation of documents, then the appellate court will not feel the same degree of inhibition as pertains where the assessment of veracity is in issue.[38] In these circumstances, there is a greater willingness to review the conclusions of the judge at first instance.[39]

OTHER STATUTORY PROVISIONS

There are a number of enactments on the statute book that make provision for the obtaining of evidence in respect of foreign law. Under the British Law Ascertainment Act 1859,[40] a court in any part of Her Majesty's dominions, may, if it thinks it necessary or expedient for the proper disposal of an action, state a case for the opinion of the court in any other part of Her Majesty's dominions in order to ascertain the view of the court as to the law applicable to the facts of the case stated.

By virtue of the Evidence (Colonial Statutes) Act 1907, copies of the Acts, ordinances and Statutes passed by or under the authority of the legislature of any British possession, if purporting to be printed by the government printer, can be received in evidence in the UK without proof that the copies were so printed.

---

35 *Bumper Development Corpn v Metropolitan Police Commissioner* [1991] 4 All ER 638; 1 WLR 1362.

36 *Di Sora v Phillips* (1863) 10 HL Cas 624; *Lazard Bros and Co v Midland Bank Ltd* [1933] AC 289; *Sinfra Akt v Sinfra Ltd* [1939] 2 All ER 675.

37 Since foreign law is a question of fact, if, at the end of the day, the court is uncertain as to a matter of foreign law, then the result of the case may be determined by the question as to which party bears the legal burden of proof; see *Rhesa Shipping Co SA v Edmunds* [1985] 1 WLR 948, p 955; 2 All ER 712, p 718, *per* Lord Brandon.

38 On the distinction between perception and evaluation, see *Benmax v Austin Motors* [1955] AC 370; *Edwards v Bairstow* [1956] AC 14; *O'Kelly v Trusthouse Forte* [1984] QB 90.

39 See *Parkasho v Singh* [1968] P 233, p 254, *per* Simon P: 'Where the inference of fact depends on the consideration of written material, an appellate court is at no particular disadvantage compared to a trial court and will regard itself as freer to review the decision of the trial court.'

40 Foreign Law Ascertainment Act 1861, which made comparable provision in respect of non-British law was never invoked and was repealed in 1973.

Thereafter, the English court may interpret the Statute and Act on its provisions without the reception of expert evidence, unless it is contended that the legislation is no longer in force.[41]

Although it is not strictly 'foreign law', Art 177 of the Treaty of Rome 1957[42] enables a court or tribunal in the UK to seek guidance on the correct interpretation[43] of European law. Any court or tribunal may make a reference but a distinction must be drawn between those courts or tribunals that have a discretion to refer[44] and those courts from which a reference is mandatory.[45] The discretion to refer is not affected by domestic rules of precedent,[46] so that any guidance given by the UK courts[47] must yield to the general principles outlined by the European Court of Justice.[48] If this was not the case, the principle of the supremacy of European law would be undermined and the objective of uniform interpretation placed in jeopardy.

---

41 See *Jasiewicz v Jasiewicz* [1962] 3 All ER 1017; 1 WLR 1426.
42 As subsequently amended by the Treaty on European Union (the Maastricht Treaty) 1993.
43 On interpretation not application; application being a matter for the national court.
44 Treaty of Rome 1957, Art 177(2).
45 *Ibid*, Art 177(3).
46 Cases 146/73; 166/73 *Rheinmühlen Düsseldorf v Einführ und Vorratstelle für Getreide und Füttermittel* [1974] ECR 33, p 139; 1 CMLR 523.
47 As in *HP Bulmer Ltd v JA Bollinger* [1974] Ch 401.
48 283/81 *CILFIT Srl v Ministro della Sanità* [1982] ECR 3415; [1983] 1 CMLR 472.

CHAPTER 9

EXCLUSION OF FOREIGN LAW

INTRODUCTION

There can be no doubt that the forum controls the cases that come before it and the forum must have power to reject suits, both domestic and foreign, which offend against some fundamental principle of its operation. The general principle was clearly expressed by Lord Parker in *Dynamit Actien Gesellschaft v Rio Tinto Zinc*,[1] where the learned judge stated:

> Whenever the courts of this country are called upon to decide as to the rights and liabilities of the parties to a contract, the effect on such a contract of the public policy of this country must necessarily be a relevant consideration. Every legal decision of our courts consists of the application of our own law to the facts of the case as ascertained by appropriate evidence. One of these facts may be the state of some foreign law, but it is not the foreign law but our own law to which effect is given ... As has often been said, private international law is really a branch of municipal law and obviously there can be no branch of law in which the general policy of such law can be properly ignored.[2]

This conventional exposition of the attitude to be adopted to foreign law has found favour in other jurisdictions, as Cardozo J observed in *Louks v Standard Oil Company of New York*:[3]

> A right of action is property. If a foreign statute gives this right, the mere fact that we do not give a like right is no reason for refusing to help the plaintiff in getting what belongs to him. We are not so provincial as to say that every solution of a problem is wrong because we deal with it otherwise at home ... the courts are not free to enforce a foreign right at the pleasure of judges, to suit the individual notion of expediency or fairness. They do not close their doors unless help would violate some fundamental principle of justice, some prevalent conception of good morals, some deep rooted tradition of the common weal.

---

1   [1918] AC 260, p 292.
2   *Dynamit Actien Gesellschaft v Rio Tinto Zinc Co* [1918] AC 260, p 292, *per* Lord Parker. The case itself concerned contractual relations with a German company during the period of World War I. At such time, it was, more than ever, important that the executive and judicial branches of Government should speak with one voice.
3   (1918) 224 NY 99, p 111.

There is some authority for the view that, in England, there are three forms of legislation that will not be enforced by English courts:[4]

(a) revenue laws;

(b) penal laws; and

(c) other public laws.

This formulation was advanced by Lord Denning MR in *AG of New Zealand v Ortiz* and his formulation has been alluded to favourably in a number of subsequent cases[5] in the UK[6] and in other jurisdictions.[7]

It is proposed to examine each of these three categories in turn before considering the particular problems that arise in respect of foreign expropriatory legislation and those laws that offend the public policy of the forum. While some order can be derived from adhering to categories, it will be appreciated that the categories are not mutually exclusive.

FOREIGN REVENUE LAWS[8]

The prohibition on direct enforcement

It has been accepted since the middle of the 18th century[9] that English courts will not enforce the revenue laws of another country. The reasons advanced of this view are less than convincing but a clear line of authority sustains the prohibition on the direct enforcement of foreign revenue laws.[10]

The expression, foreign revenue laws, has been broadly defined to mean any 'law requiring a non contractual payment to the State or some department or sub-division thereof'.[11] The revenue law may relate to direct taxes, such as

---

4 See *AG of New Zealand v Ortiz* [1984] 1 AC 1; [1982] 3 All ER 432; 3 WLR 570 (affirming the Court of Appeal at [1984] 1 AC 1); [1983] 2 All ER 93; 2 WLR 809, where Lord Denning MR drew upon the classification in the relevant edition of Dicey and Morris, *Conflict of Laws* (10th edn, 1980).

5 In the Court of Appeal: *Williams and Humbert Ltd v W and H Trade Marks (Jersey)* [1986] AC 368 and *Re State of Norway's Application* [1987] QB 433; *United States of America v Inkley* [1989] QB 255.

6 In the House of Lords: *Re State of Norway's Application (Nos 1 and 2)* [1990] 1 AC 723.

7 *AG for the United Kingdom v Heinemann Publishers Australia Pty Ltd* (1988) 165 CLR 30; *AG for the United Kingdom v Wellington Newspapers Ltd* [1988] 1 NZLR 129.

8 See Albrecht (1950) 30 BYIL 454; Mann, M (1954) 3 ICLQ 465; Webb (1965) 28 MLR 591 Stoel (1967) 16 ICLQ 663; Carter (1984) 55 BYIL 111.

9 *Holman v Johnson* (1775) 1 Cowp 341, *per* Lord Mansfield.

10 *Municipal Council of Sydney v Bull* [1909] 1 KB 7; *The Eva* [1921] P 454; *Re Visser* [1928] Ch 877; *Government of India v Taylor* [1955] AC 491.

11 Morris, *The Conflict of Laws* (4th edn, 1993), p 49.

income taxes[12] or death duties,[13] or indirect taxes, such as customs duties; the expression is wide enough to include local rates.[14]

Some writers have raised the question as to whether such an approach is damaging to international comity. However, the limited line of authority was confirmed by the House of Lords in the case of *Government of India v Taylor*,[15] where the facts were as follows: the Delhi Electric Supply and Traction Co Ltd, a company registered in England but carrying on business in India, sold its business to the Indian Government. The sum was remitted to England and the company then decided upon voluntary liquidation. The Indian Commissioners for Income Tax made a claim for income tax in respect of the capital gain on the sale of the business. The simple issue was the entitlement of the Commissioners to prove in the winding up of an English registered company for the recovery of the tax due on its trading operations in India.

The appellants argued unsuccessfully in the House of Lords that the prohibition in respect of foreign revenue laws did not apply to liquidation proceedings nor to those taxes that had an English equivalent; it was further argued that the prohibition did not apply in respect of Commonwealth countries. All such arguments were rejected. The rule was said to be based on the sound principle that to enforce such claims would permit 'an assertion of sovereign authority by one State within the territory of another ... contrary to all concepts of independent sovereignties'.[16] This justification has recently been approved in the Court of Appeal.[17]

The prohibition on indirect enforcement

That the prohibition extends to both the direct and the indirect enforcement of foreign revenue laws was illustrated by the Court of Appeal judgment in *Rossano v Manufacturers' Life Insurance Co Ltd*,[18] where the facts were as follows: the plaintiff was an Eygptian national; the defendants were an insurance company with a head office in Toronto and branches in other countries. The action was to recover money under three policies of insurance. The insurance policies involved payment in London and New York.

One of the defences raised by the defendants was that garnishee orders had been served by the Eygptian government on their offices in Cairo, so that

---

12 *USA v Harden* (1963) 41 DLR (2d) 721, Supreme Court of Canada.
13 *Re Visser* [1928] Ch 877.
14 *Municipal Council of Sydney v Bull* [1909] 1 KB 7.
15 [1955] AC 491; 1 All ER 292.
16 *Government of India v Taylor* [1955] AC 491, *per* Lord Keith of Avonholm.
17 *Camdex International Ltd v Bank of Zambia and Others (No 3)* (1997) *The Times*, 28 January; 6 Bank LR 44 (Simon Browne, Otton and Phillips LJJ).
18 [1963] 2 QB 352; [1962] 2 All ER 514.

such orders would render them liable if any payment were made to the insured before the plaintiff discharged his tax liabilities. This defence was rejected because to allow the garnishee orders, which were attributable to taxation debts, to defeat the plaintiff's claim would constitute the indirect enforcement of a foreign revenue law.

Although indirect enforcement will not be permitted, the courts will assist a foreign State to obtain evidence in a dispute with one of its taxpayers.[19]

Problems can arise, however, as to the precise nature of the claim by the State, particularly in the modern world, where the organ of State may be concerned with provision of services and the possibility of a claim based on unjust enrichment cannot be excluded. However, this was not the approach in *Municipal Council of Sydney v Bull*[20] where the plaintiff failed to recover a contribution in respect of street improvements. The difficulty of determining the nature of such a claim is illustrated by the case of *Brokaw v Seatrain UK Ltd*,[21] where the facts were as follows:

Goods were shipped by sea from the USA. While at sea, the US Treasury served a notice of levy on the shipowner in respect of unpaid taxes demanding that the goods be surrendered. On arrival at Southampton, the shipowner refused to hand over the goods to the consignees who claimed delivery.

In interpleader proceedings, the Court of Appeal rejected the claim of the US Treasury reasoning that the physical seizure of the goods would permit the indirect enforcement of a foreign revenue law.

Recognition of a foreign revenue law

While the courts have consistently refused to enforce directly or indirectly foreign revenue laws this does not prevent the recognition of such laws on the basis that public policy demands the maintenance of harmonious relations with foreign States. Sometimes the distinction between enforcement and recognition is difficult to draw and problems do arise in respect of contracts to defraud the revenue law of another jurisdiction. As Lord Simmonds observed in *Regazzoni v KC Sethia (1944) Ltd*:[22]

> It does not follow from the fact that today the court will not enforce a revenue at the suit of a foreign State that today it will enforce a contract which requires

---

19 *Re The State of Norway's Applications (Nos 1 and 2)* [1990] 1 AC 723; [1989] 1 All ER 745 (pursuant to the Evidence (Proceedings in Other Jurisdictions) Act 1975).

20 [1909] 1 KB 7.

21 [1971] 2 QB 476.

22 [1958] AC 301.

the doing of an act in a foreign country which violates the revenue laws of that country.[23]

Thus, the obligations of personal representatives to pay foreign taxes will be taken account of[24] and schemes for the evasion of foreign revenue laws will not be upheld.[25]

Contracts will not be enforced that require the doing of an act in a foreign country that violates the revenue law of that country.[26] The English courts have, in general, been more ready to scrutinise artificial attempts to avoid[27] or evade taxation obligations in a domestic setting, so that it is natural that they should be sympathetic to the attempts of foreign revenue services to prevent fraud and to collect evidence.[28] It therefore follows that the principle propounded in *Holman v Johnson*[29] does not mean that foreign revenue laws will be ignored.

FOREIGN PENAL LAWS

The prohibition on the enforcement of foreign penal laws

It has been established for over 100 years that an English court will not, directly or indirectly, aid the enforcement of a foreign penal law. The position was succinctly expressed by Marshall CJ[30] in *The Antelope*,[31] where he observed: 'The courts of no country execute the penal laws of another.'[32]

---

23 See Mann, FA (1958) 21 MLR 130; Guest (1957) 73 LQR 32.

24 *Re Lord Cable* [1976] 3 All ER 417; [1977] 1 WLR 7.

25 *Re Emery's Investment Trusts* [1959] Ch 410; 1 All ER 577.

26 The earlier view was expressed by Lord Wrenbury, in *British and Foreign Marine Insurance v Samuel Sanday and Co* [1916] AC 650, to the effect that: 'Illegality according to the law of another country does not affect the merchant.' This gives way to concerns as to international comity as reflected in *Regazzoni v KC Sethia (1944) Ltd* [1958] AC 301. This coincides with a more sceptical attitude by the English courts to artificial schemes of tax avoidance. This attitude can be traced in the 1980s as the courts moved away from the principle of non-intervention propounded in *IRC v Duke of Westminster* [1936] AC 1, towards a readiness to scrutinise the purpose of the transaction, which dates from *WT Ramsay v IRC* [1982] AC 300.

27 *Furness v Dawson* [1984] AC 300.

28 *Re State of Norway's Application (Nos 1 and 2)* [1990] 1 AC 723; [1989] 1 All ER 745.

29 (1775) 1 Cowp 341.

30 As Chief Justice of the United States (1800–35), Marshall CJ was more familiar than most with limitations on sovereign power, having himself given judgment in the case of *The Schooner Exchange v McFaddon* (1812) 7 Cranch 116, several years previously.

31 (1825) 10 What 66, p 123, *per* Marshall CJ.

32 The phrase had been used earlier by Lord Loughborough and Mr Justice Buller in *Foliot v Ogden* (1789) 1 H Bl 124.

The law has stood unchanged since the leading modern case of *Huntingdon v Attrill*[33] established that an English court will not enforce a foreign penal law.[34] The facts of the case were as follows: under a New York statute, the directors of a company who signed certificates which were false in any material representation would be jointly and severally liable for the debts of the company while they were directors. Mr Attrill was a director of the New York company and he signed a certificate which falsely stated that the entire capital stock had been paid up. Mr Huntingdon, who had lent money to the company, sued Mr Attrill in New York for the unpaid balance of his loan. He obtained judgment for $100,240 in the Supreme Court of New York. The judgment remained unsatisfied. The plaintiff then brought an action upon it in the courts of Ontario, who dismissed the claim as an attempt to enforce a penal law. The appeal was allowed by the Privy Council, who held that the statute was not penal.

In delivering the judgment of the Privy Council, Lord Watson sought to formulate the proper test for determining whether the proceedings were designed to enforce a penal law. The prohibition against such proceedings applied not only to prosecutions and sentences for crimes and misdemeanours, but to all suits in favour of the State for the recovery of pecuniary penalties for any violation of statutes, for the protection of its revenue or other municipal laws, and to all judgments for such penalties.[35] Thus, the prohibition extends to any penalty imposed by the foreign law in favour of the foreign State, but not to laws whose object is remedial, even if they are designed to benefit the general public. So, for example, a penalty clause in a contract valid by its applicable law would not be regarded as penal *per se*, nor would the prohibition prevent the enforcement in England of a foreign award of exemplary damages.[36]

Examples of the prohibition on the enforcement of a penal law

Even before the case of *Huntingdon v Attrill*, there were examples of the prohibition.[37] The case law since 1893 indicates that the prohibition extends to both direct and the indirect enforcement.[38] An example of indirect enforcement is afforded by the case of *Banco de Vizcaya v Don Alfonso de Borbon*

33 [1893] AC 150; the judgment of the Privy Council was delivered by Lord Watson.
34 See, also, *Frankfurter v WL Exner Ltd* [1947] Ch 629; *De Azucar v Industria Azucarera Nacional SA, The Playa Larga* [1983] 2 LR 171; *Williams and Humbert Ltd v W and H Trade Marks (Jersey) Ltd* [1986] AC 368.
35 Lord Watson accepted the formulation of Gray J in the US Supreme Court decision *Wisconsin v Pelican Insurance* (1888) 127 US 265.
36 *SA Consortium General Textiles v Sun and Sound Agencies Ltd* [1978] QB 279.
37 *Ogden v Folliott* (1790) 3 Term Rep 726.
38 *Banco de Vizcaya v Don Alfonso de Borbon y Austria* [1935] 1 KB 140.

y Austria,[39] where the facts were as follows: the King of Spain had deposited secuities in a London bank to be held to the order of his agents, a Spanish bank. The Spanish Republican Government later decreed the seizure of all the property of the King and ordered that all property deposited with a Spanish bank should be delivered to the Treasury. The plaintiffs claimed delivery up of the securities, on the ground that they had a right arising at the time of the original deposit.

Lawrence J, in rejecting the claim, held that the plaintiffs were not seeking to enforce their own contractual rights but were, in substance, seeking to implement the decrees of the Spanish Republic; as these decrees were penal in nature, the claim had to be rejected.

Reasoning to like effect was employed in the case of *Frankfurther v WL Exner Ltd*.[40] In recent years, claims have arisen in respect of the unlawful export of particular articles. An interesting example of the enforcement of a foreign law arose in the case of *AG of New Zealand v Ortiz*,[41] where the facts were as follows: a Maori carved door was removed from New Zealand without the permission of the appropriate authorities; it was offered for auction in London. The Attorney General of New Zealand sought an injunction claiming to restrain the sale and seeking delivery up of the chattel. The claim was based on the terms of a New Zealand statute which provided for forfeiture without compensation of historic articles.

Staughton J, at first instance, in giving judgment for the plaintiffs, did not consider the terms of the statute to be penal. The Court of Appeal[42] allowed the appeal on a point of statutory construction but chose to deal with the matter on a broad front. Ackner and O'Connor LJJ held the statute to be penal in content, while Lord Denning MR gave express approval to the threefold division of revenue laws, penal laws and other public laws.[43] In reviewing the prior case law on tangible movables confiscated by sovereign governments, the Master of Rolls observed that:

> ... the class of laws which will be enfoced are those laws which are an exercise by the sovereign government of its sovereign authority over property within its own territory or over its subjects, wherever they may be. But, other laws will not be enforced. By international law every sovereign State has no sovereignty beyond its own frontiers.

By linking this area of law with the principle of sovereignty in public international law, Lord Denning MR went on to hold that legislation

---

39 [1935] 1 KB 140.
40 [1947] Ch 629.
41 [1984] AC 1; see, also, Nott (1984) 33 ICLQ 203.
42 [1984] AC 1 (Lord Denning MR, O'Connor, Ackner LJJ).
43 As set out in the 10th edition of Dicey and Morris, *Conflict of Laws* (1980).

prohibiting exports could come within the third category of 'other public laws' which will not be enforced outside the territory of the particular State.[44]

In more recent cases, an attempt has been made to scrutinise carefully the precise nature of the claim by the foreign State. An example is afforded by the case of *United States of America v Inkley*,[45] where the facts were as follows: Inkley, having been charged with a criminal offence in the USA, was released after entering into an appearance bond. He then left for England and did not return for the remainder of the criminal proceedings. The US Government obtained a civil judgment in the USA, making Mr Inkley liable in respect of the sum stipulated in the bond. A claim was then brought in England seeking to enforce the civil judgment.

The Court of Appeal refused to enforce the judgment, arguing that it was an indirect attempt to enforce its own penal laws. Purchas LJ observed:

> ... notwithstanding its civil clothing, the purpose of the action ... was the due execution by the United States of America of a public law process aimed to ensure the attendance of persons accused of crime before the criminal courts.[46]

OTHER PUBLIC LAWS

The reference by Lord Denning MR, in *AG of New Zealand v Ortiz*,[47] to the category of 'other public laws' has given the seal of approval to this particular head as set out in Dicey and Morris.[48] The question naturally arises as to which laws fall within this specific category. This is a particular problem in the UK, where the concept of a distinct 'public law' is a matter of continuing debate. The learned authors of Dicey and Morris give as examples:

(a) import/export regulations;

(b) trading with the enemy legislation;

(c) price control legislation; and

(d) anti-trust legislation.

---

44 In an interesting judgment, Lord Denning MR drew upon *Don Alonso v Cornero* (1615) 2 Bulst 306; *King of Italy v Marquis Cosimo de Medici Tornaquinci* (1918) 34 TLR 623; *Princess Paley Olga v Weisz* [1929] 1 KB 718. One interesting feature of the judgment is that Lord Denning is anxious to reconcile the subject of non-recognition of foreign law in private international law with problems of the exercise of sovereign authority, which arise in the law of State immunity. See Carter (1989) 48 CLJ 417. As the author points out, it is worthwhile comparing the tenor of Lord Denning's judgment with both the *Emperor of Austria v Day and Kossuth* (1861) 3 De GF & J 217; *Government of India v Taylor* [1955] AC 491.

45 [1989] QB 255.

46 *United States of America v Inkley* [1989] QB 255, p 266, *per* Purchas LJ.

47 [1984] AC 1. The House of Lords dismissed the appeal from the Court of Appeal, concerning themselves, only, with the point of statutory construction, and not dealing in detail with the question of classification of foreign law, raised in the Court of Appeal.

48 Dicey and Morris, *Conflict of Laws* (10th edn, 1980), Vol 1, p 90, r 3.

Lord Denning MR admitted that the expression 'other public laws' was rather vague, but the learned judge considered that the laws that came within the expression were *eiusdem generis* with penal or revenue laws. By tracing the matter back to questions of sovereignty, Lord Denning thought that a law of State A, directed at property or non nationals beyond its territory, might in principle come within this category. The approach of the learned judge was to view this category of private international law as conditional upon the principle that a sovereign State in public international law is, in general, sovereign only within its own territory.

That a category of 'other public laws' existed was recognised in the legal proceedings in Australia and New Zealand that arose out the attempt of the UK to restrain the memoirs of Mr Peter Wright.[49] The facts of the case were simple: the Attorney General of the UK sought injunctions in Australia and New Zealand to restrain publication of the book, *Spycatcher*. It was argued that the information for the book derived from unlawful disclosure of confidential information by Peter Wright, a former member of the Security Services. One of the defences raised in the courts of Australia and New Zealand was that these courts would not recognise a foreign penal or public law.[50]

While both the Australian and the New Zealand court refused to grant the relief sought, the reasoning in respect of the private international law aspect did differ. The High Court of Australia[51] viewed the case as an attempt by the UK to employ the equitable doctrine of confidence to protect its Security Services and, thus, to sustain a governmental interest and, as such, the action fell within the category 'other public laws', while the New Zealand Court of Appeal formed the view that the purpose of the action was to protect the employer/employee relationship and, thus, the action should not be treated as an attempt to enforce 'other public laws'. In strict terms, the New Zealand approach seems more logical; the cause of action was based on a contractual duty that was owed by Mr Wright to his employers and, once that had been determined, it should have been for the court then to proceed to determine whether such rights should or should not prevail over considerations of freedom of information and freedom of expression. It is sensible to compare

---

49 The so called *Spycatcher* saga; see *AG v Guardian Newspapers Ltd (No 2)* [1990] AC 109.

50 In strict terms, the action was founded on the equitable doctrine of abuse of confidential information, which could be traced back to *Prince Albert v Strange* (1849) 1 Mac & G 25. In 1975, the decision in *AG v Jonathan Cape* [1976] QB 752, had indicated that, in certain cases, a governmental body might rely on the doctrine. This, however, failed to take account of those countries such as Australia that had enacted freedom of information legislation which limited the powers of the court to grant prohibitory injunctions where the matters were suitable for public discussion.

51 *AG for the United Kingdom v Heinemann Publishers Australia Pty* (1988) 165 CLR 30 (litigation in Australia); *AG for the United Kingdom v Wellington Newspapers Ltd* (1988) 1 NZLR 129. The judgments were subject to some criticism: see Collier (1989) 48 CLJ 33; Mann, FA (1988) 104 LQR 497.

the case to *AG of New Zealand v Ortiz*.[52] In *Ortiz*, the claim for the injunction was founded on a duty arising under a particular statute, so that the case was an attempt to enforce that specific law. In the *Spycatcher* case, the claim was based on a private duty arising from a contractual relationship, even if the motivation for bringing the case was to prevent the Official Secrets Act 1911 from being undermined.

FOREIGN EXPROPRIATION LEGISLATION

Foreign expropriatory legislation is often included within the category of public policy exclusions and may well fall within the categories of 'penal' or 'other public Laws'. In the 20th century, as governments in different parts of the world have sought to control the exercise of private property rights, this has become a specialised area subject to some fine distinctions.[53]

Before turning to the question of recognition, it is important to distinguish between the scope of such laws. As the cases indicate, such legislation may be directed against a particular individual[54] or against specific property[55] or against a particular national, ethnic or religious grouping.[56] Recent authority indicated that the form of such laws has to be carefully distinguished; past experience indicates the form of the legislation may fall within at least four broad forms:

(a) requisition: the seizure of property in the public interest for a limited period in return for compensation;[57]

(b) nationalisation: the absorbtion of property into public ownership to facilitate political objectives and in return for compensation;[58]

(c) compulsory acquisition: the permanent seizure of property usually to achieve some specific social or economic aim and in exchange for compensation;[59]

---

52 [1984] AC 1.

53 It is interesting to note the cases following the Russian Revolution of 1917, as the claims of the State to seize private property became more widespread.

54 As in *Banco de Vizcaya v Don Alfonso de Borbon y Austria* [1935] 1 KB 140.

55 As in *Attorney General of New Zealand v Ortiz* [1984] AC 1.

56 See *Oppenheimer v Cattermole* [1976] AC 249.

57 *AG v De Keyser's Royal Hotel* [1920] AC 508.

58 Coming within this category would be the programme of the Attlee Government (1945–51); the relationship with the European Convention on Human Rights and Fundamental Freedoms 1950, discussed in *Lithgow v The United Kingdom* (1986) 8 EHRR 329.

59 In the UK, the procedure is being regulated by the Acquisition of Land Act 1981; Compulsory Purchase Act 1965; and Land Compensation Act 1961.

(d) confiscation: the permanent seizure of property without regard to the payment of compensation.[60]

The central problem that arises is as to the extent to which an English court will recognise and enforce a decree of a foreign State affecting the property of nationals and aliens. The subject has become complicated because of the immunity that a State normally enjoys from the jurisdiction,[61] and because of the difficult problems that can arise as to whether a particular entity constitutes a recognised government.[62] Over the last 200 years, the case law indicates that, in addition to questions of interpretation, an English court will be concerned to inquire into three matters, namely:

(a) does the decree emanate from a recognised government?

(b) was the relevant property within the foreign jurisdiction at the time of the decree?

(c) was the foreign sovereign in possession or control of the property outside the jurisdiction at the time of the decree?

It is proposed to examine each of these questions in turn.

(a) Does the decree emanate from a recognised government?

It has been accepted for over 100 years that an unrecognised government cannot sue for the recovery of property in an English court.[63] The other side of the picture is the effect of the legislative acts of any unrecognised entity. The leading case is that of *Luther v Sagor*,[64] where the facts were as follows: timber situated in Russia belonged to the plaintiffs, who were a company incorporated in Russia. The timber was seized by the Soviet authorities, pursuant to a nationalisation decree. Part of the timber was brought to England and sold to the defendant by a Soviet agent. The plaintiffs sued for damages on the basis that the timber still belonged to them and all prior acts constituted trespass.

---

60 Any such action will almost certainly be a breach of public international law; the general principle is that any seizure should be followed by 'prompt, adequate and effective compensation', as stated by Cordell Hull (1871–1955), Secretary of State 1933–45 and Winner of the Nobel Peace Prize 1945, sometimes known as the 'Father' of the United Nations.

61 See the State Immunity Act 1978, which must be regarded as a complete code following the judgment in *Al Adsani v Government of Kuwait* (1996) 107 ILR 536, CA.

62 In respect of the recognition of governments, cases have now to be read in the light of the decision of the executive branch, in 1980, to announce that the Foreign Office would no longer make formal declarations as to recognition. The role of the executive branch would simply be to provide factual information; the new approach of the courts is set out by Hobhouse J in *Republic of Somalia v Woodhouse, Drake and Carey (Suisse) SA* [1993] QB 54, applied by Cresswell J in *Sierra Leone Telecommunications Co Ltd v Barclays Bank plc* [1998] 2 All ER 821.

63 *The City of Berne v The Bank of England* (1804) 9 Ves Jun 347; for a modern discussion, see *Gur Corporation v Trust Bank of Africa* [1987] 1 QB 599; see, also, Warbrick (1993) 56 MLR 92.

64 [1921] 1 KB 456 (Roche J); 3 KB 522, CA (Bankes, Scrutton and Warrington LJJ).

At first instance, Roche J found for the plaintiffs, on the ground that the legislative or administrative acts of an unrecognised government were of no legal effect.[65] However, subsequent to the hearing at first instance, the Foreign Office recognised the Soviet Government as the *de facto* government. On appeal to the Court of Appeal, the judgment of Roche J was reversed, on the grounds that the grant of recognition operated retrospectively to validate the legislative act in question and that the enactment had full effect since, at the operative date, the property was within the jurisdiction of the government. A strong Court of Appeal held that the courts of one sovereign State cannot sit in judgment on the legislative acts of another sovereign State, and that title to the property was to be determined by the *lex situs*.

After *Luther v Sagor*, it was reasonable to assume that the two relevant questions would be the status of the government and whether the property was within its jurisdiction at the time of the decree. These two principles were applied by the court in the subsequent case of *Princess Olga Paley v Weisz*,[66] where the facts were as follows: Princess Paley occupied the Paley Palace near St Petersburg; it was full of valuable *objets d'art*. In 1918, the revolutionaries took possession and the Princess fled to England. The Soviet Government declared all the property to be owned by the State. In 1928, it sold some of the articles to Mr Weisz, who brought them to England. The Princess sued to recover them. She failed.

In giving judgment in the Court of Appeal, Scrutton LJ expressed the position with characteristic clarity in observing:

> Our Government has recognised the present Russian Government as the *de jure* Government of Russia, and our courts are bound to give effect to the laws and acts of that Government, so far as they relate to property within that jurisdiction when it was affected by those laws and acts.

The decision of the executive branch of government to refrain from the formal recognition of governments after 1980[67] does mean that, in certain situations, the court may be required to weigh the evidence to determine whether a particular entity has the capacity both to sue and to have its legislative decrees acknowledged. Although only a limited number of cases have come before the courts since 1980, it would seem that the court, in deciding whether to regard an entity as a recognised government, will follow the criteria set out by

---

65 Following *Republic of Peru v Dreyfus* (1888) 38 Ch D 348; *City of Berne v Bank of England* (1804) 9 Ves 347.

66 [1929] 1 KB 718. See also the as yet unreported judgement of Mance J in *Kuwait Airways Corporation v Iraqi Airways Corporation* (1998) (unreported, 29 July), which was cited with approval by the House of Lords in *R v Bow Street Stipendiary Magistrate ex p Pinochet Ugarte* [1998] 3 WLR 1456, p 1494.

67 HL Deb Vol 408 Cols 1121–22, 28 April 1980 (Lord Carrington). The decision of the UK Government was in line with the decision taken by the USA in 1977 to adopt the same policy. For a discussion on the likely effects, see Crawford (1986) 57 BYIL 405; Brownlie (1982) 53 BYIL 197; Warbrick (1981) 30 ICLQ 568; Symons [1981] PL 249.

Hobhouse J in *Republic of Somalia v Woodhouse, Drake and Carey*,[68] where the learned judge observed:

> ... the factors to be taken into account in deciding whether a government exists as the government of a State are: (a) whether it is the constitutional government of the State; (b) the degree, nature and stability of administrative control, if any, that it of itself exercises over the territory of the State; (c) whether Her Majesty's Government has any dealings with it and, if so, what is the nature of those dealings; and (d) in marginal cases, the extent of international recognition that it has as the government of the State.

This test was applied in a different context by Cresswell J in *Sierra Leone Telecommunications Co Ltd v Barclays Bank plc*,[69] so that it would seem that any entity whose validity is in dispute must meet this newly formulated test both for capacity to sue and in those cases where the validity of its legislative acts is in issue.[70] On the assumption that no question of recognition of the government is in issue,[71] the court will be required to determine whether the property is within the jurisdiction of the foreign government when the decree was made, and this aspect deserves further attention.

(b) Was the relevant property within the foreign jurisdiction at the time of the decree?

As indicated above, the principle that derived from *Luther v Sagor*[72] and *Princess Paley Olga v Weisz*[73] was that a legislative decree in respect of property situated within a foreign jurisdiction would be recognised by English courts. Some doubt was cast on the principle by the case of *Anglo Iranian Oil Co v Jaffrate*,[74] where Campbell J, sitting in the Supreme Court of Aden, questioned whether the principle in *Luther v Sagor* applied to the confiscation of the property of non-nationals without compensation, as such conduct was a breach of public international law. This decision has not been followed; it was subject to criticism by Upjohn J, in *Re Helbert Wagg and Co Ltd's Claim*,[75] and cannot now be good law, having regard to the principle in *Luther v Sagor* being accepted and applied by the House of Lords in *Williams*

---

68 [1993] QB 54.

69 [1998] 2 All ER 821.

70 The link between *locus standi* to sue and recognition of legislative acts had been pointed out by Roche J, at first instance, in *Luther v Sagor* [1921] 1 KB 456.

71 In the third case to come before the courts since 1980 where *locus standi* and recognition was in issue, the court in *Gur Corporation v Trust Bank of Africa Ltd* [1987] QB 599 was able to resolve the difficulty on *locus standi* by applying the principles set out in the pre-1980 case of *Carl Zeiss Stiftung v Rayner and Keeler Ltd (No 2)* [1967] 1 AC 853. That solution will not always be open to the court; see Beck (1987) 36 ICLQ 350; Crawford (1986) 57 BYIL 405; Mann, FA (1987) 36 ICLQ 348.

72 [1921] 3 KB 532.

73 [1929] 1 KB 718.

74 [1953] 1 WLR 246 (a judgment of the Supreme Court of Aden, better known as *The Rose Mary*).

75 [1956] Ch 323; O'Connell (1955) 4 ICLQ 267; see Mann (1954) 70 LQR 181.

and Humbert Ltd v W and H Trade Marks (Jersey) Ltd.[76] In the first of these cases, *Re Helbert Wagg and Co Ltd's Claim*, Upjohn J held that a legislative enactment of the German government was to be recognised, even though it purported to confiscate the property of non-nationals without providing compensation.

Although there have been cases where such enactments have been categorised as penal,[77] the difficulty with such an approach is that it would involve an English court in analysing evidence to determine whether compensation on offer was or was not adequate. In any event, the matter must now be considered in the light of the House of Lords judgment in *Williams and Humbert Ltd v W and H Trade Marks (Jersey) Ltd*, where the facts in broad terms were as follows: in 1983, the Spanish State expropriated the shares in a Spanish Company and two banks. The Spanish company owned all the shares in the English subsidiary, W and H Ltd (the plaintiff company). In 1976, the plaintiff company had entered into an agreement to assign its valuable trade marks to the defendants, a Jersey based company, after which they allowed the plaintiffs to use the trade marks on licence. In 1983, the plaintiffs, now controlled indirectly by the Spanish State, brought an action to set aside the 1976 assignment, having been procured by the directors of the English subsidiary in breach of their fiduciary duty as directors. The defendants entered a defence asserting that the proceedings were an indirect attempt to enforce a foreign penal law. The plaintiffs asked the court, pursuant to RSC Ord 18 r 19, to strike out this defence. At first instance, Nourse J agreed to do so and his judgment was upheld by the Court of Appeal and the House of Lords.

A number of points emerge from the litigation, not all of them directly relevant to the treatment of foreign law. As Lord Templeman observed in the House of Lords, the defence pleading was misconceived because it failed to pay proper regard to the doctrine of English company law as to the separate legal personality of the company. Secondly, as the Court of Appeal observed, the cause of action was based on a 1976 assignment, itself several years prior to the legislative decrees in question. The point of interest for present purposes is that, in a scholarly reserved judgment, Nourse J tried to reduce the past case law on expropriatory laws into a number of propositions which can be summarised as follows:

> (1A) English law will not recognise foreign confiscatory laws which, by reason of their being discriminatory on grounds of race, religion or the like, constitute so grave an infringement of human rights that they ought not to be recognised as laws at all.[78]

---

76 [1986] AC 368.

77 *Frankfurther v WL Exner Ltd* [1947] Ch 629; *Novello and Co Ltd v Hinrichsen Edtions Ltd* [1951] Ch 595.

78 *Oppenheimer v Cattermole* [1976] AC 249.

(1B)   English law will not recognise foreign laws which discriminate against nationals of this country in time of war by purporting to confiscate their movable property situate in the foreign State.[79]

(2A)   English law, while recognising foreign laws not falling within class 1, which confiscate property situated within the foreign State, will not directly or indirectly enforce them here if they are also penal.[80]

(2B)   English law will not enforce foreign laws which purport to confiscate property situated in this country.[81]

(3)   English law will recognise foreign laws not falling within class 1 which confiscate property situated within a foreign State and where title is perfected there.[82] The nationality of the owner is immaterial.[83]

Having regard to the considerable volume of past case law, and the different forms of expropriatory decrees, the propositions advanced by Nourse J represent the most accurate recent summary of the law. However, the learned judge was not asked to consider the situation where the property is situated outside the jurisdiction of the government at the time of the decree and it is to that problem we must now turn.

(c) Was the foreign sovereign in possession or control of the property outside the jurisdiction at the time of the decree?

The general principle in public international law is that the legislative sovereignty of a State is territorial; in principle, the laws of State A will only operate within the territory of State A and only in certain limited circumstances will affect the citizens of State A outside the jurisdiction.

In respect of a foreign expropriatory decree that appears to affect property outside the territory of the State, the approach of the English courts has been to endeavour, as a matter of construction, to interpret the decree as not having extra-territorial effect. If such an interpretation can be given to the decree, then no question of recognition arises. This approach was adopted in the case of *Lecouturier v Rey*,[84] where the facts were as follows: a French statute declared unlicensed religious associations unlawful. The Order of Carthusian monks was disbanded and its property in France sold. The Order then re-established itself in Spain and began again to manufacture its liqueur known as Chartreuse. At a later date, a question arose as to whether the purchaser of the French business was entitled to claim ownership of the English trademarks in Chartreuse.

---

79   *Re Fried Krupp Actien Gesellschaft* [1917] 2 Ch 188.
80   *Banco de Vizcaya v Don Alfonso de Borbon y Austria* [1935] 1 KB 140.
81   *Frankfurther v WL Exner Ltd* [1947] Ch 629.
82   *AM Luther v James Sagor and Co Ltd* [1921] 3 KB 532; *Princess Paley Olga v Weisz* [1929] 1 KB 718.
83   *Re Claim by Helbert Wagg and Co Ltd* [1956] Ch 323.
84   [1910] AC 262.

The House of Lords found in favour of the monks after examining the decrees and interpreting them as only affecting property situated in France. The same willingness to employ techniques of interpretation was adopted by Maugham J in *Re Russian Bank for Foreign Trade*,[85] where the judge held that a Soviet confiscatory decree was not effective in England, even though directed against a Russian national. Problems can arise when a State seizes property beyond its own territory because, when the owner litigates in England to recover that property, he may be met by a plea of sovereign immunity.[86]

There are two cases decided on the topic that, while they may be correct on their own particular facts, are at variance with each other. In *Lorentzen v Lydden and Co*,[87] the facts were as follows: in 1940, the Norwegian Government, about to go into exile, issued a decree, the effect of which was to requisition in return for compensation all Norwegian ships in the territorial waters of the UK.

When this was later challenged in the courts, Atkinson J held that public policy demanded that, as the object was to promote the effort of Norway and the UK in a desperate war for their existence,[88] the court was obliged to recognise and enforce the decree, notwithstanding the fact that it extended to property beyond the jurisdiction of the government. This case must be regarded as decided on its own particular facts and is in line with those cases during the period of World War II, where the courts were anxious not to obstruct the executive branch in matters relating to the war effort.[89]

However, the conventional view that a decree that relates to property beyond the jurisdiction will not be recognised by the English courts was reasserted in the case of *Bank voor Handel en Scheepvaart NV v Slatford*,[90] where the facts were as follows: the Dutch Government in exile made an order requisitioning the property of Dutch citizens. The question arose after the conclusion of the war as to whether gold bars deposited in London in 1939 were subject to the decree.

In giving judgment in an action between a Dutch Bank and the Custodian of Enemy Property, Devlin J, after reviewing the prior case law, ruled that an expropriatory decree by a government will not be recognised as having extra territorial effect. The learned judge approved a statement from Dicey:

---

85 [1933] Ch 745; see, also, *The Jupiter (No 3)* [1927] P 122.

86 *Compania Naviera Vascongado v SS Cristina* [1938] AC 485; though the movement to the restrictive doctrine of State immunity will limit such situations. See the State Immunity Act 1978. See, also, *Kuwait Airways Corporation v Iraqi Airways Corporation* [1995] 1 WLR 1147, HL.

87 [1942] 2 KB 202.

88 The phrase is that of Devlin J, in *Bank voor Handel en Scheepvart NV v Slatford* [1953] 1 QB 248, who had appeared in the earlier case as counsel.

89 See *Duncan v Cammell Laird and Co* [1942] AC 624; *Liversidge v Anderson* [1942] AC 206.

90 [1953] 1 QB 248; [1951] 2 All ER 779.

A State's authority, in the eyes of other States and the courts that represent them is, speaking very generally, coincident with and limited by its power. It is territorial. It may legislate for, and give judgments affecting things and persons within its territory. It has no authority to legislate for, or adjudicate upon, things or persons not within its territory.[91]

FOREIGN LAWS CONTRARY TO ENGLISH PUBLIC POLICY

It is well settled that there will be circumstances when a foreign law or a right arising under foreign law will not be enforced in England because it offends some basic conception of public policy.[92] In reviewing the case law, it is important to pay regard to three considerations that may be expressed as follows:

(a) for what purpose was the foreign law enacted and what is it designed to prevent?

(b) does foreign law or the right arising under foreign law affect England and some domestic conception of public policy?

(c) does the foreign law or right affect some moral, economic, social or political principle that English public policy considers should be of universal application?

In the late 19th century, at the height of Empire, there tended to be an assumption that English values were superior to those of other nations and self-confident judges were much given to outlining the demands of public policy. Today, the conventional view is that the courts of State A should not hold the law or practice of State B to be wrong, simply because State B has enacted different provisions. To put the matter another way, there is today a much greater degree of judicial humility and a recognition that the doctrine of sovereignty does permit a wide margin of appreciation to individual States, having regard to their different economic and social circumstances. It should also be borne in mind that many of the earlier cases concern contractual disputes and will require reconsideration in the light of the present statutory framework.[93]

Before turning to specific heads of public policy, the general evolution in approach can be discerned by examining two cases decided in the past century, namely, *Kaufman v Gerson*[94] and the later case of *Addison v Brown*.[95]

---

91 Dicey, *Conflict of Laws* (6th edn, 1949), p 13.

92 See Scarman J in *Re Fuld's Estate* [1968] P 675.

93 Contracts (Applicable Law) Act 1990, implementing the European Convention on the Law Applicable to Contractual Obligations 1980.

94 [1904] 1 KB 591, CA.

95 [1954] 2 All ER 513; 1 WLR 779 (Streatfield J).

In the case of *Kaufman v Gerson*, the relevant facts were as follows: by a contract made in and to be performed in France, the defendant agreed to pay to the plaintiff by installments the full amount of sums misappropriated by the husband of the defendant. The consideration for the agreement was that the plaintiff would refrain from initiating criminal proceedings. At a later date, the plaintiff sued for arrears of installments.

Notwithstanding the fact that the parties were French nationals domiciled in France and that the contract was valid in France, the Court of Appeal declined to enforce it.[96] In giving judgment, Romer LJ observed that 'to enforce a contract so procured would be to contravene what by the law of this country is deemed an essential moral interest'.[97]

In the UK, where the decision to prosecute is itself discretionary, it is difficult to imagine how an agreement whereby the victim was to receive full compensation could be interpreted as violating some fundamental principle of public policy. A more sophisticated approach can be detected in the late case of *Addison v Brown*,[98] where the facts were as follows: a husband domiciled in California reached an agreement with his wife that he would pay her certain maintenance. The agreement included a term prohibiting either party from seeking to vary the agreement before any court. Ten years later, the husband secured a divorce in the courts of California and the agreement was later incorporated in the court judgment. At a later date, the wife sued for arrears under the agreement.

Since the agreement included a term to oust the jurisdiction of the court, it was arguable that this was contrary to English public policy and it was so pleaded by the defendant.

However, Streatfield J rejected the argument that the agreement was unenforceable because it included a term to oust the jurisdiction of the courts in California. Addressing the argument that a contract to oust the jurisdiction of a foreign court was void as violating public policy, the judge ruled that, if a contract is subject to a foreign law, then it will not violate English rules on public policy unless it relates to England in some particular way. It is not the purpose of public policy in the sphere of private international law to dictate to a foreign legal system as to which agreements shall be enforceable.[99]

There are a number of cases where public policy rules have operated to refuse recognition of rights acquired under a foreign legal system; no list can be comprehensive and public policy is an evolving concept according to

---

96   [1904] 1 KB 591, CA; reversing [1903] 2 KB 114 (Wright J).

97   [1904] 1 KB 591.

98   [1954] 2 All ER 513; 1 WLR 779 (Streatfield J).

99   The robust approach of *Addison v Brown* [1954] 1 WLR 779 is to be contrasted with the earlier cases of *Hope v Hope* (1857) 8 De GM & G 731 (agreement to defeat custody order) and *Rousillon v Rousillon* (1880) 14 Ch D 351 (agreement in restraint of trade).

prevailing social demands.[100] As indicated above, many of the older cases concern contractual disputes that now have to be read with caution now that choice of law has been placed on a statutory basis.[101]

Where English conceptions of morality are violated

A contract to promote sexual immorality will not be enforced in England even though a foreign legal system regards it as unobjectionable.[102] In accordance with this principle, a contract to facilitate commercial fraud will not be enforced.[103] It is also clear that a contract to be performed abroad where A, in a quasi-governmental capacity, receives a payment to ensure favourable treatment for B is objectionable.[104] Manifestly, such contractual arrangements undermine the efforts of the UK to promote open democratic and non corrupt government in other States.

Where English conceptions of justice are violated

A contract secured by coercion, duress[105] or undue influence[106] is unenforceable in England. In certain circumstances, contracts to finance litigation[107] or to assign causes of action[108] may be regarded as void or unenforceable. As will be seen later, a foreign judgment that violates natural justice or is itself based upon a contract subject to a vitiating factor will be unenforceable in England.

---

100 It is perhaps worth recalling the remarks made by Lord Wilberforce in a completely different context, namely, that of the law relating to similar fact evidence, where the learned judge observed: 'And, in matters of experience, it is for the judge to keep close to current mores. What is striking in one age is normal in another; the perversions of yesterday may be the routine or the fashion of tomorrow.' See *Boardman v DPP* [1975] AC 421, p 444; [1974] 3 All ER 887, p 898.

101 Contracts (Applicable Law) Act 1990.

102 *Robinson v Bland* (1760) 2 Burr 1077; *Pearce v Brooks* (1866) LR 1 Exch 213; *Taylor v Chester* (1869) LR 4 QB 309.

103 *Mitsubishi Corporation v Aristidis I Alafouzos* (1988) 1 LR 191.

104 *Lemenda Trading Company Ltd v African Middle Easr Petroleum Co Ltd* [1988] QB 448; [1988] 1 All ER 513; at least in those countries where such payments are prohibited.

105 *Kaufman v Gerson* [1904] 1 KB 591.

106 For the meaning of undue influence, see *National Westminster Bank plc v Morgan* [1985] AC 686; *Barclays Bank plc v O'Brien* [1994] 1 AC 180.

107 *Grell v Levy* (1864) 6 CBNS 73.

108 *Trendtex Trading Coroporation v Credit Suisse* [1982] AC 679; see Thornley (1982) 41 CLJ 29.

Where the contract prejudices the UK in its conduct of foreign affairs

As an original signatory of the United Nations Charter 1945 and as a permanent member of the Security Council, the UK is committed to the orderly and lawful conduct of foreign relations.[109] In these circumstances, transactions that seek to undermine friendly relations with other powers may be unenforceable.[110] Contracts that involve trading with an alien enemy[111] will be unenforceable, regardless of the law of the contract. In time of hostilities, the emphasis is upon the primary duty of a British national or a British based corporation not to do anything directly or indirectly to aid the enemies of the Crown; there is authority for the view that all considerations of private international law must yield to this imperative.[112]

The principle that the conduct of foreign relations should not be unduly damaged is reflected in the reluctance of the courts to enforce transactions designed to promote unrest,[113] cause damage to a friendly government[114] or to defraud its revenue.[115]

Where a foreign law or status violates English conceptions of human rights

The UK is a signatory to the European Convention on Human Rights and Fundamental Freedoms 1950 and is in the process of incorporating the contents of the Convention into domestic law.[116] In the present century, much domestic legislation has been enacted to prevent discrimination[117] and to ensure minimum standards of respect for fellow human beings.[118] It has always been the case that English courts would refuse to recognise and

---

109 In particular, the United Nations Charter 1945, Art 33, which is designed to enforce the peaceful settlement of disputes.

110 *British Nylon Spinners Ltd v ICI Ltd* [1955] Ch 37, p 52.

111 *Robson v Premier Oil and Pipe Line Co* [1915] 2 Ch 124.

112 *Dynamit Actien Gesellschaft v Rio Tinto Zinc Co Ltd* [1918] AC 260; the same reasoning appears in *Lorentzen v Lydden and Co* [1942] 2 KB 202.

113 *De Wurtz v Hendricks* (1824) 2 Bing 314; such conduct today would, of course, be a breach of the United Nations Charter.

114 *Bodley Head Ltd v Flegon* [1972] 1 WLR 680 (a case concerning the contractual capacity of those acting for the then dissident author and Nobel Prize winner, Alexander Solzhenitsyn).

115 *Re Emery's Investment Trusts* [1959] Ch 410; 1 All ER 577.

116 By virtue of the Human Rights Act 1998; the prior status of the ECHR as an unincorporated treaty is discussed in *R v Secretary of State ex p Brind* [1991] 1 AC 696. For a modern judicial opinion, see Laws [1993] PL 59.

117 Race Relations Acts 1965, 1968, 1976; Sex Discrimination Act 1975; Equal Pay Act 1970.

118 Disability Discrimination Act 1995.

enforce those foreign laws that were discriminatory or resulted in legal incapacity.[119] Difficulties have arisen in respect of 'incompetents', where the purpose of the foreign status may have been to protect the young rather than impose a burden. The three cases that have given rise to problems are *Worms v De Valdor*,[120] *Re Selot's Trusts*[121] and *Re Langley's Settlement*.[122]

In *Worms v De Valdor*,[123] the court was concerned with the French status of prodigality and whether a plaintiff subject to that status could bring an action in England. Fry J, without the benefit of expert advice as to French law, held the question to be procedural and, thus, governed by the *lex fori*; the judge concluded that the status presented no obstacle to bringing an action in England. In the later case of *Re Selot's Trusts*,[124] Farwell J was concerned with whether a person subject to the status of prodigality could petition for funds to be paid out of court; the learned judge appeared to view the status as penal and, thus, of no effect in English proceedings.

In the third case, *Re Langley's Settlement*,[125] the Court of Appeal were obliged to consider the power of a settlor to withdraw funds from a settlement governed by English law after being adjudged 'incompetent' by a court in California. On the given facts, the Court of Appeal held the joint exercise of the power by the settlor and his wife to withdraw funds to be valid. The particular relevance of the litigation is that the court appeared to be of the opinion that there was a residual discretion to refuse to recognise a foreign status conferred or imposed on an individual by virtue of the law of his domicile, if recognition would be unjust in the particular circumstances of the case.

---

119 *Sommersett's Case* (1772) 20 St Tr 1 (slavery).
120 (1880) 49 L J Ch 261 (Fry J).
121 [1902] 1 Ch 488 (Farwell J).
122 [1962] Ch 541, CA.
123 (1880) 49 LJ Ch 261.
124 [1902] 1 Ch 488.
125 [1962] Ch 541; see Grodecki (1962) 11 ICLQ 578; Collier (1962) 21 CLJ 36.

PART II

CHAPTER 10

THE JURISDICTION OF THE ENGLISH COURTS: AN INTRODUCTION

PRELIMINARY MATTERS

It is strongly arguable that the subject of jurisdiction is now the most important in the sphere of private international law. Even if this broad proposition is not fully accepted, it cannot be sensibly denied that cases giving rise to problems of jurisdiction are now much more important than they were a generation ago. The reasons for this are probably twofold. First, the development of the doctrine of *forum non conveniens,* in the case law following the judgment of the House of Lords in *The Atlantic Star,*[1] and, secondly, the statutory scheme on jurisdiction introduced by the Civil Jurisdiction and Judgments Act 1982. Possibly, in a logical world, a textbook would begin first with a treatment of the relevant principles of jurisdiction; however, questions of jurisdiction often turn on problems of domicile, so it is sensible to consider jurisdiction after the relevant general principles. However, in seriously contested litigation, today, questions of jurisdiction will often be the first matters that a judge has to consider. One party may argue that the court possesses jurisdiction and the other party will argue that even if the court does possess jurisdiction then, in the circumstances of the case, it should decline to exercise it. Unless a party establishes that a court possesses jurisdiction, then questions of choice of law will not normally arise.

Jurisdiction concerns the competence of courts and other tribunals to determine disputes with an authority which will make the decision binding and enforceable within their own system and capable of recognition and enforcement by the courts and tribunals of other countries. If a country's jurisdictional rules are too restrictive, they may result in a denial of justice as cases which ought to be justiciable before the courts are turned away; if they are lax, they may result in 'forum shopping', with an influx of cases completely unconnected with the law of the country of the 'open' forum, with the result that judgments are not respected by other countries.

The issue of jurisdiction normally involves a set of distinct but related questions which may be expressed as follows:

(a) can the plaintiff invoke the assistance of the court?

(b) has the court authority over the defendant?

(c) has the court power to determine the issue?

---

1   [1974] AC 436.

(d) must the court exercise the power or may it decline to do so?

In international cases, jurisdictional issues are particularly prominent as degrees of connection between the plaintiff and the court, the defendant and the court, and the factual connections of the legal dispute with the system of law operated by the court may in each case be close, tenuous, remote or even non-existent.

Rules of jurisdiction may be plaintiff oriented, defendant oriented or related to the cause of action invoked, and current English jurisdictional rules show the influence of all three approaches.

Courts can take, or be given, a wide or restricted jurisdictional ambit and can take, or be given, powers to exercise discretion in the cases they actually accept for trial, or they may have no choice in the matter. A wider or narrower view of jurisdiction may be taken in the light of the substance of the dispute between the parties, so that a court may have jurisdiction over a contractual dispute between A and B, but not over a matrimonial one. In broad terms, at common law, English courts tended to adopt an 'open forum' policy in personal actions, but this liberality did not extend to matrimonial causes[2] where the rules were more restrictive.

There are three matters properly within the ambit of the subject of jurisdiction, which I have chosen to treat elsewhere in the text.

(a) Jurisdiction in matrimonial causes and the recognition of foreign matrimonial decisions. Always a special case under common law, these matters are not touched (save in the special instance of maintenance) by the European Convention on Jurisdiction and the Enforcement of Judgments in Civil and Commercial Matters 1968, and are best considered under Family Law.

(b) Jurisdiction agreements. A jurisdiction agreement is a contract under English law and the matter will be considered in dealing with the law of obligations.

(c) Jurisdiction over foreign immovable property. The judgment in *British South Africa Company v Companhia de Mocambique*[3] declared the common law position that English courts would not take jurisdiction over any matter concerned with title to, or the rights to possession of, foreign immovable property. The *Mocambique* rule is mirrored in the exclusive jurisdiction provisions of the Jurisdiction Conventions.[4] It no longer

---

2   A view not helped by the silence of the Matrimonial Causes Act 1857 on the question of jurisdiction. Some confusion is demonstrated in the case law until *Le Mesurier v Le Mesurier* [1895] AC 517, which determined that only the court of the domicile had jurisdiction to dissolve a marriage.

3   [1893] AC 602; see, also, *Hesperides Hotels Ltd v Aegean Turkish Holidays Ltd* [1979] AC 508; [1978] QB 205, CA; see, also, *Pearce v Ove Arup Partnership Ltd [1997] Ch 293* (Lloyd J). For the subsequent hearing in the Court of Appeal, see (1999) *The Times*, 10 February.

4   Brussels Convention, Art 16(1)(a).

applies to simple cases of trespass or other torts to foreign land, which do not raise issues of title,[5] but it has recently been extended to foreign intellectual property rights.[6] The basis of the rule and the exceptions to it are considered in Chapter 21, 'Property'.

English law has, traditionally, adopted an 'open' forum policy for personal actions, with the result that resort is had to the English courts by parties who have no connection with this country over subject matters which are equally unconnected.[7]

This is particularly true of commercial cases, where English courts and, indeed, English law, are frequently chosen by those whose dealings are otherwise unconnected with England.[8]

Whatever this does for the esteem, self or otherwise, of English courts or for the regard in which English law is held, it is certainly good business and contributes to the UK's invisible earnings.

It is arguable that at common law there was no particular theory of jurisdiction and everything depended upon whether a plaintiff could identify a defendant and serve a writ. The liberal approach in civil and commercial matters contrasted with the restricted approach to jurisdiction in matrimonial causes.

In considering the present rules as to jurisdiction in England, one must draw a distinction not only between criminal and civil jurisdiction but, also, between the various rules applicable in civil disputes.

CRIMINAL JURISDICTION

The circumstances in which the courts of one State may exercise jurisdiction is normally considered as a topic within the sphere of public international law. Logically, this should be so since criminal proceedings are brought by an agency of the State and criminal proceedings concern other States; indeed, there may be competing claims to jurisdiction. Manifestly, if State A wishes to prosecute and State B also claims that entitlement then, clearly, that matter falls to be resolved within the ambit of public international law, not private international law. There are five principles upon which a State may exercise

---

5   Civil Jurisdiction and Judgments Act 1982, s 30(1).

6   *Tyburn Productions Ltd v Conan Doyle* [1991] Ch 75 (Vinelott J). For a more recent judicial discussion, see *Pearce v Ove Arup Partnership Ltd* [1997] 2 WLR 779; Ch 293 (Lloyd J).

7   *Buttes Gas and Oil Co v Hammer (No 3)* [1982] AC 888.

8   Clearly, the ability to conduct proceedings in England and the high reputation of the system for honesty are important considerations; the ability of the High Court to make available specialist judges encourages parties to have confidence in the system.

jurisdiction in public international law and it suffices for present purposes to outline them.

In broad terms, the courts of a particular State may exercise criminal jurisdiction on the basis of:

(a) the territorial principle;

(b) the nationality principle;

(c) the passive personality principle;

(d) the protective principle; and

(e) the universality principle.

The territorial principle asserts jurisdiction in respect of acts committed within the territory of the State, while the nationality principle focuses upon acts committed by citizens of the State. The passive personality principle enables a State to try individuals for acts committed against its citizens, while the protective principle enables a State to exercise jurisdiction where acts have been committed by aliens abroad which are damaging to the security of the State. Under the universality principle, an individual State may prosecute in respect of acts damaging to the international community as a whole. The simple point is that, in criminal law, it will be for the prosecutor to demonstrate that the court is competent to exercise jurisdiction in respect of the parties and the matter that is before the court.

CIVIL JURISDICTION IN ENGLAND

Civil actions generally

In broad terms, English law draws a distinction between a civil action *in personam* and a civil action *in rem*. An action *in personam* is one in which the plaintiff seeks a particular order against the defendant personally, for example, that he pay damages or cease certain conduct. A civil action *in personam* requires that a writ be issued and served on the plaintiff; in certain circumstances, this can be done as of right; in other circumstances, the leave of the court will be required.

The only action *in rem* known to English law is the Admiralty action[9] against a ship or some others, such as an aircraft, hovercraft or cargo or freight, connected thereto. The broad object is that the *res* should be used to satisfy the claim. Proccedings are usually started by the writ being affixed to the *res*; the plaintiff will usually seek to arrest the ship. The defendant will

---

9   The list of Admiralty actions is set out in the Supreme Court Act 1981, s 20.

normally secure the release of the ship by providing security and submitting to the jurisdiction of the court. If the action continues solely *in rem*, then the plaintiff can only claim the proceeds of the sale of the ship but, if the action proceeds *in rem* and *personam*, then the plaintiff is not so limited.[10]

The different regimes

At present, there are four sets of rules governing the exercise of civil jurisdiction. The first are the traditional common law rules of jurisdiction that have evolved since the Judicature Acts.[11]

Secondly, there are those jurisdictional rules that are established by the European Convention on Jurisdiction and the Enforcement of Judgments in Civil and Commercial Matters 1968 (the Brussels Convention).[12] Thirdly, there are those matters that are governed by the Modified Convention.[13] Fourthly, there are those matters relating to EFTA countries, that will be governed by the EEC/EFTA Convention, known as the Lugano Convention.[14] At the outset, it should be noted that three of the regimes are the direct consequence of membership of the European Community.

Moreover, while the traditional rules in England are based on the procedures of serving a writ, the European Conventions are based on a particular theory of jurisdiction that, normally, focuses upon the connection of the defendant with the forum. It is sensible at this stage to say a little about each regime.

Jurisdiction under the traditional rules

These rules will apply in all cases not covered by the Brussels Convnetion, the Modified Convention or the Lugano Convention. These rules can be traced back until the middle of the 19th century, and it is usual to refer to them as 'the traditional rules'. These rules applied in all cases prior to the coming into effect of the Civil Jurisdiction and Judgments Act 1982. In general terms, three questions would arise under the traditional rules, namely:

(a) whether the English courts had authority to hear the case. The answer to this question depended on whether a writ had been served on the defendant. A writ could be served on the defendant if he was present

---

10 *The Dictator* [1892] P 304; *The Dupleix* [1912] P 8; *The August 8* [1983] 2 AC 450; for a recent discussion of the nature of the actions, see *Republic of India v India Steamship Co Ltd* [1997] 3 WLR 818.

11 Supreme Court of Judicature Act 1873; Supreme Court of Judicature (Amendment) Act 1875.

12 Given effect to by the Civil Jurisdiction and Judgments Act 1982.

13 Civil Jurisdiction and Judgments Act 1982, Sched 4, introduces a modified version of the Brussels Convention to operate within the UK.

14 Given effect to by the Civil Jurisdiction and Judgments Act 1991.

within the jurisdiction, if there had been submission to the jurisdiction, or if the court had allowed service of the writ out of the jurisdiction under RSC Ord 11;

(b) whether the court will decline jurisdiction or stay proceedings. In certain circumstances, though the court may exercise jurisdiction, it will agree to decline jurisdiction or stay proceedings. This area has developed considerably in the last 25 years and is considered in detail below;

(c) whether there are limitations upon the exercise of jurisdiction: There are a number of situations where because of binding international obligations (for example, obligations relating to sovereign and diplomatic immunity) the court will not be competent to assume jurisdiction. These matters are considered below.

Jurisdiction under the Brussels Convention

In general terms, the rules on jurisdiction contained in the European Convention on Jurisdiction and the Enforcement of Judgments in Civil and Commercial Matters 1968 will apply where the matter is a civil and commercial matter within the meaning of the Convention and where the individual is domiciled within a European Community State, or there is an agreement to confer jurisdiction on the courts of a Contracting State.

Jurisdiction under the Modified Convention

Under the Modified Convention, introduced by the Civil Jurisdiction and Judgments Act 1982, a matter will be within the rules if it is a civil and commercial matter and the defendant is domiciled within the UK or jurisdiction arises independent of domicile, for example, due to land situated in the UK.

Jurisdiction under the Lugano Convention

In general terms, the rules set out in the Lugano Convention will be applied in the UK and other EC States where the matter is a civil and commercial matter and the defendant is domiciled in an EFTA contracting State or the matter is one that arises independent of domicile.

It is now necessary to examine each of these areas in turn. Having regard to the continuing importance of the traditional rules, it is intended to examine these first.

CHAPTER 11

JURISDICTION: THE TRADITIONAL RULES

INTRODUCTION

It is now necessary to consider the traditional or common law rules[1] that determine the jurisdiction of the High Court. As indicated earlier, the English courts adopted an 'open forum' policy; they were not preoccupied with any theory of jurisdiction and all disputes as to jurisdiction tended to be regarded as procedural in nature. There can be little doubt that, in the 19th century, there was an assumption that the justice available in the king's courts was superior to that in less fortunate lands; indeed, sometimes judges were not slow to say so.[2] Today, the emphasis is upon co-operation with courts of other jurisdictions. In examining the traditional rules, it is necessary to pay regard to three aspects of the problem:

(a) jurisdiction founded upon presence;

(b) submission to the jurisdiction; and

(c) the extended jurisdiction of the High Court arising under RSC Ord 11.

PRESENCE

Every action in the High Court must commence with the issue and service of a writ or equivalent document.[3] Where the writ has been properly served, then the court will in principle possess jurisdiction. Likewise, if the writ has not been properly served, jurisdiction cannot be exercised. It is strongly arguable that this is to confuse matters of procedure and substance. Jurisdiction is a matter of substance not procedure and judicial jurisdiction derives from the sovereignty of the State. The purpose of serving the writ is to give the defendant proper notice of a claim; whether the court has jurisdiction or not is a matter of substance rather than procedure. In a world of over 180 sovereign

---

1   It is not strictly correct to refer to them as the common law rules because they originate with the Common Law Procedure Act 1852 and the attempts to reform the superior court structure prior to the Judicature Act 1873.

2   As Shadwell VC observed: 'I consider that in the contemplation of the Court of Chancery every foreign court is an inferior court.' *Bent v Young* (1838) 9 Sim 180, p 191.

3   In many cases involving problems of private international law, the case will begin in the Chancery Division by means of originating summons; this has the advantage that the precise legal questions can be agreed by the parties prior to the hearing; the procedure is not suitable where the material facts are in dispute.

States, it is clearly desirable that there should be some form of co-operation between neighbouring States, particularly those seeking to operate a common trading market.[4] The traditional rules are open to the objection that questions of substance are determined by matters of procedure. Secondly, if jurisdiction is to be determined by presence, then there is a real risk of the limited resources of the High Court being occupied by cases that only have a limited connection with the UK. Thirdly, this concern is increased if parties to such marginal litigation then seek to avail themselves of the resources of the legal aid scheme. Such an open door policy may have been acceptable at a time when the list of pending cases was shorter but, in the post war world of civil aviation, there is a legitimate concern that individuals might seek to begin cases in the High Court that should properly be commenced elsewhere.

Common law jurisdiction, at least as far as personal actions are concerned, was, and remains, plaintiff oriented, territorially limited and procedural in essence. The basic rule therefore is that anyone can invoke the jurisdiction of the English court in a personal action by the physical service of the writ or other originating process on a defendant who is physically present in England. Neither plaintiff nor defendant need have any connection with this country, beyond the physical presence of the defendant. There is no requirement, for example, that the defendant should have assets in this country, and there is no need for the substantive dispute to have any English connection.[5]

While there is a general principle, under the traditional rules, that the service of the writ renders the person subject to the *in personam* jurisdiction of the High Court, the application of this principle differs according to whether the defendant is an individual, a partnership or a corporation.

Individuals

An individual in England may be served with a writ in an action *in personam*, however fleeting the stay. The Court of Appeal settled any doubt on this point in two cases decided within a short time of each other. In *Colt Industries Inc v Sarlie (No 1)*,[6] the facts were as follows: a New York company obtained a judgment in New York against a Frenchman and sought to enforce it in England. Proceedings were served on him at a hotel in London where he stayed for one night.

It was held that the court had jurisdiction over him. The same approach can be detected in the unusual case of *Maharanee of Baroda v Daniel Wildenstein*,[7] where the facts were as follows: both the plaintiff and the

---

4   As, indeed, envisaged in the Treaty of Rome 1957, Art 220.
5   See *Buttes Gas and Oil Co v Hammer (No 3)* [1982] AC 888.
6   [1966] 1 All ER 673; 1 WLR 440, CA (Lyell J).

defendant lived in Paris and shared an interest in art and racehorses. The defendant was the proprietor of art galleries in London, Paris and New York. Both were constant travellers and members of the 'international set'. The Maharanee bought from the defendant in Paris a painting known as 'La Poesie' by François Boucher.[8] The plaintiff later learned that it was probably a copy and not worth the original purchase price of £33,000. The plaintiff issued a writ claiming rescission of the contract and repayment of the price. The writ was served on the defendant during a visit to the racing at Ascot.

The Court of Appeal[9] refused an application by the defendant to set aside the writ, ruling that the jurisdiction had been properly invoked by the service of the writ. In giving judgment, Edmund Davies LJ recognised that the conduct of the plaintiff might be regarded as bad form, but that of itself did not constitute abuse of process. It was not in dispute that the court had acquired jurisdiction by the service of the writ.[10]

It might be argued that to allow jurisdiction to depend on personal presence, however fleeting, could lead to exaggerated claims to jurisdiction. Against this it can be argued:

(a) the rule has the virtue of certainty;

(b) the rule can now be modified by the application of the doctrine of *forum non conveniens*;[11] and

(c) where the defendant has been tricked by fraud into coming within the jurisdiction, then the rule will not apply.[12]

As a general rule, the writ must be served personally on the defendant by the plaintiff or his agent.[13] If the court considers that personal service is impracticable, then an order for substituted service can be made.[14]

---

7   [1972] QB 283; 2 All ER 689 (Bridge J in the High Court and Lord Denning MR, Edmund Davies and Stephenson LJJ in the Court of Appeal).

8   (1703–70), French court painter.

9   [1972] QB 283. The defendant argued that the action was frivolous and that, in any event, England was not a *forum conveniens*. However, the case was decided before the evolution of the modern law in *The Atlantic Star* [1974] AC 436. See, now, Brussels Convention 1968, Art 3.

10   *Carrick v Hancock* (1895) 12 TLR 59 (Englishman on short visit to Sweden).

11   In 1972, at the time of *Maharanee of Baraoda v Wildenstein*, the requirements for a stay had been set out in *St Pierre v South American Stores (Gath and Chaves) Ltd* [1936] 1 KB 382; these restrictive rules were not modified until after *The Atlantic Star* [1974] AC 436.

12   *Watkins v North American Land and Timber Company Ltd* (1904) 20 TLR 534 (Lord Davey).

13   RSC Ord 10 r 1(1); as to the elements of personal service, see RSC Ord 65 r 2.

14   RSC Ord 65 r 4; as to the circumstances when substituted service will be allowed, see *Field v Bennett* (1886) 3 TLR 239; *Wilding v Bean* [1891] 1 QB 100; *Jay v Budd* [1898] 1 QB 12; *Porter v Freudenberg* [1915] 1 KB 857.

Partnerships

A writ can be served, as of right, on any individual member of a partnership who is present in England at the time of service. RSC Ord 81 permits that partners trading in England may be sued in the name of the firm, and the order further provides that proceedings may be served on one or more partners or it may be served at the principal place of business of the partnership on the person who has control of the business.[15]

Service may be effected in this last manner even if all the partners are foreigners resident abroad.[16] If the firm is duly served in England, leave may be sought to serve a partner abroad under RSC Ord 11 r 1(1)(c) on the ground that he is a necessary and proper party to the action.[17] Service effected under RSC Ord 11 r 1(1) on one partner out of the jurisdiction is good service on all partners out of the jurisdiction.[18]

Corporations

As the corporation is an artificial legal person, one cannot speak of its nationality, domicile or residence in the same sense as one employs these expressions when considering an individual. Since the corporate form came to be widely adopted in the years after 1850, as enterprises sought a legal form in which to hold capital, and following upon the enactment of a legislative framework,[19] questions arose as to the circumstances in which a foreign corporation could be sued.

In 1872, it was established that a foreign corporation could be sued in England.[20] After this judgment it became important to establish the precise circumstances under which a foreign based corporation could be sued in England and the process to be adopted became a matter of some dispute.[21] The approach of the courts tended to be robust and impatient of technicalities. As Lord Halsbury LC observed with characteristic directness, in respect of whether a French company that leased offices in London could be sued: 'They are here, and, if they are here, they may be served.'[22] The rules relating to

---

15 RSC Ord 81 r 3.

16 *Worcester City and County Banking Co v Firbank, Pauling and Co* [1894] 1 QB 784.

17 *West of England Steamship Owners Association v John Holman and Sons* [1957] 3 All ER 421.

18 *Hobbs v Australian Press Association* [1933] 1 KB 1.

19 The legislation emerged as the Companies Act 1844; Limited Liability Act 1855; Companies Acts 1862, 1900, 1907, 1908, 1928, 1929, 1947, 1948, 1961, 1967, 1980, 1981; the present consolidation is the Companies Act 1985.

20 *Newby v Van Oppen* (1872) LR 7 QB 293.

21 See *Newby v Van Oppen* (1872) LR 7 QB 293; *Haggin v Comptoir D'Escompte de Paris* (1889) 23 QBD 519; *The Princess Clementre* [1897] P 18; *La Bourgogne* [1899] P 1; AC 431. The original rule was Ord IX r 8; see, now, RSC Ord 65 r 3.

22 *La Bourgogne* [1899] AC 431, p 433.

service of proceedings on a foreign corporation were referred to as the common law rules of service, and it was necessary for the plaintiff to demonstrate that the defendant corporation was doing business in England and that the agent in England must be operating at a fixed place of business for a definite period.[23] The courts tended to be flexible about the second requirement,[24] so that authorising an agent to occupy a stand at a motor show for nine days was sufficient to found jurisdiction.[25] On the assumption that the corporation was operating within the jurisdiction, then service could be effected under RSC Ord 65 r 3[26] by service upon a chairman, treasurer, secretary or other officer of the corporation. This particular rule was subject to the proviso that provision for service was not made by any other enactment. Thus, at common law, it was sufficient for the plaintiff to show that the company was trading within the jurisdiction and that service had been effected under RSC Ord 65 r 3.

However, domestic companies legislation[27] increased the obligations upon foreign corporations trading within the jurisdiction, and these provisions were extended in 1929.[28]

These provisions, which were re-enacted in the Companies Act 1948,[29] required a foreign corporation to file with the registrar of companies the names and addresses of one or more persons who were authorised to accept process on its behalf. Thus, the problem that arose for Brandon J in *The Theodosus*[30] was the relationship between the common law rules and the statutory provisions.[31] After forming the view that the company in question was not trading within the jurisdiction, the learned judge went on to cast doubt upon certain earlier authorities[32] and to rule that the provisions of the Companies Act 1948 must be complied with. Thus, the probable effect of *The Theodosus*[33] is that the provisions of the Companies Act 1985 represent a complete code. If the company is registered in England, then service can be effected by leaving the writ or sending it by post to the company's registered office in England.[34] If the company is registered in Scotland, then process is

---

23 *Dunlop Pneumatic Tyre Co v Actien Gessellschaft für Motor, Cudell & Co* [1902] 1 KB 342; *Okura and Co Ltd v Forsbacka Jernverks Aktiebolag* [1914] 1 KB 715; see, also, *Sacharin Corporation Ltd v Chemische Fabrik von Heyden Aktiengesellschaft* [1911] 2 KB 516.

24 The first question was one of fact, see *La Bourgogne* [1899] P 1, p 12 (AL Smith LJ).

25 *Dunlop Pneumatic Tyre Company v Actien Gessellschaft für Motor, Cudell & Co* [1902] 1 KB 342.

26 Originally Ord IX r 8 under the 1883 rules.

27 Companies Act 1907, s 35; Companies Act 1908, s 274(1), (2).

28 Companies Act 1929, s 349.

29 Companies Act 1948, ss 407(1)(c), 409(c), 412.

30 [1977] 2 LR 428.

31 The relevant provisions today are the Companies Act 1985, ss 691, 695, 744.

32 *The Lalandia* [1933] P 56; *The Holstein* (1933) 155 LT 466.

33 [1977] 2 LR 428.

34 Companies Act 1985, s 725(1).

effected by serving the writ on the principal place of business and by sending a copy to the company's registered office in Scotland.[35]

A company incorporated outside Great Britain, but establishing a place of business within the jurisdiction, will be an 'oversea company'[36] for the purposes of the Companies Act 1985. The company is obliged to file notice with the Registrar of Companies of the name and address of a person, or persons, authorised to accept service on behalf of the company.[37] If the company defaults upon its statutory obligation, or if the person dies or ceases to reside in Great Britain, then the writ can be served on the company by leaving it at or posting it to any place of business established by the company in Great Britain.[38]

As under the prior common law, the courts have required that for a business to be present it must have a degree of permanence. This is a matter of inference from the primary facts. In *South India Shipping Corporation Ltd v Export-Import Bank of Korea*,[39] the Court of Appeal held that a bank that had established a London office for promotional purposes, but which did not undertake banking business, was to be regarded as having a place of business in England.[40] At a later date, in *Cleveland Museum of Art v Capricorn Art International SA*,[41] it was held that an art gallery was carrying on business when it stored and displayed works of art in a converted church.

SUBMISSION TO THE JURISDICTION

It has long been accepted that a defendant may confer jurisdiction in respect of an action in personam by submission to the jurisdiction. The question that therefore arises is as to which acts are to be interpreted as constituting submission. Manifestly, commencing an action as a plaintiff will confer jurisdiction on the court in respect of any defence or related counterclaim.[42] Thus, in *High Commissioner for India v Ghosh*,[43] a breach of contract action by

---

35 Companies Act 1985, s 725(2), (3).

36 *Ibid*, s 744.

37 *Ibid*, s 691(1)(b)(ii); the provisions are traceable back to the Companies Act 1907, s 35.

38 *Ibid*, s 695(1); the provisions are traceable back to the Companies Act 1929, s 349.

39 [1985] 1 WLR 585; 2 All ER 219.

40 *Re Oriel Ltd* [1985] 3 All ER 216; [1986] 1 WLR 180.

41 [1990] 2 LR 166.

42 RSC Ord 15 r 2; *South African Republic v Compagnie Franco Belge Chemin de Fer du Nord* [1897] 2 Ch 487; [1898] 1 Ch 190; *Factories Insurance Co v Anglo Scottish Insurance Co* (1913) 29 TLR 312.

43 [1960] 1 QB 134 (no jurisdiction in respect of unrelated counterclaim).

the plaintiff did not confer jurisdiction on the court when the defendant filed a counterclaim founded on libel.

Clearly, a defendant who accepts service of the writ[44] or defends the case on its merits[45] will be deemed to have submitted to the jurisdiction. A defendant who acknowledges service before the actual service of the writ will also be said to have submitted to the jurisdiction.[46] Instructing a solicitor to accept the service of a writ probably constitutes submission; indeed, a defendant out of the jurisdiction who instructs his solicitor to accept service will be deemed to have submitted. Where the defendant merely acknowledges service of the writ he will be deemed to have submitted to the jurisdiction.[47]

A defendant who appears merely to contest the jurisdiction is not deemed to have submitted to the jurisdiction,[48] nor, indeed, will there be submission in circumstances where the defendant argues that there should be a stay because of proceedings elsewhere.[49] Submission to the jurisdiction may arise by agreement. If the contract contains an express clause that the parties will submit to the jurisdiction of an English court, then submission is deemed to have been made. However, there will be no submission to the jurisdiction merely because the contract contains an express choice of English law.[50]

The agreement may stipulate that in the event of a dispute service is to be made on an agent; in these circumstances, there will be submission.[51] However, where the agent resides abroad, then leave will be required under RSC Ord 11.[52]

It would seem that parties cannot by submission confer jurisdiction where the court itself lacks competence.[53] The rules as to submission to the jurisdiction only apply to actions *in personam*; they do not apply to

---

44 RSC Ord 10 r 1(4).
45 *Boyle v Sacker* (1888) 39 Ch D 249, CA.
46 RSC Ord 10 r 1(5).
47 RSC Ord 10 r 1(4).
48 *Re Dulles Settlement (No 2)* [1951] Ch 842 (for a robust assessment by Denning LJ).
49 *William and Glyn's Bank plc v Astro Dinamico Cia Naviera SA* [1984] 1 All ER 760; [1984] 1 WLR 438, where a distinction was drawn between jurisdiction to decide an action on its merits and jurisdiction to determine whether jurisdiction existed.
50 *Dunbee Ltd v Gilman and Co (Australia) Pty Ltd* (1968) 2 LR 394.
51 *Tharsis Sulphur and Copper Co Ltd v Société Industrielle et Commericale des Metaux* (1889) 58 LJQB 435; *Montgomery, Jones and Co v Liebenthal and Co* [1898] 1 QB 487.
52 RSC Ord 11 r 1(1)(d)(iv), replacing RSC Ord 11 r 2.
53 Eg, by reason of the subject matter; see *Re Paramount Airways Ltd (In Administration)* [1992] Ch 160.

matrimonial causes relating to nullity and divorce,[54] nor will they apply where statute expressly provides that no jurisdiction arises.[55]

THE EXTENDED JURISDICTION UNDER
THE RULES OF THE SUPREME COURT

The general principles

At common law, jurisdiction could only be founded upon either presence within the jurisdiction or submission to the jurisdiction. However, in the 19th century, the increasing influence of trading links and the greater incidence of travel prompted an extension of the common law position.

Sections 18 and 19 of the Common Law Procedure Act 1852 conferred on the English court a discretionary power to order the service of a writ out of the jurisdiction. This position was continued under the Judicature Act 1873–75 and the relevant law on the matter is now contained in RSC Ord 11. It will be necessary to consider in detail the specific heads of RSC Ord 11 but, before doing so, a number of general points need to be made:

(a) the present rules were drafted in 1983 and came into effect on 1 January 1987 in order to ensure conformity with the Civil Jurisdiction and Judgments Act 1982; it was hoped that the new rules would represent a more logical structure than the prior rules;[56]

(b) in broad terms, the plaintiff must meet a threefold test[57] to secure leave under RSC Ord 11: (1) as regards the merits, the plaintiff must show that there is a serious issue to be tried; (2) he must show that his claim falls within a particular head of RSC Ord 11;[58] and (3) the court must be satisfied that England is the forum conveniens;[59]

(c) the fundamental principle underlying RSC Ord 11 is that service out of the jurisdiction is not of right, but is a matter of leave to be determined by the exercise of judicial discretion;

---

54 From the Matrimonial Causes Act 1857, matrimonial causes did not come within the open forum approach; see the Domicile and Matrimonial Proceedings Act 1973, s 5(2), (3).

55 Civil Jurisdiction and Judgments Act 1982, s 30, as amended by the Civil Jurisdiction and Judgments Act 1991, Sched 2, para 13.

56 RSC (Amendment No 2) Ord 1983 SI 1983/1181.

57 *Seaconsar Far East Ltd v Bank Makazi Jomhouri Islami Iran* [1994] 1 AC 438.

58 The *onus probandi* is upon the plaintiff and, thus, any ambiguity will be resolved in favour of the defendant; *The Hagen* [1908] P 189; *The Siskina* [1979] AC 210; *EF Hutton and Co (London) Ltd v Mofarrij* [1989] 1 WLR 488.

59 *Spiliada Maritime Corporation v Cansulex Ltd* [1987] AC 460.

(d) a plaintiff may claim under more than one head of RSC Ord 11; but, if leave is granted under one head, the plaintiff may not later amend the statement of claim to permit another claim for which leave would not have been given;[60]

(e) applications for leave are normally made *ex parte* on affidavit so that the plaintiff is obliged to make full and complete disclosure of his case;[61]

(f) in cases of doubt as to whether a claim comes within a particular head, then that doubt is to be resolved in favour of the defendant;[62]

(g) the court will be minded to consider not merely whether a claim comes within a particular head of RSC Ord 11, but also whether the claim is within the spirit of the order;

(h) leave will not be granted unless 'it shall be made sufficiently to appear to the court that the case is a proper one for service out of the jurisdiction'.[63] This means that it is not enough for the plaintiff to demonstrate a *prima facie* case, he must instead show a good arguable case on the merits. This can be done by showing a serious issue to be tried in that the affidavits and exhibits thereto disclose a substantial question of fact or law or both.[64] Clearly, if the evidence of the plaintiff, taken at its highest, does not disclose a cause of action, then leave will be refused;

(i) while past case law has tended to focus on the three requirements, outlined in the second point above, the precedents provide only limited guidance and the judge in each case must ask whether the case before him is 'a proper one for service out of the jurisdiction';

(j) in exercising its discretion under RSC Ord 11, the court will be required to determine whether the English court is *forum conveniens*. While the test may be little different to when a defendant seeks a stay of domestic proceedings on grounds of *forum non conveniens*, under the RSC, the plaintiff bears the burden of proof in showing that England is *forum conveniens*.[65] In forming a view on this matter, the court will have to consider a range of practical issues such as the availability of witnesses, the need for expert evidence and questions of expense. It would seem that, as the discretion is vested in the trial judge, then an appellate court should be slow to interfere with the decision of the judge of first instance, unless it

---

60 *Whitehouse v Reid* [1938] 1 KB 743.

61 The highest duty of candour is imposed on a plaintiff in an *ex parte* application; if leave is granted, the defendant will become aware of the matter and may move to set aside the writ.

62 *EF Hutton and Co (London) Ltd v Mofarrij* [1989] 1 WLR 488.

63 RSC Ord 11 r 4(2).

64 *Seaconsar Far East Ltd v Bank Markazi Jomhouri Islami Iran* [1994] 1 AC 438; the application must be made *bona fide* with the intention of proceeding to trial and not part of some wider stratagem.

65 *Spiliada Maritime Corporation v Cansulex Ltd* [1987] AC 460.

can be shown that the discretion was exercised on manifestly wrong principles.[66] The matter was clearly expressed by Lord Templeman in *Spiliada*,[67] where the learned judge noted, 'the solution of disputes about the relative merits of trial in England and trial abroad is pre-eminently a matter for the trial judge. In nearly every case, evidence is on affidavit by witnesses of acknowledged probity. An appeal should be rare and the appellate court should be slow to interfere'.

The specific categories

Although RSC Ord 11 is not so divided, it is possible to draw a distinction between the general provisions of RSC Ord 11 r 1(1)(a)–(c) and the more specific provisions that follow thereafter.

(a) 'Relief is sought against a person domiciled within the jurisdiction.'[68]

Under the previous rule,[69] domicile was determined by reference to common law principles. The new rules require domicile to be determined by the provisions of ss 41–46 of the Civil Jurisdiction and Judgments Act 1982. In broad terms, domicile will be established if the plaintiff can demonstrate that the proposed defendant is resident within the State and the nature and circumstance of his residence indicates that he has a substantial connection with the State. The Brussels Convention and the Modified Convention will apply if the individual is domiciled in England and it is a civil and commercial matter. This head applies to cases outside the Conventions. The reference to a person will include a corporation.

(b) 'An injunction is sought ordering the defendant to do or refrain from doing anything within the jurisdiction (whether or not damages are also claimed in respect of a failure to do or the doing of that thing).'[70]

While the injunction need not be the only relief requested,[71] the injunction must be sought *bona fide* in respect of a substantial dispute. Thus, leave will not be granted if the only purpose for seeking an injunction is to bring another claim within the subheading. An injunction that would be ineffective cannot be invoked to found leave. Leave will not be granted in circumstances where the matter can be more properly dealt with before a

---

66 *Amin Rasheed Shipping Corporation v Kuwait Insurance Co* [1984] AC 50; see, also, *Spiliada Maritime Corporation v Cansulex Ltd* [1987] 1 AC 460, p 465.

67 *Spiliada Maritime Corporation v Cansulex Ltd* [1987] 1 AC 460, p 465.

68 RSC Ord 11 r 1(1)(a).

69 RSC Order 11 r 1(1)(c); the previous rule included reference to 'ordinarily resident' see *Re Liddell's Settlement Trusts* [1936] Ch 365.

70 RSC Ord 11 r 1(1)(b), previously RSC Ord 11 r 1(1)(i).

71 For prior law, see *Watson and Sons v Daily Record (Glasgow) Ltd* [1907] 1 KB 853; *Rosler v Hilberry* [1925] Ch 250.

foreign court or where there is little risk of the repetition of the offending act.

Problems began to arise under the former rule after 1975 in respect of Mareva injunctions. The House of Lords had ruled in *The Siskina*[72] that, where a plaintiff sought a Mareva injunction against a non-resident defendant, the case could not be brought under the rule in the absence of an established legal or equitable right but would need to be brought under a different head.

The ruling in *The Siskina* has been modified by s 25 of the Civil Jurisdiction and Judgments Act 1982, so that, where proceedings are in progress in a Contracting State or a relevant Order in Council has been made, then an application can be made under RSC Ord 11 r 1(1)(b) in respect of a Mareva injunction. Thus, a plaintiff, while litigating within the Brussels Convention in Germany, might seek a Mareva injunction in England to preserve assets in order to satisfy any judgment obtained in Germany.[73] The domicile of the defendant will be relevant in that leave will not be required if he is resident in a contracting State but will be if he is resident elsewhere.

(c) 'The claim is brought against a person duly served within or out of the jurisdiction, and a person out of the jurisdiction is a necessary or proper party thereto.'[74]

In its previous formulation, this subheading gave rise to much litigation.[75] It may be that this new wording will lead to less litigation, although the absence of any obvious territorial connection has always made the courts reluctant to order service out of the jurisdiction.[76] Under the former rule, if D1 had been duly served in England then D2 could be served out of the jurisdiction if a necessary or proper party;[77] much debate took place as to whether the proceedings had been properly brought.[78] Under the present rule, if D1 has been duly served either in England or under another head of RSC Ord 11, then D2 may be served if a 'necessary'or 'proper' party. The subheading will be useful in the case of claims against two defendants, for example, joint tortfeasors or where two individuals bear different liabilities in respect of the same or a related transaction. Under

---

72 *The Siskina* [1979] AC 210.

73 *Republic of Haiti v Duvalier* [1990] 1 QB 202.

74 RSC Ord 11 r 1 (1)(c), previously RSC Ord 11 r 1(1)(j).

75 The previous rule read: 'When any person out of the jurisdiction is a necessary or proper party to an action properly brought against some other person duly served within the jurisdiction.'

76 *John Russell and Co Ltd v Cayzer Irvine Co Ltd* [1916] 2 AC 298; *Multinational Gas and Petrochemical Company v Multinational Gas and Petrochemical Services Ltd* [1983] Ch 258.

77 *Derby and Co Ltd v Larsson* [1976] 1 WLR 202.

78 *The Brabo* [1949] AC 326.

this particular subheading there is a specific evidentiary requirement, namely, that the affidavit must state the grounds for the plaintiff's belief that there is a real issue between the plaintiff and D2 that it may be reasonable to ask the court to try. It will be necessary to show that D1 has been duly served. It would seem that, if D1 has a complete defence or has only been joined as a vehicle to secure jurisdiction over D2, then leave would not be granted.

(d) 'The claim is brought to enforce, rescind, dissolve, annul or otherwise affect a contract, or to recover damages to obtain other relief in respect of the breach of contract in the following cases: (i) where the contract was made within the jurisdiction; or (ii) was made by or through an agent trading or residing within the jurisdiction on behalf of a principal trading or residing out of the jurisdiction; or (iii) is by its terms, or by implication, governed by English law; or (iv) contains a term to the effect that the High Court shall have jurisdiction to hear and determine any action in respect of the contract.'[79]

This is a most important subheading and, not surprisingly, has generated a considerable volume of litigation. Difficulty has arisen in respect of the expression 'affect a contract'. It has been held that this requirement is not met by a contract that is void,[80] but is met where it is argued that a contract has been terminated by frustration;[81] indeed, an English contract is 'affected' if its obligations are substantially altered by the non-performance of a related foreign contract.[82]

Service may be ordered if the contract is substantially made within the jurisdiction; a contract made in London but amended in the USA will be a contract made within the jurisdiction.[83] Much attention under this subheading has been devoted to the question of contract formation, so that certain of the cases have emerged as leading authorities within the law of contract on the mechanics of offer and acceptance. Thus, a contract concluded by postal communication is made where the letter of acceptance is posted.[84] However, when instantaneous methods of communication are employed, then the contract will be made where the acceptance is communicated to the offeror. Thus, in *Entores v Miles Far East Corporation*,[85] the contract was made when the telex from Holland was received in London, while in the *Brinkibon*[86] case, the contract was formed

---

79 RSC Ord 11 r 1(1)(d), formerly RSC Ord 11 r 1(1)(f) and RSC Ord 11 r 2.

80 *Finnish Marine Insurance Co Ltd v Protective National Insurance Co* [1990] 1 QB 1078.

81 *BP Exploration Co (Lybia) Ltd v Hunt* [1976] 1 WLR 788.

82 *EF Hutton and Co (London) Ltd v Mofarrij* [1989] 1 WLR 488.

83 *BP Exploration Co (Lybia) Ltd v Hunt* [1976] 1 WLR 788.

84 *Benaim v Debano* [1920] AC 514.

85 *Entores Ltd v Miles Far East Corporation* [1955] 2 QB 327, approved by the House of Lords in *Brinkibon Ltd v Stahag Stahl und Stahlwarenhandelsgesellschaft mbH* [1983] 2 AC 34.

86 [1983] 2 AC 34.

when the telex of acceptance from London was received in Vienna (see below). However, if a contract is made in England but contains a foreign jurisdiction clause, then leave will not normally be granted.

In respect of subheading (ii), concerning the activities of an agent, it would seem that the activities of the agent within the jurisdiction will permit leave to be granted to serve out, even if the agent does not enjoy actual authority (express or implied) to enter into a contract.[87] Subheading (iii) was subject to interpretation at a time when the English courts were developing the doctrine of the proper law of the contract. Today, it is likely that the governing law will be determined in accordance with the Contracts (Applicable Law) Act 1990. It seems that, in cases where the English law as governing law is the only connecting factor, then the courts should exercise considerable caution before allowing leave to serve out under this subheading.[88] There may be cases where the subheading is relied upon to claim for breach of implied contractual term when the substance of the claim is for a tortious act. In such circumstances, the plaintiff can pursue alternative remedies.[89] Claims under subheading (iv) are concerned with those contracts where there is an English choice of jurisdiction clause.

(e) 'The claim is brought in respect of a breach committed within the jurisdiction of a contract made within or out of the jurisdiction, and irrespective of the fact, if such be the case, that the breach was preceded or accompanied by a breach committed out of the jurisdiction that rendered impossible the performance of so much of the contract as ought to have been performed within the jurisdiction.'[90]

A contract may be breached by a number of acts: by express or implied repudiation or by failure to perform. In cases of non-performance, it is sometimes difficult to determine where the obligation arose; this is particularly the case in situations concerning the failure to pay. In normal sale of goods transactions concerning an English seller, it will usually be the case that the obligation was to pay in England.[91] The latter part of the subheading was added in 1921 to reverse the effect of the House of Lords judgment in *Johnson v Taylor Bors and Co Ltd*.[92] In that particular case, an English buyer sought to bring himself within the subheading by arguing that a Swedish seller had breached a cif contract by failing to supply

---

87 *National Mortgage and Agency Co of New Zealand Ltd v Gosselin* (1922) 38 TLR 832, CA.

88 *Amin Rasheed Shipping Corporation v Kuwait Insurance Co* [1984] AC 50; *Spiliada Maritime Corporation v Cansulex Ltd* [1987] AC 460.

89 *Mathews v Kuwait Bechtel Corporation* [1959] 2 QB 57.

90 RSC Ord 11 r 1(1)(e), previously RSC Ord 11 r 1(1)(g).

91 *Robey and Co v Snaefell Mining Co Ltd* (1887) 20 QBD 152 (in the absence of a contractual term).

92 [1920] AC 144.

shipping documents. The House of Lords declined to grant leave to serve out of the jurisdiction, ruling that the substantial breach was committed when the seller failed to ship the goods abroad.

(f) 'The claim is founded on a tort and the damage was sustained or resulted from an act committed within the jurisdiction.'[93]

The previous subheading referred to 'a tort committed within the jurisdiction'. This caused difficulties of interpretation in the type of case where a drug was manufactured and authorised in Germany but distributed in France or England.[94] The history of the previous subrule indicated that the courts tended to interpret the rule liberally[95] unless it was evident that the case had little connection with England. For example, where a libel was published in foreign newspapers that had little circulation in England, the court refused leave to serve out of the jurisdiction.[96]

In a world in which a product is manufactured in country A, distributed in country B and consumed in country C, the widening of this subheading is designed to avoid differences of interpretation as to precisely where the tort was committed. The emphasis is upon allowing jurisdiction if the damage was sustained or the act (from which the damage resulted) was committed in England. The object of the re-drafting was to bring domestic law broadly into line with Art 5(3) of the Brussels Convention.[97] In the last two decades, the courts have moved towards a more liberal spirit of interpretation in asking not where the tort was committed but, rather, asking where in substance the cause of action arose.[98]

It is doubtful whether cases under the prior rule provide reliable guidance now that the rule has been re-drafted. It is clear that the new heading will be satisfied if significant, though not all, damage arises in England.[99] The broadening of the rule enables the court to order service if (i) the claim is founded on a tort; and (ii) damage has been sustained within the jurisdiction; or (iii) damage has resulted from an act committed within the jurisdiction. In respect of (i), the concept of a tort will not extend to a claim

---

93 RSC Ord 11 r 1(1)(f), formerly RSC Ord 11 r 1(1)(h).

94 An example of such product liability litigation being *Distillers Co (Bio-Chemicals) Ltd v Thompson* [1971] AC 458.

95 *Hobbs v Australian Press Association* [1933] 1 KB 1; *George Munro and Co Ltd v American Cyanamid Corpn* [1944] KB 232; *Bata v Bata* (1948) 92 SJ 574; *Cordova Land Co v Victor Brothers Inc* [1966] 1 WLR 793; *Diamond v Bank of London and Montreal* [1979] 1 QB 333 (substance of the tort within the jurisdiction).

96 *Kroch v Rossell et Cie* [1937] 1 All ER 725; see, also, *Shervill v Presse Alliance* [1995] AC 18.

97 Brussels Convention, Art 5(3), the test being 'where the harmful event occurred' – Case 21/76 *Bier v Mines de Potasse d'Alsace SA* [1976] ECR 1735; [1978] QB 708; [1977] 1 CMLR 284.

98 *Distillers Co (Biochemicals) Ltd v Thompson* [1971] AC 458.

99 *Metall und Rohstoff AG v Donaldson, Lufkin and Jenrette Inc* [1990] 2 QB 391.

for breach of duty by an alleged constructive trustee[100] while, in the case of (ii), significant damage within the jurisdiction is probably sufficient and, as to (iii), if there are substantial acts within the jurisdiction, the requirements of the head will be met.[101]

(g) 'The whole subject matter of the action is land situate within the jurisdiction (with or without rent or profits) or the perpetuation of testimony relating to land so situated.'[102]

This head applies to actions for the recovery of land and, in principle, applies both to disputes as to title and possession.[103]

(h) 'The claim is brought to construe, rectify, set aside or enforce an act, deed, will, contract, obligation or liability affecting land situated within the jurisdiction.'[104]

There was a tendency in the past to interpret this heading narrowly. Difficulty arose in the case of the expression 'affecting land'. The case law exhibited some uncertainty as to whether an action for rent under a lease[105] came within this head, as did an action for breach of covenant to repair[106] or an action to enforce a charging order over land.[107] A claim based on slander of title to land clearly did not.[108] There is some evidence that the modern case law favours a broader interpretation of this heading.[109]

(i) 'The claim is made for a debt secured on immovable property or is made to assert, declare or determine proprietary or possessory rights, or rights of security, in or over movable property, or to obtain authority to dispose of movable property, situate within the jurisdiction.'[110]

This subheading is wider than its predecessor and would cover, for example, non payment of a loan secured by legal mortgage.

(j) 'The claim is brought to execute the trusts of a written instrument being trusts that ought to be executed according to English law and of which the

---

100 [1990] 2 QB 391.

101 *Metall und Rohstoff AG v Donaldson, Lufkin and Jenrette* [1990] 2 QB 391.

102 RSC Ord 11 r 1(1)(g), formerly RSC Ord 11 r 1(a).

103 See *Agnew v Usher* (1884) 14 QBD 78; 51 LT 752.

104 RSC Ord 11 r 1(1)(h), formerly RSC Ord 11 r 1(1)(b).

105 *Agnew v Usher* (1884) 14 QBD 78; 51 LT 752; *Iveagh v Harris* [1929] 2 Ch 142.

106 *Tassell v Hallen* [1892] 1 QB 321.

107 *Mority v Stephen* (1888) 58 LT 850.

108 *Casey v Arnott* (1876) 2 CPD 24.

109 *Official Solicitor v Stype Investments (Jersey) Ltd* [1983] 1 All ER 629; [1983] 1 WLR 214.

110 RSC Ord 11 r 1(1)(i), being a wider version of RSC Ord 11 r 1(1)(k), which itself had been introduced to meet the lacuna revealed by *Deutsche National Bank v Paul* [1898] 1 Ch 293. The head is based on the Civil Jurisdiction and Judgments Act 1982, Art 5(8), Sched 4.

person to be served with the writ is a trustee, or for any relief or remedy which might be obtained in any such action.'[111]

Under the prior heading, leave would be refused unless there was trust property within England. Thus, in one case, leave was refused where the trustee sold the entire trust funds and left the jurisdiction with the proceeds.[112] That restriction has now been removed and under the new head there is no need for the trust property to be within the jurisdiction.

(k) 'The claim is made for the administration of the estate of a person[113] who died domiciled within the jurisdiction or for any relief or remedy which might be obtained in any such action.'[114]

(l) 'The claim is brought in a probate action within the meaning of Ord 76.'[115]

This subheading applies to actions for the grant of probate, or letters of administration of an estate or for the revocation of such a grant or for a decree pronouncin against the viability of a will.

(m) 'The claim is brought to enforce any judgment or arbitral award.'[116]

This is a new subheading. After the enactment of s 34 of the Civil Jurisdiction and Judgments Act 1982, if a foreign judgment is entitled to recognition in England, then no further proceedings can be brought on the original cause of action. The present subheading permits the plaintiff to serve a writ on the defendant to secure enforcement of the foreign judgment.

(n) 'The claim is brought against a defendant not domiciled in Scotland or Northern Ireland in respect of a claim by the Commissioners of Inland Revenue for or in relation to any of the duties or taxes which have been, or are for the time being, placed under their care and management.'[117]

Given that claims under English revenue law are unlikely to be enforceable in other jurisdictions, it is clearly sensible to enable public authorities to pursue claims in the English courts against those who have gone abroad.

(o) 'The claim is brought under the Nuclear Installations Act 1965, or in respect of contributions under the Social Security Act 1975.'[118]

---

111 RSC Ord 11 r 1(1)(j), formerly RSC Ord 11 r 1(1)(e).

112 *Winter v Winter* [1894] 1 Ch 421; see, also, *Official Solicitor v Stype Investments (Jersey) Ltd* [1983] 1 WLR 214.

113 RSC Ord 11 r 1(1)(k), formerly RSC Ord 11 r 1(1)(d).

114 The meaning of domicile to be determined in accordance with the Civil Jurisdiciton and Judgments Act 1982, ss 41–46, as amended by the Civil Jurisdiction and Judgments Act 1991, Sched 2, paras 16–21.

115 RSC Ord 11 r 1(1)(c), formerly RSC Ord 11 r 1(1)(m).

116 RSC Ord 11 r 1(1)(m).

117 RSC Ord 11 r 1(1)(n), formerly RSC Ord 11 r 1(1)(o); see *IRC v Stype Investments Ltd* [1982] Ch 456.

118 RSC Ord 11 r 1(1)(o), formerly RSC Ord 11 r 1(1)(l).

This subheading enables claims to be brought by the relevant public authorities.

(p) 'The claim is made for a sum to which the Directive of the Council of the European Communities, dated 15 March 1976, No 76/308/EEC applies, and service is to be effected in a country which is a Member State of the European Economic Community.'[119]

The directive in question concerns claims for agricultural levy and other matters relating to the European Agricultural Guidance and Guarantee Fund.

(q) 'The claim is made under the Drug Trafficking Act 1986.'[120]

This enables a claim to be made where the court has power to order the confiscation of assets considered to have been acquired as a result of offences in relation to drug trafficking.

(r) 'The claim is made under the Financial Services Act 1986 and the Banking Act 1987.'[121]

Both pieces of legislation are designed to regulate the financial markets and, in certain circumstances, the regulatory authorities may withdraw licences or impose penalties on operators within those markets. Many of those active in the London financial markets may be foreign based corporations.

(s) 'The claim is made under Part VI of the Criminal Justice Act 1988.'[122]

Part VI (ss 71–103) of the Criminal Justice Act 1988 introduced a new scheme to enable magistrates courts and the crown court to make confiscation orders in respect of the proceeds of serious crimes. The scheme itself was modelled on that operating in respect of drug trafficking under the Drug Trafficking Act 1986.

(t) 'The claim is brought for money had and received or for an account or other relief against the defendant as constructive trustee, and the defendant's alleged liability arises out of acts committed, whether by him or otherwise, within the jurisdiction.'[123]

One of the matters arising in *Metall und Rohstoff AG v Donaldson, Lufkin and Jenrette Inc*[124] was the holding that an action for breach of duty by an alleged constructive trustee[125] was not within the sixth subheading,

---

119 RSC Ord 11 r 1(1)(p), formerly RSC Ord 11 r 1(1)(p).

120 RSC Ord 11 r 1(1)(q).

121 RSC Ord 11 r 1(1)(r).

122 RSC Ord 11 r 1(1)(s).

123 RSC Ord 11 r 1(1)(t).

124 [1990] QB 391.

125 For the definition of a constructive trust, see *Carl Zeiss Stiftung v Herbert Smith and Co (No 2)* [1969] 2 Ch 276, p 301, *per* Edmund Davies LJ.

above, as 'founded on a tort' and, thus, not within any of the subheadings of RSC Ord 11. This subheading was added in 1990 to remedy that defect.[126]

(u) 'The claim is made under the Immigration (Carriers' Liability) Act 1987.'[127]

In an attempt to reduce the numbers of persons seeking asylum in the UK, the Immigration (Carriers' Liability) Act 1987[128] placed legal obligations on airlines and shipping companies to establish that they bring to the UK only those with the necessary documentation. As some of these carriers will be corporations registered abroad, leave to serve out of the jurisdiction will be required in those cases where action to enforce a financial penalty is taken.

---

126 RSC (Amendment No 2) Order 1990 SI 1990/1689.
127 RSC Ord 11 r 1(1)(u).
128 Ruff [1989] PL 222; Geneva Convention Relating to the Status of Refugees 1951, Art 31.

CHAPTER 12

STAYS OF ENGLISH PROCEEDINGS AND THE RESTRAINING OF FOREIGN PROCEEDINGS

STAYS OF ENGLISH PROCEEDINGS

We are now concerned with those situations in which an English court may possess jurisdiction but will decline to exercise it because, after weighing some other important consideration, the court decides to exercise its discretion to decline jurisdiction and stay proceedings. The plaintiff may be then forced to go abroad or to pursue the matter through arbitration. This is an area of law that has developed considerably in the last quarter of a century as international litigation has become part of the global village.[1] In general terms, two aspects of this problem need to be considered:

(a) where an English court applies the doctrine of *forum non conveniens*; and

(b) where there is a foreign jurisdiction clause.

It is necessary to consider each of these situations in turn.

Forum non conveniens

The English courts had an inherent jurisdiction, now confirmed by statute, to stay an action in England or to restrain by injunction the continuance of proceedings abroad in circumstances where it was necessary to do so in order to prevent injustice.[2] There are examples of such a power being considered in cases concerning the administration of estates[3] or in matrimonial cases where provision is made by statute.[4] However, we are concerned not with whether there is a discretion to stay, but whether this power should be exercised on the general ground of *forum non conveniens*. Such a doctrine has existed in Scotland since the middle of the 19th century and the concept is widely employed in the USA.

---

1   The reasons for this change are complex but, no doubt, some of the reasons are: (a) the effect of publicity being given to large awards in other jurisdictions; (b) advertising by lawyers; (c) the development of contingency fee agreements; (d) the development of civil aviation; (e) the pressure on court time in England, leading judges to be concerned about the hearing of cases that have little direct connection with the UK; and (f) the activities of multinational corporations.

2   See Supreme Court Act 1981, s 49(3).

3   *Ewing v Orr Ewing* (1885) 10 App Cases 453; the matter was also discussed in *Boys v Chaplin* [1971] AC 356, where it was asserted that there was a discretion in tort cases to prevent forum shopping.

4   Domicile and Matrimonial Proceedings Act 1973, s 5(6), Sched 1, para 9.

At this point, preliminary distinction should be drawn between a plea of *forum non conveniens* and a plea of *lis alibi pendens*. In the case of the former, the defendant is asserting that the action should be tried in a forum other than England for reasons that may vary. He is, thus, asserting that England is *forum non conveniens*. It might be expressed in another way by asserting that England is not an appropriate forum to determine the dispute. The second expression, *lis alibi pendens*, involves the assertion that there are concurrent proceedings in England and abroad that involve the same parties and the same cause of action.

Until 1973, it was broadly agreed that, in the absence of a plea of *lis alibi pendens* an English court would be reluctant to stay an action unless it could be shown that the action was vexatious.[5] The general position had been set out by Scott LJ in the case of *St Pierre v South American Stores (Gath and Chaves) Ltd*:[6]

> (1) A mere balance of convenience is not a sufficient ground for depriving a plaintiff of the advantages of prosecuting his action in an English court if it is otherwise properly brought. The right of access to the King's courts must not be lightly refused. (2) In order to justify a stay, two conditions must be fulfilled, one positive and the other negative: (a) the defendant must satisfy the court that the continuance of the action would work an injustice because it would be oppressive or vexatious to him or would be an abuse of the process of the court in some other way; and (b) the stay must not cause an injustice to the plaintiff ... In both, the burden of proof is on the defendant.[7]

There is little doubt that the statement by Scott LJ remained good law well into the post war period.[8] As a ruling of the Court of Appeal, it was regarded as setting out the correct approach by Lord Denning MR in *HRH Maharanee Seethadevi Gaekwar of Baroda v Wildenstein*,[9] where a strong Court of Appeal applied the principle to refuse a stay of proceedings in circumstances where jurisdiction had been founded on fleeting presence. By 1972, the law remained

---

5 See *Egbert v Short* [1907] 2 Ch 205; *In re Norton's Settlement* [1908] 1 Ch 471; *Logan v Bank of Scotland (No 2)* [1906] 1 KB 141, p 152, *per* Gorrell Barnes P.

6 [1936] 1 KB 382 (the proceedings on jurisdiction); the subsequent trial and appeal were reported at [1936] 1 All ER 206; [1937] 3 All ER 349.

7 Scott LJ stated the traditional English view of the open forum and impliedly asserting that a high standard of justice is available in England. Clearly, prior to 1945, there was an implied assertion of the superiority of the English court system, although few judges would be as blunt as Shadwell VC, who observed: 'I consider that in the contemplation of the Court of Chancery every foreign court is an inferior court.' *Bent v Young* (1838) 9 Sim 180, p 191.

8 In strict terms, Scott LJ was dealing with a case of *lis alibi pendens* (the dispute concerned rental payments due under leases granted in Chile). The learned judge had relied on the earlier authorities of *McHenry v Lewis* (1882) 22 Ch D 39; *Hyman v Helm* (1883) 23 Ch D 531; *Thornton v Thornton* (1886) 11 PD 176; *Logan v Bank of Scotland (No 2)* [1906] 1 KB 141. It should be noted that Scott LJ was referring to the Supreme Court of Judicature (Consolidation) Act 1925, s 41; see, now, Supreme Court Act 1981, s 49.

9 [1972] 2 QB 283.

that, in order to justify a stay, it was necessary that something more should exist than a mere balance of convenience in favour of proceedings in some other country.[10]

The movement towards the development of a general doctrine of *forum non conveniens* can be traced back to the judgment of the House of Lords in *The Atlantic Star*.[11] The facts of the case were as follows: the *Atlantic Star*, a Dutch container vessel, was involved in a collision in Belgian internal waters in which two barges were sunk. In consequence, several legal actions were begun in Belgium. One owner of a Dutch barge began Admiralty proceedings *in rem* in England. The owners of the *Atlantic Star* applied to have the proceedings stayed.

In reversing Brandon J and the Court of Appeal,[12] the majority in the House of Lords rejected any attempt to incorporate the Scottish doctrine of *forum non conveniens* but instead decided that the test of 'vexatious and oppressive' propounded by Scott LJ should be given a more liberal interpretation. In essence, the majority in the House of Lords felt that it was time openly to acknowledge that an equivalent level of justice might be obtainable in other jurisdictions. Lord Reid observed that it was time to develop the common law and render it less reminiscent of 'the good old days, the passing of which many may regret, when the inhabitants of this island felt an innate superiority over those unfortunate enough to belong to other races'. The majority felt that the formulation propounded by Scott LJ should remain in place but the words 'oppressive' and 'vexatious' should be given a liberal interpretation. Applying this more liberal approach, the House of Lords allowed the appeal and granted a stay.[13]

After the judgment in *The Atlantic Star*, it was clear that, even in the absence of *lis alibi pendens*, the court would adopt a more liberal approach when the defendant sought a stay. However, the question arose as to the extent of that liberality and the precise test that had to be met. The next occasion to consider the matter arose in the case of *McShannon v Rockware Glass Ltd*; this was a consolidated appeal in relation to four actions all turning on the same point: McShannon, a Scotsman, was injured in an industrial accident at a factory in Scotland owned by the defendants who were a company with the head office in England. London based solicitors acting on

---

10 See the judgment of Edmund Davies LJ (as he then was) in *HRH Maharanee Seethadevi Gaekwar of Baroda v Wildenstein* [1972] 2 QB 283, p 293.

11 [1974] AC 436; [1973] 2 All ER 175 (Lords Reid, Wilberforce and Kilbrandon forming the majority; Lords Simon and Morris in the minority).

12 [1972] All ER 705; [1975] 3 WLR 740 (Lord Denning MR, Phillimore, Cairns LJJ).

13 It is interesting to contrast the observations of Lord Reid with those of Lord Denning MR, in the Court of Appeal, who observed: 'The right to come before English courts is not confined to Englishmen ... You may call this forum shopping if you please but, if the forum is England, it is a good place to shop in, both for the quality of the goods and the speed of service.'

behalf of the plaintiff and his trade union advised the bringing of proceedings in London on the grounds that the procedure might be quicker and the damages larger. The evidence indicated that medical testimony was equally available in Scotland and that differences in costs between the two systems were minimal. An application was made to stay the proceedings in England.

The House of Lords[14] not only allowed the relevant appeals, but also decided to reformulate the test for the staying of proceedings in the absence of *lis alibi pendens*. Lord Diplock decided a modern draft of Scott LJ's judgment was required and held that the appropriate test could be formulated thus:

> In order to justify a stay two conditions must be satisfied, one positive and one negative: (a) the defendant must satisfy the court that there is another forum, to whose jurisdiction he is amenable, in which justice can be done between the parties at substantially less inconvenience or expense, and (b) the stay must not deprive the plaintiff of a legitimate personal or juridical advantage which would be available to him if he invoked the jurisdiction of the English court.

This reformulation of the test now placed the burden on the plaintiff in the second aspect unlike the original formulation by Scott LJ where the burden of proof was on the defendant at both stages. That the test was now one of judicial discretion, to be exercised where the interests of justice demand a stay, was reflected in the other speeches expressing agreement with Lord Diplock.

Although the House of Lords had the opportunity to consider questions of competing jurisdictions in 1980,[15] the next significant development in this area of law arose with the case of *The Abidin Daver*,[16] where the facts were as follows: a collision took place in the Bosphorus between two vessels, one owned by the Cuban plaintiffs and the other by the Turkish defendants, The Turkish party had the Cuban vessel arrested and they then began proceedings in the Turkish courts. Shortly after, the Cuban owners began an Admiralty action in London having served a writ on the sister ship of the defendant's vessel. The Turkish owners then applied for the English action to be stayed. The application was granted by Sheen J at first instance, but then reversed by the Court of Appeal.

In unanimously restoring the stay and approving the approach of Sheen J, the House of Lords acknowledged that the English test was now equivalent to the Scottish law of *forum non conveniens*. Lord Diplock thought that the English approach was now 'indistinguishable from the Scottish legal doctrine of *forum non conveniens*'.[17] Whether an application for a stay was granted or not was a

---

14 [1978] AC 795; 1 All ER 625 (a differently constituted House of Lords, comprising Lords Diplock, Salmon, Fraser, Keith and Russell). For the earlier Court of Appeal judgment, see [1977] 1 WLR 376; 2 All ER 449.

15 In the case of *Castanho v Brown and Root (UK) Ltd* [1981] AC 557 (a case that concerned an injunction to restrain foreign legal proceedings).

16 [1984] AC 398.

17 *The Abidin Daver* [1984] AC 398, p 411.

question of judicial discretion and that discretion could only be exercised by weighing all the relevant factors. As Lord Brandon observed in the same case, 'the exercise of the court's discretion in any particular case necessarily involves the balancing of all the relevant factors on either side, those favouring the grant of a stay on one hand, and those militating against it on the other'. In accordance with traditional principles the discretion is vested in the judge at first instance, so that the appellate court should not interfere merely because it would have weighed the evidence differently. It would seem that a decision should be set aside only if the judge at first instance has exercised the discretion on manifestly wrong principles or has reached a decision that is manifestly unreasonable.

The case law had developed incrementally in the years since 1973 and an attempt was made by Lord Goff to set out the basic principles in the case of *Spiliada Maritime Corporation v Cansulex Ltd*.[18] In allowing service of a writ out of the jurisdiction, Lord Goff embarked on a lengthy review of the English and Scottish law relating to questions pertaining to *forum non conveniens* and set out certain basic principles that have been followed in the subsequent case law. In broad terms, these principles can be expressed as follows:

(a) the basic principle is that a stay will only be granted on the ground of *forum non conveniens* where the court is satisfied that there is some other available forum, having jurisdiction, which is the appropriate forum for trial of the action, for example, in which the case may be tried more suitably for the interests of all the parties and the ends of justice;

(b) the burden of proof is on the defendant to show not only that England is not the natural or appropriate forum for the trial, but to establish that there is another available forum for the trial which is clearly or distinctly more appropriate than the English forum;

(c) in seeking to decide whether there is another forum which is clearly more appropriate, the court will seek to identify the 'natural forum' as being 'that with which the action has the most real and substantial connection' and in doing so, will examine factors such as convenience, expense, the availability of witnesses and the law governing the relevant transaction;

(d) if the court concludes that there is some other available forum which, *prima facie*, is clearly more appropriate for the trial of the action, it will ordinarily grant a stay unless there are circumstances by reason of which justice requires that a stay should nevertheless not be granted.

---

18 [1987] AC 460 (the actual case turned on whether the court should exercise its discretion to order service out of the jurisdiction under RSC Ord 11; in considering this, the court had to be persuaded that the case was a proper one for service out of the jurisdiction).

In the years since the judgment in *Spiliada*, there have been a large number of cases coming before the courts where the defendant has sought to stay proceedings.[19] In general, the principles can be reduced to three questions:

(a) is there another available forum?

(b) is the English forum or the foreign forum the appropriate forum? and

(c) if England is not the natural or appropriate forum, the court will consider whether the interests of justice require that the plaintiff should not be obliged to litigate abroad?

In respect of the first question, it is simply a question of evidence as to whether an available forum exists.[20] In respect of questions (b) and (c), the court is obliged to balance a number of competing factors with no one factor being conclusive. The approach is not dissimilar to that adopted when deciding between a licence and a lease or between a contract of service and a contract for services.

The principles outlined in *Spiliada* apply in cases other than commercial law, as was illustrated in *De Dampierre v De Dampierre*,[21] where a husband and wife, who were French nationals, married in 1977 and moved to London two years later. In 1984, the wife went to New York to establish a business and then took the child with her. When the wife refused to return, the husband began divorce proceedings in France. The wife then petitioned for divorce in London. The husband sought to stay proceedings; this was resisted by the wife, who believed that a financial settlement in London would be more favourable.

The House of Lords ordered a stay of the proceedings in England,[22] recognising that the wife had voluntarily severed her connections with the jurisdiction.

If a party has been engaged in litigation in another jurisdiction for a considerable time, then proceedings in England may be stayed. In *Cleveland Museum of Art v Capricorn Art International SA*,[23] Hirst J ordered a stay of proceedings in England where the litigation before the court of Ohio had been proceeding and where Ohio was the proper law of the agreement, and where Ohio was the most convenient forum for the witnesses.

---

19 *The Kapetan Georgis* [1988] 1 LR 352; *The Magnum* [1989] 1 LR 47; *Meadows Indemnity Co Ltd v Insurance Corporation of Ireland plc* [1989] 2 LR 298; *The Vishva Ajay* [1989] 2 LR 558 *Cleveland Museum of Art v Capricorn Art International SA* [1990] 2 LR 166; *The Golden Mariner* [1990] 2 LR 215; *Roneleigh Ltd v MII Exports Inc* [1990] 2 LR 312; *Banco Atlantico SA v The British Bank of the Middle East* [1990] 2 LR 504.

20 *Mohammed v Bank of Kuwait and the Middle East KSC* [1996] 1 WLR 1483.

21 [1988] AC 92.

22 The jurisdiction arose under the Domicile and Matrimonial Proceedings Act 1973, Sched 1, para 9.

23 [1990] 2 LR 166.

However, it would seem that no stay will be granted if the court of the alternative forum would apply the proper law of the contract or the defendant has a close connection with England.[24] The case law indicates a willingness to proceed in two steps: first, to determine the appropriate forum and, then, to consider, if England is not the appropriate forum, whether or not the plaintiff should be obliged to litigate abroad.

In respect of determining the appropriate forum, the factors to be considered will differ from case to case as, indeed, will the weight to be attached to each factor and no list can be conclusive. However, the court will consider the identity and territorial connections of the parties together with questions as to the availability of oral witnesses. If the evidence is substantially documentary, then the court will consider questions of language and translation.[25]

A second matter that is required to be considered at the first stage is whether any other proceedings are going on elsewhere; the existence of such proceedings may either point to allowing that jurisdiction to continue to deal with the matter[26] or the court may consider that related proceedings point to a particular court assuming jurisdiction.[27] In considering the other proceedings, the court will wish to consider the possibility of conflicting judgments.

In reaching a view as to the appropriate forum, it is proper for the court to consider whether all persons properly party to the proceedings can be joined.[28] In most instances, it will be proper for the court to consider whether the appropriate law will be applied by the foreign tribunal.[29] This exercise is normally performed by listing the various considerations and then forming a view as to which is the natural or appropriate forum; problems can arise as to how much weight to be given to a particular factor. This was recognised by Lord Templeman, in *Spiliada,* where he observed:

> The factors which the court is entitled to take into account in considering whether one forum is more appropriate are legion. The authorities do not, perhaps cannot, give any clear guidance as to how these factors are to be weighed in any particular case. Any dispute over the appropriate forum is complicated by the fact that each party is seeking an advantage.

In the course of his speech, Lord Templeman noted that, in forming a view as to the natural or appropriate forum, past authorities were of only limited value and that in each case it would be a matter for the trial judge to consider factors such as expense, delay and inconvenience.

---

24 *Banco Atlantico SA v The British Bank of the Middle East* [1990] 2 LR 504.

25 *The Magnum* [1989] 1 LR 47.

26 As in *Cleveland Museum of Art v Capricorn Art International SA* [1990] 2 LR 166.

27 *Spiliada Maritime Corporation v Cansulex Ltd* [1987] AC 460 (the so called Cambridgeshire factor).

28 *Meadows Indemnity Co Ltd v Insurance Group of Ireland* [1989] 2 LR 298.

29 *Banco Atlantico SA v The British Bank of the Middle East* [1990] 2 LR 504.

If the court has come to the view that England is not the appropriate or natural forum, then it will be necessary to consider whether, notwithstanding this fact, a stay should be refused on the grounds that the plaintiff should not be compelled to litigate abroad. At this stage, it will be for the court to consider whether a claim is time barred within the foreign forum. It may be appropriate to consider the effect of any possible pre-trial delay[30] or any rules of civil procedure relating to the costs that a successful plaintiff might recover,[31] and any particular rules that pertain to the assessment of damages.[32] It will also be important for the court to consider whether any trial abroad will meet minimum standards of procedural fairness[33] and this consideration may become more important in the future.[34] As part of this balancing process, the court will wish to consider whether the foreign court will consider itself bound by a choice of law rule that English law would regard as leading to injustice.[35]

Whereas, at the first stage, it will be for the defendant to show that there is another forum which is the natural forum, once that has been shown, a stay will normally be granted unless the plaintiff discharges the *onus probandi* and satisfies the court that the interests of justice require that he should not be required to litigate abroad. Thus, at the second stage, the onus is on the plaintiff. The relationship between the various questions was well illustrated by the litigation in *Connelly v RTZ Corpn plc*,[36] which has now been determined by the House of Lords. The salient facts in the litigation were as follows: the plaintiff, who was born in Scotland, travelled to South Africa in 1971 and then moved to Namibia, where he was employed by a wholly owned subsidiary of the defendants. He returned to Scotland in 1983 and, in 1986, he was discovered to be suffering form cancer of the larynx. He brought an action in England against the defendants, alleging that they were responsible for the inadequate safety precautions of their subsidiary.

At first instance, Wood J held that Namibia was the natural forum and that a stay should be granted. This decision was upheld by the Court of Appeal, who ruled that the presence or absence of legal aid in England was irrelevant to the exercise of the discretion. Instead of appealing to the House of Lords, the plaintiff entered into a conditional fee agreement and applied to the High Court to lift the stay. A differently constituted Court of Appeal then

---

30 *The Vishva Ajay* (1989) 2 LR 558 (possible delay in India of several years).
31 *Roneleigh Ltd v MII Exports Inc* [1989] 1 WLR 619.
32 *The Vishva Abha* (1990) 2 LR 312.
33 *Oppenheimer v Louis Rosenthal and Co AG* [1937] 1 All ER 23.
34 With the coming into force of the Human Rights Act 1998.
35 *Banco Atlantico SA v British Bank of the Middle East* (1990) 2 LR 504.
36 The proceedings before Wood J and the Court of Appeal (Neil, Waite, Swinton Thomas LJJ) were reported at [1996] QB 361; 1 All ER 500. The House of Lords judgment is reported at [1998] AC 854.

agreed to lift the stay.[37] The defendants then sought to appeal this judgment to the House of Lords while the plaintiff received leave to appeal the original judgment of the Court of Appeal out of time. The House of Lords allowed the appeal of the plaintiff and dismissed the appeal of the defendants.

The leading judgment of Lord Goff held that (a) the presence or absence of legal aid was a factor that could be considered in an application to stay proceedings; but (b) if, at the first stage, the defendant had demonstrated a natural or appropriate forum such as Namibia, then a stay would normally be granted and the plaintiff would have to take the foreign forum as he found it unless he could demonstrate, at the second stage, that the nature and complexity of his case was such that substantial justice could not be done in the appropriate forum. This will always be difficult and there will be many cases less pressing than *Connelly* where a destitute plaintiff was faced with calling considerable medical and scientific evidence. The judgment of the House of Lords has meant that, at the second stage, the plaintiff will bear a heavy onus in demonstrating that substantial justice cannot be done within the appropriate forum. It would seem after *Connelly* that, where, at the first stage, an appropriate foreign forum has been identified, then it would be very difficult indeed to persuade the court that, nevertheless, the plaintiffs should be allowed to proceed in England.

Where there is a foreign jurisdiction clause

At common law, if the parties had determined that a dispute was to be subject to the jurisdiction of a foreign court, then the English court would require evidence of exceptional circumstances[38] before allowing the parties to depart from their agreement. In normal circumstances, a party would be able to come to an English court and ask that the action of the plaintiff be stayed if it had been commenced in defiance of a foreign jurisdiction clause.[39] In such circumstances, the attitude of the courts was well expressed by Diplock LJ, where he observed that, 'I ... should require very strong reasons to induce me to permit one of them (that is, the parties) to go back on their word'.[40] This basic principle that a party should be held to his word was applied not only when an action was begun in defiance of a foreign jurisdiction clause, but also

---

37 Bingham MR, Evans and Ward LJJ; the House of Lords judgment is reported at [1998] AC 854. For a recent application see *Askin and Others v Absa Bank Ltd* (1999) *The Times*, 23 February, CA.

38 *Mackender v Feldia* [1967] 2 QB 590; *YTC Universal Ltd v Trans Europa Compania de Aviacion* (1968) 112 SJ 842; but, see *Evans Marshall and Co Ltd v Bertola SA* [1973] 1 All ER 992.

39 By a foreign jurisdiction clause, we normally mean an exclusive clause, namely, a clause that purports to oust the jurisdiction of all courts except the chosen one; a non-exclusive clause simply stipulates a number of courts.

40 *Mackender v Feldia AG* [1967] 2 QB 590, p 604.

where one party applied to the court for leave to serve out of the jurisdiction under RSC Ord 11.[41] The principle is also reflected in Art 17 of the Brussels Convention 1968. If a party has begun an action in defiance of a foreign jurisdiction clause, then he will bear the onus of demonstrating why the English court should not respect the foreign jurisdiction clause and grant the application of the defendant to stay the action. The modern approach is traceable to the judgment of Brandon J in *The Eleftheria*,[42] where the facts were as follows: the plaintiffs were the owners of cargo laden on the vessel, *The Eleftheria*, which was to have been carried from Romania to Hull, but was discharged at Rotterdam. The clause in the relevant bill of lading provided for the jurisdiction of the courts in Greece. The Romanian plaintiffs began an action in England, but the defendant applied for a stay of proceedings on the ground of the presence of a valid foreign jurisdiction clause.

In reviewing the authorities, Brandon J attempted to summarise the state of the law in a number of propositions, as follows:

The principles established by the authorities can, I think, be summarised as follows:

(1) where plaintiffs sue in England in breach of an agreement to refer disputes to a foreign court, and the defendants apply for a stay, the English court, assuming the claim to be otherwise within its jurisdiction, is not bound to grant a stay, but has a discretion whether to do so or not;

(2) the discretion should be exercised by granting a stay, unless strong cause for not doing so is shown;

(3) the burden of proving such strong cause is on the plaintiffs;

(4) in exercising its discretion, the court should take into account all the circumstances of the particular case;

(5) in particular, but without prejudice to (4), the following matters, where they arise, may properly be regarded:

(a) in what country the evidence on issues of fact is situated, or more readily available, and the effect of that on the relative convenience and expense of trial as between England and foreign courts;

(b) whether the law of the foreign court applies and, if so, whether it differs from English law in any material respects;

(c) with what country either party is connected, and how closely;

(d) whether the defendants genuinely desire trial in a foreign country or are only seeking procedural advantages;

(e) whether the plaintiffs would be prejudiced because they would:

(i) be deprived of security for their claim;

---

41 *Mackender v Feldia AG* [1967] 2 QB 590; *Evans Marshall and Co Ltd v Bertola SA* [1973] 1 All ER 992 (where the case was regarded as exceptional, having regard to the fact that not only was the substance of the case concerned with the UK but all the witnesses were in the jurisdiction).

42 [1970] P 94.

(ii) be unable to enforce any judgment obtained;

(iii) be faced with a time bar not applicable in England; or

(iv) for political, racial religious or other reasons be unlikely to get a fair trial.

The principles propounded by Brandon J have been accepted by the Court of Appeal[43] and the House of Lords[44] and represent a clarification of the prior law.[45] It is important to note that the principles have some affinity with the approach in *Spiliada* in that they require the court to take into account all matters in the particular case before exercising its discretion. It is also germane to observe that, under principle (3), where a valid foreign jurisdiction clause has been established, the *onus probandi* on the plaintiff is not unlike that placed on the plaintiff in the second stage of the *Spiliada* test. This is not surprising in that the object of the exercise in both cases is the same, namely, to determine whether the trial is to take place in England or elsewhere.

Difficulties will arise as to the nature of the contract containing the foreign jurisdiction clause. If the entire contract is void, then the clause will be ineffective but the clause will be operative if the contract is merely voidable.[46] At common law, the validity of the entire contract would for purposes of jurisdiction be determined by English law.[47] Under the terms of the Rome Convention 1980, the validity of the contract will be determined by the applicable law.[48] However, the Rome Convention makes no specific provision for foreign jurisdiction clauses. Thus, a question as to the validity of the contract as a whole will be determined under the Rome Convention, but a question as to the validity of a foreign jurisdiction clause will be determined under the common law rules. At common law, validity will be determined by the governing law.[49] The law which governs the validity of the foreign jurisdiction clause will also determine the ambit of the clause[50] and whether the clause is exclusive or non-exclusive.[51] If the foreign jurisdiction clause violates a rule of statutory law, then the clause will not be enforced.[52]

While a stay will normally be granted if a valid and exclusive foreign jurisdiction clause is established, the principles propounded by Brandon J in

---

43 *The El Amira* [1981] 2 LR 119.

44 *Trendtex Trading Corporation v Credit Suisse* [1982] AC 679; *The Sennar (No 2)* [1985] 1 WLR 490.

45 *The Athenee* (1922) 11 LR 6; *The Fehmarn* [1958] 1 WLR 159.

46 *Mackender v Feldia AG* [1967] 2 QB 590.

47 *Ibid.*

48 Rome Convention 1980, Art 8(1).

49 *The Iran Vojdan* [1984] 2 LR 380.

50 *The Sindh* [1975] 2 QB 590.

51 *Evans Marshall and Co Ltd v Bertola SA* [1973] 1 WLR 349.

52 *The Hollandia* [1983] 1 AC 565 (clause violated the Hague-Visby Rules given effect to by the Carriage of Goods by Sea Act 1971).

The Eleftheria[53] provide that where there is evidence of doubts as to the trial process in the foreign forum then a stay may be refused. It would seem that a fundamental change of circumstances represents a good reason for refusing to enforce a foreign jurisdiction clause. In *Carvalho v Hull, Blyth (Angola) Ltd*,[54] a foreign jurisdiction clause had stipulated that disputes were to be referred to the courts of Angola which then applied Portuguese municipal law. After the revolution of 1974, the Portuguese withdrew form Angola and the courts began to apply the rules of then revolutionary regime. In such circumstances, the plaintiff was able to persuade the English court that it would be improper to enforce the clause and order a stay. The fact that part of an agreement is unenforceable at common law is not a conclusive barrier to the enforcement of a foreign jurisdiction clause. In *Trendtex Trading Corporation v Credit Suisse*, the defendant obtained a stay in reliance on a foreign jurisdiction clause even though the agreement itself was unenforceable at common law for maintenance and champerty.[55] For a foreign jurisdiction clause to be relied upon there must be no doubt that it forms part of the contractual arrangements between the parties.[56] In cases where incorporation cannot be established, then a party may still raise the doctrine of *forum non conveniens*.[57]

While the existence of a foreign jurisdiction clause will normally be established by documentary evidence, there is no reason, in principle, why oral evidence alone should not be used to show that the parties have reached agreement that disputes are to be referred to a particular court.[58] In considering whether to enforce a foreign jurisdiction clause and allow a stay, an English court will be minded to consider the actual conduct of a trial in another jurisdiction; thus, if there is any doubt that relevant witnesses might not be permitted to give evidence then this would be a factor inclining the court to refuse a stay.[59]

THE RESTRAINING OF FOREIGN PROCEEDINGS

Introduction

In a number of situations, the English courts have been asked not to stay their own proceedings but to grant an injunction against an individual to restrain

---

53 [1970] P 94.

54 [1979] 3 All ER 280; 1 WLR 1228.

55 *Trendtex Trading Corpn v Credit Suisse* [1982] AC 679, the case itself being the sequel to *Trendtex Trading Corpn v Central Bank of Nigeria* [1977] QB 529.

56 *The Al Battani* (1993) 2 LR 219 (Sheen J).

57 *Ibid.*

58 *The Nile Rhapsody: Hamed El Chiaty v Thomas Cook Ltd* (1992) 2 LR 399.

59 *The Adolfi Warski* (1976) 2 LR 241 (a trial in Poland in the time of communist rule).

that individual from commencing or continuing with legal proceedings abroad. Such orders have come to be loosely described as anti-suit injunctions. This jurisdiction may be traced back a long way,[60] but in recent years the jurisdiction has been influenced by developments in the related but distinct area of forum non conveniens. The modern law begins with the judgment of the House of Lords in *Castanho v Brown and Root (UK) Ltd*,[61] which drew upon the case law flowing from the *Atlantic Star*.

It has always been the case that an injunction to restrain foreign proceedings should only be granted with the greatest caution.[62] Manifestly, there is a distinction between the staying of domestic proceedings and the restraining of foreign proceedings. In the latter case, the jurisdiction of the foreign court is indirectly affected and unedifying disputes can arise about competing court orders; delicate cases of sovereignty may arise. There is therefore every good reason to proceed with caution. As indicated above, the modern law originates with the judgment of the House of Lords in *Castanho v Brown and Root (UK) Ltd*. The facts of the case were as follows: the plaintiff, a Portuguese citizen, was seriously injured while employed in the UK undertaking work for the defendants, who were part of a large Texas based group of companies. After issuing a writ in England, the plaintiff was persuaded to issue proceedings in Texas. The first defendant delivered a defence admitting liability, but seeking an injunction to restrain legal proceedings in Texas.

Parker J granted an injunction, but that was set aside in the Court of Appeal and the subsequent appeal to the House of Lords was rejected.[63] The approach of the House of Lords was to the effect that an injunction restraining foreign proceedings would be granted where the interests of justice demanded it and that such an equity should be flexible and not subject to rigid rules. Secondly, in so far as there were rules, then these were broadly to be the same as those relating to the stays of domestic proceedings. Indeed, Lord Scarman observed:

> I now turn to consider what criteria should govern the exercise of the court's discretion to impose a stay or grant an injunction. It is unnecessary, now, to examine the earlier case law. The principle is the same whether the remedy sought is a stay of English proceedings or a restraint of foreign proceedings.

---

60 *Love v Baker* (1665) 1 Cas in Ch 67; *Bushby v Munday* (1821) 5 Madd 297; *Lord Portarlington v Soulby* (1834) 3 My & K 104; *The Christiansbourg* (1885) 10 PD 141; *The Hagen* [1908] P 189; *The Janera* [1928] P 55; *Ellerman Lines Ltd v Read* [1928] 2 KB 144.

61 [1981] AC 557; 1 All ER 143, where Lord Scarman considered that the case of *The Atlantic Star* [1974] AC 436 represented a fresh start and that not dissimilar principles should be applied in respect of cases seeking to restrain foreign proceedings.

62 *British Airways Board v Laker Airways Ltd* [1985] AC 58, p 95, *per* Lord Diplock.

63 [1981] AC 557. The Court of Appeal judgment was a majority verdict (Brandon and Shaw LJJ, with Lord Denning MR dissenting).

It was soon pointed out that if the test were the same for both forms of application, then as the doctrine of *forum non conveniens* began to develop after *The Abidin Daver*[64] there would be a danger that injunctions might be granted too liberally in respect of foreign proceedings. Indeed, the law might develop so that an injunction to restrain foreign proceedings would be obtainable in all cases in which England was the natural forum. To counteract such an undesirable development, the House of Lords and the Privy Council in a number of cases[65] developed clearer principles for the granting of injunctions to restrain foreign proceedings.

The principles indicated by this case law were:

(a) that an injunction to restrain foreign proceedings touched on questions of comity and, thus, had to be exercised with caution;[66]

(b) that such an injunction would only be granted when the ends of justice required it;

(c) that the injunction to restrain foreign proceedings was a different concept to the granting of a stay in respect of domestic proceedings;[67]

(d) that the ends of justice might require the granting of an injunction when the bringing of proceedings abroad might be regarded as unconscionable, oppressive or vexatious;

(e) that an injunction might be granted to restrain the bringing of proceedings abroad when such conduct threatens to invade a legal or equitable right of the other party not to be sued abroad;[68] and

(f) that an English court should have sufficient interest in, or connection with the matter in question to justify the indirect interference with a foreign court that an anti suit injunction entailed.

In these circumstances, it is proposed to examine the two broad headings under which an anti-suit injunction might be sought.

The infringement of a legal or equitable right

A defendant in an action abroad may apply to an English court for an injunction to restrain the plaintiff proceeding if the litigation in question

---

64 [1984] AC 398.

65 *British Airways Board v Laker Airways Ltd* [1985] AC 58; *South Carolina Insurance Co v Assurantie NV* [1987] AC 24; *Société Nationale Industrielle Aerospatiale v Lee Kui Jak* [1987] AC 871, PC.

66 *British Airways Board v Laker Airways* [1985] AC 58: *Cohen v Rothfield* [1919] 1 KB 410 *Settlement Coporation v Hochschild* [1966] Ch 10.

67 *Société Nationale Industrielle v Lee Kui Jak* [1987] AC 871, PC.

68 *South Carolina Insurance Co v Assurantie NV* [1987] AC 24.

violates a legal or equitable right of the defendant.[69] It may be that this right is contractual (for example, under the terms of a foreign jurisdiction clause or an arbitration clause) or it might arise by virtue of the operation of an equitable doctrine. In such cases, the court has an inherent jurisdiction to grant relief and in considering the matter the court will be mindful of the need to avoid the risk of inconsistent judgments. In recent years, it has been claimed that where foreign proceedings have been launched in flagrant defiance of an English jurisdiction clause or an arbitration clause then normally an injunction should be granted, unless there are particular countervailing factors.[70] Such an approach will apply also in any case where the Brussels Convention is in issue, since Art 17 takes precedence and it has been observed that 'there is no discretionary power in the convention itself to override the conclusive effect of an exclusive jurisdiction agreement'.[71]

Thus, in *Ultisol Transport Contractors Ltd v Bouygues Offshore SA*,[72] an injunction was granted restraining proceedings in South Africa brought in breach of an English jurisdiction clause.

However, proceedings brought abroad to obtain an advantage not available in English litigation will not normally be restrained. Thus, in *The Lisboa*,[73] shipowners in England failed to obtain an injunction to restrain proceedings by cargo owners in Italy when the purpose of the application related to an attempt to obtain security. When an injunction is sought, then there must be a close relationship between the possible English proceedings and the litigation commenced abroad; thus, if the foreign proceedings concern different issues, then an anti-suit injunction will not normally be granted.[74]

An anti-suit injunction is subject to the normal equitable principles, so that, if foreign proceedings are commenced and the defendant takes no action until the last possible moment, then an injunction will not be granted.[75]

The bringing of proceedings abroad would be unconscionable

It is well recognised that an injunction may be granted on the grounds that foreign legal proceedings constitute unconscionable conduct. The first

---

69 *Tracomin SA v Sudan Oil Seeds Company (Nos 1 and 2)* [1983] 1 WLR 1026 (where the court granted an injunction to restrain litigation in Switzerland contrary to an arbitration clause).

70 *Continental Bank NA v Aekos Compania Naviera SA* [1994] 1 WLR 558.

71 See Steyn LJ in *Contintental Bank NA v Aekos Compania Naviera SA* [1994] 1 WLR 558.

72 [1996] 2 LR 140.

73 *Mike Trading and Transport Ltd v R Pagnam and Fratelli, The Lisboa* [1980] 2 LR 546.

74 *Arab Monetary Fund v Hashim (No 6)* (1992) *The Times*, 24 July; (1992) *The Independent*, 30 July.

75 *Toepfer International GmbH v Molino Boschi SRL* (1996) 1 LR 510 (the relevant equitable maxim being *vigilantibus, non dormientibus, jura subveniunt*; see *Smith v Clay* (1768) 3 Bro CC 639, *per* Lord Camden LC).

problem is to define the expression 'unconscionable'. In *South Carolina Insurance Co v Assurantie NV*,[76] it was observed that it included 'conduct which is oppressive or vexatious or which interferes with the due process of the court'. However, even this definition may be of limited value since, as Bowen LJ observed in *McHenry v Lewis*,[77] 'it would be most unwise, unless one was actually driven to do so for the purpose of deciding this case, to lay down any definition of what is vexatious or oppressive'. It is clear that a party who asserts unconscionable conduct must produce cogent evidence. Secondly, whether conduct is unconscionable can only be determined by examining all the facts of a particular case. One of the most important facts will be whether the legal action can be brought both in England and abroad or whether the action can only be brought before a foreign court. In the latter situation, the court will be most reluctant to intervene. Thirdly, because the doctrine of the rule of law presupposes that individuals should have access to the courts, the English court must proceed cautiously before issuing an anti-suit injunction. The matter has been examined in some detail in a number of cases in the House of Lords and the Privy Council and these require consideration.

In *British Airways Board v Laker Airways Ltd*,[78] the salient facts were as follows: Laker Airways Ltd went into receivership in 1982 and the receiver began an action for multiple damages in the USA alleging conspiracy by a number of airlines and manufacturers contrary to the relevant anti trust legislation.[79] The plaintiffs sought an injunction to restrain the continuance of such proceedings. The House of Lords allowed an appeal from the Court of Appeal and restored the order of Parker J refusing the injunction.

Lord Diplock, in giving the judgment of the House of Lords, ruled that, in cases where the foreign court was the only competent court, no injunction would be granted unless the plaintiff could demonstrate the infringement of a legal or equitable right arising from a contract or from the other party's unconscionable conduct in circumstances in which it would be unjust if the defendant were not protected against the foreign claim. Since the plaintiffs could not demonstrate unconscionable conduct, no injunction was granted. In cases where there is only one possible tribunal, the English court will be slow to restrain a litigant abroad.[80]

---

76 [1987] AC 24, p 41, *per* Lord Brandon.
77 [1882] 22 Ch D 397, CA.
78 [1985] AC 58.
79 Sherman Act 1890; Clayton Act 1914.
80 In the case of *Midland Bamk plc v Laker Airways Ltd* [1986] QB 689, the Court of Appeal held that anti-trust proceedings should be subject to injunction on the basis that the plaintiff bank had conducted its dealings with Laker Airways Ltd in England. Such transactions were governed by English law, and there was little if any evidence against plaintiffs. Clearly, to begin foreign proceedings on the basis of very limited evidence might be regarded as *prima facie* offensive.

The subsequent case law[81] indicates that, while foreign proceedings may be restrained on grounds of unconscionable conduct, a plaintiff will find it very difficult to establish in circumstances where the acts of the defendant are otherwise lawful. In *South Carolina Insurance Co v Assurantie NV*,[82] the facts were as follows: the plaintiffs, an American insurance company, brought an action in England against a number of defendants on a contract of re-insurance. The defendants commenced proceedings in the USA, seeking pre-trial discovery against other persons. The plaintiffs sought an injunction restraining such litigation. The judge at first instance and the Court of Appeal agreed to an injunction. The House of Lords allowed the appeal and discharged the injunction.

The opinions delivered by the House of Lords exhibited certain differences of approach. Lord Brandon held that an anti-suit injunction could only be granted where there was an infringement of a legal[83] or equitable right or where one party had behaved or had threatened to behave in a manner that was unconscionable.[84] In contrast, Lord Goff held that the important factor was not the particular category of the injunction but whether relief was necessary both in the interests of justice and to protect the English jurisdiction. On the facts of the case, there was no threat to the English jurisdiction that would warrant the granting of an injunction. The case is also in line with the traditional reluctance of the courts to stipulate as to how a party might obtain his evidence.[85]

In any event, the entire area was reviewed by the Privy Council in *Société Nationale Industrielle Aerospatiale (SNIA) v Lee Kui Jak*.[86] The rather complex facts of the case can be summarised as follows: the plaintiffs were the widow and administrator of a businessman killed in a helicopter accident in Brunei. The helicopter was manufactured by a French company (SNIA), which had a subsidiary in Texas, but was owned by a British company and operated and serviced by its Malaysian subsidiary (M). At various times, proceedings were initiated in France, Texas and Brunei. The attractions of Texas were: (a) the

---

81 *South Carolina Insurance Co v Assurantie Maatschappij De Zeven Provincien NV* [1987] AC 24; *Société Nationale Industrielle Aerospatiale v Lee Kui Jak* [1987] AC 871, PC; *Airbus Industrie GIE v Patel* [1998] 2 WLR 686; [1999] AC 119. See Fentiman [1998] CLJ 467.

82 [1987] AC 24.

83 This approach is in line with the traditional understanding that in order to obtain an injunction the plaintiff must be able to point to actual or threatened injury to some specific legal or equitable right; see *Thorne v British Broadcasting Corporation* [1967] 1 WLR 1104; *Ex p Island Records* [1978] Ch 122; *Paton v British Pregnancy Advisory Service Trustees* [1979] QB 276; *C v S* [1988] QB 135.

84 This approach was followed by Lords Bridge and Brightman.

85 For the traditional robust approach, see Goddard LCJ in *Kuruma v R* [1955] AC 197, PC. However, whether such evidence should be admitted in criminal trials will now be subject to the exclusionary discretion under the Police and Criminal Evidence Act 1984.

86 [1987] AC 871.

content of the product liability law; (b) the possibility of higher damages; (c) the then absence of any doctrine of *forum non conveniens*; and (d) the availability of contingency fees. SNIA applied to the court in Brunei for an injunction restraining the proceedings in Texas. This was refused by the Court of Appeal in Brunei, but was allowed by the Privy Council.

In giving the judgment of the Privy Council, Lord Goff embarked on a general review of the law and attempted to set out guidelines for future cases. The learned judge indicated:

(a) that an anti-suit injunction was different from an application to stay domestic proceedings and should be subject to a more specific test;

(b) that an anti-suit injunction would not be granted merely because England (or Brunei) was the natural forum;

(c) that, in any application, a court would have to determine the natural forum for the dispute;

(d) that an injunction restraining foreign proceedings would only be granted if it could be shown that such proceedings were connected with the object of obtaining an unfair advantage (that is, they were oppressive or vexatious);

(e) that no injunction would be granted merely to deprive the plaintiff of an advantage in a foreign forum which it would be unjust to deny him;

(f) that because an anti-suit injunction gave rise to concerns as to comity then great caution would have to be shown in evaluating an application; and

(g) that, in determining whether proceedings in the foreign court were vexatious or oppressive, then regard had to be paid both to the advantages to the plaintiff in that forum and the disadvantages to the defendant in that forum.

Having set out the relevant principles, the Privy Council ruled that the action in Texas should be restrained. On the facts, all possible connecting factors were with Brunei; while proceedings in Texas might lead to higher damages for the plaintiff, they would not enable SNIA to serve a contribution notice on M. There was a risk that any judgment against SNIA in Texas would be followed by separate proceedings in Brunei as SNIA sought a contribution against M. This could lead to inconsistent findings of fact. Since SNIA had given assurances to expedite the hearing in Brunei and had made concessions on the pre-trial discovery and were prepared to afford sufficient security in Brunei, no injustice would be done to the defendant in granting the relief sought. The Brunei Court of Appeal had been influenced by *Spiliada*, an approach that is now to be seen as clearly wrong. Cases on anti-suit injunctions will now be subject to the approach set out by Lord Goff, although, as the learned judge indicated, a distinction will have to be drawn between those cases where there is only one forum[87] and those cases such as *Société Aerospatiale*,[88] where there was a choice between Brunei and Texas. In any event, the judgment in the *Société Aerospatiale* case came to be applied in subsequent cases in which anti-suit injunctions were being applied for in the High Court and the Court of Appeal.[89]

Any argument that the judgment in *Société Aerospatiale* was simply that of the Privy Council is no longer tenable, having regard to the express approval and refining of the principles in the recent House of Lords judgment, *Airbus Industrie GIE v Patel*.[90] The facts of the case were as follows: in Feruary 1990, an Airbus A320 aircraft crashed in Bangalore, India. A considerable number of passengers were killed or injured. In December 1990, a court of inquiry report in India attributed the crash to pilot error. The defendants were British citizens of Indian origin. The defendants settled any claim against the employers of the pilot. In February 1992, proceedings were issued against the plaintiffs in Texas on the basis that they were the manufacturers and had done business in the State. In December 1992, a court in India granted an injunction restraining foreign proceedings, but that was ineffective against the defendants who lived in England. The plaintiffs therefore sought an injunction in England restraining the defendants from continuing the legal action in Texas. Colman J refused an injunction,[91] but this was reversed by the Court of Appeal. The House of Lords allowed the appeal and set aside the injunction. The judgment of the House of Lords was given by Lord Goff who began his judgment by noting the differences between common law and civil law jurisdiction, observing:

> In the common law world, there was jungle of separate, broadly based jurisdictions all over the world. The potential excesses of common law jurisdictions were, generally, curtailed by the adoption of the principle of forum non conveniens, a self-denying ordinance under which the court would stay or dismiss proceedings in favour of another clearly more appropriate forum.

---

87 In *British Airways Board v Laker Airways Ltd* [1985] AC 58, the anti-trust proceedings could only be brought in the USA; In *Castanho v Brown and Root (UK) Ltd* [1981] AC 55, proceedings could be brought in England or Texas.

88 [1987] AC 871; see Kunzlik [1987] CLJ 406; Carter (1988) 59 BYIL 342.

89 *EI Du Pont and Co v IC Agnew* (1988) 2 LR 240 (injunction refused); *Hemain v Hemain* [1988] 2 FLR 388; *Re Maxwell Communications Corporation (No 2)* [1992] BCC 757; *Simon Engineering plc v Butte Mining plc* (1996) 1 LR 91. For a discussion of related matters, see *Channel Tunnel Group Ltd v Balfour Beatty Construction Ltd* [1993] AC 334.

90 *Airbus Industrie GIE v Patel* (1997) 2 LR 8, CA (Nourse, Aldous, Hobhouse LJJ); [1998] 2 WLR 686; [1999] AC 119, HL (Lords Goff, Slynn, Steyn, Clyde, Hutton). For discussion, see Fentiman [1998] CLJ 467.

91 The judge rejected an argument that the judgment of the court in India should be recognised.

His Lordship ruled that the relevant principles in respect of anti-suit injunctions must be regarded as settled following *Société Aerospatiale*.[92] The significant aspect that arose in *Airbus Industrie* was that England was not the natural forum or, indeed, even a potential forum, so the question arose as to whether an English court should grant an anti-suit injunction in circumstances where the English jurisdiction had no interest in, or connection with, the matter in question. Lord Goff answered the question in the negative, reasoning that the doctrine of comity required that an English forum should have a sufficient interest in, or connection with, the matter in question to justify the indirect interference with the foreign court that an anti-suit injunction entailed. Lord Goff considered that the Court of Appeal has been wrong to be overly influenced by the fact that, at the relevant time, Texas did not have a doctrine of *forum non conveniens*. It would therefore seem that the law on anti-suit injunctions must be regarded as settled and that any applicant to obtain such an anti suit injunction must show that he has established that the English forum has sufficient interest in the matter to act as required by *Airbus Industrie*[93] and that the balancing exercise required by *Société Aerospatiale*[94] has been complied with.

STAYS OF ENGLISH PROCEEDINGS AND RESTRAINING FOREIGN PROCEEDINGS UNDER THE TERMS OF THE BRUSSELS AND LUGANO CONVENTIONS

The matters alluded to above relate to conflicts between jurisdictions where the traditional rules are in operation. However, problems can arise if X begins an action in a Contracting State to the Brussels Convention and Y then applies to an English court for an anti-suit injunction. Manifestly, the Brussels Convention would be undermined if an English court were too ready to grant anti-suit injunctions or, indeed, stayed its own proceedings in violation of the Convention. To ensure such problems do not arise, s 49 of the Civil Jurisdiction and Judgments Act 1982 reads as follows:

> Nothing in this Act shall prevent any court in the United Kingdom from staying, sisting, striking out or dismissing any proceedings before it, on the ground of *forum non conveniens*, or otherwise, where to do so is not inconsistent with the 1968 Convention.

---

92 Noting that the principles had been followed in Australia, Canada and India.
93 *Airbus Industrie GIE v Patel* [1998] 2 WLR 686; [1999] AC 119; HL.
94 *Société Nationale Industrielle Aerospatiale v Lee Kui Jak* [1987] AC 871.

In strict terms, s 49 relates to an English court staying its own proceedings; the Convention itself, being a product of civil law jurisdictions, contains no provisions similar to the common law doctrine of *forum non conveniens*.[95]

A number of problems have arisen in the context of staying of actions and some are illustrated by *Continental Bank NA v Aeakos Compania Naviera SA*.[96] In this case, the dispute arose between a bank and its client in respect of a loan agreement. The loan agreement contained an English jurisdiction clause within the terms of Art 17. In defiance of the clause, the defendant began an action in Greece, whereupon the bank began an action in London seeking an injunction restraining the defendant from continuing with the proceedings in Greece. In defence, the client argued that the English action should be stayed in accordance with the provisions of Arts 21–22 of the proceedings. Although there was some doubt on the facts as to whether the conditions in Arts 21–22 had been satisfied, Steyn LJ in the Court of Appeal held that, in a conflict between Art 17 and Arts 21–22, the former would prevail. In consequence, an injunction was granted restraining the continuance of the proceedings and Steyn LJ observed 'that there is nothing in the Convention which is inconsistent with a power vesting in the English court to grant an injunction the objective of which is to secure enforcement of an exclusive jurisdiction agreement'.[97]

A second area where problems relating to the staying of actions has arisen concerns the provisions of Arts 21–23 of the Brussels Convention 1968. The interpretation to be placed on these provisions was recently examined by the House of Lords in *Sarrio SA v Kuwait Investment Authority*;[98] the facts of the case were as follows: in February 1993, the plaintiffs began proceedings in Spain for sums owed in relation to the sale of their paper business. At a later date, they began proceedings in London, alleging negligent misrepresentation on the sale. Mance J granted a stay under the provisions of Art 22 which was discharged by the Court of Appeal. The House of Lords allowed the appeal and granted a stay.

In giving the principal judgment, Lord Saville made clear that the purpose of Arts 21–23 is to avoid the duplication of litigation and to ensure this end the

---

95 See *Tessili v Dunlop* (Case 12/76) [1976] ECR 1473; [1977] 1 CMLR 26; *De Wolf v Cox* (Case 42/76) [1976] ECR 1759; 2 CMLR 43.

96 [1994] 1 WLR 588.

97 *Ibid*, p 597, *per* Steyn LJ; see, also, *Kloeckner and Co AG v Gatoil Overseas Inc* [1990] 1 LR 175; *IP Metal Ltd v Ruote OZ SpA* [1993] 2 LR 60. In effect, the Court of Appeal examined the basis on which the first court had assumed jurisdiction, which is contrary to the logic of the Convention; see *Overseas Union Insurance Ltd v New Hampshire Insurance Co* [1992] 1 QB 434; [1991] ECR I-3317. It is not without interest that evidence in the case of foreign law indicated that there may have been a submission to the jurisdiction of the court in Greece under Art 18.

98 *Sarrio SA v Kuwait Investment Authority* [1996] 1 LR 650 (Mance J); [1997] 1 LR 113, CA (Evans, Brooke, Peter Gibson LJJ); [1997] 3 WLR 1143; [1999] AC 32, HL (Lords Saville, Lloyd, Hope, Clyde, Goff of Chievely).

interpretation of the provisions must be broad and cover all cases where there is a risk of conflicting decisions. His Lordship ruled that an English court when receiving an application under Arts 21–22 should apply a simple broad test and not be deflected by over sophisticated linguistic analysis. Such an approach is in line with the purposive tradition of European interpretation. It seems that, following *Sarrio*, applications under Arts 21–22 will have a greater chance of success. However, for an application to succeed it must be shown that the action in England represents the same cause of action (Art 21) or a related cause of action (Art 22) to the proceedings in the other contracting State. Thus, it would be an error to stay a passing off action in England under Arts 21–22 where an action was proceeding in Germany between different parties in respect of the infringement of a trade mark.[99]

A third area of difficulty in relation to the staying of actions concerns the relationship with non-Contracting States. In *SW Berisford plc v New Hampshire Insurance Co*[100] and *Arkwright Mutual Insurance Co v Brynaston Insurance Co Ltd*,[101] it had been held that an English court had no general discretionary power to stay proceedings in England when jurisdiction had been allocated under Art 2 of the Brussels Convention. However, the correctness of this view was called into question by the subsequent Court of Appeal judgment in *Re Harrods (Buenos Aires) Ltd*,[102] where the facts were as follows: the H company was registered in London but conducted all its business in Argentina. L, a Swiss based minority shareholder, complained of the manner in which the affairs of the company were being conducted and sought an order that the defendant majority shareholder purchase his shareholding under the terms of the Companies Act 1985. The defendant argued that the proper place to resolve the dispute was in Argentina and that proceedings in England should be stayed. The Court of Appeal agreed to this course. On appeal, the House of Lords made a reference to the European Court of Justice, but the case was settled.

The Court of Appeal reasoned that the effect of s 49 of the Civil Jurisdiction and Judgments Act 1982 was to allow orders for stays to be made on grounds of *forum non conveniens*, provided that the order was not contrary to the Brussels Convention. This approach has been attacked on a number of grounds. It is argued that the Convention is not simply concerned with the allocation of jurisdiction between Contracting States, but is also concerned with the decisions Contracting States make in respect of jurisdictions that arise under the Convention. It might lead to a situation where some States decline

---

99 See *Mecklermedia Corporation and Another v DC Congress GmbH* [1997] 3 WLR 479, where Jacobs J refused a stay.

100 [1990] 2 QB 631.

101 [1990] 2 QB 649.

102 [1992] Ch 72 (Dillon LJ dissenting).

jurisdiction and others with no doctrine of forum non conveniens accept jurisdiction.

Thirdly, the case gives no indication as to the correct approach where the conflict is between Contracting State A, Contracting State B and non-Contracting State C. In any event, the judgment has been followed in subsequent cases.[103]

---

103 *The Po* (1991) 2 LR 206; *The Nile Rhapsody* (1994) 1 LR 382.

CHAPTER 13

JURISDICTION UNDER THE BRUSSELS AND LUGANO CONVENTIONS

THE BRUSSELS CONVENTION

Introduction

Under the terms of Art 220 of the Treaty of Rome 1957, the six original members[1] of the European Economic Community entered into a Convention on Jurisdiction and the Enforcement of Judgments in Civil and Commercial matters in 1968 (known as the Brussels Convention). The Convention entered into force in 1973 and was supplemented by a Protocol on Interpretation drawn up in 1971 and entering into force in 1975. The original object of the Convention was to provide for the free circulation of judgments within the Community and to this end it was considered necessary to harmonise the rules on jurisdiction. It was felt that there would be no acceptance of the free circulation of judgments unless the courts of one State had confidence in the claims to jurisdiction made by the courts of another Member State.

The UK entered the European Community on 1 January 1973 and, in 1978, signed an instrument of Accession to both the 1968 Convention and the 1971 Protocol on Interpretation. In accordance with traditional constitutional principles, domestic legislation was needed to give effect to these international obligations in municipal law. The relevant legislation was the Civil Jurisdiction and Judgments Act 1982, which came into effect on 1 January 1987. Section 2 of the legislation provides that the Conventions are to have the force of law within the UK. The expansion of the European Community has resulted in the Greek Accession Convention of 1982 and the Spanish and Portuguese Accession Convention (the San Sebastian Convention) of 1989. This resulted in a number of changes which were given effect to in the UK from 1 December 1991.[2] Thus, in respect of the Brussels Convention, the law is set out in the 1968 text and the 1971 Protocol as amended by the 1978, 1982 and 1989 Acts of Accession.

---

1 The original six signatories to the Treaty of Rome were France, Germany (then West Germany) Italy, The Netherlands, Belgium and Luxembourg. The first enlargement of 1973 brought in the UK, Ireland and Denmark. In 1979, Greece signed an instrument of accession. In 1986, Portugal and Spain joined the Community. The final round of enlargement was completed in 1995 when Sweden, Austria and Finland joined the Community.

2 See SI 1990/2591.

In the mid-1980s, the close trading links between the then EFTA[3] countries and the European Community prompted discussion as to co-operation on the matter of recognition and enforcement of judgments. At the time, the interpretative role of the European Court of Justice posed constitutional problems for those States that remained outside the European Community. Thus, in 1988, the European Community States entered into a parallel convention with the EFTA countries (known as the Lugano Convention) which has almost identical contents to the Brussels Convention.[4] In respect of the UK, the parallel convention was given effect to by the Civil Jurisdiction and Judgments Act 1991.

The recent decision of Austria, Sweden and Finland to become full members of the European Community will require them to accede to the Brussels Convention; this, in turn, will require legislation within the UK. Not all these developments have as yet filtered through the whole system. I will assume, in the remainder of this chapter, that both the San Sebastian Convention and the Lugano Convention are fully in force within their respective areas. In examining any particular case, it is important to ask what country one is dealing with and, at the operative date, to which international convention that State was a party.[5] The Lugano Convention will apply if the matter is within its scope and the defendant is domiciled within a Contracting State. However, since members of the European Community are parties to both conventions, it is provided[6] that, where the defendant is domiciled in a European Community State, then the Brussels Convention will apply but, if the defendant is domiciled in an EFTA State, then the Lugano Convention will apply.

Interpretation

In 1971, the original members of the European Community entered into the Luxembourg Protocol, which conferred jurisdiction on the European Court of Justice to enable it to give rulings on the interpretation of the Brussels Convention. The reasons for this course of action are broadly the same as the reasons for Art 177 of the Treaty of Rome, namely, to enable the European Court to give authoritative rulings on the Convention based on a broad knowledge of the aims and objectives of the Convention. As is well known,

---

3   The then EFTA States were Austria, Finland, Sweden, Iceland, Norway and Switzerland.

4   The Lugano Convention 1988 is set out in the Civil Jurisdiction and Judgments Act 1982, Sched 3C, inserted by the Civil Jurisdiction and Judgments Act 1991, s 1(1).

5   To take a fairly obvious example in relation to the UK, the case of *Maharanee of Baroda v Wildenstein* [1972] 2 QB 283 would not now be decided the same way, having regard to the scheme introduced by the Civil Jurisdiction and Judgments Act 1982.

6   Lugano Convention 1988, Art 54B.

the European Court of Justice adopts the teleological, or purposive,[7] method of interpretation and this will be applied to the text of the Brussels Convention. In giving rulings, the European Court of Justice will also be obliged to pay regard to its relationship with the Treaty of Rome 1957. The case for allowing the European Court of Justice to give rulings on interpretation was lucidly expressed by Bingham J (as he then was) in *Commissioners of Customs and Excise v Samex ApS:*[8]

> Sitting as a judge in a national court, asked to decide questions of Community law, I am conscious of the advantages enjoyed by the European Court of Justice. It has a panoramic view of the Community and its institutions, a detailed knowledge of the Treaties and of much subordinate legislation made under them, and an intimate familiarity with the functioning of the Community market which no national judge could hope to achieve.

Giving judgment more recently and speaking in the context of the Brussels Convention, Steyn LJ observed, in *Continental Bank NA v Aeakos Compania SA:*[9]

> In construing the Brussels Convention, it is important to put aside preconceptions based on traditional English rules. The Convention is a radical new regime governing the international legal relationships of the Contracting States. It is intended to eliminate obstacles to the functioning of the Common Market and to further the evolution of a vast single market. The genesis of the Convention is the jurisprudence of the civil law rather than the common law.

When a court in England is required to consider any question as to the meaning or effect of any provision of the Brussels Convention, it shall, if it does not refer to the European Court of Justice, determine the matter in accordance with the principles laid down in prior judgments of the European Court.[10] In addition and contrary to the normal tradition at common law, the legislation[11] specifically provides that the English court is to pay regard to the various reports produced by the rapporteur and the committee of experts at each stage in the evolution of the Brussels Convention.[12] In effect, there is a threefold mechanism for ensuring uniformity of interpretation; the English court will refer to past judgments of the European Court, it will refer to the specialist reports and, if further guidance is needed, it can make a reference to

---

7   A matter pointed out by Lord Denning MR in *James Buchanan and Co Ltd v Babco Forwarding and Shipping (UK) Ltd* [1978] AC 141, CA, where the learned judge draws a contrast with the common law tradition of grammatical interpretation.

8   [1983] 3 CMLR 194; 1 All ER 1042 (Bingham J was referring to the Art 177 procedure, but the same case arises under the 1971 Protocol).

9   [1994] 1 WLR 588, p 596.

10 Civil Jurisdiction and Judgments Act 1982, s 3.

11 *Ibid*, s 3(3).

12 For the 1968 Convention and 1971 Protocol, see: *The Jenard Report* OJ C 59/1, 1979; The Accession Convention 1978; *The Schlosser Report* OJ C 59/71, 1979; The Accession Convention 1982, *The Evrigenis and Kerameus Report* OJ C 298/1, 1986; The Accession Convention 1989, *The Almeida Cruz, Desantes Real and Jenard Report* OJ C 189/06, 1990; The Lugano Convention 1988, *The Jenard Moller Report* OJ C 189/57, 1990.

the European Court under the terms of the 1971 Protocol, although normally it will only be the Court of Appeal or House of Lords that will make such a reference.[13] It will therefore be the duty of the English judge when considering matters arising under the Brussels Convention to interpret the provisions by reference to the relevant European case law. In *Mecklermedia Corporation v DC Congress GmbH*,[14] the court was required to interpret Art 5(3) of the Brussels Convention and, in particular, the expression 'where the harmful event occurred' and, to do this, Jacob J was guided by the prior rulings of the European Court.[15]

Thus, the text of the Brussels Convention has nothing like the attempted precision of a UK statute. It invites the purposive rather than a literal approach to its interpretation – one which takes account of the object of the Convention as a whole, so as to inform the interpretation of particular provisions – not an easy task and one which the European Court of Justice has not always managed.[16]

Although the writ of the European Court of Justice does not run in EFTA, countries there have arrangements to ensure consistency in the interpretation of the Brussels and Lugano Conventions. Protocol 2 of the Lugano Convention requires courts in Contracting States to pay regard to the principles laid down in any relevant decision delivered by the court of another Lugano Contracting State. In the UK, s 3B(1) of the Civil Jurisdiction and Judgments Act 1982[17] requires a court to take account of any principles laid down in any relevant decision delivered by a court of any other Lugano Contracting State concerning the provisions of the Convention.

The ambit of the Conventions

The Conventions apply only to international cases; they do not seek to determine jurisdiction when there is no element foreign to the Contracting State, that is, they allocate jurisdiction among States in the international sense, they do not attempt to allocate to legal systems as such. For the UK, with its three principal legal systems, an internal system of allocation has been established by the Modified Convention and this system applies when the

---

13 Thus, the judge at first instance will have to work his way through the relevant European authorities, as Lloyd J acknowledged in *Pearce v Ove Arup Partnership* [1997] 2 WLR 779, p 783.

14 [1997] 3 WLR 479.

15 *Handelswekerij GJ Bier BV v Mines de Potasse d'Alsace SA* (Case 21/76) [1978] QB 708; [1977] 3 WLR 479; *Dumez France v Hessiche Landesbank (Helaba)* (Case C-220/88) [1990] ECR I-49.

16 See *Rosler v Rottwinkel* (Case 241/83) [1986] QB 33; [1985] 1 CMLR 806. Note the addition to Art 16 in the 1989 amendment.

17 Inserted by the Civil Jurisdiction and Judgments Act 1991, s 1(2).

defendant is domiciled in the UK and the proceedings are within the general scope of the Brussels Convention. The Modified Convention was established by s 16 and Sched 4 of the Civil Jurisdiction and Judgments Act 1968 and is dealt with later in this chapter.

The Brussels and Lugano Conventions apply only where the issue in dispute is a civil or commercial matter and either:

(a) the defendant has his domicile in a Contracting State, that is, in an European Community State (Brussels Convention) or in an EFTA State (Lugano Convention); or

(b) where a Contracting State has exclusive jurisdiction, either by reason of the subject matter in dispute (for example, real estate within the jurisdiction) or by the prior agreement of the parties.

Where the Conventions apply, the court indicated has no choice but to accept the jurisdiction, it cannot hold itself *forum non conveniens*[18] (unless, perhaps, the appropriate forum is that of a non-Contracting State)[19] and it cannot control service of process out of the jurisdiction. This does not mean that there are no choices of jurisdiction open to the parties, for there are some overlaps in the Conventions' provisions. Where these occur and multiple proceedings are instituted, the Conventions provide that, if there is identity in the roles of the parties and the cause of action, the second court in time must stay its proceedings until the court first seised has established whether or not it has jurisdiction and, if it has, the second court in time must decline jurisdiction in favour of the first.[20] Unlike the common law rules, the Conventions are defendant oriented and the domicile of the defendant is a concept key to both the application of the Conventions themselves and the jurisdictional rules they contain.

It is necessary first to examine the concept of a 'civil and commercial matter' before considering the question of domicile, after which it will be possible to examine the various bases of jurisdiction under the Conventions.

Civil and commercial matters

Article 1 of the Brussels Convention opens with the following words: 'This Convention shall apply in civil and commercial matters whatever the nature of the court or tribunal. It shall not extend, in particular, to revenue, customs

---

18 Civil Jurisdiction and Judgments Act 1982, s 49.

19 This depends on the view taken of *Re Harrods (Buenos Aires) Ltd* [1992] Ch 72, which has attracted criticism. The Court of Appeal (Stocker, Bingham, Dillon LJJ) concluded that English courts retained the power to decline jurisdiction on *forum non conveniens* where the forum was the court of a non-Contracting State.

20 Brussels Convention, Art 21; Lugano Convention, Art 21.

or administrative matters.'[21] The Conventions do not provide a specific definition of 'civil and commercial matters' but, instead, proceed by excluding certain areas of law. It is unlikely that much difficulty will be encountered in dealing with revenue and customs matters but problems may arise as to the nature of administrative law matters. In civil law jurisdictions, a rigid distinction exists between private and public law matters. In England, even though the area of judicial review has grown steadily in the last 20 years, difficulties can arise as to what is a public law body and what is a public law function. Thus, in *LTU v Eurocontrol*,[22] a question arose as to the validity of charges imposed by Eurocontrol upon an airline for the use of safety services. A Belgian court found the dispute to be commercial in nature but, when an attempt was made to enforce the judgment in Germany, a reference was made to the European Court of Justice. The Court ruled that the expression 'civil and commercial matter' required a Community meaning and a dispute with a public body as to the manner in which it had exercised its powers was not a commercial matter for the purposes of the Brussels Convention. The same approach was followed in the later case of *Netherlands State v Ruffer*,[23] where an action was brought before the Dutch civil courts by the Netherlands State, seeking financial reimbursement by a German shipowner for the cost of clearing a wreck that was obstructing a public waterway. The obligation to clear the wreck fell upon the State as a matter of international convention, but the action to reclaim monies was characterised by Dutch law as tortious in nature. The European Court of Justice held that any attempt by a public authority to recover sums for undertaking mandatory public duties should be regarded as administrative in nature and outside the definition of civil and commercial. Moreover, the Court held that the expression 'civil and commercial' within Art 1 had to be given a Community meaning and the categorisation by Dutch law was irrelevant. This is in line with the traditional view of the European Court, that Community law is an autonomous system which is not to be moulded or influenced by the provisions of a particular national law.

The expression 'civil' widens the Conventions to include matters such as employment disputes and claims for maintenance; the latter have given rise to difficulties and are dealt with later.

The text of Art 1 then proceeds to outline a number of specific exclusions; the relevant part of Art 1 of the Brussels Convention continues:

The Convention shall not apply to:

(1) the status or legal capacity of natural persons, rights in property arising out of a matrimonial relationship, wills and succession;

---

21   A similar provision appears in the Lugano Convention.
22   (Case 29/76) [1976] ECR 1541; [1977] 1 CMLR 88.
23   (Case 814/79) [1980] ECR 3807; [1981] 3 CMLR 293.

These exclusions are fairly clear and comprehend issues of majority status and the capacity of a minor to act in law, marriage and matrimonial causes, legitimacy, testate and intestate succession, and family property regimes. The expression 'rights in property arising out of a matrimonial relationship' will comprehend not only property relationships stipulated by national systems, but also proprietary relationships resulting form the matrimonial relationship or its dissolution.[24] It should be noted that the exclusion does not include maintenance for which there is a separate provision.[25] It does not exclude matters which are related to, but do not expressly raise, the excluded issues. So, for example, an international legal action brought by a disappointed beneficiary against the testator's legal adviser over the negligent drafting of the will, or an action by a wife who has lost her interest in the matrimonial home as a result of a surety agreement which she had entered without warning of the consequences, are not excluded:[26]

(2) bankruptcy, proceedings relating to the winding up of insolvent companies or other legal persons, judicial arrangements, compositions and analogous proceedings;

The intention was that matters directly related to and consequential upon bankruptcy or insolvency should be excluded from the Brussels Convention:[27]

(3) Social Security;

This is not an exclusion that has resulted in any difficulty; since social security benefits are paid by governmental organs, the rights arising are traditionally viewed as public law rights and, in many cases, are subject to the exercise of discretion by governmental bodies:

(4) arbitration.

Arbitration awards cannot be enforced under the Convention. There are a number of matters that can arise in respect of arbitration, including questions as to the law governing the agreement and the law governing the proceedings; it would seem that this particular exclusion is to be widely interpreted. In *Marc Rich and Co v Società Italiana Impianti PA*,[28] the European Court of Justice held that the exclusion was total and this would include a dispute before an English court as to the appointment of an arbitrator. The reason for the exclusion was that all the original Member States had participated in other international conventions relating to arbitration and it was felt that community provision was not needed.

---

24 *De Cavel v De Cavel (No 1)* (Case 143/78) [1979] ECR 1055; [1979] 2 CMLR 547.
25 See Art 5(2); *De Cavel v De Cavel (No 2)* (Case 120/79) [1980] ECR 731; 3 CMLR 1.
26 Eg, *Ross v Caunters* [1980] Ch 297.
27 The original intention was to produce a distinct Bankruptcy Convention, although the drafts of 1970 and 1980 met with little enthusiasm; see Hunter (1972) 21 ICLQ 682; (1976) 26 ICLQ 310; *Gourdain v Nadler* (Case 133/78) [1979] ECR 733; 3 CMLR 180.
28 (Case C-190/89) [1992] 1 LR 342.

The domicile of the defendant

Although the Brussels Convention adopts the concept of domicile as a central tenet, no definition of domicile appears within the Convention. Article 52 provides: 'In order to determine whether a party is domiciled in the Contracting State, whose courts are seised of the matter, the court shall apply its internal Law.' Thus, an English court will apply domestic law to determine whether X is domiciled in the UK. However, if the question for the English court is whether X is domiciled in France, then Art 52(2) requires the English court to apply the law of France. It needs to be noted at this point that domicile under the Brussels and Lugano Conventions is related to a State, not a country or law district. The object of the exercise is to link the defendant with the UK as a whole; special rules apply if further localisation is required.[29]

However, the traditional English concept of domicile developed in the 19th century was considerably at variance with that employed in civil law jurisdictions. Such a divergence would have undermined the working of the Convention, so that, for the purpose of the Brussels and Lugano Convention, ss 41–45 of the Civil Jurisdiction and Judgments Act 1982 introduced a particular definition designed to promote harmony with the other Contracting States. The simplified code of domicile, which applies only for the purpose of the Brussels and Lugano Conventions, enables a person's domicile in the UK to be established if it can be shown that:

(a) he is resident in the UK; and

(b) the nature and circumstances of his residence indicate that he has a substantial connection with the UK.[30]

This second requirement will be rebuttably presumed if the person has been resident in the UK for the last three months.[31]

If the defendant is not domiciled in the UK or in another Contracting State, it must follow that he is domiciled in a non-Contracting State. If, however, it is necessary positively to establish that a person is domiciled in a non-Contracting State, as it is to allow the English courts to take jurisdiction at common law rather than under the Conventions, the same test as for UK domicile under the Conventions is applied.[32] But, in these cases there is no presumption raised by three months residence and no attempt either to take account of the non-Contracting State's concept of domicile, if it has one. This special test of domicile for the purposes of the Conventions can have odd results. Suppose an English court takes jurisdiction at common law, having satisfied itself that the defendant is domiciled in State X, a non-Contracting

29 Civil Jurisdiction and Judgments Act 1982, s 41(3), (5).
30 *Ibid*, s 41(2)(a), (b).
31 *Ibid*, s 41(6).
32 *Ibid*, s 41(7).

State. When it proceeds to the substantive issues, its choice of law rules might involve a reference to the defendant's *lex domicilii*. Now, of course, the English court will apply its ordinary test of domicile for choice of law purposes. This could result in a finding that the defendant was domiciled in State Y. State Y could be either a Contracting or a non-Contracting State.

The domicile of a company or an unincorporated association[33] is identified with its seat and it is for the national court seised of the case to determine where that is by the use of its own conflict rules.[34] The Civil Jurisdiction and Judgments Act 1982[35] provides that a company has its seat and, therefore, its domicile in the UK if:

(a) it was incorporated or formed under a law of part of the UK and has its registered office or some other official address in the UK; or

(b) its central management or control is exercised in the UK.[36]

The same test is applied to establish if such a body is domiciled in a State other than the UK.[37] If the foreign State indicated by the test is a non-Contracting State the common law rules on jurisdiction will be applied. If, however, the State indicated is a Contracting State, the company or association will only be domiciled there if it is so regarded by the law of that State.[38] Where the matter concerns the exclusive jurisdiction under Art 16(2) of the Brussels Convention 1968, a modified version of these domicile tests is applied.[39]

The domicile of a trust is left by the Brussels and Lugano Conventions to the conflict rules of the court which is seised of the case.[40] For the UK, a trust will only be domiciled in the UK if it is domiciled in a part of the UK. It will be domiciled in that part of the UK whose legal system has the closest and most real connection with it.[41]

The general basis of jurisdiction under the Brussels Convention 1968 and the Lugano Convention 1988

The Conventions apply whenever the defendant is domiciled in a Convention State, and the basic jurisdictional rule is that a defendant must be sued in the

---

33 The nature of an unincorporated association, discussed in *Leahy v AG of New South Wales* [1959] AC 457; *Neville Estates Ltd v Madden* [1962] Ch 832; *Re Recher's Will Trusts* [1972] Ch 526.

34 Brussels Convention 1968, Art 53.

35 Civil Jurisdiction and Judgments Act 1982, s 42.

36 *Ibid*, s 42(3).

37 *Ibid*, s 42(6).

38 *Ibid*, s 42(7).

39 *Ibid*, s 43.

40 Brussels Convention 1968, Art 53; Lugano Convention 1988, Art 53.

41 Civil Jurisdiction and Judgments Act 1982, s 45.

State in which he is domiciled.[42] Thus, where the defendant is domiciled in a Contracting State, the bases of jurisdiction are those under the Convention and not the traditional rules of the forum. It is also clear that the principle that the defendant should be sued in the courts of his domicile is the central point of the Convention. While there are other bases of jurisdiction, it is clear that these are to be construed restrictively, having regard to the fact that they are derogations from the basic principle.[43] Special rules apply to cases where there are multiple defendants, third party proceedings or counterclaims,[44] in order to avoid multiplicity of proceedings, but these do not significantly detract from the basic principle.

Where the defendant is domiciled in a Contracting State, the Conventions override the ordinary jurisdictional rules of the national courts, which means, under English law, that the jurisdiction based on presence or permissive service out of the jurisdiction has no application.[45] However, where the defendant is not domiciled in a Contracting State, then Art 4 permits jurisdiction to be assumed under the traditional English rules. Thus, if an English company wished to sue a Texan domicilary on a fleeting visit to England or to serve out under RSC Ord 11, these would be matters governed by the traditional rules. Thus, the traditional rules which provide for exorbitant jurisdiction and are favourable to the plaintiff provide a basis for jurisdiction in certain cases. This can have important consequences in respect of the recognition of judgments and, where jurisdiction arises under Art 4, there may be problems about the status of the doctrine of *forum non conveniens*.[46]

In order to determine whether a person is domiciled in a Contracting State, an English court will follow the provisions of ss 41 and 42 of the Civil Jurisdiction and Judgments Act 1982 and Art 52 of the Conventions. In cases where it is important to know where in the UK a particular person is domiciled reference will be made to the Modified Convention.[47]

---

42 Brussels Convention 1968, Art 2; Lugano Convention 1988, Art 2.

43 See the scholarly judgment of Lord Goff in *Kleinwort Benson Ltd v Glasgow City Council* [1997] 3 WLR 923, p 927; *Martin Peters Bauunternehmung GmbH v Zuid Nederlandse Aannemers Vernigung* (Case 34/82) [1983] ECR 897; *Kalfelis v Bankhaus Schroder, Munchmeyer, Hengst and Co* (Case 189/87) [1988] ECR 5565.

44 Brussels Convention 1968, Art 6; Lugano Convention 1988, Art 6.

45 *Ibid*, Art 3; Art 3.

46 See the Court of Appeal judgment in *Sarrio SA v Kuuwait Investment Authority* [1997] 1 LR 113, where the defendant raised not only a plea of *lis alibi pendens* under Arts 21 and 22 but, also, argued that the doctrine of *forum non conveniens* could be invoked in cases where jurisdiction was assumed under Art 4; see the judgment of Evans LJ. As the House of Lords allowed the appeal under the first head, there was no need for this matter to be explored further. See Harris (1997) 113 LQR 557.

47 Civil Jurisdiction and Judgments Act 1982, Sched 4; this will be discussed further at the conclusion of the chapter.

To the basic jurisdictional rules under the Conventions – that a defendant who is domiciled in a Contracting State must be sued in the courts of his domicile – there are some additions and exceptions. These will be explored in the next sections, but they can be listed here:

(a) special jurisdiction: the Brussels and Lugano Conventions provide that certain courts shall have jurisdiction over particular types of cases. In such cases, the defendant may be sued either in the courts of his domicile or in the courts which have special jurisdiction;[48]

(b) exclusive jurisdiction: the Conventions confer exclusive jurisdiction on some courts for some matters. In these cases, litigation must come before the courts so designated and the defendant cannot be sued in the courts of his domicile unless, of course, the two happen to coincide;[49]

(c) jurisdiction agreements: a valid jurisdiction agreement may confer jurisdiction on a court which is not the court of the defendant's domicile;[50] and

(d) submission to the jurisdiction: except in the cases covered by the exclusive jurisdiction provisions, the defendant can empower a court to hear the case by submitting to the jurisdiction of that court.[51]

It is now necessary to examine each of these particular bases of jurisdiction.

Special jurisdiction under the Brussels Convention 1968 and the Lugano Convention 1988

The Conventions have a number of special provisions which confer jurisdiction on courts additional to those of the defendant's domicile. Where these apply, the plaintiff is free to select the forum he prefers. Where actions between the same parties and over the same subject matter are brought in the courts of different Contracting States, it is the policy of the Conventions to give precedence to the court first seised.[52]

A domiciliary of one Contracting States may be sued in the courts of another Contracting State in the following cases:

---

48 Brussels Convention 1968, Arts 5–15; Lugano Convention 1988, Arts 5–15.
49 *Ibid*, Art 16; Art 16.
50 *Ibid*, Art 17; Art 17.
51 *Ibid*, Art 18; Art 18.
52 *Ibid*, Arts 21 and 22; Arts 21 and 22. For a discussion as to the correct approach to these Articles, see *Sarrio SA v Kuwait Investment Authoirty* [1997] 3 WLR 1143; [1999] AC 32, HL.

Contracts

Article 5(1) of the Brussels Convention reads as follows:

> A person domiciled in a Contracting State may, in another Contracting State, be sued:
>
> (1) in matters relating to a contract, in the court for the performance of the obligation in question; in matters relating to individual contracts of employment, this place is where the employee habitually carries out his work, or if the employee does not habitually carry out his work in any one country, this place shall be the place of business through which he was engaged.

In matters relating to a contract, an action may be brought before the courts of the place of performance of the contract.[53] Despite the generality of the phrase 'matters relating to a contract', it would seem that the action must itself be contractual. So, an action by a buyer against the manufacturer, rather than the seller, of a defective componnent has been held not to fall within the provision.[54] An action for restitution of money paid under a void contract will not fall within the provision.[55]

In an international contract, the 'place of performance' may not, of course, be in a single country; the contract may require acts of performance to be made in several different countries. Where this is the case, the plaintiff has a choice, but the country chosen must relate to the particular dispute, that is, he cannot invoke the jurisdiction in a place where the contract has been satisfactorily performed in order to litigate his claim that the contract was not properly performed somewhere else.[56] It should be noted here that, although the place of performance has a strong connection with the contract, neither it nor the law of the defendant's domicile have particular claims to the applicable law under the Rome Convention 1980. It may well be the case, therefore, that a country which has jurisdiction under the Conventions will be required to apply a foreign law under the Rome Convention.

An analysis of the case law indicates that the European Court of Justice has consistently refused to broaden the scope of Art 5(1): the obligation must be 'the contractual obligation forming the basis of the legal proceedings'.[57] Or,

---

53 Art 51.

54 *Handte (Jacob) and Co GmbH v Traitements Mecano-chemiques des Surfaces SA* (Case C-26/91) [1992] ECR I-3967.

55 *Kleinwort Benson Ltd v Glasgow City Council* [1993] QB 429 (Hirst J); [1994] QB 404, CA; (Case 346/93) [1996] QB 57, ECJ; [1996] QB 678, CA (Roch and Millett LJJ, with Legatt LJ dissenting); [1997] 3 WLR 923, HL (Lords Goff, Mustill, Nicholls, Clyde, Hutton). This is an unusual example of a case under Sched 4.

56 *Ets A de Bloos SPRL v Société en commandité par actions Bouyer* (Case 14/76) [1976] ECR 1497.

57 *Ibid.*

to put the matter another way, the obligation is the obligation on which the plaintiff's action is based. The important question concerns 'the place where the obligation which constitutes the basis of the claim was, or ought to be, performed'. The obligation 'cannot be interpreted as referring to any obligation whatsoever arising under the contract in question, but is rather that which corresponds to the contractual right on which the plaintiff's action is based'.[58] If a question arises as to whether a contract is in existence at all, then the court may examine the question as to whether there is a valid contract as one of the pre conditions of jurisdiction.[59] In *Boss Group Ltd v Boss France SA*,[60] it was held by the Court of Appeal that Art 5(1) applies even where the plaintiff alleges that no contract exists between the parties. It has to be borne in mind that Art 5(1) is part of Art 5 and the general position as to Art 5 is that it is to be interpreted restrictively as a derogation from the general principle of domicile in Art 2.[61]

In cases where there is more than one obligation in issue, then the European Court of Justice has tended to follow the rule of *accessorium sequitur principale*, namely, that jurisdiction will be determined by the place of the principal obligation. Thus, in *Union Transport plc v Continental Lines SA*,[62] the House of Lords held that failure to nominate a vessel in London, under a charterparty agreement, was sufficient grounds for jurisdiction under Art 5(1), even though the cargo of telegraph poles were to be carried from Floirda to Bangladesh and the obligation to provide the vessel arose in Florida. As regards the place of performance, the European Court held, in *Industrie Tessli v Dunlop AG*,[63] that it will be for each national court to apply its own rules of private international law to determine where the obligation in question is to be performed. Although some have criticised this approach as placing too much emphasis on the national court, the European Court has recently affirmed this approach.[64]

Since the 1989 Accession Convention, the Conventions make special provision for the identification of the place of performance of an individual employment contract.[65] However, a distinction has to be drawn between an individual contract of employment and contracts for services and collective agreements; in principle, the special provisions will only apply to the

---

58 *Custom Made Commercial Ltd v Stawa Metallbau GmbH* (Case C-288/92) [1994] I-2913.

59 *Effer SpA v Kantner* (Case 38/81) [1982] ECR 825.

60 [1996] 4 All ER 970.

61 *Kalfelis v Bankhaus Schroder, Munchmeyer, Hengst and Co* (Case 189/97) [1988] ECR 5565.

62 [1992] 1 WLR 15; 1 All ER 161; 1 LR 229.

63 (Case 12/76) [1976] ECR 1473.

64 *Custom Made Commercial Ltd v Stawa Metallbau GmbH* (Case C-288/92) [1994] ECR I-2913.

65 Giving effect to the broad outlines of the approach in *Ivenel v Schwab* (Case 133/81) [1982] ECR 1891 and *Shenavai v Kreischer* (Case 266/85) [1987] ECR 239.

individual contract of employment.[66] Article 5(1) provides that, in the case of the individual contract of employment, the place of performance will be where the employee habitually carries out his work or, if there is no such place, the place of business through which he was engaged. It should be noted here that there is a difference between the Brussels Convention and the Lugano Convention on this matter. Under the Lugano Convention, both the employer and the employee can, in default of an habitual workplace, sue in the place of business but, under the amended Brussels Convention, only the employee has this additional option. It is also worth noting here that both the law of the country where the employee habitually works and the default provision are significant in the worker protection provisions of the Rome Convention. The justification for these provisions is founded on the view that an employment contract is a particular type of contract, often of long duration and under which the subordinate employee is regarded as part of the business of the employer.

If a contractual action also involves rights *in rem*, the courts of the *situs* will also have jurisdiction.[67]

Maintenance

Article 5(2) of the Brussels Convention reads:

> (2) in matters relating to maintenance, in the courts for the place where the maintenance creditor is domiciled or habitually resident or, if the matter is ancillary to proceedings concerning the status of a person, in the court which, according to its own law, has jurisdiction to entertain those proceedings, unless that jurisdiction is based solely on the nationality of one of the parties.

A maintenance creditor has the option of suing in the courts of his own domicile or habitual residence or in the courts of the defendant's domicile. This provision favours the plaintiff, who will normally be a woman and the weaker party economically. A problem has arisen in respect of the combination of maintenance claims with actions for divorce.

Maintenance claims alone are within the Convention; divorce claims are outside the Convention. However, in *De Cavel v De Cavel*,[68] it was held that the Convention can apply in relation to maintenance awards ancillary to divorce proceedings. It seems that the expression 'maintenance creditor' is to be given a liberal interpretation, following the ruling in *Farrell v Long*:[69] the applicant, an unmarried woman resident in Ireland, claimed that the

---

66 *Shenavai v Kreischer* (Case 266/85) [1987] ECR 239; 3 CMLR 782.
67 Brussels Convention 1968, Art 6(4).
68 (Case 120/79) [1980] ECR 731; 3 CMLR 1.
69 (Case C-295/95) [1997] 3 WLR 613, ECJ.

respondent was the father of her child. The respondent, a married man habitually resident in Belgium, denied the claim. The applicant applied for a maintenance order in Dublin; the respondent argued that the court did not have jurisdiction under Art 5(2) because the term 'maintenance creditor' applied to a person in possession of a maintenance order and not a person seeking such an order.

On a reference from the court in Dublin, the European Court of Justice ruled that the term 'maintenance creditor' was not restricted to a person who had previously obtained a judicial decision but covered any person applying for maintenance. In reviewing the broad purpose of Art 5(2), the court noted that the maintenance creditor is, in most cases, the more impecunious of the parties, so that it is fair that he or she should be spared the costs of an action abroad. Secondly, the court reasoned that the tribunal for the place where the applicant is domiciled or resident is best placed, by reason of its familiarity with the economic and social climate in which the applicant lives, to make findings as to the needs expressed.

Torts

Article 5(3) of the Brussels Convention reads as follows:[70]

> (3) in matters relating to tort, delict or quasi delict, in the courts for the place where the harmful event occurred.

The expression 'tort, delict or quasi delict'[71] refers to Convention concepts which are not to be determined under national law. Article 5(3) is drafted in the past tense, so that it would seem that it does not cover actions to prevent a threatened wrong. The first difficulty arises as to the distinction between where the initiating act arose and where the damage took place. In a simple case of a road accident, the place will be the same in respect of both matters. However, in more complex situations, difficulties can arise. In *Bier BV v Mines de Potasse D'Alsace SA*,[72] the facts were as follows: the plaintiff claimed that French defendants had polluted the Rhine in France. It was claimed that the waters had flowed into the Netherlands and damaged their horticultural business. The plaintiffs wished to proceed in the Netherlands, so it was necessary to determine where harmful event occurred.

On a reference from the Dutch court, the European Court held that the expression 'where the harmful event occurred' embraced both where the act was done and where the damage was suffered. The Court justified this decision on the basis that the object of the provision was to provide an

---

70 A similar provision exists in the Lugano Convention, Art 5(3).

71 *The Netherlands v Ruffer* (Case 814/79) [1980] ECR 3807.

72 (Case 21/76) [1978] QB 708; [1976] ECR 1735. For a recent application of the case, see *Reunion Europeene SA v Spliethoff's Berachtingskantoor BV* (Case 51/97) (1998) *The Times*, 11 November, ECJ.

appropriate forum other than that provided under Art 2. If the expression was confined to the place of the act rather than also the place of the damage then no proper alternative would arise. While the court has insisted that Art 5(3) should be interpreted restrictively, it has been held that the expression 'matters relating to tort, delict or quasi delict' in Art 5(3) must be regarded as an independent concept covering all actions which seek to establish the liability of a defendant and which are not related to a contract.[73]

The European Court of Justice has been obliged to consider Art 5(3) in the context of particular torts. In the case of *Shevill v Presse Alliance*,[74] upon a reference from the House of Lords, the court ruled that, in a case where a libelous article was distributed in more than one Contracting State, the plaintiff could bring an action, either where the publisher was established or where the article was distributed and where the plaintiff claimed to have suffered damage to his reputation. However, if he sues where the publisher is established, he may recover for all the loss he has suffered but, if he sues in a country of distribution, he may only recover for the loss of reputation in that particular Contracting State. This does open up the possibility of forum shopping in libel cases, so that, if a newspaper is published in Germany and distributed in France, Italy and England, the potential plaintiff has a choice of four jurisdictions in which to proceed. It does not, at present, matter that the circulation of the newspaper may only be to a small group of expatriates.[75]

Examples abound of the conventional application of Art 5(3) in the English courts. In *Minster Investments Ltd v Hyundai Precision Industry*,[76] Steyn J held that Art 5(3) gave rise to jurisdiction in the English courts where an English plaintiff alleged that a French company had been in breach of duty in issuing certificates as to the quality of containers manufactured in Korea, in circumstances where they knew that the English company would place reliance upon them. Difficulties can arise as to the damage suffered by the plaintiff in respect of financial torts. In *Dumez France and Tracoba v Hessische Landesbank*,[77] the European Court of Justice decided no action could be brought in France in respect of the alleged tortious termination of loans to certain German companies; the losses felt by the German subsidiary companies gave rise to loss in the French parent. The court ruled that no direct financial loss had been caused to the French parent to entitle the French court to assume jurisdiction under Art 5(3). The court has shown a reluctance to

---

73 *Kalfelis v Bankhaus Schroder, Munchmeyer, Hengst and Co* (Case 189/97) [1988] ECR 5565.

74 *Shevill v Presse Alliance SA* (Case C-68/93) [1995] 2 AC 18; ECR I-415.

75 In *Shevill*, the newspaper had difficulty selling 250 copies in England, but sold 200,000 copies in France. For a recent example of an application to stay libel proceedings under the traditional rules, see *Berezovsky v Forbes Inc* (1998) *The Times*, 19 January (Popplewell J); (1998) *The Times*, 27 November, CA, where the action was allowed to proceed in England on the basis that the plaintiff had sufficient reputation within the jurisdiction.

76 [1988] 2 LR 621 (Steyn J).

77 (Case C-220/88) [1990] ECR I-49.

extend the principles of *Bier v Mines de Potasse D'Alsace*[78] in cases involving financial loss. If the act take place in State A and the damage is caused in State A, the fact that there is consequential loss in State B will not suffice to confer jurisdiction on the courts of State B. Thus, in *Marinari v Lloyds Bank plc*,[79] an Italian plaintiff who had his property confiscated in London was not able to sue in the Italian courts under Art 5(3) on the basis that he had suffered consequential financial loss in Italy. On a reference by the Italian courts, the European Court of Justice held that the expression 'the place where the harmful event occurred' did not cover consequential financial loss in State B where the act and the damage had arisen and been suffered in State A.

One of the difficulties under Art 5(3) has been to try and produce principles that make sense in respect of torts concerning personal injury, torts entailing property damage and torts resulting in financial loss.

Compensation orders from criminal courts

Article 5(4) reads as follows:

> (4) as regards a civil claim for damages or restitution which is based on an act giving rise to criminal proceedings, in the court seised of those proceedings, to the extent that the court has jurisdiction under its own law to entertain civil proceedings.

Although the Conventions are confined to 'civil or commercial matters, they apply 'whatever the nature of the court or tribunal' and extend to criminal courts. In many European countries, the victim of a crime may intervene in the criminal proceedings in order to claim damages arising from the offence. The *locus standi* of the victim under the civil law is acknowledged and the criminal court will make an award of damages.[80] This procedure is common in the case of road accidents, where an injured party will intervene in the criminal prosecution for dangerous driving to obtain an ancillary award of damages. Thus, under Art 5(4), the victim of a criminal act can seek compensation or restitution from a criminal court, if it has the power to make such orders under its own internal law, even though the defendant happens to be domiciled in a Contracting State other than one dealing with his criminal offence.

---

78 [1976] ECR 1735, which holds that a plaintiff may sue: (a) where the defendant is domiciled; (b) where the act giving rise to the damage took place; and (c) where the damage occurred.

79 (Case C-364/93) [1995] ECR I-2719; [1996] 2 WLR 159.

80 An example being the judgment of Hamilton J in *Raulin v Fischer* [1911] 2 KB 93, which concerned the attempt to enforce a civil award in England.

Disputes arising out of the operation of a branch or agency or other establishment[81]

Article 5(5) reads as follows:

> (5) as regards a dispute arising out of the operations of a branch, agency or other establishment, in the courts for the place in which the branch, agency or other establishment is situated;

This is not as wide an extension of jurisdiction as it may appear. Before the courts of the place where the branch is situated can assume jurisdiction, it has to be shown that there is a fixed permanent place of business, not simply a stall at a market fair or the presence of a sales representative[82] or even an independent commercial agency if it is not under the direction and control of the 'parent' company. As regards legal personality, a branch will not normally have separate legal personality, but an agency or establishment may. The matter has been examined by the European Court of Justice in four important cases, each examining a facet of the problem.[83] The case law indicates that the evidence will need to establish that the entity:

(a) has a fixed permanent place of business;[84]

(b) is given a degree of direction and control by the parent company;[85]

(c) enjoys a certain autonomy;

(d) acts on behalf of and is capable of binding the parent.

The case law further indicates that the legal relationship between parent and branch is only one factor to consider and that is will also be necessary to evaluate the conduct and in particular how it appeared to third parties. Although it has been denied in the case law, this looks to the common lawyer very much like the doctrines of apparent authority, ostensible authority and holding out. Indeed, in cases where the personnel and operations of parent and subsidiary have become inextricably interlinked, the court has shown flexibility in the interpretation of Art 5(5).[86]

---

81 Art 5(5).

82 *Somafer v Saar Ferngas* (Case 33/78) [1978] ECR 2183; [1979] 1 CMLR 490.

83 *De Bloos v Bouyer* (Case 14/76) [1976] ECR 1497; [1977] 1 CMLR 60; *Somafer v Saar Ferngas* (Case 33/78) [1978] ECR 2183; [1979] 1 CMLR 490; *Blanckaert and Williams v Trost* (Case 139/80) [1981] ECR 819; [1982] 2 CMLR 1; *Sar Schotte GmbH v Parfums Rothschild SARL* [1987] ECR 4905.

84 *Somafer v Saar Ferngas* (Case 33/78) [1978] ECR 2183; [1979] 1 CMLR 490 (where there was no office or furniture).

85 *De Bloos v Bouyer* (Case 14/76) [1976] ECR 1497; [1977] 1 CMLR 60 (holder of exclusive sales concession not subject to direction); Case 139/80 (an autonomous commercial agent not subject to direction).

86 See *Sar Schotte GmbH v Parfums Rothschild SARL* [1987] ECR 4905 (probably best regarded as a case confined to its own particular facts).

Trusts

Article 5(6) reads as follows:

(6) as settlor, trustee or beneficiary of a trust created by the operation of a statute, or by written instrument, or created orally and evidenced in writing, in the courts of the Contracting State in which the trust is domiciled.

This provision, which was of particular interest to the UK, was added by Art 5(4) of the 1978 Accession Convention and enables a person domiciled in one Contracting State to be sued in the Contracting State in which the trust is domiciled. These provisions need to be read with Art 53(2), which was added by Art 23 of the 1978 Convention and provides that, in order to determine whether a trust is domiciled in a particular Contracting State, that State must apply its own law.

Multiple defendants

The relevant part of Art 6 reads as follows:

A person domiciled in a Contracting State may also be sued:

(1) where he is one of a number of defendants, in the courts for the place where any one of them is domiciled;

(2) as a third party in an action on a warranty or guarantee or in any other third party proceedings, in the court seised of the original proceedings, unless these were instituted solely with the objective of removing him from the jurisdiction of the court which would be competent in his case;

(3) on the counterclaim arising from the same contract or facts on which the original claim was based, in the court in which the original claim is pending.

Article 6(1) deals with the situation in which the plaintiff has claims against two defendants, either because they are individually liable or jointly liable. Thus, if a plaintiff wishes to sue D1, who is domiciled in England, and D2, who is domiciled in Germany, he may be minded to seek to sue both in England. The first can be sued under Art 2 and the latter under Art 6(1). It is clear that a person may proceed under Art 6(1) as a matter of discretion, having regard to the use of the word 'may'; secondly, the ambit of Art 6(1) is not to be artificially broadened so as to undermine Art 2. In *Kalfelis v Bankhaus Schroder, Munchmeyer, Hengst and Co*,[87] the European Court of Justice indicated that the cardinal question under Art 6(1) was whether the claims should be tried together to avoid irreconcilable findings of fact or law. Such a ruling is in line with the approach under Art 22 in seeking to avoid the multiplicity of proceedings. It would seem that the plaintiff cannot rely on

---

87 (Case 189/87) [1988] ECR 5565.

Art 6(1) to proceed against the foreign based defendant in England when there is no legal or evidentiary case against D1.[88]

The provisions of Art 6(2) concern the situation in which the defendant seeks to add other parties to the action. In the most obvious example, X might sue Y, who then wishes to serve a third party proceedings on Z. In *Kongress Agentur Hagen GmbH v Zeehage BV*,[89] a Dutch company sued a German company in the Netherlands pursuant to Art 5(1) and the German company sought to issue a third party notice under Art 6(2). On a reference from the courts in the Netherlands, the European Court of Justice stressed the discretionary nature of Art 6(2), but ruled that a third party notice could be issued even where jurisdiction was assumed under Art 5(1) if the national court, in following its own rules of procedure, considered that the objectives of the Convention could be achieved by this course. The approach to Art 6(2) was considered by Phillips J in *Kinnear v Falconfilms NV*,[90] where the salient facts were as follows: the film actor, Roy Kinnear, was injured when he fell from a horse while filming in Spain. He died in a Madrid hospital the following day. The administrators of his estate brought an action against the film company for negligence and breach of contract. The film company sought to serve a third party notice on the hospital and the surgeon. The hospital sought to have the notice set aside.

In refusing to do so, Phillips J observed:

> Where one tortfeasor wishes to reduce his liability to reflect the fact that another tortfeasor shares responsibility for the plaintiff's damage, it may be impossible to do this unless all three parties are brought before the same tribunal.

Problems can arise as to the relationship between Art 6(2) and the choice of jurisdiction provisions contained in Art 17; the accepted view is that the provisions of Art 17 prevail over those of Art 6(2).[91] This was the view taken by Rix J in *Hough v P & O Containers Ltd*,[92] where the facts were as follows: the plaintiff brought a personal injury action against the defendants in respect of an accident during ship repair works in a German dry dock. The defendants sought to serve a third party notice on the owners, Blohm and Voss Holdings AG. The German shipyard owners were successful in having the third party notice set aside on grounds of an exclusive jurisdiction clause.

In giving judgment, Rix J held that the mandatory provisions of Art 17 prevailed over the permissive provisions of Art 6(2) even if such a result exposed the defendants to litigation in two different forums.

---

88 *The Xing Su Hai* [1995] 2 LR 15; see, also, *Aiglon Ltd and L'Aiglon SA v Gau Shan Ltd* [1993] 1 LR 164; *Gascoine v Pyrah* [1994] ILPr 82.

89 (Case C-365/88) [1990] ECR 88.

90 [1994] 3 All ER 42; [1996] 1 WLR 920.

91 *Karl Schaeff GmbH and Co KG v Société Patrymat* (1990) ILPr 381.

92 [1998] 3 WLR 851; a judgment conspicuous by its clarity and careful attention to detail.

The third element of Art 6 is Art 6(3), which provides that the court which has jurisdiction over the claim of the plaintiff will also have jurisdiction over the counterclaim of the defendant, so long as the counterclaim arises out of the same agreement or facts in issue in the claim of the plaintiff.[93]

Insurance

The Brussels Convention contains special provisions in relation to insurance because it is felt that the individual policyholder is in a weaker economic position than the financial institutions responsible for insurance business. The relevant provisions are set out in Arts 7–12A. By Art 8, an insurance company domiciled in a Contracting State may be sued in that State or in the State in which the policyholder is domiciled. Further, the article provides that an insurer not domiciled in a Contracting State will be deemed to be domiciled in the State in which he has a branch or agency for the purposes of disputes concerning the operation that agency. In respect of liability insurance concerning immovable property, the insurer may be sued in the State in which the harmful event occurred (Art 9). In respect of proceedings by an insurer, these proceedings can normally only be brought in the State in which the policyholder is domiciled. The purpose of these provisions is to prevent the policyholder having to go abroad to sue, although a policyholder does not have to show any form of economic disability to take advantage of the provisions.

The second element of the provisions relating to insurance is to limit the use of jurisdiction clauses by the economically stronger party to five situations:[94]

(1) where the agreement was entered into after the dispute arose;

(2) where the agreement allows a wider choice than under the Convention;

(3) where the agreement confers jurisdiction on the courts of the Contracting State in which the policy holder and the insurer are domiciled;

(4) where the policy holder is not domiciled in a Contracting State;

(5) the agreement forms part of a contract of insurance dealing with major risks as set out in Art 12A.

The detailed provisions in relation to jurisdiction agreements are attributable, partly, to the decision to modify the original provisions to meet concerns of British insurers who, with world wide insurance businesses, were unhappy with the original provisions of the Brussels Convention 1968; thus, Arts 12(4), 12(5) and 12A derive from the 1978 Accession Convention. Although the

---

93 *Danvaern Productions A/s v Schuhfabriken Otterbeck GmbH & Co* (Case C-341/93) [1995] ECR I-2053.

94 As set out in Art 12(1)–(5).

original provisions were designed to protect the single policyholder of limited means, no such qualifications are contained in the text.[95]

Consumer contracts

As with insurance contracts, special provision exists in the Brussels Convention 1968 to protect consumers on the basis that they represent a weaker contracting party. The special provisions in regard to consumer contracts are contained within Arts 13–15. The present text derives from the 1978 Accession Convention and a consumer contract is one which a person enters 'for a purpose which can be regarded as being outside his trade or profession' if it is:

(1) a contract for the sale of goods on installment credit terms;[96] or

(2) a contract for a loan repayable by installments, or for any other form of credit made to finance the sale of goods; or

(3) any other contract for the supply of goods or a contact for the supply of services (but not transport) and (a) in the State of the consumer's domicile the conclusion of the contract was preceded by a special invitation addressed to him by advertising; and (b) the consumer took in that State the steps necessary for the conclusion of the contract.

If the contract is a consumer contract as defined by Art 13 (subject to the branch agency or other establishment jurisdictional basis which is specifically preserved by the scheme and which enables a supplier in a non-Contracting State, who has a branch in a Contracting State, to be deemed to be domiciled there),[97] the consumer can sue the supplier either in the courts of the supplier's domicile or in those of his own, whereas the supplier can sue only in the courts of the consumer's domicile.[98] If a supplier wishes to sue a consumer, Art 14(2) requires the action to be brought before the courts of the Member State in which the consumer is domiciled. The supplier may counterclaim in a court in which the consumer has brought an action against him in respect of the same transaction.[99]

There are limitations on the effects of jurisdiction agreements in the case of those consumer contracts to which the special jurisdiction provisions of the Convention apply. The agreement will be recognised only if: (1) it was concluded after the dispute had arisen; (2) the agreement permits the

---

95 *New Hampshire Insurance Co v Strabag Bau AG* [1992] 1 LR 361. For a discussion as to the territorial scope of Arts 8 and 11, see, also, *Jordan Grand Prix Ltd v Baltic Insurance Group and Others* [1998] 1 WLR 1049, CA; [1999] 2 WLR 134, HL.

96 Brussels Convention 1968, Art 13(1).

97 *Ibid*, Art 13.

98 *Ibid*, Art 14.

99 *Ibid*, Arts 6(3), 14(3).

consumer to bring proceedings in courts other than those indicated in the Convention; (3) the agreement is made between parties who are domiciled or habitually resident in the same Contracting State and confers jurisdiction on the courts of that State.[100]

It is to be noted that the provisions of Art 13 apply without prejudice to the provisions of Art 4 and Art 5(5), so that, in *Brenner and Noller v Dean Witter Reynolds Inc,*[101] where two German domiciliaries speculated in commodity futures with a USA domiciled broker (without a branch in Germany), Art 13 could not be invoked to establish jurisdiction in Germany. It would seem that being a consumer is a matter of personal status that arises under the original contract. Thus, if X a consumer enters into a contract with Y and then assigns his right to Z, the latter does not become a consumer and cannot rely on the consumer contract provisions against Y, notwithstanding the fact that X can do so.[102]

Exclusive jurisdiction

Article 16 of the Brussels and Lugano Conventions provides for exclusive jurisdiction of the courts of Contracting States in certain limited cases. These situations are exceptional in two respects:

(a) they derogate from the general rule that the defendant always can, and generally must, be sued in the State of his domicile. Where exclusive jurisdiction applies, the courts of the defendant's domicile must decline jurisdiction unless, of course, they happen to be the designated courts under Art 16;

(b) they apply whether or not the defendant is domiciled in a Contracting State.

All other Contracting States must decline jurisdiction on their own motion if another Contracting State has jurisdiction under Art 16.

Article 16 reads as follows:

The following courts shall have exclusive jurisdiction, regardless of domicile

(1)(a) in proceedings which have as their object rights *in rem* in immovable property or tenancies of immovable property, the court of the Contracting State in which the property is situated.

This provision is in line with the position of the English court at common law. English courts have traditionally declined jurisdiction where the dispute involved the question of title to or rights to possession of foreign immovable

---

100 Art 15.

101 (Case C-318/93) [1994] I-EECR 4275.

102 *Shearson Lehman Hutton v TVB Treuhandgesellschaft für Vermogensverwaltung und Beteiligungen mbH* (Case C-89/91) [1993] ECR I-139.

property. Experience has demonstrated that only the courts of the *situs* can effectively deal with immovable property within their territory. Thus, if the immovable property is situated in England, then the English court will have jurisdiction regardless of where the defendant is domiciled. In similar terms, if the property is situated abroad, then the English court will not assume jurisdiction even if the defendant is domiciled in England. Thus, in *Re Hayward (Deceased)*,[103] an application by a trustee in bankruptcy to determine title to a villa situated in Minorca, Spain and appearing on the local property register was rejected by Rattee J as being at variance with Art 16(1)(a) and Art 16(3).

The rationale of the inclusion of tenancies, beyond the obvious factual control of the officials of the *situs*, is that social legislation to protect the weaker members of a society would focus, *inter alia*, on the supply of housing and the protection afforded might be ineffective if disputes about it were to be litigated in foreign courts.[104]

The immovable property must be situated in a Contracting State; if it is not, then Art 16 has no application though, of course, some other provision of the Convention might. This could present a problem for English courts. Suppose the defendant, who is domiciled in England, is sued here over immovable property situated in a non-Contracting State. The English courts would have jurisdiction under the Conventions but not under the *Mocambique* rule which is confirmed by statute;[105] but made subject to the Conventions.[106] It would seem that, in such circumstances, the English would decide jurisdiction by reference to common law principles.

Rights *in rem* include matters of title or possession and interests in and over the immovable, and the tenancy interests will include possession, repossession and damage to the property. It is not clear whether unpaid rent itself, as opposed to the landlord's rights to the property when the rent is unpaid, falls within the exclusive jurisdiction. An action which is a personal action, although related to an immovable, will not be subject to the exclusive jurisdiction so, for example, a petition for a decree of specific performance will fall outside the provision, as will one which is based on a resulting trust. Thus, in *Webb v Webb*,[107] the European Court of Justice ruled that an action by A, seeking a declaration that a property was held by B on trust for himself was not an action *in rem*, but an action *in personam* and, thus, outside Art 16. The

---

103 [1997] Ch 45; 1 All ER 32; [1996] 3 WLR 674.

104 To some extent, the Brussels Convention reflects a desire to afford some protection to weaker parties, ie, tenants in respect of landlords, employees in respect of employers, consumers in respect of suppliers and, in regard to the provisions on maintenance, the protection of women against male wage earners.

105 Civil Jurisdiction and Judgments Act 1982, s 30(1).

106 *Ibid*, s 30(2).

107 *Webb v Webb* [1991] 1 WLR 1410 (Judge Baker QC); (Case 294/92) [1994] QB 696, ECJ.

judgment was followed in *Jarrett v Barclays Bank plc*,[108] where the Court of Appeal concluded that actions for breach of contract in relation to annual timeshares in Portugal and Spain were outside Art 16 (1)(a). In giving judgment, Morritt LJ, after a careful review of the authorities, accepted that Art 16 was to be interpreted narrowly so as to do no more than achieve its objective of giving exclusive jurisdiction to the courts of States in which immovable property was situated. In *Reichert v Dresdner Bank*,[109] the European Court of Justice ruled that the expression 'in proceedings which have as their object rights *in rem* in immovable property' must be given an independent definition within Community law. One of the questions that has given rise to problems is 'what is a tenancy for the purpose of Art 16?' This has been considered in three cases.[110] In *Sanders v van der Putte*,[111] it was held that Art 16 had no application where B entered into an agreement to transfer to C the leasehold interest that he held from A. In the following case of *Rosler v Rottwinkel*,[112] the facts were as follows: two Germans, Rosler and Rottwinkel, agreed that Rosler would let a holiday villa in Italy to Rottwinkel for a period of three weeks. The parties had agreed to refer any dispute to the German courts. Rosler commenced proceedings in Berlin in respect of breaches of the agreement concerning the number of occupants and also claimed in respect of damage to the property and failure to pay relevant electricity bills. The landlord also claimed damages for disappointment over a spoiled holiday (landlord and tenant were both on holiday at the Italian house at the same time). The matter was referred by the Bundesgerichtshof to the European Court of Justice.

The European Court held that proceedings that concerned tenancies of immovable property including disputes as to short term holiday lets fell within Art 16. The court held that the Italian courts had exclusive jurisdiction over the claim for payment of sums due in relation to the let, but not over the landlord's action for disappointment. Such an approach, which in no way advanced the purpose of Art 16, was widely felt to be unsatisfactory and out of line with the more liberal approach in *Sanders v van der Putte*. Thus, Art 16(1) was subsequently amended by the Lugano Convention, as set out in Sched 3C of the 1982 Act, so as to exclude short term holiday lets. The 1989 Accession Convention follows the 1988 Lugano Convention.

Article 16(1)(b) reads:

(1)(b) however, in proceedings which have as their object tenancies of
immovable property concluded for temporary private use for a

---

108 [1997] 3 WLR 654.
109 (Case C-115/88) [1990] ECR 2383.
110 *Sanders v van der Putte* (Case 73/77) [1977] ECR 2383; *Rosler v Rottwinkel* (Case 241/83) [1986] QB 33; [1985] ECR 99; *Hacker v Euro-Relais* (Case C-280/90) [1992] ECR I-1111.
111 (Case 73/77) [1977] ECR 2383.
112 (Case 241/83) [1986] QB 33; [1985] ECR 99.

maximum period of six consecutive months, the courts of the Contracting
State in which the defendant is domiciled shall also have jurisdiction,
provided that the landlord and tenant are natural persons and are
domiciled in the same Contracting States.

The effect of this is that while the court of the *situs* retains jurisdiction, the
court of the common domicile of the landlord and tenant, provided that they
are both natural persons and the other conditions are met, shall also have
jurisdiction. In the event of proceedings being begun in both courts, the usual
rule of first seisure will apply.[113] Thus, the plaintiff in the *Rosler* case could
now sue in Germany if he wished. It would seem that, for Art 16(1)(b) to
apply, four requirements must be met, namely, (a) the proceedings must
concern tenancies of immovable property; (b) it must concern a short term let;
(c) the landlord and tenant must be natural persons; and (d) both must be
domiciled in the same Contracting State.

A more liberal approach to the interpretation of Art 16 is to be found in the
third case, *Hacker v Euro Relais GmbH*, where the facts were as follows:[114] the
plaintiff, Mrs Hacker, was domiciled in Germany and entered into a contract
(*meitvertrag* – tenancy contract) with the defendants a German travel agency.
The contract provided that the plaintiff would have the use of a holiday home
in the Netherlands owned by a third party. The contract made provision for
the payment of travel expenses. The plaintiff claimed that there had been a
breach of contract in respect of the quality of the accommodation. The matter
was referred to the European Court of Justice.

The European Court ruled that 'a complex contract of the type which
concerns a range of services provided in return for a lump sum paid by the
customer, is outside the scope within which the exclusive jurisdiction laid
down by Art 16(1) finds its *raison d'être*'. The amendment to Art 16 is clearly
sensible. The Lugano Convention has treated the same problem in a rather
more liberal way. Following the same limitation to temporary private
tenancies, it provides that the courts of the defendant's domicile shall have
jurisdiction provided that the tenant is a natural person and that neither party
is domiciled in the *situs* of the immovable property.

Both versions of the amendment to the original Art 16 are clearly
influenced by the judgment in *Rosler v Rottwinkel*;[115] neither address the wider
issues of exclusive jurisdiction. Clearly, it is generally to be hoped that that a
single court and a single piece of litigation will determine the parties'
dispute.[116] For the Italian courts to have jurisdiction over one element of the

---

113 Art 21.

114 *Hacker v Euro Relais GmbH* (Case C-280/90) [1992] ECR I-1111.

115 (Case 241/83) [1986] QB 33; [1985] 1 CMLR 806.

116 The general philosophy of the Brussels Convention 1968 is to avoid multiple litigation; a
matter that influenced the House of Lords in *Sarrio SA v Kuwait Investment Authority*
[1997] 3 WLR 1143; [1999] AC 119.

case and the German courts another seems ridiculous but, unless the plaintiff instituted the process in Italy on his claim for damages for disappointment and the defendant submitted to the Italian jurisdiction on that claim it is difficult to see how the matter could be resolved. The German court could, if it wished, stay the action[117] but only if action on the same claim was pending in the Italian courts. The problem cannot be resolved unless all matters connected with the immovable are subject to the exclusive jurisdiction of the courts of the *situs*, which would make far too much of the exception.

On the other hand, too narrow a view of the concept of a right *in rem* would destroy the purpose of the exclusive jurisdiction. The equitable jurisdiction of the English courts goes a long way down the road of undermining the concept, as might a vigorous use of the lease/licence distinction, another English peculiarity.

Before leaving the issues of rights *in rem*,[118] it should be remembered that, though not concerned with exclusive jurisdiction, if a contractual action also involves rights *in rem*, the courts of the *situs*, along with those of the defendant's domicile, will have jurisdiction.

The second aspect of Art 16 relates to corporations. The provisions of Art 16(2) read as follows:

> (2) in proceedings which have as their object the validity of the constitution, the nullity or the dissolution of companies or other legal persons or associations of natural or legal persons, or the decisions of their organs, the courts of the Contracting State in which the company, legal person or association has its seat.

For the purpose of this provision, the UK has adopted a modified version of corporate domicile from that used for other parts the Brussels Convention. The corporation or association has its 'seat' in the UK if, and only if,[119] it was incorporated or formed under the law of part of the UK or its central management and control is exercised in the UK. It is further provided that a company has its seat in part of the UK if: (a) it has its seat in the UK; (b) it was incorporated or formed under the law of that part; and (c) being incorporated or formed under the law of a State other than the UK, its central management and control is exercised in that part. In respect of a corporation formed under an enactment that applies throughout the UK, such a corporation will be 'seated' where it has its registered office.

The provisions of Art 16(2) have been considered in a number of cases in England and the emphasis has been on a detailed analysis of the claim that is

---

117 Art 23.

118 See, also, *Scherrens v Maenhout* (Case 158/87) [1988] ECR 3791; *Reichert v Dresdner Bank* (Case 115/88) [1990] ECR 27.

119 Civil Jurisdiction and Judgments Act 1982, s 43.

before the court. In *Newtherapeutics Ltd v Katz*,[120] a UK company[121] which conducted all its business in France brought a claim against a former director who was domiciled in France. One of the allegations concerned the validity of acts undertaken by a director in the absence of the authority of the full board. Knox J ruled that a question as to the validity of a directors powers was within the terms of Art 16(2).[122] The same emphasis on the analysis of the cause of action was displayed in *Grupo Torras Sa v Sheik Fahad Mohammed al Sabah*,[123] where a Spanish company and its English subsidiary brought an action against the defendant, who was a director of the company in England. The defendant argued that the Spanish court had jurisdiction under Art 16(2). The Court of Appeal rejected this argument, holding that what was in issue was not the 'decisions of the company organs' but individual fraud and breach of a duty personally owed. Thus, Art 16(2) did not apply and no stay was granted. In principle, the provisions of Art 16(2) apply also to partnerships. It should also be noted that, under Art 1(2), proceedings relating to the winding up of insolvent companies and analogous proceedings are outside the scope of the Convention. There may still be cases of *lis alibi pendens* under Art 16(2). By the terms of Art 53, the seat of a corporation is to be determined by the rules of private international law of that particular State; there is, thus, a possibility that a company may be deemed to have a seat in more than one Contracting State.

Article 16(3) reads as follows:

(3) in proceedings which have as their object the validity of entries in public registers, the courts of the Contracting State where the register is kept.

Where the validity of entries in published registers is in issue, only the courts of the Contracting State will have jurisdiction. This is clearly sensible because if any court order has to be given for the rectification of the register it must be made by a court that the registry is empowered to recognise. The 19th century saw the establishment of registers for both land law and company law; in principle, both would come within the definition of a public register.[124] As will be indicated below, there are particular difficulties in the context of the register of patents.

Article 16(4) reads:

(4) in proceedings concerned with the registration or validity of patents, trade marks designs, or other similar rights required to be deposited or registered, the courts of the Contracting State, in which the deposit or registration has been applied for, has taken place or is under the terms of an international convention deemed to have taken place.

---

120 [1991] Ch 226; 2 All ER 151.

121 Within the terms of the Civil Jurisdiction and Judgments Act 1982, s 43(2).

122 Although leave was refused under RSC Ord 11 because the company had granted a waiver, so any action was bound to fail.

123 [1996] 1 LR 7.

124 *Re Hayward* [1997] Ch 45.

It has to be admitted that the position as regards intellectual property is less than clear. In *Coin Controls Ltd v Suzo International (UK) Ltd*,[125] Laddie J, basing himself upon Art 16(4) and Art 19, concluded that, where validity and infringement of a registered patent were in issue, this matter had to be determined in the court of the State in which the patent was registered.[126] This is not accepted by courts in the Netherlands, who have begun to grant injunctions to restrain Dutch nationals from infringing a UK patent. The relationship between the jurisdiction arising under Art 2 and that arising under Art 16(4) is less than clear and the Dutch approach has been followed in Germany. The English view is that proceedings for infringement for a patent, even if not involving questions of validity, should only be brought in the courts of the State whose patent is said to be infringed.[127] The division of opinion between different courts was well illustrated by the case of *In re a Petition by Fort Dodge Animal Health Ltd*,[128] where the substance of the application was a request to an English court to restrain proceeding in the Netherlands on the basis that the courts might misinterpret the Convention. In a thoughtful judgment, Laddie J drew attention to the differences of opinion in respect of patent litigation and invited the European Court to consider the matter at the earliest opportunity.

Article 16(5) reads:

(5) in proceedings concerned with the enforcement of judgments, the courts of the Contracting State in which the judgment has been or is to be enforced.

This provision indicates that proceedings concerned with the enforcement of judgments fall within the exclusive jurisdiction of the Contracting State in which the judgment has been or is to be enforced.

Prorogation of jurisdiction

As a broad principle, a party may agree or consent to the jurisdiction of the court. The Brussels Convention provides that consent may be given in two circumstances. First, a party may consent in the form of a formal agreement that, in the event of a dispute, a particular court will have jurisdiction. Secondly, the plaintiff may begin proceedings and the defendant may submit to the jurisdiction of the court. The former situation is referred to as a 'jurisdiction agreement' and is provided for in Art 17, while the situation of submission to jurisdiction is dealt with under Art 18. It is necessary to take each in turn.

---

125 [1997] 3 All ER 45.
126 See, also, *Pearce v Ove Arup Partnership Ltd* [1997] 3 All ER 310 (copyright); *Mecklermedia v DC Congress* [1997] FSR 627 (trade marks).
127 *Molnlycke AB v Proctor and Gamble Ltd* [1992] 1 WLR 1112, pp 1117–18.
128 (1997) *The Times*, 24 October, Chancery Division (Laddie J).

Submission

Except where the exclusive jurisdiction rules of Art 16 apply, a court of a Contracting State will have jurisdiction if the defendant submits to the jurisdiction of that court by entering an appearance, unless he does so to contest the jurisdiction.[129] Clearly, he must contest jurisdiction at the outset; he cannot wait to see how things go on the substantive dispute before he makes up his mind. In English civil procedure, there will be submission to jurisdiction if the defendant instructs a solicitor to accept service on his behalf and he then does so. If the defendant appears to contest the jurisdiction but, also, with the intention of defending on the merits if his objection is rejected, then this is not submission. From the perspective of the court, two matters have to be kept separate: (a) the jurisdiction of the court to determine the scope of its jurisdiction; and (b) the jurisdiction of the court on the merits.

There are a number of points of interpretation that arise in respect of Art 18. The first question is whether there is a requirement that the defendant be domiciled in a Contracting State; this argument depends on reading Art 18 as subordinate to the wording of Arts 3–4. It is open to argument that the text of Arts 16–17 indicate expressly that they are to apply regardless of domicile and it is argued that the omission of such words from Art 18 is significant. Against this, it is open to argument that, as Art 17 applies regardless of domicile and as Arts 17–18 are part of s 6 and concerned with the same topic, then Art 18 should be read in the same light as Art 17.

Secondly, the question of entering an appearance is to be determined under the rules of civil procedure of the court in question[130] and this will involve examining the conduct of the defendant and his advisers and drawing the appropriate inferences. The third difficulty concerns the meaning to be attached to the word 'solely' in the text; this acquires significance because of the absence of an equivalent expression from the French text. It would appear, from *Elefanten Schuh GmbH v Jacqmain*,[131] that a defendant who appears to contest the jurisdiction but, also, addresses arguments on the merits, is not to be considered to have submitted, provided that the arguments on jurisdiction are made *bona fide* and are preliminary to any discussion of the merits. Moreover, there may be cases where an argument as to jurisdiction cannot be fully developed unless the court is prepared to absorb certain factual material inextricably linked with the merits.

The words of Art 18 make it clear that it is subordinate to Art 16; however, where there has been submission, then that will prevail over Art 17 on the basis that later agreement will prevail over earlier selection.[132] So, if the

---

129 Art 18.
130 *Jenard Report* OJ C 59/1, p 38, 1979.
131 (Case 150/80) [1981] ECR 1671.
132 *Elefanten Schuh v Jacqmain* (Case 150/80) [1981] ECR 1671.

English court has exclusive jurisdiction under Art 16, a defendant cannot confer jurisdiction on the German court by submitting to the jurisdiction when the plaintiff begins proceedings. However, if the parties have agreed to litigate in France, a defendant may submit to proceedings begun in England.

Agreements on jurisdiction

Article 17 deals with the situation where the parties have entered into an agreement about which courts are to have jurisdiction over their disputes. Jurisdiction agreements are common in commercial contracts and can generally be regarded as a prudent step for the parties to take. Many such agreements, are however, agreements in the legal sense only. It is the stronger party which stipulates which court is to have jurisdiction or the jurisdiction provision may be one of the terms of a standard form contract to which one or even both of the parties have given little heed in the making of the contract. The Brussels Convention seeks to deal with these problems in two ways: first, by stipulating the form of the jurisdiction agreement and, secondly, by restricting the ambit of the agreement or making it work only in the interests or supposed interests of the party who is assumed to be the weaker. Two of these restrictions relate to insurance contracts[133] and consumer contracts.[134] There is one further restriction under Art 17 itself which relates to individual employment contracts.

Article 17 provides that jurisdiction agreements shall have no legal force if they are contrary to the provisions of Art 12 or Art 15. Nor will a jurisdiction agreement oust the jurisdiction of a court which has exclusive jurisdiction under Art 16, even if, as can be the case under Art 16(1)(b), two courts simultaneously have jurisdiction and the agreement relates to one of them.

In all other cases (except individual employment contacts), a jurisdiction agreement can be effective provided it satisfies the formal requirements set out in the Article.[135] The agreement must be:

(1) in writing or evidenced in writing;

(2) in a form which accords with practices which the parties have established between themselves; or

(3) in international trade or commerce, in a form which accords with a usage of which the parties are or ought to have been aware and which in such trade or commerce is widely known to, and regularly observed by, parties to contracts of the type involved in the particular trade or commerce concerned.

---

133 Art 12.
134 Art 15.
135 Art 17, para 1.

The purpose of these stipulations is to ensure that there is sufficient evidence to justify concluding that the parties did reach agreement.

Where such an agreement is made by parties one of whom is domiciled in a Contracting State, or if a trust instrument has conferred such jurisdiction,[136] the courts of the Contracting State chosen have exclusive jurisdiction over the actions. This means that the courts chosen must accept jurisdiction (there is no basis under the Conventions which allows them to decline it) and that the courts of other Contracting States must refuse jurisdiction.

If a jurisdiction agreement to which Art 17 applies is made between parties none of whom is domiciled in a Contracting State, the courts of other Contracting States shall have no jurisdiction unless the chosen courts decline it.[137]

The provisions of Art 17 concern formality; if a challenge is made to the validity of the clause, then that is a matter to be determined by the rules of private international law of the court in which jurisdiction is sought. It is clear that the clause may relate to more than one court,[138] although, in such cases, the second court will defer to the court that is first seised.[139] A clause may be drafted to cover contingencies, for example, if X sues Y the Italian court will have jurisdiction, but if Y sues X the German court will have jurisdiction.

If a clause is contained within a document signed by both parties, then Art 17(1)(a) will be satisfied.[140] The original approach to Art 17(1)(a) was strict and technical, so a choice of jurisdiction clause printed on the reverse of a contract did not meet the requirements of Art 17[141] while, in *Segoura v Bonakdarian*,[142] an oral agreement followed by transmission of standard business terms was insufficient. There is evidence, however, that the judgment in *F Berghoefer GmbH and Co KG v ASA SA*[143] represents a more liberal approach. In this case, the European Court of Justice considered that the requirements of Art 17 would be satisfied if there had been an oral agreement on jurisdiction followed by the transmission of a standard agreement which was not objected to by the other side. The same principle would apply if the transmission had been by fax and not letter.[144] The interpretation of Art 17 has become more liberal, so that Art 17(1)(b), while

---

136 Art 17, para 2.
137 Art 17, para 1.
138 *Meeth v Glacetal Sarl* (Case 23/78) [1978] ECR 2133.
139 Art 23.
140 *Partenreederei ms Tilly Russ v NV Haven and Vervoerbedriff Nova* (Case 71/83) [1984] ECR 2417.
141 *Estasis Salotti di Colzani Aimo v RUWA Polstereimaschinen GmbH* (Case 24/76) [1976] ECR 1831.
142 (Case 25/76) [1976] ECR 1851.
143 (Case 221/84) [1985] ECR 2699.
144 *IP Metal Ltd v Route OZ SpA* [1993] 2 LR 60.

added by the 1989 Accession Convention, represents a codification of the position reached by the European Court of Justice.[145] Article 17(1)(c) was added by the 1978 Accession Convention to meet concerns that original interpretation had been too strict; the references to wide knowledge and regular observance were added by the 1989 Accession Convention. It seems that, in appropriate cases, the provisions may be inserted to benefit a third party to the contract.[146]

In respect of the Convention as a whole, it is clear that the provisions of Art 17 yield to those of Art 16 and Art 18. Article 17 itself provides that if the jurisdiction agreement is for the benefit of one party only, that party is free to bring proceedings in any other court which has jurisdiction under the Convention.[147] It must be clear from the express terms of the agreement that it is for the benefit of one party alone.[148] To allow the party who has the benefit of the agreement to waive that benefit is clear enough, but the determination of benefit is formal not substantial, that is, it would be shown by a statement that one party could bring proceedings in State X or that proceedings must be brought in State X. There will be no attempt antecedently to find out who might be advantaged by litigation in one place, even less to determine who would benefit in the dispute resolution.

Article 17(5)[149] contains provisions relating to individual employment contracts. In individual employment contracts, a jurisdiction agreement will only have effect if it is made after the dispute has arisen or the employee invokes it to seise courts other than those specified in Art 5(1). This new limitation was introduced by the 1989 Accession Convention. Under the Brussels Convention, an employer, whether acting as plaintiff or defendant, can only rely on an agreement conferring jurisdiction entered into after the dispute has arisen. Although there are differences between the Brussels and Lugano Conventions on Art 5(1), they agree on this point that the employee can sue in the place where he habitually works or, if there is no such place, in the place where the business through which he was engaged is located.

The role of the court under the Brussels Convention

Unlike the position at common law, where the court operates on the basis of the submissions made by the parties, courts under the Conventions are expected to take an active role over jurisdictional issues. At common law, a party who wishes to argue that the English court is not the appropriate forum

---

145 (Case 71/83) [1984] ECR 2417.
146 *Gerling v Italian Treasury* (Case 201/82) [1983] ECR 2503.
147 Art 17(4).
148 *Anterist v Credit Lyonnais* (Case 22/85) [1986] ECR 1951.
149 In strict terms, the paras of Art 17 are not numbered.

must appeal against the leave given to serve out of the jurisdiction or apply for a stay of proceedings, as appropriate, and the burden is on him to establish at least a *prima facie* case for a refusal of jurisdiction. Under the Conventions, the court itself has to examine its jurisdictional position in a number of situations.

It is provided[150] that a court in the UK may stay or dismiss actions on the ground of *forum non conveniens* or otherwise, where to do so is not inconsistent with the Conventions. A court cannot, it seems, decline to take jurisdiction which the Conventions confer on the basis that it regards another court as the more appropriate forum but whether this applies when the *forum conveniens* is a non-Contracting State is the subject of some controversy.[151]

A court seised of a case which is principally concerned with a matter covered by the exclusive provisions of Art 16, unless, of course, it is a court given exclusive jurisdiction under that article, must declare, of its own motion, that it has no jurisdiction.[152]

Similarly, the court of a Contracting State before which the domiciliary of another Contracting State is sued must, unless it has jurisdiction under one of the special jurisdictional rules or the defendant submits to the jurisdiction, declare, of its own motion, that it has no jurisdiction.

Where the proceedings have been brought between the same parties and over the same cause of action in different Contracting States, both of which have or may have jurisdiction under the Conventions, the court which regards itself as the court second seized of the issue must, of its own motion, stay the proceedings until the jurisdiction of the court first seized has been established. If and when it is established, all courts in other Contracting States must decline jurisdiction.[153] If both courts have exclusive jurisdiction under Art 16 the second court must defer to the court first seised.[154]

Where actions are not identical but are related, that is, are so closely connected that 'it is expedient to hear and determine them together to avoid the risks of irreconcilable judgments', the court second seised may stay its proceedings and, at the request of one of the parties, decline jurisdiction, if its rules of court permit consolidation of such actions and the court first seised has jurisdiction to determine the whole issue.[155]

---

150 Civil Jurisdiction and Judgments Act 1982, s 49.

151 *Re Harrods (Buenos Aires) Ltd* [1992] Ch 72.

152 Art 19.

153 Art 21.

154 Art 23.

155 Art 22; See *Sarrio SA v Kuwait Investment Authority* [1997] 3 WLR 1143; *Mecklermedia Corporation and Another v DC Congress GmbH* [1997] 3 WLR 479 (Jacob J).

THE MODIFIED CONVENTION: ALLOCATION OF JURISDICTION WITHIN THE UK

The parties to the Brussels Convention are States in the sense of international law and, thus, jurisdiction is allocated to the courts of international States rather than to individual legal systems. For the UK, therefore, the Conventions do not distinguish English law, Scots law or the law of Northern Ireland. In some cases, for example, where the special jurisdictional rules apply, the localising job may have been done incidentally but, in other cases, for example, where jurisdiction is based on the wide concept of domicile used in the Conventions, it will not. To deal with these issues, the Modified Convention was introduced.[156] This goes further than was necessary simply to make the Brussels Convention operative within the UK and, in effect, produces a code for the general allocation of conflict cases based on the Brussels model.

The Modified Convention applies to:

(a) internal UK cases which would otherwise be outside the Conventions but only to matters which are civil or commercial within the meaning of the Conventions; and

(b) situations where the defendant is domiciled in the UK in the sense of domicile as used for the Conventions; or

(c) situations where the UK courts have exclusive jurisdiction under the Conventions.

Thus, where Art 2 of the Brussels Convention specifies that a defendant, if domiciled in the UK, may be sued in the UK, the effect of Art 2 of the Modified Convention is to specify that the defendant be sued in the appropriate part of the UK. The effect of the Modified Convention from the perspective of England is to treat Northern Ireland and Scotland as if they were distinct contracting States.

The code of domicile introduced for the international purposes of the Conventions has been adapted to deal with the internal allocation of jurisdiction within the UK.[157] It is now clear that the European Court of Justice has no jurisdiction under the Luxembourg Protocol to give rulings on the interpretation of the Modified Convention even in respect of those provisions that are identical to the provisions in the Brussels Convention. The Modified Convention is a creature of domestic law designed to regulate conflicts between jurisdictions, while the role of the Brussels Convention is to

---

156 See the Civil Jurisdiction and Judgments Act 1982, s 16, Sched 4, as amended.

157 *Ibid*, s 41(3)–(6) (individuals); s 42(4)–(5) (corporations); s 43(3)–(6) (corporate domicile for Art 16(2)); and s 45(3) (trusts).

158 See *Kleinwort Benson Ltd v City of Glasgow District Council* (Case C-346/93) [1995] ECR I-615; All ER 514; [1996] QB 57, ECJ. See also the subsequent application of this ruling by the House of Lords, [1997] 3 WLR 923.

regulate conflicts between Contracting States.[158] However, while the European Court of Justice has declined to provide guidance on the interpretation of the Modified Convention, it is clear that English courts, in considering questions under Sched 4, must, under s 16(3)(a) of the Civil Jurisdiction and Judgments Act 1982, have regard to the principles laid down by the European Court of Justice in relation to Title II of the Brussels Convention and to any relevant decision of the court as to the meaning and effect of any provision.[159]

An example may be used to illustrate this. Suppose the plaintiff wishes to sue the defendant in England on a matter which is within the scope of the Conventions but to which the UK, localised to England, has no special or exclusive jurisdiction. It will have to be established that the defendant is domiciled in England or in a non-Contracting State. If the defendant is domiciled in Scotland, France or Switzerland, the English court will not have jurisdiction (under the Modified Brussels and Lugano Conventions, respectively) and the proper forum will be the courts of the defendant's domicile. If, however, the defendant is domiciled in New York, Japan or India, the Conventions will have no operation and the English court can take jurisdiction under the common law rules. It must be remembered that it is the special not the traditional rules of domicile which will determine whether the defendant is domiciled in England, Scotland, Japan, New York or India, but it is the French and Swiss laws of domicile which have to be applied by the English court under the Conventions to determine the defendant's domicile there.

THE LUGANO CONVENTION

It is necessary to say a little on the differences between the Brussels Convention 1968 and the Lugano Convention 1988. The Lugano Convention was drawn up in 1988 to facilitate closer co-operation with the then EFTA countries.[160] The text of the Lugano Convention was based upon the Brussels Convention as it stood prior to the 1989 Accession Conventions. The Convention only operates between those States that have signed and ratified it. The provisions of the Lugano Convention are broadly similar to those of the Brussels Convention.

In the UK, domestic legislation was needed to implement the Convention. The Civil Jurisdiction and Judgments Act 1991 was passed to implement the Lugano Convention. This legislation operates by amending the Civil Jurisdiction and Judgments Act 1982.[161]

---

159 See *Kleinwort Benson Ltd v Glasgow City Council* [1997] 3 WLR 923, p 927, *per* Lord Goff.

160 The then States were Austria, Finland, Norway, Iceland, Sweden and Switzerland.

161 By inserting a new s 3A into the 1982 legislation; the text of the Lugano Convention is set out in Sched 3C.

It is important to note that the Lugano Convention permits the accession of States that are not members of either EFTA or the EC; it will, therefore, be possible for those States not ready for full EC membership to begin by seeking accession to the Lugano Convention. Those States that proceed to full membership of the EC will be required to accede to the Brussels Convention.[162]

The Lugano Convention operates in the same manner as the Brussels Convention but, as there are certain differences of detail, it is important to know which Convention applies in any particular case. This matter is regulated by Art 54B of the Lugano Convention, which provides that, from the perspective of an EC Contracting State (such as the UK):

(a) if the defendant is domiciled in an EC Contracting State, then the Brussels Convention will apply;

(b) if the defendant is domiciled in an EFTA Contracting State, then the Lugano Convention will apply;

(c) the Lugano Convention will also apply where jurisdiction is given to an EFTA Contracting State under Arts 16 and 17.

In the UK, the scheme pertaining to domicile under the Brussels Convention will also apply in respect of the Lugano Convention.[163]

No procedure exists under the Lugano Convention for rulings on interpretation to be obtained from the European Court of Justice. However, there remains the need to ensure uniform interpretation. Protocol 2 of the Lugano Convention requires courts to pay regard to the decisions of other courts in Lugano Contracting States in respect of the provisions of the Convention. In the UK, s 3B of the Civil Jurisdiction and Judgments Act 1982 requires the court to pay regard to judgments within the scope of Protocol 2 and to the *Jenard Moller Report* on the Lugano Convention.[164]

The drafters of the Lugano Convention were aware of the need to amend some of the provisions of the Brussels Convention but they were at the same time anxious to avoid two Conventions with different provisions. In the original draft, there were changes to Arts 5(1), 6, 16, 17, 21 and 52. However, many of these changes were then adopted in 1989 version of the Brussels Convention, so the question arises as to differences that exist between the 1989 version of the Brussels Convention and the Lugano Convention. In broad terms, the differences are as follows:

(a) Under Art 5(1), there are differences as regards the treatment of individual employment contracts. The revised version of the Brussels Convention provides that the 'employer may also be sued in the courts for the place

---

162 Since 1988, Austria, Finland and Sweden have joined the EC.
163 Civil Jurisdiction and Judgments Act 1982, ss 41–45.
164 *Jenard Moller Report* OJ C 189/57, 1990.

where the business which engaged the employee was or is now situated. The provision in the Lugano Convention declares that jurisdiction shall be in the courts of 'the place of business through which (the employee) was engaged'. The Lugano Convention is, thus, broader in providing that employer or employee may be sued. However, the Convention is less clear when the location of the business has changed between the time of engagement and the time of action.

(b) Article 16(1)(b) of the Brussels Convention provides that 'the landlord and tenant are natural persons and are domiciled in the same Contracting State'. In contrast, the provision in the Lugano Convention is broader providing that jurisdiction will arise as long as that 'the tenant is a natural person and neither party is domiciled in the Contracting State in which the property is situated'. A further difference is that the Lugano Convention, but not the Brussels Convention, permits a State to enter a reservation not to recognise a judgment based on Art 16(1)(b).[165]

(c) Article 17(5). In respect of choice of jurisdiction clauses concerning individual employment contracts, the provisions of the Lugano Convention are very specific, stipulating: 'In matters relating to individual contracts of employment, an agreement conferring jurisdiction shall have legal force only if it is entered into after the dispute has arisen.' A problem can arise in respect of clauses negotiated prior to the dispute and the provision in the Brussels Convention is wider, concluding with the words 'or if the employee invokes it to seise courts other than those for the defendant's domicile or those specified in Art 5(1)'.

In the context of the texts taken as a whole, these are small differences of detail. The philosophy of both documents is the same and most of the provisions are identical.

---

165 Lugano Convention 1988, Protocol 1, Art 1b.

CHAPTER 14

RECOGNITION AND ENFORCEMENT OF FOREIGN JUDGMENTS: THE TRADITIONAL RULES

INTRODUCTION

The powers of a court are territorially limited; their judgments have no effect beyond the jurisdiction in which they are given unless other countries agree to accept them.

A person who has obtained a judgment from a court of one system may wish that judgment to be recognised or enforced in another. Recognition alone, without any further action to enforce the judgment, may be sought when, for example, a defendant has been found not liable in an action brought by a plaintiff in one jurisdiction and wants to stop the plaintiff trying again in an another, or a party may want his divorce or nullity decree granted in one country to be recognised in another so that he can remarry there.

A person might seek to have a foreign judgment recognised and enforced in England if, say, the judgment debt has not been satisfied out of the foreign assets of the defendant and there are assets in this country against which he wants to proceed. Thus, a preliminary distinction has to be drawn between enforcement and recognition. An Englishman may obtain a judgment in Germany against a German company, but finds that the company has insufficient assets there and he may then wish to enforce the judgment against the defendant's assets in England. The question naturally arises as to whether he can enforce the original judgment in England or whether he needs to bring a fresh action.

A distinction also requires to be drawn between judgments *in personam* and judgments *in rem*; in the former, the obligation is addressed to a particular individual. The obligation may be to pay money or to refrain for a particular act. In the case of a judgment *in rem*, the judgment normally has the effect of creating a status that will be binding upon third parties. For example, the judgment may determine the ownership of a ship or it may declare whether an individual is divorced or not.

Thirdly, the recognition and enforcement of foreign judgments in England is subject to a number of different legal regimes, so that it is important to ask in which country the judgment was given before selecting the appropriate legal regime. Thus, a judgment given in France will be subject to a different legal regime to one awarded in Morocco. In broad terms, the following are legal regimes applicable to foreign judgments:

(a) foreign judgments subject to the common law rules. The common law rules apply to all countries that are outside the statutory or Convention rules.[1] This would include the countries of Eastern Europe, the Middle East and countries in Africa Asia and the Americas;

(b) the Administration of Justice Act 1920 applies to the enforcement of some Commonwealth judgments;

(c) the Foreign Judgments (Reciprocal Enforcement) Act 1933 governs the enforcement and recognition of the judgments of some Commonwealth countries and some non-Commonwealth countries (including Western Europe and Israel);

(d) as regards Western Europe, judgments in civil and commercial matters will be governed by the Brussels and Lugano Conventions. In broad terms, these rules will apply to countries within the EC or EFTA;

(e) the Civil Jurisdiction and Judgments Act 1982 provides for the recognition and enforcement of judgments given by the courts of Scotland and Northern Ireland.

In principle, there are five possible frameworks regulating the recognition and enforcement of judgments. A distinction can be drawn between the common law regime, where an action needs to be brought to enforce the foreign judgment, and the statutory scheme, where the emphasis is upon registration and enforcement of the foreign judgment.

At this stage, a preliminary point should be made. In England, it is a rule of domestic law that a plaintiff who has obtained judgment against a defendant is normally debarred from litigating upon the original cause of action.[2] This rule did not apply in the case of foreign judgments because it was argued that the foreign court was not a court of record;[3] thus, in the past, the plaintiff who was successful in a foreign court had the choice of either bringing an action in England against the defendant based on the foreign judgment or commencing litigation in England based on the same cause of action. This state of affairs was subject to criticism[4] and so the law has been changed, by s 34 of the Civil Jurisdiction and Judgments Act 1982, to provide that foreign judgments and domestic judgments should be subject to the same treatment. The section reads as follows:

> No proceedings may be brought by a person in England and Wales or Northern Ireland on a cause of action in respect of which a judgment has been given in his favour in proceedings between the same parties, or their privies, in a court in another part of the United Kingdom or in a court of an overseas

---

1 The rules stipulated in the Brussels and Lugano Conventions.

2 *Interest rei publicae ut sit finis litum* (it is for the common good that there should be an end to litigation). *Henderson v Henderson* (1843) 3 Hare 100; *Brisbane City Council v AG for Queensland* [1979] AC 411; *Arnold v National Westminster Bank Ltd* [1991] 2 AC 93.

3 *Smith v Nicolls* (1839) 5 Bing NC 208; *Bank of Australasia v Harding* (1850) 9 CB 661.

4 See *Carl Zeiss Stiftung v Rayner and Keeler Ltd (No 2)* [1967] 1 AC 853, p 966.

country, unless that judgment is not enforceable or entitled to recognition in England and Wales or, as the case may be, in Northern Ireland.[5]

Before turning to the particular schemes of recognition and enforcement, it is sensible to consider the theoretical basis for the recognition and enforcement of foreign judgments.

THE THEORETICAL BASIS FOR RECOGNITION AND ENFORCEMENT

One possibility would be for the English court to recognise all foreign judgments, while an alternative would be to recognise none at all. The first course would lead to individual injustice and might bring discredit on English law, while the second course would, in all probability, lead to considerable practical inconvenience. Common sense and practical considerations indicate that a middle course should be pursued, namely, that foreign judgments should be recognised if they meet certain criteria. The element of practical convenience has played a considerable part in the development of this area of law; as Slade LJ observed in *Adams v Cape Industries plc*,[6] the law is founded on:

> ... an acknowledgment that the society of nations will work better if some foreign judgments are taken to create rights which supersede the underlying cause of action, and which may be directly enforced in countries where the defendant or his assets are to be found.

However, before examining the particular criteria for recognition, it is important to note that the criteria embody a particular philosophy. In general terms, two theoretical justifications have been advanced for the recognition of foreign judgments.

The first justification was advanced in the 18th century and was based on the idea of comity;[7] however, comity is a rather vague concept and is more appropriate to the relations between sovereigns.[8] Closely linked to ideas of comity is the concept of reciprocity. There are some cases that favour reciprocity as a justification for recognition; the doctrine of reciprocity holds that the courts of country A should recognise and enforce the judgments of country B if country B is prepared to offer like treatment. The doctrine of

---

5   The provisions are effective from 24 August 1982 and are not retrospective, so it does not apply to prior foreign judgments (Civil Jurisdiction and Judgments Act 1982, Sched 13, para 10). For judicial consideration, see *Black v Yates* [1992] QB 526; *Republic of India v India SS Co Ltd* [1993] AC 410.

6   [1990] Ch 433.

7   *Geyer v Aguilar* (1798) 7 Term Rep 681.

8   May have been a consequence of the writings of Ulrich Huber (1636–94).

reciprocity has exercised some influence in the area of recognition of foreign divorces prior to the enactment of statutory reform.[9]

By the middle of the 19th century, English courts had adopted the doctrine of obligation as the justification for the recognition and enforcement of foreign judgments.[10] The doctrine held that, if the courts of country A have properly assumed jurisdiction, then the resulting judgment should be regarded as creating an obligation between the parties which an English court ought to recognise. Thus, if a foreign court orders X to pay damages to Y, then it is argued that this creates a legal obligation that may be enforced by Y as an action for debt. Later in the century, this became the governing orthodoxy, the position being expressed by Blackburn J[11] in *Schibsby v Westenholz*,[12] where the learned judge expressed the matter thus:

> We think that ... the true principle on which the judgments of foreign tribunals are enforced in England is ... that the judgment of a court of competent jurisdiction over the defendant imposes a duty or obligation on the defendant to pay the sum for which judgment is given, which the courts in this country are bound to enforce; and consequently that anything which negatives that duty, or forms a legal excuse for not performing it, is a defence to the action.[13]

The advantages of grounding recognition on the concept of obligation are that, first, it removes the necessity to investigate questions of reciprocity and, secondly, when the defendant contests the recognition of the judgment if evidence can be shown disproving the obligation, then the course open to the English court is clear.

THE RECOGNITION AND ENFORCEMENT OF JUDGMENTS AT COMMON LAW

In order for a judgment to be recocognised and enforced at common law, three main grounds need to be established. In broad terms, these are:

(a) that the foreign court must have been a competent court of jurisdiction;

(b) that the judgment must be final and conclusive; and

(c) that the judgment must be for a fixed sum not itself a tax or penalty.

In general terms, if the judgment creditor can establish these three elements then, *prima facie*, the judgment is entitled to be recognised; it is then the duty of

---

9 *Travers v Holley* [1953] P 246; see, also, *Indyka v Indyka* [1969] 1 AC 33 and the Recognition of Divorces and Legal Separations Act 1971.

10 *Russell v Smyth* (1842) 9 M & W 810; *Williams v Jones* (1845) 13 M & W 628.

11 As he then was.

12 (1870) LR 6 QB 155, p 159; see, also, *Godard v Gray* (1870) LR 6 QB 139.

13 Accepted as an accurate statement of the position in *Adams v Cape Industries plc* [1990] Ch 433.

the defendant to bring forward evidence relating to one of the accepted defences, if he wishes, to persuade the court that the judgment should not be recognised.

It is necessary to examine each of these elements in turn but, before doing so, it is helpful to dispose of a preliminary point. In the case of *Emanuel v Symon*,[14] Buckley LJ made a statement which has been cited in many subsequent cases; the learned judge observed:

> In actions *in personam*, there are five cases in which the courts of this country will enforce a foreign judgment:
>
> (1) where the defendant is a subject of the foreign country in which the judgment has been obtained;
>
> (2) where he was resident in the foreign country when the action began;
>
> (3) where the defendant in the character of a plaintiff has selected the forum in which he is afterwards sued;
>
> (4) where he has voluntarily appeared; and
>
> (5) where he has contracted to submit himself to the forum in which the judgment was obtained.

This statement has to be taken with a degree of caution. In so far as the first element is founded on nationality, this cannot be taken to be the law today;[15] the second element, relating to residence, is clearly correct and elements three, four and five are all variations on the theme of submission. Thus, it is the case that, in considering the jurisdiction of the foreign court, it is necessary to consider the elements of residence and submission. In general, the plaintiff with an enforceable judgement proceeds as he would for an ordinary claim in debt, within the limitation period of six years and with the possible benefit, if he seeks it, of summary judgment under RSC Ord 14 procedure, on the basis that the defendant has no defence to the claim.

With that qualification noted, it is now necessary to consider further the three elements noted above as required for the recognition of a foreign judgment.

There must be a court of competent jurisdiction

Introduction

For a foreign judgment to be recognised in England, it must have been given by a court of competent jurisdiction. By this, one means not that the court of

---

14 [1908] KB 302 (Lord Alverstone CJ, Kennedy, Buckley LJJ).

15 *Sirdar Gurdyal Singh v Rajah of Faridkote* [1894] AC 670; *Blohn v Desser* [1962] 2 QB 116; *Rossano v Manufacturers Life Insurance Co Ltd* [1963] 2 QB 352; *Vogel v RA Kohnstamm Ltd* [1973] 1 QB 133.

country A considers itself to have jurisdiction but that the rules of English private international law indicate that the foreign court is competent to exercise jurisdiction.

This principle can be traced back to the case of *Buchanan v Rucker*,[16] where the facts were as follows: the plaintiff brought an action in England to enforce a judgment given by a court in the island of Tobago. The defendant had never been to the island, nor had he submitted to the jurisdiction. Substituted service had been made by nailing a copy of the writ to the courthouse door. That was valid service by the law of Tobago.

In refusing to recognise and enforce the judgment, Lord Ellenborough observed: 'Can the island of Tobago pass a law to bind the whole world? Would the world submit to such an assumed jurisdiction?' Since that date, the question has arisen as to the precise criteria that need to be established to demonstrate the international competence of the foreign court. The case law indicates that it is normally necessary to show presence or residence by the defendant or submission to the jurisdiction. It is probably the case that no other ground will suffice.

Residence

It is generally assumed that the residence[17] of the defendant within the territory of the court will suffice. In *Carrick v Hancock*,[18] the temporary presence of an Englishman in Sweden was sufficient to confer jurisdiction on the Swedish court. This case, to some extent, typifies the 19th century emphasis on territorial jurisdiction. As Lord Russell of Killowen CJ observed, 'all persons within any territorial dominion owe their allegiance to its sovereign power and obedience to all its laws and the lawful jurisdiction of its courts'.[19] That there is a minimum requirement of presence was illustrated by the case of *Sirdar Gurdyal Singh v Rajah of Faridkote*,[20] where the facts were as follows: the Rajah obtained two *ex parte* judgments against the appellant in the courts of Faridkote. The appellant had not lived there for five years and was domiciled in Lahore. The Rajah sought to enforce the judgment in the State of Lahore (another country for the purpose of jurisdiction).

On appeal, the Privy Council ruled that the foreign judgment could not be recognised as the defendant was not resident in Faridkote and had not, on the evidence, submitted to the jurisdiction.

---

16   (1809) 9 East 192.

17   There is some doubt as to whether the requirement is presence or residence; this has been explored in greater detail in those cases concerning corporations.

18   (1895) 12 TLR 59.

19   *Carrick v Hancock* (1895) 12 TLR 59, p 60; it is interesting to contrast the remarks on jurisdiction made in this case with the similar emphasis on territorial jurisdiction in *AG for New South Wales v Macleoad* [1891] AC 455; 117 Cox CC 341, PC.

20   [1894] AC 670.

Applying this principle, it is argued that the English courts will not recognise a judgment where a foreign court has claimed jurisdiction in circumstances where leave to serve a writ out of the jurisdiction under RSC Ord 11 might be granted;[21] there is, thus, in this area, a tension between wide claims to national jurisdiction and narrow rules as to the recognition of judgments.

Presence or residence of corporations

Difficulties have arisen as to whether a company is resident in a particular jurisdiction when proceedings are initiated. In *Littauer Glove Company v F W Millington (1920) Ltd*,[22] the question arose as to whether the company was resident in New York when a writ was served on its managing director while visiting a customer's office.[23] Salter J held that the proper test to apply was to ask whether there was 'some carrying on of business at a definite and, to some reasonable extent, permanent place'. Applying this test, the learned judge concluded that the New York court did not have jurisdiction. In relation to companies, a common problem arises as to whether the activities of a foreign agent can render the company liable. In *Sfeir v National Insurance Company of New Zealand*,[24] a New Zealand insurance company was held not to be resident in Ghana when it engaged an agent there; the agent did little business for the company and was free to engage with other clients. In like terms, in *Vogel v R and A Kohnstamm Ltd*,[25] a question arose as to whether a judgment given in Israel should be recognised. The company in question had no office in Israel and engaged a 'contact man' to seek out possible business; this individual did not have the power to enter into contracts on behalf of the company. In these circumstances, Ashworth J rejected the argument that the company was present in Israel and further rejected the assertion that there had been an implied submission to the jurisdiction.

The question of the residence of a company was considered in the case of *Adams v Cape Industries plc*,[26] where the facts, in summary form, were as follows: an English company, which had been involved through a subsidiary and an associated company in the mining and sale of asbestos, was the defendant in two personal injury actions brought in Tyler, Texas by plaintiffs

---

21   *Schibsby v Westenholz* (1870) LR 6 QB 155; *Turnbull v Walker* (1892) 67 LT 769; although see *obiter* remarks to the contrary by Denning LJ in *Re Dulles Settlement (No 2)* [1951] Ch 842.

22   (1928) 44 TLR 746.

23   The Managing Director was on a visit to New York and staying in a hotel.

24   [1964] 1 LR 330 (a judgment on the Administration of Justice Act 1920).

25   [1973] 1 QB 133 (Ashworth J); see Cohn (1972) 21 ICLQ 157.

26   [1990] Ch 433, CA (Scott J).

alleging that their health had been damaged by exposure to asbestos. The defendants participated in the first action (*Tyler (No 1)*) which was settled; in respect of *Tyler (No 2)*, they contested the jurisdiction of the court but then took no part in the action. Thereafter, a default judgment was made against them and damages were assessed on a lump sum sliding scale basis, without any objective judicial determination on the evidence of each individual case.

Scott J rejected an attempt to enforce the judgment and his ruling was upheld by the Court of Appeal. Among the many points discussed in the case the following are pertinent:

(a) the argument that a holding company, a subsidiary company and an associated company could form a single economic unit for the purposes of jurisdiction was rejected;

(b) the argument that defendants had submitted to the jurisdiction in the second legal action, *Tyler (No 2)*, by participating in *Tyler (No 1)* was rejected;

(c) the argument that submission could be implied by appearing to contest the jurisdiction of the court was rejected.[27]

In dealing with the question as to whether a company was present or resident in another jurisdiction, Slade LJ expressed the matter as follows:

> The English courts will be likely to treat a trading corporation incorporated under the law of one country ('an overseas corporation') as present within the jurisdiction of the courts of another country only if either (i) it has established and maintained ... a fixed place of business of its own in the other country and for more than a minimal period of time has carried on its own business at or form such premises by its servants or agents ... or (ii) a representative of the overseas corporation has for more than a minimal period of time been carrying on the overseas corporation's business in the other country at or from some fixed place of business.

The learned judge then proceeded to outline the variety of facts that might be looked at when considering whether a company was resident in a particular jurisdiction by virtue of having a representative there. One particular point that was stressed was that the fact that the representative lacked contractual capacity did not necessarily lead to the conclusion that the company was not resident there. The tone of the judgments at first instance and in the Court of Appeal is to the effect that questions of the residence of a company and the relationship between a holding company and any other company are to be settled by recourse to the traditional principles of English company law, which proceed on the basis of the separate legal personality of the company. If a foreign subsidiary or a foreign representative is to render the holding company resident, then there will have to be a detailed investigation of factors

---

27 See the Civil Jurisdiction and Judgments Act 1982, s 33.

such as (a) the ownership of business premises; (b) the payment of wages; (c) the degree of control; and (d) the degree of contractual capacity.

Submission

A foreign judgment will be enforced in England if the defendant submitted to the jurisdiction of the foreign court. Submission to the jurisdiction may take many forms and it is hardly surprising that there has been considerable litigation as to whether the defendant submitted to the jurisdiction.

Manifestly, if the defendant began proceedings as plaintiff, then there will have been submission;[28] but, there will be no submission if the defendant appeared as a result of duress or undue influence.[29] Whether such pressure was exerted is a question to be determined in accordance with English law.[30]

At common law, if the defendant entered into an agreement to submit to the jurisdiction of a foreign court, then he will be deemed to have submitted to that jurisdiction.[31] By virtue of s 32 of the Civil Jurisdiction and Judgments Act 1982, a judgment given by country A in defiance of a valid jurisdiction agreement in favour of country B will be refused recognition in England.[32]

A difficult question arises as to whether there can be implied submission by conduct; the older authorities are against it but, in recent years, there have been some equivocal statements.[33]

Another area of difficulty at common law was whether a defendant could be said to have submitted to the jurisdiction when he appeared voluntarily in the foreign court to contest the jurisdiction. In *Harris v Taylor*,[34] this was held to constitute submission but the judgment was not welcomed and was subject to criticism in subsequent case law.[35] However, in the case of *Henry v Geoprosco International Ltd*,[36] the Court of Appeal ruled that submission to the

---

28 *Emanuel v Symons* [1908] 1 KB 302. For a recent discussion of the scope of submission, see *Murthy v Sivajothi* (1998) *The Times*, 11 November, CA.

29 *Israel Discount Bank of New York v Hadjipateras* [1984] 1 WLR 137.

30 *Desert Sun Loan Corporation v Hill* [1996] 2 All ER 847.

31 *Copin v Adamson* (1875) 1 Ex D 17 (agreement in articles of association of company); *Feyerick v Hubbard* [1902] LJ KB 509 (agreement on sale of patent rights).

32 For a case concerning the transitional provisions in relation to the Civil Jurisdiction and Judgments Act 1982, ss 32–33, see *Trancomin SA v Sudan Oil Seeds Company (Nos 1 and 2)* [1983] 1 WLR 1026.

33 *Sirdar Gurdyal Singh v Rajah of Faridkote* [1894] AC 670; *Emanuel v Symon* [1908] 1 KB 302; but, see *Blohn v Desser* [1962] 2 QB 116; *Sfeir and Co v National Insurance Company of New Zealand* [1964] 1 LR 330.

34 [1915] 2 KB 580.

35 *Re Dulles Settlement (No 2)* [1951] Ch 842; *Daarnhouwer and Co Handelmaatschappij v Boulos* [1968] 2 LR 259 (Megaw J). Criticised by Dicey and Morris (9th edn, 1973), p 638.

36 [1976] QB 726; see Collier [1975] CLJ 219; Collins (1976) 92 LQR 268.

jurisdiction was not limited to cases of disputing the merits[37] but extended to a situation where a defendant appeared before a foreign court and asked it to decline jurisdiction. In considering cases where a dispute arises as to whether the defendant entered an appearance under protest, then a distinction can be drawn between a number of situations:

(a) where the defendant alleges that the foreign court has no jurisdiction;

(b) where a defendant asks a foreign court to set aside service out of the jurisdiction;

(c) where a defendant requests a stay of proceedings on the basis of the doctrine of *forum non conveniens*;

(d) where the defendant asks for a stay because of a valid foreign jurisdiction agreement;

(e) where the defendant argues that the court should stay the proceedings because of an arbitration agreement;

(f) where the defendant asks for a stay to give effect to a *Scott v Avery*[38] clause.

Following criticism of the reasoning in *Henry v Geoprosco International Ltd*, s 33 of the Civil Jurisdiction and Judgments Act 1982 was enacted; the operative provisions are as follows:

> For the purposes of determining whether a judgment given by a court of an overseas country should be recognised or enforced in England and Wales or Northern Ireland, the person against whom the judgment was given shall not be regarded as having submitted to the jurisdiction of the court by reason only of the fact that he appeared (conditionally or otherwise) in the proceedings for all or any one or more of the following purposes, namely:
>
> (a) to contest the jurisdiction of the court;
>
> (b) to ask the court to dismiss or stay the proceedings on the ground that the dispute in question should be submitted to arbitration or to the determination of the courts of another country;
>
> (c) to protect or obtain the release of property seized or threatened with seizure in the proceedings.

The legislation does not define the expression 'to contest the jurisdiction' and, having regard to the distinctions that can be drawn between the existence of jurisdiction and the exercise of jurisdiction, there may be room for argument. In respect of specific repeals, it is clear that s 33(1)(a) reverses the judgment in *Harris v Taylor*;[39] it must be unclear whether s 33(1)(a) incorporates (a) and (b) above, but that may be of only academic interest because the ruling in *Henry v*

---

37 *Boissiere and Co v Brockner* (1889) 6 TLR 85.

38 (1885) 5 HL Cas 811.

39 [1915] 2 KB 580.

Geopresco International Ltd (where a stay was sought to enable arbitration to take place) is reversed by s 33(1)(b). This interpretation was followed by Staughton J in *Tracomin SA v Sudan Oil Seeds Co Ltd (No 1)*,[40] where the learned judge held that sellers who appeared before a Swiss court to ask for a stay on grounds of an arbitration clause had not submitted to the jurisdiction of the Swiss courts.

In respect of s 33(1)(c), it would seem that the object of the sub-section is to reverse those common law authorities where the jurisdiction of the foreign court is established by the seizure of property.[41]

The judgment must be final and conclusive

It is not enough that the foreign court is competent it must be shown that the judgment is final and conclusive.[42] As Lord Herschell expressed the matter:

> It must be shown that in the court in which it was produced, it conclusively, finally and for ever established the existence of the debt of which it is sought to be made conclusive evidence in this country, so as to make it res judicata between the parties.[43]

Thus, where court A has given a summary judgment in proceedings in which limited defences may be raised, but the losing party may request a full hearing before the same court at which all defences can be raised, it cannot be said that the judgment is final and conclusive.[44] The same would apply to the situation where of a judgment in default of appearance is given and the defendant is allowed within a certain time to move to set aside the judgment. The reasoning is that at common law the court is concerned to enforce the debt or obligation arising the foreign judgment. As Lord Herschell explained:

> I do not, therefore, see that there is any wrong or any hardship done by holding that a judgment which does not conclusively and for ever as between the parties establish the existence of a debt in that court cannot be looked upon as sufficient evidence of it in the courts of this country ...[45]

Careful attention has to be paid to the precise legal person against whom the judgment is obtained. In *Blohn v Desser*,[46] a judgment was obtained in Austria against a firm but it was sought to enforce the judgment in England against

---

40 [1983] 1 WLR 662; 1 WLR 1026.
41 *Vionet v Barrett* (1885) 55 LJQB 39; *Guiard v De Clermont* [1914] 3 KB 145.
42 *Nouvion v Freeman* (1889) 15 App Cas 1.
43 *Ibid*, p 9.
44 *Ibid*.
45 *Ibid*, p 9 (Lords Herschell, Watson, Bramwell and Ashbourne concurring).
46 [1962] 2 QB 116 (Diplock J).

the defendant personally. Personal proceedings could have been iniated in Austria against the defendant but were not; if such proceedings had been initiated, then the defendant would have been able to raise a number of specific defences. In such circumstances, Diplock J[47] ruled that, even if the judgment could be regarded as against the defendant personally, it could not be recognised because it was not 'final'.

Problems arise when a judgment is given in court A, but there is a right of appeal to court B. In principle, the existence of a right of appeal will not prevent a judgment being final and conclusive[48] but, if an appeal is in process, then the English court will normally stay proceedings until a decision is known.[49] The requirement that the judgment be final and conclusive has given rise to difficulties in respect of maintenance awards because of the power of the court to vary such awards.[50] In cases under foreign law where the exercise of a right of appeal has the effect of automatically suspending the judgment, then it would seem that the judgment should not be recognised in England.[51] Indeed, any indication in the text of the foreign judgment that it is provisional or interim will normally be fatal to recognition.[52]

The judgment must be for a fixed sum

The plaintiff seeking to enforce the judgment in England is treated as if his action was based on debt; thus, he can claim only for a fixed sum and, unless the foreign court has finally determined the amount, there is nothing to enforce.[53] A sum that requires the deduction of sums in taxation of costs will not be regarded as fixed.[54] In principle, it does not matter that damages are exemplary or punitive.[55] It follows from this that foreign judgments which do not take the form of a fixed monetary sum cannot be enforced at common law. Injunctions, decrees of specific performance or any judgment which requires the defendant to do more then pay a certain amount are not enforceable.

Even where the foreign judgment is for a fixed sum, it can only be enforced if it has been made in favour of an individual or corporate legal

---

47 As he then was.

48 *Colt Industries Inc v Sarlie (No 2)* [1966] 1 WLR 1287.

49 *Scott v Pilkington* (1862) 2 B & S 11; *Colt Industries Inc v Sarlie (No 2)* [1966] 1 WLR 1287.

50 *Harrop v Harrop* [1920] 3 KB 386; *Beatty v Beatty* [1924] 1 KB 807. The recognition of maintenance awards is now regulated by statute – see the Maintenance Orders (Facilities for Enforcement) Act 1920; Maintenance Orders Acts 1950, 1958; Maintenance Orders (Reciprocal Enforcement) Act 1972.

51 *Patrick v Schedden* (1853) 2 E & B 14.

52 *Desert Sun Loan Corporation v Hill* [1996] 2 All ER 847.

53 *Sadler v Robins* (1808) 1 Camp 253.

54 *Ibid.*

55 *SA Consortium General Textiles v Sun and Sand Agencies Ltd* [1978] QB 279.

person. The general principle that English courts will not act as the policeman of foreign States nor as their tax gatherers precludes the recognition of judgments for tax arrears or fines.[56] But, a compensation order made by a criminal court, for the benefit of a victim, may be enforceable at the suit of that victim[57] as may an award of exemplary or aggravated damages, even if described as a penalty.[58] An example is afforded by the case of *Raulin v Fischer*, where the facts were as follows: the defendant was involved in a riding accident in the Bois de Boulogne in Paris. Criminal proceedings were begun against her under Art 320 of the Penal Code; the plaintiff then joined in the proceedings to claim compensation. The court, at different sittings, imposed a fine on the defendant of 100 francs and ordered her to pay the sum of 15,000 francs in compensation to the plaintiff. The plaintiff sought to enforce the judgment in England.

Hamilton J, after hearing evidence both as to French law and as to the nature of the legal proceedings, ruled that, while recognition would be withheld in respect of the fine, the judgment could be severed and the sum of 15,000 could be the subject of enforcement proceedings.

While English law is not minded to form a view as to the sums awarded by foreign courts,[59] it should be noted that legislation has been passed to prevent the enforcement of the most controversial of the punitive damages cases, that is, those arising from the multiple damages award of the United States anti-trust laws.[60] An example of the refusal to enforce penalties arose in the case of *United States of America v Inkley*,[61] where a judgment had been given in civil proceedings in Florida to enforce payment of a sum under an appearance bond relating to non-appearance in a criminal case. The Court of Appeal, in rejecting an application to enforce the judgment, held that, although civil proceedings had been invoked, the overall purpose of the legal action and the nature of the sum claimed related to criminal proceedings. Purchas LJ, in giving judgment, explained:

> ... notwithstanding its civil clothing, the purpose of the action ... was the due execution by the United States of America of a public law process aimed to ensure the attendance of persons accused of crime before the criminal courts.

This is consistent with the approach propounded in *Huntington v Atrill*[62] of looking not at the name of the law or proceeding, but at its substance and intent.

---

56 See, generally, under recognition of foreign law in Chapter 9.
57 *Raulin v Fischer* [1911] 2 KB 92 (Hamilton J).
58 *Huntingdon v Attrill* [1893] AC 150, PC.
59 Unless, of course, they were not awarded on consideration of the evidence; see *Adams v Cape Industries plc* [1990] Ch 433.
60 Protection of Trading Interests Act 1980, s 5(2).
61 [1989] QB 255.
62 [1893] AC 150.

DEFENCES AND NON-DEFENCES TO RECOGNITON AND ENFORCEMENT

Introduction

There are few defences which the defendant can raise. It will not influence the English court that the foreign judgment was based on mistaken facts[63] or that the wrong law was applied, or the right law was applied wrongly.[64] Such matters are for the internal system which produced the original judgment. A question that has raised difficulties concerns whether the foreign court may lack internal competence, that is, may lack jurisdiction under its own internal system of law. In terms of strict logic, it might be argued that that such a judgment would be void within its own system and ought not to be recognised. There is some authority to support this view in matrimonial cases, where the recognition rules are different.[65] There is a *dictum* by Lindley MR in *Pemberton v Hughes*[66] which has been much commented upon; the learned judge observed:

> But, the jurisdiction which alone is important in these matters is the competence of the court in an international sense, that is, its territorial competence over the subject matter and over the defendant. Its competence or jurisdiction in any other sense is not regarded as material by the courts of this country.

The learned judge was making the remarks in the context of a case turning on a procedural mistake by the foreign court. It would seem that a correct reading of the case and a prior ruling of the Court of Exchequer Chamber,[67] is that procedural errors do not constitute substantial injustice, and will not act as a defence to an action for enforcement. The value of the *dictum* by Lindley MR lies in drawing the proper distinction between matters of internal competence and matters of international jurisdiction.

The principle that English courts will not allow the defendant to attack the foreign judgment on the merits extends to a refusal to allow him to argue a defence to the original claim. In *Ellis v M'Henry*,[68] a judgment had been

---

63 *Bank of Australasia v Nias* (1851) 16 QB 717; *Bank of Australasia v Harding* (1850) 9 CB 661; *De Cosse Brissac v Rathbone* (1861) 6 H & N 301.

64 *Goddard v Gray* (1870) LR 6 QB 139 (Blackburn, Mellor, Hannen JJ) (where the interpretation of a penalty clause in a charterparty (whose proper law was English) by a French court was at variance with the probable interpretation by an English court – it was held that the plea failed).

65 *Papadopoulos v Papadopoulos* [1930] P 55; *Adams v Adams* [1971] P 188 (an exceptional case, turning on the legal status of the judiciary in the then Southern Rhodesia).

66 [1899] 1 Ch 781 (Lindley MR, Rigby, Vaughan Williams LJJ).

67 For the effect of procedural errors in the foreign court, see *Vanquelin v Bouard* (1863) 15 CBNS 341.

68 (1871) 3 LR 6 CP 228.

obtained in Canada in an action that would have failed had the defendant pleaded a particular deed of composition. The plaintiff sued to enforce the judgment in England and the court held that he could do so and rejected the attempt by the defendant to set up the composition deed as a defence. In ruling against the defendant, Bovill CJ observed that to do so would 'go to impeach the propriety and correctness of the judgment, and is a matter which cannot be gone into after the judgment has been obtained'. The view that the English courts will not allow a defendant to argue a defence that was factually and legally available to him at trial or on appeal in the courts which gave judgment was echoed by Stephenson LJ in *Israel Discount Bank of New York v Hadjipateras*,[69] where the learned judge observed that 'a defendant must take all available defences in a foreign country'.

Even where the defence was not available to him in the foreign proceedings, the general principle of not retrying foreign cases should prevent the defendant raising the matter before the English court, unless some fundamental principle of English public policy would be offended. The other side of this coin is that, unless the foreign judgment was given on the merits, there is nothing for an English court to recognise. So, if a foreign court dismissed the plaintiff's action for want of jurisdiction, or for some other reason unrelated to the merits of the case, the defendant cannot raise the judgment as the basis of an estoppel *per rem judicatem* in subsequent English proceedings. At one time, dismissal of an action as time barred was not regarded as a judgment on the merits by English courts, as time bars, at least when they barred the action without extinguishing the right of action itself, were regarded as procedural – but that position has now been altered by statute.[70]

Despite the general principle that an English court will not investigate the substantive judgment of a foreign court, there are some defences open to a party opposing the recognition and enforcement of a judgment in the English court. It is proposed now to examine each of these heads, although it may, of course, be the case that a defence is raised under more than one head.

Natural justice

While the refusal to recognise or enforce a foreign judgment inevitably affects the substantive rights of the parties to get what they want, the argument about natural justice goes not to the merits of the case, but to the procedure by which the foreign court arrived at its judgment. Although cases on aspects of natural

---

69   [1984] 1 WLR 137; see Collier [1984] CLJ 47.
70   Foreign Limitation Periods Act 1984, s 3.

justice can be identified in the domestic law from the 17th century,[71] there is little doubt that interest in this area of law increased with the important House of Lords judgment in *Ridge v Baldwin*.[72] Since that date, there has been a greater degree of judicial activism in cases concerned with procedural fairness. In broad terms, the rules of natural justice embrace two basic ideas.

The first element is that an individual be given adequate notice of the charge and that he be given a proper hearing (*audi alteram partem*); the second element is that the adjudicator or judge be unbiased (*nemo judex in causa sua*). While the rules of natural justice are easy enough to state, the difficulty arises in applying them to different factual situations, so much so that the more recent case law is replete with references to the duty to act fairly.[73] In the context of a foreign court, the defendant is entitled to proper notice of the hearing and an opportunity to properly present his case. This can raise difficulties because the nature of a hearing depends on the rules of evidence of the forum and these are, therefore, matters for the procedure of the foreign court; in these circumstances, English courts have been slow to find fault with the rules of evidence of a foreign court.[74]

Clearly, if the conduct of the foreign court should 'offend against English views of substantial justice',[75] then the judgment will not be recognised. It would seem that the litigant must be given notice of the hearing;[76] however, there will be no intervention simply because the result may be wrong[77] and, where the defendant has contracted to submit to the jurisdiction of a foreign court, then the English court will be reluctant to find that there has been procedural impropriety.[78]

While attention has tended to focus on practical problems such as the notice of the hearing or the presentation of evidence, there is no doubt that compliance with the rules of natural justice extends to all participants in the hearing. As Shadwell VC observed, in *Price v Dewhurst*,[79] 'whenever it is manifest that justice has been disregarded, the court is bound to treat the decision as a matter of no value and no substance'. Thus, it can probably be

---

71 See *Bagg's Case* (1615) 11 Co Rep 93b; *R v Chancellor of the University of Cambridge* (1723) 1 Str 557; *Cooper v Wandsworth Board of Works* (1863) 14 CBNS 180.

72 [1964] AC 40.

73 A concept that emerges in the judgment of Lord Parker CJ in *Re HK* [1967] 2 QB 617; a detailed analysis of procedural fairness is contained in the important judgment of Megarry VC in *McInnes v Onslow Fane* [1978] 1 WLR 1520. The importance of the rules of natural justice was emphasised by the House of Lords in *Re Pinochet Ugarte (No 2)* (1999) *The Times*, 18 January, and by Lord Browne-Wilkinson in particular.

74 *Scarpetta v Lowenfeld* (1911) 27 TLR 509.

75 *Pemberton v Hughes* [1899] 1 Ch 781 at 790.

76 *Jacobson v Frachon* (1927) 138 LT 386.

77 *Robinson v Fenner* [1913] 3 KB 835.

78 *Vallee v Dumergue* (1849) 4 Exch 290; *Feyerick v Hubbard* (1902) 71 LJKB 509.

79 (1837) 8 Sim 279.

said that the test is either the disregarding of justice or that substantial justice has not been done. The Court of Appeal, in *Adams v Cape Industries plc*,[80] were minded to focus on the second formulation when considering an argument raised in that case. It was argued by the defendants that, at the conclusion of the trial, the award of damages had been arrived at not by objective judicial determination of the evidence but by allowing the plaintiffs to claim a sliding scale of award. Clearly, this is a matter of discretion but it would seem, after *Adams v Cape Industries plc*, that English courts will be inclined to the view that the rule of law demands that the principles by which damages have been assessed should be clearly identified by the foreign court. Any situation in which the plaintiff determines the level of the award would appear to constitute an abdication of the judicial function and a breach of the rules of natural justice.

Fraud

A fraud going to the jurisdiction or the merits of the case, in a manner which materially affected the result, may provide a case for the non-recognition of a judgment in circumstances where an English judgment would be sacrosanct. Under domestic English law, a high regard is paid to the principle of finality in litigation. The principle of estoppel *per rem judicatem*, or cause of action estoppel as it is sometimes referred to as, provides for the merger of the cause of action in the judgment. The rule is designed to promote finality and to prevent essentially the same matter being litigated twice.

If one party brings an action against another for a particular cause and judgment is given on it, there is a strict rule of law that he cannot bring another action against the same party for the same cause.[81]

The principal exception to this strict rule is that a party may move to set aside a judgment on the ground that it was secured by fraud.[82] The courts are very reluctant to admit such actions and any applicant faces a very difficult task, needing:

(a) to meet a demanding standard of proof;

(b) to show that he is in possession of new factual material;

(c) to show that this factual material was not available nor reasonably discoverable at the time of the original trial;

(d) to show that, if such factual material had been available at the time of trial, it would have materially affected the result.

---

80 [1990] Ch 433.

81 *Fidelitas Shipping Co Ltd v V/O Exportchleb* [1966] 1 QB 630, p 640.

82 *Flower v Lloyd* (1877) 6 Ch D 297; *Flower v Lloyd (No 2)* (1879) 10 Ch D 327; *Jonesco v Beard* [1930] AC 298.

These are very demanding criteria and are intended to be so and, in certain circumstances, the court may consider an attempt to reopen a judgment as an abuse of process.[83]

The purpose of outlining the position under domestic law is to note the contrast with the rules in respect of foreign judgments, where it is firmly established that a defendant may raise the question of fraud. He can raise the issue even if it was decided against him in the foreign litigation or he can raise it for the first time in the enforcement proceedings. The practical effect is that it will then be necessary for the English court to investigate the merits of the action. In four judgments over the last century, the Court of Appeal have ruled that the court should investigate allegations of fraud in enforcement proceedings even though such allegations have been investigated and dismissed at the original foreign trial.

The first case that raised the difference between domestic rules and conflict rules in relation to fraud was *Abouloff v Oppenheimer*,[84] where the facts were as follows: an action was brought in the Russian courts for the return of certain goods or the payment of their value. The plaintiff obtained judgment in the Russian court and then sought to enforce it in England. The defendant argued that the claim was tainted by fraud because the goods in question had been in the possession of the plaintiff and he had misled the Russian court. The plaintiff argued this defence was bad because the matter had been investigated by the Russian court and been rejected.

The question at issue was whether the English court should embark on an investigation of matters said to constitute fraud, even when they had been raised and rejected before the foreign court. The Court of Appeal declined to apply the strict demands of domestic law and ruled that an investigation should proceed. Brett LJ was not concerned that this might traverse the same ground and he observed:

> I will assume that, in the suit in the Russian courts, the plaintiff's fraud was alleged by the defendants and that they gave evidence in support of the charge: I will assume even that the defendants gave the very same evidence which they propose to adduce in this action; nevertheless, the defendants will not be debarred at trial from making the same charge of fraud and adducing the same evidence in support of it.[85]

Within a few years, a very strong Court of Appeal ruled, in *Vadala v Lawes*,[86] that it did not matter that the English court on enforcement proceedings would investigate the same issues as the foreign court had investigated or that the evidence would be same; the court ordered that a new trial should take

---

83 *Hunter v Chief Constable of the West Midlands* [1982] AC 459.
84 (1882) 10 QBD 295 (Lord Coleridge CJ, Brett, Baggallay LJJ).
85 *Abouloff v Oppenheimer and Co* (1882) 10 QBD 295, p 306.
86 (1890) 25 QBD 310 (Lindley, Bowen LJJ).

place to determine whether there had been fraud. In giving judgment, Lindley LJ identified the difficulty of striking a balance between two principles, observing:

> There are two rules relating to these matters which have to be borne in mind, and the joint operation of which gives rise to the difficulty. First of all, there is the rule which is perfectly well established and well known, that a party to an action can impeach the judgment in it for fraud ... Another general proposition, which, speaking in equally general language, is perfectly well settled, is, when you bring an action on a foreign judgment, you cannot go into the merits which have been tried in the foreign court.

The two Court of Appeal judgments had been concerned with the defendant who had raised the matter before the foreign court and then wished to raise it as a defence to enforcement. In the subsequent case of *Syal v Heyward*,[87] the court was confronted with the problem of the defendant who chose to wait. The facts of *Syal v Heyward* were as follows: the plaintiff, an Indian moneylender, obtained judgment in India against the defendant in respect of monies lent pursuant to a promissory note. The defendant chose not to defend the action. The plaintiff then sought to register the judgment under the Foreign Judgments (Reciprocal Enforcement) Act 1933. The defendant moved to set aside the registration. The defendant alleged that (a) there had been fraud in relation to the issue of the promissory note; and (b) while he had known about matters at the time of trial, that was not itself a barrier to demanding that the issue of fraud be investigated in England. Jones J, in overruling the master, ordered the issue of fraud to be tried and this judgment was upheld on appeal.

Cohen LJ, in delivering the judgment of the Court of Appeal, expressly approved the earlier judgments in *Abouloff v Oppenheimer* and *Vadala v Lawes*. The court accepted that a defendant could resist enforcement in England if he could produce *prima facie* evidence of fraud, and it did not matter whether the allegations of fraud had been investigated and rejected by the foreign court or, as in this case, whether the defendant could have raised the matter before the foreign court, but chose not to do so. This line of authority was approved and to some extent extended in the subsequent case of *Jet Holdings Inc v Patel*,[88] where an action was brought to enforce a judgment given in the superior court of California. The defence included the contention that the judgment had been obtained by fraud. The Court of Appeal ordered that the allegations of fraud would have to be investigated at trial in England. Staughton LJ noted:

> The decisions in *Abouloff* ... and *Vandala* ... show that a foreign judgment cannot be enforced if it was obtained by fraud, even though the allegation of fraud was investigated and rejected by the foreign court.

---

87 [1948] 2 KB 443 (Cohen, Scott, Wrottesley LJJ).
88 [1990] 1 QB 335, CA. It is arguable that this represents an extension because the allegation of fraud related to a collateral matter rather than to the cause of action itself.

This stream of authority admitted of no real dispute that, in cases of fraud, the courts were prepared to review the merits of the original judgment. The only case contrary to this approach was that of *House of Spring Gardens Ltd v Waite*,[89] where a judgment had been obtained in Ireland (action *No 1*) and then some of the defendants had moved to have the judgment set aside on the specific ground of fraud; this matter was then investigated before the courts in Ireland (action *No 2*) and the allegations were rejected. When enforcement was sought in England, the Court of Appeal upheld the ruling of Pain J that the second action created an issue estoppel in respect of fraud and so, in the absence of fresh evidence, the repeated allegation of fraud represented an abuse of process.

The entire stream of case law was reviewed by the House of Lords in *Owens Bank Ltd v Bracco*,[90] where the facts, in simplified form, were as follows: the plaintiff bank claimed to have lent nine million Swiss francs to the defendant, who received the money in cash against certain signed documents. The defendant resisted the claim in the courts of St Vincent and denied that he had ever entered the transaction. The bank succeeded before the courts of St Vincent and sought registration of the judgment under the Administration of Justice Act 1920. The defendant applied to resist registration on the grounds of fraud by the bank. Pain J ordered that the issue of fraud be tried. This ruling was upheld by the Court of Appeal and by the House of Lords.

In the House of Lords, counsel for the bank[91] mounted an attack on the case law originating with *Abouloff v Oppenheimer*; he argued that the decisions were wrong at the time they were given and, even if not, the rule they established was inconsistent with the modern principle of non reviewability of foreign judgments and conceptions of judicial comity. In giving judgment for the House of Lords, Lord Bridge, while acknowledging that criticisms that could be made of the common law rules, felt that the Administration of Justice Act 1920 had adopted the principle of fraud at common law and that now reform would have to be for the legislature. He observed:

> But, enforcement of overseas judgments is now primarily governed by the statutory codes of 1920 and 1933. Since these cannot be altered except by further legislation, it seems to me out of the question to alter the common law rules by overruling *Abouloff v Oppenheimer* and *Vadala v Lawes*. To do so would produce the absurd result that an overseas judgment creditor, denied statutory enforcement on the ground that he had obtained his judgment by fraud, could succeed in a common law action to enforce his judgment because the evidence on which the judgment debtor relied did not satisfy the English rule.

---

89 [1991] 1 QB 241; the judgment in the case had been given prior to entry into force of the Brussels Convention between the UK and the Republic of Ireland.

90 [1992] AC 443.

91 Martin Mann QC.

Accordingly, the whole field is now governed by statute and, if the law is now in need of reform, it is for the legislature not the judiciary to effect it.

Recognition contrary to public policy

A foreign judgment will not be recognised and enforced in England if it is considered to be contrary to public policy. While fraud and denial of natural justice have been taken as separate heads, they are equally capable of being subsumed under this head, along with duress, coercion or undue influence[92] or, perhaps, a bizarre mode of trial or an idiosyncratic method of assessing damages.[93] However, it will not be contrary to public policy to enforce a judgment which orders the defendant to pay exemplary damages.[94]

One of the advantages of a public policy head is flexibility, although, to some, such flexibility may constitute vagueness and uncertainty. The approach has varied over the years and, apart from cases in family law, it is rare for an argument based on public policy to prevail. In *Re Macartney*,[95] Astbury J refused to recognise a Maltese judgment on grounds of public policy because he felt both that the cause of action was unknown to English law and that an indefinite award against the estate of a deceased putative father was contrary to public policy. In respect of the first ground, this cannot now stand in the light of subsequent authority.[96] In the later case of *Israel Discount Bank v Hadjipateras*,[97] it was argued that to enforce a judgment in respect of a contract procured by undue influence would be contrary to public policy. However, the court, in accepting the principle, ruled that such a defence should be raised first in the foreign court where it was equally available. It is also clear that complaints about the procedure of a foreign court which do not constitute an allegation of denial of natural justice are unlikely to find favour under this head[98] and that only allegations of criminal conduct are likely to find favour with an English court.[99]

---

92 *Israel Discount Bank of New York v Hadjipateras* [1984] 1 WLR 137.
93 *Adams v Cape Industries plc* [1990] Ch 433.
94 *SA Consortium General Textiles v Sun and Sand Agencies Ltd* [1978] QB 279.
95 [1921] 1 Ch 522 (Astbury J).
96 *Phrantzes v Argenti* [1960] 2 QB 19.
97 [1984] 1 WLR 137.
98 *Armitage v Nanchen* (1983) 4 FLR 293.
99 See *Soleimany v Soleimany* (1998) (unreported, 4 March, CA) (where, on grounds of public policy, the court refused to enforce an arbitration award vitiated by illegality).

Conflicting judgments

It is well established that an English court will not recognise and enforce a foreign judgment if it is contrary to a prior English judgment on the same subject. That such a principle exists was established conclusively in *Vervaeke v Smith*,[100] where the House of Lords upheld the refusal of Waterhouse J and the Court of Appeal to recognise a Belgian decree of nullity on the ground that it conflicted with a prior ruling of the High Court in the same matter.[101] The same principle was applied in the commercial law context in the convoluted case of *EF Man (Sugar) Ltd v Haryanto (No 2)*,[102] where the Court of Appeal ruled that it could not recognise an Indonesian judgment as being contrary to a prior ruling of an English court. In a situation where there are two conflicting foreign judgments, then it would seem that the first in time should be recognised.[103] A problem that awaits determination is the attitude the court should adopt where an English ruling is made subsequent to the foreign judgment for which recognition is sought. As a matter of principle, the English judge, if he were minded to refuse recognition, might be able to fall back upon some ground of public policy.

Judgment invalid under foreign law because of lack of internal competence

As indicated above, the state of authority on the subject of internal competence is less than harmonious. The reasons for this are probably threefold. First, several authorities have experienced difficulty with the distinction between international competence and internal competence.[104] Secondly, there has been some difference of opinion as to whether lack of internal competence renders an order void or voidable and, thirdly, there has been a willingness to characterise many defects as procedural and, thus, matters for the foreign court.

It cannot, therefore, be said that the authorities can be easily reconciled. In the case of *Vanquelin v Brouard*,[105] it was a condition precedent to the jurisdiction of the French court that the defendant was a trader; notwithstanding that the defendant was not a trader, the English court upheld

---

100 [1983] 1 AC 145.

101 *Messina v Smith* [1971] P 322; see Jaffey (1983) 32 ICLQ 500; Smart (1983) 99 LQR 24; see, also, the Family Law Act 1986, s 51.

102 (1994) 1 LR 429.

103 *Showlag v Mansour* [1995] 1 AC 431, PC (the first judgment being that of an English court).

104 At least before *Pemberton v Hughes* [1899] 1 Ch 781.

105 (1863) 15 CBNS 341.

the judgment, reasoning that the limitation relating to jurisdiction was a matter for the French court to determine; this may, indeed, reflect the 19th century approach to jurisdiction, so that, if the court was properly seized of the overall matter, it did not forfeit jurisdiction if it made an error of law. On the other hand, there are remarks by Blackburn J, in *Castrique v Imrie*,[106] that can be read as requiring internal competence. In the later case of *Pemberton v Hughes*, the judgment of Lindley MR can be read as requiring international competence, so that, if the foreign court has international competence, any subsequent error by the foreign court renders the decision no more than voidable. It would seem that, if the foreign court enjoys international competence, then any subsequent conduct will not be a defence unless it is more than a mere matter of procedure and is such a serious defect as to render the decision a nullity under the relevant foreign law.

A foreign judgment given in breach of an arbitration or jurisdiction clause

A foreign judgment will not be enforced in England if the plaintiff began proceedings in a foreign country in breach of an arbitration or jurisdiction clause. This defence arises under the terms of s 32 of the Civil Jurisdiction and Judgments Act 1982. For this particular defence to operate, the following sub-sections of s 32(1) stipulate that three conditions must be met:

(a) the bringing of the proceedings in the foreign court must be in breach of an agreement between the parties to settle the dispute otherwise than in the courts of that country;

(b) the person against whom the proceedings were brought must have neither brought nor agreed to the bringing of those proceedings; and

(c) the person against whom the proceedings were brought must not have counterclaimed or otherwise submitted to the jurisdiction of the foreign court.

The operation of s 32 was considered in the case of *Tracomin SA v Sudan Oil Seeds Co Ltd (No 1)*,[107] where the facts were as follows: a dispute arose between the Sudanese sellers of ground nuts and Swiss buyers. The contracts provided they should be governed by English law and that any dispute should be resolved by arbitration in London. Notwithstanding the terms of the contract, the buyers brought an action for damages in the Swiss courts. The sellers were unsuccessful in contesting the jurisdiction of the court on the basis of the arbitration clause. The Swiss court ruled that the arbitration clause

---

106 (1870) LR 4 HL 414, p 429.
107 [1983] 1 WLR 1026.

was invalid as not having been incorporated into the contract. No evidence was heard as to English law; by English law the arbitration clause was valid. The buyers then sought an injunction in England to restrain an arbitration in London on the basis that the judgment of the Swiss court had determined the status of the arbitration clause and effected an estoppel *per rem judicatem*.

The application was rejected by Staughton J and his judgment was upheld by the Court of Appeal.[108] The reasoning of Staughton J was that the contract contained a valid arbitration clause and that the proceedings before the Swiss court were not brought with the consent of the sellers. Having regard to the terms of s 33 of the Civil Jurisdiction and Judgments Act 1982, the conduct of the sellers in seeking to contest the jurisdiction did not constitute a submission to the jurisdiction of the court. In these circumstances, the Swiss judgment would not be recognised and no injunction should be granted.[109]

Multiple damages

The Protection of Trading Interests Act 1980[110] was passed to counter the extra territorial effect of the anti-trust legislation of the USA.[111] One of the elements of the US legislation is that a defendant may be required to pay to the plaintiff multiple damages in respect of anti-competitive conduct.[112] Under s 5(2) of the legislation, a UK court cannot enforce a judgment for multiple damages or a judgment based on a competition law specified by statutory instrument made by the Secretary of State under s 5(4).[113]

Discovery of fresh evidence

The normal rule is that the defendant must call all relevant evidence at the time of trial[114] but it is possible for a situation to arise where material evidence was discovered after the trial. In such circumstances, the defendant

---

108 [1983] 1 WLR 662 (Staughton J); 1 WLR 1026 (Donaldson MR, Fox, Ackner LJJ).
109 In *Tracomin SA v Sudan Oil Seeds Co Ltd (No 2)* [1983] 1 WLR 1026, the Court of Appeal granted the sellers an injunction to restrain the buyers litigating in Switzerland.
110 See *Re Westinghouse Electric Corporation* [1978] AC 547.
111 See Huntley (1981) 30 ICLQ 213; Jones [1981] CLJ 41; Lowe (1981) 75 AJIL 257; Blythe (1983) 31 AJCL 99.
112 Under the Protection of Trading Interests Act 1980, s 5(3), a judgment for multiple damages means a judgment for an amount arrived at by doubling, trebling or otherwise multiplying a sum assessed as compensation for the loss or damage sustained by the person in whose favour judgment is given.
113 See the Protection of Trading Interests (US Anti-Trust Measures) Order 1983 SI 1983/900; Protection of Trading Interests (Australian Trade Practices) Order 1988 SI 1988/569.
114 *Henderson v Henderson* (1844) 6 QB 288.

might not wish to assert fraud or infringement of the rules of natural justice; instead, he might seek to demonstrate that material evidence not available at the time of trial has come to light. Such assertions are normally greeted with a degree of judicial scepticism and, although such an argument was rejected in *De Cosse Brissac v Rathbone*,[115] there seems no reason, in theory, why it should not be advanced.

STATUTORY REGIMES FOUNDED UPON COMMON LAW

Introduction

At common law, the enforcement of a foreign judgment requires an action to be brought by writ in England.[116] The common law doctrine is that while the foreign judgment creates an obligation and is actionable in England it cannot be enforced without the bringing of a new legal action in England. In normal circumstances, the plaintiff will seek summary judgment under RSC Ord 14.[116a] The prior rule that the plaintiff had the option of suing in England on the original cause of action was abolished by s 34 of the Civil Jurisdiction and Judgments Act. Such a system of fresh legal action should be contrasted with the system of direct enforcement of judgments through registration. Two statutes make provision for enforcement by registration, namely, the Administration of Justice Act 1920 and the Foreign Judgments (Reciprocal Enforcement) Act 1933. The other two statutes which provide for registration of foreign judgments are the Civil Jurisdiction and Judgments Acts 1982 and 1991, which will be dealt with separately.

Administration of Justice Act 1920

This legislation originated with a proposal tabled at the Imperial Conference of 1911 for the reciprocal enforcement of judgments within the British Empire. A Bill based upon the Judgments Extension Act 1868[117] was prepared and circulated in 1916. However, several governments objected to strict reciprocity extending to all countries within the Empire; such proposals would have given all judgments within the Empire an equal status and this was objected to by some governments. In the event, the Lord Chancellor established a

---

115 (1861) 6 H & N 301.

116 The basis of the action being *indebitatus assumpsit; Grant v Easton* (1883) 13 QBD 302.

116a A recent example being *Murthy v Sivajothi* (1998) *The Times*, 11 November, CA.

117 Under the terms of the Judgments Extension Act 1868, the judgments of a superior court in England, Scotland and Ireland became reciprocally registrable on satisfying certain formal criteria and could be enforced as if it were a judgment of the court where it was registered.

committee under Lord Sumner[118] to investigate the problem and it produced its report in 1919.[119] The Committee recommended a cautious approach and its recommendations formed the basis of Part II of the Administration of Justice Act 1920.

When Part II of the Administration of Justice Act 1920 has been extended by Order in Council to any Commonwealth country outside the UK,[120] then a judgment creditor of a superior court may, provided the judgment is for a fixed sum of money[121] and the application is made within 12 months of the original judgment,[122] apply to the High Court in England or Northern Ireland or the Court of Session in Scotland[123] to have the judgment registered in that court. Registration is not automatic and depends on the discretion of the court, which must be satisfied that it is just and convenient that the judgment be enforced.[124] If the judgment is so registered, then the judgment shall from the date of registration have the same force and effect as if it were a judgment of a court of the country in which it was registered.[125]

The Act was extended to a large number of Commonwealth countries and will continue to apply even if they cease to be members of the Commonwealth. However, the legislation only applies to those countries that have established reciprocal arrangements for the recognition of judgments given in the courts of the UK. The list of countries to which the legislation applies is a long one;[126] it cannot be extended to any further country following the coming into effect of the Foreign Judgments (Reciprocal Enforcement) Act 1933.

The original court must have jurisdiction under its own internal rules[127] and the court must possess international jurisdiction in the sense understood at common law. In particular, the defendant, individual or corporate, must have been ordinarily resident or carrying on business or have submitted to the jurisdiction.[128]

---

118 *Report of the Committee Appointed by the Lord Chancellor to Consider the Conduct of Legal Proceedings Between Parties in this Country and Parties Abroad and the Enforcement of Judgments and Awards* (Cmnd 251, 1919).

119 Reporting to the then Lord Chancellor, Lord Birkenhead (1919–22).

120 Administration of Justice Act 1920, s 14.

121 *Ibid*, s 12.

122 *Ibid*, s 9(1).

123 *Ibid*, s 9(1).

124 *Ibid*, s 9(1).

125 *Ibid*, s 9(3)(a).

126 Reciprocal Enforcement of Judgments (Administration of Justice Act 1920, Pt II) (Consolidation) Order 1984 SI 1984/129, as amended by 1985 SI 1985/1994.

127 Administration of Justice Act 1920, s 9(2)(a).

128 *Ibid*, s 9(2)(b).

The basic defences at common law are given statutory expression, but the common law cases will provide authority as to the nature of each defence.[129] Thus, no judgment can be registered if vitiated by fraud[130] or has been secured as an infringement of the rules of natural justice[131] or would be contrary to public policy.[132] Registration will not be granted if an appeal is pending or if the court is persuaded that the defendant intends to appeal.[133]

A foreign judgment will not be recognised if given in an action brought in defiance of a jurisdiction or arbitration agreement unless the defendant submitted to the jurisdiction.[134]

A plaintiff is not deprived of his entitlement to enforce at common law,[135] but if he chooses to do so, in respect of a judgment capable of registration, then he will be subject to a penalty as to costs, unless an application for registration has previously been refused or unless the court otherwise orders.[136]

Foreign Judgments (Reciprocal Enforcement) Act 1933

The twin objectives of promoting the direct enforcement of foreign judgments and facilitating the enforcement of English judgments was taken further by the enactment of Part I of the Foreign Judgments (Reciprocal Enforcement) Act 1933.[137] In similar terms to Part II of the Administration of Justice Act 1920, the legislation only pertains to those countries to which its provisions have been extended by Order in Council on the basis of reciprocity.[138] The legislation has been extended only to a limited number of countries.[139]

When an Order in Council has been made, then a judgment creditor[140] may apply to the High Court in England or Northern Ireland or the Court of Session in Scotland at any time within six years of the original final

---

129 *Owens Bank Ltd v Bracco* [1992] 2 AC 443.

130 Administration of Justice Act 1920, s 9(2)(a).

131 *Ibid*, s 9(2)(c).

132 *Ibid*, s 9(2)(f).

133 *Ibid*, s 9(2)(e).

134 Civil Jurisdiction and Judgments Act 1982, s 32.

135 *Yukon Consolidated Gold Corporation v Clark* [1938] 2 KB 241.

136 Administration of Justice Act 1920, s 9(5).

137 For background, see Gutteridge (1932) 13 BYIL 61; *Report of the Foreign Judgments (Reciprocal Enforcement) Committee* (Cmnd 4213, 1932).

138 Foreign Judgments (Reciprocal Enforcement) Act 1933, s 1(1).

139 The legislation has been extended to Australian Capital Territory, Bangladesh, Canada, Guernsey, India, Israel, Jersey, Pakistan, Surinam and Tonga. Although the legislation was also extended to a number of European countries (Austria, France, Germany, Belgium, Netherlands and Norway), this is of limited relevance in the light of the Brussels and Lugano Conventions.

140 Applies also to arbitration awards; see the Foreign Judgments (Reciprocal Enforcement) Act 1933, s 10A.

judgment[141] for the judgment to be registered.[142] As under the 1920 Act, a registered judgment shall, for the purposes of execution, be of the same force and effect as one given in the registering court.[143] Unlike the 1920 Act, there is no discretion to refuse registration to a judgment which falls within the terms of the Act. Though registration cannot be refused, it can, on the application of the judgment debtor, be set aside.

Registration will be set aside if the judgment is not a recognised judgment or the court did not have jurisdiction.[144] In respect of actions *in personam*, jurisdiction will be established if the individual defendant was resident within the jurisdiction or the corporate defendant had its principal place of business there.[145] If the defendant, whether individual or corporate, had a place of business in the country of the original court and the dispute related to a transaction effected through that place of business, the court will have jurisdiction on that basis.[146] Submission to the jurisdiction by agreement, by taking advantage of the process there, whether as plaintiff or counterclaimant or otherwise[147] voluntarily appearing, will also confer jurisdiction.[148]

The registration must be set aside if the judgment was obtained by fraud[149] or if the defendant did not receive sufficient notice of the proceedings and did not appear in them,[150] or if the enforcement of the judgment would be contrary to public policy,[151] or the action in the original court was brought in breach of a jurisdiction or arbitration agreement.[152] The registering court has a discretion to set aside the registration if it is satisfied that there is a previous final and conclusive judgment on the identical dispute by a jurisdictionally competent court.[153]

By virtue of the provisions of s 6, no action at common law could be brought to enforce a judgment that was registrable under the Act. Because of the non-merger rule, this did not prevent a plaintiff suing on the original

---

141 Has to be a judgment of a recognised court or tribunal: Foreign Judgments (Reciprocal Enforcement) Act 1933, ss 10–11.

142 Foreign Judgments (Reciprocal Enforcement) Act 1933, s 2.

143 *Ibid*, s 2.

144 *Ibid*, s 4(1)(a)(i), (ii).

145 *Ibid*, s 4(2)(a)(iv).

146 *Ibid*, s 4(2)(a)(v).

147 Including participating in an appeal; *SA Consortium General Textiles v Sun and Sand Agencies Ltd* [1978] QB 279.

148 Foreign Judgments (Reciprocal Enforcement) Act 1933, s 4(2)(a)(i), (ii), (iii).

149 *Ibid*, s 4(1)(a)(iv); *Syal v Heyward* [1948] 2 KB 443.

150 *Ibid*, s 4(1)(a)(iii).

151 *Ibid*, s 4(1)(a)(v).

152 Civil Jurisdiction and Judgments Act 1982, s 32.

153 Foreign Judgments (Reciprocal Enforcement) Act 1933, s 4(1)(b); see *Vervaeke v Smith* [1983] 1 AC 145.

cause of action; this course is no longer open, having regard to the provisions of s 34 of the Civil Jurisdiction and Judgments Act 1982. No foreign judgment can be registered and enforced that is at variance with the provisions of the Protection of Trading Interests Act 1980 in relation to the award of multiple damages.

The legislation contains, in Part II, provisions[154] relating to recognition and, while the provisions of s 8 are not confined to where there has been a money judgment, it would seem that recognition can only be accorded to a judgment on the merits[155] and matrimonial proceedings are unlikely to be within the ambit of the section.[156]

---

154 Foreign Judgments (Reciprocal Enforcement) Act 1933, s 8.
155 *Black Clawson International Ltd v Papierwerke Waldhof Aschaffenburg AG* [1975] AC 591.
156 *Maples v Maples* [1988] Fam 14.

CHAPTER 15

RECOGNITION AND ENFORCEMENT UNDER THE BRUSSELS AND LUGANO CONVENTIONS

INTRODUCTION

The provisions of Art 220 of the Treaty of Rome 1957[1] committed Member States to enter into negotiations to secure 'the simplification of formalities governing the reciprocal recognition and enforcement of judgments of courts or tribunals and of arbitration awards'. Thus, the original initiative which gave rise to the Brussels Convention on Jurisdiction and the Enforcement of Judgments in Civil and Commercial Matters 1968 was not prompted by the varying bases of jurisdiction employed by the six Member States of the then European Economic Community but by the need to establish community wide recognition of the judgments of individual States.

In the course of preparing the Brussels Convention 1968, the draftsmen concluded that the Convention would not endure unless there was trust and confidence between the various jurisdictions. In particular, it was necessary to ensure that courts did not assume jurisdiction upon too wide a basis; thus, it was decided that strict and detailed provisions on jurisdiction were a precondition to a liberal regime on the recognition and enforcement of judgments. This has had the consequence that an individual is now unlikely to ignore legal proceedings in Country A, intending only to dispute the matter when an attempt is made to enforce the judgment in Country B.[2] The liberal regime on recognition has tended to lead to more attempts being made to question jurisdiction; this is, indeed, as the draftsmen had intended. The Convention adopts a particular theory and detailed rules as to jurisdiction; the intention is that the defendant should contest the matter at the earliest opportunity. If he is unsuccessful in persuading the court to decline jurisdiction, then he will be prompted to contest the matter vigorously on the merits, knowing that any judgment given will be, in principle, recognised and enforceable elsewhere. Under the common law system, a defendant might be minded to ignore the proceedings elsewhere so that he could raise enough points to re-open the entire matter when an attempt was made to enforce the judgment. Thus, one should approach the Brussels Convention as a document that attempts to provide for a system of jurisdiction (strict and designed to avoid a multiplicity of proceedings) with a system of recognition and

---

1   These are part of the original Treaty of Rome 1957, drawn up by the drafting committee 1955–57.

2   As, indeed, was the case in *Syal v Heyward* [1948] 2 KB 443.

enforcement of judgments (liberal and designed to avoid the reopening of the same case).

The European scheme, in respect of the recognition of judgments, is alien to traditional English ways in two particular respects, namely, that the concept of a judgment extends beyond the purely money judgment recognised at common law; and, as a broad principle, the court which is asked to recognise and enforce the judgment cannot investigate the jurisdiction of the original court.

A second important matter to bear in mind is that questions on interpretation of the Convention will be referred to the European Court of Justice, who, in producing an answer to any reference, will be influenced not by the details of a single dispute, but a desire to ensure that the Convention constitutes a coherent scheme in respect of both jurisdiction and enforcement.[3]

The first part of the Brussels Convention is divided into three parts, namely: (a) Title I (the scope of the convention); (b) Title II (the provisions relating to jurisdiction); and (c) Title III (the provisions relating to the recognition and enforcement of judgments); as the case law indicates, these three parts relate closely to each other. As regards recognition, the philosophy of Title III is well expressed by the first paragraph of Art 26, which reads 'A judgment given in a Contracting State shall be recognised in other Contracting States without any special procedure being required'. In respect of enforcement, the matter is clearly set out in the first paragraph of Art 31, which reads:

> A judgment given in a Contracting State and enforceable in that State shall be enforced in another Contracting State when, on the application of any interested party, it has been declared enforceable there.

This broad principle requires some, though not much, qualification and some explanation of the mechanisms for recognition and enforcement which the Convention seeks to establish. The first matter that requires consideration is the concept of a 'judgment' and it is to this matter one must now turn.

JUDGMENTS FALLING WITHIN TITLE III

Article 25 of the Brussels Convention contains a broad definition of a 'judgment' and reads as follows:

> For the purposes of this Convention, 'judgment' means any judgment given by a court or tribunal of a Contracting State, whatever the judgment may be called, including a decree, order, decision or writ of execution, as well as the determination of costs or expenses by an officer of the court.

---

3   As an example of the approach, see *De Wolf v Cox* (Case 42/76) [1976] ECR 1759; [1977] 2 CMLR 43; Hartley [1977] 2 ELR 146.

This definition requires a degree of amplification.

First, for a judgment to fall within the terms of Title III it must be given 'by a court or tribunal of a Contracting State' and then provision is made for it to 'be recognised in the other Contracting State'.[4] Thus, the provisions only apply to international recognition so that from the perspective of an English court a judgment given by a court in Northern Ireland or Scotland does not meet this requirement.[5] Secondly, the judgment must relate to a matter within the scope of Title I; thus, while the Brussels Convention applies to civil and commercial matters a number of areas are excluded from its application, for example, wills and succession, personal status and matrimonial property.[6] Where a case falls outside the Convention, any recognition and enforcement of the judgment in England will depend on the common law rules or on the bilateral treaties which the UK may have with other Contracting States.[7]

There are other international conventions which are expressly preserved by the Convention. Thus, if a convention exists in respect of a specific matter and it has rules on recognition and enforcement of judgments, then those rules will apply rather than the rules stipulated in Title III.

Thirdly, a judgment under the Convention, that is, one relating to a civil or commercial matter, will be recognised and enforced in other Contracting States irrespective of whether the defendant is domiciled in a Contracting State. So, a judgment given against an 'outsider', whether or not at the suit of an 'insider', and whether or not within the exclusive jurisdiction rule of Art 16 or the jurisdiction agreement provisions of Art 17, is subject to the recognition rules of the Conventions.[8] If, therefore, an English court takes jurisdiction at common law in a contractual action between a New York domiciliary and a Japanese domiciliary, whose only connection with England is that they expressed a choice of English law as the governing law of the contract, the English judgment would be entitled to recognition and enforcement in, say, France. Equally, an English court has to recognise and enforce a judgment of a French court, which has taken jurisdiction on some 'exorbitant' ground of its own, provided that the subject matter of the case falls within the Conventions.

A fourth qualification arises as to the nature of the judgment; unlike at common law, there is no requirement that the judgment be final and

---

4   See the text of the Brussels Convention 1968, Arts 25, 26, when read together.
5   This matter is dealt with in domestic legislation; see the Civil Jurisdiction and Judgments Act 1982, s 18, Scheds 6, 7.
6   Brussels Convention 1968, Title I, Art 1.
7   *Ibid*, Art 56.
8   The provision for the automatic recognition of judgments in respect of defendants domiciled in non-Contracting States has attracted some comment; see Nadelmann [1967] 5 CMLR 409; Nadelmann (1967) 64 Col Law Rev 995; Bartlett (1975) 25 ICLQ 44; Von Mehren (1981) 81 Col Law Rev 1044.

conclusive. In *De Cavel v De Cavel*,[9] the European Court of Justice held that the Brussels Convention could apply to an interlocutory order made by a French judge in the course of divorce proceedings. Thus, in principle, a provisional or protective order is enforceable. However, by virtue of Art 27(2) of the Brussels Convention (1968) where an order is granted *ex parte* or for some other reason the defendant is not heard, then recognition will be denied.[10] A consistent theme of the jurisprudence of the European Court of Justice has been the desire to preserve the rights of the defendant to be heard, so that in the case of default judgments particular defences arise and specific evidentiary burdens are placed on the party seeking to enforce.[11] Thus, a Mareva injunction[12] or Anton Piller order[13] will normally fall foul of the defence afforded by Art 27(2). The objection to enforcement relates to whether the defendant had a chance to be represented at the hearing, not whether the injunction granted was provisional, interim or permanent.[14]

Thus, in *EMI Records v Modern Music Karl-Ulrich Walterbach GmbH*, Hobhouse J refused recognition to a judgment by way of injunction where the defendant had not been given prior notice of the proceedings and no documents had been served.[15] If the intention is to prevent the removal of assets, then an application for protective measures can be made in each of the Contracting States in which the defendant holds assets.[16]

RECOGNITION AND ENFORCEMENT

The essence of the Brussels Convention is summed up in the first paragraph of Art 26, which reads 'A judgment given in a Contracting State shall be recognised in a Contracting State without any special procedure being required'. Section 1 (Arts 26–30) contains no particular provisions relating to recognition. However, if enforcement is desired, then the provisions under s 2

---

9   *De Cavel v De Cavel* (Case 143/78) [1979] ECR 1055; 2 CMLR 547; *De Cavel v De Cavel (No 2)* (Case 120/79) [1980] ECR 731; 3 CMLR 1.

10 Brussels Convention 1968, Art 27(2); see *Denilaouler v SNC; Couchet Frères* (Case 125/79) [1980] ECR 1553; [1981] 1 CMLR 62.

11 *Klomps v Michel* (Case 166/80) [1981] ECR 1593; [1982] 2 CMLR 773; Hartley (1982) 7 ELR 419.

12 Such injunctions emerged in the mid-1970s, granted by an English court to restrain a defendant disposing of assets in advance of judgment: *Nippon Yusen Kaisha v Karagorgis* [1975] 1 WLR 1093; *Mareva v International Bulkcarriers* [1975] 2 LR 509.

13 An order granted normally *ex parte* in the Chancery Division to enable the plaintiff to enter premises and inspect documents; first granted in *EMI Ltd v Pandit* [1975] 1 WLR 302, the process was validated in *Anton Piller KG v Manufacturing Processes Ltd* [1976] Ch 55.

14 *EMI Records v Modern Music Karl-Ulrich Walterbach GmbH* [1992] 1 QB 115.

15 [1992] 1 QB 115.

16 Brussels Convention 1968, Art 24; see, also, the Civil Jurisdiction and Judgments Act 1982, ss 24–25.

(Arts 31–45) will become relevant. The European Court of Justice has ruled that, if enforcement is sought under the Convention, then the relevant rules as to enforcement must be observed; there is no option of using informal, cheaper national rules. This principle emerged from the ruling in *De Wolf v Cox*.[17]

De Wolf had obtained judgment in Belgium against the defendant. Instead of seeking to enforce judgment in the Netherlands under the terms of the Convention, the defendant brought a fresh legal action because the procedure under the recovery of small debts procedure was cheaper. On appeal, the *Hoge Raad* (the Supreme Court of the Netherlands) made a reference to the European court of Justice to determine whether Art 31 precluded other methods of enforcement.

The European Court of Justice ruled that, once a judgment had been given within the scope of the Convention, then enforcement was required to be under the terms of the Convention alone. In reviewing the broad policy of the Convention, the European Court considered that, if the rule were otherwise, then a number of undesirable consequences might arise. First, the court of the enforcing State might be tempted to examine the merits of the original judgment;[18] secondly, there was a danger of producing a conflicting judgment that would thwart recognition of the original judgment. As is common with the European Court, the judges considered the overall objectives of the entire Convention and noted that the draftsmen had gone to considerable lengths in Arts 21–23 to reduce the risk of conflicting judgments by restricting the possibility of two sets of proceedings in respect of the same matter. Moreover, if individual national methods of enforcement were allowed to pertain alongside the Convention and there was a risk that a creditor might be able to obtain two orders of enforcement in respect of the same debt.

Thus, enforcement is required to be in accordance with ss 2 and 3 (Arts 31–49) of the Conventions as implemented in the UK and given effect to by the Civil Jurisdiction and Judgments Act 1982.[19] In England, an application to register a judgment will be made to a Master of the Queen's Bench Division;[20] the Convention stipulates the documentation that is required to be produced by an applicant[21] and, in the case of default judgments, requires evidence that the party in default was served with the document instituting the proceedings.[22]

---

17 *De Wolf v Cox* (Case 42/76) [1976] ECR 1759; [1977] 2 CMLR 43; Hartley (1977) 2 ELR 146.

18 A course that is prohibited under Art 29.

19 Civil Jurisdiction and Judgments Act 1982, ss 4–8; RSC Ord 71.

20 *Ibid*, s 4; Brussels Convention 1968, Art 32.

21 Brussels Convention 1968, Arts 33, 46, 47.

22 *Ibid*, Art 46(2).

The application for registration will be made *ex parte* to the Master.[23] At this stage, the defendant has no entitlement to be heard and no right to be informed of the registration proceedings. The object of providing for an *ex parte* procedure is to prevent the defendant acquiring notice so that he might be tempted to remove his assets from the jurisdiction. If the application to register is granted, then notice must be served on the affected person. By virtue of Art 36, if the party is domiciled in that State, then he has one month in which to lodge an appeal against registration; if he is domiciled in another Contracting State, then an appeal must be lodged within two months. In England, an appeal will be to a single judge of the Queen's Bench Division.[24] The Brussels Convention provides that thereafter there can only be one further appeal on point of law; it can be either to the Court of Appeal (Civil Division) or direct to the House of Lords under the terms the Administration of Justice Act 1969.[25] In like terms, where a Master refuses registration there is an appeal against a refusal to enforce[26] and one further appeal thereafter on a point of law.[27] Interest is recoverable on money judgments provided that it was recoverable in the Contracting State in which judgment was given.[28]

DEFENCES TO RECOGNITION AND ENFORCEMENT

The Brussels Convention lists a limited number of matters that can be raised as defences to recognition[29] and enforcement[30] of a judgment.

Public policy[31]

A judgment will not be recognised if is contrary to the public policy of the recognising State. It has to be acknowledged at the outset that the public policy defence is narrower than that available at common law and is subject to the limitations on its exercise as declared by the European Court of Justice. This head cannot be used to criticise the judgment of the original court[32] nor, indeed, save in limited circumstances, should it be employed to review the

---

23 Brussels Convention 1968, Art 34(1).
24 *Ibid*, Art 37; see, also, RSC Ord 71, stipulating details of appeal.
25 See the Civil Jurisdiction and Judgments Act 1982, s 6; Administration of Justice Act 1969, Pt II.
26 Brussels Convention 1968, Art 40.
27 *Ibid*, Art 41.
28 Civil Jurisdiction and Judgments Act 1982, s 7.
29 Brussels Convention 1968, Arts 27, 28.
30 *Ibid*, Art 34.
31 *Ibid*, Art 27(1).
32 *Ibid*, Arts 29, 34, para 3.

jurisdiction of the original court.[33] Whether the court making the original judgment was exercising jurisdiction under the Convention or not, the recognising court cannot, in most cases, question the court's jurisdiction or apply the public policy defence to recognition on the basis of an objection to the original court's jurisdictional process.[34]

It can, of course, as we have seen, question whether the judgment comes within the terms of the Conventions, that is, whether or not it is upon a civil or commercial matter. The original court's jurisdiction may be questioned, however, if it was taken in defiance of the special jurisdictional rules applicable to insurance or consumer contracts or the exclusive jurisdiction provisions of Art 16, or if jurisdiction was taken contrary to the provisions of another convention protected under Art 59. So, for example, a court of a Contracting State, which was not a court of the *situs* of the property, which took jurisdiction in a case falling under Art 16(1), relating to immovable property, could not expect its judgment to be recognised or enforced under the Convention. Similarly, an original court which took jurisdiction in an action brought by a supplier against the consumer on the sole basis of Art 5(1) – place of performance – would be acting outside the Conventions. Even here, however, the recognising court would be bound by any finding of fact made by the original court.[35] The distinction made between a finding of fact and a ruling of law in the area of jurisdiction is not an easy distinction to make. Suppose the original court in the consumer case above took jurisdiction under Art 5(1) because it did not regard the contract as a consumer contract. Suppose it decided that the unpaid Cannes hotel bill related to a contract which, while it fulfilled all the other requirements of a consumer contract, was made within a 'resting' film actor's trade or profession when he went to the film festival in the hope of being noticed and offered employment. Is this a finding of fact or a ruling of law?

Although there is no express reference within the Brussels Convention, it has always been assumed that a judgment obtained by fraud can be raised under the public policy objection. However, not only is this objection narrower than at common law, it would seem that the circumstances in which a case of fraud can be sustained will be very limited indeed. This emerged from the case of *Interdesco SA v Nullifire Ltd*,[36] where the facts were as follows: the plaintiffs had obtained judgment in France in respect of claims under a distribution agreement. The defendants lodged an appeal in France alleging fraud while seeking to stay enforcement provisions in England under Art 38.

---

33 Brussels Convention 1968, Art 28, para 3.
34 *Ibid*, Art 28, para 3.
35 *Ibid*, Art 28, para 2.
36 (1992) 1 LR 180 (Phillips J).

In refusing the application of the defendants, Phillips J made a number of points in the course of his judgment that indicated the limited circumstances in which fraud can be invoked. The learned judge observed (a) that in normal circumstances an English court will not act on evidence of fraud if it has been before the original court and rejected by it; (b) if new material comes to light subsequent to the original trial, then, in normal circumstances, this should be raised in the courts of State of trial not before the enforcing court; (c) that an enforcing court in England could not act to refuse registration on evidence less demanding than that to set aside an English judgment. It would seem, therefore, that enforcement can only be resisted by unambiguous evidence of fraud that emerges so late that it cannot be considered by any trial or appeal court in the original State.

As a public policy objection to the original court's jurisdictional rules is expressly ruled out[37] and as 'under no circumstances may a foreign judgment be reviewed as to its substance'[38] and as a denial of natural justice is otherwise catered for,[39] it is difficult to imagine, other than fraud, what content the public policy objection might have or what form it might take. In these circumstances, it would seem that claims are likely to be based on either fraud, an offensive procedure or an extravagant award of damages.

Natural justice

Article 27(2) provides that a judgment shall not be recognised 'where it was given in default of appearance, if the defendant was not duly served with the document which instituted the proceedings or with an equivalent document in sufficient time to enable him to arrange for his defence'. These provisions complement the provisions set out in Art 20 that concern the obligations of the original court in respect of natural justice. The fact that the original court considers the defendant to have been validly served does not preclude the enforcing court from reaching a different conclusion. Thus, in *Pendy Plastic Products v Pluspunkt*[40] the European Court of Justice observed on a reference from Germany:

> The court of the State in which enforcement is sought may, if it considers that the conditions laid down by Art 27(2) of the Brussels Convention are fulfilled, refuse to grant recognition and enforcement of a judgment, even though the court of the State in which the judgment was given regarded it as proven ... that the defendant, who failed to enter an appearance, had an opportunity to receive service of the document in sufficient time to enable him to make arrangements for his defence.

37 Brussels Convention 1968, Art 28, para 3.
38 *Ibid*, Art 29; Art 34, para 3.
39 *Ibid*, Art 27(2).
40 (Case 228/81) [1982] ECR 2723.

Allegations of non-compliance with rules of procedural justice have formed a significant number of references to the European Court of Justice. The wording of Art 27(2) embraces a number of elements, namely:

(a) the giving of a judgment in default;

(b) the failure to serve the defendant:

- with the document which instituted the proceedings or with an equivalent document; and

- in sufficient time for him to arrange for his defence.

The European Court of Justice has taken the general approach that the letter and spirit of procedural justice must be observed; this is evidenced by a large number of cases[41] and it is consistent with the approach of the European Court of Justice in other areas of community law.[42] In broad terms, the cases will be either that the defendant was not served or properly served or, if he was served, he did not have sufficient time to arrange for his defence.

The case law indicates that a defendant cannot rely on Art 27(2) if he participated fully in the original hearing on the merits.[43] However, he can rely on the defence if he merely made an application to set aside a judgment already given.[44] Whether a defendant has been served at all is a matter to be determined by examining the relevant facts and the contents of the rules of civil procedure of the State in question.[45] In the context of sufficiency of service, it is important for the court to take a broad view of the matter; normally, time will run from the date that service has been effected, but it would seem from the judgments in *Klomps v Michel* and *Debaeker v Bowman*[46] that the court must look at the entire history of the matter and this may involve reviewing conduct subsequent to service. This is illustrated by *Debaeker v Bowman* where the facts were as follows: the plaintiff and defendant were in dispute about a flat in Antwerp. The defendant left without leaving a forwarding address. The plaintiff, in accordance with Belgian law, served proceedings at the local police station. At a later date, the defendant sent his actual address. The plaintiff did not respond, but instead obtained judgment in default. When the plaintiff applied to enforce the judgment in the Netherlands, the defendant argued that he had insufficient time to arrange his defence.

---

41 For various aspects, see *Klomps v Michel* (Case 166/80) [1981] ECR 1593; [1982] 2 CMLR 773; *Pendy Plastic Products v Pluspunkt GmbH* (Case 228/81) [1982] ECR 2723; [1981] 1 CMLR 665; *Debaeker v Bowman* (Case 49/84) [1985] ECR 1779; [1986] 2 CMLR 400; *Isabelle Lancray SA v Peters und Sichert KG* (Case 305/88) [1990] ECR 2725.

42 *British Aerospace plc and Rover Group Holdings plc v E Commission* (Case 292/90) [1992] 1 CMLR 853, in the context of Arts 92–94.

43 *Sontag v Waidman* (Case 172/91) [1993] ECR 1693.

44 *Klomps v Michel* (Case 166/80) [1981] ECR 1593; [1982] 2 CMLR 773.

45 *Ibid.*

46 *Ibid* and *Debaeker v Bowman* [1985] ECR 1779.

In responding to the reference, the European Court of Justice ruled that the enforcing court was obliged to review the entire facts, paying regard to the conduct of both plaintiff and defendant. It would seem that sufficiency of time is a factual matter and this will involve reviewing the evidence and considering whether the proper inference is that the defendant did or did not have sufficient time to arrange his defence.[47] In normal cases, this will involve sufficient time to consult a lawyer and for that lawyer to absorb the central elements of the case and to advise. In a complicated and technical case with large volumes of documentary evidence, then more time will be needed than in a case where the history of the matter is brief and the legal issues straightforward.

Procedural justice involves not only being aware of the fact of proceedings but, also, of the detailed allegations made. In *Isabelle Lancray v Peters und Sichert KG*,[48] the defendant objected that service had not been made in German or, as a minimum, the French documentation had not been accompanied by a translation. The court in France disregarded the objections of the defendant because they had been written in German and judgment was entered. The enforcing court in Germany made a reference to the European Court of Justice which held that, where the local rules of civil procedure embrace a requirement as to translation of documents, then that must be strictly complied with; otherwise, to countenance such omissions would be to undermine the ideal of due and proper service. The judgment reveals the traditional approach of the European Court of Justice in asking whether the scheme and philosophy of the Convention would be undermined if the individual conduct in issue were to become common.

In most cases, it will not be difficult to establish the document 'which institutes the proceedings'; but, in cases of doubt, it has been ruled that it is the document which, when served on the defendant, enables him to assert his rights before an enforceable judgment is given.[49] At first blush, it might be thought that the European Court of Justice has been unduly favourable in respect of references under Art 27(2). However, it should be borne in mind that procedural justice is regarded as an aspect of the doctrine of the rule of law and the European Court of Justice has never hesitated to stress the importance of European integration being based upon the rule of law. In a different context to the enforcement of judgments, the court alluded to 'the general principle of good administration to the effect that an administration which has to take decisions, even legally, which cause serious detriment to the

---

47   *Klomps v Michel* (Case 166/80) [1981] ECR 1593.
48   (Case 305/88) [1990] ECR I-2725.
49   *Minalmet GmbH v Brandeis Ltd* (Case 123/91) [1992] 1 ECR 5661.

person concerned, must allow the latter to make known their point of view, unless there is a serious reason for not doing so'.[50]

Irreconcilable judgments

Article 27(3) provides that the recognising court shall refuse recognition if the judgment of the original court, given in a dispute between the same parties, is irreconcilable with one of its own. The operative provision affords a defence 'if the judgment is irreconcilable with a judgment given in a dispute between the same parties in the State in which recognition is sought'. There is no first come first served rule here, so that judgments may be in either order or contemporaneous. Certain provisions of Title II relating to *lis pendens* and related actions are designed to prevent a situation arising in which there are multiple proceedings and irreconcilable judgments[51] but even actions which are neither the same nor related may produce judgments which conflict. Irreconcilable judgments may also arise, either because related proceedings are being conducted in a non-Contracting State or because proceedings in a Contracting State are outside the scope of Title I. Under Art 27(3), irreconcilability must be between the original judgment and a judgment of the recognising court – irreconcilability between two judgments of different original courts which the recognising court is asked to recognise, or between two judgments of the same original court, is not addressed by the provision. The European Court has ruled in *Hoffman v Krieg*[52] that the enforcing court must examine the text of the judgments to determine whether they indicate legal consequences which are mutually exclusive. Such would be the case in *Hoffman v Krieg*,[53] where a German court had ordered a husband to maintain his wife as part of his conjugal obligations while a subsequent judgment in Holland had pronounced a divorce.

It should be noted that the provisions of Art 27(3) relate to 'a dispute between the same parties in the State in which recognition is sought.' Thus, an attempt to register an Italian judgment that is incompatible with a judgment in Scotland will be rejected by a court in England. There may be difficulties about the precise meaning of the word 'given'; it is possible to conceive of a situation in which a judgment is given in State A and recognised in State B and then, at a later date, a judgment is given in State C and recognition and enforcement is sought in State B. Does the recognition of the earlier judgment

---

50 *Kuhner* (Cases 33 and 75/79) [1980] ECR 1671, p 1698; see, also, *Transocean Marine Paint Association v Commission* (Case 17/74) [1974] ECR 1063; 2 CMLR 459.

51 Brussels Convention 1968, Arts 6, 21–23.

52 (Case 145/86) [1988] ECR 645; Hartley (1991) 16 ELR 64.

53 The case was followed in England in *Macaulay v Macaulay* [1991] 1 All ER 866, where an English court failed to recognise an Irish maintenance order.

in State B constitute a giving of judgment? Common sense and the strict wording of Art 27(3) would appear to indicate otherwise.

A further problem arises in respect of judgments given in non-Contracting States and this is addressed by Art 27(5), which provides that a judgment shall not be recognised 'if the judgment is irreconcilable with an earlier judgment given in a non-Contracting State involving the same cause of action and between the same parties, provided that this latter judgment fulfills the conditions necessary for its recognition in the State addressed'. Thus, if there is an existing judgment by a court of a non-Contracting State on the same cause of action between the same parties, the recognising State is obliged to go through the process required by Art 27(5). To take an example: suppose there are judgments in civil and commercial matters given by a court in California and a court in Germany, which appear to be irreconcilable. The recognising court will have to consider whether the judgment given in California meets the common law requirements for recognition and then it will determine whether the judgment is *prima facie* enforceable under the Brussels Convention. If the answer to both questions is in the affirmative and the judgment in California was given first, then the German judgment will be refused recognition. Thus, for Art 27(5) to arise, it must be demonstrated:

(a) the judgment given in the non-Contracting State was first in time;

(b) that it is entitled to recognition in England;

(c) that it is irreconcilable with the later judgment given in a Contracting state;

(d) that it involves the same cause of action and the same parties.

The Convention itself is silent on the question of conflicting judgments given by the courts of Contracting States; the hope of the draftsmen was that proper application of the jurisdictional provisions in Arts 21–23 would prevent the matter arising.

Rulings on preliminary issues

A particular defence arises under Art 27(4) in respect to preliminary rulings as to status. The defence in Art 27(4) allows any court outside the State of origin to make its own determination of status:

> ... if the court of the State of origin ... has decided a preliminary question concerning the status or legal capacity of natural persons, rights in property arising out of a matrimonial relationship, wills or succession in a way that conflicts with a rule of the private international law of the State in which recognition is sought, unless the same result would have been reached by the application of the rules of private international law of that State.

The effect of the provision is that each State reserves the right to determine the status of persons under its own rules of private international law. The provision will not arise very often but it could arise where, say, a German court held A and B to be married and made a maintenance order in favour of B; such an order would not be recognised if English rules of private international law held that A and B were not married.

Appeals and other matters

There are no other bases for refusing recognition or enforcement.[54] The fact that a judgment is subject to appeal is not a reason for refusing recognition or enforcement. However, the recognising court may stay the proceedings if an appeal has been lodged in the original court system[55] and the person against whom the judgment is intended to be enforced may apply for a stay if an appeal has been lodged or the time for lodging one has not yet elapsed.[56] Where appeal against enforcement has been made, the recognising court must delay enforcement measures, other than those of a purely protective nature, until the appeal has been determined.

The fact that the original court assumed jurisdiction despite an agreement to refer the dispute to another court or to arbitration will probably not be a basis for refusing to recognise the judgment.[57]

Relationship with other conventions

The Brussels Convention does not affect other intentional conventions to which the UK is a party and which may provide for the recognition and enforcement of judgments.[58] Thus, defences particular to such conventions may be raised. Moreover, a judgment will not be recognised that infringes the provisions of Art 59. This Article permits the UK to enter into international agreements with non-Contracting States in relation to reciprocal arrangements for jurisdiction. Thus, the UK might agree with China not to recognise judgments given in third States based on the exorbitant bases of jurisdiction set out in Art 3. Thus, if a German court (a third State) were to give judgment against a Chinese domiciliary where jurisdiction had been assumed on that basis, then an English court would not be obliged to recognise the judgment.

---

54   Brussels Convention 1968, Art 34, para 2.

55   *Ibid*, Art 30. However, such an appeal has to be an ordinary appeal, being one that arises out of the action itself and is not a request to reopen the entire case: *Industrial Diamond Supplies v Riva* [1977] ECR 2175.

56   Brussels Convention 1968, Art 38.

57   But, see the provisions of the Civil Jurisdiction and Judgments Act 1982, s 32(4)(a).

58   Brussels Convention 1968, Art 57.

THE LUGANO CONVENTION[59]

The Lugano Convention is designed to extend the principle of the free circulation of judgments to EFTA bloc countries; the Convention has been in force since 1 January 1992 but it only applies to those States that have signed and ratified it. An important matter in relation to the recogniton of judgments is that, under the Convention, provision is made for the accession not only of future EC/EFTA Member States but also for the accession of third States. The provisions of the Lugano Convention are broadly similar to those of the Brussels Convention and it is, for that reason, sometimes referred to as the Parallel Convention.[60] One important distinction between the two instruments is that the Lugano Convention does not contain provision for references to the European Court of Justice.

In relation to the recognition of judgments, a problem arises as to the relationship between the Brussels Convention and the Lugano Convention. Article 54B of the Lugano Convention provides that, if either the original State or the addressed State is not a member of the European Community, then the Lugano Convention rather than the Brussels Convention will apply. However, if both States are members of the European Community then the Brussels Convention will govern relations *inter se*.

Although the contents of the two Conventions are, to a large extent, similar, there are a number of provisions in the Lugano Convention that might arise as defences in an enforcement action. Under Art 54B, para 3, there is a discretionary power to refuse recognition if the court in an EC State has assumed jurisdiction under a differently worded provision of the Brussels Convention. Secondly, Art 57, para 4 of the Lugano Convention restricts the operation of Art 57 of the Brussels Convention, the reason being that EFTA States were unhappy with the operation of such liberal rules. A third modification is contained in Protocol 1 of the Lugano Convention which introduces restrictions in relation to the operation of Art 16(1)(b), concerning tenancies of immovable property.

---

59 The Lugano Convention means the Convention on Jurisdiction and the Enforcement of Judgments in Civil and Commercial Matters (including the Protocols annexed to that Convention), opened for signature at Lugano on 16 September 1988 and signed by the UK on 18 September 1989.

60 The Convention was given effect in the UK by the Civil Jurisdiction and Judgments Act 1991, which became effective on 1 May 1992. In 1988, at the time of signature, the EFTA bloc countries comprised Austria, Finland, Iceland, Norway, Sweden, Switzerland.

THE RECOGNITION AND ENFORCEMENT OF JUDGMENTS WITHIN THE UK

The Brussels Convention is concerned with the relations between Contracting States and not with matters internal to a State. As has been seen earlier, separate provision has been made in respect of questions of jurisdiction arising within the UK.[61] In like terms, Parliament has made provision for the recognition and enforcement of judgments given by courts within the UK. The relevant provisions are contained in s 18 of the Civil Jurisdiction and Judgments Act 1982[62] and the Schedules thereto. The provisions of s 18 apply[63] only to civil proceedings and do not pertain to maintenance orders[64] or matters of bankruptcy or liquidation.[65] The applicant applies for a certificate from the original court (be it superior or inferior) and then seeks to register it with the superior court in the recognising jurisdiction. In respect of money judgments, the detailed procedure is set out in Sched 6 while the procedure in respect of non-money judgments is set out in Sched 7. There are limited grounds for setting aside the registration but the legislation follows the 1868 and 1882 Acts in providing that registration cannot be set aside on the basis of fraud, abuse of natural justice or on public policy grounds. A judgment falling within s 18 cannot be enforced in another part of the UK save by virtue of the registration scheme set out in Scheds 6 and 7.

Section 19 provides for the recognition of judgments given by courts in other parts of the UK; the section provides that recognition cannot be withheld on the ground that the court in question may have lacked jurisdiction according to the rules of private international law pertaining in another part of the UK.

---

61 Civil Jurisdiction and Judgments Act 1982, s 16, Sched 4.
62 Together with s 19, Scheds 6, 7.
63 Replacing the Judgments Extension Act 1868 and the Inferior Courts Judgments Extension Act 1882.
64 Civil Jurisdiction and Judgments Act 1982, s 18(3).
65 See, instead, the Insolvency Act 1986.

PART III

CHAPTER 16

THE LAW OF CONTRACT

INTRODUCTION

The approach of English conflict law to international contracts was greatly influenced by its largely laissez faire attitude to contractual terms in domestic law. The 19th century position[1] was expressed with characteristic candour by Jessel MR in *Printing and Numerical Registering Co v Sampson*, when he observed:

> ... if there is one thing more than another which public policy requires, it is that men of full age and competent understanding shall have the utmost liberty in contracting, and that their contracts, when entered into freely and voluntarily, shall be held sacred and shall be enforced by Courts of Justice.[2]

The model was an agreement freely negotiated between economic equals and the philosophy was that agreements must be honoured. Such an approach did not endure long into the 20th century as the State came under pressure to redress imbalances in bargaining power in areas such as housing[3] employment[4] and consumer contracts.[5] To suggest that the modern English law of contract is an area of non-regulation would be false.[6] Nevertheless, the business contract is not closely regulated and that was the model for, and often the reality of, international contracts.

English law leaves business parties largely free to determine the content of their contracts. Wise contracting parties will make provision for as many contingencies as they can foresee in order to minimise the disruption of the operation of the agreement and they can, if they wish, produce their own set of rules to deal with those contingencies and to dispose of any disputes that

---

1   For the relationship between 19th century political philosophy and the law of contract, see Atiyah, *The Rise and Fall of Freedom of Contract* (1979).

2   *Printing and Numerical Registering Co v Sampson* (1875) LR 19 Eq 462, p 465. George Jessel had himself served as a Liberal MP and Solicitor General in the first administration of WE Gladstone (1868–74).

3   See the Housing of the Working Classes Act 1890, leading to the Increase of Rent and Mortagage Interest (War Restrictions) Act 1915 and the volume of legislation that subsequently followed, culminating in the Rent Act 1977.

4   See the Workmen's Compensation Acts 1897, 1906; Coal Mines Regulation Act 1908; Trade Boards Act 1909; however, the subject was only to expand in the post-war period, with the Contracts of Employment Act 1963 and the Redundancy Payments Act 1965.

5   Although the courts had tried to restrict the scope of exclusion clauses prior to 1945, the central division between consumer contracts and commercial contracts was given effect to in the Supply of Goods (Implied Terms) Act 1973.

6   As illustrated by the Consumer Credit Act 1974.

may arise between them. It would be wrong to pretend that many contracts are self-governing in this full sense or that, even if they were, this would obviate the need for a court to try an issue but the possibilities are there – possibilities which English law positively encourages.

Where a contract is truly international, among the matters which prudent contractors should bear in mind are the location of, and the law to be applied in, any litigation. As an ordinary part of the agreement, a term can specify where any dispute is to be brought.

Such a term, known as a choice of jurisdiction clause, can provide that all disputes shall be litigated in the courts of a particular system and English courts are frequently chosen even by contractors who have no connection with this country. Alternatively, the parties may agree that disputes between them will be arbitrated and they proceed to specify the form and place of the arbitration. The parties can also agree the rules to govern any dispute by incorporating into the contract rules of their own invention, rules derived from an existing legal system or, more succinctly, by identifying the system of law that they wish to be applied. Such a term, known as a choice of law clause, derives its validity from the general contractual agreement but, even if it did not, it would be a contract in its own right by English law as the mutual agreement implies mutual forbearances and, thereby, satisfies the requirement of consideration. As a general proposition, then, the parties to a contract are free to include legal stipulations in precisely the same way as they include any other stipulations which determine what is to be done in the fulfillment of the agreement or what is to happen in the event of its breach or failure.

Just as many contractors are not astute enough or sufficiently well advised to make detailed contingency plans, many parties to international contracts will not advert to the issues of choice of jurisdiction or choice of law. A conflict system must, therefore, provide rules for the determination of the governing law, both for those cases in which the parties have indicated the system of law which they wish to govern their contract and for those cases where they have not.

At common law, the judges[7] developed a number of rules to determine the law to be applied to an international contract. The common law rules in private international law centred on the proper law of the contract, which was the law chosen by the parties or, in default of choice, the legal system with which the contract had the closest and most real connection.[8]

It is proposed to examine the common law rules before turning to the changes introduced into English law by the Rome Convention on the Law Applicable to Contractual Obligations 1980.[9]

---

7   In the years after 1850, with the trend becoming more pronounced after the judgment in
    P & O Steam Navigation Co v Shand (1865) 3 Moo PC (NS) 272.

8   See Mann, FA (1991) 107 LQR 353.

9   Given effect to in English law by the Contracts (Applicable Law) Act 1990, in force from
    1 April 1991.

THE COMMON LAW APPROACH

At common law, judges were confronted from the end of the 18th century with questions as to which law was to govern contractual disputes that involved a foreign element. To be more precise, the question was not 'which law is to govern the contract?' but 'which law is to govern the particular contractual issue that is before the court?'. It would have been possible to select the *lex loci contractus*,[10] but that could have been fraudulently chosen or it might have little connection with the substance of the contract and the precise *locus* might be difficult to determine until the contract had been concluded. The *lex loci solutionis* might be attractive, but it can cause difficulties if the contract is bilateral and each party has to perform in a different country. English law endeavoured to avoid rigid criteria and sought flexibility. The general approach was explained by Lord Wright in *Mount Albert Borough Council v Australasian Temperance and General Assurance Society*:[11]

> English law, in deciding these matters, has refused to treat as conclusive rigid or arbitrary criteria such as *lex loci celebrationis* or *lex loci solutionis* and has treated the matter as depending on the intention of the parties to be ascertained in each case on a consideration of the terms of the contract, the situation of the parties and generally on all the surrounding facts.

From the middle of the 19th century, English judges began to seek the proper law of the contract as the law to govern most of the questions arising under a contract containing a foreign element. In many cases, there would be an express choice of law but, in other cases, the choice of law would have to be inferred. In broad terms, this flexible approach grounded in the real or presumed intentions of the parties was consistent with the laissez faire traditions of the age. The case law that began to develop after the middle of the 19th century concerned three possible approaches, namely, (a) where there had been an express choice of law; (b) where the court could infer an implied choice of law; and (c) those situations where the court would select the proper law based on the closest and most real connection with the transaction. It is proposed to examine each of these situations in turn.

Express choice of law

At common law, it was recognised from the 18th century that parties might expressly select the law to govern a particular dispute.[12] Such a degree of

---

10 Where there had been no express choice of law, the *lex loci contractus* had been adopted prior to the judgments in *P & O Steam Navigation Co v Shand* (1865) 3 Moo PC (NS) 272 and *Lloyd v Guibert* (1865) LR 1 QB 115.

11 [1938] AC 224, p 240.

12 *Gienar v Meyer* (1796) 2 Hy Bl 603.

freedom was consistent with the theory that contractual obligations were founded upon agreement and that the courts should have recognised the intention of the parties as manifested by the terms of the contract.[13] The principal question that arose was as to whether there were any limits to the parties' freedom of choice.

The matter fell to be determined in the case of *Vita Food Products Incorporated v Unus Shipping Company Limited*,[14] where the salient facts were as follows: by Newfoundland law, all bills of lading were required expressly to incorporate the Hague Rules. A cargo of herrings was sent from Nova Scotia to New York. The bill of lading did not incorporate the local law but merely stated that the bill was to be governed by English law. Both the Rules and the bills of lading provided for exclusion clauses in favour of the shipowner. The ship and its cargo were damaged off Nova Scotia. The consignees of the herrings brought an action against the shipowners.

The Privy Council held that the action of the consignees failed by virtue not of the exclusions under the Hague Rules, but by reason of the terms of the bill of lading. In dealing with the argument that there were limits upon parties to select the governing law, Lord Wright began by noting that the proper law of the contract is 'the law which the parties intended to apply'[15] and he then observed:

> ... where the English rule that intention is the test applies, and where there is an express statement by the parties of their intention to select the law of the contract, it is difficult to see what qualifications are possible, provided the intention expressed is *bona fide* and legal, and provided there is no reason for avoiding the choice on the ground of public policy.[16]

It was therefore the case that the courts would respect an express selection that was *bona fide* and legal, although there were *dicta* in the cases that indicated that a legal system unconnected with the contract, save for the choice of law clause, might be subject to close judicial scrutiny.[17] Moreover, in accordance with the normal domestic rule as to certainty of contractual terms, there was some authority for the assertion that an express selection clause that was vague might be regarded as meaningless and incapable of enforcement. An example of this approach is illustrated by the Court of Appeal judgment in *Compagnie d'Armement Maritime SA v Compagnie Tunisienne de Navigation SA*[18]

---

13 *Mount Albert BC v Australasian Temperance and General Assurance Society* [1938] AC 224.

14 [1939] AC 277.

15 *R v International Trustee for the Bondholders AG* [1937] AC 500.

16 *Vita Food Products Incorporated v Unus Shipping Co Ltd* [1939] AC 227, p 290.

17 *Boissevain v Weil* [1949] 1 KB 482; *Re Helbert Wagg and Co Ltd's Claim* [1956] Ch 323 *Tzortzis v Monarch Line A/B* [1968] 1 WLR 406.

18 [1969] 3 All ER 589; 1 WLR 1338.

where a clause that stipulated that 'the contract shall be governed by the laws of the flag of the vessel carrying the goods' was regarded as too vague when the parties contemplated that more than one vessel might be used.

In respect of the express selection of the proper law, it was important to distinguish such a clear choice from the situation where the parties had simply incorporated within the contract certain domestic provisions of a foreign law.[19]

Implied choice of law

Where there was no express selection of the proper law, the courts were prepared to infer that there had been an implied choice of law by reason of the presence of particular contractual terms. As Bowen LJ observed in *Jacobs v Credit Lyonnais*,[20] the process was one of 'applying sound ideas of business, convenience and sense'. Thus, a clause indicating that disputes were to be submitted to the courts of, or arbitration in, a particular country was often considered to represent an implied choice of law[21] – the rationale being the principle *qui elegit iudicium elegit ius*. The high water mark of this approach is illustrated by *Tzortzis v Monark Line A/B*,[22] where, although all the indications pointed to the law of Sweden, the Court of Appeal considered that the choice of English arbitration raised a conclusive inference in favour of English law.

However, this principle could be overstated, as was illustrated by the House of Lords judgment in *Compagnie D'Armement Maritime SA v Compagnie Tunisienne de Navigation SA*,[23] where the facts were as follows: French shipowners contracted with a Tunisian company for the shipment of oil from one Tunisian port to another. Clause 13 of the contract declared that the contract was to be governed 'by the laws of the flag of the vessel carrying the goods'[24] and cl 18 required that disputes were to be settled in London.

By a majority, the House of Lords concluded that cl 13 was not meaningless and could be interpreted as a reference to French law, and they further held that, if cl 13 had been inapplicable, the arbitration clause would not have been decisive. Lord Diplock considered that the implication arising from an arbitration clause might be rebutted by other indications of intention, while Lord Wilberforce noted that such a clause 'must be considered as an

---

19 Mann, FA (1939) 18 BYIL 97.
20 (1884) 12 QBD 589, CA (Brett MR, Bowen LJ) (a case turning on non-performance).
21 *Hamlyn and Co v Talisker Distillery* [1894] AC 202; *NV Kwik Hoo Tong Handel; Maatschappij v James Findlay and Co* [1927] AC 604; *Makender v Feldia AG* [1967] 2 QB 590.
22 [1968] 1 All ER 949; 1 WLR 406.
23 [1971] AC 572.
24 Several vessels and several flags were involved.

indication, to be considered together with the rest of the contract and relevant surrounding facts'.

Apart from choice of jurisdiction and arbitration clauses, the courts have been prepared to infer the intention of the parties from the language[25] or the style[26] of the document. In some instances the courts have paid regard to the nationality[27] or the residence[28] of the parties.

Closest and most real connection[29]

In those cases where the evidence was not sufficient for the court to determine that there had been an express or implied choice of law, it was necessary to determine the governing law by identifying the system of law that had the closest and most real connection with the transaction.[30] In attempting this task, the court was required to review and weigh a number of factors,[31] including the place of contracting, the place of performance, and the residence of the parties. By looking at a range of factors, the approach was not unlike the exercise performed by the courts to determine whether an agreement created a licence or a lease or where the distinction between a contract of service and a contract for services was in issue.

In performing this task, some difference of opinion existed as to whether the court was seeking to determine what the intention of the parties would have been[32] had they considered the matter or merely what they ought to have intended.[33] A third approach was advanced by Lord Denning MR, when he argued that determination was not based on any presumed intention; the learned judge observed that the determination:

> is not dependent on the intention of the parties. They never thought about it. They had no intentions upon it. We have to study every circumstance connected with the contract and come to a conclusion.[34]

---

25 *The Leon XIII* (1883) 8 PD 121.

26 *Rossano v Manufacturers' Life Insurance Co* [1963] 2 QB 352.

27 *Re Missouri Steamship Co* (1889) 42 Ch D 32.

28 *Jacobs v Credit Lyonnais* (1884) 12 QBD 589.

29 *Bonython v Commonwealth of Australia* [1951] AC 201.

30 *The Assunzione* [1954] P 150.

31 *Re United Rlys of Havana and Regla Warehouses Ltd* [1960] Ch 52; *Tomkinson v Forst Pennsylvania Banking and Trust Co* [1961] AC 1007; *James Miller and Partners Ltd v Whitworth Street Estates (Manchester) Ltd* [1970] AC 583.

32 *Lloyd v Guibert* [1865] 1 QB 115, *per* Willes J.

33 *Bonython v Commonwealth of Australia* [1951] AC 201; *The Assunzione* [1954] P 150; *Re United Railways of Havana and Regla Warehouses Ltd* [1960] Ch 52.

34 *Coast Lines Ltd v Hudig and Veder Chartering NV* [1972] 2 QB 34.

The process is well illustrated by the course adopted in the case of *The Assunzione*,[35] where the facts were as follows: an Italian vessel had been chartered by French shipowners for the carriage of wheat. The charterparty was concluded in Paris, but written in both French and English. The bills of lading were written in French. Freight and demurrage were payable in Italian currency in Italy. The ship flew the Italian flag and the bills of lading were endorsed to consignees in Italy. In an action by the charterers against the shipowners for damage to the cargo, the Court of Appeal[36] was required to determine whether French or Italian law was to be applied.

The court found no particular factor to be decisive, but concluded that the payment of freight and demurrage in Italian tilted the balance in favour of Italian law. Singleton LJ expressed the principle thus: 'One must look at all the circumstances and seek to find what just and reasonable persons ought to have intended if they had thought about the matter at the time when they made the contract.'

Conclusion

The common law rules outlined above were developed in the years after 1865; they apply to contracts concluded prior to 1 April 1991[37] and they remain in force in many Commonwealth jurisdictions. Although they have now been replaced by the rules set out in the Rome Convention on the Law Applicable to Contractual Obligations 1980, this was not without a degree of controversy. Since the Convention was based on the agreement of Member States of the European Community, some questioned whether it was sensible to disregard the corpus of law built up by experience and found to have been consistent with business needs. There was considerable debate as to whether the flexibility of the prior rules would be loss under the dictates of an international convention.[38]

---

35 [1954] P 150, CA.

36 *Ibid*, Hodson, Singleton, Birkett LJJ, upholding a determination of Wilmer J.

37 The date of the coming into effect of the Contracts (Applicable Law) Act 1990.

38 See Mann, FA (1991) 107 LQR 353; also Mann, FA (1982) 32 ICLQ 265; Mann, FA (1989) 38 ICLQ 715; Briggs (1990) LMCLQ 192; Jaffey (1984) 33 ICLQ 531.

THE ROME CONVENTION[39]

The Contracts (Applicable Law) Act 1990 gives effect in the UK to the Rome Convention on the Law Applicable to Contractual Obligations.[40] The Rome Convention is a further move towards the harmonisation of the laws of the Member States of the European Union.[41] Work on the Convention began in 1969 after the completion of the Brussels Convention on Jurisdiction and Judgments[42] in 1968. The Contracts (Applicable Law) Act came into force on 1 April 1991 and, thus, the Rome Convention applies to contracts made after that date.[43] It puts the English conflict of laws on contracts on to a statutory basis for the first time, replacing the common law rules. It has been argued, on the one hand that the greatest contribution of English law to the conflict of laws was the development of the doctrine of the proper law of the contract; indeed, some writers have even asserted that there is no need to alter this area of law.[44] Moreover, there were fears that foreign litigants might lose confidence in the Commercial Court's ability to deal with non-European cases if an essentially European model replaced the common law rules. It can be argued, on the other hand, that the Convention adopts many of the principles of the English conflict of laws, including the right of contracting parties to select the law to govern their dealings free from any requirement that the chosen law be factually connected with the contract. Initially, at least, there is not likely to be any major change in the approach of English courts to the disposition of contract conflict cases except, possibly, in the areas of employment and consumer contracts for which the Convention makes special provision where the common law had none.

As the Convention has no retrospective effect,[45] for the next few years, there will be some litigation under the former common law rules. Although the Rome Convention does not require its application to internal conflicts within Contracting States,[46] the Contracts (Applicable Law) Act 1990 applies the Convention to all cases coming before the courts in the UK.[47] It applies

---

39 See North (1980) JBL 382; Bennett (1980) 17 CMLR 269.

40 Rome Convention on the Law Applicable to Contractual Obligations 1980.

41 As provided under the original Art 220 of the Treaty of Rome 1957, although it should be noted that the terms of the original article do not extend to choice of law.

42 European Convention on Jurisdiction and the Enforcement of Judgments in Civil and Commercial Matters 1968.

43 So that, not being retrospective, the common law rules will continue to apply to contracts made prior to that date.

44 See Mann, FA (1991) 107 LQR 353; see, also, Lord Chancellor, HL Deb Vol 518 Col 439, 24 April 1990.

45 See the Rome Convention 1980, Art 17.

46 *Ibid*, Art 19(2).

47 Contracts (Applicable Law) Act 1990, s 2(3).

equally, therefore, to cases involving choices of law between countries within the UK, for example, English and Scots law, as to cases involving the laws of other countries.

The Rome Convention is a further move towards the harmonisation of the laws of the Member States of the European Community and ties in with the European Convention on Jurisdiction and the Enforcement of Judgments (1968). By standardising the choice of law rules within the European Community, the Convention seeks to further the aims of the single market and to minimise the advantages of forum shopping, in that, wherever the action is brought, the same governing law should be applied.

It is a 'universal' convention, however, in that its operation is not confined to choice of law problems arising between Contracting States. Courts in the Contracting States must apply the Convention to all cases coming before them. It follows from this that the applicable law under the Convention can be that of any legal system in the world[48] and that it can be applied to parties who are residents, domiciliaries or nationals of any country irrespective of whether those countries are parties to the Convention, members of the European Community or neither.

The convention establishes uniform rules for the determination of contract conflicts. Its fundamental principles may be conveniently summarised as follows:

(a) that the parties are free to choose the law to govern their contracts;[49]

(b) that, in default of choice by the parties, the contract should be governed by the legal system with which it is most closely connected;[50]

(c) that some contracts are characterised by such imbalances of power that the weaker party is in need of special protection and, hence, special provision is made for certain consumer contracts[51] and individual employment contracts.[52]

It is necessary to explore the implementation of these principles in some detail.

The scope of the Rome Convention

The Rome Convention applies to 'contractual obligations in any situation involving a choice between the laws of different countries'.[53] The choice does

---

48 Rome Convention 1980, Art 2.
49 *Ibid*, Art 3.
50 *Ibid*, Art 4.
51 *Ibid*, Art 5.
52 *Ibid*, Art 6.
53 *Ibid*, Art 1(1).

not have to be a difficult or nicely balanced one. A contract wholly connected with one country which contains a choice of another country's law is clearly within the Convention.[54] A contract wholly connected with one country which contains a choice of jurisdiction clause in favour of another or happens to be litigated in a foreign country should equally attract the application of the Convention.

It is, of course, under English law, for the litigant who seeks to rely upon a foreign law to plead and prove it as a matter of fact before an English court. This principle equally applies under the Convention, so that, if a litigant fails to plead foreign law, the hearing will proceed on the basis of English law alone; and, if foreign law is pleaded but not proved, the case will proceed on the assumption that the foreign law has the same content as English law.[55]

The Convention applies only to contracts and, initially, English courts will use their own concept of contract for this purpose. This does not mean that they will apply only their domestic rules, they will apply the concept as it operates in the conflict system. Technical rules govern the recognition of contracts under English domestic law and it would be silly to deny a foreign contract recognition simply because it did not correspond to the English model. A good illustration of the English court going about the matter in the right way is afforded by *Re Bonacina*[56] where the relevant facts were as follows: an Italian, trading in England, incurred a debt to another Italian who was resident in Italy. When the trader was adjudged bankrupt his Italian creditor failed to prove his debt in bankruptcy because he was ignorant of the proceedings. The trader subsequently obtained his discharge from bankruptcy and signed a document (*privata scrittura*) whereby he promised to pay off the debt within five years. Before he could do so, he died and an English court was faced with a claim by the Italian creditor in the administration of the estate.

Under Italian law, the promise was enforceable as it had been made by *privata scrittura* and this formality sufficed – in a manner similar to, but not as formal as, an English deed – to make the promise binding by Italian law. At trial, Eve J[57] dismissed the claim on the basis of lack of consideration for the promise. This judgment was reversed by the Court of Appeal.[58] In giving judgment in the Court of Appeal, Cozens-Hardy MR noted that the proper law of the contract was Italian and that, under Italian law, the promise constituted a binding promise, even though consideration was absent.

---

54 Rome Convention 1980, Art 3(3).

55 Although not in all cases – see *R v Brixton Prison Governor ex p Coldough* [1961] 1 All ER 606; *Österreichische Landerbank v S'Elite Ltd* [1981] QB 565.

56 [1912] 2 Ch 394, CA.

57 The judgment of Eve J is reported at [1912] 2 Ch 394, p 395.

58 The judgment of the Court of Appeal (Cozens-Hardy MR, Farwell, Kennedy LJJ) is reported at [1912] 2 Ch 394.

The learned judge observed:

> ... according to the law of Italy, the English doctrine of consideration, being necessary to support a contract, has no application, and further that the moral obligation to pay the debt is sufficient to found a legal obligation if a document such as the *'privata scrittura'* has been executed. It seems to me, therefore, that the claimant is in precisely the same position in this country as he would have been if there had been an English contract of the same date with a new and valuable consideration.[59]

Despite wide variations in different legal systems' recognition rules for contracts, and the very different incidents attending valid contracts, English conflict law has had less trouble with the concepts of the law of contract than with most of the concepts upon which the conflict of laws depends.

Where the plaintiff has a choice of cause of action, that is, where the case can be pleaded in more than one way, for example, a negligently injured employee can decide to sue for breach of contract or in the tort of negligence, a decision to sue in negligence will take the case out of the operation of the Convention, notwithstanding that a contractual action would be within it.

The Rome Convention sets out a list of matters to which the uniform rules do not apply.[60] These continue to be governed, as far as English law is concerned, by the common law rules relating to contract, insofar as English law sees them as contractual, or by the choice of law rules applicable to the other classifications into which English law puts them.

The exceptions have very limited contractual significance for the most part and do not detract from the wide operation of the Rome Convention. Article 1(2) of the Rome Convention provides that the rules of the Convention:

> ... shall not apply to:
>
> (a) questions involving the status or legal capacity of natural persons, without prejudice to Art 11;
>
> (b) contractual obligations relating to wills and succession, rights in property arising out of a matrimonial relationship, rights and duties arising out of a family relationship, parentage, marriage or affinity, including maintenance obligations in respect of children who are not legitimate;
>
> (c) obligations arising under bills of exchange, cheques and promissory notes and other negotiable instruments to the extent that the obligations under such other negotiable instruments arise out of their negotiable character;
>
> (d) arbitration agreements and agreements on the choice of court;
>
> (e) questions governed by the law of companies and other bodies corporate or unincorporate such as the creation, by registration or otherwise, legal capacity, internal organisation or winding up of companies and other

---

59 *Re Bonacina* [1912] 2 Ch 394, p 400.
60 Rome Convention 1980, Art 1(2).

bodies corporate or unincorporate and the personal liability of officers and members as such for the obligations of the company or body;

(f) the question whether an agent is liable to bind a principal, or an organ to bind a company or body corporate or unincorporate, to a third party;

(g) the constitution of trusts and the relationship between settlors, trustees and beneficiaries;

(h) evidence and procedure, without prejudice to Art 14.

In addition, the Rome Convention 1980 does not affect the operation of other international conventions which lay down choice of law rules in particular areas,[61] nor does it affect European Community legislation establishing specific choice of law rules in particular situations.[62]

The Convention does not apply, as far as UK courts are concerned, to matters relating to the consequences of a contract being held void.[63]

It is necessary to say a little at this stage about the scope of the various exclusions.

Questions involving the status or legal capacity of natural persons, without prejudice to Art 11

Whether a minor, or anyone else, is capable of entering contracts generally or contracts of a particular description is not a matter which has much troubled the English conflict of laws,[64] so uncertainty remains over the choice of law. The personal law, which is referred to for other types of capacity, for example, to marry or to make a will, would not seem to have a strong case in contract, especially where the contract is made outside the home country. The *lex loci contractus* – the law of the place where the contract is made – has some support in a very old and uncertain authority[65] and in more modern *dicta*,[66] but suffers form the lack of any necessary connection with the parties or the substance of the contract. It could be subject to the exploitation of the stronger party in establishing the locus contractus in a country where the protection of the party whose capacity is in doubt is weakest. The putative applicable law – that which would be the applicable law of the contract if the capacity issue is determined affirmatively – is, in its chosen form, equally unsatisfactory, as it

---

61 Rome Convention 1980, Art 21.

62 *Ibid*, Art 20.

63 *Ibid*, Art 10(1)(e); Contracts (Applicable Law) Act 1990, s 2(2).

64 *Bodley Head Ltd v Flegon* [1972] 1 WLR 680 (where Brightman J considered contractual capacity to be governed by the proper law of the contract).

65 *Male v Roberts* (1790) 3 Esp 165 (where Lord Eldon considered that whether infancy could be raised as a defence depended on the *lex loci contractus*).

66 *Baindail v Baindail* [1946] P 122, p 128, *per* Lord Greene MR (in the context of capacity to marry).

enables the stronger party to stipulate a law which, in effect, removes the protection which the weaker might otherwise enjoy. The putative applicable law in the objective sense – the law which would apply to the contract in default of choice by the parties – is probably the safest bet as it avoids both accident and machination. But, it does not, of course, ensure the protection of the weaker party as a reference to his personal law might. As the matter appears to raise few issues in practice, there is no need to dwell upon it here.

There is, however, a special provision contained in Art 11 of the Rome Convention 1980 which provides that, where the parties are in the same country when the contract is made, a party who has capacity by that law can invoke his incapacity by another law only if the other party knew of, or was negligent in not knowing about, the incapacity. In these limited circumstances, the party who acts in good faith and without negligence will be protected from a subsequent claim of incapacity by the other party, based on his personal law before a court whose conflict of law rules would look to the domiciliary or national law to determine his capacity. The provision does not affect the ability of the party with capacity from raising the incapacity of the other party.

I have used the term putative applicable law – that which would be the applicable law if the contract was not affected by the incapacity. Strictly, as the issue of capacity is outside the Convention, it would be more correct to speak of the putative proper law. There are several differences between the proper law and the applicable law under the Convention and it would be possible for the court using the proper law test to identify a law different from that indicated by the Convention. It would seem that there is little merit in maintaining this distinction for the purpose of contractual capacity.

Matters relating to wills, succession, matrimonial property and family relationships

This provision mirrors the wording in the Brussels Convention 1968.[67] The clear intention is to exclude non commercial agreements from the uniform rules on the grounds that they are viewed as essentially matters of family law. An agreement between husband and wife for the division of property on divorce, the agreement between father and mother for the maintenance of their illegitimate child, an agreement with respect to the destination of property on death are the types of arrangement that the provision contemplates. In some of these instances, the parties could have obtained a court order for the financial provision concerned and it may be that the disappointed party will have a choice between seeking the enforcement of the

---

67 Brussels Convention 1968, Art 1.

agreement or seeking a court order to establish his claim against the defaulter. The overlap of these proceedings is the reason for the exclusion. Such an exclusion was also justified on the grounds that many States were signatories of the Hague Convention on the Recognition and Enforcement of Decisions Relating to Maintenance Obligations 1973. One of the objectives of the draftsmen of the Rome Convention 1980 was to avoid any action that would frustrate the work of the Hague Conference on Private International Law.

Most situations covered by the exclusion would not be regarded as contractual matters under English law, but the following example is worthy of consideration. In the well known case of *De Nicols v Curlier*,[68] the husband and wife, who were French domiciliaries, were married in France. They made no specific agreement about the matrimonial property as they could have done and, therefore, by French law at that time, a community property regime applied automatically to them. The husband died domiciled in England and his will sought to dispose of the property to which his wife had a claim if the community property regime still applied. English law was the *lex successionis*, the general law governing the succession and would, *prima facie*, have seen the husband as free to dispose of all the property in the will unfettered by the wife's claim to community, which was a concept unknown to English domestic law. The House of Lords, in reversing the Court of Appeal, held that the parties, having failed to reach a specific agreement on differential allocation of the matrimonial property, must be assumed to have tacitly agreed to the regime of community.[69] Thus, the wife had a contractual right to half the matrimonial property which the English court would recognise.

A contract which does not arise from the legal relationships which are excluded, for example, an agreement among children for the maintenance of their parents, is governed by the ordinary rules of the Convention.

Bills of Exchange, cheques and negotiable instruments

Article 1(2)(c) of the Rome Convention excludes obligations arising under bills of exchange, cheques and negotiable instruments. The important concept is that of negotiability; the Giuliano and Lagarde report[70] states that it is for the private international law of the forum to determine whether the instrument is to be characterised as negotiable. Such documents run counter to the ordinary rules of contract under English law in two respects. First, there is no necessary

---

68 [1898] 2 Ch 60, CA; [1900] AC 21, HL (a case in which a certain AV Dicey QC appeared as counsel).

69 The Court of Appeal had been bound by authority to hold that any implied agreement was nullified by by a subsequent change of domicile.

70 Giuliano and Lagarde, *Report on the Rome Convention* OJ C 282, 1980, p 11; for the report, see below under 'Interpretation', p 319.

relationship of privity between the holder of such a document and the person responsible under it and, secondly, a holder in due course who is *bona fide* and who has given consideration is capable of having a better title than his transferor had – an exception, in other words, to the general principle of *nemo dat quod non habet*.

One reason for the exclusion was that most Member States (but not the UK) were parties to the two relevant Geneva Conventions of 1930 and 1931.[71] Thus, the vast majority of questions in this area coming before English courts will be governed by the Bills of Exchange Act 1882.[72]

The exclusion relates to the issue of negotiability alone. It does not mean that a contract is outside the convention simply because payment is to be made by cheque.

Arbitration agreements and agreements on the choice of court

Article 1(2)(d) of the Rome Convention excludes arbitration agreements and agreements on the choice of court from the scope of the Convention. Under the common law rules, arbitration agreements and agreements over jurisdiction, whether contained in the main contract or not, gave rise to no classificatory problems – they were contract terms or separate contracts, the mutual forbearance of the parties constituting the consideration for a perfectly bilateral contract.

Just as the parties were free under the common law to select the governing law for their contract, they were free also to decide whether disputes would, in the last resort, go to court or arbitration and where that should be. Like choice of law clauses, choice of jurisdiction clauses are frequently contained within standard form contracts. The close connection between choice of jurisdiction and choice of law was marked by the presumption that a choice of jurisdiction clause, in the absence of an effective choice of law clause, could be taken as an implied choice of the legal system under which the court or arbitrator operated – *qui elegit iudicium elegit ius*.

This particular exclusion attracted a degree of controversy. It was argued that Art 17 of the Brussels Convention on Jurisdiction and the Enforcement of Judgments already made adequate provision for questions of validity and form in respect of jurisdiction agreements. Secondly, it was claimed that many

---

71 Convention of 7 June 1930 for the Settlement of Certain Conflicts of Laws in Connection with Bills of Exchange and Promissory Notes; and Convention of 19 March 1931 for the Settlement of Certain Conflicts of Laws in Connection with Cheques.

72 See the Bills of Exchange Act 1882, s 72, which stipulates that formal validity of a bill drawn in one country and accepted in another shall be determined by the law of the place of issue.

matters pertaining to arbitration were already subject to international conventions.[73]

The decision to exclude arbitration awards was opposed by the UK delegation. An arbitration agreement in English domestic law is subject to the doctrine of separability. This doctrine had been developed in the case law[74] and has now been given statutory force.[75] In principle, the doctrine holds that the arbitration agreement constitutes an agreement distinct from the wider agreement in which it is included. In England, this means that the common law rules of private international law will apply to the arbitration agreement or choice of court while the remainder of contract will be subject to the law arising under the Convention. The fear of the UK delegation was that such an approach could lead to different conclusions in respect of the arbitration agreement and the contract taken as a whole.

Corporate and incorporate status

The full text of the exclusion in Art 1(2)(e) reads:

> ... questions governed by the law of companies and other bodies corporate or unincorporate such as the creation, by registration or otherwise, legal capacity, internal organisation or winding up of companies and other bodies corporate or unincorporate and the personal liability of officers and members as such for the obligations of the company or body.

Whether a corporation or unincorporated body has the capacity to enter a contract and what effect any such contract may have on the relations between the members of the corporation or unincorporated association is not the concern of the Convention. Although the importance of this area was recognised, it was felt that any inclusion might be at variance with the work of the European Commission.[76] The general sense was that company law matters should be dealt with separately outside a convention devoted to

---

73 Geneva Protocol on Arbitration Clauses 1923; Geneva Convention on the Execution of Foreign Arbitral Awards 1927, given effect to by the Arbitration Act 1950; New York Convention on the Recognition and Enforcement of Foreign Arbitral Awards 1958, given effect to by the Arbitration Act 1975. For the present law, see the Arbitration Act 1996, Pt III, ss 99–104. It is relevant to add that the New York Convention has been ratified by a very large number of States.

74 *Harbour Assurance Co (UK) Ltd v Kansa General International Insurance Co Ltd* [1993] QB 701; 1 LR 455; 3 All ER 897.

75 Arbitration Act 1996, s 7.

76 The Commission had been active from the outset in: (a) directives issued under Art 54(3)(g); (b) treaties drawn up under Art 220; and (c) attempts to provide a draft statute for a European company under Art 235. The first company law directive had been issued as early as March 1968 (68/151/EEC).

general contracts. It would seem that agreements between promoters prior to the formation of a company are outside the exclusion.[77]

Agency

Article 1(2)(f) excludes from the Convention questions as to whether an agent can bind his principal, or the organ of a company can bind that company, to a third party. It therefore follows that any dispute between principal and agent or between agent and third party is outside the terms of the exclusion. However, the exclusion will cover disputes as to whether a company is bound by an act of its directors or whether the activities of a single officer can bind the company. These are regarded as matters of company law and will be subject to the domestic legislation affecting potentially *ultra vires* activities.[78] Thus, under English law, the question of whether a principal is bound by a contract concluded between agent and third party will depend on the proper law of that contract.

It is arguable that such an exclusion is not required and that questions of actual authority (express or implied) should be governed by the law which governs the contract between principal and agent, while questions as to ostensible or apparent authority should be governed by the law of the place where the principal did the acts that are relied upon as creating the impression of authority.[79]

Trusts

The exclusion of matters relating to trusts in Art 1(2)(g) is justified partly on grounds of clarity and partly on the basis that questions pertaining to the law of trusts are part of the law of property and not of the law of obligations. The constitution of trusts and the relations between settlors, trustees and beneficiaries will be governed by the Hague Convention on the Law Applicable to Trusts and on their Recognition 1986 introduced into English law by the Recognition of Trusts Act 1987. These matters will be considered in the context of property law.

---

77 An area that has given rise to much litigation in domestic company law; see *Erlanger v New Sombrero Phosphate Co* (1878) 3 App Cas 1218; *Gluckstein v Barnes* [1900] AC 240; *Re Leeds and Hanley Theatres of Varieties Ltd* [1902] 2 Ch 809. See Giuliano and Lagarde, *Report on the Rome Convention* OJ C 282, 1980, p 12.

78 The European Commission dealt with *ultra vires* in the First Directive on Company Law (68/151/EEC); European Communities Act 1972, s 9; Companies Act 1985, ss 35, 35A; Prentice (1973) 89 LQR 518; Farrar and Powles (1973) 36 MLR 270; Collier and Sealy (1973) CLJ 1.

79 See Lasok and Bridge, *Conflict of Laws in the European Community* (1987), p 354.

Evidence and procedure, without prejudice to Art 14

Evidence and procedure remain matters for the law of the forum, whatever the applicable law of the contract, and are, therefore, excluded from the operation of the Convention.

The exclusion is subject to Art 14, which introduces two qualifications to the broad exclusion by stating:

(1) the law governing the contract under the Convention applies to the extent that it contains, in the law of contract, rules which raise presumptions of law or determine the burdens of proof;

(2) a contract or an act intended to have legal effect may be proved by any mode of proof recognised by the law of the forum or by any of the laws referred to in Art 9 (formal validity) under which that contract or act is formally valid, provided that such mode of proof can be administered by the forum.

The effect of Art 14 is to provide for two situations where the applicable law under the Convention will apply to matters of proof which would otherwise appear to fall under the exception. First, where the applicable law under the Convention contains, as part of its law of contract, rules which raise presumptions of law to determine the burden of proof, those presumptions shall have effect. So, for example, under English law and aside from the operation of the Unfair Contract Terms Act 1977, where a person signs a contractual document he will be deemed to know and be bound by its contents unless he establishes some ground, for example, *non est factum* to afford him relief. A further example that might come within Art 14(1) would be those cases in equity of presumed undue influence where the onus is upon the party taking the benefit to demonstrate that advantage was not obtained by undue influence.[80] In respect of Art 14(2), a contract or other act intended to have legal effect may be proved by any mode of proof allowed by the forum, or by any of the laws identified by Art 9 on formal validity, provided, in the latter case, that the mode of proof can be administered by the forum, that is, is physically possible there and not repugnant to the forum's policy on proof.

Contracts of insurance covering risks in the European Community

Article 1(3) has the effect of excluding contracts of insurance which cover risks situated within a Member State of the European Community. Article 1(4) provides that this exclusion shall not apply to contracts of reinsurance. Thus, the process of reinsurance, whereby the primary insurer lays off the risk or

---

80   *Allcard v Skinner* (1887) 36 Ch D 145; *National Westminster Bank v Morgan* [1985] AC 686.

part of it by contract to others, is covered by the Convention. It was argued that contracts of reinsurance do not raise the same problems as contracts of insurance where there is a need to protect the weaker party.

The exclusion is therefore confined to direct insurance. Whether a risk falls within a Member State is a matter to be determined by the trial judge using his own internal law.

The reason for the exclusion of contracts of insurance was that the European Community had been legislating in the area of insurance.[81] Another difficulty was that after the UK became a member of the European Community the need to strike a balance between individual policyholders and the interests of corporate insurers became more acute.[82]

Nullity

Article 10 of the Rome Convention 1980, which is concerned with the scope of the applicable law, provides, in Art 10(1)(e), that the applicable law shall govern 'the consequences of nullity of the contract'. A difficulty arises in that English law regards the effects of nullity not as a matter of contract law but as a matter pertaining to the law of quasi-contract or restitution.[83] There was some opposition at the time of drafting, so that Art 22 entitled a Member State to enter a reservation in respect of Art 10(1)(e). The UK entered such a reservation and this is given effect to by s 2(2) of the Contracts (Applicable Law) Act 1990. Although this approach is supported by logic, it may lead to interesting results. Suppose a contract is governed, under the terms of the Rome Convention, by German law and, under that law, it is void; it should be held void in any Contracting State. However, the consequences of that finding of nullity will differ according to the State in which the litigation takes place.

An attempt has been made to set out the principal exclusions from the Rome Convention. Before turning to the central provisions, it is sensible to say a little about problems of interpretation.

Interpretation

It was always intended that the European Court of Justice should have the same powers of interpretation in respect of the Rome Convention 1980 as it enjoyed in respect of the Brussels Convention 1968. Being a legal instrument

---

81 See Directive 88/357/EEC; Insurance Companies Act 1982; Directive 90/619/EEC; Friendly Societies Act 1992.

82 As indicated by the 1978 Accession Convention.

83 An example being *Kleinwort Benson Ltd v Glasgow City Council* [1997] 3 WLR 923 (where the original proceedings before Hirst J were brought on the basis of seeking restitution of sums paid on the ground of unjust enrichment); see *Barclays Bank plc v Glasgow CC* [1993] QB 429.

designed to serve the interests of a single market there is the same need for uniformity and consistency of interpretation. This is made clear by Art 18 of the Rome Convention, which stipulates that:

> In the interpretation and application of the preceding uniform rules, regard shall be had to their international character and to the desirability of achieving uniformity in their interpretation and application

After considerable deliberation, two protocols were drawn up in 1988 to regulate references to the European Court of Justice. The First Protocol defines the scope of the jurisdiction of the European Court and appears in the schedule to the Contracts (Applicable Law) Act 1990.[84] The Second Protocol conferred power on the European Court to give rulings. The protocols cannot come into force until the requisite number of documents of ratification have been received. At the time of writing, the protocols are not in force. When the protocols come into force, a reference will be discretionary and only the appellate courts will be able to make a reference.[85]

In respect of English courts, s 3(1) of the Contracts (Applicable Law) Act 1990 requires conformity with European law in requiring that:

> Any question as to the meaning or effect of any provision of the Conventions shall, if not referred to the European Court in accordance with the Brussels Protocol, be determined in accordance with the principles laid down by, and any relevant decision of, the European Court.

It is strongly arguable that this provision is wide enough not only to embrace judgments given in respect of references under the Brussels Convention 1968[86] but, also, to those judgments given in the context of other references, having regard to the general principle of the supremacy of European Community Law and the duties falling upon an English court under the European Communities Act 1972.

In considering the interpretation of the Rome Convention (1980), an English Court will be guided by past relevant judgments of the European Court of Justice[87] and by the *Report on the Rome Convention* by Professor Mario Giuliano and Professor Paul Lagarde of 31 October 1980[88] and the *Report on the Protocols of Interpretation* by Professor Tizzano of 3 September 1990.[89] It is also clear that decisions of the courts in other Contracting States will constitute persuasive authority in the English courts on the interpretation of the Convention.

---

84 Contracts (Applicable Law) Act 1990, Sched 3 (known as the Brussels Protocol).
85 *Ibid*, Sched 3, Art 2.
86 Civil Jurisdiction and Judgments Act 1982, s 3(1).
87 Contracts (Applicable Law) Act 1990, s 3(1), (2).
88 OJ 282/1 1980; Contracts (Applicable Law) Act 1990, s 3(3)(a).
89 OJ 219/1 1990; Contracts (Applicable Law) Act 1990, s 3(3)(b).

The universal nature of the Rome Convention

The Rome Convention is universal in its geographical scope; it does not depend on the residence, nationality or domicile of the parties. Article 1 reads:

> The rules of this Convention shall apply to contractual obligations in any situation involving a choice between the laws of different countries.

That the Convention is to be wide in scope is made abundantly clear by Article 2, which reads:

> Any law specified by this Convention shall be applied whether or not it is the law of a Contracting State.

Thus, the Rome Convention will apply not only to contracts with Contracting States, but it will also apply to contracts that have no connection with the European Community save that the litigation arising from the contract has been commenced in a Contracting State. Thus, a contractual dispute between a Japanese resident and a Californian resident that is litigated in England will be subject to the Rome Convention.

The potentially broad sweep of the Rome Convention attracted criticism when the Contracts (Applicable Law) Bill was passing through Parliament in the spring of 1990;[90] this criticism was linked to an objection in principle to the Rome Convention. A number of distinguished scholars and judges questioned the necessity of incorporation;[91] they were concerned that the body of case law and experience that that had been developed at common law in the years since 1865[92] was to be set aside when all the evidence indicated that these common law rules were acceptable to a considerable part of the common law world. There was a concern that, if an English judge was compelled to apply the Rome Convention, litigation might move form London to other non-Contracting States. In the House of Lords, these concerns took the form of an amendment to the Bill indicating that the Convention would only apply where the contract had some specific European connection. The amendment was defeated and the Contracts (Applicable Law) Act 1990 proceeded to the statute book.[93]

The UK comprises three distinct jurisdictions (England, Scotland, Northern Ireland); the Rome Convention does not require that the terms of the Convention should operate for internal conflicts. Article 19(2) reads:

---

90 It received Royal Assent on 26 July 1990.
91 See Mann, FA (1983) 32 ICLQ 265; Mann, FA (1989) *The Times*, 14 December; Mann, FA (1991) 107 LQR 353. In the House of Lords, both Lord Wilberforce and Lord Goff of Chieveley expressed considerable reservations.
92 From *P & O Steam Navigation Co v Shand* (1865) 3 Moo PC (NS) 272.
93 The case for the legislation was put by Dr P North (part of the UK team in the negotiations for the Rome Convention) in a letter to (1989) *The Times*, 19 December.

A State within which different territorial units have their own rules of law in respect of contractual obligations shall not be bound to apply this Convention to conflicts solely between the laws of such units.

However, Parliament decided to fully implement the Convention so that s 2(3) of the Contracts (Applicable Law) Act 1990 requires that the Convention 'shall apply in the case of conflicts between the laws of different parts of the UK'.[94]

THE CHOICE OF THE GOVERNING LAW

Express choice

The fundamental provisions of the Rome Convention 1980 are set out in Arts 3 and 4 and these provisions give effect to the general principle that the parties should be free to select the law to govern their contact. To this extent the Rome Convention 1980 confirms the position which had been reached by the English common law. The leading pre-Convention authority was the judgment of the Privy Council in *Vita Food Products Inc v Unus Shipping Co Ltd*,[95] which established that the parties were free to select any governing law they wished, irrespective of any connection with the contract, provided that the choice was *bona fide*, legal and not contrary to English public policy. There is no reported decision of the English courts in which a choice of law clause was struck down, though there is one Australian case where the choice of law was not held to be *bona fide*.[96] The conflict laws of the other Contracting States contained similar freedoms, though perhaps not quite the same enthusiasm for unrestricted choice as English law displayed, in particular, with regard to the choice of a wholly unconnected law. London's historical place in international commodity exchanges, in shipping and in marine insurance encouraged the English courts to look positively on choice of law clauses and, indeed, choice of jurisdiction clauses, which selected English law, English courts or, commonly, both. There remain many standard forms of contract which lead to the choice of English law, English courts or English arbitration as parts of their standard terms and there are important financial benefits to this country in the continuance of this practice.

The first important provision for determining the law to govern a contract is contained in Art 3(1):

---

94 It would seem that when the scheme for references to the European Court of Justice is fully operational, it will not extend to internal conflicts: see *Kleinwort Benson Ltd v Glasgow City Council* [1997] 3 WLR 923.

95 [1939] AC 277; 1 All ER 513; see, also, *R v International Trustee for the Protection of Bonholders AG* [1937] AC 500, p 529, *per* Lord Atkin; *Compagnie d'Armement Maritime SA v Compagnie Tunisienne de Navigation SA* [1971] AC 572, *per* Lord Diplock.

96 *Golden Acres Ltd v Queensland Estates* [1969] Qd R 378; *Freehold Land Investments v Queensland Estates Ltd* (1970) 123 CLR 418.

A contract shall be governed by the law chosen by the parties. The choice must be express or demonstrated with reasonable certainty by the terms of the contract or the circumstances of the case. By their choice the parties can select the law applicable to the whole or a part only of the contract.

It is important to note as a preliminary point that by virtue of Art 15 the governing law is the internal law of the relevant country; the Rome Convention 1980 accords with the position that had been reached at common law.[97]

The common law did not require that the law chosen by the parties should have a significant connection with the contract or, indeed, any connection at all. The parties freedom extended beyond a selection among the laws, which might have been objectively determined to be the proper law, to a free choice of any legal system they wished to use. The Rome Convention adopts the same philosophy.

The law chosen by the parties will govern the substance of their contractual relationship subject to the mandatory rules of the *lex fori*[98] and to its public policy.[99] There are three situations, however, where the Rome Convention makes the parties choice of the applicable law subject to the mandatory rules of another connected system, they are:

(a) contracts wholly connected to a single country;[100]

(b) certain consumer contracts;[101] and

(c) individual employment contracts.[102]

Every choice of law in a contract which is genuinely international inevitably avoids the operation of the laws of other connected systems. Whether that avoidance is material to the validity of the contract itself or significant to the rights and duties of the parties to it will obviously depend on the content of the legal rules of those systems. Where the avoidance is not merely incidental but is intentional, that is, the parties consciously choose one system in order to avoid another, the matter may take on a different complexion. Suppose the applicable law of the contract, objectively ascertained, could be either English or French law – the connections being so nicely balanced that one would need a court ruling to determine the answer definitively – there is no objection to the parties making up their own minds in advance of any dispute arising. Suppose in the same example, however, the parties select Italian law to govern their contract and thereby avoid the provisions of French law and

---

97   *Amin Rasheed Shipping Corpn v Kuwait Insurance Co* [1984] AC 50; [1983] 2 All ER 884.

98   Rome Convention 1980, Art 7 (discussed below).

99   *Ibid*, Art 16 (discussed below).

100 *Ibid*, Art 3(3) (discussed below).

101 *Ibid*, Art 5 (discussed below).

102 *Ibid*, Art 6 (discussed below).

English law, which would materially alter the legal view of the contract. There is a slide from inevitable avoidance to deliberate evasion. Should evasion be prevented? Some evasions are controlled by the use of the concept of the mandatory rule. A mandatory rule is a rule of the law of the country which cannot be derogated from by contract. This important concept, which appears in several of the Convention's provisions, will be considered later.

The parties may expressly choose, by a term in their contract or a separate agreement, a law to govern their contract. The most obvious way to do this would be to insert a simple statement that the contract shall be governed by the law of the designated country. Wording such as 'this contract shall be governed by English law' or 'any dispute arising out of this contract shall be decided under Italian law' would be sufficient. Such a wording indicates a distinct territorial legal system and is probably the wisest choice. Many standard form contracts include such clauses.

Unless the clause indicates a distinct territorial system of law, there will be problems. Suppose the parties were to agree on 'British law' or 'American law'; it would be necessary to determine whether that choice could be given meaning by further localisation, for example, as between Scots law and English law, though it could be argued that, in so far as English law and Scots law were the same on the particular point in issue, it did not matter.

The power of the parties to invent their own legal rules within the contract or to incorporate sets of rules from any legal system they chose led the late FA Mann to suggest that the parties could avoid the Rome Convention altogether by a properly worded choice of law clause selecting the common law rules. While there may be no reason in principle to oppose the selection of the common law rules, or classical Roman law for that matter, such a choice could only work within the Rome Convention itself[103] in providing for an express choice of law. Article 3(1) will not include those situations where parties simply incorporate certain provisions of a foreign legal system into their contract; in such a situation, the provisions are merely additional contractual terms and the applicable law still has to be determined by applying the rules of the Convention.

---

103 See Mann, FA (1991) 107 LQR 353. It is difficult to understand how this proposal would withstand scrutiny in the High Court, as: (a) such a proposal violates the spirit if not the letter of the Contracts (Applicable Law) Act 1990, s 3(1), (2), (3); (b) there might well be difficulties with the Rome Convention, Art 16; (c) under Art 1 it might well be argued that common law rules did not exist and therefore could not be chosen or if chosen cannot be applied under Art 2; and (d) the proposal is at variance with the fundamental duty of an English court to comply with the principle of the supremacy of European law.

Choice demonstrated with reasonable certainty

There may be circumstances where the parties have made no express choice of law so that Art 3(1) permits the court to find that a choice has been 'demonstrated with reasonable certainty by the terms of the contract or the circumstances of the case'. The concept of looking at the conduct of the parties and seeking to determine their actual intentions as a matter of inference was well known to the common law. However, prior common law cases must be regarded with a degree of caution, having regard to Art 18 of the Rome Convention.[104] Secondly, it is well established in European Community law that community treaties are to be interpreted in a manner consistent with policy objectives and not in accordance with the traditions of the legislation. The Giuliano and Lagarde report contains a number of instances where a choice of law might be inferred; examples might include:

(a) where a standard form of contract is employed;

(b) where there are previous dealings between the parties;

(c) where a jurisdiction clause or arbitration clause has been used;

(d) where a connected transaction includes an express choice of law; and

(e) where a contract expressly incorporates the rules of a foreign legal system.

It is necessary to say a little about these possibilities.

The use of a standard form contract

The use of a particular standard form contract might properly give rise to the inference that a particular law was impliedly chosen. In *Amin Rasheed Shipping Corporation v Kuwait Insurance Co*,[105] the use of a Lloyd's SG form of policy modelled on that contained in a schedule to the Marine Insurance Act 1906 persuaded the House of Lords that English law was the impliedly chosen law by the parties, a Liberian company and a Kuwait insurance company. At the time of contracting, Kuwait had no developed law on marine insurance. There is every reason to believe that the same result would have been reached under the Rome Convention.

Where there are previous dealings between the parties

The Giuliano and Lagarde report acknowledges that, where there have been previous dealings between the parties embodying an express choice of law, then it might be proper to infer a choice in a subsequent contract. However,

---

104 Rome Convention 1980, Art 18 reads: 'In the interpretation and application of the preceding uniform rules, regard shall be had to their international character and to the desirability of achieving uniformity in their interpretation and application.'

105 [1984] AC 50.

such an inference is not automatic and much would depend on the surrounding circumstances and, in particular, whether the subsequent contract was similar in character to previous dealings

Where there is a jurisdiction or arbitration clause

The Giuliano and Lagarde report recognises that a choice of forum may be a strong indication of an implied choice but it is not conclusive and all the circumstances of the contract have to be considered and there may be conflicting *indicia* that have to be weighed. This is not any different from the prior position at common law. In *Compagnie Tunisienne de Navigation SA v Companie d'Armement*,[106] the House of Lords concluded that the presence of a choice of forum clause raised a strong inference but it could be set aside by other indicators. It would seem that the position under the Rome Convention is unlikely to be different to that at common law.

Some indication of this emerged in *Egon Oldendorff v Liberia Corpn*[107] where the plaintiff, a German company, secured leave under RSC Ord 11 r 1(1)(d)(iii) to serve a writ on the defendant, a Japanese company, on the basis that the contract was governed by English law, having regard to the inclusion of a clause providing for arbitration in England.

Where a connected transaction includes an express choice of law

At common law, when one transaction contains an express choice of law, it may be possible to imply a choice of law in a related transaction. Where a contract between A and B contains an express choice of English law, it may be possible to imply a choice of English law where C undertakes to guarantee the obligations of A.[108] The same principle has been extended to a situation where a charterparty includes an express choice of law and the court then finds that related bills of lading give rise to an implied choice of law.[109] There is some indication from the Giuliano and Lagarde report that the matter will be no different under the Rome Convention. However, it will be necessary, in each case, to examine the events to determine whether the transactions can be categorised as related or connecting.

---

106 [1971] AC 572.

107 [1995] 2 LR 64 (Mance J). In subsequent proceedings reported at [1996] 1 LR 380, Clarke J observed that, while the test under the Convention might be different, the factors set out in the *Compagnie Tunisienne* case were of continuing relevance.

108 See *Broken Hill Proprietary Co Ltd v Xenakis* [1982] 2 LR 304.

109 See *The Njegos* [1936] P 90.

Where a contract expressly incorporates the rules of a foreign legal system

At common law, there was a clear distinction between a choice of law and the incorporation of the provisions of a foreign legal system[110] as contractual terms. The distinction is important if the foreign law changes between the time of making the contract and the time of performance; where a choice of law has been made, then subsequent changes may operate to the benefit of a particular party.[111] However, if the provisions have merely been incorporated they remain as contractual terms even if repealed within that particular legal system.

Although there is no ruling on the matter, the Giuliano and Lagarde report appears to indicate that the adoption of particular articles (for example, French Civil Code) might lead to an implied choice of law. It remains to be seen whether the European Court of Justice favour this approach.

If the parties are unable to bring themselves within either of the heads of Art 3(1), it will be necessary to consider the provisions of Art 4(1). However, before doing that, it is important to pay regard to the remaining provisions of Art 3.

Splitting the applicable law[112]

The final sentence of Art 3(1) reads: 'By their choice the parties can select the law applicable to the whole or part only of the contract.' The effect of this provision is to recognise the process of *depecage*.

The parties are free to select the law to govern the whole of their contract or a part of it only, or, indeed, to have a series of choices for different parts. A multifaceted international contract requiring performances in various countries might be one reason for the parties wishing to split up the whole into component parts or the parties might wish to select one law to interpret the contract and another to implement the terms so interpreted. The working group drawing up the Rome Convention rejected the principle that the law chosen for one part of the contract should govern the whole; they considered that the main argument against severability, or *depecage*, that it might be used to avoid mandatory rules, was reduced by the inclusion of Art 7. The doctrine of depecage has a long history in English private international law[113] but the

---

110 *Dobell v SS Rossmore Co Ltd* [1895] 2 QB 408; *Stafford Allen and Sons Ltd v Pacific Steam Navigation Co* [1956] 1 WLR 629.

111 *R v International Trustee for the Protection of Bondholders AG* [1937] AC 500.

112 See Lando (1987) 24 CMLR 159; McLachlan (1990) 51 BYIL 311.

113 The authority cited in the first edition of Dicey, *The Conflict of Laws* (1896) was *Hamlyn v Talisker Distillery* [1894] AC 202; but, see *Kahler v Midland Bank* [1950] AC 24; *Forsikringsaktieselskapet Vesta v Butcher* [1989] AC 852, HL and CA, affirming [1986] 2 All ER 488 (Hobhouse J); *Libyan Arab Foreign Bank v Bankers Trust Co* [1988] 1 LR 259.

Giuliano and Lagarde report indicates that the doctrine is only to be applied where severability does not lead to inconsistency. The problem with *depecage* has been to find a balance between the principle of party autonomy and the need to respect the claims of those legal systems that have a close connection with the contract. The inclusion of an express provision in the Rome Convention may lead to an increase in the number of cases in this area.

Variation of choice

Article 3(2) provides:

> The parties may at any time agree to subject the contract to a law other than that which previously governed it, whether as a result of an earlier choice under this Article or of other provisions of this Convention. Any variation by the parties of the law to be applied, made after the conclusion of the contract, shall not prejudice its formal validity under Art 9 or adversely affect the rights of third parties.

The principle of party autonomy is demonstrated by Art 3(2) of the Rome Convention. This enables the parties at any time to alter the applicable law, whether they are revising an earlier choice, have discovered the benefits of choice after the contract is under way, or have decided that they don't wish to be subjected to the law which the Convention would impose on them. The new or revised choice may apply to the contract as a whole or to any severable part of it. While the Convention permits changes to be made at any time, the effect of any agreement between the parties which is made after the dispute has come to litigation will depend on the attitude of the forum and its rules about amending pleadings. There are four potential dangers in respect of a change of applicable law: (a) the new law might contain requirements for formal validity not present under the prior law; (b) the rights of third parties might be affected; (c) attempts might be made to avoid mandatory rules arising under the prior applicable law; and (d) under the newly chosen law, the contract might be invalid.[114]

Thus, no change in the applicable law can adversely affect the formal validity of the contract or operate to the prejudice of third party rights acquired under the former applicable law. Where, in consumer contracts and individual employment contracts, the Convention imports mandatory provisions of a law other than the one chosen by the parties, this importation is not affected by a change in the applicable law.[115] So, for example, in an individual employment contract, the mandatory rules of the law of the country where the employee habitually carries out his work will apply

---

114 See the Rome Convention 1980, Art 8, below.
115 *Ibid*, Art 3(3), below.

whatever the choice of law and will persist through any change in the applicable law which the parties may subsequently agree.

Limitation on choice – single country contracts

Article 3(3) introduces a restriction to the principle of freedom of choice. The operative provisions read:

> The fact that the parties have chosen a foreign law, whether or not accompanied by the choice of the foreign tribunal, shall not, where all the other elements relevant to the situation at the time of the choice are connected with one country only, prejudice the application of rules of the law of that country which cannot be derogated from by contract, hereinafter called 'mandatory rules'.

Suppose a contract was made by parties who were Italian, to be performed in Italy and all other relevant contacts were with Italy. Suppose, further, that the parties chose German law and consented to the jurisdiction of the German courts. Article 3(3) requires the German court to apply the mandatory rules of Italian law. In such a situation, the probability is that the parties only chose German law to avoid such mandatory rules. While the law of Germany will be the governing law, it will only be applied to the extent that it does not violate the mandatory rules of Italian law. If we change the facts slightly and replace Germany with England then the position will be the same under the Rome Convention. However, at common law, there was no such doctrine of evasion of law and the courts would have applied English law at the expense of the Italian rules unless objection could have been taken under the terms of *Vita Food Products Inc v Unus Shipping Co Ltd*.[116]

Thus, under the provisions of Art 3(3), where all the other elements relevant to the situation at the time of the choice are connected with one country only, a choice of a foreign law, whether or not accompanied by a foreign jurisdiction clause, will not prejudice the application of the mandatory rules of the solely connected system. The Rome Convention 1980 applies only to contracts which involve a choice between the laws of different countries[117] and the situation envisaged here is not such a case as, on the facts, all the connections are with a single country. What brings it within the Rome Convention is the selection by the parties of a governing legal system which is factually unconnected with the contract. The Giuliano and Lagarde report makes it clear that the UK, in particular, was insistent that the parties' freedom to select the governing law should not be confined to contracts which

---

116 [1939] AC 277 (where objection could be taken on grounds that the choice was not *bona fide*, legal or consistent with public policy). Whether an unconnected law was open to objection was the subject of conflicting *dicta* – see *Boissevain v Weil* [1949] 1 KB 482; *Tzortzis v Monark Line* [1968] 1 WLR 406; *Re Helbert Wagg and Co Ltd's Claim* [1956] Ch 323.

117 Rome Convention 1980, Art 1(1).

inherently contained a potential choice between connected laws. There were interests to be protected here, as choices, particularly of English law, are often made in contracts which not only have no factual connection with England, but are wholly connected to a single foreign system. As the Rome Convention has universal application, that is, the countries which adopt it are to apply it to all cases coming before their courts, the omission of this freedom would have been detrimental to the business of English courts. The *quid pro quo* for this concession is that the selection of a governing law in such cases will not avoid the application of the mandatory rules of the system with which the contract is solely connected. There is not much ground given here, for, under the common law rules, the choice of a proper law had to be *bona fide*, legal and not contrary to public policy.[118] A choice of law unconnected to the contract which had the effect of evading the mandatory rules of the solely connected system might well be regarded as *prima facie* evidence of bad faith. Article 3(3) avoids any need to look into the minds of the contracting parties by providing that any pertinent rule of the legal system solely connected to the contract which that system regards as obligatory will be inserted into the contract, notwithstanding the choice of a foreign applicable law.

There are a number of points that arise on the wording of Art 3(3). First, what is the meaning of the expression 'all the other elements relevant to the situation'? Can, for example, a choice of law avoid the mandatory provisions of the almost solely connected law simply because there is some connection, however slight, with a third legal system?

Secondly, it would seem that the expression 'foreign law' relates to the parties and the contract. So, if a contract is made between two Japanese residents but with a choice of English law, then, even though the matter is litigated in England, English law will be regarded as foreign, notwithstanding that it is the law of the forum. Thirdly, Art 3(3) is only concerned with mandatory rules, so that, if all the connections are with country A and there is a choice of law of country B, then that choice will operate in respect of non mandatory rules. In the example cited above, Italian mandatory rules will apply, notwithstanding the choice of German law. However, German law will apply in respect of all matters not covered by mandatory rules. Fourthly, Art 3(3) is part of Art 3 and this Article proceeds from a general principle of freedom of choice; it would, therefore, seem that a party seeking to invoke Art 3(3) should bear the *onus probandi*. Finally, Art 3(3) falls to be read with Art 7 and will be touched on again under that head.

Although the common law did not establish a doctrine of evasion of law in the area of international contracts beyond the qualifications established in *Vita Foods Products Inc v Unus Shipping Co Ltd*,[119] there are statutory provisions

---

118 *Vita Food Products Inc v Unus Shipping Co Ltd* [1939] AC 277; 1 All ER 513.
119 *Ibid.*

which do. Most prominently, the Unfair Contract Terms Act 1977 deals with the choice of a foreign law where the contract has a substantial connection with a legal system within the UK. The purpose of the Unfair Contract Terms Act 1977 is to introduce detailed legislative controls in respect of exclusion clauses contained in contracts; the legislation will apply notwithstanding the choice of a foreign law if it comes within the scope of s 27(2) of the Act. Section 27(2) of the Unfair Contract Terms Act 1977 reads as follows:

> (2) This Act has effect notwithstanding any contract term which applies or purports to apply the law of some other country outside the UK, where (either or both):
>
> (a) the term appears to the court, or arbitrator or arbiter to have been imposed wholly or mainly for the purpose of enabling a party imposing it to evade the operation of this Act; or
>
> (b) in the making of the contract one of the parties dealt as a consumer, and he was then habitually resident in the UK, and the essential steps necessary for the making of the contract were taken there, whether by him or by others on his behalf ...

As there appear to be no reported cases involving the application of this provision, it may be concluded, either, that there was no problem or that the precautionary measures have been effective. It may be useful, however, to use this provision as an illustration of the relationship between the Rome Convention and a domestic system.

By way of illustration, I want to look, first, at a contract unconnected with the UK where the parties have chosen English law and, then, at a contract connected with England where the parties have chosen a governing law which is not a UK legal system.

Where the parties have chosen English law to govern a contract which is wholly unconnected with any part of the UK, their choice will be the applicable law under the Convention, and English law will be applied to determine all matters of substance at issue between them. This does not mean that every rule of English law will be applied. It must always be determined whether a rule of a domestic legal system extends to an international contract. For example, the Unfair Contract Terms Act 1977[120] provides that, where the law of any part of the UK applies to the contract solely by reason of the parties' choice and, but for that choice, the contract would be governed by the law of a country outside the UK, the protection provided by the Act,[121] which includes some rules which are undoubtedly mandatory, has no application. The purpose of this provision is to protect the position of English law as a commonly chosen governing law by parties whose contracts have no connection with England. No mandatory provision of any other law will be applicable unless:

---

120 Unfair Contract Terms Act 1977, s 27(1).
121 *Ibid*, ss 2–7 (for English law); ss 17–21 (for Scots law).

(a) the contract is wholly connected to a single foreign country;

(b) the contract is a consumer contract as provided for in Art 5;

(c) the contract is an individual employment contract which is subject to Art 6;

(d) there is a mandatory rule of the forum[122] or there is a rule of the forum's public policy which is imperative;[123]

(e) the case is brought before a non-UK forum which applies a mandatory rule of another system under the terms of Art 7(1).[124]

This list appears lengthy, but length should not be confused with importance and several of these limitations have themselves very limited effect.

In the second situation, where the contract is connected with England and subjected to a chosen foreign law, there must be a strong connection with a UK law against which the choice of a foreign law contrasts. Section 27(2)(b) of the Unfair Contract Terms Act 1977 stipulates the connection and s 27(2)(a) assumes it, for one cannot evade that which would not otherwise apply. So we can assume that the contract either is wholly connected with a UK legal system or is sufficiently connected with one to make it at least more probable than not that the applicable law in default of choice would be the law of some part of the UK. In such a situation, the choice of the applicable law under the Rome Convention will be effective in a UK court unless there is a finding that the choice of law was designed to evade or that the contract was a consumer contract with the connections being specified in the section. In the event of either of these being established, the chosen applicable law will still govern the contract, but it will do so subject to the application of the provisions of the Act.

Suppose, however, that the case is brought not before a UK court, where the provisions of the Statute cannot possibly be ignored, but before a foreign tribunal. If the contract were wholly connected with England, the foreign tribunal would be bound by Art 3(3) to apply the mandatory rules of English law and, as by English law the mandatory rules do not apply automatically but only on the basis of a finding, the foreign court would have to determine whether the case fell within the provisions.

If the facts of the case are not wholly connected with the UK, the problem becomes more difficult as, by definition, it does not fall within Art 3(3). In such a situation, the choice of law will be effective and wholly exclude the possibility of the application of the Unfair Contract Terms Act 1977, unless either the case falls within the special consumer[125] or employment categories[126] or the foreign court is prepared to invoke Art 7(1).

---

122 Rome Convention 1980, Art 7(2), discussed below.

123 *Ibid*, Art 16.

124 But, contracted out of by the UK; see the Contracts (Applicable Law) Act 1990, s 2(2).

125 Rome Convention 1980, Art 5.

126 *Ibid*, Art 6.

Having considered the provisions of Art 3 concerning an express choice of law, it is now necessary to examine the provisions of the Rome Convention 1980 where no express choice has been made.

THE APPLICABLE LAW IN DEFAULT OF CHOICE

In the event that no express choice has been made under Art 3, it is necessary to consider Art 4. The basic principle is set out in Art 4(1), which provides:

> To the extent that the law applicable in the contract has not been chosen in accordance with Art 3, the contract shall be governed by the law of the country with which it is most closely connected. Nevertheless, a severable part of the contract which has a closer connection with another country may by way of exception be governed by the law of that other country.

In default of choice of a governing law by the parties, the Rome Convention seeks the law which is most closely connected with the contract. The basic principle here is exactly that of the common law, which involved a quest for the system of law with which the contract was most closely connected. The test here is an objective one and depends on establishing the 'centre of gravity' or 'grouping of contacts' of the contract, rather than an attempt to discover what the parties would have chosen had they thought about the matter.[127] It is important to note that Art 4(1) requires that the connection must be with a country; at common law, some judges referred to the country and others to the system of law. Some have indicated that the two concepts could be combined.[128] However, it is arguable that the emphasis on the country is less precise, since it leads to undue weight being placed on matters such as the place of contracting or the place of performance, which may be arbitrary. It is arguable that to connect with a system of law is preferable, since emphasis is placed on factors such as the legal terminology and the form of the contract.

In searching for the proper law under the common law rules, the better approach of the English court was to have regard to all the connections such as: (a) the place of contracting; (b) the place of performance; (c) the language of the contract; (d) the money of the account; (e) the personal law of the parties; and (f) all the circumstances surrounding the contract. This was not done with a view to comparing the lengths of the lists of contacts, but to weigh the various connections in order to determine the country most significantly connected.[129] The Rome Convention 1980 involves the same approach.

---

127 For the approach at common law, see *The Assunzione* [1954] P 150; 1 All ER 278.
128 *James Miller and Partners Ltd v Whitworth Street Estates (Manchester) Ltd* [1970] AC 583.
129 *The Assunzione* [1954] P 150; 1 All ER 278.

The final sentence of Art 4(1) reads:

> Nevertheless, a severable part of the contract which has a closer connection with another country may by way of exception be governed by the law of that other country.

This provision is designed to emphasise that the process of *depecage*, by which parts of the contract are referred to different systems of law, is to be confined to very limited circumstances.[130]

The common law had not developed a set of presumptions to identify the proper law, though there was a marked preference for the *lex loci solutionis*. In contrast, Art 4 of the Rome Convention contains one general presumption (Art 4(2)) and two specific presumptions (Art 4(3), (4)); these are then followed by a provision (Art 4(5)) that might be conveniently described as a general sweep up provision. The structure of Art 4 has not escaped criticism[131] but it does seem that it makes sense to regard the principle in Art 4(1) as being followed by a general and then two specific presumptions, followed by a sweep up provision.

Presumption one – characteristic performance

Article 4(2) provides:

> Subject to the provisions of para 5 of this Article, it shall be presumed that the contract is most closely connected with the country where the party who is to effect the performance which is characteristic of the contract has, at the time of conclusion of the contract, his habitual residence, or, in the case of a body corporate or unincorporate, its central administration. However, if the contract is entered into in the course of that party's trade or profession, that country shall be the country in which the principal place of business is situated or, where under the terms of the contract the performance is to be effected through a place of business other than the principal place of business, the country in which that other place of business is situate.

Article 4(2) operates in two stages; first the characteristic performance under the contract is identified and then an attempt is made to provide a geographical location. The doctrine of characteristic performance is a novel and somewhat controversial aspect of the Rome Convention 1980 deriving from Swiss law.[132] The first difficulty is that the expression is not defined in the convention itself. The common law was familiar with the concept of the law of the place of performance (*lex loci solutionis*) but the problem was that, in

---

130 For a non-Convention example, see *Libyan Arab Foreign Bank v Bankers Trust Co* [1989] QB 728 (Staughton J).

131 See Mann, FA (1991) 107 LQR 353, p 354, the learned author regretting the 'obfuscating verbosity' of the Rome Convention and the 'almost bizarre' provisions of Art 4.

132 Collins (1976) 25 ICLQ 35; D'Oliviera (1977) 25 AJCL 303; Mann, FA (1982) 32 ICLQ 265.

a normal bilateral contract, there may be two places of performance; one in respect of the delivery of the goods and another in respect of the place where payment is to be made. The Giuliano and Lagarde report does not itself define 'characteristic performance' but identifies it as the performance 'which usually constitutes the centre of gravity and the socioeconomic purpose of the contractual transaction'. A common lawyer might be inclined to phrase this as 'what the fundamental purpose of the transaction was'. Indeed, as the report indicates, in modern society, many contracts can be reduced to A making payment for goods or services provided by B.[133] In such circumstances, the characteristic performance will be the work done under the contract rather than the payment for that work, so that, in a sale contract, it will be the seller's law (the law of the country of his place of business) rather than the buyer's law which will apply. The report gives other instances; the characteristic performance of an agency contract will relate to the law of the agent; a banking contract to the law of the bank; a building contract to the law of the builder; and a hire contract to the to the law of the hirer out. The report proceeds on the basis that one party has an active duty to deliver goods or perform a service while the other party is nearly passive in simply making payment. The report suggests that the presumption relates the contract to the law of its socioeconomic function but that assertion is far from convincing.

If the characteristic performance cannot be located (for example, in a contract which involves the exchange of goods or reciprocal services), the applicable law will be the law of the country with which the contract is most closely connected.[134] Even if a characteristic performance can be found, the presumption will not apply if the contract is more closely connected with another country. The law of that other country will apply instead.[135]

Suppose the contract requires the English manufacturer to build a machine and ship it to his customers in Hong Kong. The characteristic performance is the work to be done in England – obviously. What if, however, the contract was made in Hong Kong and payment is to be made there in Hong Kong dollars upon delivery and the contract is written in Chinese? It is open to the court to take a wide or narrow view of the presumption, just as it is left to the court to decide whether another law is more closely connected to the contract than the system indicated by the presumptions.

The text of Art 4(2) has been subject to criticism not only on grounds of its complexity but also, having regard to the manner in which characteristic performance is determined, the law will normally be that of the seller and therefore the balance is tilted in favour of the supplier of goods and services and, thus, the larger economic unit. There is also clear room for difficulties in

---

133 *Report on the Rome Convention* OJ C 282, 1980, p 80.
134 *Ibid*, Art 4 (5).
135 *Ibid*, Art 4 (5).

cases concerning more complex contracts such as distributorship agreements or joint venture transactions.[136]

As the second limb of Art 4(2) makes clear, it is necessary to identify a link between the characteristic performer and a country. This will be the characteristic performer's: (a) habitual residence; or (b) its central administration; or (c) its principal place of business; or (d) a place of business other than its principal place of business.

It might be argued that habitual residence is not appropriate in the context of commercial transactions. However, it has to be noted that it is residence at the time of the contract that is important.

Thus, if an English company were to sell furniture to a German customer the applicable law would be English, being the law of the principal place of business. However, if an English company were to agree with a foreign company to hire an offshore oil rig through its Texas branch, then Art 4(2) would point towards the law of Texas as the applicable law.[137]

The main criticism raised in respect of Art 4(2) is that the object of a presumption is to provide certainty by the operation of a rule that is simple to apply; whether this can be said of the two limb process under Art 4(2) is a moot point.

Presumption two – immovable property

The second presumption contained in Art 4(3) is of a specific nature. Article 4(3) reads:

> Notwithstanding the provisions of para 2 of this Article, to the extent that the subject matter of the contract is a right in immovable property or a right to use immovable property, it shall be presumed that the contract is most closely connected with the country where the immovable property is situated.

One of the objectives of the Rome Convention 1980 is to operate alongside the Brussels Convention on Jurisdiction and the Enforcement of Judgments 1968. The Brussels Convention establishes exclusive jurisdiction, where the issue is the right to immovable property, for the courts of the *situs* – where the immovable property is situated – and those courts have exclusive, though not sole, jurisdiction over tenancy agreements.[138]

English courts apply the *lex situs* to govern the proprietary effects of real estate contracts, so the reference to the *lex situs* as the governing law in default of choice is not surprising.

---

136 Lando (1987) 24 CMLR 159.
137 See *Bank of Baroda v Vysya Bank* [1994] 2 LR 87; Morse [1994] LMCLQ 560.
138 Brussels Convention 1968, Art 16(1)(a), (b).

The problem that arises here is the ambit of the presumption. It clearly extends to the sale of immovable property and tenancy agreements and other rights over immovable property, and clearly does not extend to ordinary personal contracts which merely relate to the immovable – to work on it, design it, repair it or clean it. The inclusion of the words 'right to use' seems to take us well beyond rights *in rem* to include arrangements which English law would regard as licences – so, short term holiday lets or hotel accommodation are within the terms of the presumption. There is an aspect of overkill here. To take an example: suppose an English holiday company takes a lease of an hotel in Miami owned by a New York company. Certainly the proprietary effects of the contract should be governed by the law of Florida, but there appears no special reason to subject the contract itself to the law of Florida.

Suppose further that a French holidaymaker were to contract with that same English company to stay for a week in a Miami hotel. Unless the agreement was a package tour and, thus, came under the special provisions relating to consumer contracts,[139] this contract would also fall to be governed by the law of Florida unless the parties chose otherwise.

This presumption, like the others, will not apply if the contract is more closely connected with another country.[140] The Giuliano and Lagarde report gives the example of two Belgians agreeing on the holiday rental of property belonging to one of them on the Elba and offers the opinion that Belgian law rather than Italian law would govern in each case but, in the examples I have used, there is no such easy rebuttal to the presumption.

Although the formal validity of a contract concerning immovables is subject to the general provisions on formal validity contained in Art 9, in so far as the *lex situs* has formal requirements which it regards as mandatory, irrespective of where the contract was made or what law governs its substance, those formal requirements have to be complied with.

Presumption three – carriage of goods

Article 4(4) stipulates:

> ... a contract for the carriage of goods shall not be subject to the presumption in para 2. In such a contract, if the country in which, at the time the contract is concluded, the carrier has his principal place of business is also the country in which the place of loading or the place of discharge or the principal place of business of the consignor is situated, it shall presumed that the contract is most closely connected with that country. In applying this paragraph, single voyage charterparties and other contracts the main purpose of which is the carriage of goods shall be treated as contracts for the carriage of goods.

---

139 Rome Convention 1980, Art 5(4)(b), 5(5).
140 *Ibid*, Art 4(5).

For carriage of goods contracts – and the provision extends to all modes of carriage – the presumption relating to characteristic performance is expressly excluded and a special set of connections is provided.[141]

In default of choice, the applicable law will be presumed to be the law of the country where the carrier had, at the time the contract was made, his principal place of business, provided that such place is also the place of loading or unloading or the principal place of business of the consignor.

The carrier for this purpose is the party who undertakes the carriage whether he does any carrying himself or arranges for someone else to do it.

The presumption applies only to carriage of goods, not passengers. The likelihood that this would separate the passenger from his baggage in legal terms was felt to be less objectionable than that the passengers on the same journey with the same carrier should be subject to different legal regimes.

If the coincidences are not present, the courts must search for the most connected country without further help from the Convention.

The Rome Convention, here as elsewhere, is displaced by other international conventions which Contracting States have entered or may in future enter.[142] So, for example, as far as the UK is concerned, the international carriage of goods by sea remains subject to the Hague-Visby Rules.[143]

Non-application of the presumptions

Article 4(5) reads as follows:

> Paragraph 2 shall not apply if the characteristic performance cannot be determined, and the presumptions in paras 2, 3 and 4 shall be disregarded if it appears from the circumstances as a whole that the contract is more closely connected with another country.

Article 4(5) is designed to deal with two different situations. The first situation is where characteristic performance cannot be determined; the second situation is where the contract is more closely connected with another country.

If characteristic performance cannot be determined, then Art 4(5) indicates that the court is thrown back to the general provision in Art 4(1); the judge will then be required to weigh the various factors to determine the country with which the contract is most closely connected. This is not unlike the objective determination of the proper law of the contract at common law. In

---

141 Rome Convention 1980, Art 4(4).
142 *Ibid*, Art 21.
143 Carriage of Goods by Sea Act 1971.

such a case, a judge will proceed from Art 4(1) to Art 4(2) and then Art 4(5) and back to Art 4(1).

The second part of Art 4(5) provides that none of the presumptions are to apply if the contract is more closely connected with another country. As a matter of application, it is difficult to know how a judge is to determine this until he weighs the various contacts. The purpose of Art 4(5) was to provide a degree of flexibility alongside the presumptions. Some writers have speculated that Art 4(5) might be used by English courts to continue the common law approach of seeking the objective law of the contract. It would seem that a judge in such a situation should proceed to Art 4(1) and then apply any of the relevant presumptions in Art 4(2), (3) and (4) before moving to Art 4(5) and then listing and weighing the relevant contacts to determine whether the test in the second limb of Art 4(5) has been met, namely, that the contract is more closely connected with another country. If this interpretation is correct, then it would seem that the presumption is being rebutted rather disregarded.

As indicated above, the wording of Art 4 has attracted comment; it remains to be seen how effective the presumptions will be in practice and what effect the European Court of Justice will have upon their operation when the interpretative jurisdiction under the Brussels Protocol becomes fully operational.

THE SCOPE OF THE APPLICABLE LAW

Article 10 of the Rome Convention provides:

1   The law applicable to a contract ... shall govern in particular:

(a) interpretation;[144]

(b) performance;

(c) within the limits of the powers conferred on the court by its procedural law, the consequences of the breach, including the assessment of damages in so far as it is governed by rules of law;

(d) the various ways of extinguishing obligations and prescription and limitation of actions;

(e) the consequences of nullity of the contract.

2   In relation to the manner of performance and the steps to be taken in the event of defective performance, regard shall be had to the law of the country in which performance takes place.

---

144 This is in line with the common law position that questions of interpretation of the contract were normally matters for the proper law: *Bonython v Commonwealth of Australia* [1951] AC 201, PC.

The law applicable to the contract under the Rome Convention, whether chosen by the parties or found in default of choice and including any mandatory rules imported into it, governs the substance of the obligation between the parties. The interpretation of the contract, its performance, frustration, the ways in which the obligations may be extinguished, prescription and the limitations of actions are all matters for the applicable law.[145] Of course, under Art 3, the parties are free to subject different parts of their contract to different governing laws so, for example, they can subject the interpretation of the contract to a separate system of law if they wish.

The Rome Convention's provisions much resemble those which the common law had established. One provision, however, seems peculiar to the English lawyer. The applicable law also governs 'within the limits of the powers conferred on the court by its procedural law, the consequences of the breach, including the assessment of damages in so far as it is governed by rules of law'.[146] This goes beyond the decision that the contract has been broken and that consequently the defendant is to pay damages, to the assessment of those damages. The assessment of damages includes the heads of recoverable damages, whether, for example, the plaintiff can recover for disappointment or anguish at the breach of the contract, and the issues of causation and remoteness of damage. It does not, under English law, extend to the quantification of damages, which is seen as a matter wholly within the realm of the *lex fori*.

The references to performance in Art 10(1)(b) and (2) bear some comparison with the position at common law. At common law, there was a distinction as regards performance between 'the substance of the performance' and the 'method and manner of performance'. It was well established that the former aspect was governed by the proper law. Thus, in *Jacobs v Credit Lyonnais*,[147] the question of whether a defendant could raise a defence of *force majeure* was to be determined by the proper law of the contract. In *Mount Albert Borough Council v Australasian Temperance and General Assurance Society*,[148] the interpretation as to the correct rate of interest to be paid under a debenture deed was a matter of substance and thus to be determined by the proper law of the contract.

In respect of the relationship between Art 10(1)(b) and Art 10(2), it is clear that performance is to be governed by the applicable law. However, it would seem, in respect of Art 10(2), that this is intended to be confined to the details of performance rather than the substance of the obligation. So, for example, if

---

145 Rome Convention 1980, Art 10(1)(a), (b), (d).
146 *Ibid*, Art 10(1)(c).
147 (1884) 12 QBD 589.
148 [1938] AC 224.

delivery has to be made during normal business hours, or notice has to be given within seven working days, the local law's rules on these will be taken into account. It should not follow that the law of the place of performance has any say in the substantial performance of the obligation or that a defence for non-performance, which is more than technical and which exists in the local law but not in the applicable law, can be pleaded.[149] Article 10(2) will arise where the law of the country in which performance is to take place is different from the country whose law is applicable. It is clear that the court does not have to apply the *lex loci solutionis* but is simply to pay regard to it; this means that the court is to have a discretion whether to apply it or not. This differs from the position at common law in that, if a matter was related to the mode and manner of performance, then the law of the place of performance was applied.

In respect of Art 10(1)(d), the sub-Article deals with the extinguishing of obligations (for example, by adjudication in bankruptcy) and the issue of limitation. The requirement that the issue of limitation is governed not by the procedural law of the forum but by the applicable law is consistent with the approach of the Foreign Limitation Periods Act 1984.[150]

As regards Art 10(1)(e), which deals with the consequences of nullity, the UK entered a reservation under Art 22 and this is given effect to in domestic law by s 2(2) of the Contracts (Applicable Law) Act 1990. This provides that Art 10(1)(e) 'shall not have the force of law in the UK'. This exclusion is a result of the fact that English law takes the view that the consequences of nullity are a matter for the law of restitution rather than the law of contract.

PARTICULAR ASPECTS OF THE CONTRACT

Although the applicable law as identified under Arts 3–6 is the central concept within the Rome Convention, it does not determine all issues arising under a contract. There are a number of specific issues that require particular attention.

Material validity

Article 8 is concerned with the issue of material validity and reads as follows:

1   The existence and validity of a contract, or of any term of a contract, shall be determined by the law which would govern it under this Convention if the contract or term were valid.

---

149 *Jacobs v Credit Lyonnais* (1884) 12 QBD 589.

150 The awareness of provisions in the Rome Convention 1980 paved the way for the Foreign Limitation Periods Act 1984.

2 Nevertheless, a party may rely upon the law of the country in which he has his habitual residence to establish that he did not consent if it appears from the circumstances that it would not be reasonable to determine the effect of his conduct in accordance with the law specified in a preceding paragraph.

The existence and validity of the contract, or of a term of it, is governed by the putative applicable law, that is, the law which would be the applicable law if the contract existed and was valid. At common law, in the absence of clear authority, the better view was that the existence of the contract should be governed by the putative proper law but whether this was the chosen proper law or the objective proper law was open to contention.[151] There was a general preference for the objective proper law, as that would defeat a self-validating choice in the face of objective invalidity. The solution adopted by the Convention is more liberal – the putative applicable law can as equally be the chosen law as the law found in default of choice. The putative applicable law will determine whether an offer has been accepted, whether the agreement is, if it needs to be, supported by consideration and whether the consent to the contract has been obtained by fraud, duress, misrepresentation or undue influence. These matters relate to the formation of the agreement itself not to its subsequent functioning. Suppose the plaintiff contends that his entry into the contract was induced by a misrepresentation, such that, had he known the truth, he would not have entered the contract at all. What remedy he seeks will depend on the position he is in at the time of the discovery of the misrepresentation. He may want to contest the validity of the contract, seek rescission of the contract or obtain damages for the effect of the misrepresentation on his performance of the contract. All these are matters for the applicable law – the putative applicable law if the plea goes to the existence or validity of the contract, the actual applicable law if the complaint goes to the performance of an existing contract.[152]

Similarly, the common law has tended towards the objective putative proper law to determine the issue of the consent of the parties. Again, the solution adopted by the Convention is the putative applicable law, whether chosen or found in default, but with the proviso that a party can also rely on the law of his habitual residence to establish that he did not consent.[153] To take a simple example, suppose the alleged contract resulted from the offeror presuming the offeree's agreement unless he heard to the contrary. Unless it had previously been agreed by the parties that such an inference could be drawn, English law would not allow the offeror to bind the offeree in this way. If the applicable law would infer consent in these circumstances, an offeree habitually resident in England could use English law to counteract that

---

151 *Albeko Schuhmaschinen v The Kamborian Shoe Machine Co Ltd* (1961) 111 LJ 519.
152 Rome Convention 1980, Art 10.
153 *Ibid*, Art 8(2).

inference. In considering whether a claim is made out under Art 8(1) or 8(2), the court is obliged to consider the matter from an international perspective and weigh the factors to determine reasonableness under Art 8(2).[154]

Formal validity

The provisions in respect of formal validity are set out in Art 9 of the Rome Convention; the scheme of the article is to set out general rules and particular rules in respect of consumer contracts and contracts in respect of immovable property.

English law has few requirements for the formal validity of contracts and those there are generally go to the enforceability of the contract rather than to its validity. The specialty contract or deed is an obvious example of a contract which derives its validity from its form but the requirements relating to surety agreements or contracts for the sale of land survive from procedural restrictions. Procedural matters are, according to the English conflict of laws, wholly within the control of the forum. In the absence of authority, the English common law rules would probably have allowed a contract to be formally valid if it satisfied the formal requirements of either the *lex loci contractus* or the proper law. Authority on this point is limited because modern legal systems impose little in the way of formalities; contract law in advanced societies is founded upon the consent of the parties not compliance with formalities.

Other Contracting States have more elaborate rules of formal validity and their interest in this matter can be shown by the rules contained in the Convention. A contract will be formally valid:

(a) if, the parties being in the same country when the contract was made, it satisfies the formal requirements of the applicable law or of the law of the place where it is made;[155]

(b) if, the parties being in different countries when the contract is made, it satisfies the formal requirements of the applicable law or those of either place of presence;[156]

(c) for the purpose of these rules, where the contract is concluded by an agent, the country in which the agent acts is the relevant country;[157]

---

154 See *Egon Oldendorf v Liberia Corpn* [1995] 2 LR 64 (where Mance J was influenced by the presence of an arbitration clause to reject a defence based on Art 8(2)).
155 Rome Convention 1980, Art 9(1).
156 *Ibid*, Art 9(2).
157 *Ibid*, Art 9(3).

(d) the above rules do not apply in respect of a consumer contract which fall under Art 5. Their formal validity is tested by reference to the law of the country of the consumer's habitual residence;[158]

(e) contracts for rights to, or to use, immovable property, while subject to the general rules on formal validity, will have to comply with any formal requirements of the *lex situs* which the law regards as mandatory, irrespective of the applicable law or of the *lex loci contractus*.[159]

Any later change in the applicable law bought about by the parties' agreement will not prejudice the formal validity of the contract.[160]

Although English law placed little emphasis on matters of form, in contrast to civil law, there was a pronounced tendency to treat many matters of form as those of procedure.[161] This approach now has to be modified in the light of Art 14(2) which has to be read with Art 9 and reads:

> A contract or an act intended to have legal effect may be proved by any mode of proof recognised by the law of the forum or by any of the laws referred to in Art 9 under which that contract or act is formally valid, provided that such mode of proof can be administered by the forum.

Capacity

In general, questions of capacity are excluded from the Convention because, in civil law, questions of capacity are regarded as matters of status not contract. However, attention needs to be paid to Art 11, which reads:

> In a contract concluded between persons who are in the same country, a natural person who would have capacity under the law of that country may invoke his incapacity resulting from another law only if the other party to the contract was aware of this incapacity at the time of the conclusion of the contract or was not aware thereof as a result of negligence.

It has to be remarked at the outset that the cases on capacity at common law were very limited.[162]

This is an unusual provision and derives from civil law. It is concerned with the situation when A contracts with a party B and B is himself unaware of his own incapacity. Article 11 only applies when both A and B contract in the same country and, further, it requires B to be a natural person. Thus, suppose A, from England, enters into a contract with B in country C when A is only 17 (but has capacity under the law of C because he is married); suppose, further, that B then sues A on the contract in England. Can A rely on

---

158 Rome Convention 1980, Art 9(5).

159 *Ibid*, Art 9(6).

160 *Ibid*, Art 3(2).

161 *Leroux v Brown* (1852) 12 CB 801.

162 *Male v Roberts* (1800) 3 Esp 163 (Lord Eldon LC); *Bodley Head v Flegon* [1972] 1 WLR 680.

any incapacity under English law? According to the Giuliano and Lagarde *Report*, the provision operates only in the conflict of laws, so that A will have capacity both under the law of C and the private international rules of England (which would regard the law of C as the objective proper law) and any incapacity under English law could only be raised in the circumstances indicated in Art 11.

MANDATORY RULES AND PUBLIC POLICY

Mandatory rules

Article 7 of the Rome Convention contains two provisions in respect of mandatory rules. The full text of Art 7 reads as follows:

1   When applying under this Convention the law of a country, effect may be given to mandatory rules of the law of another country with which the situation has a close connection, if, and so far as, under the law of the latter country, those rules must be applied whatever the law applicable to the contract. In considering whether to give effect to these mandatory rules, regard shall be had to their nature and purpose and to the consequences of their application or non-application.

2   Nothing in this Convention shall restrict the application of the rules of the law of the forum in a situation where they are mandatory, irrespective of the law otherwise applicable to the contract.

One of the main concepts of the Rome Convention, which runs through many of its provisions, is that of the mandatory rule.

A mandatory rule is a rule of a domestic legal system which cannot be derogated from by contract. The Convention seeks to preserve applicable mandatory rules against casual avoidance or deliberate evasion. For example, under English domestic law, the implied term that the seller has the right to sell the goods, unless he makes it clear that he is selling a limited interest only, cannot be excluded or limited by any contract term. It is applicable under the Convention, whatever law has been chosen by the parties, if the contract is connected with English law in a manner which triggers the operation of the Convention's rules.

There are three situations where the mandatory rules of a domestic legal system will apply under the Convention, irrespective of the choice of law by parties, and two others where mandatory rules may be applied whether the applicable law is chosen by the parties or determined by the rules of the Convention in default of choice. The situations are as follows:

(a) where the contract is wholly connected with a single country and the parties have chosen a different law as its applicable law;[163]

---

163 Rome Convention 1980, Art 3(3).

(b) where there is a consumer contract within the provisions of Art 5;

(c) in the case of an individual employment contract under Art 6;

(d) where there is an applicable mandatory rule of the forum under Art 7(2); and

(e) where the forum chooses to apply the mandatory rule of a system other than that of the applicable law or of its own law.[164]

Where a mandatory rule of a legal system other than the applicable law is applied under the Convention, it does not mean that the parties' choice of applicable law or the law applicable in default of choice is invalidated. The law remains effective for the whole of the parties' substantive relationship, except for the matters covered by the mandatory rule. In other words, the mandatory rule is incorporated into the contract and trumps any contract term, express or implied, or any legal rule of the applicable law which would have a different effect. To take a simple example, suppose that, in an individual employment contract, the terms specify a minimum two week period of notice to be given to the employee in the event of his dismissal and that the contract is expressed to be governed by the law of Country X, which would regard it as entirely valid. If the employee habitually carries out his work in Country Y, where the minimum period of notice is one month, and the provision in Country Y cannot, according to the law of Y, be reduced by agreement – it is, in other words, a mandatory provision – any dispute involving the period of notice would be resolved by reference to the law of Country Y; any dispute not involving that issue, and indeed the implementation of the four week period, would remain subject to the law of Country X – the law chosen by the parties.

Of course, the mandatory rule imported into the contract may be crucial in the resolution of the particular dispute – there is no need to import it unless it is to have some effect – but we are not only concerned with litigation. The importation by the Convention of the mandatory rules of connected legal systems enables the parties to be clear about their position well in advance of any dispute between them actually arising.

Article 7 concerns a category of overriding or mandatory rules that must be applied even in the case of an international contract. Whether a rule is mandatory or not is a question of interpretation. Article 3(3) is concerned with the relationship between mandatory rules and an express choice of law, while Art 7 applies in the wider category of case where the choice of law may have been determined under Art 4. The idea behind Art 7 is that it is not only the country of the applicable law that may have an interest in the contractual relationship. It is sensible to take Art 7(1) and 7(2) in turn.

---

164 Rome Convention 1980, Art 7(1).

Article 7(1)

The purpose of Art 7(1) is to enable the court, in limited circumstances, to apply a mandatory rule which is neither one of the forum nor one of the applicable law, nor one imported into the contract by Arts 3, 5 or 6. Thus, where the applicable law is the law of country A but the facts have a close connection with country B, then a court may give effect to the mandatory rules of country B. The second limb of Art 7(1) requires that the court, in considering whether to give effect to the mandatory rules, shall pay regard to the nature, purpose and consequences of their application or non-application. Thus, to stand a chance of application, the rule must be part of a closely connected legal system and must not only be mandatory in nature but must be one which the system which contains it would apply in the particular case in hand. Even then, the forum has a discretion over whether or not to apply it and, in the exercise of that discretion, should take account of its nature and purpose. Although English courts do not have this power under the Convention, there is some indication at common law that a mandatory rule of the *lex loci contractus* could be applicable whatever the proper law of the contract[165] but there are no unequivocal decisions in favour of the overriding effect of the *lex loci contractus*. There is more certain authority in favour of a rule of the *lex loci solutionis* having a say, but the cases turn on illegality by the *lex loci* and are equally, and more convincingly, explicable in terms of the application of English public policy.[166] Presumably, it would have to be something on these lines, or a mandatory rule of one of the contracting parties' 'home' countries to trigger the application of the provision.

Regardless of the above considerations, an English court will not be concerned with the above considerations under Art 7(1). The UK considered the provision to be too vague and productive of uncertainty; in consequence, a reservation was entered under Art 22. Section 2(2) of the Contracts (Applicable Law) Act 1990 provides that the provisions have not been incorporated into English law.

It is, however, useful to speculate on how the provision would work. Suppose a foreign supplier agrees to sell to a commercial buyer, resident in England, a quantity of goods which are to be delivered to the buyer in England. The contract is in the supplier's standard form of contract and contains a choice of law clause in favour of an unconnected law, which leaves the supplier free to exclude or limit his liability in a manner that would be at variance with the Unfair Contract Terms Act 1977. In such circumstances, a foreign forum where Art 7(1) applied would have to decide the following:

---

165 Where a contract is void on the ground of immorality or is contrary to such positive law as as would prohibit the making of such a contract at all, then the contract would be void all the world over (*Re Missouri SS Co* (1889) 42 Ch D 321).

166 *Ralli Bros v Companhia Naviera Sota y Aznar* [1920] 2 KB 287 (actions under contract unlawful by *lex lcoi solutionis*); *Regazzoni v KC Sethia (1944) Ltd* [1958] AC 301 (action unlawful under *lex loci solutionis*); *Sharif v Azad* [1967] 1 QB 605; [1966] 3 All ER 785.

(a) whether delivery in England to an English commercial customer was a sufficiently close connection to carry the potential application of a rule of English law – I think the answer to this is probably in the affirmative;

(b) whether the English rule is mandatory – under the Unfair Contract Terms Act 1977, it clearly is;

(c) whether the English rule applies to a case with a non-English applicable law – again, clearly it does, subject to the appearance of evasion; and

(d) whether, in the light of its nature and purpose, the court ought to apply it; it would be difficult, having found evasion, not to apply the remedy prescribed for it.

While the operation of Art 7(1) seems, in this case, to provide a desirable result, it is questionable whether the potential for complexity and time wasting in such cases does not detract from the general clarity that the Convention seeks to establish. After all, the example cited was a commercial model and it might be argued that commercial contractors should take care to ascertain their positions before they accept standard terms presented by the other side. It would certainly seem doubtful as to whether there should be a wide use of Art 7(1) when there has been a *bona fide* choice of law by parties of equal bargaining strength.

As the UK has opted out of this provision, UK courts will only take account of the rules of a foreign legal system which is not the applicable law if required to do so under the Convention or in the exercise of their own public policy.

Article 7(2)

Article 7(2) provides for the application of the mandatory rules of the forum. The provision will be operative in respect of any choice of law arising under Art 3 or Art 4. To come within Art 7(2), the rule must not merely be one that cannot be derogated from by contract (as in Art 3(3)) but must be a rule that is regarded as overriding by the forum, regardless of the applicable law. In practical terms, this means that, in respect of cases coming before the English courts, the judge will have power to determine whether fundamental or overriding statutory provisions apply to the contractual claim. The sequence of events in an English courts might be as follows. Suppose an English judge was faced with a contractual claim where all the relevant connections were with Argentina but a clause provided for litigation in London under Chilean law. In such circumstances, the judge would be required: (a) to determine whether the English court had jurisdiction; (b) to determine whether there had been an express choice of law under Art 3(1) – clearly this is Chilean law; (c) to determine whether the Chilean law should be set aside in respect of the mandatory rules of Argentina under Art 3(3); (d) to determine whether there are any mandatory rules of English law under Art 7(2); and (e) in the event of a conflict between the mandatory rules of Argentina and those of England, to apply those of the forum.

It would seem that extreme caution should be shown in this area in respect of prior common law decisions, since the insistence on English law might arise either: (a) by asserting the matter was procedural;[167] (b) by asserting that the matter was covered by a rule of public policy;[168] or (c) that there was a mandatory rule of the *lex fori*.[169] Having regard to the fact that the Rome Convention represents a new code and having regard to the fact that it contains a distinct provision in respect of public policy, it would seem that prior common law decisions can provide little guidance as to the correct approach to Art 7(2).

If we confine ourselves for the moment to the precise power conferred under Art 7(2), we should expect an application of the mandatory rules of the forum only when:

(a) the contract, though the applicable law is foreign, has a close connection with England or with English law;

(b) there is a clear substantive rule of English law which applies irrespective of the foreign governing law, that is, a rule of English law which requires its own application despite the foreign applicable law; and

(c) justice demands its application on the facts of the particular case.

This is a minimising view of the provision, which suggests that the forum should not apply its own rules to a contract governed by a foreign law unless there is an overwhelming reason for doing so. It recognises that the application of English rules will, on the particular issue in dispute, displace the rules of the applicable law, including the mandatory ones, and, indeed, displace any mandatory rules which are read into the applicable law in Arts 3, 5 and 6.

A maximising interpretation of Art 7(2) would hold the whole of the Convention to be subject to the forum rules. Taken literally, Art 7(2) allows the forum to ignore the whole legal regime under the Convention and apply its own exclusions, choice rules and any other provision it had a mind to, provided that it regards them as mandatory. The Giuliano and Lagarde report suggests that this provision was included to take account of concerns some States felt about their rules relating to cartels, competition and restrictive practices, consumer protection and certain aspects of carriage. The inference is, and the object of the Convention must require, that this aspect of forum power be used sparingly.

---

167 As in *Leroux v Brown* (1852) 12 CB 801.
168 *Zivnostenska Banka v Frankman* [1950] AC 57.
169 *Boissevain v Weil* [1950] AC 327; 1 All ER 728.

Under the Convention, a mandatory rule is one that cannot be derogated from by contract.[170] What is important is to identify those statutory rules that might come within Art 7(2). In respect of statutory provisions, it is important to draw a distinction between provisions that describe the territorial ambit of a statute and provisions in a statute that apply to contracts governed by a law other than English. At common law where the terms of an English statute applied where the proper law of the contract was not English, the statute was said to include an overriding rule.[171]

Every case will depend on the words of the particular statute, but it would seem that certain general classes can be identified.

Where the statute contains no express provision as to territorial ambit and no express provision as to overriding rules

In such a case, the presumption is that the statute normally only operates within the territory and it will be difficult to deduce any overriding rules. However, in *English v Donnelly*,[172] the Inner House in Scotland was prepared to accept that that provisions of the Hire Purchase and Small Debts (Scotland) Act 1932, which applied only in Scotland, could be invoked in respect of a contract where the finance company had accepted the offer in England and the contract was both to be performed in England and subject to a choice of English law clause.

Where the statute expressly indicates that it is not to have an overriding effect

In such a case, the provisions of Art 7(2) would have no application.

Where the statute has an express provision as to its territorial scope but has no reference to overriding effect

In such a situation, it will be a matter of statutory construction. In *Boissevan v Weil*,[173] the relevant legislation[174] made it a criminal offence for a British subject to carry out certain currency transactions. The defendant, when involuntarily resident in Morocco during German occupation, borrowed French francs from a Dutchman also resident, on the basis that the sum would be repaid in sterling when permitted by English law. In an action for recovery

---

170 Rome Convention 1980, Art 3(3).
171 Normally, the mandatory rule is a rule of social policy and, thus, likely to be found within a statute.
172 1958 SC 494.
173 [1950] AC 327; 1 All ER 728.
174 Emergency Powers (Defence Act) 1939; Defence (Finance) Regulations 1939 SI 1939/1620

of the money, the House of Lords held that, if the act were a criminal offence, then no action would lie regardless of the proper law. The position would be the same under Art 7(2).

Where the statute expressly provides that the overriding effect is subject to limits

An example of such a provision is contained in the Unfair Contract Terms Act 1977.[175] The legislation had extended the restrictions on exclusion clauses that had been imposed in the Supply of Goods (Implied Terms) Act 1973. The restrictions in the legislation cannot be contracted out of;[176] to prevent contracting parties evading the law by a choice of foreign law, s 27(2) of the Unfair Contract Terms Act 1977 provides that the legislation has effect, notwithstanding the choice of foreign law, if the term appears to have been imposed wholly or mainly for the purpose of enabling the party imposing it to evade the application of the Act or, in the making of the contract, one of the parties dealt as a consumer[177] and was then habitually resident in the UK and the essential steps necessary for the contract were taken there. Such a provision would probably not come within Art 7(2) because the sub-section is directed to the express choice of foreign law and cannot be said to be 'mandatory irrespective of the law otherwise applicable to the contract'.

Where the statute expressly provides that the overriding effect is absolute

A statute may be so widely drawn that it applies regardless of whether the applicable law has been the subject of express choice or where the case is one of the applicable law objectively determined. An example is provided by the Employment Rights Act 1996 which provides that, save in the case where the employee ordinarily works outside Great Britain, it is immaterial whether the law which governs the contract is that of the UK or that of another country.[178] This is an example of a rule coming within Art 7(2) as it applies 'in a situation where they are mandatory irrespective of the law otherwise applicable to the contract'.

---

175 See, also, now, the Unfair Terms in the Consumer Contracts Regulations 1994 SI 1994/3159, giving effect to the Council Directive OJ L 95/29, 1993.

176 Although, by s 26, the legislation does not apply to an international supply contract.

177 See the Rome Convention 1980, Art 5.

178 Employment Rights Act 1996, ss 196, 204; see prior provisions in the Employment Protection (Consolidation) Act 1978, ss 141, 153(5); such special treatment is traceable back to the Contracts of Employment Act 1963 and the Redundancy Payments Act 1965. See Mann, FA (1966) 82 LQR 316; Hughes (1967) 83 LQR 180; Unger (1967) 83 LQR 427.

Public policy

Article 16 of the Rome Convention provides that:

> The application of a rule of law of any country specified by this Convention may be refused only if such application is manifestly incompatible with public policy (*'ordre public'*) of the forum.

It needs to be noted at the outset that the public policy exception to the application of a rule of the applicable law is intended to be of very limited scope. Objection cannot be taken to the foreign law itself, but only to its application by the forum in the particular case in hand. So an objectionable foreign law which operates, in the particular case, in an acceptable way is not to be ruled out under this provision.

The objection has to be a strong one – 'manifestly incompatible' – much more than the recognition of a difference or a mild distaste for the result, it requires that the forum cannot in conscience give effect to the foreign law without doing great disservice to its own fundamental principles.

Where the applicable law, whether chosen or found, is English, the case will, for most purposes, be treated as a domestic one by the English forum. This means, *inter alia*, that English morality and English public policy will be applied as appropriate. Even where the case is governed by a foreign applicable law, similar standards of English law will be applied.

It would seem that the common law cases would have been decided in much the same manner had the provisions of Art 16 been operative. While it is established that rules of public policy will apply even when the proper law is a foreign law, complete agreement does not exist as to the categories. At a risk of oversimplification, the following have been thought to violate public policy:

(a) contracts to commit crimes or tortious acts;[179]

(b) contracts prejudicial to public safety;[180]

(c) contracts to promote sexual immorality;[181]

(d) contracts that interfere with the administration of justice;

(e) contracts that tend to defraud the revenue;

(f) contracts that tend to the corruption of public life; and

(g) contracts in restraint of trade.

It is well established that a contract governed by foreign law will not be enforced if it falls within a particular head of public policy. In *Kaufman v*

---

179 *Allen v Resocus* (1676) 2 Lev 174; *Fores v Johnes* (1802) 4 Esp 97.
180 *Ertel Bieber and Co v Rio Tinto Co* [1918] AC 260.
181 *Jones v Randall* (1774) 1 Cowp 37.

Gerson,[182] a contract procured by pressure to restrain criminal proceedings was refused enforcement in England, even though it was valid by French law. In like terms, a contract valid by its own proper law will be refused enforcement if it infringes the doctrine of restraint of trade.[183]

In *Regazzoni v KC Sethia* (1944) Ltd,[184] the contract was made in Germany between Swiss and English parties. The deal involved the seller delivering jute bags to the buyer in Genoa. The buyer knew that the seller was to obtain the jute from India, the seller knew that the buyer intended to transport the jute to South Africa and both knew that Indian law forbade the direct or indirect export of Indian goods to South Africa. The seller failed to supply and relied on the illegality of the transaction by Indian law as a basis for the contract being unenforceable in the English courts. The contract included a clause choosing English law as the law to govern it, but nothing turns upon this, the attitude of the English court would have been exactly the same if the clause had chosen some other system of law. Why? While an obvious case can be made for the non-enforcement in England of a contract which requires the breach of criminal laws of foreign States,[185] at least where those laws are not themselves repugnant, the better basis for the decision is the public policy of English law, not the illegality by the *lex loci solutionis* as such.[186] In *Regazzoni*, illegality by the *lex loci solutionis* was a red herring – a false issue as there was no evidence that the Indian supplier was aware of the ultimate destination of the goods and the main parties to the transaction were not subject to Indian jurisdiction. The real issue in the case was how far the English court should go in enforcing, or giving damages for the breach of, a contract which interfered with the good relations between the UK and India. An English court trying an ordinary action in contract is clearly not the place for the formulation of foreign policy and it would not be proper for the court to give its view of the rights and wrongs of the dispute between India and South Africa which gave rise to the embargo. The principle that emerges from *Regazzoni* is that any contract which envisages the performance in a friendly foreign country of an act damaging to the welfare of that country is a breach of international comity and will be regarded as illegal and unenforceable in an English court. In recent years, problems have arisen where A enters into a contract with B to help B secure a contract in country C; normally this involves A making improper payments to public officials in country C. Such a contract will not be enforceable in England, either, because it breaches a head of public policy or it violates the principles of international comity.[187]

---

182 [1904] 1 KB 591.
183 *Rousillon v Rousillon* (1880) 14 Ch D 351.
184 [1958] AC 301; [1957] 3 All ER 286.
185 *Ralli Bros v Companhia Naviera* [1920] 2 KB 287; *Foster v Driscoll* [1929] 1 KB 470.
186 See *Howard v Shirlstar Container Transport Ltd* [1990] 3 All ER 366; 1 WLR 1292.
187 *Lemenda Trading Co Ltd v African Middle East Petroleum Co Ltd* [1988] QB 4489.

The affront to the sovereignty of a foreign State, the prejudice to the relations with that State which might follow the decision of an English court upholding the contract, or simply the offence to domestic policy in allowing an action on such a basis justifies the refusal. It should be noted, however, that the basis for the English court's policy intervention will be the plea of one of the parties, who is seeking, perhaps in a rather dishonourable way, to avoid the consequences of his agreement. In *Regazzoni*,[188] both parties were aware of the circumstances when they made their contract. Had that not been the case, the problem might have been resolved without reference to public policy. In cases where one party has been duped by the other, the matter would be referable to the applicable law's misrepresentation rules under which, of course, the contract might be rescindable, unilaterally enforceable or remediable in some other way. If both parties were innocent or if the illegality or other difficulty occurred after the contract was made, the applicable law's rules on mistake or frustration[189] would be relevant and the case might be resolved without reference to public policy.

There is little reason to believe that the incorporation of Art 16 will cause any great difference as to how English judges approach cases giving rise to problems of public policy. It is a little difficult to discern a clear dividing line between Art 7(2) and Art 16; it might be argued that the former is positive in substance while the latter is negative. In any event, the mandatory rules in England are likely to be statutory and consistent with well established principles of public policy at common law. In the circumstances, this is unlikely to be a source of difficulty.

PARTICULAR CONTRACTS

In many legal systems, there has been a move away from 19th century doctrines of freedom of contract towards a recognition that, in certain circumstances, the legislature may be required to intervene to redress an inherent inequality of bargaining power. In the UK, legislation has been passed to protect tenants, employees and consumers. This tendency increased in the years after 1945 and the Rome Convention of 1980 adopts the same approach by making special provision for consumer contracts and individual employment contracts. It is necessary to examine each in turn.

---

188 *Regazzoni v KC Sethia* [1958] AC 301.
189 *Ralli Bros v Companhia Naviera* [1920] 2 KB 287.

Consumer contracts

The Rome Convention establishes a rather complex regime for the treatment of certain consumer contracts. For this purpose, a consumer contract is defined by Art 5(1), which reads:

> This article applies to a contract the object of which is the supply of goods or services to a person ('the consumer') for a purpose which can be regarded as being outside his trade or profession, or a contract for the provision of credit for that object.

There is nothing in the Convention to suggest that the supplier must be a business or that he must know or believe that he is dealing with a consumer. It would seem likely that the first of these must be the case and the second probably so; the Giuliano and Lagarde report assumes both. If a consumer pretended to buy by way of trade, say, to obtain a trade discount, he should lose the protection of the special provisions. There is also no definition of what is 'outside his trade or profession' and it may be contentious when the goods have a dual function, for example, the doctor's motor car. The report suggests that regard should be had to the primary purpose of the transaction.

The consumer movement has been one of the most effective lobbying groups throughout Europe in recent decades and national responses have not been uniform. The lack of a more precise definition is due to the impossibility of finding an agreed solution and mirrors that in the Brussels Convention 1968. It should be noted that the special rules in Art 5 apply to both contracts for the sale of goods and to those for the provision of services (the report instances insurance) and extend to the supply of credit for both of these but do not extend to the purchase of securities or unlinked credit transactions.

> The first form of protection is afforded by Art 5(2), which reads:
>
> Notwithstanding the provisions of Art 3, a choice of law made by the parties shall not have the result of depriving the consumer of the protection afforded to him by the mandatory rules of the law of the country in which he has his habitual residence.

Thus, if the parties have chosen the law to govern the contract (which means, in effect, if the supplier has stipulated a governing law) the contract will be governed by that law. But, the chosen law will apply only to the extent that the consumer does not lose the benefits of the mandatory protection laws of his principal residence, provided that certain alternative connections with the country can be established. Those connections are set out in the remainder of Art 5(2) and read as follows:

> (i) if in that country the conclusion of the contract was preceded by a specific invitation addressed to him or by advertising, and he had taken in that country all the steps necessary on his part for the conclusion of the contract; or
>
> (ii) if the other party or his agent received the customer's order in that country; or

(iii) if the contract is for the sale of goods and the consumer travelled from that country to another country and there gave his order, provided that the consumer's journey was arranged by the seller for the purpose of inducing the consumer to buy.

The first connection covers doorstep selling and mail order in the sense of replying to an individual mail shot or clipping a coupon in a newspaper or magazine (though only if the publication was specifically targeted at consumers in the country concerned). It also covers cases where a consumer responds to a general advertisement in any media but, again, only if the advertisement was directed at consumers in that country.

The formulation 'all the steps necessary on his part for the conclusion of the contract' is a device to prevent technical arguments about the actual place of contracting which otherwise might arise from, for example, the peculiar distinction in English law between postal and instantaneous communications;[190] the *lex loci contractus* is not pertinent to the issue of consumer protection.

The second connection covers cases where the consumer approaches the foreign seller, for example, at an exhibition or trade fair or gets in touch with the seller's branch office in the country of the consumer's habitual residence.

The third connection applies only to contracts for the sale of goods and attempts to deal with 'cross border excursion selling', where the seller takes or arranges the carriage of the consumer from the country of his habitual residence to another country as part of the inducement to buy. The protection afforded by the Convention would apply whether or not the seller had a place of business in the country of sale and irrespective of whether the chosen law was the law of the country where the sale took place or any other law.

Of course, most consumer transactions will take place in the country of the consumer's habitual residence and most of his consumer purchases will take place in retail shops in that country. In most cases, there will not be any foreign element at all and the domestic law of that country will apply.[191] Where a choice of law is made in the context of a transaction wholly connected to a single country, the chosen law will apply but will be subject to all the mandatory provisions of the law of the wholly connected country.[192] So, an English supplier in such a case cannot avoid the protectionary provisions of English law simply by stipulating a foreign law to govern the contract.

---

190 *Adams v Lindsell* (1818) 1 B & Ald 681; *Byrne v Van Tienhoven* (1880) 5 CPD 344; *Entores Ltd v Miles Far East Corpn* [1955] 2 QB 327; *Brinkibon v Stahag Stahl GmbH* [1983] 2 AC 34.
191 In England, it will normally be governed by the Consumer Credit Act 1974 and regulations made thereunder.
192 Rome Convention 1980, Art 3(3).

When a consumer buys directly from a retailer in reliance on the manufacturer's advertisement, the ordinary rules of privity exclude any connection in contract between the manufacturer and the consumer and the Convention does not alter that position.

Where the parties to a consumer contract which falls within Art 5 have not made a choice of governing law, the applicable law will be that of the consumer's habitual residence.[193]

So, whenever the special circumstances expressed in the article apply, the consumer will enjoy the protection of the mandatory rules of his habitual residence. For, in default of choice, the law will be the applicable law under the Convention and, if there is a choice of another law, the effect of the choice will not deprive the consumer of the protection of his 'home' law.

The Convention does not deal with the situation where the provisions of the chosen law are more favourable[194] on the particular issue in dispute, than the mandatory rules of the law of the law of the country of the consumer's habitual residence. It must surely be the case that the consumer can have the benefit of the more favourable provisions. For, although the Convention operates by importing the mandatory rules of the law of the habitual residence into the chosen law, the purpose of the special provisions on consumer contracts is the protection of consumers and this purpose would be defeated if less favourable rules were allowed to replace more favourable ones.

In such a dispute, the consumer would plead the chosen law and the supplier would be prevented from setting up the less favourable mandatory rule of the law of the consumer's habitual residence in opposition to the law which he himself has stipulated as the contract's governing law.

Although this means that the consumer can blow hot and cold, using the chosen law when it suits him and relying on the mandatory rules of the law of his habitual residence when they are more favourable, so be it.

The special consumer provisions do not apply to contracts of carriage nor to contracts for the supply of services where the services are to be supplied to the consumer exclusively in a country other than that in which he has his habitual residence.[195] So, if a consumer makes his own separate foreign travel and accommodation arrangements, his contracts will not come under Art 5. In default of choice or the application of other international conventions, the travel contract will be rebuttably presumed to be governed by the law of the country of the carrier's principal or subsidiary place of business[196] and the

---

193 Rome Convention 1980, Art 5(3).
194 Note the words of the Rome Convention 1980, Art 5(2): 'a choice of law made by the parties shall not have the result of depriving the consumer of the protection ...'
195 Rome Convention 1980, Art 5(4).
196 *Ibid*, Art 4(2).

accommodation contract will be rebuttably presumed to be governed by the *lex situs*.[197] But, a 'package tour' arrangement, that is, a contract which, for an inclusive price, provides for a combination of travel and accommodation, is covered by the special provisions if the connections are present.[198]

A European Community directive on package tours[199] has recently been implemented in the UK[200] and applies to any packages sold or offered for sale in the UK.[201] Any terms which the Regulations imply into the package contract are expressed to be mandatory: 'it is so implied irrespective of the law which governs the contract.'[202]

It has been argued that Art 5 is a rather heavy handed attempt to protect consumers from certain malpractices rather than to recognise consumer rights. The protection afforded to the consumer extends only to the mandatory rules of the legal system of his country of habitual residence and only where the particular, limited, connections exist. It operates in limited circumstances on fairly uncommon transactions.

Examples of mandatory rules in this area in English law range from the implied terms on title, correspondence with description and fitness for purpose under the Sale of Goods Act 1979, to the narrow regulations aimed at particular types of transactions such as the cooling off period for timeshare agreements[203] and the unenforceability of one off doorstep sales of goods or services where the consumer has not been given notice of his right to cancel.[204]

Consumer contracts which do not fall within the narrow range of Art 5 are governed by the general Convention rules and, thereby, lose any special quality as consumer contracts.

The Convention applies, of course, only to contractual obligations; the English consumer's remedies for personal injury or damage to property under the Consumer Protection Act 1987[205] or his prospects of a claim in the tort of negligence against the manufacturer of a defective product are unaffected by it.

---

197 Rome Convention 1980, Art 4(3).

198 *Ibid*, Art 5(1).

199 Council Directive 90/314/EEC.

200 Package Travel, Package Holidays and Package Tours Regulations 1992 SI 1992/3288.

201 SI 1992/3288, reg 3(1).

202 *Ibid*, reg 28.

203 Timeshare Act 1992, s 5.

204 Consumer Protection (Cancellation of Contracts Concluded Away from Business Premises) Regulations 1987 SI 1987/2117.

205 Consumer Protection Act 1987, itself implementing Directive 85/374/EEC on Product Liability.

There is a special rule relating to the formal validity of those consumer contracts covered by Art 5. Their formal validity is governed solely by the law of the country in which the consumer has his habitual residence.[206]

The rules on consumer contracts are subject to the general rules of the Convention: so, if litigation takes place in England, the consumer will be able to claim the protection of any mandatory rules under Art 7(2). However, in many cases this will be otiose because the consumer will receive protection under Art 5 of the mandatory rules of the country where he is habitually resident. In a case in which Art 5 did not apply, the consumer might rely on Art 7(2) to apply the Unfair Contract Terms Act 1977 if the purpose of the choice of law was to avoid the operation of the legislation. This would be a rare case indeed, so much so that some writers argue that the exhaustive nature of Art 5 impliedly excludes the operation of Art 7.[207]

Individual employment contracts

Unlike the common law rules, which treated employment contracts along with all other contracts despite their rather special circumstances and sometimes with results which are hard to justify,[208] the Convention introduces special rules for employment contracts.[209] The full text of Art 6(1) reads as follows:

> Notwithstanding the provisions of Art 3, in a contract of employment a choice of law made by the parties shall not have the result of depriving the employee of the protection afforded to him by the mandatory rules of law which would be applicable under para 2 in the absence of choice.

By default, the applicable law will be 'the law of the country in which the employee habitually carries out his work in performance of the contract, even if he is temporarily employed in another country'.[210] If there is no place of habitual work, the applicable law will be the law of the country in which the place of business through which the employee was engaged is situated. In either event,[211] if 'it appears from the circumstances as a whole that the contract is more closely connected with another country, the contract shall be governed by the law of that country'.[212]

---

206 Rome Convention 1980, Art 9(5).
207 See Morse (1992) 41 ICLQ 1, p 10.
208 See, eg, *Sayers v International Drilling Co NV* [1971] 1 WLR 1176, CA (Lord Denning MR, Stamp and Salmon LJJ); see, also, Smith (1972) 21 ICLQ 164.
209 Art 6.
210 Art 6(2)(a).
211 Art 6(2)(b).
212 Art 6(2)(b).

The Rome Convention does not define the term 'employment', and it cannot be assumed that the English distinction between contracts of service and contracts for services is universally known.[213] Ultimately, when the Court is given that power, reference may be made to the European Court of Justice for definitive rulings on the expression; there are already some rulings from the European Court of Justice on the term which have arisen from references under the Brussels Convention.[214] For the time being, national courts will apply their own tests to distinguish employees from independent contractors. English courts will continue to apply a purposive approach rather than rely on mechanical tests, and it is reasonable to anticipate that the European Court of Justice will adopt the same approach.

Although there is no definition of 'habitual' in the Convention, there is no reason to suppose that its interpretation will differ from the 'ordinarily employed' test applied under existing British legislation[215]. It does not prevent occasional or periodic employment elsewhere, provided that the employment is temporary.

The protection of the Convention extends only to the mandatory rules of the identified system; these are defined[216] as rules of a domestic legal system which cannot be derogated from by contract. For States have recognised the imbalance between the bargaining power of the individual worker and that of the employer, and this has caused them to make special provisions for employment contracts which establish minimum standards of protection for employees.

Examples of mandatory protection rules under English law include the rights to a minimum period of notice,[217] to claim that a dismissal was unfair,[218] to maternity pay,[219] to return to work after pregnancy,[220] and to redundancy payments.[221] Although these rights can properly be described as mandatory because they cannot be abrogated by contract, it does not follow that they are universally applicable. So, for example, there is a qualification

---

213 *Stevenson Jordan & Harrison Ltd v McDonald and Evans* [1952] 1 TLR 101; *Ready Mixed Concrete (South East) Ltd v Minister of Pensions and National Insurance* [1968] 2 QB 497; *O'Kelly v Trusthouse Forte plc* [1983] ICR 728; [1983] IRLR 369.

214 *Shenavi v Kreischer* Case 266/85 [1987] ECR 239; [1987] 3 CMLR 782.

215 See *Wilson v Maynard Shipbuilding Consultants AB* [1978] QB 665.

216 In Art 3(3).

217 Employment Protection (Consolidation) Act 1978, s 49; see, now, Employment Rights Act 1996, s 86.

218 *Ibid*, s 54; see, now, Employment Rights Act 1996, s 94; the statutory protection against unfair dismissal being traceable back to the Industrial Relations Act 1971.

219 Social Security Contribution and Benefits Act 1992, s 164.

220 Employment Protection (Consolidation) Act 1978, s 45; see, now, Employment Rights Act 1996, s 79.

221 *Ibid*, s 81; see, now, Employment Rights Act 1996, s 135.

period – the employee must have worked continuously for the same employer for two years;[222] there is a geographical limitation – the employee must 'ordinarily' work within Great Britain;[223] and there is a limited power of waiver.[224]

The Rome Convention, by establishing a special regime for individual employment contracts, seeks to ensure that the employee does not lose the benefit of the protection simply by being a party to an international contract. It would make nonsense of any domestic protection provisions if the employer could circumvent them by adding a choice of law clause to the terms of the contract in order to make them mandatory.[225] When the contract is genuinely international, the problems of evasion are joined by those of avoidance if the choice of law process fails to recognise the need to protect.

While the principle of freedom of choice is preserved by the Rome Convention, the employee will always have the benefit of the mandatory rules of the law applicable. The chosen law will be respected with regard to all the conditions of employment which are not subject to the mandatory controls – depending on which system of law is applicable; this might amount to most of it.

Effectively, the employer, characteristically the party to stipulate the choice of law in the contract, is prevented from derogating from the employee's protections in two ways. In line with the general restriction, he cannot turn a domestic contract into an international one simply by stipulating a foreign governing law.[226] The choice will be respected but the mandatory provisions of the domestic law will be imported into it. Where the contract is genuinely international, any choice of law will not oust the mandatory provisions of the law which would be the applicable law of the contract if no choice had been made. So in each case of dispute, it will be necessary to examine the law applicable by default, for obviously that will be the governing law if no choice has been made, but also the mandatory provisions of that law will apply even where there has been a choice.

An international company which uses a standard form of employment contract which stipulates that the governing law of the contract as the law of the country where the employee works will have no difficulty with the Rome

---

222 With regard to unfair dismissal, see the Employment Protection (Consolidation) Act 1978, s 64, the provisions having been re-enacted in Employment Rights Act 1996, s 110.

223 See Employment Protection (Consolidation) Act 1978, s 141, as subsequently amended; see, also, Employment Rights Act 1996, s 196.

224 For unfair dismissal by reason only of the non renewal of a fixed term contract, see Employment Protection (Consolidation) Act 1978, s 142(1); see, now, Employment Rights Act 1996, s 197(1).

225 Employment Protection (Consolidation) Act 1978, ss 140(1) and 153(5); see, now, Employment Rights Act 1996, ss 203(1) and 204.

226 Rome Convention 1980, Art 3(3).

Convention as long as the employee 'habitually' works there. However, a contract which selects the law of the country of the company's headquarters for all its employees worldwide will not achieve the standardisation of the terms and conditions of employment if the mandatory laws of the country where the employee habitually works are more favourable, in any regard, than the chosen law. Arguments of business efficiency, equality of treatment among employees, or the overall quality of the employment contract, will not prevail if, in any particular case which an individual employee can raise, the provisions of what would be the applicable law by default under the Convention are more favourable to that particular employee than the terms of his contract.

A typical international employment dispute will involve the employee asserting either a contractual or a non-contractual right which he alleges his employer is infringing. If he asserts a right under the employment contract, there will be a dispute about the applicable law only if different potentially applicable laws would interpret the contract differently. Unless the parties have agree otherwise, the interpretation of the contract will be governed by the applicable law.[227]

The assertion of a right which his employment contract does not give him will always involve the determination of the applicable law. The employee will have to establish his right by reference to a mandatory rule of the legal system which is the applicable law under Art 6. If he can do this, he has a trump card which will defeat his employer's reliance on the terms of their contract, including the term, if there is one, that the contract shall be governed by another system of law.

Under English law it is the practice to sue for damages for personal injuries arising out of the employment relationship in tort rather than in contract, although an action for the breach of an express or implied term in the contract is also available. In all cases where there is a choice of the cause of action, it is for the plaintiff to select the one he wants.[228]

Given that the Convention is concerned only with contractual obligations, a decision by the employee to sue in tort takes the case outside the Convention, and the particular rules for the choice of law in tort will be applied by the forum selected to hear the case. So, an employee injured in the course of his employment may need to consider whether to sue in contract or in tort. The choice in contract may turn upon the content of the chosen governing law or the mandatory rules of the country where he habitually works. The choice in tort may depend upon the *lex loci delicti* (being the actual place of injury or the place where the employer failed to take the steps

---

227 Rome Convention (1980), Art 10.

228 *Coupland v Arabian Gulf Petroleum Co* [1983] 2 All ER 434 (Hodgson J); affirmed [1983] 3 All ER 226, CA (Waller, Oliver and Robert Goff LJJ).

necessary to protect the safety of his employee). There are more issues here than what is the governing law, and the matter will be considered further in Chapter 17.

It seems reasonable to suppose that the mandatory protection rules can be avoided if the protection afforded by the chosen law is greater. The employer should be estopped from setting up the terms of the Convention against the law which has been stipulated in the employment contract. The purpose of the special rules in the Convention is to protect employees and it would be a meaningless exercise for a court to insist on the letter of the Convention with the result that a less favourable law was applied to the employee. But all this turns upon the particular issue in dispute. Generalities cannot be argued. So, for example, an employer cannot argue that the employee gets a good deal from the contract as a whole (such as better pay, or more generous leave, or greater fringe benefits) if, in the specifics of the actual dispute, the employee would be deprived of the basic protection of the mandatory rules of the applicable law.

A posted worker is one who is sent by his employer to work abroad on his employer's business, or who is recruited by an employment agency in one country to work in another country, or who is seconded by his multinational employer for a period of work in a connected company abroad. The Rome Convention 1980 provides for the temporary posting of workers abroad only to the extent that such a removal from the habitual workplace provided that it is only 'temporary' does not break the link with it.[229] A posted worker can have the benefit of the superior protections of the 'host' country, assuming that another law is the applicable law under the Convention, in only two situations. If he can bring his action before the courts of the 'host' country and the forum applies its own mandatory rules,[230] or if he sues in a forum (not in the UK) which is prepared to apply the mandatory rules of the 'host country'.[231]

229 Rome Convention 1980, Art 6(2)(a).
230 *Ibid*, Art 7(2).
231 *Ibid*, Art 7(1).

CHAPTER 17

THE LAW OF TORT

INTRODUCTION

More energy has been expended in the discussion of tort cases in private international law in the common law world than on any other area of the subject.[1] For English law, this was somewhat surprising,[2] as the number of cases in the law of tort giving rise to conflicts problems had, until recently, been very limited indeed. However, it was accepted that the common law choice of law rules in respect of tort claims were one of the least satisfactory parts of the conflict system.[3] The problems in this area are considerable and it remains to be seen if the recent legislative changes will provide a more satisfactory legal framework.[4]

Since the middle of the 19th century, if not earlier, the choice of law rules in the law of tort were governed by a number of leading judgments.[5] The general view was that, even if the cases were correctly decided on their own particular facts, the underlying general principles were difficult to deduce.[6]

Following two reports by the Law Commission, Parliament legislated and the common law rules[7] were replaced by Part III of the Private International Law (Miscellaneous Provisions) Act 1995. The enactment received the Royal Assent on 8 November 1995 and the relevant provisions came into effect on 1 May 1996.[8]

---

1   Road accidents abroad, product liability claims and civil aviation litigation have all contributed to need for clearer principles in this area of law.

2   Little attention was directed at the subject in the years prior to 1945; the final edition of Westlake, *Private International Law* (1925), devoted only seven pages to the subject.

3   The area was dominated by the so called rule of double actionability propounded in the 19th century case of *Phillips v Eyre* (1870) 6 QB 1; this rule admitted of a number of interpretations and, even if the interpretation could be agreed, there were difficulties of application.

4   For the Private International Law (Miscellaneous Provisions) Act 1995, see below.

5   The most celebrated is *Phillips v Eyre* (1870) LR 6 QB 1 (a judgment of the Court of Exchequer Chamber delivered by Willis J); at the time, the only authors available to counsel were Blackstone, Kent, Story and Savigny.

6   The relevant cases are, in chronological order, *The Halley* (1866) LR 2 PC 193; *Phillips v Eyre* (1870) 6 QB 1; and *Machado v Fontes* [1897] 2 QB 231.

7   The two relevant reports are: Law Commission Working Paper No 87 (1984); and Law Commission Report No 193 (1990), which itself included a Draft Bill.

8   See the Private International Law (Miscellaneous Provisions) Act (Commencement No 2) Order 1996 SI 1996/995, as noted by Lloyd J in *Pearce v Ove Arup Partnership Ltd* [1997] 2 WLR 779; Ch 293.

However, none of the provisions of Part III[9] of the Private International Law (Miscellaneous Provisions) Act 1995 apply in respect of acts or omissions giving rise to claims before that date.[10] The practical consequence of this is that, in respect of torts committed abroad, there will be two sets of rules, namely, (a) the common law rules applicable in respect of acts or omissions prior to 1 May 1996; and (b) the statutory rules in respect of acts or omissions arising after that date.

A second reason for the continuing relevance of the common law rules is that claims in respect of defamation[11] are specifically excluded from the legislation and, thus, remain subject to the common law rules. It will therefore be necessary to continue to have a knowledge of the common law background.

THE NATURE OF TORTIOUS LIABILITY

Common lawyers have long abandoned the attempt to produce an overall definition of tortious liability, realising that the subject matter defies any unitary treatment. Not only do torts cover a great variety of wrongs, but they also cover a variety of ways of doing wrongs and a wide realm of social purposes. There is very little in common among, say, an unintentional defamation, a deliberate assault, a negligent running down and the incursion into another's air space – yet all these need to be subsumed under a single dispositive rule if the traditional methodology of the English conflict of laws is to be preserved.

Policing policies in the area of trespass, the protection of the use and enjoyment of property, the picking up of the legal pieces after a road accident, the protection of the consumer, the control of industrial safety and the security of commercial transactions are all tasks which the tort system is given to do alongside its traditional role as the means to the vindication of civil liberties. With such an heterogeneous collection of aims, methods and techniques, it is little wonder that no satisfactory rule emerged at common law and that the courts have been influenced by the particular examples of tortious liability with which they happen to have been faced.

Let us explore some of these examples a little further to show both the complexity of the problems and the likelihood that different societies will adopt different methods of dealing with them. What any society has to work out are the interests which are to be protected and the nature of the harms

---

9   Private International Law (Miscellaneous Provisions) Act 1995, ss 9–15.
10   *Ibid*, s 14(1).
11   Excluded by the Private International Law (Miscellaneous Provisions) Act 1995, s 13.

which are to be controlled. The common law, for example, has long protected the person from crude physical aggression but has hesitated over the range of those who can seek compensation for carelessly inflicted emotional distress.[12] The protection of the individual's property rights is also a long standing area of tort law but what is to count as a property right and what sort of interference is to give rise to an action? Whether the injured consumer of a product should be expected to seek his remedy from the seller or manufacturer and on what basis, and whether the liability of a driver who has injured another road user should depend on fault or trigger strict liability are also matters of contention.

The common origin of tort and crime involves a residual public involvement in the tort system, whether the tort is mirrored by potential criminal liability or is purely a matter for private litigation. Tort law protects the basic personal rights which a citizen has, not only against other persons but against the State itself. The recognition and enforcement of exotic tortious duties may, thus, be seen as a more difficult task for the conflict system to achieve than, say, the recognition of a foreign institution of marriage or the acceptance of foreign rules for the recognition of contracts.

THE POSSIBLE APPROACHES

If tort is seen as a sub-species of crime, as in some cases it can be, there might be reason to apply the local law to its commission in the same way as a criminal system is seen applying only within a defined territory.

The local law, although it may be the only 'common' law between strangers, may fly in the face of a pre-existing relationship, a common personal law or a concurrence of legal rules. There are some spectacular cases in which the application of the *lex loci delicti commissi* has led to bizarre results. In *Walton v Arabian American Oil Co*,[13] the law of Saudi Arabia was applied to the personal injury claim of one US citizen against his employer for a motor accident occurring on the US company's property in Saudi Arabia; while, in *Mackinnon v Iberia Shipping Co*,[14] the Court of Session applied the law of the Dominican Republic to the personal injury claim of a Scottish seaman against a Scottish shipowner simply because, at the time of the accident, the ship was in the territorial waters of that country. Nor should it be thought that the

---

12 A head of claim that only fully emerged after 1945 following developments in psychiatric medicine; see *Victorian Rly Commissioners v Coultas* (1883) 13 App Cas 222, PC; *Dulieu v White and Sons* [1901] 2 KB 669; *Hambrook v Stokes Bros* [1925] 1 KB 141; *Bourhill v Young* [1943] AC 92; *McLoughlin v O'Brian* [1983] 1 AC 410; *Alcock v Chief Constable of West Yorkshire* [1992] 1 AC 310.

13 (1956) 233 F (2d) 541.

14 1955 SC 20.

adoption of a crude localising rule necessarily leads to the simple mechanical identification of a single legal system, as arguments for the law of the place where the wrongful act was done can be matched by those in favour of the different place where the harm resulted.

The personal law which, if it is common, provides a standard reason against the application of the local law, is of little help if the parties are from different countries with differing legal rules covering the matter in dispute. There is no general case for applying the defendant's law rather than the plaintiff's law to the determination of the issue.

The law of the forum is unacceptable, as the forum is generally a matter for the plaintiff's choice and may well have no contact with the issue.[15]

One solution to some of the difficulties which arise when all the material facts relate to one country and it is only the occurrence of the accident in another which makes the case a conflict case at all, is to apply the law of the social environment or the law which has the closest and most real connection with the parties and the issue. This 'proper law' of the tort[16] has, in various guises, had considerable influence[17] in the decisions of US courts[18] and in the terms of the Law Commission proposals that formed the basis for the reforms introduced in Part III of the Private International Law (Miscellaneous Provisions) Act 1995.[19]

It would be possible to devise a system which contained not one but a number of conflict rules for tort, each one directed at a particular manifestation of wrong. So, for example, one might have one rule for consumer/manufacturer cases, another for passenger/carrier cases, another for general road accidents, another for defamation and so on. While such a system would have the obvious advantage of recognising that unlike things are best kept separate, it would not take us very far forward unless we could characterise an action as definitively connected with a particular legal system.

To take what might seem an easy example first: the protection of reputation is covered to a limited degree in English law by the tort of defamation.[20] It might be argued that such a suitable disposition of the case

---

15 See *Machado v Fontes* [1897] 2 QB 231.

16 The test of the 'proper law' of the tort began to be discussed after the judgment of the Court of Session in *M'Elroy v M'Allister* 1949 SC 110, in particular, in articles by Dr JH Morris (1949) 12 MLR 248; (1951) 64 HLR 881.

17 See Lord Denning MR in *Chaplin v Boys* [1968] 2 QB 1.

18 A matter discussed by the House of Lords in *Chaplin v Boys* [1971] AC 356.

19 The proposals of the Law Commission are now given effect to, for the most part, in the Private International Law (Miscellaneous Provisions) Act 1995. Note, in particular, s 12, where the *lex loci delicti* will be displaced by the proper law in circumstances where it is 'substantially more appropriate'.

20 The tort of defamation will continue to be governed by common law rules as to choice of law; see the Private International Law (Miscellaneous Provisions) Act 1995, s 13.

could be made if the court applied the law of the place where the injury to the reputation was felt.[21] But, the idea of the injury to the reputation, rather than the affront to the dignity of the defamed individual, as the essence of the action, is a common law concept; a civil lawyer might concentrate on the personal affront. In the more complex case of consumer protection, should liability depend on where the defective product was designed, made, marketed, bought, consumed, where the injury was caused by its use or consumption, or where the harm actually manifested itself? And would it make any difference whether the manufacturer targeted his product to the country of buying, using or harm, or not?

What makes the production of separate rules for different cases even more difficult is the personal law – where the parties come from the same legal system, it seems artificial to apply a law which may have no more than an accidental connection with the dispute. The same can be said of the situation where the parties, though from different countries, have in common the rules which would dispose of a purely domestic case.

TORTS COMMITTED IN ENGLAND

If the tort was committed in England, there was no doubt at common law that English law applied and the rule in *Phillips v Eyre*[22] had no application. Even if there had been any doubt about this proposition, it could not be open to further argument after the case of *Szalatnay-Stacho v Fink,*[23] where the facts were as follows: the Czech Government was in exile in England during World War II. The defendant, an official of that Government, sent documents to the President of the Czech Republic who was himself resident in England. The documents were, *prima facie*, defamatory of the plaintiff. Under the law of Czechoslovakia, the documents were absolutely privileged while, under English law, only the defence of qualified privilege was available.[24]

The Court of Appeal, in upholding the judgment of Henn Collins J, ruled that, as the libel had been published in England, then the tort had been committed in England and English law applied. In the later case of *Metall und Rohstoff AG v Donaldson Lufkin and Jenrette Inc,*[25] the Court of Appeal appeared to accept that if the tort had been committed in England then the rule in *Phillips v Eyre* had no application and that English law applied.

---

21   For the jurisdictional problems arising where material is published in more than one country, see *Shevill v Presse Alliance SA* [1996] AC 359; 3 All ER 929.

22   (1870) LR 6 QB 1.

23   [1947] 1 KB 1 (Scott, Somervell, Cohen LJJ).

24   Ie, information passed on by a person acting under a duty; see *R v Rule* [1937] 2 QB 375 *Lincoln v Daniels* [1962] 1 QB 237; *Beach v Freeson* [1972] 1 QB 14.

25   [1990] 1 QB 391; this was, in fact, a case turning on RSC Ord 11.

In the recent review of the law by the Law Commission,[26] the proposal was made that, in respect of torts that 'relate to, or the consequences of any conduct the most significant elements of which took place in a part of the UK',[27] the law of that part of the UK should apply.

However, the view that only English law applied to torts committed in England[28] remained the position prior to the enactment of the Private International Law (Miscellaneous Provisions) Act 1995. The possible relevance of new legislative provisions will be discussed later in the chapter.

THE PLACE WHERE THE TORT WAS COMMITTED AND THE POSSIBLE LAWS

At common law, there were two practical problems for the court, namely: (a) to formulate a test as to where the tort had been committed; and (b) having determined the location of the tort, to determine the relevant applicable law. It is necessary to say a little as to the background to these problems.

The place where the tort is committed

At common law, there was some discussion in the case law as to the precise place that the tort was committed. This problem normally arose at the jurisdiction stage and, in most cases, there was no problem. However, in the modern world, it is not difficult to imagine cases of a libel broadcast on television in more than one country or a book published in New York but sold in London. Indeed, in the area of product liability, it is quite possible to have a product manufactured in country A and sold to a wholesaler in country B, who then distributes it to a retailer in country C, where it is then purchased by a person on holiday who lives in country D. In the 20th century, developments in travel, the carriage of goods and the transmission of information have given rise to much discussion in this area. This is particularly true in the USA, where there has been considerable debate as to the precise place of the tort, although opinion varies from State to State. In the remainder of the common law world, the problem has arisen when a plaintiff has sought leave to serve out of the jurisdiction. In this context, it is interesting

---

26 In the original document, the Law Commission observed 'it appears to be universally agreed that, notwithstanding the existence of a foreign element, a tort committed in England and Wales will, in an action in England and Wales, be governed by English law only'; Law Commission Working Paper No 87 (1984), para 2. 47.

27 Law Commission Report No 193 (1990), para 3.14.

28 *Arab Monetary Fund v Hashim* (1996) 1 LR 589, p 597, *per* Saville LJ.

to compare the original RSC Ord 11 r 1(1)(h), which allowed service out of the jurisdiction 'where the action is founded on a tort committed within the jurisdiction',[29] with the present rule contained in RSC Ord 11 r 1(1)(f), which permits service when 'the claim is founded on a tort and the damage was sustained, or resulted from an act committed, within the jurisdiction'.

It is very doubtful whether any guidance can be derived in respect of choice of law from considering cases that turned on whether the court had jurisdiction. Indeed, following the enactment of the Private International Law (Miscellaneous Provisions) Act 1995, this is probably only of academic interest.[30] However, at common law, there were three possible approaches as to how a court might identify the place of the tort. A court might rule that:

(a) the tort was committed where the defendant did the acts from which the harm resulted; or

(b) the tort was committed in the country in which the harm was suffered; or

(c) the tort should be deemed to have taken place in the legal system most favourable to the innocent party.

There is only limited value in considering cases on jurisdiction but such prior case law does indicate that the courts have sought to identify the elements of a tort and then formulate a particular question. In *Metall und Rohstoff AG v Donaldson Lufkin and Jenrette Inc*,[31] the question posed was: 'Where in substance did the cause of action arise?'

Somewhat earlier, in *George Munro Ltd v American Cyanamid Corporation*,[32] the Court of Appeal posed the question as: 'Where was the wrongful act, from which the damage flows, in fact done?' The modern tendency has been to favour the substance test and this was applied by the Privy Council in *Distillers Co (Bio-Chemicals) Ltd v Thompson*[33] and, later, by the Court of Appeal in *Castree v Squibb Ltd*.[34]

In the case of some torts, the place of the tort was determined by locating the cardinal element of the tort. Thus, in *Bata v Bata*,[35] where defamatory correspondence was written in Switzerland but published in England, the Court of Appeal held that the tort had been committed where publication

---

29 See *George Munro Ltd v American Cyanamid Corporation* [1944] KB 432; *Cordova Land Co v Victor Brothers Inc* [1966] 1 WLR 793; *Distillers Co (Bio-Chemicals) Ltd v Thompson* [1971] AC 458.

30 Because the Private International Law (Miscellaneous Provisions) Act 1995, s 11 makes specific provision as to where the events constituting the tort take place in more than one country.

31 [1990] 1 QB 391.

32 [1944] KB 432.

33 [1971] AC 458.

34 [1980] 1 WLR 1248.

35 [1948] WN 366; 92 SJ 574.

took place. In the later case of *Church of Scientology of California v Commissioner of the Metropolitan Police*,[36] where the allegation was that defamatory material had been passed by English officers to the Federal Criminal Police Authority of West Germany, the Court of Appeal assumed, for the purpose of a striking out action, that the tort was committed in West Germany, where the material was published.

While, in the tort of libel, the emphasis has been upon identifying the place of publication, a different approach has been used in other torts. However, the cases reveal that there is a similar emphasis on analysing the component events of the unlawful conduct. Thus, in *Metall und Rohstoff AG v Donaldson Lufkin and Jenrette*, the Court of Appeal held that the tort of inducing a breach of contract should be regarded as taking place in the country in which the contract was breached.[37] In cases turning on forms of fraudulent misrepresentation, the courts have been prepared to rely on basic concepts drawn form the law of contract to determine where the tort was committed. Thus, in *Diamond v Bank of London and Montreal Ltd*,[38] the Court of Appeal ruled that a fraudulent misrepresentation made by telephone or telex would be made where the message is received and relied upon.[39] This approach found favour with the House of Lords in the subsequent case of *Armagas Ltd v Mundogas SA*,[40] where it was assumed that a fraudulent misrepresentation would be committed in Denmark if it was both communicated and acted upon in that country.

The case law demonstrates that in certain instances it is important to be able to locate the country in which the tort was committed. At common law this normally arose at the jurisdiction stage when the plaintiff was seeking to serve out of the jurisdiction under the terms of RSC Ord 11. However, because of the operation of the rule in *Phillips v Eyre*[41] it was unusual for questions as to the location of the tort to arise in the choice of law context.[42]

Theories as to the appropriate law

As indicated above, once an English court has come to the conclusion that the tort was committed abroad there are a number of theories as to the law that an

---

36 (1976) 120 SJ 690 (Bridge and Cairns LJJ, Talbot J).

37 [1990] 1 QB 391.

38 [1979] QB 333.

39 See also, *Entores v Miles Far East Corporation* [1955] 2 QB 327; *Brinkibon v Stahag Stahl und Stahlwarenhandelsgesellschaft GmbH* [1983] 2 AC 34.

40 [1986] AC 717.

41 [1870] 6 QB 1 (on which, see below).

42 An example would be *Church of Scientology of California v Commissioner of the Metropolitan Police* (1976) 120 SJ 690, where it was assumed that the tort had taken place in West Germany.

English court should apply in respect of the foreign tort. It is sensible to say a little about each at this point.

The law of the forum (lex fori)

An English court could simply apply the law of the forum and, indeed, this was advocated by Savigny in the 19th century.[43] The difficulty with this course is that a defendant might be held liable by the *lex fori* for an act or omission that was itself not tortious in the foreign country. Such a consequence is at variance with traditional concepts of justice. Secondly, such an approach appears to indicate that the forum feels a degree of cultural superiority over other lands.[44] The original justification was that the law of tort was closely associated with criminal law and, thus, a legitimate concern of the forum. However, it is now well recognised that the law of tort is increasingly based on policy considerations where there may be differences of approach between different jurisdictions. As Cardozo J observed: 'We are not so provincial as to say that every solution of a problem is wrong because we deal with it otherwise at home.'[45] The third problem with such an approach is that with liberal jurisdictional rules there is every incentive for forum shopping, which is itself now a problem in the modern world.

The law of the place of the tort (lex loci delicti commissi)

The second possibility is to apply the law of the place where the tort was committed. As indicated above, this may involve an analysis as to where the tort was committed. However, it is claimed that the *lex loci delicti commissi* leads to both certainty and justice. In the modern world, when A visits State X on holiday, he is well aware that he must observe the criminal law of State X; so, it is argued, there is little that is objectionable in holding A to the law of tort of that State. Those who advocate this approach argue: (a) that the theory has been accepted in Europe and large parts of the USA; (b) that it promotes certainty and uniformity and reduces the risk of forum shopping; (c) that it has attracted the support in the past of some of the most distinguished jurists;[46] (d) that it is consistent with the principle of territorial sovereignty; (e) that it does not involve assumptions of cultural superiority by the courts of the forum; and (f) that it corresponds to the reasonable expectations of the parties. Thus, if I decide to drive to Germany, I am agreeing to accept the duties that Germany demands of all drivers on its roads and I am implieldy agreeing to conform to that standard.

---

43   Savigny, *System des Heutigen Romischen Rechts* (1849).
44   See the dissenting speech of van Voorhis and Scileppi JJ in *Babcock v Jackson* [1963] 2 LR 286.
45   *Loucks v Standard Oil Co of New York* (1918) 224 NY 99; 120 NE 198.
46   *Slater v Mexican National Rly* 194 US 120 (1904), *per* Holmes J.

The arguments advanced against the *lex loci delicti* are: (a) that the place of the tort may be random (for example, an accident in Madrid between a German driver and an Italian tourist has little specific connection with Spain); (b) the *lex loci* may be outside the reasonable contemplation of the parties (for example, if A, domiciled in State B, agrees to fly to State C but, *en route*, the aircraft veers off course and crashes in State D, it is a little difficult to find any particular nexus with the law of State D); and (c) it is argued that, in some cases, where the *lex loci delicti commissi* has been followed, rights that would normally arise under the *lex fori* may be negated.[47] It is for these reasons that some writers argue that one could adopt the *lex loci delicti* but confer on the court the power to set it aside in cases where the facts require some other approach.[48]

The proper law of the tort

After 1949, and partly as a result of the writings of Dr Morris,[49] the theory of the proper law of the tort acquired an increasing degree of prominence. In broad terms, it was argued that in most instances one would not need to go beyond the place of the wrong, but in certain cases one should 'choose the law which, on policy grounds, seems to have the most significant connection with the chain of acts and circumstances in the particular situation'.[50] It was argued that such an approach would be more flexible and it was claimed that experience with the doctrine of the proper law of the contract had shown that the concept was workable. Further, it was argued that the expansion in the forms of tortious action in the post-war period made it an appropriate model because of its inherent flexibility. The approach was followed by the American Law Institute, which advocated that 'the law of the State which had the most significant relationship with the occurrence and the parties determines their rights and liabilities'.[51] Thus, in a typical case, the law chosen would be dependent on the social environment and this would be determined by weighing a number of factors such as: (a) the place of the injury; (b) the domicile and nationality of the parties; (c) the place of incorporation and the place of business; and (d) the place where the event causing the injury occurred. To an English lawyer, this looks very much like how an English court might differentiate between a licence and a lease or a contract of service and a contract for services; in short, it appears uncertain and likely to undermine uniformity of approach. More particularly, it is likely to make it

---

47 Some writers point to *M'Elroy v M'Allister* 1949 SC 110 (a result that does not bring any credit on a civilised legal system).

48 See the Private International Law (Miscellaneous Provisions) Act 1995, below.

49 Morris (1949) 12 MLR 248; (1951) 64 HLR 881. Dr Morris was the general editor of Dicey from 1949 until his death in 1984.

50 Morris (1951) 64 HLR 881, p 888.

51 American Law Institute Draft Restatement (2d) Conflict of Laws 1963, alluded to with approval by Fuld J in *Babcock v Jackson* (1963) 2 LR 286.

difficult for a lawyer to advise a client in advance of litigation as to the applicable law. Some critics argue that analogies drawn with the law of contract are inappropriate, having regard to the fact that, in a contractual relationship, the parties are free to expressly select the proper law.[52]

A further point that needs to be noted is that discussion of the proper law of the tort began to be extended in the USA and became closely linked with those writers favouring the approach of the governmental interest analysis,[53] that is, where a case arises giving rise to a conflict between two State's laws, the court should apply the law of the State whose interest would be most impaired if it were not applied.[54] A variant of this approach is familiar in the USA in cases where a number of State's laws appear to be in conflict and the court of the forum selects the law of the State most appropriate to the facts of the instant case.

It is doubtful whether approaches in the USA[55] could be applied so easily in the UK; it may be appropriate within a federal system, where individual States share the same values within the umbrella of a written constitution, but many of the cases coming before English courts concern conflicts with the laws of other independent States that have a different history and culture. In such circumstances, an English court would need to receive considerable evidence of foreign law and would be placed in the unenviable position of evaluating the social context of the laws of another sovereign State. There is little evidence of English judges in the years after 1949 being attracted by the approach of certain American writers[56] and, in any event, the English courts were bound to follow the rule in *Phillips v Eyre*.[57] Now that choice of law in the law of tort has been placed on a statutory basis, there is little reason to believe English courts will be attracted to developments in the USA.

FOREIGN TORTS: THE POSITION AT COMMON LAW

English law did not manage to establish a satisfactory method of dealing with tort problems in the conflict of laws after over a century of trying.[58] Unlike the

---

52 A point made by a number of the judges in *Boys v Chaplin* [1971] AC 356.

53 See Cavers, *The Choice of Law Process* (1965); Currie, *Selected Essays on the Conflict of Laws* (1963).

54 *Bernhard v Harrah's Club* (1976) 16 Cal 3d 313; 546 P 2d 719, Supreme Court of California.

55 Particularly not after the Private International Law (Miscellaneous Provisions) Act 1995.

56 The matter was discussed in *Boys v Chaplin* [1971] AC 356, on which, see below.

57 (1870) LR 6 QB 1.

58 However, it has to be recognised that, before 1945, only a very limited number of cases concerning foreign torts came before the English courts. The leading authorities are: *The Halley* (1866) LR 2 PC 193 (Selwyn LJ); *Phillips v Eyre* (1870) LR 6 QB 1 (Willes J); *The Mary Moxham* (1876) 1 PD 107 (Sir Robert Phillimore) *Machado v Fontes* [1897] 2 QB 231 (Lopes, Rigby LJJ).

USA and most of continental Europe, English law refused to accept the law of the place where the tort was committed as the basic governing law and preferred instead a mixture of the *lex fori* and the *lex loci delicti.*

The prominence of the forum was explicable in terms of the rights thesis of tort, that is, when the English court provides a remedy for a tort, it is acknowledging that a recognised interest of the plaintiff has been invaded and that this right should be vindicated by the award of damages. To recognise an exotic 'right' does not fit into this pattern. For example, English law does not recognise a right to privacy as such.[59] In so far as privacy is protected at all,[60] the plaintiff must establish the commission of some specific tort, for instance, that his property has been invaded or that his reputation has been injured. Suppose that a plaintiff from a country which gave a right to privacy *per se* were to sue in England for the breach of that right and an English court were to give him damages in compensation. It might be thought that the decision had established a precedent for such a right in a purely domestic case. There is no need for fears of this type. When an English court recognises a foreign law to the extent of giving a remedy based upon its content, it does not thereby make an extension to the domestic law of England and there are no grounds for seeing tort as an exception to this.

If the application of the law of the forum to the disposition of tort cases undermines the whole idea of the conflict of laws and the *lex loci* imports adventitious elements, the amalgamation of the two would not appear promising. In fact, the English way has been to make the forum law dominant but to require that the wrong[61] complained of before the English court should have at least some quality of wrongfulness by the law of the place where it was done. The *lex loci delicti* was merely required to indicate that an unjustified act had been done and, then, it was for English law to deal with the matter in its own way.

---

59 *Kaye v Robertson* [1991] FSR 62; at least, this represents the present state of the law. See Younger Committee (Cmnd 5012, 1972); Markesinis (1992) 55 MLR 118.

60 The position will change when the European Convention on Human Rights and Fundamental Freedoms is incorporated into domestic law by the Human Rights Act 1998. By Art 8(1), 'Everyone has the right to respect for his private and family life, his home and his correspondence ...'.

61 This may be a reflection of the self-confidence of Victorian England, which manifested itself in the view that the quality of justice available in England was superior to that available in other less fortunate lands. This view was alluded to by the House of Lords in moving towards a doctrine of *forum non conveniens.* See, in particular, *The Atlantic Star* [1974] AC 436, p 453, where Lord Reid made reference to 'the good old days, the passing of which many may regret, when the inhabitants of this island felt an innate superiority over those unfortunate enough to belong to other races ... The time is ripe for a re-examination of this rather insular doctrine'.

The common law approach can be traced to the judgment of Willes J in *Phillips v Eyre*,[62] which, unfortunately, but such is the accident of litigation, was an atypical tort case. The facts of the case were as follows: Eyre was the Governor of Jamaica at a time of rebellion in the colony. In putting down the rebellion, he contravened the civil liberties of the plaintiff. At a later date, the legislature retrospectively validated the action of the Governor by passing an Act of Indemnity. The plaintiff's action for assault and false imprisonment was dismissed by the Court of Exchequer Chamber.[63]

It is unlikely that the case would have attracted much legal notice[64] had it not been for the attempt of Willes J to state a general rule. His words have been scrutinised by generations of commentators as if he were seeking to legislate for all time. The central passage, which became known as the rule in *Phillips v Eyre*, reads as follows:

> As a general rule, in order to found a suit in England for a wrong alleged to have been committed abroad, two conditions must be fulfilled. First, the wrong must be of such a character that it would have been actionable if committed in England. Secondly, the act must not have been justifiable by the law of the place where it was done.[65]

Authority for the first limb of the rule, that the wrong complained of must be a tort by English domestic law, is provided alone by the judgment of the Judicial Committee of the Privy Council in *The Halley*.[66] The facts of this case were as follows: foreign shipowners sued the owners of a British steamer in respect of collision damage caused by the negligent navigation of a compulsory pilot in Belgian territorial waters. The defendants contended that they were obliged, by Belgian law, to employ a pilot[67] but were not liable for his negligence. English law, at that time, differed from Belgian law, the *lex loci delicti*, in holding that a shipowner was not liable for the negligence of a compulsory pilot.

---

62 (1870) LR 6 QB 1. The rule in *Phillips v Eyre* came to be described as the 'double actionability' rule but was abolished with effect from 1 May 1996 by virtue of the Public International Law (Miscellaneous Provisions) Act 1995, s 10(1)(a).

63 The Court of Exchequer Chamber confirmed the earlier judgment of the Court of Queen's Bench at (1869) LR 4 QB 225; the judgment of the court had been reserved for several months and was delivered by Willes J on behalf of all seven judges of the Court of Exchequer Chamber.

64 Indeed, it is arguable that the law reporter in the headnote and two of the leading counsel (Mellish QC, Giffard QC) considered that the main point of interest in the case related to the precise legislative powers of a subordinate colonial legislature.

65 *Phillips v Eyre* (1870) LR 6 QB 1, p 28; the passage appears in a paragraph where the learned judge appears initially to be dealing with jurisdiction in respect of foreign causes.

66 (1868) LR 2 PC 193; the full title is *The Liverpool, Brazil and River Plate Steam Navigation Co Ltd v Henry Benham*.

67 The law is set out in the Merchant Shipping Act 1854, s 388; for the present law, see the Pilotage Act 1983.

The Privy Council[68] allowed an appeal from the Court of Admiralty and dismissed the action of the foreign shipowners, holding that it would be contrary both to principle and authority to award a remedy for an act that constituted no wrong by English law. Selwyn LJ expressed the matter in robust terms, asserting that it would be:[69]

> ... contrary to principle and to authority to hold that an English Court of Justice will enforce a foreign municipal law, and will give a remedy in the shape of damages in respect of an act which, according to its own principles, imposes no liability on the person from whom the damages are claimed.

It has been argued that the decision is explicable on the basis that the court was minded to uphold English rules relating to pilotage as set out in the Maritime Shipping Act 1854.[70]

However, a close reading of the case indicates that the successful appellants were determined to advocate the general proposition that an English court of law should not entertain a cause of action arising in a foreign country that would not lie in England. As counsel expressed the matter,[71] 'no authority can be found to show that there is a remedy here for a tort abroad which is not a tort here'.[72]

It is arguable that the judgment in *The Halley*,[73] adopted in *Phillips v Eyre*,[74] was a product of the tradition of maritime superiority asserted by English law. In any event, it had a disastrous effect on the development of a satisfactory system of choice of law in tort because it prevented any claim in England for any wrong which did not have its precise counterpart in English law.

The language used for the second limb of the rule – that the act must not have been justifiable by the *lex loci delicti* – fits the facts of *Phillips v Eyre* but the word 'justifiable' is an odd one in the context of most tort actions and its use has caused a great deal of difficulty. It was clearly intended, quite properly, to cover the situation where the act was not wrongful by the *locus delicti*, where it was lawfully authorised, in advance or retrospectively, or where the defendant had, by that law, a complete defence to the plaintiff's

---

68 In the years prior to the Judicature Acts 1873–75, Admiralty and Prize appeals were taken by the Judicial Committee of the Privy Council.

69 See Selwyn LJ in *The Halley* (1868) LR 2 PC 193, p 204.

70 In so far as the merchant shipping legislation was part of the law of the sea, this was a particularly sensitive topic. England had played a considerable part in building up the relevant rules of maritime law and was unlikely in the 19th century to defer to the legal regime of a newly created State such as Belgium.

71 It is not without interest that counsel for the successful appellants was the then Solicitor General, Sir William Baliol Brett QC, who, two years later (in July 1870), as Brett J, would contribute to the judgment in *Phillips v Eyre* (1870) LR 6 QB 1.

72 (1868) LR 2 PC 193, p 195, *per* Brett QC.

73 *The Liverpool, Brazil and River Plate Steam Navigation Co v Benham* (1868) LR 2 PC 193.

74 (1870) LR 2 PC 193.

claim. Whether it was intended to require actionability in the *locus delicti* is more dubious.

Indeed, the assumption that the rule relates to the choice of law is open to question. A review of the language indicates that three possible interpretations can be advanced: (a) that it provides a double barrelled choice of law rule and has nothing to say about jurisdiction; (b) that it is a double barrelled jurisdictional rule leaving open the choice of law; and (c) that the first part of the rule is jurisdictional, whilst the second part constitutes a choice of law rule in favour of the *lex loci delicti*.

The subsequent decisions showed a willingness to follow the rule in *Phillips v Eyre*. An example is afforded by *The Mary Moxham*,[75] where the facts were as follows: the plaintiffs, an English company, owned a pier in Spain. The plaintiffs brought an action in England in respect of collision damage caused by a vessel owned by the defendants. In England, the shipowners would have been vicariously liable; in Spain, liability would fall on the masters and crew alone.

The plaintiffs failed in their action in England against the shipowners as Spanish law did not apply the doctrine of vicarious liability and would regard the proper defendants to be the master and crew.

Within a short period of time, the second limb of the rule[76] in *Phillips v Eyre* was given a very liberal interpretation by the Court of Appeal, in the case of *Machado v Fontes*,[77] where the facts were as follows: the plaintiff sued the defendant in England in respect of a libel contained in a pamphlet published in the Portuguese language by the defendant in Brazil. As his defence, the defendant contended that, as the act was not subject to civil liability in Brazil, it was not actionable in England. The plaintiff contended that as the act could be the subject of criminal prosecution in Brazil it was not justifiable and, thus, actionable in England.

The Court of Appeal,[78] in allowing the appeal and giving judgment for the plaintiff on a question of pleading, ruled that the second limb of the rule in *Phillips v Eyre* would be satisfied unless it could be demonstrated that the act in question was authorised, innocent or excusable in the country in which it was committed.[79] Thus, in fitting the case within the rule in *Phillips v Eyre*, there was no problem over the first limb of the rule – had the libel been published in England, it would have given rise to a successful action here.

---

75 (1876) 1 PD 107.

76 Ie, that the act must not have been justifiable by the law of the place where it was done.

77 [1897] 2 QB 231.

78 *Machado v Fontes* [1897] 2 QB 231, where the court applied *Phillips v Eyre* (1870) LR 6 QB 1 and *The Mary Moxham* (1876) 1 PD 107.

79 The formulation adopted by Rigby LJ in *Machado v Fontes* [1897] 2 QB 231, p 236.

With regard to the second, the fact that there was a possibility of criminal proceedings in Brazil was regarded as sufficient to make the wrong non-justifiable by that law.

The judgment in *Phillips v Eyre* was subject to criticism because it made the whole substance of the obligation turn upon English law, a legal system which is involved in the case solely because the plaintiff decided to bring his action in England.

The willingness to extend the second limb of *Phillips v Eyre* was not confined to the UK. A Quebec court went one step further in allowing a personal injury claim brought by a gratuitous passenger against his host driver for an accident in Ontario, although the Ontarian 'guest statute' prevented the passenger's recovery. Though there was no civil liability by the *locus delicti*, there was potential criminal liability for careless driving; the Quebec court latched onto this, notwithstanding that an Ontarian criminal court had acquitted the driver of the offence.[80] The conflict here was a false one. Both parties were domiciled in Quebec and only the fact of the accident happening in Ontario brought that system's law into consideration.[81]

Despite these examples, which give the impression that the rule in *Phillips v Eyre* is plaintiff oriented, the reverse is the case as the plaintiff had to satisfy a double test, the most formidable of which is that of English law as the *lex fori*.[82] Nevertheless, although the traditional interpretation of *Phillips v Eyre* reduced the *lex loci delicti* to a very minor role, it would deny the action in a number of situations. Where the defendant could show that his act was justified or not in any way wrongful (that is, gave rise to no civil action of any description and could not be made the subject of any criminal process) by the *lex loci delicti* or could establish that he had a complete defence to the action by that law, the second limb of the rule in *Phillips v Eyre* would not be satisfied. The defendant would also escape liability if he could show that he was not liable in the same capacity under two legal systems. Only the last of these needs amplification here. The rule in *Phillips v Eyre* requires that the parties be involved in the same capacities and that the claim is the same under both legal systems. An object lesson here, though not actually following *Phillips v Eyre*, as

---

80 *McLean v Pettigrew* (1945) 2 DLR 65; it is difficult to imagine how there could be potential criminal liability at a time and in a jurisdiction in which the doctrine of *autrefois acquit* operated.

81 Compare with *Babcock v Jackson* (1963) 12 NY 2d 473; 2 LR 286.

82 A point made by Lord Mackay LC in the Special Bill Committee of the Private International Law (Miscellaneous Provisions) Act 1995: 'A general rule such as the rule of double actionability, which imposes the use of the law of the forum as an additional limitation to an action, is parochial in appearance in that it presupposes that it is inherently just for the rules of the English or Scottish law of tort or delict to be indiscriminately applied regardless of the foreign elements of the relevant facts.'

it is a Scottish case, is afforded by the litigation in *M'Elroy v M'Allister*.[82a] The facts of the case were as follows: the pursuer's husband was killed on an English road in Cumbria. At the time of the accident, the husband was a passenger in a lorry owned by his employer's and driven by their servant the defender. All the involved parties were natives of and resident in Glasgow.

If the accident had happened in Scotland, then the widow would have been able to recover a substantial sum for *solatium*. In respect of an accident before the English courts, a widow would have had: (a) a claim under the Fatal Accidents Act 1846; (b) a claim for the deceased's expectation of life under the Law Reform (Miscellaneous Provisions) Act 1934; and (c) a claim for funeral expenses. The claim for *solatium* failed because it was not available under the *lex loci delicti*. The claim under the Fatal Accidents Act 1846 failed because it was beyond the relevant English limitation period and such a bar was regarded as a rule of substantive law. Thirdly, the claim under the Law Reform (Miscellaneous Provisions) Act 1934 failed because, under the then Scottish law, all rights of action in respect of personal injuries due to negligence died with the injured person. Thus, the pursuer was entitled to claim only £40 of funeral expenses, a remedy common to both systems.

In every case before 1969, where the rule in *Phillips v Eyre* had been followed, the result was the application of English domestic law to the substantive issue between the parties. It has been suggested that the rule is not a choice of law rule at all, but a further jurisdictional hurdle which has to be surmounted before English law is applied as *lex fori*. In other words, the rule in *Phillips v Eyre* was not a double barrelled choice of law rule which happened to lead to the application of English law as *lex causae*, but a test which, once completed, leads to the application of English law as *lex fori*. As English law was applied in every case, it could be argued that it really did not matter whether it was applied as *lex causae* or as *lex fori*. However, if the rule in *Phillips v Eyre* is seen as a jurisdictional rule which leaves open the choice of law, it may at least be argued that, once the rule has been satisfied, the court is left with the freedom to determine the appropriate governing law, even if in every case so far it has chosen English law for that role.[83]

The defects in a system which always leads to the application of the forum law, like the wooden application of the *lex loci delicti*, can result in an entirely artificial connection which bears little or no relation to the parties or the facts of the case. It has the additional disadvantage that the plaintiff can, by selecting his jurisdiction, create a right which he did not possess under any other legal system or greatly increase the effect of any right which he did

---

[82a] 1949 SC 110.

[83] While the rule in *Phillips v Eyre* (1870) LR 6 QB 1 is abrogated by the Private International Law (Miscellaneous Provisions) Act 1995, s 10, it is clear that, by virtue of s 14(1), there could still be cases concerning the rule in respect of acts and omissions arising prior to 1 May 1996.

have. The criticisms founded on these difficulties – the artificiality of the *locus delicti*, already considered, the development of other theories, not least that of the law of the social environment developed by the late Dr JH Morris,[84] and the abandonment of the rigid adherence to the *lex loci* by American courts (manifested for English lawyers primarily by the judgment in *Babcock v Jackson*)[85] – created a mood for change in English law. The litigation in *Boys v Chaplin*[86] provided just the opportunity.

THE JUDGMENT IN *BOYS V CHAPLIN*

Since the judgment in *Phillips v Eyre*,[87] no case had gone as far as the House of Lords in which the question of choice of law in respect of an exclusively foreign tort was directly in issue. The rather mundane facts of *Boys v Chaplin*[88] provided such an opportunity for the House of Lords to consider this entire area of law.

The plaintiff and the defendant, both normally resident in England, were temporarily stationed in Malta as members of the British forces. While both were off duty, the plaintiff, riding as a passenger on a motor scooter, was seriously injured in a collision in Malta with a motor car driven by the defendant. There was no dispute as to liability. However, under the law in Malta, the plaintiff could only recover special damages, being out of pocket expenses and proved loss of earnings. In the circumstances of the case, this was £53. However, by English law a claim for general damages was available for pain, loss and suffering of £2,250.

At first instance, Milmo J,[89] following *Machado v Fontes*, held that the plaintiff could recover £2,250 in general damages, notwithstanding the fact that such a sum could not be recovered in the *lex loci delicti*. This decision was supported by the Court of Appeal[90] and by the House of Lords.[91] However, the judgments contain such a wide ranging discussion of the problems that many have questioned whether any clear *ratio decidendi* can be identified. At the risk of over simplification, the following questions arose for decision:

(a) was the rule in *Phillips v Eyre* a rule of general application or was it subject to particular exceptions?

---

84 Morris (1949) 12 MLR 248; (1951) 64 HLR 881.
85 (1963) 12 NY 2d 473; 2 LR 286.
86 [1971] AC 356; [1969] 2 All ER 1085.
87 (1870) LR 6 QB 1.
88 [1971] AC 356.
89 [1968] 2 QB 1; [1967] 2 All ER 665.
90 [1968] 2 QB 1; 1 All ER 283 (Lord Denning MR, Lord Upjohn, Diplock LJ).
91 [1971] AC 356; [1969] 2 All ER 1085.

(b) is the rule in *Phillips v Eyre*, as extended in *Machado v Fontes*, still good law?

(c) are questions of heads of damage matters of substantive or procedural law? and

(d) should English law move towards the principle that the proper law of the tort should be the general governing law for tort?

Before looking at the choice of law issue, it is necessary to consider the matter of damages. The quantification of damages, that is, how much in money terms the plaintiff shall be awarded for his injury, is incontrovertibly a matter for the *lex fori*. One cannot claim that broken legs are more valuable in California than they are in Bangladesh and that, therefore, the forum should make the necessary adjustment in the particular case (hence the importance of forum selection).

If you sue in England, you get the English going rate for the injury you have sustained. But, while quantification is a matter for the *lex fori*, is the question of the heads of damage recoverable similarly a matter for the law of the forum? With varying degrees of precision, legal systems use separate bases of claims which are then quantified. So, to take the example of a personal injury claim, the allowable heads of damage would include medical and other out of pocket expenses, damages for pain and suffering, for losses of amenity, future earnings and so on. It does not follow that the court, in making an overall award of general damages, will specify the amount awarded under each of the allowable heads. English judges have resisted the invitation to make their awards specifically itemised as they are very far from dealing with a precise process. But, the ability to award at least notionally under the specific heads is part of the nature of the action. If the refusal of Maltese law to award damages for pain and suffering – not in this case specifically, but as a general policy of Maltese law – was seen as a matter of quantification only, there would be no problem, as the case was being brought before the English court which allows such awards. If, however, the claim for general damages is seen as part of the substantive right, then, according to one view of the rule in *Phillips v Eyre*, there must be a match between the plaintiff's claim in English and in the *locus delicti*. If the English law does, and the Maltese law does not, recognise the claim, then the action must fail. It needs to be emphasised that this is true only on one view of *Phillips v Eyre*. The view that any unjustifiable act in the *locus delicti* satisfies the second limb of the rule, or even that the second limb requires civil actionability of some sort, would allow application of English law.

It has generally been supposed, and the better judgments in *Chaplin v Boys* bear this out, that the proper classification is that the heads of damage are matters of substantive right and not merely matters of quantification. If this is so, there is a real conflict between English and Maltese law and not merely an artificial one.

wondered whether that this is indeed the better view. Suppose like Malta in this case, decides not to allow compensation to be awarded for harms of a particular type while another decides to confine such awards within narrow monetary limits. An example of this would be English law's attitude to the, now defunct, action for loss of expectation of life, where awards were limited to a conventional, if not token, amount; another would be the practice of some States in the USA of putting a ceiling on personal injury awards. The operation of the rule in *Phillips v Eyre* meant that, where the *lex loci delicti* had no remedy for the plaintiff's claim, there could be no successful claim in England. But, if it has a remedy, however conventional or token it might be, not only did an action lie in England but it lay to the full extent of English law, that is, free from the restrictions of the *locus delicti*, because English law governs the issue of quantification. The distinction, then, between the procedural issue of quantification and the substantive issue of heads of damage ultimately comes down to the difference between nought and one!

At trial,[92] Milmo J felt obliged to follow the judgment of the Court of Appeal in *Machado v Fontes*. It followed from that case, inevitably as there was no law of the *locus delicti* on the matter of civil compensation for libel, that English law governed the heads of damage as well as the quantification of damages awarded under any head. The Court of Appeal,[93] arguably not bound by the decision in *Machado v Fontes,* could explore the various possibilities. Lord Denning MR, showing his characteristic impatience with old decisions which stood in the way of his view of justice, was prepared to set aside *Machado v Fontes* as wrongly decided and to come out fully in favour of the application of the proper law of the tort, both to the cause of action and to the heads of damage also, as these were substantive matters.

Lord Upjohn, in the Court of Appeal, took a very traditional view of the rule in *Phillips v Eyre*, which left the *lex loci delicti* with the very minor role of establishing unjustifiability and made the *lex fori* paramount. He wanted nothing to do with the proper law of the tort, which he considered totally unsuited to English conditions. Diplock LJ, in a dissenting judgment, recognised that the question of heads of damage was a matter of substantive law but he took an historical view, not entirely borne out by the authorities, that the *lex causae* was the *lex loci delicti*. As Maltese law was the *lex causae*, it followed that the plaintiff had no right before the English courts to any more than the damages allowed by Maltese law, to be quantified, if anything turned on it, by the English court. He rejected the proper law of the tort as being a retrograde step, at least outside passenger/carrier, driver/guest cases. It is also worthy of note that Diplock LJ appeared to be of the opinion that the first limb of the rule was directed to jurisdiction rather than choice of law. It is

---

92 *Boys v Chaplin* [1968] 2 QB 1; [1967] 2 All ER 665.
93 *Boys v Chaplin* [1968] 1 All ER 283.

clear that the extract from Willes J was included in a paragraph which commenced with remarks about jurisdiction and the matter had been canvassed by academic writers notwithstanding the absence of direct authority.[94]

The case was then appealed to the House of Lords[95] with all the options still open and, while their lordships were unanimous that English law should govern the case, the lack of agreement on exactly why it should do so continued.

Lord Hodson favoured overruling *Machado v Fontes*, regarded the issue of heads of damage as matters of substance and rejected the proper law of the tort, as a general dispositive law, as too uncertain. He did adopt a form of reasoning which supporters of the proper law can pray in aid of their arguments. The rule in *Phillips v Eyre*, he said, was only a general rule, as Willes J himself had stated, and, therefore, it was subject to exceptions based on public policy and, if controlling effect is given to the law of the jurisdiction which, because of its relationship with the occurrence and the parties, has the greatest concern with the specific issue raised in the litigation, the ends of justice are likely to be achieved.

Lord Guest took the view that the rule in *Phillips v Eyre* was a rule of double actionability – that the plaintiff had to show that his action, while it would give rise to an action in England had it happened there, would also give rise to civil liability by the *lex loci delicti*, thereby avoiding abuses like *Machado v Fontes*. As the plaintiff could establish that he had a remedy, albeit a limited one, under Maltese law, that would suffice as he believed damages for pain and suffering did not depend on a substantive right but were part and parcel of the right to damages for personal injury and, thus, procedural matters for the *lex fori*. He roundly rejected the suggestion that the court might apply the proper law of the tort.

Lord Donovan took an even more traditional line; he was not prepared to go even as far as to interpret the rule in *Phillips v Eyre* as requiring double actionability, though he did concede that the decision in *Machado v Fontes* was an abuse. If the word 'justifiable' was to be given its ordinary meaning, the plaintiff's case was secure, as there was clearly a wrong done him under Maltese law. As the English court was competent to entertain the action under the rule in *Phillips v Eyre*, it was right that it should award its own remedies. His rejection of the proper law of the tort was even more vigorous than that of Lord Guest.

Lord Wilberforce gave a judgment that attracted considerable interest, partly because the learned judge explored the approach in other jurisdictions.

---

94 Yntema (1949) 27 Can Bar Rev 116.
95 [1971] AC 356; [1969] 2 All ER 1085.

His Lordship had no hesitation in condemning the decision in *Machado v Fontes*, which he thought ought to be overruled. *Phillips v Eyre* involved, he asserted, double actionability. He was not in favour of adopting the proper law of the tort as a general choice of law rule but *Phillips v Eyre* should be applied with some flexibility, subject to exceptions along the lines of the American Law Institute's Restatement,[96] which would enable the court, in a suitable case, to proceed:

> ... by segregation of the relevant issue and consideration whether, in relation to that issue, the relevant foreign rule ought, as a matter of policy, to be applied. For this purpose, it is necessary to identify the policy of the rule, to inquire in what situations, and with what contacts, it was intended to apply; whether not to apply it, in the circumstances of the instant case, would serve any interest which the rule was devised to meet ... The rule limiting damages is the creation of the law of Malta, a place where both respondent and appellant were temporally stationed ... Nothing suggests that the Maltese State have any interest in applying this rule to persons resident outside it, or in denying the application of the English rule to these parties ... No argument has been suggested why an English court, if free to do so, should renounce its own rule. That rule ought, in my opinion, to apply.[97]

Lord Pearson delivered the final judgment in the House of Lords and he regarded the issue of pain and suffering to be a substantive matter, but rejected any requirement of double actionability. In his view, the rule in *Phillips v Eyre* applied directly, that is, the *lex fori* became the *lex causae* once non-justifiability by the *lex loci delicti* had been established. He recognised, however, that there was a problem of forum shopping inherent in the English system, as evidenced by the decision in *Machado v Fontes*, and that this should be controlled by public policy and by the application of the proper law, at least in the identification of the natural forum.

The outcome of the litigation was that English law was applied to the issue of heads of damage and the plaintiff obtained his English award. Only Diplock LJ, in the Court of Appeal, had opposed this result but there was nothing like unanimity on the basis of the adjudication. Indeed, it is not easy to find a clear majority in favour of any particular important position. If we examine the particular issues, the division of opinion is clear.

(a) In favour of the proposition that heads of damage are matters of substantive law, the opinions of Lord Denning MR, Diplock LJ, Lord Hodson, Lord Wilberforce and Lord Pearson were in favour. Milmo J, Lord Upjohn, Lord Guest and Lord Donovan were against.

(b) Of the view that *Machado v Fontes* remained good law, Milmo J (though this is perhaps unfair, as he felt bound by the decision of a higher court)

---

96 See, now, the American Law Institute Restatement (2d) Conflict of Laws 1971.
97 [1971] AC 356, p 391; [1969] 2 All ER 1085, p 1104.

and Lord Upjohn, Lord Donovan and Lord Pearson were in favour. However, those against it were Lord Denning MR, Diplock LJ, and Lord Hodson, Lord Wilberforce and Lord Guest.

(c) In respect of the proposition that the doctrine of the proper law of the tort should be the general governing law for tort, we have the sole voice of Lord Denning MR. Opposing it, we have the express statements of all other judges concerned with the litigation, though Lord Pearson did suggest the use of the proper law to prevent forum shopping and Lord Wilberforce did in fact apply, in his use of interest analysis, a rather sophisticated proper law approach.

(d) If we consider the place of the rule in *Phillips v Eyre* after the judgment in *Boys v Chaplin*, we find that Lord Denning MR, Lords Hodson and Lord Wilberforce would regard it as a general rule only, to which there were exceptions; in the case of Lord Denning MR, the exceptions would be numerous. Taking the traditional view that the rule required the application of English law as *lex fori*, we have Lord Upjohn, Lord Donovan and Lord Pearson, while Diplock LJ alone took the view that the rule required the application of the *lex loci delicti commissi*. Lord Denning MR, Lord Hodson, Lord Wilberforce and Lord Guest can be assumed to regard the rule as now requiring double actionability.

The position after *Boys v Chaplin* appeared to be that the rule in *Phillips v Eyre* required double actionability – the particular plaintiff must show that he has a cause of action against the particular defendant under both English law and the *lex loci delicti*. While the wrong must be actionable as a tort by English law, it would seem that the cause of action does not need to be categorised in the same way, provided that it is the same claim against the same defendant in the same capacity. It must be a claim based on the wrongful act of the defendant and not a claim which is merely triggered by it. This can be illustrated by a couple of old cases which came before the Privy Council on appeal from Canada. In *McMillan v Canadian Northern Railways*,[98] an action was brought in Saskatchewan against his employer by a workman who had been injured by a fellow employee in Ontario. By Ontarian law, employers were not liable to employees who had been injured by those in common employment with them. While this rule did not apply in Saskatchewan, it provided a complete defence by the *lex loci* and, thus, prevented satisfaction of the second limb of the rule in *Phillips v Eyre*. The accident entitled the employee to compensation under a workmen's compensation fund, but that was not accepted as satisfying the second limb of the rule, as the entitlement under that fund was a statutory right which was not dependent on the fault of the employer. The same would apply if, in the *lex loci*, the right to claim damages in a running down case had been replaced by a State compensation

---

98 *McMillan v Canadian Northern Rlys* [1923] AC 120; *Walpole v Canadian National Rly* [1923] AC 120.

scheme which was available on the basis of injury rather than fault or by the system under German law covering injured workers.

The judgment in *Boys v Chaplin* was followed by a flood of academic literature[99] in which it has to be admitted that writers complained that it was difficult to extract a precise *ratio* from the case, having regard to the differing judgments. In any event, much would depend on how the case was interpreted in subsequent litigation and that is a matter to which we must now turn.

THE COMMON LAW AFTER *BOYS V CHAPLIN*

After *Boys v Chaplin*, the question arose as to the precise *ratio* of the case and how it should be applied in subsequent litigation. In broad terms, it seemed to be clear that the doctrine of the proper law of the tort had been rejected and the rule in *Phillips v Eyre* remained good law and represented a general rule. However, the conduct had to be actionable, not merely justifiable, by the *lex loci deliciti* and the rule was one to which there might be exceptions and which, in any event, was to be applied with flexibility.

It was unclear what ambit the flexibility introduced by Lord Wilberforce was to have. After 1970, it was used only to apply English law and it is unclear whether it could have been used to apply a foreign law, though, in principle, that was possible. It was intended to apply only to displace the second limb of the rule in *Phillips v Eyre* and does not affect the rule in *The Halley*. Where all the other connections are with England, then flexibility provides a suitable escape device from the *lex loci*. Whether it would apply in the event of less significant connections was unclear.

That the judgment in *Boys v Chaplin* was open to differing interpretations was evident after *Sayers v International Drilling Co NV*,[100] as Lord Denning MR, in giving judgment, indicated that *Boys v Chaplin* was an authority for the doctrine of the proper law of the tort.[101] It is difficult to read all the judgments in the House of Lords and find such a degree of enthusiasm for the proper law of the tort theory.

---

99 Graveson (1969) 85 LQR 505; McGregor (1970) 33 MLR 1; Shapira (1970) 33 MLR 27 North and Webb (1970) 19 ICLQ 24; Karsten (1970) 19 ICLQ 35.

100 [1971] 1 WLR 1176 (Lord Denning MR, Salmon, Stamp LJJ). As the case gives rise to problems in the law of contract, it is discussed below, p 395ff.

101 *Ibid*, p 1180 (Lord Denning MR noted: 'the claim by the plaintiff is founded on tort. In considering that claim, we must apply the proper law of the tort, that is, the law of the country with which the parties and the acts done have the most significant connection. That is how I put it in *Boys v Chaplin* [1968] 2 QB 1, p 20. I think it is confirmed by what Lord Wilberforce said in [1971] AC 356, p 391–92, in the House of Lords.').

The interpretation of *Boys v Chaplin* received a more orthodox treatment in the Court of Appeal in the *Church of Scientology of California v Commissioner of the Metropolitan Police*.[102] The facts of the case were that the plaintiff was seeking to sue the defendant in England on the basis that he was vicariously liable[103] for a libel committed abroad by officers under his command. The defendant had persuaded Boreham J that the action should be struck out as an abuse of process. The plaintiff successfully appealed to the Court of Appeal, arguing that he had produced affidavit evidence to satisfy both heads of *Phillips v Eyre* and that, in any event, after *Boys v Chaplin*, the rule was to be applied with flexibility. In giving judgment, Bridge LJ noted that *Boys v Chaplin* had established the rule of double actionability subject to a limited exception and the learned judge then noted:

> This is an extremely uncertain subject. The exception to the general rule of double actionability is one newly enunciated by their Lordships in *Boys v Chaplin*. Its true limits will no doubt become clearer as more cases are decided in the courts.

A broadly similar conclusion was reached by Hodgson J in *Coupland v Arabian Gulf Oil*,[104] where the facts were as follows: the plaintiff, a resident in Scotland, brought an action in England against the defendant, a Libyan national oil company, in respect of personal injuries arising from his employment in Lybia.

In ruling on a number of preliminary issues, Hodgson J held: (a) that the effect of *Boys v Chaplin* was to restate the rule in *Phillips v Eyre*; (b) that, while the true *ratio* of *Boys v Chaplin* was difficult to determine, it was, in fact, stated in the speech of Lord Wilberforce;[105] (c) that, in the instant case of a personal injury abroad, as the act was actionable in both Lybia and England, then the action could proceed to trial. This conclusion was supported by the Court of Appeal where Robert Goff LJ noted that the principles in *Boys v Chaplin* required that 'the claim must be actionable by the *lex fori* and also actionable by the *lex delicti*'.[106]

The legacy of *Boys v Chaplin* was considered further in *Johnson v Coventry Churchill International Ltd*,[107] where the facts were as follows: the plaintiff was engaged by the defendants in England to travel to West Germany, in order that he might work on various building sites. While working there, he suffered injury and, at a later date, began a legal action against the defendants.

---

102 (1970) 120 SJ 690.

103 Under the terms of the then Police Act 1964, s 48; see, now, Police Act 1996, s 88.

104 [1983] 1 WLR 1136 (Hodgson J, HC; Waller, Oliver and Robert Goff LJJ, CA).

105 Hodgson J considered that the *ratio* was that of double actionability, subject to a limited exception to the general rule; see *ibid*, p 1146.

106 The aspect of the case involving the law of contract is dealt with below, p 395ff.

107 [1994] 3 All ER 14.

The judge at first instance[108] ruled that, as no action could be taken in West Germany[109] against an employer in such circumstances for negligence, then the strict terms of the double actionability rule had not been complied with but the claim fell within an exception to the double actionability rule and English law should be applied because England was the country which had the most significant relationship with the occurrence and the parties. The learned judge considered that the case fell within the exception because the parties were both English, the contract was made subject to English law and the defendants had taken out insurance to cover themselves against claims by English workers who suffered injury abroad.[110] In *Coupland*, both limbs of *Phillips v Eyre* had been complied with but, in *Johnson*, it was clear that the second limb had not been met and it was therefore correct to consider whether an exception to the rule arose.

The precise scope of the exception was considered by the Privy Council in giving judgment in *Red Sea Insurance Co v Bouygues SA*.[111] The facts of the case were complex, but can be summarised as follows: the dispute between the parties arose out of the building of the University of Riyah in Saudi Arabia. The plaintiffs (split into two groups, that is, Group 1 and Group 2) sued the defendants, an insurance company based in both Hong Kong and Saudi Arabia, in respect of losses arising out of the repair of structural damage. The defendants filed various defences in the courts of Hong Kong but then counterclaimed against Group 2, alleging the losses were caused by their supply of faulty pre-cast concrete units. The legal basis for this counterclaim was either (a) indirectly under the principle of subrogation recognised in the law of insurance in Hong Kong; or (b) directly under the right of action arising under the law of Saudi Arabia. The problem in respect of (a) was that the right of action did not arise in Hong Kong law until Group 1 had been paid; they had not been paid. The Court of Appeal in Hong Kong, in considering an action to strike out the counterclaim, ruled that the defendant could proceed with action (a) under Saudi Arabian law but not action (b). The defendant appealed, arguing that he should be allowed to rely on the *lex delicti*. The Privy Council allowed the appeal, permitting the defendant to rely on the *lex delicti*, even though the *lex fori* did not recognise the action.

Although the Privy Council rejected the doctrine of the proper law of the tort, there is no doubt that the exception had been widened and, in an appropriate case, a party might rely on a cause of action not permitted by the *lex fori* and, further, that the exception in favour of the *lex delicti* might arise in

---

108 JW Kay QC, sitting as a Deputy Judge of the High Court.

109 The matter would have been dealt with through the social security system of the Reichsversicherungsordnung, s 656.

110 As in *Coupland*, this case gave rise to problems in the law of contract and that is discussed below, p 395ff.

111 [1995] 1 AC 190.

respect of the entire case not merely of an issue arising. On the facts of the case, such flexibility was justified because all the factual links were with Saudi Arabia. It was therefore clear that, in an appropriate case, the first limb of the double actionability rule might be departed from.

Thus, in the years after *Boys v Chaplin*, the law had evolved so that, although the double actionability rule was still law, it might, in exceptional cases, be departed from. Whether it was departed from would depend on the factual links. In *Johnson v Coventry Churchill International Ltd*,[112] the rule was departed from because most of the relevant factors pointed to the *lex fori* while, in *Red Sea Insurance Co Ltd v Bouygues SA*,[113] the nexus with Saudi Arabia was described by the Privy Council as overwhelming.

THE CASE FOR REFORM

The judgment in *Boys v Chaplin* was not well received and many academic articles appeared indicating that the judgment would probably not conclude debate.[114] In the subsequent case law, two experienced judges had confessed to difficulty in respect of the correct *ratio decidendi*.[115] It was argued that the law was still extremely parochial as the first rule of *Phillips v Eyre*, based on *The Halley*, still required that the action satisfied the test of English domestic tort law.

It was argued that even the reformed law swung the balance too much in favour of the the defendant as the plaintiff had to establish his cause of action by both the *lex fori* and the *lex loci delicti*, with the concomitant advantage to the defendant, who can defeat the claim by a defence open to him under either. The result was that the plaintiff, if he succeeded at all, achieved the lowest common level of relief. Even though the flexibility introduced by Lord Wilberforce in *Chaplin v Boys* avoided some of the greatest injustices, it was far from clear whether it would result in the application of anything other than English law.[116]

---

112 [1992] 3 All ER 14.

113 [1995] 1 AC 190.

114 McGregor (1970) 33 MLR 1; North and Webb (1970) 19 ICLQ 24; Karsten (1970) 19 ICLQ 35; Carter (1970) 44 BYIL 222; Reese (1970) 18 AJCL 189.

115 In *Coupland v Arabian Gulf Oil* [1983] 1 WLR 1136, Hodgson J observed: 'one must accept that the true *ratio* of the decision is not without its difficulties.' While, in the *Church of Scientology of California v Commissioner of the Metropolitan Police* (1976) 120 SJ 690, Bridge LJ observed, in respect of the exceptions to the double actionability rule, 'This is an extremely uncertain subject'.

116 At least until *Red Sea Insurance Co v Bouygues SA* [1995] 1 AC 190.

After *Red Sea Insurance,* it became clear that, if all the significant contacts were with the *lex delicti,* that law might be applied to the exclusion of the *lex fori.* However, Lord Slynn, in giving judgment, admitted that there were a number of unresolved questions as to the ambit of the exception. For example, could the *lex fori* and the *lex loci* be displaced in favour of some third system? It was argued that the choice of law rules were anomalous in that, in other spheres of private international law, provision was made for the exclusive application of the appropriate foreign law rather than concurrent application with *lex fori.* The central role of the *lex fori* was seen at being at variance with the fundamental principles of private international law.

It was argued that the rule in *Phillips v Eyre* was the product of 19th century conditions and that, with more citizens travelling abroad and more goods being sold across frontiers, modifying a 19th century rule was insufficient. It was contended that a high proportion of tort cases involve insurance and that there is always the possibility of a settlement if the basis of liability is clear. By placing the law on a clear statutory basis, a greater degree of certainty would be achieved and it would be easier for settlements to be achieved.

The process of reform had three stages. In the mid-1970s, attempts were made to secure reform at the European level; however, attempts to draft an EEC Convention on both non-contractual and contractual obligations was abandoned. The parties then proceeded to draw up the Rome Convention on the Law Applicable to Contractual Obligations 1980. The matter was then taken up by the Law Commission, who produced their Working Paper and Consultative Memorandum on *Choice of Law in Tort and Delict* in 1984.[117] In broad terms, the document set out four possible options for reform, namely: (a) the law of the forum; (b) a rule selection approach, selecting the applicable law on the basis of the specific issue in question, in the light of the various countries whose laws fell to be considered; (c) the law of the place of the wrong, the *lex loci delicti,* with a proper law (that is, the law of the place with the closest and most real connection) exception – Model 1; and (d) the proper law of the tort, subject to presumptions in certain cases – Model 2. Options (a) and (b) were rejected leaving only Model 1 and Model 2 as serious contenders. The Law Commission indicated that any reform would need to balance the need for certainty and predictability with the requirement that the law be flexible enough to do justice in any particular case. The Report indicated that any reform would have to include the abolition of the first limb of the rule in *Phillips v Eyre.* The Report acknowledged that it was difficult to point to any particular case where the common law rules had led to injustice[118] but they

---

117 Law Commission Working Paper No 87 (1984); Scottish Law Commission Consultative Memorandum No 62 (1984).

118 *M'Elroy v M'Allister* 1949 SC 110 was not an English case and is not one that would be decided the same way after *Boys v Chaplin.*

indicated that the degree of uncertainty and complexity revealed by the decided cases showed that statutory reform was desirable.

The concluded views of the Law Commission were set out in the *Report on Choice of Law in Tort and Delict*[119] and the report included a Draft Tort and Delict (Applicable Law) Bill. The final report recommended that option (c), Model 1, should be the basis of any law reform. In general terms, the basis of the applicable law would be the *lex loci delicti*, with a proper law exception. It was suggested that such a solution would combine the need for certainty with the requirement of flexibility in appropriate cases.

The proposals would lead to the removal of the rule in *The Halley*, so that, for the first time in the English conflict of laws, the existence of the cause of action will not be dependent on English law as the *lex fori*. Of course, it would remain for English law to determine what constituted an action in tort. The initial classification would remain with the *lex fori* but that classification would no longer be confined to the domestic model.[120]

Given the classification of the matter by the forum court as tort, the proposals provided presumptions for the identification of the applicable law. Thus, in the case of personal injury or death, the applicable law will, *prima facie*, be the law of the country where the injury was sustained.[121] In the case of damage to property, the *prima facie* applicable law will be the law of the country where the property was when it was damaged.[122]

In all other cases, the *prima facie* applicable law will be the law of the country 'where the most significant elements of the events constituting the subject matter of the proceedings took place'.[123]

The proposals in the final report envisaged a situation where 'the most significant element of the events' test does not identify a country and, in such cases, the test of the 'most real and substantial connection' is substituted.[124]

The law of the country indicated by the presumptions can, in all cases, be displaced if, comparatively, the connections with the country indicated by the presumptions and those constituting a real and substantial connection with another country demonstrate that it would be more appropriate for the law of the latter country to be applied.[125]

The proposal that the displacement of the *prima facie* applicable law should occur only where the court concludes that it is 'substantially more

---

119 Law Commission Report No 193 (1990); Scottish Law Commission Report No 129 (1990).

120 Draft Tort and Delict (Applicable Law) Bill 1990, cl 1(4).

121 *Ibid*, cl 2(1).

122 *Ibid*, cl 2(2).

123 *Ibid*, cl 2(3)(a).

124 *Ibid*, cl 2(3)(b).

125 *Ibid*, cl 2(4).

appropriate' to apply another law might cause difficulty and much would depend on the precise drafting.

The Law Commission proposals attempted to clarify a number of other potential difficulties. Reference to the applicable law is a reference to the domestic rules only – the doctrine of *renvoi* shall continue to have no application to torts.[126] The forum's principles of public policy are preserved[127] and the application of foreign 'penal, revenue or other public law'.[128]

Savings were also made for UK statutes and the forum's procedural rules.[129]

PRIVATE INTERNATIONAL LAW (MISCELLANEOUS PROVISIONS) ACT 1995[130]

The new legislative code in respect of choice of law in tort is contained in Part III (ss 9–15) of the Private International Law (Miscellaneous Provisions) Act 1995. In broad terms, the legislation builds upon the prior work of the Law Commission, as published in 1984 and 1990. The legislative provisions depart in matters of detail from the prior draft bill of the Law Commission but the broad objectives of the legislation are in line with the extensive preparatory work undertaken by the Law Commission.

The scope of Part III

The legislation is not retrospective. Section 14(1) of the legislation makes clear that the provisions of Part III do not apply in respect of acts or omissions arising prior to the date of commencement of the Act. The legislation came into effect on 1 May 1996.[131]

It therefore follows that the common law rules will apply in respect of causes of action arising prior to that date.

---

126 Draft Tort and Delict (Applicable Law) Bill 1990, cl 2(6).

127 *Ibid*, cl 4(1).

128 *Ibid*, cl 4(2).

129 *Ibid*, cl 4(3), (4).

130 For a discussion of the new legislative provisions, see Briggs (1995) LMCLQ 519; Morse (1996) 45 ICLQ 888; Reed (1996) 15 CJQ 305.

131 See the Private International Law (Miscellaneous Provisions) Act 1995 (Commencement Order) 1996 SI 1996 995, made under the terms of Public International Law (Miscellaneous Provisions) Act 1995, s 16. The legislation received the Royal Assent on 8 November 1995.

Section 14(2) indicates that the legislation is only to apply in respect of those common law rules abolished by s 10 of the legislation. It therefore follows that, where a matter was covered by a common law rule outside the ambit of s 10, then it remains unaffected by new statutory code.

The first question that arises is as to whether the claim is one in tort. By the terms of s 9(2), 'the characterisation for the purposes of private international law of issues arising in a claim as issues relating to tort ... is a matter for the courts of the forum'. It has been suggested that the use of the expression 'for the purposes of private international law' requires the court to approach the matter in a liberal internationalist spirit.[132] However, such a wide interpretation must only extend to matters of substantive law since the legislation specifically excludes matters of procedure.[133] The rules introduced do not apply to claims of defamation, which are specifically excluded.[134]

The provisions of s 9(4) provide:

> The applicable law shall be used for determining the issues arising in a claim, including, in particular, the question of whether an actionable tort or delict has occurred.

The effect of this provision is that, once the court has classified an issue as relating to tort,[135] the applicable law will be used to determine whether a tort has occurred and any other substantive issue. The applicable law is the internal law of the relevant country and the doctrine of *renvoi* is specifically excluded.[136]

The provisions of Part III apply where the events which constitute the tort take place in a part of the UK which is also the forum for the action and they also apply where events occurring in one part of the UK (for example, Scotland) are the subject of litigation in another part.[137]

The choice of law rules

Section 10 of the Act reads:

> The rules of common law, in so far as they–
>
> (a) require actionability under both the law of the forum and the law of another country for the purpose of determining whether a tort or delict is actionable; or

---

132 See Morse (1996) 45 ICLQ 888 (the writer was a member of the 1984 Law Commission Working Party).

133 Private International Law (Miscellaneous Provisions) Act 1995, s 14(3)(b).

134 *Ibid*, ss 9(3), 13; see below for defamation.

135 *Ibid*, s 9(2).

136 *Ibid*, s 9(5).

137 *Ibid*, s 9(5), (6).

(b) allow (as an exception from the rules falling within paragraph (a) above) for the law of a single country to be applied for the purpose of determining the issues, or any of the issues, arising in the case in question, are hereby abolished so far as they apply to any claim in tort or delict which is not excluded from the operation of this Part by s 10 below.

This is the central provision in Part III of the legislation. The purpose of s 10(a) is to abolish the rule best known as the double actionability rule or the rule in *Phillips v Eyre*.[138] The purpose of s 10(b) is to make clear that modified forms of the double actionability rule, as set out in both *Boys v Chaplin*[139] and *Red Sea Insurance Co v Bouygues SA*,[140] are abolished. One area of difficulty would seem to be that those common law rules that were outside the ambit of *Phillips v Eyre* (for example, rules relating to aerial and maritime torts) are unaffected by the repeal and remain governed by the common law; this is confirmed not only by the provisions of s 14(2) but by the reference to 'abolition of certain common law rules' preceding the words of s 10.

The new legal provisions are set out in ss 11 and 12. In respect of s 11, the words of the provision are:

(1) The general rule is that the applicable law is the law of the country in which the events constituting the tort or delict in question occur.

(2) Where elements of those events occur in different countries, the applicable law under the general rule is to be taken as being–

(a) for a cause of action in respect of personal injury caused to an individual or death resulting from personal injury, the law of the country where the individual was when he sustained the injury;

(b) for a cause of action in respect of damage to property, the law of the country where the property was when it was damaged; and

(c) in any other case, the law of the country in which the most significant element or elements of those events occurred.

(3) In this section, 'personal injury' includes disease or any impairment of physical or mental condition.

The purpose of s 11 is to establish a general rule in favour of the *lex loci delicti*. The emphasis of the draftsman is upon the 'events' and, if such events take place in more than one country, then the general rule in s 11(1) will be subject to the more detailed provisions set out in s 11(2). There is every reason to believe that, in the normal case of personal injury, death or damage to property, identification of the applicable law should not be unduly difficult. Section 11(2)(c) might apply to those difficult cases where a parent in England watches on television a serious injury to a child in Scotland and then suffers nervous shock. It would seem that the applicable law in respect of the third

---

138 (1870) LR 6 QB 1.
139 [1971] AC 356.
140 [1995] 1 AC 190.

party suffering the shock would be England, even if the applicable law for the primary victim was Scotland.[141]

One of the criticisms made of the double actionability rule prior to *Boys v Chaplin* is that it was insufficiently flexible to meet the wide variety cases that might come before the courts. To meet this objection, s 12 provides that the general rule in s 11 may be displaced when it appear substantially more appropriate for the governing law to be that of another country. The wording of s 12 would appear to indicate that those seeking to rely on it will face an uphill task:

(1) If it appears, in all the circumstances, from a comparison of–

    (a) the significance of the factors which connect a tort or delict with the country whose law would be the applicable law under the general rule; and

    (b) the significance of any factors connecting the tort or delict with another country,

that it is substantially more appropriate for the applicable law for determining the issues arising in the case, or any of those issues, to be the law of the other country, the general rule is displaced and the applicable law for determining those issues or that issue (as the case may be) is the law of that other country.

The factors that may be taken into account as connecting a tort or delict with a country for the purposes of this section include, in particular, factors relating to the parties, to any of the events which constitute the tort or delict in question or to any of the circumstances or consequences of those events.

One of the most important matters in Part III will be the precise relationship between the general rule in s 11 and the 'proper law' exception in s 12. It would seem, on the basis of the drafting, that it would be difficult indeed for a party to demonstrate that 'it appears in all the circumstances ... that it is substantially more appropriate' that the general law should be displaced. The section gives some indication of the factors that may be taken into account. The Working Paper of 1984 was of the opinion that displacement should only take place if the connection with the applicable law was minimal. The list of factors that may be taken into account is not exhaustive. However, any factor must be legally relevant. From the wording of the section it would appear that the judge will be required to engage in a comparison of the relevant factors before proceeding to determine whether it is substantially more appropriate that the law of some other country should apply. It was argued, during the passage of the Bill, that the use of the word 'substantially'[142] served to indicate that displacement under s 12 would be rare indeed. The wording of the section refers to 'issues' so that it might be possible to identify a particular issue for the purpose of the section.[143]

---

141 See *Alcock v Chief Constable of South Yorkshire Police* [1992] 1 AC 310.

142 HL Deb Col 833, 6 December 1994, *per* Lord Mackay LC.

143 Morse (1996) 45 ICLQ 888 takes the example of heads of damages in *Boys v Chaplin* [1971] AC 356.

The exclusion of defamation

One of the most contentious issues during the passage of the Bill related to claims for defamation; such special provision had not been included in the original Bill. During the passage of the legislation through Parliament, newspaper editorials raised questions as to press freedom.[144] The argument appeared to be that, since the first limb of *Phillips v Eyre* was to be repealed, a London newspaper might be exposed to libel proceedings in London where the applicable foreign law did not allow the defendant to raise defences that might be available under the English law of defamation. Secondly, it was argued that such a course might undermine press freedom and was at variance with the UK's international obligations under Art 10 of the European Convention on Human Rights and Fundamental Freedoms 1950. In any event, the exception is confined to actions for defamation and, in such cases, the common law rules will continue to apply.

It must be open to doubt as to whether such an express exclusion was necessary; other countries in the democratic world preserve press and media freedom without resorting to the double actionability rule. It may be that the absence of written constitutional guarantees made media interests more concerned in the UK.[145]

Public policy

The legislation contains a number of provisions consistent with the general principles of private international law. First, the legislation is not retrospective[146] and the new choice of law rules extend only to those matters abolished by s 10.[147] It would therefore seem that maritime and aerial torts are outside the scope of the Act. The legislation provides that nothing shall be done that will conflict with principles of public policy or that would allow the enforcement of any penal revenue or public law that is unenforceable by the laws of the forum.[148] This is broadly in line with the accepted principles of private international law. An interesting provision is s 14(4), which provides that Part III of the Act 'has effect without prejudice to the operation of any rule of law which either has effect notwithstanding the rules of private international law applicable in the particular circumstances or modifies the rules of private international law that would otherwise be so applicable'. It

---

144 See (1995) *The Times*, 19 January; (1995) *The Evening Standard*, 19 January. Evidence was taken by the Special Public Bill Committee; see Carter (1996) 112 LQR 190.

145 *Tolofson v Jensen* (1994) 120 DLR (4th) 289.

146 Private International Law (Miscellaneous Provisions) Act 1995, s 14(1).

147 *Ibid*, s 14(2).

148 *Ibid*, s 14(3)(a), (b).

would seem that this provision is wide enough to permit the application of a mandatory rule other than those of the forum, such as those of a third country.[149]

Conclusion

Since the provisions of the legislation operate only in respect of acts or omissions after 1 May 1996, it will be some time before a fully argued case on Part III reaches the higher courts.[150] Some writers argue that legislation is, in general, undesirable in the field of private international law as it is a subject more suitable for gradual judicial development.[151] Other writers argue that such legislation is not warranted in the field of the law of tort because there is no evidence that the common law has given rise to injustice or is itself a source of uncertainty.[152] However, against this, it must be admitted that, in the case law after *Boys v Chaplin*, a number of judges confessed to difficulties in determining the scope of any exception. A further point that deserves attention is whether Part III contains enough escape devices to permit the law of the forum to return through the back door.[153] It would seem that the legislative history clearly indicates that the general rule in s 11 should normally apply, save in the most exceptional circumstances. It would be surprising if this is not the approach of the higher courts when the matter first comes before them.

THE RELATIONS BETWEEN CONTRACT AND TORT

As the English conflict of laws is based on the conceptual classifications of English domestic law and those classifications are too crude to embrace all the types of relation within the domestic law, so its deficiencies are equally apparent in the conflict of laws. To take a couple of obvious examples of the limitations of traditional conceptual classifications: a contract may contain a clause which seeks to limit or exclude liability for matters, such as personal injury or damage to property, which are not part of the express contractual terms and arise either as implied terms in the contract or by the operation of the general law of tort. If the injured party sues in tort, the contractual aspect

---

149 See Law Commission Working Paper No 87 (1984), para 4.5; Law Commission Report No 193 (1990), para 3.55.

150 Lloyd J made reference in passing to the new legislation in *Pearce v Ove Arup Partnership* [1997] 2 WLR 779; [1997] Ch 293.

151 Mann, FA (1991) 107 LQR 353 (in the context of the law of contract).

152 Carter (1991) 107 LQR 405.

153 Carter (1996) 112 LQR 190 draws attention to the provisions of ss 9(2), 11(2)(c), 12 and 14(3)(a).

of his relationship with the defendant must be taken into account. Similarly, the employment relationship does not fit easily into either of the conceptual categories of tort or contract.

Certainly the relationship is contractual and there are some matters which are exclusively such, for example, pay rates and working hours (though, of course, both could be controlled by statutory rules as well). Other matters, say, concerning the health and safety of employees, can be seen as implied terms in the contract, statutory obligations which, if broken, will give rise to an action for breach of statutory duty or matters redressible by an action in the tort of negligence. For English domestic law, the niceties of possible classifications are rarely of much concern but, for the conflict of laws, they are crucial, as the choice of law rules depend on the initial classification of the subject matter. The issue is made more relevant for the English conflict of laws than for some others because it is the practice in England to sue for personal injuries in tort rather than in contract, even where the tortious duty relied on can be seen as an implied term in the contract itself.[154]

There are a number of cases that have arisen in England where a claim is brought based on tort and a defence is filed based on the existence of a contract between the parties. Normally it will be argued that the contract contains an exclusion clause that is both valid under the applicable law and effective in respect of the tort. The leading case remains *Sayers v International Drilling Co NV*[155] where the facts were as follows: an English plaintiff was injured by a fellow worker when working for a Dutch company on an oil rig in Nigerian territorial waters. The defendant company had issued a contract of employment which contained an exclusion clause; such a clause was valid under Dutch law but was void under English law under the Law Reform (Personal Injuries) Act 1948.

The Court of Appeal upheld the judgment of Bean J and rejected the claim for damages. However, the approaches of the judges differed. Lord Denning MR analysed the claim as one in tort and the defence as one based on contract, he then proceeded to identify a proper law of the issues as being Dutch law, thus enabling him to uphold the exclusion clause. Salmon LJ acknowledged that the claim was based on tort, but that the exclusion clause was valid under Dutch law and should prevail. Stamp LJ appeared to regard the matter as one where the duties were stipulated under the contract and that the exclusion clause was valid under the proper law of the contract. The differing judicial opinions caused some academic comment.[156] It is arguable that the important questions in such a case are: (a) is the claim based on tort? (b) what is the applicable law of the tort? (c) is the defence based on contract? (d) is the

---

154 *Coupland v Arabian Gulf Petroleum Co* [1982] 2 All ER 434; [1983] 1 WLR 1136; 3 All ER 226, CA, *per* Waller, Oliver, Robert Goff LJJ.
155 [1971] 3 All ER 163; 1 WLR 1176, CA, *per* Lord Denning MR, Salmon, Stamp LJJ.
156 Smith (1972) 21 ICLQ 164; Collins (1972) 21 ICLQ 320; Carter (1971) 45 BYIL 404.

applicable law of the contract to be determined by the conflict rules of the forum or the law of the place of the tort? (e) in any event, is the exclusion clause valid by its applicable law? (f) is the exclusion clause effective by the law governing the tort? and (g) in any event, should the exclusion clause be refused recognition as violating a mandatory rule of the forum?[157]

In the later case of *Coupland v Arabian Gulf Oil Co*, a Scotsman working abroad brought a case in the English courts in respect of personal injury. Hodgson J determined that the claim was brought in tort and held that any contract was only relevant to a claim in tort where, in accordance with its own proper law, it had the effect of excluding or restricting the tortious claim. As there was no attempt to raise a contractual defence, it was not necessary to consider the matter any further.

The relationship between a claim in tort and a contractual defence was considered by the Law Commission in the 1984 Working Paper. The Law Commission considered that English law probably was that the validity of an exclusion clause would be determined by the law applicable to the contract, but its effectiveness as a defence to a claim in tort was to be determined by the law governing the tort.[158] The final *Report* did not contain any specific recommendations on this point.[159] Now that the Private International Law (Miscellaneous Provisions) Act 1995 is in force, there will be no need in the future for the plaintiff in tort to establish his cause of action by domestic English law and there will only be a single system, the applicable law under the code, to deal with. A defendant seeking to rely on a contractual defence will have to establish his right by the law governing the contract, which, if it is an international one, will be determined under the Rome Convention 1980 as implemented by the Contracts (Applicable Law) Act 1990. Unless he can do that, he will have no defence. If he can, then the effect of the exclusion clause as a defence will be a matter for the applicable law of the tort.

A defence, valid under the contract's applicable law, will not be available, of course, if it offends the public policy of the forum or conflicts with a mandatory rule of the forum which is applicable to the contract under Art 7(2) of the Rome Convention 1980.[160]

---

157 It is arguable that this could have been the case in *Sayers* in respect of the 1948 Act.

158 Law Commission Working Paper No 87 (1984), paras 2.87–2.101.

159 Law Commission Report No 193 (1990), paras 3.49–3.50.

160 Thus, if a case such as *Sayers* were to arise after 1996, the court would be obliged to consider: (a) the Rome Convention 1980; (b) the Unfair Contract Terms Act 1977; (c) the Law Reform (Personal Injuries) Act 1948; and (d) the Private International Law (Miscellaneous Provisions) Act 1995, s 14(3), (4).

CHAPTER 18

MARRIAGE

INTRODUCTION

It has often been observed that, while marriage[1] may be based on agreement, it is an agreement *sui generis,* in that it confers on the parties a particular status.[2] Marriage provides an excellent counter example to the notion that classifications can be made on the basis of analytical jurisprudence and comparative law. While it is a universal institution, in that all societies have a concept of marriage, very different cultural traditions have influenced the development of the concept in the various countries of the world. So that, while the institution can be recognised easily enough, its attendant incidents vary considerably. Even within the Western Christian cultural tradition, different rules on capacity and form and different attitudes to the termination of marriage produce important variations from the core of monogamy.

There are many occasions when an English court might have to consider whether the parties are in fact married. In the criminal law, a question might arise in the event of a prosecution for bigamy;[3] in the law of inheritance, the claims of a surviving spouse might depend on being able to establish marital status.[4] Indeed, in the law of evidence, particular provisions exist in respect of the compellability of a spouse as a witness.[5]

The task of the conflict of laws in respect of marriage is very much greater than simply to take account of the minor adjustments necessary in order to recognise the validity of established relationships between people from different countries; there are issues about the very nature of the institution itself which require consideration.

The conceptual approach which English law has adopted in this, as in most other areas of the conflict of laws, requires that a positive approach is

---

1   The classic definition is that of Lord Penzance in *Hyde v Hyde* (1866) LR 1 P & D 130, on which, see below.

2   At common law, the parties are a man and a woman; see *Corbett v Corbett (orse Ashley)* [1971] P 83.

3   *Macleod v AG for New South Wales* [1891] AC 455, PC; 7 TLR 703.

4   As illustrated by the long drawn out litigation in *Vervaeke v Smith* [1983] 1 AC 145, where the plaintiff sought to show the second marriage was valid in order to inherit a large sum of money.

5   See *Hoskyn v Metropolitan Police Commissioner* [1979] AC 474, for the status of the spouse at common law; the judgment of the majority of the House of Lords was reversed by statute. See the Police and Criminal Evidence Act 1984, s 80, for the present law.

taken and that this approach is one that is sufficiently flexible to accommodate the foreign institutions of marriage.

English law was, for example, slow to come to terms with judicial divorce.[6] Even more difficult was the problem of the institution of polygamy.[7] Monogamy was essential to the Western Christian concept of marriage. Though it was never the case that recognition was confined to Christian marriages,[8] the exclusivity of the relationship was its fundamental characteristic. Yet it could not be denied that polygamous relationships had social significance, legal implications and, often, deep religious importance.

In this chapter, it is intended to examine the English conflict rules, nearly all common law rules, on the recognition of valid marriages.

THE CONCEPT OF MARRIAGE

Until the Court for Divorce and Matrimonial Causes was established in 1857,[9] the civil courts, in so far as they had to deal indirectly with marriages, had operated upon an ill defined, though widely assumed, understanding of the Christian marriage. The transfer of the jurisdiction from ecclesiastical courts and the introduction of the new powers to make financial orders[10] made the need for a clear statement of the concept of marriage as understood in English law all the more pressing. The issue arose in the celebrated case of *Hyde v Hyde*,[11] where the facts were as follows: an Englishman, who had embraced the Mormon faith, married a Mormon lady in Utah according to Mormon rites. After living with her for three years and having children by her, he renounced the Mormon faith and, soon afterwards, became a minister of a dissenting chapel in England. He petitioned for a divorce in England after his wife had contracted another marriage in Utah according to the Mormon faith.

---

6   Judicial divorce was introduced into England in the Matrimonial Causes Act 1857; judicial divorce had been available in Scotland prior to that date. Pressure for judicial divorce had been growing gradually as Benthamite arguments began to appeal to the legislature., although not to WE Gladstone, who opposed the Matrimonial Causes Bill clause by clause. Although the grounds for divorce were equalised in the Matrimonial Causes Act 1923, there was no general extension until the Matrimonial Causes Act 1937.

7   The jurisdiction of the courts was limited until the Matrimonial Proceedings (Polygamous Marriages) Act 1972; see, now, the Matrimonial Causes Act 1973, s 47.

8   *Isaak Penhas v Tan Soo Eng* [1953] AC 304 (marriage celebrated in Singapore in 1937 between a Jew and a non-Christian according to mixed Chinese and Jewish rites in an area where priests were few and no parochial system existed; marriage held valid at common law).

9   Under the terms of the Matrimonial Causes Act 1857. The court formed part of the Probate, Divorce and Admiralty Division of the High Court in 1875. In 1972, it was reconstituted as the Family Division of the High Court.

10   Matrimonial Causes Act 1857, ss 32, 35.

11   (1866) LR 1 P & D 130.

In giving the judgment of the court, Lord Penzance[12] assumed that the Mormon marriage was potentially polygamous and he refused to dissolve the marriage. The laws of England, the judge thought, were not adapted for polygamy and the parties to a polygamous marriage were 'not entitled to the remedies, the adjudication, or the relief of the matrimonial law of England'. In the course of giving his judgment, Lord Penzance sought to define marriage for the purpose of 'the remedies, the adjudication and the relief of the matrimonial law of England' as being 'marriage as understood in Christendom ... as the voluntary union for life of one man and one woman to the exclusion of all others'.[13] It was not his object to define marriage for any other purpose but his definition characterises the basic concept of marriage in English law and a starting point for the conflict of laws. If we analyse this definition and examine its components, we can see that there are a number of difficulties.

We are concerned at the moment with the concept of marriage for the purpose of the English conflict of laws. Once a relationship has been accepted by an English court as falling within the definition, the rules of choice of law on marriage come into play and they may involve reference to a foreign law which takes a different view of the nature of the institution of marriage. The foreign law may require, for instance, that, for a marriage to be valid, the parties must intend at the time of the marriage to establish a genuine matrimonial relationship.[14] Where this is the case, it will be for the English court to decide whether account is to be taken of the foreign law and this may well involve issues of English public policy. For the present, we are concerned only with the identification of those relationships which will trigger the application of the English conflict of law's rules on marriage.

Voluntary

The idea of romantic love generally displaced arranged marriages in Europe[15] but they lingered on in the dynasties and have come to the fore in recent years in marriages arranged for their children by parents who have emigrated from the Indian subcontinent.

---

12 In actual fact, at that stage, Sir James Wilde (1816–99) (Judge, P & D 1863–74), as he was not ennobled as Lord Penzance until 1869; there is reason to believe that much of the speech drew upon remarks of Lord Brougham in *Warrender v Warrender* (1835) 2 Cl & F 488. These remarks were inappropriate, as they had been made prior to the Marriage Act 1836.

13 (1866) LR 1 P & D 130, p 133; the historical background to the case is discussed in Poulter (1976) 25 ICLQ 475.

14 See *Vervaeke v Smith* [1983] 1 AC 145; note the attitude of Belgian law.

15 The right of a person above a stipulated age to marry an unmarried person of his or her own choosing is protected under the European Convention on Human Rights 1950, Art 12.

There is little doubt that a marriage founded on duress[16] or other forms of lack of consent would not be recognised in the English courts.[17] A shotgun marriage with real shotguns would not be recognised under English conflict law; but, where the forces used to overcome the free will are more subtle, where it takes the form of appeals to filial duty or to family honour or cultural tradition, the response is less clear cut.[18] It should be noted that English domestic law provides that a marriage shall be voidable for lack of consent whatever the cause of failure.[19] The approach of the English courts is illustrated by *Szechter v Szechter*,[20] where the facts were as follows: a husband, his first wife and secretary were all domiciled in Poland. The secretary was in ill health and in prison, having been convicted of 'anti-State activities'. To secure her release, the husband divorced his first wife and married his secretary. The parties left Poland and came to England, where the secretary petitioned for a decree of nullity on grounds of lack of consent; the object of the petition was to enable the husband and his first wife to resume their married life.

The facts gave rise to choice of law problems. Polish law was the *lex loci celebrationis* and the law of the domicile of both parties. English law was the *lex fori* and the law of the domicile at the time of proceedings. Simon P held that the marriage was invalid under Polish law, invalid under English domestic law and would have been invalid under English conflicts rules even if it had been valid under Polish law. In giving judgment, the learned judge was influenced by the proposition stated in Dicey and Morris that 'no marriage is valid if, by the law of either party's domicile, one party does not consent to marry the other'.[21] Simon P expressed the test of voluntariness in the following manner:

> In order for the impediment of duress to vitiate an otherwise valid marriage, it must, in my judgment, be proved that the will of one of the parties has been overborne by genuine and reasonably held fear caused by threat of immediate

---

16 Matrimonial Causes Act 1973, s 12(c).

17 *Parojcic v Parojcic* [1958] 1 WLR 128 (marriage in England voidable because of coercion by father of bride); *Buckland v Buckland* [1968] P 296 (bridegroom threatened with prosecution).

18 For earlier cases on various forms of influence, see *Scott v Sebright* (1886) 12 PD 21 (allegations of seduction); *Cooper v Crane* [1891] P 369 (bridegroom threatened to commit suicide); *Bartlett v Rice* (1894) 72 LT 122 (bridegroom threatened to shoot bride); *Ford v Stier* [1896] P 1 (mistake as to ceremony); *H v H* [1954] P 258 (escaping from Hungary).

19 Matrimonial Causes Act 1973, s 12(c).

20 [1971] P 286; [1970] 3 All ER 905.

21 Dicey and Morris, *The Conflict of Laws* (8th edn, 1967), p 271; the proposition is stated in similar terms in subsequent editions. The judgment of Simon P was approved by the Court of Appeal in *Singh v Singh* [1971] P 226, in particular, the observations of judge as to voluntariness.

danger, for which the party is not himself responsible, to life, limb or liberty, so that the constraint destroys the reality of consent to ordinary wedlock.[22]

The emphasis in English law on the consent of the parties accords with the international obligations of the UK.[23] It would seem that two obvious cases of mistake – where one party fails to understand the nature of the ceremony or is mistaken about the identity of the other party – ought, in principle, to render the marriage voidable under English domestic and English conflict law.[24]

Union

English law does not require a marriage to be a sexual relationship, although it gives relief where the marriage has not been consummated by sexual intercourse.[25] Such a petition under English domestic law is a claim that the marriage is voidable not that it is void *ab initio* and, as far as the English conflict of laws is concerned, a marriage between parties who are too old or infirm or otherwise incapable of sexual relations remains capable of being recognised as a marriage. One qualification and one observation here – although sexual intercourse is not essential for the validity of a marriage, it remains the case that, though the parties need not wish or be capable of consummating the marriage, they must be male and female.[26] There is no requirement under English law that the parties intend to live together as husband and wife or, indeed, have any serious intention to make the marriage any sort of relationship – so marriages entered into for the purpose of conferring nationality or enabling immigration or preventing the deportation of a prostitute as an undesirable alien[27] have all been upheld as valid under English law and would fall within the concept for the purposes of English conflict law.

For life

The introduction of judicial divorce into English law[28] necessarily involved the acceptance that any marriage might be terminated before the death of one of the parties; this was known to Lord Penzance at the time that he formulated

---

22 [1971] P 226, pp 297–98.
23 Universal Declaration of Human Rights 1948, Art 16(2); International Covenant on Civil and Political Rights 1966, Art 23.
24 However, any action will have to meet the tests set out in the Matrimonial Causes Act 1973, s 13, ie, that there has been no waiver, that it would not be unjust and that proceedings have been brought within the time period.
25 Matrimonial Causes Act 1973, s 12(a), (b).
26 *Ibid*, s 11(c).
27 *Vervaeke v Smith* [1983] 1 AC 145.
28 Matrimonial Causes Act 1857.

his definition. What it could only mean then, and what it clearly means now, is that the relationship must be potentially for life and a 'marriage' delimited at its inception cannot be recognised as a marriage for the purpose of the conflict of laws. That this is the case is clear after *Nachimson v Nachimson*,[29] where the facts were as follows: the parties were married in the USSR under the Bolshevik Law of 1918. This provided for dissolution by mutual consent through an administrative process. In the event of no consent, dissolution could be granted by a judge. Hill J refused an application for judicial separation, arguing that the marriage was terminable at will.

In reversing the judgment of Hill J, the Court of Appeal held that a distinction had to be drawn between the essence of marriage and its dissolubility.[30] It might be argued that it would be more realistic to expand the definition to include the words 'for life (or until the grant of a decree of annulment or divorce)'. Be that as it may, *Nachimson v Nachimson* holds that, if a marriage is potentially for life, then the ease of its termination is not a relevant consideration.

Of one man and one woman

This raises three issues. First, age. Although Lord Penzance might just as well have said one male and one female, the issue of the age of the parties ought not to be ignored. Different societies have different views on the minimum age of marriage. At common law, the rule was 14 for boys and 12 for girls; a marriage contracted before this legal age of puberty could be avoided. The law was changed in the Age of Marriage Act 1929, whereby s 1 stipulated that a valid marriage could not be contracted unless both parties had reached the age of 16.[31] The philosophy behind the change was set out by Pearce J (as he then was) in *Pugh v Pugh*:[32]

> According to modern thought it is considered socially and morally wrong that persons of an age, at which we now believe them to be immature and provide for their education, should have the stresses, responsibilities and sexual freedom of marriage and the physical strain of childbirth. Child marriages by common consent are believed to be bad for the participants and bad for the institution of marriage.

The age of consent to sexual intercourse does not have to be the same as the age for marriage but, in the past at least, it would have been unthinkable for the legislature to have decriminalised unmarried sexual intercourse at an age

---

29 [1930] P 217; 46 TLR 444.
30 The Court of Appeal (Lord Hanworth MR, Romer, Lawrence LJJ) stressed that the evidence indicated that the parties intended the marriage to be for life.
31 The provisions are now in the Marriage Act 1949, s 2.
32 [1951] P 482.

lower than it permitted marriage. Recognition that marriage below the English age of sexual consent is permitted abroad is evidenced in domestic criminal legislation, which assumes as an answer to a charge of unlawful sexual intercourse with a girl under the age of 13 that the defendant was married to the victim and that, therefore, the intercourse was lawful.[33] In cultures where marriages are arranged for infant children, it is the practice only to allow them to become physical unions when both parties have reached puberty. It remains to be seen what the lower limit on public policy will be on marriages where one party is very young.

Secondly, it is clear that, under English law, a marriage has to be between a man and a woman[34] and a homosexual relationship cannot be accepted for the purpose of the English conflict of laws. In recent years, pressure has grown in certain European States to permit the legal recognition of homosexual relationships;[35] the question arises as to the reaction of English law. It is clear that English law would not recognise such a relationship as falling within the concept of marriage. Whether it would take account of any special rules applicable to it under the foreign law would be a matter of public policy[36] – in principle, there is no reason why certain rights should not be acknowledged and given effect in England just as we recognise foreign companies and partnerships. English law has not faced the palimony litigation[37] which has become prominent in the USA in recent years – were it to do so, there is, again, no reason why such claims, in so far as they are based on agreements rather than status, and provided they do not offend English public policy in their detail, should not be accepted as valid contracts.

The third problem which arises here is polygamy. Clearly, the institutions of English law were directed at monogamous relationships and so, not only with regard to marriage itself, but for all related purposes, for example, legitimacy and succession, the monogamous marriage was the model. The expansion of trade, and, more significantly, the expansion of Empire, brought English law in touch with vast numbers of peoples who lived under regimes where polygamy, if not the norm, was a legitimate form of relationship. The

---

33 Sexual Offences Act 1956; *Mohamed v Knott* [1969] 1 QB 1 (26 year old man married to 13 year old girl).

34 Matrimonial Causes Act 1973, s 11(c); *Corbett v Corbett* [1971] P 83. This approach has been upheld by the European Court of Human Rights: *Rees v The United Kingdom* (1986) 9 EHRR 56; *Cossey v The United Kingdom* (1991) 13 EHRR 622; *Re P and G (Transexuals)* [1996] 2 FLR 90; *X, Y and Z v The United Kingdom* [1997] Fam Law 605.

35 Denmark enacted the Registered Partnership Act 1989, which allows homosexual couples (one of whom must be of Danish nationality) to register their relationships after a civil ceremony. Apart from adoption and custody the legal consequences are similar to that of marriage.

36 The matter was considered in the context of the armed forces in *R v Ministry of Defence ex p Smith* [1996] QB 517, where the Court of Appeal noted 'the progressive development and refinement of public and professional opinion at home and abroad'.

37 *Windeler v Whitehall* [1990] 2 FLR 505.

initial reaction was to deny to these relationships the status of marriage and this rejection of them was often accompanied by vituperative and chauvinistic ignorance[38] yet, throughout the world, there were many peoples who accepted the institution and were prepared to defend its social function. When *Hyde v Hyde*[39] was decided, polygamous marriages could be found not only among Muslims, the most obvious group today, but among Hindus, Jews and those living under African and Chinese customary laws.

Nowadays, polygamous marriages, with the exception of capacity, are subjected to the same basic conflict rules as monogamous marriages and English law allows those polygamously married to invoke the matrimonial jurisdiction of the English courts.[40]

To the exclusion of all others

Although, at the time of the judgment in *Hyde v Hyde*, adultery was the main basis for judicial divorce, this part of the definition reinforces the point about polygamy and is not a requirement of sexual continence. The adultery of one party, or, indeed, of both, never resulted in the invalidity of a marriage but only in grounds which might allow one party to petition for its termination. A polygamous marriage cannot take place in England, since the rules on formalities set out in the Marriage Act 1949 prohibit such a course.[41] A person who is already lawfully married cannot contract a second valid marriage in England during the subsistence of the first.[42] Thus, this aspect of Lord Penzance's definition is accurate in respect of marriages contracted in England.

Having said a little about the broad definition of marriage under English law, it is now necessary to devote some attention to problems of classification.

CLASSIFICATION AND DEFECTS

The status of marriage has a wide range of implications under systems of domestic law. Under English law, for example, marriage is significant, *inter alia*, for succession, social security, damages for bereavement, immigration, taxation and legitimacy, as well as the more obvious issues of the special relationship between the parties themselves.

---

38 *Warrender v Warrender* (1835) 2 Cl & Fin 288.
39 (1866) 1 LR P & D 130.
40 Matrimonial Proceedings (Polygamous Marriages) Act 1972; see, now, Matrimonial Causes Act 1973, s 47.
41 *R v Bham* [1966] 1 QB 159.
42 Matrimonial Causes Act 1973, s 11(b).

For all these purposes, the key distinction is between those marriages which are void and those which are not. Whatever defects a marriage might have, unless it is void, it counts as valid for all purposes. The only concern about defects in a marriage which is not void arise when it is sought to terminate the marriage – only at that stage, when the question is whether to petition for nullity or divorce do they come into play.

Usually, the defects which make marriage void are easily established, for example, formal defects, non-age, prohibited degrees of relationship; though the determination of the status of a former marriage may involve complex conflict problems. The assertion that no decree is necessary when a marriage is void and that all the world can treat it as such, needs to be treated with caution.

In some cases of a marriage which is void by English or foreign law, there will be triable issues, for example, a lack of consent which renders the marriage void by the foreign law; the matter may have to be tested by trial even if, in the result, the marriage is void and no decree would actually have been needed to make it so.

In cases where the marriage is voidable, the problem does not arise in the same way because a decree is always necessary to change the status. Such a decree operates prospectively under English law.[43] It would be logical, therefore, to postpone all discussion of defects which render a marriage voidable to the consideration of matrimonial causes, for it is only in that context that they have any significance. It is not practical to do so, however, as there are defects which, though English law treats them as matters of voidability, may be regarded by foreign law as defects rendering the marriage void *ab initio*, for example, impotence, lack of consent, mistake of quality. They will, therefore, be treated in this section.

Void and voidable marriages

Under English law, a marriage will be void if the required formalities have not been observed,[44] the parties are within the prohibited degrees of relationship,[45] either of them is under the age of 16[46] or already lawfully married,[47] or they are not respectively male and female.[48]

---

43 Matrimonial Causes Act 1973, s 16.

44 *Ibid*, s 11(a)(iii). The provisions on void and voidable marriages are set out in the Matrimonial Causes Act 1973 which re-enact the provisions contained in the Nullity of Marriage Act 1971; this legislation had followed a review of the law of nullity in Law Commission Report No 33 (1970).

45 *Ibid*, s 11(a)(i).

46 *Ibid*, s 11(a)(ii).

47 *Ibid*, s 11(b).

48 *Ibid*, s 11(c).

Under English law, a marriage will be voidable and will, therefore, be regarded as valid until one of the parties to it obtains a decree, if it has not been consummated as a result either of impotence or wilful refusal,[49] if either party did not validly consent to it[50] or was suffering such mental disorder as to make him or her unfitted for marriage,[51] if the respondent was suffering at the time of the marriage from communicable venereal disease[52] or the wife was, at the time of the marriage, pregnant by another man.[52a] There are bars to the award of a nullity decree for a voidable marriage in all cases.[53] The court will not make the award if the respondent satisfies it that the petitioner knew of the effect of the defect but behaved in such a way as to lead the respondent reasonably to believe that he would not act on it, or that it would be unjust to the respondent to grant the decree.[54] In all cases, except failure to consummate, the proceedings have to be brought within three years of marriage[55] and, in cases of venereal disease and pregnancy, the court must be satisfied that, at the time of the marriage, the petitioner was ignorant of the facts.[56]

It would be naive to suppose that foreign systems of law would be likely to have precisely the same taxonomy and, although some defects, like lack of age, failure to observe formalities, and prohibited degrees, might be expected to be common, others, like lack of consent or mistake of quality, cannot be expected either to have the same content or, even if they have, the same effect. Foreign systems may have additional grounds or may restrict defects to a narrower field.

There is more pragmatism than principle in the distinction between void and voidable marriages under English law and, indeed, the whole concept of a marriage being voidable for an initial defect lacks in logic what it gains in predictability.

So, when English conflict law is faced with a marriage which is argued to be defective under a foreign law, it cannot be assumed that foreign defects have their English counterparts or that, even if they have, they will be categorised in the same way, that is, as having the same effect upon the marriage. Nor should it be assumed that the only classification to be made is that of English law.

---

49 Matrimonial Causes Act 1973, s 12 (a), (b).
50 *Ibid*, s 12(c).
51 *Ibid*, s 12(d).
52 *Ibid*, s 12(e).
52a *Ibid*, s 12(f).
53 *Ibid*, s 13.
54 *Ibid*, s 13(1)(a), (b).
55 *Ibid*, s 13(2).
56 *Ibid*, s 13(3).

The matter of a foreign marriage may come before the English courts in a number of ways. The question of the validity of a marriage may be raised incidentally in proceedings which are not primarily directed to its validity, for example, in a succession case. In such cases, the issue will be whether the marriage was or was not valid at its inception or whether, if valid, it was still subsisting at the time in question or had been validly terminated by a divorce or an annulment. More directly, the English court may be asked to dissolve or annul the marriage or make a declaration of its validity,[57] subsistence or termination.

In nullity proceedings, the English court has only two responses available to it. An invalid marriage can be void *ab initio* or voidable, and the decrees involved are different; one is effective from the date of the void marriage, the other prospective from the date of the decree. When a foreign defect does not match a defect under English law or operates in a different way, the English court has to decide into which of its two categories the matter falls.

Distinctions

It has been well established since the middle of the 19th century that English conflict law draws a fundamental distinction in questions of validity of a marriage between those matters that pertain to formal validity and those matters that concern the capacity of the parties to marry or the essential validity of the marriage. The distinction between formal validity and essential validity derives form the case of *Brook v Brook*.[58] The salient facts of the case were: a man married his deceased wife's sister in Denmark in 1850. Both parties to the marriage were British subjects domiciled in England. At the time, the marriage was lawful under Danish law but prohibited on grounds of affinity under English law.[59]

In holding the marriage to be void,[60] the House of Lords drew a distinction between matters of formal validity which would continue to be governed by the *lex loci celebrationis* and matters of essential validity. Lord Campbell LC, in giving judgment, observed that 'while forms of entering into

---

57 Family Law Act 1986, ss 55–60.

58 The position at common law prior to *Brook v Brook* (1861) 9 HLC 193 was that all questions as to validity of a marriage were governed by the *lex loci celebrationis*: *Scrimshire v Scrimshire* (1752) 2 Hagg Con 395; *Compton v Bearcroft* (1769) 2 Hagg Con 444n; *Dalrymple v Dalrymple* (1811) 2 Hagg Con 54; *Warrender v Warrender* (1835) 2 Cl & Fin 488.

59 The Marriage Act 1835 (Lord Lyndhurst's Act) rendered such a marriage void.

60 The Deceased Wife's Sister's Act 1907 made such a marriage lawful. In 1921, the Deceased Brother's Widow's Marriage Act 1921 was enacted. See, also, the Marriage (Prohibited Degrees of Relationship) Act 1931. The relevant legislation is now contained in the Marriage (Enabling) Act 1960.

the contract of marriage are to be regulated by the *lex loci contractus*, the law of the country in which it is celebrated, the essentials of the marriage depend on the *lex domicilii*, the law of the country in which the parties are domiciled at the time of the marriage and in which the matrimonial residence is contemplated'.[61] Thus, from the middle of the 19th century, it has been important to determine whether a defect is a matter of formal validity or a matter of essential validity as the choice of law rule will differ.

In many situations, therefore, problems will arise as to how a particular defect is to be classified and, having been classified, it will then have to be determined whether it is a matter of formal or essential validity. In respect of the law which should classify the defect, there is some support for the view that the legal system which imposes the defect should also classify it. Some support for this view was expressed by Lord Greene MR in *De Reneville v De Reneville*,[62] where the facts were as follows: a domiciled Englishwoman married a domiciled Frenchman in France and lived with him there for some years. She then returned to England and presented a nullity petition on grounds of wilful refusal to consummate. No evidence of French law was produced at trial.

The Court of Appeal dismissed an appeal from the trial judge holding that the court did not have jurisdiction to hear the petition as the woman was resident, but not domiciled, within the jurisdiction. Lord Greene MR, having observed that impotence and wilful refusal might not be classified in the same way, gave the opinion that it would be for French law to determine the effect of either defect as making the marriage void or voidable 'not merely in the verbal sense, but in the sense of the words as understood in this country, that is, as indicating, as the case might be, that the marriage might be regarded in France as a nullity without the necessity of a decree annulling it'.

This test presupposes that foreign systems of law operate on the basis that there are some defects so fundamental that their presence renders the purported marriage a total nullity, so that any resort to the courts for a judgment to that effect is legally unnecessary, and there are other defects which require the court's active involvement. It assumes, in short, that other systems have something akin to the two fold classification of English domestic law. Such a presupposition may not be well founded.

Although there are some *dicta* in the cases favouring classification by the *lex causae*, this approach is not borne out by an examination of the case law. The normal course has been for an English judge to examine the evidence of the alleged defect and to decide whether the defect is one of formal validity or essential validity and then apply the appropriate choice of law rule. Before

---

61 *Brook v Brook* (1861) 9 HL 193, p 207.
62 [1948] P 100.

turning to these particular categories, it is proposed to examine two specific situations where difficulties have arisen.

Particular cases

It is proposed to examine two specific areas where difficulties have arisen before proceeding to the general categories of formal validity and essential validity.

Parental consent to marry

With the general reduction in the age of majority, the issue of parental consent has ceased to be a matter of significance to the validity of marriages. It is included here as another example of the workings of the conflict process and to illustrate the need to understand a problem before resolving it.

The law in this area has had to steer a course between the principle of the autonomy of young persons and the principle of parental authority. The Western idea of romantic love would suggest that the parties, once they are of an age to marry, should be able freely to decide whom they wish to marry. The contrary view is that marriage is more socially significant than the decision to have sexual intercourse and that parental guidance, in the interests of the child, is something which should be taken sufficiently seriously to justify a parental veto for the two years, in the case of English law, between the age of sexual consent and the age of majority. A different version of this view would be advocated by the culture of the arranged marriage, where the whole matter is put in charge of the parents and elders, whose job it is to arrange a suitable match.

It is difficult to avoid the conclusion that this particular problem has been unduly influenced by domestic considerations. Lord Hardwicke's Act of 1753 introduced the requirement that a minor should have parental consent to marry. The legislation required a licence to be obtained and banns to be published. In the event that these requirements were not observed, there was a risk that the marriage would be held to be void. However, the legislation did not apply to Scotland, so there was an understandable temptation for young persons, unable to obtain parental consent, to travel to Scotland and marry there without consent.[63] The English conflict of laws established early on that the issue was one of formal validity to be governed by the *lex loci celebrationis*; hence, the practice of couples eloping to Gretna Green, just over the border in Scotland, to marry there, after a short period of residence, without hindrance, as Scots law has no requirement of parental consent.

---

63   The so called Gretna Green marriage.

In the years after Lord Hardwicke's Act, questions arose as to the validity of these marriages. At that time, the courts referred all questions to the *lex loci celebrationis* and did not draw a distinction between matters of formal validity and essential validity; the marriages were held valid.[64]

While the English requirements as to parental consent had proved irksome, more extensive requirements were set out in the French Civil Code. In *Simonin v Mallac*,[65] the question arose as to the validity of a marriage celebrated, in England, between a Frenchman of 29 and a Frenchwoman of 22. Such a marriage was contrary to the provisions of Arts 151 and 152 of the Civil Code. The marriage was held lawful in England on the basis that questions of validity were to be determined by the *lex loci celebrationis*.

At a later date, the House of Lords, in *Brook v Brook*,[66] introduced the distinction between matters of form and matters of capacity or essential validity. To ensure that the prior case law was not redundant, the House of Lords asserted that matters of parental consent are to be regarded as part of the marriage ceremony and, thus, matters of formal validity.[67]

The tendency to see questions of parental consent as a matter of form was placed beyond doubt after the Court of Appeal judgment in *Ogden v Ogden*.[68] In that case, a domiciled Frenchman of 19 married a domiciled Englishwoman without having obtained the consent of his parents as required by Art 148 of the Civil Code.[69] The Court of Appeal held: (a) that questions of parental consent were matters of formality; (b) that formality was governed by the *lex loci celebrationis*; and (c) that, in any event, the marriage was valid under the principle in *Sottomayor v De Barros (No 2)*.[70] The correctness of this decision[71] was highly questionable because the operative provision of the French Civil Code quite clearly made the issue one of capacity; a French court had granted a decree of nullity in respect of the marriage and a remarriage had taken place on the strength of it. The result of the decision was to set at nought, as far as

---

64 *Compton v Bearcroft* (1769) 2 Hagg Cons 430; *Grierson v Grierson* (1781) 2 Hagg Cons 86 *Beamish v Beamish* (1788) 2 Hagg Cons 83.

65 (1860) 2 Sw & Tr 67.

66 (1861) 9 HLC 193.

67 A trend that was developed further by Hannen P in *Sottomayor v De Barros (No 2)* (1879) 5 PD 94, on which, see below.

68 [1908] P 46.

69 The operative provision of the Civil Code, Art 148 is, in absolute terms, in contrast to the qualified provisions of Arts 151 and 152, dealing with a person, as in *Simonin v Mallac* (1860) 2 Sw & Tr 67, who had obtained the age of majority.

70 (1879) 5 PD 94; on this aspect, see below.

71 It is arguable that the Court of Appeal (Gorrel Barnes P, Cozens Hardy MR, Kennedy LJ) went wrong early on by rejecting the submission of Sir Edward Clarke QC; the interventions of Gorrel Barnes P at [1908] P 46, p 52 make it clear: (a) that the court considered the defect as one of formality; and (b) that they considered *Brook v Brook* (1861) 2 SW & Tr 67 as being restricted to cases on the prohibited degrees and not as stating a general rule.

English law was concerned, the French decree, and the remarriage which had followed it, and to affirm the validity of the initial English marriage. If one needed a stark example of the advantage of the test propounded by Lord Greene MR in *De Reneville v De Reneville, Ogden v Ogden* provides it. Despite widespread academic criticism of the decision English courts still classify all cases of parental consent as matters of form to be referred to the *lex loci celebrationis* alone.[72]

Proxy marriages

English law requires both parties to be present at the marriage ceremony.[73] However, in some countries, proxy marriages are permitted and questions can arise as to validity. In *Apt v Apt*,[74] an English domiciliary authorised a representative to go through a marriage on her behalf with an Argentinian domiciliary in Buenos Aires. Proxy marriages are lawful under Argentinian law but not under English law. In upholding the validity of the marriage, the Court of Appeal drew a distinction between the method of giving consent and the fact of consent. The employment of a proxy was within the former category and, thus, part of the method by which the ceremony was performed; in such circumstances, it was a matter of formality and, thus, fell within the *lex loci celebrationis*. The same approach was followed in *McCabe v McCabe*,[75] where an Irish and Ghanaian domiciliary were absent from the ceremony, but the marriage was held to be formally valid because the conduct of the ceremony complied with the relevant customary law.

In most cases, it will not be difficult to determine whether a defect relates to formality or essential validity and it is to these two general categories that we must now turn.

FORMAL VALIDITY

The general principle in favour of the *lex loci celebrationis*

Probably the oldest rule in English private international law derives from the general principle – *locus regit actum*: the law of the place rules the deed – that

---

72 *Lodge v Lodge* (1963) 107 SJ 437 (Hewson J); *Bliersbach v McEwan* [1959] SC 43 (same approach in Scotland).
73 Marriage Act 1949, s 44(3), which requires 'each of the persons contracting the marriage' to make various declarations.
74 [1948] P 83.
75 [1994] 1 FLR 410.

the formal validity of a marriage is governed by the *lex loci celebrationis* (the law of the place of celebration).[76]

A marriage will be formally valid if the formalities required by the law of the place where it was celebrated have been observed. It does not matter whether these formalities are wholly secular, wholly religious or a mixture of the two, provided that whatever is done has the effect under the law of the place of celebration[77] of establishing the relationship as marriage. If the local law has special rules for foreigners, compliance with these rules will be required.[78]

Formalities include the licensing, certification and publicity requirements, the form of ceremony, what has to be said, number of witnesses, officials present and whether proxies can be used.[79] Other matters are more controversial: whether a marriage can take place without the parental consents required by the underage party's domiciliary law[80] or whether a party can marry contrary to the ritual required by his domiciliary law[81] may well be viewed differently by different systems. English law has treated them as formal matters and it is quite clear that the initial classification of an alleged defect, as relating to formal or essential validity will be made by English law, as *lex fori*, and not be the foreign law which imposes it.

As form is governed by the *lex loci celebrationis* and parties can marry where they wish, it follows that couples can evade the formal requirements of their 'home' laws by marrying abroad.

It is clear that formal validity should be determined according to the *lex loci celebrationis* at the time the marriage takes place. In certain circumstances there might be a case for accepting retrospective legislation which makes up for a technical defect and repairs it before anyone has acted in reliance on the formal invalidity. The willingness of English courts to approach matters in a liberal spirit was illustrated by the case of *Starkowski v AG*, where the facts were as follows:[82] a Polish man and woman married on 19 May 1945 in a religious ceremony in Austria. At the time, the marriage was void in Austria. On 12 June 1945, a child, Barbara, was born. On 30 June 1945, an Austrian

---

76 *Scrimshire v Scrimshire* (1752) 2 Hag Con 395; *Dalrymple v Dalrymple* (1811) 2 Hag Con 54; *Warrender v Warrender* (1835) 2 Cl & Fin 488.

77 *Berthiaume v Dastous* [1930] AC 79.

78 *Hooper v Hooper* [1959] 1 WLR 1021 (man and woman marry in Iraq, where *lex loci celebrationis* refers to *lex nationalis*).

79 *Apt v Apt* [1948] P 83 (marriage by proxy in Argentina); *Ponticelli v Ponticelli* [1958] P 204 (marriage by proxy in Italy).

80 *Ogden v Ogden* [1908] P 46, p 52, *per* Gorell Barnes: 'The want of consent is not incapacity; it is want of compliance with a formality.'

81 *Papadopoulos v Papadopoulos* [1930] P 55 (Greek Orthodox); *Gray v Formosa* [1963] P 259 (Roman Catholic); *Lee v Lepre* [1965] P 52 (Roman Catholic).

82 [1954] AC 155; [1953] 2 All ER 1272; see Sinclair (1952) 29 BYIL 479; Sinclair (1953) 30 BYIL 523; Thomas (1954) 3 ICLQ 353.

statute retrospectively validated religious ceremonies provided that they were registered. The couple failed to register the marriage until 1949, by which date they were resident in England. In 1950, the wife went through a ceremony of marriage in Croydon, London with another man. They had a son, Christopher, born before the marriage.

The narrow issue before the House of Lords was whether Christopher was legitimate or not;[83] this question could only be resolved by determining whether the 1945 marriage was still valid in 1950. The House of Lords ruled that the first marriage was valid, being retrospectively validated by the statute of 30 June 1945, and that legislation had been complied with by registration even though the parties were neither domiciled nor resident in Austria at the time of registration. It therefore followed that the second marriage was void and Christopher illegitimate.

Although the rule that questions of formality are subject to the *lex loci celebrationis* has existed since the middle of the 18th century, it has been subject to modern approval. The leading contemporary authority is *Berthiaume v Dastous*[84] where the facts were as follows: a French Canadian woman met a French Canadian man in Paris and the parties were married there in a Roman Catholic ceremony. Because of an oversight by the priest, the religious ceremony was not preceded by the civil ceremony that French law requires. At a later date, in divorce proceedings in Quebec, Canada, questions arose as to the status of the marriage.

The Privy Council, in allowing an appeal from the Court of King's Bench for Quebec, ruled that the marriage was a nullity because the formal requirements of the *lex loci celebrationis* had not been complied with. Viscount Dunedin expressed the mater in robust terms:

> If there is one question better settled than any other in international law, it is that as regards marriage – putting aside the question of capacity – *locus regit actum*. If a marriage is good by the laws of the country where it is effected, it is good all the world over, no matter whether the proceeding or ceremony which constituted the marriage according to the law of the place would or would not constitute marriage in the country of the domicile of one or other of the spouses.[85]

Although the rule that questions of formality are governed by the *lex loci celebrationis* is a rule of long duration and supported by the clearest authority, there are a number of exceptions to the general principle that need to be examined.

---

83 The proceedings were for a declaration of legitimacy under the Legitimacy Act 1926 and the Matrimonial Causes Act 1950, s 17.

84 [1930] AC 79, PC.

85 *Ibid*, p 83.

Common law exceptions to compliance with the *lex loci celebrationis*

It is normal to divide the exceptions to the rule into those existing at common law and those created by statute. It is proposed to examine the common law exceptions first.

There are certain circumstances where parties may demonstrate formal validity not on the basis of compliance with the *lex loci* but by asserting a 'common law marriage'. In strict terms, a common law marriage is one that met the requirements that pertained prior to the enactment of Lord Hardwicke's Act of 1753. The parties were required to declare themselves husband and wife in each others presence *per verba de praesenti*; at a later date, the House of Lords declared that this would have to be before an episcopally ordained clergyman.[86] However, it came to be accepted by judges that the qualification added by *R v Millis* did not apply where the marriage was contracted abroad and no parochial system had been established.[87]

It is arguable whether this is an actual exception to the *lex loci celebrationis* since it was based on the theory that when Englishmen went abroad to colonise they would take the common law with them in so far as it was not inconsistent with the local law. If there was no clear local law, then the common law was deemed to be part of the *lex loci*. This accorded with the Victorian conception of the civilising force of the common law and it was also in harmony with the desire of the courts to hold a marriage valid if at all possible, particularly when entered into in good faith by both parities. Thus, in *Wolfenden v Wolfenden*,[88] a marriage between an English and Canadian domiciliary in the Hupeh province of China before a local minister of the Church of Scotland was held valid on the basis that it complied with minimum common law requirements and that, though the 'colonists take the law of England with them to their new home, they only take so much of it as is applicable to their situation and condition'.[89]

There are two situations where reliance has been placed on the concept of the common law marriage: (a) where there are insuperable difficulties in complying with the local law; and (b) where the marriage has been contracted in a country under belligerent occupation.

---

86 *R v Millis* (1844) 10 Cl & Fin 534.

87 *Beamish v Beamish* (1861) 9 HL Cas 274, 348; *Lightbody v West* (1903) 18 TLR 526 *Wolfenden v Wolfenden* [1946] P 61; *Penhas v Tan Soo Eng* [1953] AC 304.

88 [1946] P 61; where Lord Merriman P, in reliance on *Catterall v Catterall* (1847) 1 Rob Eccl 580 and *Maclean v Cristall* (1849) Perry's Oriental Cases 75, held that an episcopally ordained clergyman was not required. The minister was not episcopally ordained nor authorised under the Foreign Marriages Act 1892.

89 *Wolfenden v Wolfenden* [1946] P 61, *per* Lord Merriman.

Where there are insuperable difficulties in complying with the local law

There are a number of situations where a valid common law marriage is found not because the territory is deemed subject to the common law but because the demands of the *lex loci* were impossible for the parties to fulfil. Lord Eldon held that a common law marriage had been established where two Protestants had been married in Rome before a Protestant clergyman when the court received evidence that no Roman Catholic priest would perform the ceremony.[90] In like terms, Lord Stowell held that a marriage celebrated in the Cape of Good Hope was valid where one party was unable to obtain the consent of a guardian resident in England.[91] There must be some evidence of insuperable difficulty not mere inconvenience, so that failure to meet a residence requirement of the *lex loci* will not normally be sufficient.[92]

Marriages in countries under belligerent occupation

A particular problem was raised by the large numbers of religious marriages which had taken place at the end of World War II in parts of Europe recently liberated from German control between couples who had been displaced by the upheavals of war. These marriages were formally invalid as there had been a failure or a refusal to comply with the German marriage laws. To deal with this problem, the English courts adapted an old institution – the common law marriage (the marriage *per verba de praesenti*) – in order to give these marriages formal validity by English law, although the marriages, at the time they took place, had not the slightest connection with England. There is little to be said for the reasoning in these cases and much for the good will of the courts in seeking to resolve a serious problem. It is best to regard the cases[93] as a particular response to what one hopes is a one off problem and it is unlikely that there will be any further development of the concept.

The stream of case law commences with *Taczanowska v Taczanowski*,[94] where the facts were as follows: two domiciled Polish nationals were married in Italy in 1946 by a Polish army chaplain who was an episcopally ordained clergyman of the Roman Catholic church. The husband was a serving soldier and the wife a civilian refugee. The marriage was formally invalid by both Italian domestic law and Polish domestic law. In 1955, the wife petitioned for a decree of nullity in England on the basis of non-compliance with local forms.

---

90 *Lord Cloncurry's Case* (1811); see Westlake, *Private International Law* (7th edn, 1925), section 26.

91 *Ruding v Smith* (1821) 2 Hag Con 371.

92 *Kent v Smith* (1821) 11 Sim 361.

93 The leading cases are *Taczanowska v Taczanowski* [1957] P 301; 2 All ER 563 (Poles in Italy); *Kochanski v Kochanska* [1958] P 147 (Poles in Germany); *Merker v Merker* [1963] P 283; [1962] 3 All ER 928 (Poles in Germany); *Preston v Preston* [1963] P 411; 2 All ER 405 (Poles in Germany).

94 [1957] P 301, CA.

The Court of Appeal, aware of a number of other situations, held that the marriage was valid as a common law marriage. The primacy of the *lex loci celebrationis* was grounded on the principle that the parties were presumed to submit to the local law; such a presumption could not arise in the case of conquering forces. Thus, a marriage that was formally invalid both by the *lex loci celebrationis* and the personal law of the parties was validated on the basis of compliance with forms existing in England prior to 1753; a country which, at the time, the parties had not even visited. The principle of presumed submission was taken up by Sachs J in *Kochanski v Kochanska*[95] to validate a marriage entered into in Germany between displaced Polish persons. The learned judge held that presumed submission was rebutted and the marriage was validated as a common law marriage.

In later cases, attempts were made by judges to ensure that the principle was drawn no wider than was absolutely necessary. In *Lazarewicz v Lazarewicz*,[96] Phillimore J held that the principle in *Taczanowska v Taczanowski* could not apply where the parties had expressly intended to comply with local law, while, in *Merker v Merker*,[97] Simon P, in applying the principle, defined it as being restricted to marriages within the lines of a foreign army of occupation and this approach was followed by the Court of Appeal in *Preston v Preston*,[98] where the court asserted that those who marry abroad will be presumed to have submitted to the local law save in the case of members of occupying forces. As indicated above, this stream of case law was prompted by the devastation and dislocation existing in Europe in 1945 and is unlikely to be subject to any judicial extension.

Marriages on the high seas

The general principle is that the high seas are not subject to the sovereignty of any single State[99] and that jurisdiction is normally exercised by the Flag State over the ship. In the 19th century, it was common to hold that a British ship was a floating island in which British law applied.[100] The problem that arises is that there is no legal system common to those countries that display a British flag. Secondly, there is no specific statute that applies to the situation,

---

95 [1958] P 147.

96 [1962] P 171 (Phillimore J).

97 [1963] P 283 (Simon P).

98 [1963] P 411.

99 Geneva Convention on the High Seas 1958, Art 2; Law of the Sea Convention 1982, Art 89.

100 See Byles J in *R v Anderson* (1868) 1 Cox CC 198 (the case itself concerned an American accused of manslaughter on a British vessel in French internal waters).

so it would seem that the matter is governed by common law.[101] It would seem that, in principle, a common law marriage can be effected on a vessel by analogy with *Wolfenden v Wolfenden*. Although the matter is not free from doubt, it would seem that an episcopally ordained clergyman is not required.[102]

Statutory exceptions

There are two statutory exceptions to the general rule that that the *lex loci celebrationis* governs questions of formality.

Consular marriages

The first statutory exception derives from the Foreign Marriage Act 1892 (as amended by the Foreign Marriage Act 1947 and the Foreign Marriage (Amendment) Act 1988), which provides that a marriage where one party is a British subject conducted by a marriage officer in a foreign country in the manner set out in the legislation shall be as valid as if the same had been solemnised in the UK. Such marriages are often referred to as consular marriages in that, while Ambassadors or High Commissioners may serve as marriage officers, the task is normally regarded as a consular function.

The legislation includes provision as to the giving of notice,[103] parental consent[104] and those who can act as marriage officers. By s 8 of the Act, the marriage is to be conducted at the official house of the marriage officer.[105] The legislation has to be read with the Foreign Marriage Order of 1970,[106] which stipulates that a marriage is not to be solemnised in a foreign country unless there is evidence: (a) that the authorities of that country will not object; (b) that there are insufficient facilities for the marriage of parties in that country; and (c) that the parties will be regarded as validly married by the law of the country in which each party is domiciled. In a rather curious provision, the Act lays down that no marriage is to be celebrated where it would be a breach of international law,[107] while s 23 provides that the provisions of the legislation are not to affect the validity of other marriages celebrated abroad.

---

101 The provisions of the Merchant Shipping Act 1854 that marriages should be entered in the official log book have now been repealed.
102 *Wolfenden v Wolfenden* [1946] P 61.
103 Foreign Marriage Act 1892, s 2.
104 *Ibid*, s 4.
105 *Collett v Collett* [1968] P 482; see, also, *Hay v Northcote* [1900] 2 Ch 262.
106 SI 1970/1539, as amended by SI 1990/598.
107 Foreign Marriage Act 1892, s 22.

Marriages of members of British forces serving abroad

Section 22 of the Foreign Marriage Act 1892 (as substituted and amended by the legislation of 1947 and 1988) makes provision for marriage abroad where one person is a member of HM Forces serving in foreign territory or employed within categories to be specified by Order in Council or is a child of a person falling within that category.[108] The expression 'foreign territory' will not include any part of the Commonwealth[109] but it does include a ship in foreign waters.[110] The provisions of s 22 are largely declaratory of common law.

Renvoi

Before leaving the subject of formal validity, it is necessary to make mention of the doctrine of *renvoi*. In most cases, reference to the *lex loci celebrationis* will mean a reference to the domestic law of that particular country. However, there is some evidence in the authorities to the effect that the *lex loci* should include reference to the relevant rules of private international law. In *Taczanowska v Taczanowski*,[111] the question at issue was the formal validity of a marriage between domiciled Poles at a military camp in Italy in 1946; the marriage was invalid under the rules of domestic Italian law but the court appeared to indicate that, if it had been valid by the legal system identified by the rules of Italian private international law (that is, Polish law), then that would have been acceptable. In the event, the marriage was invalid under Polish law and validated as a common law marriage. In the subsequent case of *Hooper v Hooper*,[112] it would seem that the doctrine of *renvoi* would have been applied to validate the marriage by the *lex nationalis* if the formalities had been complied with.

Those who argue for the use of the doctrine of *renvoi* in the area of formal invalidity claim that it will lead to less 'limping marriages'; however, as *Taczanowska v Taczanowski*[113] illustrates, marriages can still be validated on other grounds. Secondly, it is argued that the English courts do try to uphold a marriage if at all possible and that the doctrine of *renvoi* has a role to play in providing flexibility. Against this, it might be argued that the rule of compliance with the *lex loci celebrationis* is too narrow and that the rule should

---

108 Foreign Marriage Act 1892, s 22; see the Foreign Marriage (Armed Forces) Order 1964 SI 1964/1000, as amended by SI 1965/137; SI 1990/2592.

109 *Ibid*, s 22(2).

110 *Ibid*, s 22(3).

111 [1957] P 301.

112 [1959] 1 WLR 1021 (unclear whether the domestic law of Iraq was considered; it was clear that under the Iraq choice of law rule (the *lex nationalis*) the marriage was invalid).

113 [1957] P 301.

be extended so that a marriage will be formally valid if it complies with either the *lex loci celebrationis* or the personal law of the parties.

These various arguments were considered by the Law Commission in its Working Paper in 1985, where it indicated a certain sympathy for the employment of *renvoi* in cases of formal invalidity in the interests of upholding a marriage.[114] However, after consultation, there was less enthusiasm and the conclusion was that the mischief of rare invalidity in which *renvoi* might be helpful was outweighed by the complexity of the operation of the doctrine and the proposals were dropped.[115] The Law Commission were not anxious to promote a reform that could lead to a marriage being formally valid in an English court but not so in the place of celebration.

The role of the *lex loci celebrationis*

While the job of the *lex loci celebrationis* is to control the formal validity of marriage, it is undoubtedly the case that, where marriages are closely regulated by the *lex loci*, that law will police its country's capacity rules. So, for example, parties, whatever their personal laws may permit, will not be able to get the necessary permission to marry in England if they are under the age or within the prohibited degrees by English law. Were they to slip through the net and celebrate their marriage in England, it is unlikely that the marriage would be upheld. However, this is probably not the case if the *lex loci* is foreign and the parties manage to marry there despite that law's view of their capacity. A reference to the foreign *lex loci* will probably be confined to the question of formal validity only and its view of the essential validity of the marriage is ignored.

ESSENTIAL VALIDITY

Although it might seem logical to distinguish the issues of capacity and essential validity, as we do, for example, in the law of contract, the issues are conventionally treated together for two reasons. The choice of law rules are the same and, more importantly, the issues are harder to separate here than elsewhere. While there are some matters, age, for example, or existing marriage, which quite obviously affect an individual's capacity to marry as such, there are others which relate not to the individual's personal capacity directly but to his or her ability to enter a particular marriage. For example,

---

114 Law Commission Working Paper No 89 (1985).
115 Law Commission Report No 165 (1987).

rules of exogamy, consanguinity or affinity concern the proposed relationship. The two parties, single and of full age and status, may be able to marry whomsoever they wish except each other, because they stand in a relationship which the system of law will not allow as a marriage. It is equally correct to describe, say, the Portuguese prohibition on the marriage of cousins as a matter of the essential validity of the marriage or as an incapacity on the part of a Portuguese domiciliary to marry a cousin.

The choice of law rules in respect of essential validity

There is no doubt that the essential validity of marriage is governed by the personal law. While the English conflict of laws retains domicile as the determinant of the personal law, all questions of the capacities of the parties to marry one another will be referred to the *lex domicilii*. The reference is to the internal law of the chosen system not to its conflict rules,[116] so no issue of *renvoi* arises. The Law Commission suggested the incorporation of *renvoi* into the basic rule of reference[117] but did not propose legislative changes to this effect.[118] If the personal law did not play a role in questions of essential validity, it would be open to parties simply to travel to other countries to avoid restrictions imposed by their own law.[119] However, beyond the general statement that essential validity is linked to the personal law, there is considerable room for debate; although one test enjoys a wide degree of support in the academic literature and the case law, a number of other possible tests have been put forward. In England, at least six possible tests can be identified and it is necessary to say a little about each; it is proposed to examine each test in turn.

The dual domicile doctrine

According to the dual domicile doctrine, a marriage will only be valid if each party has capacity under the law of his or her domicile to contract the marriage. To put the matter another way, the essential validity of the marriage is tested by reference to the laws of the ante-nuptial domicile of both parties and only if there is capacity under both will the marriage be valid. Suppose an English court had to rule on the validity of a marriage conducted in Paris between A and B, who are first cousins. A is domiciled in Germany, whose laws place no restrictions on the marriage, and B is domiciled in Portugal, whose law regards first cousins as within the prohibited degrees of

---

116 But, see *R v Brentwood Superintendent Registrar of Marriages ex p Arias* [1968] 2 QB 956.
117 Law Commission Working Paper No 89 (1985).
118 Law Commission Report No 165 (1987).
119 As, indeed, was the case in *Brook v Brook* (1861) 9 HL Cas 193.

relationship. If an English court were to apply the dual domicile doctrine then the marriage would be invalid. The question posed to both A and B is not only whether the individual has capacity to marry but whether this particular person can marry the intended partner.

The dual domicile test was advocated by Professor Dicey[120] and probably has more support than any other test in the case law. The advantages of the dual domicile test are considerable. First, as a matter of principle, it identifies the legal system with which a party has the closest legal connection – it is the legal system to which he or she has 'belonged' for a substantial part of his life. Secondly, as a test, it can be applied on the day that the marriage takes place.[121] Thirdly, it puts the parties on an equal footing and does not prefer the husband's law to that of his wife.[122] Fourthly, because it enables the validity of the marriage to be established prior to the ceremony, it can be used by officials concerned with administration and solemnisation of marriages.

In respect of disadvantages, it can be argued, first, that it makes reference to legal systems which may have no further interest in the future of the individuals or their marriage. It also tends to invalidity by making the marriage subject to two legal tests, which might be argued to be contrary to the traditional common law policy of seeking to uphold the validity of a marriage. Suppose H and W are domiciled in Country X, where they are regarded as being within the prohibited degrees of marriage as they are cousins. They decide that they will make their home in Country Y, which has a less restrictive regime on consanguinity, and they go through the marriage ceremony there. If a question arises about the validity of their marriage, the court will have to determine whether they had acquired a domicile in Country Y before they married or only subsequently. If before, their capacity will be determined by the law of Y and their marriage will be valid. If after, their capacity will be determined by the law of X and their marriage will be void. The same problem would arise if their ante-nuptial domiciles were in different countries, only one of which regarded them as within the prohibited degrees. It would be easy enough to advise them to avoid any problems by the simple expedient of establishing domiciles in Y before getting married and we may suppose the acquisition of such a domicile would be a simple and easy process; but no advice may be sought, not least because the parties may not be aware of either the prohibition or, indeed, of their relationship.

---

120 AV Dicey (1835–1922). The publication of *The Conflict of Laws* (1st edn, 1896) played some part in this, as did the fact that, in the second half of the 19th century, domicile had emerged as the dominant test for the personal law. At the same time, it should not be forgotten that Dicey was probably the most influential legal writer of the time having consolidated his reputation with *The Law of the Constitution* (1885).

121 See Law Commission Working Paper No 89 (1985).

122 Of more importance since the Domicile and Matrimonial Proceedings Act 1973, s 1.

The intended matrimonial home doctrine

The second test to govern the essential validity of a marriage is that propounded by Professor Cheshire.[123] The intended matrimonial home test (sometimes described as the matrimonial domicile doctrine) holds that the law of the intended matrimonial domicile is to govern the validity of the marriage, with the proviso that, if no matrimonial home could be discovered, reference should be made to the husband's ante-nuptial domiciliary law.

Professor Cheshire had been influenced by the writings of Savigny and Cook and the test must be judged against the social conditions early in the century. The normal circumstance would be for the woman to marry the man and then go and live in the matrimonial home. If it was in a new country, then the intended matrimonial home test would have been met. However, it might be that the woman (normally the non-working, economically inferior of the two) would move to the home of the husband and, in any event, would acquire the husband's domicile on marriage. Since the enactment of the Domicile and Matrimonial Proceedings Act 1973, this form of reasoning is outdated.

It is argued that the intended matrimonial home test enables the country with the closest interest in the marriage to determine the validity of the marriage; some argue, by analogy with company law, that it enables the legal system to identify the 'true seat' of the marriage. Thirdly, it is argued that by testing the validity of the marriage against a single legal system one is more likely to validate the marriage.

However, it has to be admitted that the test has a number of disadvantages. First, A and B may not immediately establish a matrimonial home, in which case, the validity of the marriage would remain in suspense. Secondly, the test assumes that a matrimonial home will be established within a reasonable time but such a phrase is vague and difficult to apply in practice. Thirdly, in a world of job mobility and advanced systems of civil aviation, A and B may marry and move to Country X but, after a year, move to Country Y; in such circumstances, one might then have the absurd situation of the validity of the marriage changing with any change of domicile. Such a situation would be impractical, uncertain and unjust. Fourthly, many of the rules relating to marriage concern the protection of young persons and will be of concern to their parents within the country of the ante-nuptial domicile. An English parent concerned that his daughter of 12 is about to marry in Uruguay is likely to demand that validity be judged by the law of England rather than

---

123 GC Cheshire (1886–1978) produced the first edition of his *Private International Law* in 1935 admitting that his views on some matters departed from those of Dicey and Westlake. The editors of recent editions of the textbook have taken a more neutral position. For the two tests, see Cumming Bruce J in *Radwan v Radwan (No 2)* [1973] Fam 35.

Uruguay.[124] Fifthly, the test can only be applied after the event and is of little practical value to those public officials concerned with the administration of marriages. Sixthly, the argument that capacity to contract should be judged in the same manner as commercial contracts pays insufficient regard to the status created by marriage and its effect on third parties, including the State and its organs; it also fails to give proper weight to the ethical, eugenic and religious reasons that determine the law on prohibited degrees.

Finally, any rule of law that might lead to suspending judgment on the validity of a marriage would lead to uncertainty in other related area, for example, the property or social security rights of the wife. Moreover, it is argued that the rule might cause difficulties in public international law; the pattern of emigration in the modern world tends to be from the poorer States to the richer States. In prosperous, advanced societies, the normal rule is of monogamy and a high minimum age for lawful marriage; to adopt the intended matrimonial home test would run the risk of invalidating the marriage of those who marry in a poor country and emigrate to a richer one.[125]

In broad terms, when Professor Cheshire propounded the test, the law of domicile still made wives dependant on their husbands – they acquired their husband's domicile as a domicile of dependency upon the marriage and had no power to change it while the marriage lasted. There was, therefore, a unity of domicile between husband and wife and, therefore, one could speak correctly of a matrimonial domicile even if there was no matrimonial home. The Domicile and Matrimonial Proceedings Act 1973 liberated married woman from domiciliary dependence and, by so doing, put an end to the concept of an automatic matrimonial domicile. Of course, the vast majority of cohabiting married couples will share the same domicile but they share it as a matter of individual autonomy not as the operation of a legal process. There is no reason for preferring the husband's domicile to that of the wife either in law or in logic and, while it may be true that, where the couple come from different countries, it is more common for the matrimonial home to be established in the husband's country than the wife's, this does not help when no such home has been established nor justify such discriminatory treatment.

It might have been thought that the passing of the Marriage (Enabling) Act 1960[126] and the Domicile and Matrimonial Proceedings Act 1973 would have

---

124 A girl of 12 may lawfully marry in Uruguay.

125 While, of course, immigration laws in the richer countries have tended to be strengthened, the test does involve sitting in judgment on the marriage laws of another country.

126 Removing the prohibition on marriages between parties related by affinity after divorce had severed the connection, provided that, under s 1(3), no such marriage would be valid if either of the parties was, at the time of the marriage, domiciled in a country which did not allow such relationships.

decided the issue in favour of the dual domicile test once and for all. However, although there is no doubt that the dual domicile test is the one most commonly applied and, indeed, the issue normally goes in its favour by default, a few recent cases have chosen to apply the Cheshire test, so, to that extent the issue remains a live one. However, the fact that the Law Commission[127] considered the intended matrimonial home test to be found wanting and advocated the adoption of the dual domicile test is likely to mean that the former doctrine is unlikely to be adopted one a wide scale .

Combining the tests[128]

There is some support in the authorities for the view that a marriage might be valid if it meets either the dual domicile test or the intended matrimonial home test; in some cases, this would mean that the marriage was valid if it complied with one of three possible laws. The argument in favour of this approach is that enables the court to uphold the validity of the marriage if at all possible. However, the support in the authorities is limited and equivocal. Attention has focused on the judgment of Lincoln J at first instance in *Lawrence v Lawrence*.[129] In this case, the facts were that a Brazilian domiciliary obtained a divorce in Nevada and then married a domiciled Englishman there, with whom she came to live in England. The Nevada divorce was not recognised in Brazil so that, under the standard dual domicile test, the second marriage would have been void for bigamy. At a later date, the wife petitioned for a decree of nullity in England. Lincoln J, in holding the second marriage to be valid, reasoned that compliance with either test was sufficient.[130]

However, this is but a first instance judgment and it is strongly arguable that the main issue in the case was not the capacity to contract the second marriage but the recognition of the foreign divorce.[131] Secondly, the judgment of Lincoln J can equally be read as favouring the real and substantial connection approach.[132] Thirdly, such an approach represents the abandonment of a choice of law rule in favour of the principle that the validity of the marriage should be upheld if at all possible. Fourthly, some of the writers argue that the test should only be used in respect of some incapacities and not others; this involves making judgments about the purpose of individual invalidating rules. Fifthly, it is very difficult to imagine how the

---

127 Law Commission Report No 165 (1987), para 2.6.

128 Jaffey (1978) 41 MLR 38; (1982) 2 OJLS 368; Hartley (1972) 35 MLR 571.

129 [1985] Fam 106, CA (Lincoln J).

130 Support for Lincoln J was expressed in the Court of Appeal by Sir David Cairns but not by Ackner or Purchas LJJ.

131 See the Family Law Act 1986, s 50.

132 See below.

test could be used prospectively by registrars and administrative officials. Finally, such an approach has been rejected by the Law Commission,[133] not least because it involves determining the validity of the marriage with reference to three possible laws.

Real and substantial connection

Another view is that the essential validity of a marriage should be determined by the law of the country with which it has the most real and substantial connection. At various times, this approach has been described as the 'proper law of the marriage'[134] but there is little direct support in the cases. The idea of a real and substantial connection which can be found in some obsolete cases on the recognition of foreign decrees[135] clearly has, like the matrimonial home test itself, certain attractions in those cases where the premarital domiciliary law is remote from the marriage but, again, like the matrimonial home test, it cannot be applied universally. There are certain remarks of Lord Simon in *Vervaeke v Smith*[136] that might be cited in support but they can be no more than *obiter*, having regard to the unusual nature of the litigation and the fact that the main issues concerned the fraudulent nature of the claim and the role of public policy where two legal systems were in conflict. These remarks were taken up by Lincoln J in *Lawrence v Lawrence*, where the learned judge considered the country with the most real and substantial connection to be the country of the intended matrimonial home. It is unlikely that this test will attract much future support as it was criticised by the Law Commission as being too vague and only applicable retrospectively and, thus, of limited use in matters of public administration.[137]

Validity under a single law

It has been contended that a marriage might be considered valid if it met the requirements of the ante-nuptial domiciliary laws of one of the parties. There is no indication in the case law of acceptance of this principle and it was rejected by the Law Commission. It involves ignoring a relevant law of one of the parties and, while it might lead to marginally more marriages being validated, it would also lead to an increase in the number of limping relationships. It is difficult to imagine what advantage might arise from the adoption of this rule.

---

133 Law Commission Working Paper No 89 (1985).
134 Sykes (1955) 4 ICLQ 159; Fentiman (1985) CLJ 256; Fentiman (1986) 6 OJLS 353.
135 *Indyka v Indyka* [1969] 1 AC 33.
136 [1983] AC 145; see, however, *Padolechia v Padolechia* [1968] P 314, p 336, *per* Simon P.
137 Law Commission Working Paper No 89 (1985).

A variable rather than a single rule

For the purposes of the present discussion, it has been assumed that once a matter has been classified as a matter of essential validity, then a single choice of law rule should be applied to determine the validity of the marriage. However, there are a wide category of incapacities and judges have raised the question as to whether the same rule should apply in all circumstances. The concern was expressed by Cumming Bruce J in *Radwan v Radwan (No 2)*, where the judge observed:

> It is arguable that it is an oversimplification of the common law to assume that the same test for purposes of choice of law applies to every kind of incapacity – non-age, affinity, prohibition of monogamous contract by virtue of existing spouse, and capacity for polygamy. Different public and social factors are relevant to each of these types of incapacity.[138]

Those who favour a varying rule argue that incapacities can be divided into: (a) those imposed to protect a particular interest of society (for example, prohibition against polygamy); and (b) those imposed to protect the individual parties (for example, minimum age). On the assumption that such clear cut distinctions can be made, proponents argue that the former should be regulated by the intended matrimonial home, while the latter should be determined by the ante-nuptial domicile.[139]

There are, however, a number of criticisms that have been levelled. First, it is argued that legal advice can only be confidently given on the basis of a general rule and limited exceptions. Secondly, it is argued that the attempt to distinguish types of incapacity would prove difficult in practice. Thirdly, a case in which there was more than one form of incapacity might give rise to conflicting indications. Fourthly, it is argued that Parliament has already made particular provision in the case of capacity to marry after a foreign divorce. Finally, it is argued that it incorporates a philosophy of 'rule scepticism' which may be necessary in the USA but is alien to the tradition of English private international law.

After considering the various theories that have been advanced as to the choice of law rule that should govern the essential validity of a marriage, it is logical to move on and examine the case law. However, it is sensible to examine these matters after considering the particular role of *lex fori*.

---

138 *Radwan v Radwan (No 2)* [1973] Fam 35, p 51 (this interesting and much criticised judgment is discussed below in the context of polygamy).
139 Jaffey (1982) 2 OJLS 368.

The *lex fori* and essential validity

Even if agreement can be reached as to the choice of law rule to govern questions of essential validity, it is clear that there is a significant exception to that rule. This is because of the judgment in *Sottomayor v De Barros (No 2)* which holds that the essential validity of a marriage celebrated in England where one party is an English domiciliary is to be governed by English law.[140] It is sensible to outline the facts of this unusual litigation: the petitioner and the respondent were first cousins born in Portugal. They came to England in 1858. In 1866, when the petitioner was 14 and the respondent 16, they went through a ceremony of marriage at a registry office in London. From 1866 until 1872, they lived under the same roof but the marriage was not consummated. In 1873, the petitioner returned to Portugal and, in 1874, the respondent returned. The petitioner then filed a claim for a decree of nullity, claiming the parties lacked capacity under Portuguese law. The Queen's Proctor argued that the marriage was to be governed by English law. The first hearing before Phillimore J proceeded on the unwise basis of seeking to determine the legal question before a full finding of facts had been made.

Phillimore J, considering himself bound by *Simonin v Mallac*,[141] dismissed the petition. The Court of Appeal distinguished *Simonin v Mallac* and ruled that 'personal capacity must depend on the law of the domicile' Thus, the judgment of the Court of Appeal constitutes some support for the dual domicile theory. However, the Court of Appeal sent the case back to the Divorce Division so that a determination could be made of the domicile of the parties. In the subsequent hearing, Hannen P concluded that the respondent was domiciled in England and he then went on to assume that capacity to marry was governed by the *lex loci celebrationis*. This seems to have been based on a misunderstanding of the prior Court of Appeal judgment, which had sought to draw a distinction between questions of form and questions of capacity.[142] However, the judgment of Hannen P was never overruled and it was necessary for Dicey to incorporate the case as an exception to the general rule that domicile determined capacity. Thus, the case came to be authority for the proposition that, where a marriage was celebrated in England between a person domiciled in England and a person domiciled abroad, the marriage will not be invalidated by an incapacity which, though existing under a

---

140 The litigation was *Sottomayor v De Barros (No 1)* (1877) 2 PD 81 (Phillimore J); on appeal, *Sottomayor v De Barros (No 1)* (1877) 3 PD 1 (Cotton, Baggallay, James LJJ); on remission to PDA, *Sottomayor v De Barros (No 2)* (1879) 5 PD 94 (Hannen P).

141 (1860) 2 Sw & Tr 67.

142 Cotton LJ, in the Court of Appeal, could not have been clearer when he observed: 'The law of a country where a marriage is solemnised must alone decide all questions relating to the validity of the ceremony by which the marriage is alleged to have been constituted; but, as in other contracts, so in that of marriage, personal capacity must depend on the law of the domicile.

foreign law, does not exist in England. The judgment of Hannen P was approved as one of the grounds for the decision in *Ogden v Ogden*.[143]

Although the judgment has been variously attacked as 'wrong' and 'xenophobic', arguments have been advanced in its support, such as: (a) it represents a mandatory rule of the *lex fori*; (b) that it is an aspect of public policy; (c) that it promotes conformity; and (d) that it protects the legitimate interests of the English domiciliary who marries in England. The Law Commission[144] concluded that, on balance, the rule should be abolished but did admit that: (a) it had not caused hardship in the past 100 years; (b) it promoted the validity of marriage; (c) the policy was followed in other countries; and (d) it did justice to the English domiciliary marrying in England.

Defects and impediments

It is now necessary to examine the various defects and impediments and to determine which choice of law rule applies in each particular instance.

Consent of the parties

The effect that a lack of consent by one of the parties should have was a matter of controversy in domestic English law for some time. The arguments are fairly evenly balanced between regarding the marriage as void *ab initio* for the lack of an essential ingredient and treating it as voidable on the basis that, despite the reluctance of one of the parties to enter into the marriage, the relationship might work out and, therefore, leaving it to one of the parties to bring a petition if it does not. The matter was finally resolved in favour of voidability by the Nullity of Marriage Act 1971[145] and the same provision is re-enacted as sub-s 12(c) of the Matrimonial Causes Act 1973, which provides that a marriage will be voidable if:

> ... either party to the marriage did not validly consent to it, whether in consequence of duress, mistake, unsoundness of mind or otherwise.

Despite the completeness of the provision, there are some mistakes – mistake about the nature of the ceremony or mistake about the identity of the other

---

143 [1908] P 46.

144 Law Commission Working Paper No 89 (1985), para 3.48. For an interesting review of the arguments for and against, see Clarkson (1990) 10 LS 80.

145 The Nullity of Marriage Act 1971 is based upon the Law Commission Report No 33 (1970); see s 2(c) of the 1971 Act. The position prior to the Act was that such a marriage was void but capable of ratification; see Hall (1971) CLJ 208; Cretney (1972) 35 MLR 57.

party – which would seem to be too fundamental to leave to the wait and see principle.

The uncertainty over the position as to mistake in domestic law was reflected in the English conflict of laws by uncertainty over the choice of law rule to be applied. Cheshire favoured the *lex loci celebrationis* and there is some authority to support this view.[146] Dicey took the view that consent, like capacity, should be governed by the dual domicile test.[147] The modern authorities, such as they are, are not helpful. English law has been applied to a case involving a mistake going to the nature of the foreign ceremony[148] and English law as the *lex loci celebrationis* to a case of duress[149] but there is strong support for Dicey's view,[150] although it can be argued that only the non-consenting party's law should be applied and that, if he or she consented by that law, a lack of consent by the other party's law is irrelevant. We might notice here the effect of the ease of divorce on nullity of marriage. Where divorces are difficult to obtain or cannot be granted at all, for example, in some countries where the constitution adopts the Roman Catholic teaching on marriage, then the regime of nullity appears to have been extended in order to offer relief from marriages that don't work. So, for example, the concept of mistake may be extended to mistakes about the attributes of the other party which would not be regarded as vitiating consent under English domestic law. That the husband falsely believed that his wife was a virgin at the time of the marriage or that the wife had been misled into believing that the husband was a member of the aristocracy would have no effect under English domestic law but might be grounds for nullity elsewhere. Again, any petition in England would be subject to English public policy and a trivial ground might well not be recognised. Were a ground unknown to English law to be accepted, then the usual question which has been mooted before recurs – what law is to determine the effect of the defect?

The same question arises when a common defect has a different effect in different legal systems. Under Scots law, for example, a lack of consent renders the marriage void; under English law, the same defect renders the marriage voidable. The application of the dual domicile test, in such a case, might reveal that both parties were, say, under an operative mistake by their own premarital domiciliary laws or that only one of them was.

---

146 *Mehta v Mehta* [1945] 2 All ER 690 (mistake as to whether marriage in India was monogamous or not); *Parojcic v Parojcic* [1958] 1 WLR 1280 (Davies J) (coercion of a refugee in England).

147 Important to note the distinction between the fact of consent and the method of giving consent as noted in *Apt v Apt* [1948] P 83.

148 *Mehta v Mehta* [1945] 2 All ER 690 (the woman had an English ante-nuptial domicile while the ceremony was in pre-independence India).

149 *Parojcic v Parojcic* [1958] 1 WLR 1280.

150 *Szechter v Szechter* [1971] P 286 (both parties had an ante-nuptial domicile in Poland).

Alternatively, it is possible that one of the parties could be found to be under an operative mistake by the other party's law but not by his or her own. Whether we apply both parties' laws to each party's mistake or only the mistaken party's own law to his or her error, there is a case for determining the result by the application of the law which recognises the mistake as a ground of nullity. That law should be allowed to determine whether the mistake makes the marriage void or voidable. In the case of a common operative mistake, where both parties' laws regard the marriage as defective, it would seem appropriate to apply the law which gives the greatest effect to the mistake, that is, to the law which makes the marriage void rather than to the law which makes it voidable.

While the past case law does not enable one to identify a clear and unambiguous authority, it does seem that the law is best stated by combining the proposition of Dicey and Morris with that of Cheshire, as follows: (a) that no marriage is valid if, by the law of either party's domicile, one party does not consent to marry the other;[151] and (b) that references to domicile should be construed as references to the individual's ante-nuptial domiciliary law and not to that of both parties. On this basis, one can explain the remaining prior case law.[152]

Impotence and wilful refusal to consummate

This, the most common ground for nullity petitions in England, presents special problems for the conflict of laws, as for domestic law. First, it is not one ground but two; but, although the matters can be considered separately, they are commonly pleaded together. Technically, they are distinct in that impotence involves the physical or psychological inability to consummate the marriage and is an existing state at the time the marriage takes place, whereas wilful refusal involves the psychological or other dispositional refusal of sexual intercourse with the marriage partner and does not preclude the possibility of sexual intercourse *per se*. Secondly, wilful refusal is, logically, a post marital defect and its relation back to the inception of the marriage is a fiction.

The common merger of impotence and wilful refusal under English law in practice, though they are separate heads of nullity in the statute,[153] does not obviate the need to treat them as distinct when applying the foreign law.[154]

---

151 See *Szechter v Szechter* [1971] P 286, where Simon P approved this proposition.

152 *Kenward v Kenward* [1951] P 71 (marriage void for non-compliance with formalities of *lex loci celebrationis*); *Szechter v Szechter* [1971] P 286 (parties had common ante-nuptial domicile); *Vervaeke v Smith* [1981] Fam 77 (first marriage validated on basis of the rule in *Sottomayor v De Barros (No 2)* (1879) 5 PD 94).

153 Matrimonial Causes Act 1973, s 12(a), (b).

154 As indicated by Lord Greene MR in *De Reneville v De Reneville* [1948] P 100.

Some of the early authorities were inconclusive on the choice of law and support could be found for the *lex fori*[155]and the *lex loci celebrationis*.[156] However, since the judgment of Lord Greene MR in *De Reneville v De Reneville*,[157] it seems to be accepted that such matters should be governed either by the law of the husband's domicile at the time of the marriage or the law of the matrimonial domicile.

If the issues are separated, there is every reason to apply the dual domicile test or the matrimonial home test to impotence, as that is a premarital defect. It could be argued with regard to the dual domicile test that one law only should be applied but there seems no reason to prefer the impotent party's law to that of the other. For wilful refusal, however, there is no reason to apply the premarital domiciliary law for what is a post marital defect which could, equally well, be the basis for an English divorce. Wilful refusal might have been taken out of the nullity category had it not been regarded as socially desirable that those whose religious sensitivities made the divorce option ineligible should retain some way of getting out of an unsatisfactory marriage. Viewed in this light, the case for the application of a post marital domiciliary law, that of the common matrimonial domicile, if there is one, would be the obvious choice. However, if the matter is to be wedded to the issue of impotence, then there is reason in using a common choice of law rule with this distinction. It may be acceptable for a party to plead his own impotence, but not his own wilful refusal.

An example of the resolution of these problems is afforded by *Ponticelli v Ponticelli*,[158] where the facts were as follows: the husband was domiciled in England and the wife in Italy. The parties married by proxy in Italy. At a later date, the husband petitioned for a decree of nullity on the basis of wilful refusal to consummate; this was not a ground for a decree of nullity under Italian law.

Sachs J rejected an argument that wilful refusal should be governed by the *lex loci celebrationis* and applied the law of the husband's ante-nuptial domicile, which was also his personal law at the time of the petition. Interestingly, in contrast to the view stated above, the learned judge was inclined to view both impotence and wilful refusal as personal defects to be determined by the law of the domicile. At the time of *Ponticelli*, there was no problem about the married woman's independent domicile. While the decision of the judge was correct on its facts, it does leave open the question of whether the relevant

---

155 *Easterbrook v Easterbrook* [1944] P 10 (here, the *lex fori* and the *lex loci celebrationis* were English and the domicile of the respondent was England).

156 *Robert v Robert* [1947] P 164.

157 [1948] P 100. The case itself turned on a point of jurisdiction; the petitioner not being resident in England, the court had no jurisdiction.

158 [1958] P 204 (Sachs J).

domicile is that of the husband or the wife, the petitioner or the respondent, or the domicile of the party who is *capax*. It has been proposed that the rule should be that a party should be entitled to a nullity decree if he is so entitled by the law of his domicile at the time of the marriage.[159]

It need hardly be said that the defect here is a failure to consummate the marriage, not a post consummation failure or refusal of sexual intercourse. No pretence can be made that such a later lack of sexual intercourse is related to the inception of the marriage and English law would neither grant a nullity decree in such circumstances nor recognise an annulment based on such a ground, though it could, in appropriate circumstances, both grant and recognise a divorce.

Parental consent

As has been stated above, the consistent trend of English courts has been to classify rules of foreign law relating to parental consent as matters of formality to be governed by the *lex loci celebrationis*. The reason for this is probably historical accident. In the years after Lord Hardwicke's Act of 1753, English law did not draw a clear distinction between matters of form and matters of essential validity; all matters were referred to the *lex loci celebrationis*. It was on this basis that the court found the marriage to be valid in *Simonin v Mallac*,[160] notwithstanding its non-compliance with provisions of the French Civil Code. At a later date, when *Brook v Brook*[161] introduced the distinction between matters of formal validity and matters of essential validity, the earlier case law on parental consent was explained away as turning on matters of formal validity. Thus, Cotton LJ, in *Sottomayor v De Barros (No 1)*,[162] was able to observe: 'In our opinion, this consent [parental consent] must be considered a part of the ceremony of marriage and not a matter affecting the personal capacity of the parties.' Any attempt to draw a distinction between foreign rules of law that required qualified parental consent and those that imposed an absolute prohibition was ignored in *Ogden v Ogden*[163] and the absolute provisions of Art 148 of the French Civil Code were treated as matters of formality in the same way as the qualified provisions of Arts 151 and 152 had been treated in *Simonin v Mallac*. In *Ogden v Ogden*, Gorrell Barnes P was able to assert: 'The want of consent is not incapacity; it is want of compliance with formality.' Thus, after *Ogden v Ogden*, it would seem that any foreign rule of

---

159 Jaffey (1978) 41 MLR 38, p 49.

160 (1860) 2 Sw & Tr 67; rejecting a submission by Dr Phillimore that an English court should recognise incapacities arising under the law of domicile. Recalled by Phillimore J in *Sottomayor v De Barros* (1877) 2 PD 81.

161 (1861) 9 HLC 193.

162 (1877) 3 PD 1, p 7.

163 [1908] P 46.

law making provision for obtaining parental consent is likely to be treated as a matter of formality rather than essential validity.[164]

Lack of age

In the 20th century, English law has placed clear statutory restrictions on the age at which parties can marry in England. Section 2 of the Marriage Act 1949 provides that: 'A marriage solemnised between persons either of whom is under the age of 16 shall be void.'[165] The philosophy behind such an approach was set out in an often cited quotation from the judgment of Pearce J (as he then was) in *Pugh v Pugh*, where the learned judge expressed the matter as follows:

> According to modern thought, it is considered socially and morally wrong that persons of an age at which we now believe them to be immature and provide for education should have the stresses, responsibilities and sexual freedom of marriage and the physical strain of childbirth.

In respect of lack of age, there are three factual situations that require to be distinguished. They are: (a) where the parties marry in England and one is below the age of 16; (b) where parties marry abroad when one is below the age of 16 and then come to England; and (c) where an English person goes abroad and contracts a marriage with a person below the age of 16.

In respect of the first situation, it would seem clear, even though direct authority is lacking, that parties that marry in England must comply with English law not only as to formalities but, also, as to essential validity, regardless of the personal law of the parties.[166]

In respect of the situation where parties marry abroad, English law regards the matter as governed by the dual domicile rule. Clearly, in other countries, children will develop at different rates and, while English law may set the age of capacity at 16, it is proper to take the view that another country is in a better position to set the appropriate age of capacity for its own children. Secondly, it would be a return to the judicial chauvinism of the 19th century if an English court were to sit in judgment on the age limits set down by an independent country. As Cardozo J observed: 'We are not so provincial as to say that every solution of a problem is wrong because we deal with it otherwise at home.'[167] Any doubt in the matter must have been resolved by *Alhaji Mohamed v Knott*,[168] where the facts were as follows: a man of 26

---

164 *Lodge v Lodge* (1963) 107 SJ 437.

165 Re-enacting provisions first contained in the Age of Marriage Act 1929, s 1.

166 *Pugh v Pugh* [1951] P 492; *Padolechia v Padolechia* [1968] P 314; *Vervaeke v Smith* [1983] 1 AC 145; in all three cases, it emerges as a matter of inference. See Marriage (Scotland) Act 1977, ss 1(2), 2(1)(a); see Clarkson (1990) 10 LS 80.

167 *Louks v Standard Oil Co of New York* (1918) 224 NY 99, p 111.

168 [1969] 1 QB 1 (Lord Parker LCJ; Ashworth, Blain JJ).

married a girl of 13 in Nigeria. Both parties were domiciled in Nigeria and the marriage was valid in Nigerian law. Four months later, the parties came to England. A bench of magistrates ordered that the girl was exposed to moral danger and should be taken into care under the Children and Young Persons Act 1933.

In allowing the appeal and setting aside the care order, Lord Parker CJ accepted that the marriage was valid because the girl had reached the age stipulated by Nigerian law, even though that was not an age at which she could lawfully marry in England. In giving judgment, Lord Parker observed that it was only as recently as 1929 that Parliament had set a statutory age for marriage.

A third situation that arises is the problem of the English person who goes abroad and contracts a marriage with a person below the age of 16; it would seem, following the judgment in *Pugh v Pugh*,[169] that the matter is governed by the dual domicile theory. The facts in the case were as follows: an English officer went through a Roman Catholic ceremony in Austria with a girl of 15 who had a Hungarian domicile of origin. The girl had capacity under both Hungarian and Austrian law. In 1950, after the parties had come to live in England, the wife brought a petition for nullity on grounds of non-age.

Pearce J granted the petition, reasoning that the central question was one of statutory interpretation and that the Age of Marriage Act 1929 (now, s 2 of the Marriage Act 1949) was intended to regulate the capacity to marry of all persons domiciled in the UK, wherever the marriage might be celebrated. The judgment has been attacked on the ground that the husband had capacity to contract a marriage by his *lex domicilii*, as, indeed, did the wife. However, capacity has two elements: capacity to marry and capacity to marry a particular individual; Pearce J held that this was a marriage which the man could not lawfully enter by reason of the statutory provisions. In *Pugh v Pugh*, the court was upholding the intention of the legislature to exercise a degree of control over child marriages entered into by English domiciliaries; in the earlier case of *Alhaji Mohamed v Knott*, even though the girl was 13, there was no direct connection with England or an English domiciliary. It is perfectly consistent with international law for a legislature to seek some control over the activities of its nationals or domiciliaries beyond its own territory;[170] it is quite another matter to seek to impose one's own standards and values upon the citizens of an independent State.

---

169 [1951] P 482.

170 Sexual Offences (Conspiracy and Incitement) Act 1996 (directed to the protection of children in foreign countries in respect of conduct initiated in England).

Prohibited degrees of relationship

Most legal systems impose some restrictions on who X can marry. The restriction may be based on blood relationship (consanguinity) or relationship by marriage (affinity). The former is dictated by eugenic considerations and the latter is determined by religious, ethical or sociological considerations. The broad tendency has been to liberalise the restrictions in the last 150 years.[171] The modern law commences with *Brook v Brook*,[172] where a man seeking to marry his deceased wife's sister went to Denmark and went through a ceremony of marriage. Such a marriage was valid in Denmark but unlawful in England and, at a later date, the marriage was held void by the House of Lords. Two propositions emerge from the judgments: (a) that there is a distinction between questions of formal validity and essential validity; and (b) that questions relating to the prohibited degrees are matters of essential validity to be determined by the ante-nuptial domicile of the parties. It has been pointed out that the text of this judgment and that of *Mette v Mette*[173] are not conclusive in the controversy between the dual domicile doctrine and that of the intended matrimonial home doctrine; be that as it may, after *Brook v Brook*, it became usual to interpret the case as having decided in favour of the ante-nuptial domicile. In *Sottomayor v De Barros*,[174] Cotton LJ considered that questions relating to the prohibited degrees were governed by the ante-nuptial domicile and that would appear to have been the opinion of Gorrell Barnes P in the less than satisfactory judgment in *Ogden v Ogden*.[175]

The subsequent case law appears to indicate that the ante-nuptial domicile test is applied to matters of consanguinity and affinity. Thus, in *Re Paine*,[176] where a marriage was celebrated in Germany between a man domiciled in Germany and his deceased wife's sister, who was domiciled in England, the dual domicile doctrine was applied to hold the marriage void.[177] In the later case of *Cheni v Cheni*,[178] a marriage between an uncle and niece that was lawful by the law of both parties' ante-nuptial domicile was held valid in England. Simon P rejected the argument that because the marriage would have been within the prohibited degrees by English domestic law it should therefore be held to violate public policy.

---

171 See the Marriage Act 1949, Sched 1; Marriage (Enabling) Act 1960, replacing the Deceased Wife's Sister's Marriage Act 1907; Deceased Brother's Widow's Marriage Act 1921; Marriage (Prohibited Degrees of Relationship) Act 1931. See, also, Marriage (Prohibited Degrees of Relationship) Act 1986.

172 (1861) 9 HLC 193.

173 (1859) 1 Sw & Tr 416 (domiciled Englishman marries his deceased wife's half sister in Frankfurt; marriage held invalid).

174 (1877) 3 PD 1, p 7.

175 [1908] P 46.

176 [1940] Ch 46.

177 The marriage was entered into prior to the Deceased Wife's Sister's Marriage Act 1907.

178 [1965] P 85.

An implied recognition that matters of consanguinity and affinity are governed by the ante-nuptial domicile is afforded by the Marriage (Enabling) Act 1960. The overall object of the legislation is to further reduce the prohibited degrees under English law so as to permit a man to marry his divorced or deceased wife's sister, niece or aunt. However, s 1(3) of the legislation provides:

> ... this section does not validate a marriage if either party to it is at the time of the marriage domiciled in a country outside Great Britain and, under the law of that country, there cannot be a valid marriage between the parties.

Thus, if X were to marry in England or outside England his deceased wife's sister, Y, who was domiciled in a country where such a marriage was prohibited, then s 1(3) requires the court to apply the law of both parities' ante-nuptial domicile; in this particular case, the marriage would be invalid even if the intended matrimonial home was in England.

Therefore, in respect of consanguinity and affinity the preponderance of the authority and statutory provision supports the doctrine of the ante nuptial domicile.

Previous marriage

The difficulties that might arise in respect of capacity and prior marriage have been obvious from the time of *Shaw v Gould*.[179] Clearly, questions can arise if X wishes to marry Y in England and the prior divorce of Y is not recognised in England or, indeed, in the ante-nuptial domicile of Y. In such circumstances, questions naturally arise as to whether Y has capacity under her ante-nuptial domiciliary law. An example of the practical difficulties that can arise is provided by *Padolechia v Padolechia*,[180] where the facts were as follows: a man who was domiciled in Italy married a woman who was domiciled there. At a later date, he obtained a divorce in Mexico. This was not recognised in Italy. He then went to live in Denmark. He came to London on a day trip and married a woman domiciled in Denmark and then returned to live there. At a later date, he sought a decree of nullity, asserting that he lacked capacity under Italian law.

Simon P applied the ante-nuptial domicile test and concluded that the husband lacked capacity to enter into the second marriage; a decree of nullity was therefore granted. No attempt was made to apply the test of the intended matrimonial home.

In considering previous marriages, three factual situations need to be considered, namely:

---

179 (1868) LR 3 HL 55.
180 [1968] P 314.

(a) where the divorce or annulment is recognised by English law but not by the law of the domicile;

(b) where the divorce or annulment is recognised by the law of the domicile but not by English law; and

(c) where there is a restriction on the remarriage of divorced persons.

It is proposed to examine each of these in turn.

Where the divorce is recognised in England but not by the law of the domicile

The earliest cases indicate that the courts regarded capacity to marry as the principal question and this would be referred to the ante-nuptial domicile. If a problem arose as to the recognition of a prior divorce, then this was regarded as an incidental question, to be determined by the ante nuptial domicile (the *lex causae*) rather than the *lex fori*. This was illustrated by *R v Brentwood Superintendent Registrar of Marriages ex p Arais*,[181] where the facts were: an Italian man, domiciled in Switzerland, married a Swiss woman. The parties were then divorced and the wife remarried. The divorce was not recognised in Italy. The man could not remarry in Switzerland because Swiss law referred the matter to the *lex nationalis*. The Divisional Court held that he could not remarry in England because he lacked capacity under the law of his ante-nuptial domicile.

In this case, the primary question is that of capacity to marry, but the secondary or incidental question, the recognition of the divorce, is determined by *the lex causae* (the law of the ante-nuptial domicile) and not the *lex fori*.[182] The inconvenience of this result was removed by s 7 of the Recognition of Divorces and Legal Separations Act 1971, which provided that 'where the validity of a divorce obtained in any country is entitled to recognition ... neither spouse shall be precluded from remarrying on the ground that the validity of the divorce would not be recognised in any other country'. The present relevance of *Padolechia v Padolechia* and *R v Brentwood Superintendent Registrar of Marriages ex p Arias* is that, in both cases, capacity to marry was determined by recourse to the law of the ante-nuptial domicile.

By the mid 1970s, the attention of the courts had been directed to the problems posed by the recognition of divorces and decrees of nullity and a slightly different approach is indicated by *Perrini v Perrini*,[183] where the facts were as follows: an American woman, X, domiciled in New Jersey, married a domiciled Italian in Italy. The marriage was not consummated, so X returned to New Jersey and obtained a decree of nullity. The Italian man then came to

---

181 [1968] 2 QB 956.

182 The approach also adopted in *Padolechia v Padolechia* [1968] P 314.

183 [1979] Fam 84 (Sir George Baker P).

England, where he married Y, a domiciled Englishwoman. At a later date, Y sought a decree of nullity, claiming that the husband was still married.

Baker P rejected the petition for nullity and ruled that the marriage was valid. Although the judgment is open to a number of interpretations,[184] it would seem that the learned judge held the marriage to be valid either because the decree of nullity was recognised in England or because there had been compliance with the intended matrimonial home test. This flexible approach was to some extent followed in the case of *Lawrence v Lawrence*,[185] where the facts were: a woman domiciled in Brazil obtained a divorce in Nevada, USA, and thereafter married an Englishman. The divorce was not recognised in Brazil but was recognised in England. At a later date, an English court was required to determine the validity of the second marriage.

Anthony Lincoln J and the Court of Appeal upheld the validity of the marriage by reference to a considerable number of reasons. Among these were: (a) the principle that recognition of the divorce entailed the right to remarry; (b) that capacity should be determined either by the law of the intended matrimonial home or the law of the country with which the marriage had the closest and most real connection; and (c) by a judicial extension of s 7 of the Recognition of Divorces and Legal Separations Act 1971.[186]

The review by the Law Commission resulted in a proposal that the law should be the same in respect of prior divorces, regardless of whether the divorce is followed by a remarriage in England or abroad. The relevant provision is set out in s 50 of the Family Law Act 1986, which reads:

(1) Where, in any part of the UK–

    (a) a divorce or annulment has been granted by a court of civil jurisdiction; or

    (b) the validity of a divorce or annulment is recognised by virtue of this Part, the fact that the divorce or annulment would not be recognised elsewhere shall not preclude either party to the marriage from re-marrying in that part of the UK or cause the remarriage of either party (wherever the remarriage takes place) to be treated as invalid in that part.

The effect of this provision is that any incapacity under the personal law is set aside and the remarriage is valid.

---

184 The judgment could be supported either (a) because the decree of nullity was recognised; or (b) under the rule in *Sottomayor v De Barros (No 2)* (1879) 5 PD 94.

185 [1985] Fam 106.

186 See Jaffey (1985) 48 MLR 465; Carter (1985) 101 LQR 496.

Where the divorce is recognised by the law of the domicile but not by English law

Having regard to the liberal rules on the recognition of foreign decrees, this is not likely to be a common occurrence. An illustration is afforded by the Canadian case of *Schwebel v Ungar*,[187] where the facts were as follows: a husband and wife, who were domiciled in Hungary, decided to settle in Israel. The husband divorced the wife by Jewish *ghet* (that is, extra-judicial divorce) in Italy. Both parties then acquired a separate domicile in Israel. The wife then, on a short visit to Ontario, married a man. At a later date, the man sought a decree of nullity, claiming the first marriage had not been ended. The *ghet* was not recognised in Hungary or Ontario but was recognised in Israel.

The Ontario Court of Appeal ruled that the second marriage was valid because the woman had obtained a divorce and it was recognised by the law of her domicile; at the time of the second marriage, she was regarded as a single person by the law of her domicile, so, by applying the test of the ante-nuptial domicile, the marriage was valid. Such a case is the converse of *Lawrence v Lawrence*, in that the divorce is not recognised by the *lex fori* but is recognised by the *lex causae*.

Restrictions on the marriage of divorced persons

In the normal situation, when a decree of divorce has been made absolute, the two parties will be free to remarry. However, there are a limited number of cases in the books where restrictions have been placed on one or other party. Such cases are unlikely to arise today as they are at variance with contemporary views as to personal autonomy and the equality of the sexes; they are also a legacy of a time when divorce proceedings were concerned to determine fault.

In *Scott v AG*,[188] a husband obtained a divorce in Cape Colony, where he was domiciled. By the law of Cape Colony, the guilty party was not permitted to marry until the innocent party had remarried. The wife came to England and married a second husband. Hannen P held that the effect of the divorce was to make the wife a single woman who was capable of coming to England and acquiring a distinct domicile and, thus, remarrying. However, in the later case of *Warter v Warter*,[189] Hannen P explained that, in the earlier decision, the restriction was imposed on only one party and would therefore not be recognised in England because it was penal in substance. In *Warter v Warter*, a wife, having been divorced on grounds of adultery, was subject to a restriction under the Indian Divorce Act 1869, which provided that neither party should

---

187 (1963) 42 DLR (2d) 622, Ontario Court of Appeal; (1964) 48 DLR (2d) 644, Supreme Court of Canada.

188 (1886) 11 PD 128 (Hannen P).

189 (1890) 15 PD 152 (Hannen P).

remarry within six months of the decree absolute. The restriction was upheld and the marriage declared invalid.

It would seem from the decided cases that if the incapacity arises from the divorce proceedings themselves then it will be respected by the English courts, but if it is a restriction imposed on a single party then it will be classified as penal and unenforceable on grounds of public policy.

Capacity to contract a polygamous marriage

Problems sometimes arise because some countries permit polygamous marriages while others do not. The topic of capacity to enter into a polygamous marriage belongs within the general area of essential validity. Having regard to the problems posed by polygamous marriages, it is proposed to deal with this matter in detail below. It should be noted here that, in the much discussed case of *Radwan v Radwan (No 2)*,[190] Cumming-Bruce J held that capacity to contract a polygamous marriage should be governed by the intended matrimonial home doctrine. Although the judgment of Cumming-Bruce J was much criticised, the learned judge did raise the question in the course of his judgment as to whether the common law should openly recognise that there might have to be different tests for choice of law purposes according to the type of incapacity involved and that it was a slightly artificial exercise to try and divide all cases into those favouring the dual domicile approach and those within the scope of the intended matrimonial home.

POLYGAMOUS MARRIAGES

Introduction

There are a number of countries in the world which permit polygamy.[191] In broad terms, a polygamous marriage is a marriage under which a man is permitted to take more than one wife. To be more accurate, where a man may have more than one wife, the marriage is said to polygamous; where the wife may have more than one husband, the marriage is said to be polyandrous. However, because the latter is rare, it is normal to refer to both situations as polygamy.

---

190 [1973] Fam 35.

191 The most significant are African countries under systems of customary law and those countries that operate under a system of Islamic law.

The approach of the English courts can be traced back to the judgment of Lord Penzance in *Hyde v Hyde*;[192] it will be recalled that this case concerned an Englishman who had gone through a Mormon ceremony of marriage in 1853 and, in 1866, filed a divorce petition in England. In the course of giving judgment, Lord Penzance ruled that a potentially polygamous marriage such as Hyde's was to be equated with an actually polygamous marriage and that such unions were excluded form the remedial jurisdiction of the matrimonial courts. The rule in *Hyde v Hyde* did not prevent such marriages from being recognised but it prevented applications being made for decrees of divorce, nullity or judicial separation.

After 1866, it became important to determine whether a union was monogamous or not and, while each case turned on the inferences to be drawn from the facts, the case law did enable a number of propositions to be stated with a reasonable degree of confidence.

(a) the nature of the marriage was not influenced by the fact that the husband did not exercise his right to select a second wife – a potentially polygamous union was in the same position as an actually polygamous marriage;[193]

(b) the court would normally seek to identify the nature of the marriage at the time of its inception;[194]

(c) if a husband took a second or third wife, no distinction was to be made between them;

(d) the fact that the marriage was not according to Christian rite does not prevent the marriage being monogamous;[195]

(e) it is for the *lex loci celebrationis* to determine the nature and incidents of the union and then for English law to adjudge whether the union is monogamous or polygamous;[196]

(f) the nature of the marriage is not determined by the personal law of the parties;[197]

(g) the nature of a marriage is not determined by the procedures available for its dissolution;[198] and

---

192 (1866) LR 1 P & D 130. On the social background to the case, see Bartholomew (1952) 15 MLR 35; Poulter (1976) 25 ICLQ 475. Interestingly, the wedding was celebrated by Brigham Young (1801–77), who had led the Mormon migration to Utah in 1846.

193 *Hyde v Hyde* (1866) LR 1 P & D 130.

194 *Sowa v Sowa* [1961] P 70.

195 *Brinkley v AG* (1890) 15 PD 76; *Spivack v Spivack* (1930) 46 TLR 243; *Penhas v Tan Soo Eng* [1953] AC 304.

196 *Lee v Lau* [1967] P 14.

197 *Chetti v Chetti* [1909] P 67; *R v Hammersmith Marriage Registrar* [1917] 1 KB 634; *Quereshi v Quereshi* [1972] Fam 173.

198 *Nachimson v Nachimson* [1930] P 217.

(h) it is now recognised that a marriage can change its nature. Thus, a potentially polygamous marriage may become polygamous if the parties acquire an English domicile.[199] In many cases, it will be necessary to determine the nature of the marriage at the time of the court proceedings.[200]

Before turning to a number of substantive issues, it is important to note that a valid polygamous marriage cannot be lawfully contracted in England. A marriage celebrated in polygamous form without a civil ceremony would be invalid.[201] The formalities adopted by the Marriage Act 1949 are not adapted to the polygamous marriage. Thus, in *Quereshi v Quereshi*,[202] where a civil ceremony was followed by a ceremony according to Islamic rites, it was accepted that the civil ceremony created a valid monogamous union.

This state of affairs is clearly defensible. English law accords respect and recognition to polygamous unions contracted abroad but, in respect of marriages contracted within England, the legislature is entitled to set out its own conditions. Most marriages contracted in countries where polygamy is permitted are actually monogamous. But, English law has worked on the basis that the distinction lies not between the actually monogamous and the actually polygamous but between those which are *de jure* monogamous marriages and those which are not so.

Capacity of persons domiciled in England to contract polygamous marriages

The main problem in the area of polygamy arises where a person whose personal law does not permit him or her to marry polygamously marries one whose personal law does allow it, in a country where polygamy is recognised and according to a form suitable to it.

As indicated above, questions of capacity to marry are normally governed by the dual domicile rule. It would therefore follow from this that, if an Englishman contracted a polygamous marriage abroad, then this would normally be void. Thus, in *Re Bethell*,[203] a domiciled Englishman contracted a marriage in Bechuanaland (now Botswana) with a woman of the Barolong tribe; under the native law, he was entitled to take other secondary wives. Stirling J held the marriage to be void, partly on the basis that the English domiciliary lacked capacity to enter into such a marriage.

---

199 *Ali v Ali* [1968] P 564.
200 *Parkasho v Singh* [1968] P 223.
201 Marriage Act 1949; *R v Bham* [1966] 1 QB 159; *Quereshi v Quereshi* [1972] Fam 173, p 182.
202 [1972] Fam 173.
203 (1888) 38 Ch D 220.

In considering this issue further, it is necessary to refer to a number of statutory provisions. Sections 11 and 14 of the Matrimonial Causes Act 1973 read, in part, as follows:

(11) A marriage celebrated after 31 July 1971 shall be void on the following grounds only, that is to say–

...

(b) that at the time of the marriage either party was already lawfully married;

...

(d) in the case of a polygamous marriage entered into outside England and Wales, that either party was at the time of the marriage domiciled in England and Wales.

For the purposes of paragraph (d) of this sub-section, a marriage may be polygamous although at its inception neither party has any spouse additional to the other.

...

(14) Where, apart from this Act, any matter affecting the validity of a marriage would fall to be determined (in accordance with the rules of private international law) by reference to the law of a country outside England and Wales, nothing in s 11 ... above shall–

(a) preclude the determination of that matter as aforesaid; or

(b) require the application to the marriage of the grounds ... there mentioned except as so far as applicable in accordance with those rules.

In considering these sub-sections, it is important to pay regard to the legislative history of these provisions.[204]

Against this statutory background, it is important to consider the judgment in *Radwan v Radwan (No 2)*,[204a] where the facts were as follows: W2, a woman domiciled in England, contracted a polygamous marriage in 1951 at the Egyptian Consulate in Paris with H, who had a wife in Egypt. The matrimonial home was established in Egypt and, in 1952, H divorced W1 by *talaq*. Subsequently, the parties came to live in England and, during divorce proceedings, the Family Division was required *inter alia* to rule on the validity of the 1950 marriage and whether W2 had capacity to enter into a polygamous marriage.

Cumming-Bruce J held that since the evidence on French law was, at best, equivocal, it must be presumed that the ceremony was valid by the *lex loci celebrationis*. In respect of the question as to whether the woman domiciled in

204 Matrimonial Causes Act 1973, s 14 derives from the Nullity of Marriage Act 1971, s 4; s 11 derives from the Nullity of Marriage Act 1971, s 1, but s 11(d) derives from the Matrimonial Proceedings (Polygamous Marriages) Act 1972, s 4, which inserted a new para (d) into the Nullity of Marriage Act 1971, s 1.

204a [1973] Fam 35 (Cumming-Bruce J).

England had capacity to enter into a polygamous marriage, the learned judge concluded that the matter was free from direct and binding authority and that capacity was to be determined by the law of the intended matrimonial home. The judgment was then subject to some criticism[205] in various legal journals. It should be noted that, while Cumming-Bruce J considered the effect of the legislative changes, they were not binding in respect of a marriage concluded in 1950.

After 1973, if *Radwan v Radwan (No 2)* was correctly decided, then, if a person domiciled in England contracts a polygamous marriage abroad, s 11(d)[206] will not apply if the intention is to establish a matrimonial home abroad; this is because s 14 gives precedence to any relevant rule of private international law. However, in respect of a person domiciled in England contracting a polygamous marriage abroad with the intention of residing in England, there was a risk that the marriage would be held void. This could operate harshly in respect of a person of Indian or Pakistani origin who went to Pakistan or India and went through a marriage in Islamic form and then brought his wife to live in England and might then find that the marriage was regarded as void.

Not surprisingly, this attracted a degree of criticism[207] and so the Law Commission proceeded to investigate the matter. However, before the Law Commission report was published, the Court of Appeal gave judgment in the case of *Hussain v Hussain*.[208] The facts of the case were in line with the difficulties predicted in the literature: H, domiciled in England, married in Moslem form in Pakistan in 1979 Although the marriage was in polygamous form, it was, at all times, monogamous. At a later date, when the wife petitioned for judicial separation, the husband asserted that the marriage was void under s 11(d) of the Matrimonial Causes Act 1973.

The Court of Appeal,[209] after noting the unusual legislative history of s 11(d), ruled that the marriage in question was not void and that the subsection should be given a very narrow interpretation. It was argued: (a) that

---

205 Against: Karsten (1973) 36 MLR 291; Pearl (1973) CLJ 43; Wade [1973] 22 ICLQ 571. For: Stone [1983] Fam Law 76; Jaffey (1978) 41 MLR 38. It should be borne in mind that (a) the judgment turned on the common law position in 1950; and (b) the learned judge had the benefit of full argument from two senior counsel who would later serve as High Court judges (Ewbank QC and Davies QC) and, after full consideration of the prior authorities, the learned judge concluded: (1) that there was no prior authority that asserted that the dual domicile doctrine applied in all cases of capacity; (2) that the premise upon which subsequent legislative changes had been made was not conclusive as to the common law position; and (3) that there was nothing objectionable in individual aspects of capacity being subject to different choice of law rules.

206 Inserted into the Nullity of Marriage Act 1971 by the Matrimonial Proceedings (Polygamous Marriages) Act 1972, s 4.

207 Cretney (1972) 116 SJ 654; Poulter (1976) ICLQ 475, pp 503–08 (a detailed account of the likely difficulties); James (1979) 42 MLR 533.

208 [1983] Fam 26.

209 *Ibid* (Ormrod, Griffiths, Slade LJJ).

the sub-section only applied to the marriage in question; (b) that it did not apply in respect of a marriage that was incapable at the time of its inception of becoming actually polygamous by virtue of the personal laws of the parties; and (c) that the husband lacked capacity by virtue of the provisions of s 11(b). One feature of Ormrod LJ's judgment that attracted criticism was that the learned judge appeared to cast doubt on the principle that the nature of the ceremony according to the *lex loci celebrationis* and not the law of the parties' domicile should determine whether a marriage was monogamous or polygamous.[210] It may be that, in *Hussain v Hussain*, the important fact was not the reasoning but the result; there is some indication that the Court of Appeal decided on the necessary result and then produced reasons to justify it. As Ormrod LJ observed, in respect of a decision in favour of the husband:

> It would mean that all marriages contracted abroad by persons domiciled in the country, in accordance with the local law, would be void if that law permitted polygamy in any form. The repercussions on the Muslim community alone in this country would be widespread and profound.

The other feature of *Hussain* that gave rise to concern was that, if the facts had been that the woman had travelled to Pakistan and married a local man whose personal law allowed him to have more than one wife, then the marriage would have been actually polygamous and void and under s 11(d).[211] Despite the obvious sense of *Hussain*, it worked only in the case of a domiciled Englishman marrying in a country which allows polygamy, not of a domiciled Englishwoman marrying in a country doing the same thing, even if she and her new husband intend to make England their permanent home. The man's marriage is valid and the woman's marriage is void because the basis of the *Hussain* judgment is that the marriage is monogamous because the husband is domiciled in England and cannot, therefore, take any further wives.

The question of capacity to enter into a polygamous marriage was investigated by the Law Commission in two reports.[212] The recommendation was that s 11(d) of the Matrimonial Causes Act 1973 should be repealed and replaced with a provision that made clear that men and women domiciled in the UK had the capacity to enter into a potentially polygamous marriage (that is, one polygamous in form but monogamous in fact) outside the UK. The recommendations formed the basis of Part II of the Private International Law (Miscellaneous Provisions) Act 1995.[213]

---

210 Schuz (1983) 46 MLR 653; Pearl [1983] CLJ 26; Briggs (1983) 32 ICLQ 737; Carter (1982) 53 BYIL 298.

211 Assuming that capacity is governed by the dual domicile rule; the approach of the Court of Appeal in *Hussain* is difficult to reconcile with *Radwan v Radwan (No 2)* [1973] Fam 35.

212 Law Commission Working Paper No 83 (1982); Law Commission Report No 146 (1985).

213 Private International Law (Miscellaneous Provisions) Act 1995, ss 5–8.

The central provision is s 5(1), which reads:

> A marriage entered into outside England and Wales between parties, neither of whom is already married, is not void under the law of England and Wales on the ground that it is entered into under a law which permits polygamy and that either party is domiciled in England and Wales.

The effect of this provision is to give effect to the spirit of the *Hussain*[214] judgment; the provisions are extended to Scotland by s 7. The combined effect of s 5(1) and s 7 is that persons of either sex domiciled in England, Wales or Scotland now have legal capacity to enter into a marriage outside the UK which, although celebrated in a polygamous form, is not actually polygamous. To ensure this objective is achieved, s 11(d) of the Matrimonial Causes Act has been amended[215] to read:

> For the purposes of para (d) of this sub-section, a marriage is not polygamous if at its inception neither party has any spouse additional to the other.

It is important to note that s 5(1) is directed to the parties, 'neither of whom is already married'; thus, it will not affect the domiciled Englishwoman who goes to Egypt and intentionally and knowingly goes through a polygamous form of marriage with a man already married with the intention of settling in Egypt.[216]

The provisions of s 5(1) are wider than *Hussain*, in that protection is accorded to both women and men. Thus, if an English domiciled woman married in Pakistan a man domiciled there, then such a marriage (a) would have been void as polygamous under both *Hussain* and the former s 11(d); but (b) the marriage will now be valid under s 5(1). The reform ends any discriminatory treatment of women under the prior law.

Section 5(2) of the legislation provides that

> ... this section shall not affect the determination of the validity of a marriage by reference to the law of another country to the extent that it falls to be so determined in accordance with the rules of private international law.

The Law Commission were of the opinion that the purpose of this clause was to be similar to that of s 14 of the Matrimonial Causes Act 1973. However, there must be some doubt as to whether this is correct since, if the intended matrimonial home doctrine were adopted, s 14 would enable a court to bypass s 11. It would seem that the purpose of s 5(2) is to limit s 5(1) to questions of capacity to contract a polygamous marriage and that any other questions relating to validity (formal or essential) continue to be governed by the appropriate rule of private international law. Thus, if an unmarried English domiciliary were to marry in Pakistan, then any aspect relating to polygamy

---

214 *Hussain v Hussain* [1983] Fam 26.
215 Private International Law (Miscellaneous Provisions) Act 1995, s 8(2), Sched 1, para 2.
216 It would not come within the proviso to the Matrimonial Causes Act 1973, s 11(d).

would be validated under s 5(1) but any difficulty as to the form of the ceremony or essential validity (for example, lack of age) would continue to be governed by the appropriate rule of English private international law.

The provisions of s 5 are for the most part made retrospective in England and Wales[217] by the operation of s 6. Thus, if a woman domiciled in England were to marry by Islamic rights an unmarried Pakistani in Pakistan in 1993, it is probable that such a marriage would have been declared void. However, such a marriage is now to be regarded as valid under s 6. By s 6(2), a marriage outside the scope of *Hussain v Hussain* (that is, before 31 July 1971 or in the case of a domiciled woman marrying a man whose law permits polygamy) will not be retrospectively validated if it has been followed by a subsequent valid marriage.[218] There will be no retrospective validation in respect of a marriage that has been annulled[219] and any retrospective effect will not extend to matters of succession, benefits, pension rights or tax.[220]

Change in the nature of the marriage

Just as the dissolubility of a marriage can be changed by a change of domicile or habitual residence – for example, a couple domiciled and marrying in Ireland, where divorce was restricted, can change the dissolubility of their marriage by either of them becoming domiciled or habitually resident in England and, thus, obtaining access to the divorce jurisdiction of the English court – so a marriage originally polygamous or potentially polygamous, can become monogamous. Before the passing of the Matrimonial Proceedings (Polygamous Marriage) Act 1972,[221] there was an incentive for the court to find that a potentially polygamous marriage had been converted into a monogamous one as only then could the parties have recourse to the English matrimonial law. The issue also arose in succession cases and in criminal proceedings for bigamy.

Polygamy to monogamy

At one time, it appears to have been the law that the nature of a marriage was fixed irrevocably at the time of its inception.[222]

However, now there is no doubt that a marriage that is potentially polygamous at its inception may become monogamous as a result of a

---

217 Scotland was omitted because it was felt that its law did not need correction.
218 Private International Law (Miscellaneous Provisions) Act 1995, s 6(2).
219 *Ibid*, s 6(3)–(5).
220 *Ibid*, s 6(6).
221 See, now, the Matrimonial Causes Act 1973, s 47.
222 *Hyde v Hyde* (1866) LR 1 P & M 130.

subsequent event or a change in the law. There are a number of authorities in which the court has been obliged to consider whether the event in question was sufficient to change the nature of the marriage. Thus, in *The Sinha Peerage Claim*, the court was prepared to accept that, where the husband had joined a Hindu sect that practised monogamy, that was sufficient for the potentially polygamous marriage to be regarded as monogamous.[223] Conversion may be the consequence of non-compliance with a religious requirement; thus, in *Cheni v Cheni*,[224] a potentially polygamous marriage would be regarded as monogamous if it were no longer childless. The act that effects the conversion may be independent of the parties; a change in the law of the country to prohibit polygamy will be sufficient to convert a potentially polygamous marriage into a monogamous union. An example is provided by the case of *Parkasho v Singh*, where the potentially polygamous marriage was regarded as monogamous after the Hindu Marriage Act 1955 prohibited the husband from taking further wives.[225]

There is little doubt that a change in domicile can result in a change in the nature of the marriage. This was illustrated by the judgment in *Ali v Ali*, where the facts were as follows: H and W entered a potentially polygamous marriage in India. In 1961, H acquired an English domicile and W left him. H petitioned for divorce on the grounds of desertion. W cross-petitioned on the basis of H's adultery since 1964. The jurisdiction of the court at that time depended on whether the marriage was monogamous or not.

Cumming-Bruce J held that the court had jurisdiction. The learned judge considered that, by acquiring an English domicile, the husband had agreed to submit to English matrimonial law and its restriction upon taking a second wife during the subsistence of the marriage. Such conduct, the judge considered, was sufficient to confer upon the marriage a monogamous character. The emphasis on domicile at the relevant date and submission to English matrimonial law by virtue of English domicile appears again in *Hussain v Hussain*.

It is arguable that the distinction is not so important after the enactment of the Matrimonial Proceedings (Polygamous Marriages) Act 1972 and that any case prior to that date should be read with a degree of caution.[226]

---

223 *The Sinha Peerage Claim* [1946] 1 All ER 348 (House of Lord Committee of Privileges).

224 [1965] P 85 (Simon P).

225 *Parkasho v Singh* [1968] P 233; see, also, *R v Sagoo* [1975] QB 885 (Kenya Sikh Marriage Ordinance 1960).

226 That would seem to have been the view of Ormrod LJ in *Hussain v Hussain* [1983] Fam 26.

Monogamy to polygamy

Even though direct authority[227] is lacking, it would seem that a marriage that is monogamous at inception does not change its status even though the husband may subsequently go through a polygamous ceremony of marriage. Although there would seem to be no direct authority in the English courts, the matter was examined in detail by the Privy Council in *AG of Ceylon v Read,*[228] where the facts were as follows: Alan and Edna Reid contracted a monogamous Roman Catholic marriage in 1933. In 1957, the parties ceased living together. In June 1959, Mr Reid converted to the Muslim faith. In July 1959, he was married by the Registrar of Muslim Marriages to one Fatima Pansy. In 1961, he was charged with bigamy.

The Privy Council upheld the judgment of the Supreme Court of Ceylon in quashing the conviction for bigamy and, in doing so, impliedly recognised that the second marriage was a valid polygamous marriage. The Privy Council accepted the argument of counsel for Mr Reid that: (a) the second marriage was a valid marriage by reason of compliance with personal and religious law; but (b) from the perspective of Mrs Reid, the conduct of her husband was adultery, entitling her to a dissolution of the first marriage. Such a set of facts could not arise in England, although the status of the first marriage is important because intercourse with a second wife under a polygamous marriage will not constitute adultery.[229] So, a husband might well be found to be validly married to a second wife and, thus, have a defence to a charge of adultery yet at the same time, from the perspective of the prior, monogamous first wife, would be committing adultery. Although examples in England are rare, the case of *Nabi v Heaton*[230] is illustrative, in that a monogamous marriage in England was followed by a polygamous marriage in Pakistan.

It would seem, as a matter of principle, that the status of the wife under the first monogamous marriage is unaffected by any ceremony of a polygamous nature that her husband may choose to go through. The status of the first monogamous marriage does not change.

---

227 Doubtless because any marriage would be void under the Matrimonial Causes Act 1973, s 11(b).

228 [1965] AC 720; 1 All ER 812.

229 *Onobrauche v Onobrauche* [1978] 8 Fam Law 107.

230 [1981] 1 WLR 1052 (Vinelott J); [1983] 1 WLR 626 (appeal allowed by consent).

Recognition of polygamous marriage

The general principle today is that a polygamous marriage will be recognised unless there is some good public policy reason to the contrary. It has to be borne in mind that the original remarks made by Lord Penzance were carefully restricted to the question of polygamous marriages and matrimonial relief. There is some reason to believe that the remarks were taken out of context and used to assert that polygamous marriages should, in general, be unrecognised.[231] This was noted by Lord Greene MR in *Baindail v Baindail*,[232] where he observed:

> Lord Penzance quite clearly saw how undesirable it would be to attempt to lay down any comprehensive rule as to the manner in which a polygamous marriage ought to be regarded by the courts of this country for purposes different from that with which he was immediately concerned.

> In each case one has to pay proper regard to the relevant statutory provision and to the question as to whether there is any legitimate issue of public policy.[233]

The original obstacle to matrimonial relief was ended by the Matrimonial Proceedings (Polygamous Marriages) Act 1972,[234] and these provisions are now contained in s 47 of the Matrimonial Causes Act 1973[235] which provides that matrimonial relief shall be available in respect of a polygamous marriage.

It has long been accepted that a polygamous marriage is a barrier to a subsequent monogamous marriage in England. In *Baindail v Baindail*,[236] the respondent, having gone through a potentially polygamous marriage in India in 1928, then went through a ceremony at Holborn Registry Office in 1939 with the petitioner. Lord Greene MR held that an English court would recognise the polygamous marriage as a barrier to a subsequent monogamous marriage, even though the prior marriage might not be accorded full recognition for all purposes. In such circumstances, the second marriage was bigamous and the petitioner was entitled to a decree of nullity.

Secondly, there is little doubt that the children of a polygamous marriage will be regarded as legitimate[237] and will be entitled to succeed to property,

---

231 *Re Bethell* (1887) 38 Ch D 220; *R v Hammersmith Marriage Registrar* [1917] 1 KB 634; *R v Naguib* [1917] 1 KB 359.

232 [1946] 1 All ER 342, p 345.

233 *Mohamed v Knott* [1969] 1 QB 1.

234 Matrimonial Proceedings (Polygamous Marriages) Act 1972, s 1; for the prior law, see *Risk v Risk* [1951] P 50.

235 As amended by the Private International Law (Miscellaneous Provisions) Act 1995, Sched 1, para 2.

236 [1946] P 122; 1 All ER, CA (Lord Greene MR, Bucknill and Morton LJJ), upholding [1945] 2 All ER 374 (Barnard J).

237 *The Sinha Peerage Claim* [1946] 1 All ER 348 (decided by the House of Lords Committee of Privileges in 1939, *per* Lord Maugham LC).

save in respect of some entailed interests and titles of honour.[238] Thus, in *Bamgbose v Daniel*,[239] it was held that the children of nine polygamous marriages were entitled to succeed after the death of their father. Thirdly, there is no doubt that a spouse under a polygamous marriage is entitled to succeed on intestacy[240] and the Privy Council has accepted that, where there is more than one wife, then the entitlement is proportionate.[241]

In cases where the claim is made under the terms of the Inheritance (Provision for Family and Dependants) Act 1975, a wife under a polygamous marriage has *locus standi* to claim. In *In re Sahota*,[242] the deceased left his entire estate to the second of his polygamous wives. Foster J, at a preliminary hearing, determined that the first wife was entitled to claim as a 'wife' under the legislation. In reaching this conclusion, the learned judge followed the approach of Dunn J in *Chaudhry v Chaudhry*,[243] who had ruled that a spouse under a polygamous marriage was entitled to claim under the Married Women's Property Act 1882. In like terms, the wife under a polygamous marriage was accorded protection in respect of the family home and domestic violence under the terms of the Family Law Act 1996.[244]

The extent to which a polygamous marriage is now recognised is well illustrated by the judgment of the Divisional Court in *Mohamed v Knott*, where the court quashed an order made under the Children and Young Person's Act 1933 upon evidence of a valid polygamous marriage with a girl of 13, notwithstanding the concerns of the court as to the welfare of the young person.[245]

In respect of social security legislation, the original approach of the National Insurance Commissioner was that the word 'wife' did not extend to the polygamous marriage, actual or potential, because it was argued that Parliament did not intend the single contributor to be able to claim for more than one wife. However, it was clearly unfair to discriminate where there was only one wife, so, by virtue of regulations made under s 162(b) of the Social Security Act 1975 and s 9(2)(a) of the Child Benefit Act 1976, a polygamous marriage is to be treated for the purposes of the legislation as if it were a

---

238 *The Sinha Peerage Claim* [1946] 1 All ER 348; see the Legitimacy Act 1976, Sched 1, para 4.

239 [1955] AC 107, PC, applying *Re Goodman's Trusts* (1881) 17 Ch D 266: 'if a child is legitimate by the law of the country where at the time of its birth its parents were domiciled, the law of England ... recognises and acts on the status thus declared by the law of the domicile.'

240 *Coleman v Shang* [1961] AC 481, PC.

241 *Cheang Thye Phin v Tan Ah Loy* [1920] AC 369, PC.

242 [1978] 3 All ER 385; 1 WLR 1506; see, also, the Inheritance (Provision for Family and Dependants) Act 1975, s 1A, as added by the Law Reform (Succession) Act 1995, s 2(3).

243 [1976] Fam 148.

244 Family Law Act 1996, s 63(5); see, previously, Matrimonial Homes Act 1983, s 10(2).

245 *Mohamed v Knott* [1969] 1 QB 1.

monogamous union for as long as it was in fact monogamous.[246] In respect of means tested benefits, it was determined in *Iman Din v National Assistance Board*[247] that a husband was bound to support his polygamous wife and children and that sums paid on their behalf by the National Assistance Board were recoverable from him.[248] Under the present regulations relating to income support the central question is not whether the parties are married, but whether they are partners and members of the same household; a 'partner' includes a polygamous wife.[249]

Thus, in respect of the recognition of polygamous marriages, there are three broad points that emerge: (a) that the original remarks of Lord Penzance in *Hyde v Hyde* were misconstrued and not intended to apply beyond the area of matrimonial relief, and, in any event, after 1972 no longer represent the law; (b) that a polygamous marriage will be recognised unless there is some good public policy reason to the contrary; and (c) that the extent of that recognition will vary with the context.

---

246 The legislation originates with the Family Allowances and National Insurance Act 1956, s 3; Social Security and Family Allowances (Polygamous Marriages) Regulations 1975 SI 1975/561 (as amended SI 1989/1642). See, also, the Social Security Contributions and Benefits Act 1992, s 121(b); for child benefit, see the Child Benefit (General) Regulations 1976 SI 1976/965, reg 12.

247 [1967] 2 QB 213.

248 National assistance being replaced by supplementary benefit and, since 1988, income support.

249 Income Support (General) Regulations 1987 SI 1987/1967.

CHAPTER 19

MATRIMONIAL CAUSES

The purpose of this chapter is to examine a number of matters, namely: (a) the jurisdiction of the English courts to entertain proceedings for divorce, separation and nullity; (b) the choice of law in suits for divorce, separation and nullity; (c) the extent to which the orders of foreign courts are recognised; and (d) the power of English courts to grant financial relief and recognise foreign maintenance orders.

JURISDICTION OF THE ENGLISH COURTS

Introduction

At common law, there were different rules governing the jurisdiction of the court depending on whether the petitioner was seeking a divorce, a decree of judicial separation or an annulment. The Matrimonial Causes Act 1857 had been silent on the question so that, in the late 19th century, judges fluctuated between residence and domicile.[1] However, at the end of the century, when domicile was beginning to become the dominant concept in determining the personal law, the Privy Council in *Le Mesurier v Le Mesurier*[2] ruled that the only court that had jurisdiction to grant a decree of divorce was that of the parties' domicile. As the domicile of the wife was that of the husband, considerable practical difficulties arose if a wife sought a divorce in England after her husband had deserted her and found a new domicile abroad. It is arguable that this narrow test for jurisdiction was in line with the reluctance to extend the grounds for divorce set out in 1857.[3]

The grounds were extended by s 13 of the Matrimonial Causes Act 1937 to enable the wife who had been deserted to file a petition if her husband had been domiciled in England prior to the desertion. This was extended by s 1 of the Law Reform (Miscellaneous Provisions) Act 1949, which enabled a petition to be filed on the basis that a wife had been ordinarily resident for three years.

---

1 *Wilson v Wilson* (1872) LR 1 P&D 435 (domicile); *Niboyet v Niboyet* (1878) 4 PD 1 (residence).
2 [1895] AC 517.
3 *Stathatos v Stathatos* [1913] P 46; *De Montaigu v De Montaigu* [1913] P 154; *H v H* [1928] P 206; *Herd v Herd* [1936] P 205. The Matrimonial Causes Act 1923 would equalise the grounds but there was no extension of the grounds until the Matrimonial Causes Act 1937. Lord Merrivale (President, PDA 1919–33) had not been enthusiastic.

In 1972, the Law Commission produced recommendations[4] which formed the basis of the Domicile and Matrimonial Proceedings Act 1973; the legislation provided that, in respect of petitions for divorce, separation or nullity, there should be two broad bases of jurisdiction – domicile and habitual residence. The philosophy behind the legislation was that at least one of the parties should have sufficient nexus with England to make it reasonable for an English court to deal with the matter with a probability that any order would be recognised in other countries.

The Domicile and Matrimonial Proceedings Act 1973 provided that the court would have jurisdiction in respect of divorce and judicial separation if either party were domiciled in England and Wales or was habitually resident and had been so resident for the preceding year.[5] These provisions have now been carried forward into s 19(2) of the Family Law Act 1996, which provides that the court will have jurisdiction if, on the statement date, one of the parties is domiciled in England and Wales, habitually resident for a year prior to that date or nullity proceedings are pending in relation to the marriage.[6]

The grounds in respect of nullity are set out in s 5(3) and are broadly the same as those for divorce, namely, domicile of one of the parties or habitual residence for a period of one year. In addition, the court will have jurisdiction where one of the parties has died and, at death, was either domiciled in England and Wales or habitually resident for the preceding year.[7] Section 5(5) of the legislation further provides that the court will have jurisdiction to entertain proceedings for divorce, judicial separation or nullity of marriage, notwithstanding that the jurisdictional requirements of the section are not satisfied, if they are begun at a time when proceedings which the court has jurisdiction to entertain by virtue of sub-ss (2), (3) or (5) are pending in respect of the same marriage. The jurisdiction is not tested with regard to the petitioner or the respondent as such but by the parties to the marriage. So, a petitioner who is neither domiciled nor resident in England and Wales can invoke the jurisdiction on the basis of the respondent's connection and, in the case of a void marriage, any interested party can invoke the jurisdiction based on the life or death connection of either of the parties to the marriage.

The connections of domicile and habitual residence are the ordinary ones employed by English conflict law. As habitual residence is tested, like domicile, at the time of the institution of the proceedings, it follows that, if the proceedings are begun a year after one of the parties came to England and

---

4 Law Commission Report No 48 (1972).

5 Domicile and Matrimonial Proceedings Act 1973, s 5(2)(a), (b).

6 Under the Family Law Act 1996, there is only one ground for divorce, ie, irretrievable breakdown, and this is only to be established by a statement made by one of the parties that they believe the marriage to have broken down (see the Family Law Act 1996, ss 3 and 5).

7 Domicile and Matrimonial Proceedings Act 1973, s 5(3).

habitual residence is found to exist, then that party was habitually resident here on day one of the residence. It is clear that residence does not have to be married residence and that pre-marriage residence will count.

The clear statutory grounds are an improvement on the prior law. The rules on jurisdiction are unaffected by the Brussels and Lugano Conventions, which do not apply to matters relating to 'status or legal capacity of natural persons'.[8]

Staying proceedings

The purpose of the new jurisdictional rules was to produce clear but demanding criteria. The Law Commission, in their report,[9] had already addressed the problem posed by wide criteria. If the requirements had been loosely drawn, then there was a danger of parties litigating matrimonial problems before the courts of England and Wales. In general, as indicated elsewhere, the English courts prefer commercial disputes that belong abroad to be litigated abroad. In the case of matrimonial litigation, the legislature is anxious to avoid any form of forum shopping because matrimonial litigation involves difficult questions about care of children and financial support that are best adjudicated upon by the courts of the country where the parties have the closest connections. Having regard to the level of formality and expense within the English system, it is highly unlikely that England and Wales would ever develop into a Nevada style divorce venue. However, this is a problem that has to be guarded against.

Secondly, there is a real problem of matrimonial proceedings being conducted in more than one country. Because different countries have different jurisdictional criteria for matrimonial causes, it is possible that there may be legal proceedings launched in more than one country. To take a simple example, if a domiciled English woman began divorce proceedings in England, it is possible that her Italian husband might begin proceedings in Italy. In a world in which some countries adopt domicile or habitual residence as jurisdictional criteria, there are others which will accept jurisdiction on the basis of residence or nationality. Clearly, one party might select a country because he or she imagines that they will obtain a more favourable financial settlement or that they will receive a more sympathetic hearing in respect of questions concerning the children. In these circumstances, the Domicile and Matrimonial Proceedings Act 1973, as amended by the Family Law Act 1996, makes provision for the court to stay proceedings when there are proceedings pending before a foreign court. The legislation provides that a stay may be either obligatory or discretionary.

---

8   Brussels Convention 1968, Art 1.
9   Law Commission Report No 48 (1972).

Obligatory

The Domicile and Matrimonial Proceedings Act 1973 provides that, if an English court is about to try a matter relating to divorce, then, if proceedings are continuing in another part of the British Isles and the parties had resided in that jurisdiction together when the English proceedings were begun or, if not together, the place where they last resided was in that jurisdiction and either of the parties was habitually resident in that jurisdiction throughout the year ending on the date on which they last resided together before the initiation of the English proceedings, then the proceedings shall be stayed.[10] If the criteria set out are not met (because, for example, the English proceedings concern separation) it will be open to a party to seek a discretionary stay.

Discretionary

The Domicile and Matrimonial Proceedings Act 1973 provides that before the trial in England of any matter in matrimonial proceedings the court may stay proceedings if: (a) any proceedings in respect of the marriage in question are continuing within another jurisdiction; and (b) it appears to the court that the balance of fairness (including convenience) between the parties is such that the proceedings in the other jurisdiction should be disposed of before any further step is taken in the English proceedings.[11] This discretion extends to all forms of matrimonial proceedings, not merely divorce proceedings. It is important to note that this statutory discretion operates alongside the inherent discretion which has been expressly preserved by s 5(6)(b) of the Act which reads: 'nothing in the Schedule prejudices any power to stay proceedings which is exercisable by the court apart from the Schedule'.

It should be borne in mind that, since matrimonial jurisdiction is based on statutory criteria, the role of the discretionary stay will be different to that in the general law of *forum non conveniens*, where the objective is to mitigate the exorbitant jurisdiction based on presence. In matrimonial cases, the court is trying to strike a practical balance between two competing jurisdictions, both of which have some connection with the parties. A second important factor is that many of the general cases on *forum non conveniens* concern large corporations where duplication of litigation may simply be the inevitable consequence of multinational operations. However, in matrimonial matters, the consequences of duplication are more serious, as Holman J observed:[12]

---

10 Domicile and Matrimonial Proceedings Act 1973, s 5(6), Sched 1, paras 3(2), 8, as amended by the Family Law Act 1996, Sched 3, para 6.

11 Domicile and Matrimonial Proceedings Act 1973, Sched 1, para 9(1), as amended by the Family Law Act 1996, Sched 3, para 7.

12 *W v W* [1997] 1 FLR 257, p 269 (a case on inherent jurisdiction).

Where spouses or former spouses are litigating about the division of their assets and, directly or indirectly, almost certainly paying for the litigation out of those very assets, the financial drain and the emotional strain are intolerable.

As the general common law doctrine of *forum non conveniens* began to develop in the late 1970s and early 1980s, questions arose as to the relationship between the general doctrine and the statutory discretion under the Domicile and Matrimonial Proceedings Act 1973.[13] It is arguable that, in *Spiliada Maritime Corp v Cansulex*,[14] both Lord Goff and Lord Templeman considered that they regarded the case as of equal application to matrimonial and commercial cases. In any event, the matter fell to be decided by the House of Lords shortly afterwards, in *De Dampierre v De Dampierre*,[15] where the facts were as follows: the parties were French nationals who came to England in 1979. The husband was concerned with marketing cognac produced at the family estate in France. Some years later, the wife went to live in New York and established a business there; she took the child of the marriage to live with her. She told the husband she did not intend to return. The husband instituted divorce proceedings in France and, shortly after, the wife began proceedings in England. The husband applied for a stay under s 5(6) and Sched 1 of the 1973 Act. The application was dismissed at first instance and by the Court of Appeal.

The House of Lords allowed the appeal and granted a stay. Their Lordships concluded that on the evidence France was the appropriate forum and that, while the wife might lose certain advantages from proceeding in England, after *Spiliada*, this was not the determining factor. It was for the wife to demonstrate that she would not receive substantial justice before the French courts so as to displace France as the appropriate forum and, as she could not do this on the evidence, no stay should be granted. Lord Goff indicated:

> ... that judges of first instance should approach their task in cases under the 1973 statute in the same way as they now do in cases of *forum non conveniens* where there is a *lis alibi pendens* and the court should not, as a general rule, be deterred from granting a stay of proceedings simply because the plaintiff in this country will be deprived of such ... advantage, provided that the court is satisfied that substantial justice will be done in the appropriate overseas forum.

Where the statutory discretion is being relied upon, there will have to be concurrent proceedings elsewhere.[16] Normally, one party will be resisting a stay of the English proceedings on the basis that the foreign proceedings are

---

13 *Shemsford v Shemsford* [1981] 1 All ER 726; *Gadd v Gadd* [1985] 1 FLR 220; *Thyssen-Bornemisza v Thyssen-Bornemisza* [1986] Fam 1; *K v K* [1986] 2 FLR 411; *De Dampierre v De Dampierre* [1987] 1 FLR 51.

14 [1987] AC 460.

15 [1988] 1 AC 92.

16 Domicile and Matrimonial Proceedings Act 1973, s 5(6).

likely to award a less generous level of financial relief. Thus, in *Gadd v Gadd*,[17] the absence of financial relief in Monaco was influential in refusing a stay while, in the earlier case of *Shemshadfard v Shemshadfard*,[18] Purchas J placed stress on the range of matrimonial remedies available in the Iranian proceedings. Since the application to stay will often be heard before all the evidence is presented, then the judge will be looking at the heads or structure of matrimonial remedies in the foreign forum rather than the actual sum a party may be awarded. If an appropriate foreign forum cannot be shown or the range of matrimonial relief is limited, then a stay will be refused.[19] In respect of the nature of proceedings abroad, a duty is placed upon the parties to ensure that an English judge is given full particulars of any foreign proceedings relating to the marriage.[20] As to the time limit for exercising the discretion, para 9 indicates that it can be exercised 'before the beginning of the trial or first trial in any matrimonial proceedings'; such a discretion can be exercised any time until the commencement of the main hearing and will not be lost by the making of interim orders.[21]

Since the principles underlying the statutory discretion have been brought into line with the general common law discretion, it will be rare when the court might need to rely on any inherent discretion to stay. There is authority that such a discretion exists[22] and it was clearly preserved by statute.[23] However, such a discretion might be relied upon when, as in *W v W*,[24] there are no concurrent proceedings and the application was made late in the day, after the divorce had been granted. In exceptional cases, an English court might consider whether to restrain a party from continuing matrimonial proceedings abroad. In *Hemain v Hemain*,[25] it was recognised that such a power existed and that the appropriate test was that formulated for civil proceedings.[26]

17 [1985] 1 FLR 220.
18 [1981] 1 All ER 726.
19 *R v R* [1994] 2 FLR 1036.
20 Domicile and Matrimonial Proceedings Act 1973, Sched 1, para 7
21 *Thyssen-Bornemisza v Thyssen-Bornemisza* [1986] Fam 1 (divorce within the jet set super rich).
22 *Sealey v Callan* [1953] P 135.
23 Domicile and Matrimonial Proceedings Act 1973, s 5(6)(b).
24 [1997] 2 FLR 257 (stay granted even though jurisdiction of foreign court uncertain).
25 *Hemain v Hemain* [1988] 2 FLR 388.
26 *Société Nationale Industrielle Aerospatiale v Lee Kui Jak* [1987] AC 871; accepted by Holman J in *W v W* [1997] 1 FLR 257, p 273.

CHOICE OF LAW

Divorce and separation

In broad terms, there is no choice of law in divorce; the English court always applies English law as the *lex fori*.

To obtain a divorce in an English court, the petitioner must establish that the marriage has irretrievably broken down according to the criteria established in the legislation.[27] Under the Family Law Act 1996, provided that the requirements for information meetings and arrangements for the future have been met, then the divorce is granted on the basis that the marriage has irretrievably broken down and this is established by a statement of marital breakdown made by one or both of the parties and complying with ss 5 and 6 of the legislation. Nothing less than the requirements under English law will do and, while the petitioner is free to rely on any facts which support the contention, including those facts which would sustain a foreign petition based on the concept of the matrimonial offence or on a different concept of breakdown, the position under any foreign law is irrelevant.

The application of English law as the *lex fori* can be rationalised by the assertion that what is being sought is an English judgment *in rem* definitively affecting the status of the parties to the marriage and that, therefore, it is only right that English law should govern exclusively. Such an assertion is not compelling. Every litigant in an English court is seeking the exercise of the authority of that court and the proposition could be extended to the universal application of English law in all cases coming before the English courts. This would render the whole conflict of laws redundant, at a considerable cost to justice. Certainly, the argument could be extended with pretty well equal force to nullity proceedings and, indeed, it was thought at one time that there was no choice of law issue in nullity proceedings. The contrary has been clearly established by the legislation.[28] A second argument is that, although family law is a matter of private law, it has effects upon third parties (that is, children and State institutions), so that it is a matter of legitimate public policy that the dissolution of marriage should be in accordance with domestic procedures and traditions. Thirdly, as a practical matter, matrimonial disputes comprise a high proportion of civil disputes in England and, although most divorces are undefended,[29] it would be highly inconvenient if the largely administrative nature of divorce were to be disrupted by the need to plead and prove difficult questions of foreign law.

---

27 See the Matrimonial Causes Act 1973, s 1, as amended.
28 *Ibid*, s 14(1).
29 Law Commission Report No 170 (1988).

Aside from these considerations, a better explanation is available from the history of the development of divorce jurisdiction in England. When the Matrimonial Causes Act 1857 established the Court for Divorce and Matrimonial Causes, no express provision was made defining the jurisdiction of the court. The court gradually established its own rules for jurisdiction based on the domicile of the parties. At that time, of course, the parties would have the same domicile, as it has always been a precondition for granting the divorce that the parties were validly married in the eyes of English law, and valid marriage communicated the husband's current domicile of choice to the wife as a domicile of dependency.[30] Such being the case, the Privy Council in *Le Mesurier v Le Mesurier*[31] arrived at a neat and simple proposition that, for every marriage, there would be one court and only one court which was competent to grant a dissolution. This line, could it have been held, would at once have dealt with jurisdiction, choice of law and the recognition of foreign divorce decrees. There would have been one competent court for every marriage, that court could apply its own domestic law, as that would simultaneously be the *lex fori* and the *lex domicilii*, and its decrees would have been entitled to universal recognition. But, the line could not be held. It became apparent that using domicile as the sole jurisdictional basis was capable of working great hardship, particularly to wives who had been deserted by their husbands and who found themselves, by reason of their husband's acquisition of a new domicile abroad, with a domicile of dependency in a country with which they had no connection. Their only hope of matrimonial relief was to resort to the courts of that country, a resort which, for legal or financial reasons, was often unrealistic. A series of measures aimed at relieving such hardship put an end to the exclusive jurisdiction of the domicile.[32] In consequence, the question of whether, in granting a divorce, the English court was applying English law as *lex fori* or *lex domicilii*, a question which had always existed but was not worth asking before as it made not the slightest difference one way or the other, became a matter of significance. In *Zanelli v Zanelli*,[33] where a petition was filed under s 13 of the Matrimonial Causes Act 1937, the Court of Appeal accepted that English law was still applicable, even though the rules on jurisdiction had been modified. The decision in favour of English law was given statutory force by s 1(4) of the Law Reform (Miscellaneous Provisions) Act 1949, which provided that the court should apply English law, whatever the jurisdictional base, the court being required to proceed on the same basis as if both parties had been domiciled in England.[34] This provision precluded a choice of law rather than

---

30 See, now, the Domicile and Matrimonial Proceedings Act 1973, s 1(1).
31 [1895] AC 517 (Lord Watson).
32 Matrimonial Causes Act 1937, s 13.
33 (1948) 64 TLR 556.
34 The provisions were continued in the Matrimonial Causes Act 1973, s 46(2), but repealed by the Domicile and Matrimonial Proceedings Act 1973, s 17(2), Sched 6.

suggesting that the *lex domicilii* was applicable and, then, pretending that all parties were domiciled in England.

The exclusive operation of English law as *lex fori* does not mean that there are no conflict problems associated with the grant of English divorces. Clearly, the concepts of domicile and habitual residence are pertinent, even if they are being applied for purely domestic purposes. It is preconditional to the grant of an English divorce that the parties to the proceedings are validly married – an issue which could take the court into some difficult conflict territory. Questions might arise which involve a decision about the validity of a foreign marriage or of the effect to be given to foreign decrees or annulments. As the number of divorce petitions rose after the Divorce Law Reform Act 1969 and the defended divorce became a creature of the past, it was simply not practical to expect English judges to conduct lengthy inquiries as to the relevant foreign law of the parties. Indeed, to require English judges to give effect to exotic foreign grounds of divorce might be objectionable to public opinion and, in the future, might give rise to difficulties under the Human Rights Act 1998.

A decree of judicial separation[35] is very rarely sought today and it is accepted that English law should be applied in respect of any application.[36]

Nullity

If a marriage is void by English conflict law, there is no need for a decree annulling it; the parties and the rest of the world can behave as if the marriage had never taken place (though the status of any children of the marriage may be protected). Nevertheless, prudent parties may seek a decree to keep the record straight and there will be some cases where the issue is controversial and an authoritative determination of the question is needed. For example, an allegation that a marriage is void for bigamy may depend on the disputed status of an acknowledged prior marriage. Although the position of a remarriage after a recognised divorce or annulment is now clear,[37] if there has been no annulment of a first marriage claimed to be void, there may be difficult questions to answer.

It was thought, for some time, that the award of a nullity decree, like a divorce, was a matter for the exclusive authority of the granting court which should apply its own domestic law to the matter. Such a proposition may seem strange, as it is a recipe for inconsistency, but inconsistency is sometimes

---

35 The former divorce *a mensa et thoro* of the ecclesiastical courts – the order simply allowed the petitioner and the respondent to live apart.

36 The traditional English expression is 'judicial separation' but, in Europe, it is usual to refer to 'legal separation'; the Family Law Act 1986 refers to both judicial separation (s 44) and legal separation (ss 46–52), while the Family Law Act 1996 provides for separation orders (ss 2, 4).

37 Family Law Act 1986, s 50.

inevitable, as the choice of law rules for marriage may be applied for a whole host of reasons unconnected with the nullity decree. Suppose, for example, an English court has jurisdiction over a succession case and it has, incidentally, to decide the validity of a marriage; it cannot avoid making its decision, say, that the marriage is void, simply because it lacks jurisdiction, because neither of the parties to the marriage is habitually resident or domiciled in England, to grant a decree to that effect. This is so, even if the courts which are competent to grant a decree would not see the marriage as defective. Questions about the validity of a marriage may arise in all manner of cases, from taxation and immigration to legitimacy and damages for bereavement, so that a conflict system might have a developed set of choice of law rules, even if it never granted a nullity decree to any foreign marriage. However, where the court has nullity jurisdiction, it is obviously preferable that it applies the choice of law rules which it ordinarily uses.

Since 1971,[38] it is clear that issues of choice of law are raised by nullity petitions with foreign contacts but there are few clear decisions on choice of law. The older authorities, especially where they lead to the application of the *lex fori*, must now be treated with caution.

We have already seen the choice of law rules that English courts have produced to determine the formal and essential validity of a marriage and it would seem obvious that these rules should be applied to the question of whether a decree of nullity should be granted. Such is the case. So that a marriage might be annulled for failure to comply with the rules of the *lex loci celebrationis*, even though such formalities might be sufficient by English domestic law.[39] Similarly, a marriage might be void within the prohibited degrees of the law of the ante-nuptial domicile, even though the same parties might have full capacity under English domestic law.[40]

However, the English courts have only two nullity options to play with – voidness and voidability[41] – and, if the foreign defect does not have its analogue in English domestic law or a convenient category cannot be found for it, there may be problems. English courts could avoid these problems by classifying foreign defects in a way which prevents difficulties for themselves, as they have with foreign parental consents, or apply public policy to reject defences which do not fit the domestic mould. But, suppose they act within the spirit of the legislation. It may happen either that there is an operative

---

38 See the Nullity of Marriage Act 1971, s 4(1), which stipulates that, where English rules of private international law so require, the validity of a marriage may be determined in accordance with the law of a foreign country. See, now, the Matrimonial Causes Act 1973, s 14(1).

39 *Berthiaume v Dastous* [1930] AC 79, PC (absence of civil ceremony).

40 *Sottomayor v De Barros (No 1)* (1877) 3 PD 1 (marriage of first cousins).

41 See the Matrimonial Causes Act 1973, s 11 (void) and s 12 (voidable).

defect unknown to English law, or that the foreign law, while it has the same defect as English law, gives it a different effect. The foreign law could treat the defect as rendering the marriage void (lack of consent by one of the parties has this effect under Scots law) or voidable (non-age could be a candidate here – a foreign law might say that a marriage above a minimum age, but below the age for marriage, would be voidable at the option of the under age party, provided that he or she acted within a time limit); or it could classify a defect, which English law recognises as a matter of nullity, as a matter of divorce (wilful refusal to consummate would be an obvious candidate). In these cases, the English courts should give effect to the foreign law, including its limitations or bars to relief, for example, that a complaint can only be made by one party or must be brought within a certain time, unless to do so would offend public policy. It is clear that the limitations and bars of English law do not have to be applied where the position is governed by a foreign *lex causae*[42] and the inference, clearly, is that the foreign qualifications may be so applied.

The converse case, where English law sees the marriage as defective in some way but the *lex causae* does not, is covered adequately by the legislation[43] and English courts should not intrude except in those cases, for example, single sex marriage, where English public policy would prevail. If the foreign law regards the alleged defect, say, wilful refusal to consummate the marriage, not as a marriage defect, but as a ground of divorce, there would seem to be no justification for the English court to grant a decree of nullity at all. However, it can be argued, in this particular case, that this defect, as a post marital one, might be referable to a law other than the ante-nuptial domiciliary law of the petitioner.

A further refinement could be a situation where both English law and the *lex causae* regard the marriage as voidable but the foreign law would regard a decree for such a marriage as having retrospective effect, whereas English law, since 1971,[44] has given such a decree prospective effect only. There is nothing to stop a foreign court qualifying the recognition of an English decree and giving what effect, if any, to it which it wants; however, it is difficult to see how an English court can modify the type of decree it gives to accommodate the *lex causae* in such a case and, anyway, little is likely to turn on the distinction.

---

42 Matrimonial Causes Act 1973, s 14(1).

43 *Ibid*, s 14(1).

44 Nullity of Marriage Act 1971, s 5; now, the Matrimonial Causes Act 1973, s 16, implementing Law Commission Report No 33 (1970). For prior law, see *Re Wombell's Settlement* [1922] 2 Ch 298; *Newbould v AG* [1931] P 75; *Re D'Altroy's Will Trusts* [1968] 1 AER 181; *Re Rodwell* [1970] Ch 726.

THE RECOGNITION OF DIVORCES AND LEGAL SEPARATIONS

Introduction

The rules for recognition of divorces and legal separations are the same. To avoid repetition of cumbersome expressions, the word 'divorce' will be used to include the other form of relief and may be understood to do so unless the contrary is stated. The simple question that we are concerned with is whether a divorce granted by a foreign court is to be recognised in England. English law has to strike a balance between two extreme positions. It would be possible to have a situation in which the criteria for the recognition of divorces granted by country X were so demanding that few divorces were recognised. There would then be a large number of situations in which parties were divorced in country X but the divorce was not recognised in England. The disadvantages and practical inconvenience that may arise from such an increase in 'limping marriages' are obvious. The second possible situation is where the rules of recognition are so liberal that A may leave country B, secure a divorce in country C and return to country B expecting that the divorce will be recognised; such a liberal regime, where effectively all foreign divorces are recognised, will only serve to undermine the jurisdictional rules of country B, as its citizens will seek to secure abroad that which they cannot obtain at home. English law, as in so many areas, has to find a sensible balance midway between two undesirable extremes.

Recognition of divorces is entirely statutory and is exclusively contained in Part II of the Family Law Act 1986. As in the case of the recognition of foreign judgments in non-matrimonial cases, the basic issue is the jurisdictional competence of the court whose decision is under consideration. If the court is regarded by English law as competent to make the decision, then the decision will be recognised in England without investigation of its merits, unless there are overwhelming reasons of public policy against doing so.

The statute, however, applies not only to judicial awards but extends to divorces, annulments and legal separations, which are not made by courts at all and may be no more than the individual exercise of power by a party to the marriage. It therefore covers, for example, what are called 'bare' *talaqs* – Islamic divorces which are not based on any proceedings. Before turning to the present legislation, it is necessary to say a little of the historical background.

The historical background

Judicial divorce has been available in England since 1858 and in Northern Ireland since 1939.[45] However, because of the different impact of the

---

45 Matrimonial Causes Act 1857; Matrimonial Causes Act (NI) 1939.

Reformation, it was available in Scotland from the 16th century. There was a natural temptation for Englishmen to travel to Scotland and, after securing a divorce, seek to remarry. The question of the recognition of divorces therefore arose first in the context of the circumstances in which an English court would recognise a Scottish decree. In *R v Lolley*,[46] an Englishman induced his wife to divorce him in Scotland after a residence of 40 days; he then returned to England and went through a ceremony of marriage with another woman. The response of the English authorities was to charge and convict him of bigamy and impose a sentence of transportation.

When divorce was made available in England, it came to be accepted that jurisdiction would be exercised on the basis of domicile. At the same time, a series of cases towards the end of the 19th century held that the English courts would only recognise a divorce if the parties were domiciled in Scotland at the outset of the proceedings but in no other circumstances.[47] If there was any doubt that the requirement was that the parties should be domiciled in the country, it was settled by *Le Mesurier v Le Mesurier*,[48] where Lord Watson, in giving the judgment of the Privy Council, observed: 'According to international law, the domicile for the time being of the married pair affords the only true test of jurisdiction to dissolve the marriage'. A decade later, it was accepted, in *Armitage v AG*,[49] that a divorce could be recognised in England if it would be recognised in the *lex domicilii* of the parties – the relevant principle being that, if a change of status had been recognised in the parties' domicile, then it should be recognised in England.

As has been noted elsewhere, English law extended jurisdiction in s 13 of the Matrimonial Causes Act 1937 and s 1 of the Law Reform (Miscellaneous Provisions) Act 1949 to permit a wife to bring proceedings when the husband had been domiciled in England immediately prior to deserting her or she had been resident in England for a period of three years. In consequence, in *Travers v Holley*,[50] the Court of Appeal ruled that an English court will recognise a foreign decree of divorce if it is granted in circumstances where, *mutatis mutandis*, an English court would itself have exercised jurisdiction, the principle being that it would be at variance with comity if an English court were to refuse to recognise a jurisdiction that, *mutatis mutandis*, it claimed for itself.

---

46 (1812) Russ & Ry 237.

47 *Dolphin v Robins* (1859) 7 HLC 390; *Shaw v Gould* (1868) LR 3 HL 55; *Harvey v Farnie* (1882) 8 App Cas 43.

48 [1895] AC 517; the case itself turned on jurisdiction to grant a divorce rather than recognition of a grant, however: (a) the judgment was widely drawn and taken to refer to recognition; (b) an attempt had been made to link the two areas of jurisdiction and recognition; and (c) the judgment of the Privy Council was delivered by Lord Watson, a scholarly and highly regarded Law Lord.

49 [1906] P 135 (husband domiciled in New York while wife settled in South Dakota and obtained divorce there that was recognised in New York – see US Constitution 1787, Art IV, s 1).

50 [1953] P 246.

This remained the position until the House of Lords, in *Indyka v Indyka*,[51] in reviewing the general state of the law, held that a foreign decree should be recognised in England if there was a 'real and substantial connection' between either the petitioner or the respondent and the foreign country in which the divorce was obtained. This was not a very precise test and gave rise to litigation as to whether a real and substantial connection was to be demonstrated on the basis of residence, nationality or even the place of the celebration of the marriage.[52]

In any event, the common law rules became of less importance because the Hague Conference on Private International Law produced a Convention on the Recognition of Divorces and Legal Separations 1970, which was signed by the UK on 1 June 1970. The Convention was given effect to in the Recognition of Divorces and Legal Separations Act 1971,[53] which came into effect on 1 January 1972. The legislation provided for the recognition of divorces and legal separations granted in different parts of the UK[54] and overseas.[55] In respect of overseas divorces, recognition would be accorded on the basis of habitual residence or nationality.[56] The common law rules were abolished, save as they were expressly preserved. The legislation was amended by the Domicile and Matrimonial Proceedings Act 1973 and attracted criticism both on grounds of its drafting and also in respect of its treatment of Islamic divorces.[57] A further element of concern was that the legislation did not extend to nullity decrees. The Law Commission had been asked to report on the recognition of nullity decrees and, in the *Report on the Recognition of Nullity Decrees and Related Matters*,[58] it recommended that recognition of nullity decrees should be placed on the same statutory basis as that for divorce. However, they recommended a number of changes to the divorce legislation. The recommendations were accepted and a new statutory code emerged in the form of Part II of the Family Law Act 1986, which now constitutes the basis of the present law.

---

51   [1969] 1 AC 33.
52   *Peters v Peters* [1968] P 275; *Angelo v Angelo* [1968] 1 WLR 401; *Blair v Blair* [1969] 1 WLR 221; *Mayfield v Mayfield* [1969] P 119.
53   See, also, Law Commission Report No 34 (1970).
54   Recognition of Divorces and Legal Separations Act 1971, s 1 (but not retrospectively).
55   *Ibid*, s 2 (not subject to restriction on time).
56   *Ibid*, s 3.
57   For the case law, see *Torok v Torok* [1973] 1 WLR 1066 (Ormrod J); *Radwan v Radwan* [1973] Fam 24 (Cumming-Bruce J); *Cruse v Chittum* [1974] 2 All ER 940 (Lane J); *Kendall v Kendall* [1977] Fam 208 (Hollings J); *Quazi v Quazi* [1980] AC 744.
58   Law Commission Report No 137 (1984).

Judicial divorces under the Family Law Act 1986

In broad terms, the legislation draws a distinction between: (a) divorces granted in the British Islands; (b) overseas divorces obtained by proceedings outside the British Islands; and (c) overseas divorces not obtained by proceedings.

UK divorces

A divorce granted by a court of civil jurisdiction in any part of the British Islands[59] will be recognised throughout the UK.[60] Only divorces which have been obtained in the UK by civil proceedings are capable of recognition,[61] so unilateral and non-judicial divorces obtained here will not have any effect unless obtained before 1 January 1974[62] and recognised by rules of law applicable before that date.

An English court may refuse recognition only if the decree is irreconcilable with an earlier decision of an English court on the subsistence or the validity of the marriage, or with an earlier decision of a foreign court which has been recognised or is capable of recognition by the English court.[63]

A divorce or legal separation (though not, obviously, an annulment) may be refused recognition by the English courts if there was no subsisting marriage between the parties in the eyes of English law, including its conflict rules.[64]

Overseas divorces

Section 45 of the Family Law Act 1986 defines an overseas divorce as a divorce obtained in a country outside the British Islands and specifies that such a divorce is to be recognised in the UK if and only if it meets the requirements of Part II of the legislation. In respect of overseas divorces, s 46 of the Family Law Act 1986 then draws a distinction between those divorces obtained by proceedings and those not.[65] This distinction will be returned to below but, for present purposes, it can be assumed that a judicial divorce is one obtained by proceedings.

---

59 Which include England and Wales, Scotland, Northern Ireland, the Channel Islands and the Isle of Man but not, of course, the Irish Republic; see the Interpretation Act 1978, Sched 1.
60 Family Law Act 1986, s 44(2).
61 *Ibid*, s 44(1).
62 *Ibid*, s 55(5)(a).
63 *Ibid*, s 51(1).
64 *Ibid*, s 51(2).
65 See *Ibid*, s 46(1) (by proceedings), s 46(2) (otherwise than by proceedings).

For a divorce obtained by proceedings to be recognised, s 46 requires that it be effective under the law of the country in which it was obtained[66] and that, at the date of the commencement of the proceedings, either party was: (a) habitually resident in the country in which the divorce was obtained; (b) domiciled in that country according to either English law or the law of that country; or (c) a national of that country. To put the matter another way, s 46 of the Family Law Act 1986 involves consideration of: (a) the appropriate connecting factor; (b) the concept of country; and (c) the concept of effectiveness.

Under the legislation, nationality and habitual residence are to be determined by English law but the domiciliary connection can be established either by English law or by the law of the domicile as used for family law matters in the country concerned.[67]

In respect of habitual residence, it will be a question of examining the evidence and drawing the appropriate inferences. The alternative of nationality was included to meet the concerns of the Hague Conference and those European States that use nationality as a connecting factor. In such cases evidence of citizenship would have to be before the court; it would seem that, in cases where a person has dual nationality, this will not be an obstacle.[68]

Particular attention should be devoted to the extended definition of domicile in s 46(5); a party may demonstrate that they were domiciled within the country in accordance with the demands of English law or they may show that they were domiciled in the country 'according to the law of that country in family matters'. The purpose of this provision is to make provision for those federal States where there may be more than one form of domicile.[69] To take an example, a divorce may be granted in New South Wales, Australia and the parties may have been domiciled in New South Wales under normal principles. However, it may be that their precise domicile was uncertain and the New South Wales court may have assumed jurisdiction on the basis of domicile under federal legislation which provides that a person may be domiciled within Australia for the purposes of divorce and related matters. A divorce granted in these circumstances will come within s 46(5).

A further aspect that requires attention is the concept of 'country'.[70] Detailed provisions are contained in s 49 of the Family Law Act 1986. The reason for their inclusion depends on the distinction between a 'country' and a 'State'. Throughout this book, the expression 'country' has been used to identify a single territorial system of law, a law district, as the Americans call

---

66   *D v D* [1994] 1 FLR 38 (possibility of an appeal in Ghana); on effectiveness, see below.
67   Family Law Act 1986, s 46(5).
68   *Torok v Torok* [1973] 1 WLR 1066 (Ormrod J).
69   Australian Family Law Act 1975; Canadian Divorce Act 1968.
70   The failure to provide a precise definition was the subject of criticism under the Recognition of Divorces and Legal Separations Act 1971; see s 10(3).

it, as opposed to a State, which is an internationally recognised political unit. Several States, the UK itself being one, have a number of countries within the political unit, which have their own legal systems. When it comes to applying this distinction to the recognition of foreign divorces, there can be problems.

There is no difficulty where the country is also the political State – France, Japan, Saudi Arabia and, indeed, most States in the world – both the question of the effectiveness of the divorce and that of the jurisdictional nexus are referable to a single legal system.

The next group are federal States which have separate countries within them for most conflict purposes but which have a unitary law on family matters – Australia and Canada, for example. While, for other conflict purposes, it is necessary to decide where a person is domiciled, say, in Queensland or New South Wales, Ontario or Quebec, for the purpose of the recognition of divorces, it is possible to be domiciled or habitually resident in Australia or Canada, just as one can obviously be a national of those States. So, the question of effectiveness[71] and the jurisdictional nexus are referable to the federal State as a whole.

The third group are the federal States whose separate countries remain distinct for the purpose of all conflict matters. The USA is the obvious example; one cannot be a domiciliary of the USA any more than one can be a national of Texas or Nebraska. The jurisdictional connection based on domicile, whether the English or local interpretation of that concept is applied, and the habitual residence must relate to the individual law district.[72] The connection based on nationality must, of course, relate to the international State but what about effectiveness? To take an example, a divorce might be granted in Texas simply on the basis that one of the parties was an American citizen. It should go without saying that the divorce must be recognised in Texas where it was granted, for, if it isn't, there is nothing to be recognised. But, must it be effective in the eyes of the federal unit? If it must, does that depend on whether the jurisdictional connection is based on domicile or habitual residence or only if it is based on nationality? Where, and only where, the jurisdictional connection is nationality, the divorce must be effective not only in the law district where it was obtained but throughout the federal unit.[73] So, in the example indicated, the Texas divorce would be recognised in England if it is effective throughout the USA.

---

71 See below.

72 Family Law Act 1986, s 49(2). For examples, see *Messina v Smith* [1971] P 322 (Nevada); *Lawrence v Lawrence* [1985] Fam 106.

73 Family Law Act 1986, s 49(3).

Not only must the jurisdictional requirements be satisfied, but the divorce decree must be effective under s 46 of the Family Law Act 1986.[74] The principle of 'effectiveness' can be traced back to the Recognition of Divorces and Legal Separations Act 1971.[75] It would seem that, in the context of divorce, the decree should be 'legally effective to dissolve the marriage'. This expression is wide enough to encompass situations where there have been procedural irregularities as to service[76] or where the foreign court lacked internal competence or the decree was suspended pending appeal. It would seem that a decree will be ineffective until it becomes absolute.

One of the problems for any regime of recognition is to prevent improper attempts to reopen issues already decided by the foreign court. The basis of recognition of judicial divorces is the international competence of the court where the divorce was obtained. An English court is concerned neither with the grounds on which the divorce was granted nor with the jurisdictional basis on which the foreign court itself took jurisdiction.

However, insofar as the foreign court made, expressly or by implication, a finding of fact on the basis of which it assumed jurisdiction, including a finding that either party to the marriage was a national of, or domiciled or habitually resident in, the country where the divorce was obtained, such a finding will be conclusive evidence of that fact if both parties took part in the proceedings. If only the petitioner took part in the proceedings, such a finding will be sufficient evidence of that fact, that is, it will stand unless the contrary is shown.[77] So, if a foreign court were to find that X was present in the country and that the court was entitled to assume jurisdiction on the basis of habitual residence, then the prior finding as to presence would have presumptive evidentiary effect for the English court.

Extra-judicial divorces under the Family Law Act 1986

The institution of judicial divorce under the Matrimonial Causes Act 1857 was a secular phenomenon; while the ecclesiastical courts had power to make an order of judicial separation or divorce *a mensa et thoro* (from bed and board), they had no power to make a full order of divorce itself (*a vinculo matrimonii*). Thus, from 1858 divorce in England was a matter of civil jurisdiction obtainable by formal procedures in the civil courts.[78]

---

74 The actual expression in the legislation is that the 'divorce ... is effective under the law of the country in which it was obtained'.

75 See Recognition of Divorces and Legal Separations Act 1971, s 2(b).

76 *D v D* [1994] 1 FLR 38.

77 Family Law Act 1986, s 48.

78 Indeed, from 1857 until 1969, traditional Church of England teaching had not been enthusiastic about extending the grounds for civil divorce and had stressed the orthodox Christian position of the indissolubility of marriage.

However, there are a number of religions in the world that make some provision for divorce; sometimes, this is by means of a unilateral act by one or other party to the marriage. Probably best known in England is the Islamic *talaq* divorce. Under classical Islamic tradition, a man might divorce his wife by pronouncing once or more (usually three times) words which can be translated as 'I divorce you'.[79] In principle, the procedure is both unilateral and irrevocable and, because there are no procedures of an administrative or judicial nature, the basic procedure has come to be known as the bare *talaq*.

However, in some States, where the legal system is founded on or closely linked with Islamic principles, administrative or judicial procedures have been introduced without which the *talaq* may or may not be effective from the perspective of the State. The State may require registration with a court;[80] however, the best known procedure is that in Pakistan under the Muslim Family Laws Ordinance of 1961, where there is a requirement for suspension of the *talaq* for 90 days while conciliation procedures may take place. Indeed, if written notice of the *talaq* is not given, it would appear that the *talaq* does not take effect.[81]

A second form of religious divorce is that of the Jewish *ghet*.[82] Under Jewish Rabbinical law, where there is agreement of both parties, the husband might divorce his wife by the delivery of a *ghet* document. Although the husband is required to appear before the Beth Din, there is no judicial finding of fact and it is the delivery of the *ghet* to the wife that severs the marital bonds. Even though the *talaq* and the *ghet* are both religious forms of divorce, there are significant differences between them and both have given rise to case law before the English courts.[83]

It is important to note that religious divorces differ in procedure and there is a fundamental distinction between those religious divorces that may be valid in themselves (for example, the so called bare *talaq*) and those religious procedures which operate within countries where the legislature has required some additional administrative act (for example, in Pakistan, under the terms of the Muslim Family Laws Ordinance 1961).[84]

---

79 The procedure is analysed in some detail by Lord Diplock in *Quazi v Quazi* [1980] AC 744. It should be noted that there is also the consensual Muslim divorce, the *khula*. If the procedure is in writing, then it is described as *talaqnama*.

80 *Russ v Russ* [1963] P 87; [1964] P 315 (expert evidence received that, in Egypt, there had to be registration with a court, although failure to do so did not affect validity).

81 See *Quazi v Quazi* [1980] AC 744; *Quereshi v Quereshi* [1972] Fam 173. The conciliation procedures could take place in Pakistan or at a Pakistani Embassy abroad.

82 The word *ghet* is the Aramaic translation of the Hebrew word for book or bill of divorcement; the procedure is explained by Berkovits (1988) 104 LQR 60.

83 *Har Shefi v Har Shefi (No 2)* [1953] P 220 (effect of a letter of divorce given to wife in London – effective on basis that it was recognised in Israel).

84 Thus giving rise to the distinction between the bare *talaq* and the procedural *talaq*.

At first, English law was reluctant to recognise the validity of the extra-judicial divorce.[85]

However, within a generation, that approach had changed[86] and recognition would be accorded provided that the parties were domiciled in a country where the laws would allow or recognise such a method (for example, Pakistan, Egypt or Israel). Recognition would not be denied even if the *ghet* was obtained[87] or the *talaq* was delivered in England. In 1971, in the Recognition of Divorces and Legal Separations Act, new grounds of recognition (habitual residence and nationality) were added but these grounds only applied to divorces obtained by proceedings.[88] Further, limits were introduced in s 16 of the Domicile and Matrimonial Proceedings Act 1973, which provided that no extra-judicial divorce obtained in the UK would be recognised if both parties were habitually resident here.[89]

In the years after 1971, a number of cases came before the courts involving different aspects of divorce by *talaq*[90] and the entire area was reviewed by the House of Lords in *Quazi v Quazi*,[91] where the facts were as follows: both parties were nationals of Pakistan. The husband pronounced a *talaq* in Pakistan in accordance with the laws of Pakistan and then complied with the terms as to written notice under the Muslim Family Ordinance 1961. This provided that the *talaq* would be suspended for a 90 day period but would then take effect unless revoked. At a later date, the wife sought a divorce in England and the husband argued that the *talaq* divorce should be recognised under s 2(a) of the Recognition of Divorces and Legal Separations Act 1971.

The House of Lords, in reversing the Court of Appeal, held that the *talaq* divorce was entitled to recognition and that the expression 'other proceedings' did not require judicial proceedings involving findings of fact but extended to any proceedings which could be considered officially recognised. Since the proceedings under the 1961 Ordinance were official and attracted a criminal sanction, they were within the definition. When the Law Commission came to produce their report, they followed the approach of Lord Scarman in *Quazi* and recommended that 'judicial or other proceedings' should include 'acts

---

85 *R v Hammersmith Marriage Registrar ex p Mir-Anwarrudin* [1917] 1 KB 634.

86 *Sasson v Sasson* [1924] AC 1007, PC; *Har Shefi v Har Shefi (No 2)* [1953] P 200; *Russ v Russ* [1963] P 87 (Scarman J); [1964] P 315; *Lee v Lau* [1967] P 14; *Quereshi v Quereshi* [1972] Fam 173; *Quazi v Quazi* [1980] AC 744.

87 *Har Shefi v Har Shefi (No 2)* [1953] P 200.

88 Recognition of Divorces and Legal Separations Act 1971, s 3.

89 Thus, reversing *Quereshi v Quereshi* [1972] Fam 173.

90 *Radwan v Radwan* [1973] Fam 24 (divorce by *talaq* at Egyptian Consulate in London – was this overseas for purpose of 1971 Act?); *Chaudhry v Chaudhry* [1976] Fam 148 (divorce by *talaq* at Pakistani Embassy in London).

91 [1980] AC 744.

which constitute the means by which a divorce may be obtained in a country and are done in compliance with the law of that country'.[92] This would have included the bare *talaq* but this approach was not adopted in the Family Law Act 1986 or in the subsequent cases. Instead, the draftsman of s 46 of the Family Law Act 1986 drew a distinction between divorces 'obtained by means of proceedings'[93] and divorces obtained 'otherwise than by means of proceedings'.[94] This contrasted with the provision under the Recognition of Divorces and Legal Separations Act 1971 which referred to 'judicial or other proceedings'.[95]

In respect of the *talaq*, it was held by the Court of Appeal, in *Chaudhary v Chaudhary*,[96] that a bare *talaq* did not constitute proceedings and could not be recognised. There is, thus, a distinction between a bare *talaq* and a procedural *talaq* where there has been compliance with administrative forms. The former is not 'by way of proceedings' but the latter might be.[97]

If the extra-judicial divorce is obtained by means of proceedings, then it will be recognised in England and Wales if it is effective in that country and either party was habitually resident in, domiciled[98] in or a national of that country. There is some indication in the case law that English domiciliaries who went abroad and executed a procedural *talaq* might be denied recognition on grounds of public policy, even though the terms of the relevant legislation had been complied with.[99] These concerns were no doubt stimulated by a fear that the parties might seek to divorce abroad and deprive the weaker party of the ancillary relief under the Matrimonial Causes Act 1973. That concern has been remedied to some extent by the Matrimonial and Family Proceedings Act 1984 which permitted English courts to award financial relief when recognising foreign decrees. If the extra-judicial divorce has been obtained otherwise than by proceedings, then the grounds of recognition are set out under s 46(2) of the Family Law Act 1986:

(2) The validity of an overseas divorce, annulment or legal separation obtained otherwise than by means of proceedings shall be recognised if–

(a) the divorce, annulment or legal separation is effective under the law of the country in which it was obtained;

---

92 Law Commission Report No 137 (1984), p 122.

93 Family Law Act 1986, s 46(1).

94 *Ibid*, s 46(2).

95 Recognition of Divorces and Legal Separations Act 1971, s 2.

96 [1985] Fam 19 (oral *talaq* obtained in Kashmir but not subject to the 1961 Ordinance).

97 The other distinction emerging in the case law was as to whether any of the steps took place in England; in which case, the divorce will be treated as transnational; on which, see below.

98 Domiciled either according to foreign law or that of the relevant part of the UK; see the Family Law Act 1946, s 46(1), (5).

99 *Chaudhary v Chaudhary* [1985] Fam 19; *R v Secretary of State for the Home Department ex p Ghulam Fatima* [1986] AC 527.

(b) at the relevant date –

   (i) each part to the marriage was domiciled in that country; or

   (ii) either party to the marriage was domiciled in that country and the other party was domiciled in a country under whose law the divorce, annulment or legal separation is recognised as valid; and

(c) neither party to the marriage was habitually resident in the UK throughout the period of one year immediately preceding that date.

These grounds are narrower than those in respect of extra-judicial divorces obtained by proceedings. The reason for sub-s 46(2)(c) is that those habitually resident for one year will be entitled to seek a divorce in the English courts. The provision is designed to bolster the prohibition on extra-judicial divorces in England, so that English domiciliaries obtaining an extra-judicial divorcee during a short period abroad are likely to find that it is not recognised.[100]

In respect of the recognition of extra-judicial divorces, it is clear that the Pakistani *talaq* may come within s 46(1), that a Jewish *ghet* may also come within s 46(1) but that a bare *talaq*, if it is to be recognised at all, must come within s 46(2). However, beyond these general statements, one must be cautious because much of the case law has arisen in circumstances where some of the relevant steps have taken place in England and the case has turned on the point concerning where the divorce was actually obtained.[101] In reviewing the past case law, one must be careful as to the precise recognition regime that was in place and the specific question that fell to be addressed. Much of the relevant case law arose under regimes prior to the 1986 Act and can only be of limited value because of the need to follow the precise words of the 1986 legislation, although past authorities are of value, particularly in the attempts made to analyse the steps in an extra-judicial divorce.[102]

---

100 Family Law Act 1986, ss 46(2)(c), 44(1), 51(3)(c).

101 In looking at the prior case law, one must bear in mind the various recognition regimes that have operated in the last 30 years, namely: (a) the common law rules; (b) the 1971 Act; (c) the 1971 Act, as amended by the 1973 Act; and (d) the 1986 Act. Secondly, one must note the number of legally relevant questions that might arise, of which some are: (a) where was the divorce obtained? (b) was the divorce judicial? (c) was the divorce obtained by means of proceedings? and (d) did any part of the proceedings or procedure take place in England and Wales? It is only by keeping these questions distinct that one can rationalise the prior case law.

102 The relevant authorities are *Quereshi v Quereshi* [1972] Fam 173 (*talaq* recognised when husband domiciled in Pakistan); *Sharif v Sharif* [1980] 10 Fam Law 216 (Wood J) (bare *talaq* not proceedings for 1971 Act); *Quazi v Quazi* [1980] AC 744 (*talaq* divorce in Pakistan recognised); *Zaal v Zaal* [1983] 4 FLR 284 (Bush J) (bare *talaq* recognised); *Chaudhary v Chaudhary* [1985] Fam 19 (bare *talaq* in England at variance with the 1971 Act as amended by s 16 of the 1973 Act); *R v Secretary of State for the Home Department ex p Ghulam Fatima* [1986] AC 527 (proceedings in more than one country outside the 1971 Act).

Transnational divorces

A transnational divorce[103] is a divorce where some of the relevant acts are performed in country A and some in country B. The expression transnational divorce does not appear in the Recognition of Divorces and Legal Separations Act 1971 or the Family Law Act 1986. For example, a husband having Pakistani nationality might pronounce the *talaq* in England and then send the relevant details to Pakistan to comply with Muslim Family Ordinance 1961; such a form of divorce might be described as a transnational divorce.

It has been the case that a number of problems have arisen in respect of transnational divorces where some of the acts have taken place in England and the remaining acts have taken place abroad. Secondly, statutory provisions have existed since 1973, placing restrictions on those resident in the UK as to how they obtain a divorce.[104]

Section 44(1) of the Family Law Act 1986 reads, in part:

... no divorce or annulment obtained in any part of the British Islands shall be regarded as effective in any part of the UK unless granted by a court of civil jurisdiction.

These provisions repeat, in substance, the provisions of s 16 of the Domicile and Matrimonial Proceedings Act 1973; such provisions have clearly been dictated by social policy considerations.

After the judgment in *Quereshi v Quereshi*,[105] it was clear that a person resident in the UK but domiciled elsewhere (for, example, in Pakistan, as in *Quereshi*) might avoid UK divorce law by taking advantage of the common law domicile basis of recognition that had been expressly preserved by the 1971 Act.[106] However, there was every incentive to do so because, until the enactment of the Matrimonial and Family Proceedings Act 1984, the financial orders that an English court could make after a foreign divorce were strictly limited. Although there is a natural concern to avoid limping marriages, the case law on transnational divorces does indicate that the courts are anxious to ensure there is no attempt to by pass the UK divorce laws. Thus, in *Chaudhary v Chaudhary*,[107] the Court of Appeal ruled that a bare *talaq* pronounced in England and communicated to a wife in Pakistan was not entitled to recognition.

---

103 The phrase appears to have originated with *In re Fatima* [1985] QB 190, p 207, *per* Slade LJ and is normally taken to denote an extra-judicial divorce in which the relevant acts or procedure takes place in more than one country.

104 Domicile and Matrimonial Proceedings Act 1973, s 16.

105 [1972] Fam 173.

106 Recognition of Divorces and Legal Separations Act 1971, s 6.

107 [1985] Fam 19.

The problems posed by transnational divorces were considered by the House of Lords in *R v Secretary of Secretary of State for the Home Department ex p Ghulam Fatima*,[108] where the facts were as follows: a Pakistani national, resident in England, pronounced a *talaq* in England in order to divorce his wife who lived in Pakistan. In 1978, he complied with the 1961 Muslim Family Ordinance by sending the relevant written notice to Pakistan. In 1982, his fiancée, Ghulam Fatima, was refused entry to the UK on the basis that the immigration rules had not been complied with because no valid marriage could take place within a reasonable period of time. The immigration officer was not convinced that the prior marriage had been validly terminated. This conclusion was challenged by judicial review. Taylor J and the Court of Appeal upheld the ruling of the immigration officer.

The issue for the House of Lords was whether the divorce was entitled to recognition under the Recognition of Divorces and Legal Separations Act 1971 as being one 'obtained by means of judicial or other proceedings in any country outside the British Isles'. The House of Lords, in upholding the judgment of the lower courts, ruled that a divorce merely concluded abroad would not be recognised. Lord Ackner, in giving judgment, held that ss 2 and 3 of the Recognition of Divorces and Legal Separations Act 1971 required 'a single set of proceedings which have to be instituted in the same country as that in which the relevant divorce was ultimately obtained'. While this question of statutory construction was sufficient to dispose of the appeal, Lord Ackner made reference to the social policy behind s 16 of the Domicile and Matrimonial Proceedings Act 1973[109] when he observed:

> It is, thus, clearly the policy of the legislature to deny recognition to divorces obtained by persons within the jurisdiction, and, therefore, subject to the law of the UK, by any proceedings other than in a UK court. It would seem contrary to that policy to encourage the obtaining of divorces essentially by post by Pakistani nationals resident in this country by means of the *talaq* procedure.

Broadly, the same approach was followed in *Berkovits v Grinberg*,[110] where Wall J refused to recognise a divorce under s 46(1) of the Family Law Act 1986 where a Jewish *ghet* had been written in England but delivered in Israel. Wall J reasoned that obtaining a divorce involved going through a process or procedure and that, if any part of the process took part in England, then the legislation would not be complied with. It would certainly seem that, in respect of a transnational divorce, recognition will be denied if any aspect of the proceedings took place in England.[111] The learned judge accepted the

---

108 [1986] AC 527.
109 See, now, Family Law Act 1986, s 44.
110 [1995] Fam 142.
111 Young (1987) 7 LS 78; Pilkington (1988) 37 ICLQ 131; Berkovits (1988) 104 LQR 60.

approach in *Ex p Ghulam Fatima*[112] but acknowledged that a rich man could avoid its effects by flying to Pakistan to pronounce a *talaq*, whilst a poor man could not. Although the judge rejected a petition that the divorce was valid,[113] he ended his judgment by observing: 'the question as to whether or not, in an increasingly multiracial and multi-ethnic society, the refusal to recognise the transnational divorce can or should continue is a matter for Parliament'.

RECOGNITION OF FOREIGN NULLITY DECREES

Until the enactment of Part II of the Family Law Act 1986, the recognition of foreign nullity decrees was governed by the common law rules.[114] As indicated above, the Law Commission had indicated that recognition of nullity decrees should be placed on a statutory basis.[115] This was effected by Part II of the Family Law Act 1986; it is to be noted that, by s 52(1) of the Family Law Act 1986, the provisions of the legislation will apply to decrees of nullity granted before the date of commencement.[116] However, any such recognition will not affect any property rights that a person became entitled to prior to that date.[117]

As in the case of overseas divorces, the legislation differentiates between nullity decrees obtained by means of proceedings and those not the subject of proceedings. It is difficult to imagine a nullity decree not being the subject of proceedings. A nullity decree obtained by means of proceedings will be entitled to recognition if: (a) it is effective under the law of the country in which it was obtained; and (b) at the date of the commencement of the proceedings, either party to the marriage was habitually resident or domiciled in or was a national of that country.[118] The provisions for a nullity decree obtained other than proceedings are the same as for those in respect of a divorce decree obtained otherwise than by proceedings.[119] In cases where there has been a death, then recognition will be accorded if either party was habitually resident in, domiciled in or a national of that country at the relevant date.[120] The provisions of s 46(4) are necessary because, while there can be no

---

112 *R v Secretary of Secretary of State for the Home Department ex p Ghulam Fatima* [1985] QB 190.

113 The case had come before the Family Division in the form of a petition under the Family Law Act 1986 seeking a declaration that the divorce be recognised as valid.

114 *Salvesen v Austrian Property Administrator* [1927] AC 641.

115 Law Commission Report No 137 (1984).

116 4 April 1988.

117 Family Law Act 1986, s 52(2)(a).

118 *Ibid*, s 46(1).

119 *Ibid*, s 46(2).

120 *Ibid*, s 46(4).

divorce after death,[121] different considerations apply in respect of nullity decrees.

It should be noted that the provisions in respect of the proof of facts and the provisions in relation to the application of recognition rules in foreign and federal States apply equally in the context of nullity decrees.

REFUSAL OF RECOGNITION OF FOREIGN DIVORCES, ANNULMENTS AND LEGAL SEPARATIONS

There are a number of grounds on which a divorce, annulment or legal separation obtained abroad may be refused recognition. Those grounds are set out in Part II of the Family Law Act 1986.[122] The different types of decree may lead to slight variations as regards the precise effect. It is now necessary to review the various heads under which recognition may be refused.

Res judicata

A divorce, legal separation or decree of nullity may be refused recognition if it is inconsistent with a judgment of an English court or of a court elsewhere in the UK which is itself entitled to recognition.[123] This gives effect to the broad principle enunciated by the House of Lords in *Vervaeke v Smith*,[124] where one of the reasons for not recognising a Belgian nullity decree was that the entire matter was subject to estoppel *per rem judicatem*.[125] It should be noted that the refusal of recognition under s 51(1)(b) is discretionary and that the prior judgment may be that of an English court, as in *Vervaeke v Smith*, or that of a foreign court which is itself entitled to recognition under the terms of the legislation. The section, therefore, gives effect in respect of divorces and legal separations to the terms of Art 9 of the Hague Convention on the Recognition of Divorces and Legal Separations 1970 and, in respect of decrees of nullity, is in line with the common law position as set out in *Vervaeke v Smith*.

---

121 For an interesting case in domestic law, see *Harris v Goddard* [1983] 1 WLR 1203.

122 Family Law Act 1986, ss 45–54, replacing the Recognition of Divorces and Legal Separations Act 1971, s 8.

123 Family Law Act 1986, s 51(1)(b).

124 [1983] 1 AC 145 (to have done otherwise would have involved setting aside an earlier judgment of Ormrod J (a specialist Family Law judge) in *Messina v Smith* [1971] P 322, where the learned judge had not only dismissed the earlier case but made a finding that the claim was fraudulent.

125 See, in particular, the speech of Lord Simon; the application for recognition was also rejected on the grounds of public policy.

No subsisting marriage

This ground applies only to decrees of divorce and orders of legal separation. According to s 52(2), the English court has a discretion to refuse to recognise such decrees where the decree is inconsistent with a prior holding by an English court or a foreign court under the rules of private international law that the marriage is itself a nullity. Clearly, a marriage cannot be terminated by divorce after it has previously been declared to be a nullity. Manifestly, there is some overlap between this provision and that of *res judicata*. For example, if a nullity decree is pronounced in country A and a divorce is granted in country B, then any attempt to seek recognition of the divorce would be met by an assertion that the matter was not only *res judicata* but, also, at variance with the prior nullity decree. It is possible to imagine circumstances coming within this head where a divorce is granted in country A in respect of matters which, in England, would be grounds for a decree of nullity.

Want of notice of the proceedings

An overseas divorce, annulment or judicial separation may be refused recognition if the decree was obtained without steps having been taken for giving notice of proceedings which, having regard to the nature of proceedings, should reasonably have been given.[126] This ground of refusal is discretionary and will normally involve three elements, namely: (a) an inquiry into whether the rules of the foreign court have been complied with; (b) a determination as to whether the rules themselves are reasonable; and (c) a determination as to whether the discretion to refuse recognition should be exercised. Thus, in *Sabbagh v Sabbagh*, a wife was held not to have received proper notice of an appeal in Brazil even though the notice had been published in accordance with Brazilian law. However, Balcombe J did not exercise the discretion to refuse recognition of the decree of judicial separation, as the wife had already chosen not to take part in the proceedings.[127] A similar general approach was followed by Wall J in *D v D*,[128] where the judge refused recognition of a decree obtained in Ghana in circumstances where the wife had not been informed of the proceedings and the expert evidence indicated that the judgment would have been set aside by the High Court of Ghana.[129]

---

126 Family Law Act 1986, s 51(3)(a)(i).

127 *Sabbagh v Sabbagh* [1985] FLR 29 (the court was not prepared to accept that the Official Gazette published in Brazil was likely to be supplied by newsagents even in cosmopolitan London NW4!).

128 [1994] 1 FLR 38 (the court took the view that it was insufficient to inform the mother-in-law and make her a party to proceedings).

129 The judgment was not effective under the law of the country in which it was obtained, so s 46(1)(a) had not been complied with.

Denial of an opportunity to take part in proceedings[130]

An overseas decree of divorce, nullity or separation may be refused recognition if it was obtained without a party having been given such opportunity to take part in the proceedings as, having regard to these matters, he or she should reasonably have been given. Thus, if a party is prohibited from participating by external events, this might be a ground for refusing recognition.[131] Recognition will be refused if the failure of one party to participate was directly attributable to the deception of another party[132] or if the foreign court has assumed jurisdiction solely on the basis of false evidence provided by the petitioner.[133] Where full participation in the foreign proceedings has been frustrated partly because of the conduct of legal advisers, then recognition may be refused if it would be of practical advantage to an innocent party.[134]

Difficult questions may arise where a party does not participate in foreign proceedings simply because of lack of financial resources. It is certainly true that the absence of financial resources may be a relevant factor to weigh in the balance when exercising the discretion but much will depend on the context. The court will be concerned to investigate whether the party could have participated in the foreign proceedings by correspondence and, while the absence of legal aid is a factor, the court will wish to investigate whether the party had access to other resources (for example, parents or relatives) or whether an individual had been rendered destitute by the failure of the other party to provide financial support.[135]

Absence of documentation in non-proceedings cases

In the cases of decrees of divorce, annulment or separation obtained other than by proceedings, recognition may be denied if there is no official document certifying that the decree is effective under the law of the country in which it was obtained.[136] In cases where either party to the marriage was domiciled in another country at the relevant date, then there is to be no recognition unless there is an official document certifying that the decree is

---

130 Family Law Act 1986, s 51(3)(a)(ii).

131 *Mitford v Mitford* [1923] P 130 (Duke P) (in any event, the absence of natural justice did not arise on the facts).

132 *Macalpine v Macalpine* [1958] P 35 (husband induced foreign court to dispense with service by false evidence).

133 *Middleton v Middleton* [1967] P 62.

134 *Newmarch v Newmarch* [1978] Fam 79; *Joyce v Joyce* [1979] Fam 93.

135 *Joyce v Joyce* [1979] Fam 93 (Lane J); *Mamdani v Mamdani* [1984] FLR 699, CA; *Sabbagh v Sabbagh* [1985] FLR 29.

136 Family Law Act 1986, s 51(3)(b)(i).

recognised as valid under the law of that other country.[137] It should be noted that the absence of the requisite documentary evidence is only a discretionary ground for refusal of recognition.

Recognition contrary to public policy[138]

There is a statutory discretion to refuse recognition where it would be manifestly contrary to public policy. It would seem that the word 'manifestly' has been inserted in order to demonstrate that recognition will only be refused in circumstances where the facts plainly violate an identifiable head of public policy. Obviously, an English court cannot be used as an 'engine of fraud' so recognition would, in principle, be refused under this head where there was unambiguous evidence of duress or deception of another party.[139] Thus, in *Kendall v Kendall*,[140] Hollings J had no hesitation in refusing recognition of a Bolivian decree where a husband had deceived his wife into signing divorce papers. In that case, the documents were in a language the wife did not understand and the evidence of deception could not have been clearer. In such a case, the deception of a party will also involve the deception of the court. However, it is clear that the crucial question is whether the other party has been deceived. In *Eroglu v Eroglu*,[141] the husband and wife deceived a Turkish court into granting a divorce in 1976 on grounds of extreme incompatibility. The motive for the deception was to secure an abbreviated period of national service for the husband. The parties were far from incompatible and lived together until 1988, during which period two children were born. At a later date, the wife petitioned an English court for a dissolution; the husband, in reply, argued that the Turkish divorce should be recognised. Thorpe J distinguished *Kendall v Kendall* by pointing out that, in the case before him, the wife had joined with the husband to deceive the Turkish court. Secondly, the judge indicated that the discretion under s 51(3)(c) was to be exercised sparingly. Thirdly, the judge appeared to indicate that, where parties collude to deceive a foreign court, a form of estoppel will arise, so that: 'Those who play games with divorce decrees ... cannot reorder their status now that they have fallen out.' In respect of nullity decrees, where the position was until recently governed by common law, there were a number of judgments in which an English court had held a foreign nullity decree to be contrary to public policy. In *Gray v Formosa*,[142] a

---

137 Family Law Act 1986, s 51(3)(b)(ii).
138 *Ibid*, s 51(3)(c); see the Recognition of Divorces and Legal Separations Act 1971, s 8(2)(b).
139 *Re Meyer* [1971] P 278 (Jewish divorce in Germany in 1938).
140 [1977] Fam 208.
141 [1994] 2 FLR 287 (Thorpe J).
142 [1963] P 259 (Lord Denning MR, Pearson, Donovan LJJ).

Maltese court had declared a marriage in an English registry office to be null and void because, under Maltese law, such a marriage should be in accordance with canon law. The Court of Appeal declined to recognise the nullity decree, partly because it attempted to introduce an extra-territorial element into questions of formality and partly because the court considered that to do so would be flagrantly unjust. In the subsequent case of *Lepre v Lepre*,[143] where a Maltese court had granted a decree of nullity on the basis of an incapacity arising from creed, Simon P, after reviewing the prior case law, held that an English court at common law would refuse to recognise a decree of nullity if it 'offended intolerably against the concept of justice which prevails in our courts'. Thus, a foreign nullity decree might be refused recognition if it was contrary to English conceptions of substantial justice; in both cases, the effect of recognition would have been to retrospectively invalidate a marriage that was valid by the English choice of law rules. That such a discretion existed at common law was affirmed by the House of Lords in *Vervaeke v Smith*,[144] where one of the grounds for refusing to recognise the Belgian decree of nullity was that it was based on the Belgian view (but not the English) that a marriage was void where there was no intention to cohabit.

---

143 [1965] P 52 (Simon P).
144 [1983] 1 AC 145.

CHAPTER 20

CHILDREN

INTRODUCTION

We are concerned, in this chapter, with questions that arise in the conflict of laws concerning children. English law has a very large volume of legislation concerning children;[1] the legislation concerns not only the status of children and their relationship with their parents but, also, the duties and responsibilities of State agencies.This legislation has been growing in volume and importance in the 20th century.[2] In the conflict of laws, we are concerned with questions about the status of the child and where the child should live. A number of problems concerning children arise in the context of disputes about succession. It is intended, in this chapter, to examine five topics, namely: (a) legitimacy; (b) legitimation; (c) adoption; (d) custody; and (e) declarations. Although there are detailed statutory rules in respect of each of these matters, it should be borne in mind that, in most questions directly relating to children, the judge in England will normally be obliged to regard the welfare of the child as the paramount consideration;[3] where a different statutory provision has been enacted, then it is often indistinguishable from this general principle.[4]

LEGITIMACY

Introduction

At common law, a child born or conceived during marriage was presumed to be legitimate.[5] Thus, legitimacy was a legal status that the child acquired at the time of his birth. Illegitimacy (bastardy) attracted a considerable social

---

1   The most important being the Children Act 1989; but see, also, Child Abduction Act 1984 and Child Abduction and Custody Act 1985.

2   See, eg, Children Act 1948; Children and Young Persons Act 1963; Children Act 1975; and Child Care Act 1980.

3   See Children Act 1989, s 1; manifestly, this does not extend to cases concerning property rights.

4   See, eg, the Adoption Act 1976, s 6, which reads, in part: 'In reaching any decision relating to the adoption of a child, a court or adoption agency shall have regard to all the circumstances, first consideration being given to the need to safeguard and promote the welfare of the child throughout his childhood ...'

5   *Banbury Peerage Case* (1811) 1 Sim & St 153; *Morris v Davies* (1837) 5 Cl & Fin 163; *Cope v Cope* (1833) 5 C & P 604; *Hawes v Drager* (1883) 23 Ch D 173; *Re Bozelli's Settlement* (1902) 1 Ch 751; *Gordon v Gordon* (1903) P 141.

stigma and was subject to severe restrictions in respect of succession to property.[6] Although the law on legitimacy has been subject to three major statutory reforms in the present century,[7] the rules on succession to property reflect the common law history.[8]

Despite the efforts which have been belatedly made in English domestic law to remove the stigma of illegitimacy and to treat all children equally,[9] it remains the case that it may be necessary for conflict purposes, particularly in cases of succession, to distinguish the legitimate child from the illegitimate one. Even in domestic law, despite the reversal in 1969[10] of the traditional interpretation of words such as 'children' or 'issue' in wills and trusts, so that they now include all children, and the further extension of that principle in ss 18 and 19 of the Family Law Reform Act 1987, the testator or settlor remains free to distinguish his beneficiaries on the basis of their legitimacy, although now he has to be clear in his rebuttal of the inference of equality.

Historically, the exercise of establishing legitimacy has been the need to connect the child with his father, on the basis that motherhood is a fact but fatherhood is never more than a hypothesis, and this historical approach permeates the current law.

Traditionally, and still most commonly, legitimacy is solely determined by the validity of the parental marriage. However, there is another basis. Even if a child is illegitimate at birth, there is the process of legitimation, by which he can become legitimate. Also, there is the process of adoption, by which the legal links with the natural parents are severed and replaced by a new set of family relations.

The issues arising here are matters of status. The effect to be given to the status will vary according to the *lex causae* of the issue which gives rise to the enquiry. So, for example, whether illegitimate children or those legitimated or adopted can succeed on intestacy or can share in a testamentary or trust gift to 'children' will depend, respectively, on the *lex successionis* of the intestacy, the law governing the interpretation of the will and the *lex successionis*, and the law governing the interpretation and effect of the trust.

A child born or conceived during a marriage is presumed to be a legitimate child of the marriage[11] but the marriage must be valid by English conflict law. If the marriage is not valid on that basis, its validity by another

---

6   *Birtwhistle v Vardill* (1840) 7 Cl & F 895; *Re Goodman's Trusts* (1881) 17 Ch D 266; *Re Grey's Trusts* (1892) 3 Ch 288.

7   Legitimacy Act 1926; Legitimacy Act 1959; Legitimacy Act 1976.

8   See Family Law Reform Act 1969; Family Law Reform Act 1987.

9   The legislation is based, in a large part, on two Law Commission reports, Law Commission Report No 118 (1982) and Law Commission Report No 157 (1986), the general principle being set out in the Family Law Act 1987, s 1 (on which, see below).

10 Family Law Reform Act 1969, s 15.

11 *Re Bozelli's Settlement* (1902) 1 Ch 751.

system of law is for this purpose irrelevant. The two propositions are not, however, mutually exclusive. If the parental marriage is not valid by the English conflict of laws, the child's legitimacy cannot be based upon it, but that does not mean that the child is illegitimate. In general terms there are two broad questions that concern us, in particular, (a) whether a child should be recognised as legitimate; and (b) the effect of any such status upon succession.

The recognition of the status of legitimacy

It has to be admitted, at the outset, the there is no commonly agreed rule in private international law as to how the status of legitimacy is to be determined. In broad terms, there are three theories.

The first and oldest theory holds that a child is only to be recognised as legitimate if he is born or conceived during a marriage regarded as valid by the rules of the English conflict of laws. According to this theory, the role of the court is to determine whether there is a valid marriage and, if there is, then legitimacy follows by operation of the normal evidentiary presumptions. This approach had the virtue of simplicity, which was of some importance in the 19th century, when the status of illegitimacy could have serious social consequences. All the case law prior to 1945 is consistent with this theory. Thus, in *Brook v Brook*,[12] the determination that the marriage was invalid as within the prohibited degrees led inexorably to the conclusion that a child was illegitimate and that his property rights passed to the Crown.

Seven years later, a differently constituted House of Lords[13] adopted the same approach in the leading case of *Shaw v Gould*.[14] The facts of the case were as follows: a testator domiciled in England devised land on trust for the sons 'lawfully begotten' of his great niece Elizabeth Hickson. In 1828, at the age of 16, Elizabeth had gone through a ceremony of marriage with one Thomas Buxton. The marriage was never consummated. Both parties were domiciled in England. In 1844, Elizabeth fell in love with one John Shaw and wished to marry him. So, she paid Thomas Buxton to travel to Scotland and reside there for 40 days, so as to confer jurisdiction on the Scottish courts. A divorce was obtained in Scotland. In 1846, Elizabeth went through a ceremony of marriage with John Shaw. The parties resided and became domiciled in Scotland. There were three children of the marriage. Elizabeth died in 1863 and the three children then applied to the Court of Chancery for maintenance under the will of the testator.

---

12 *Brook v Brook* (1861) 9 HLC 193.
13 Apart from Lord Cranworth, who sat on both appeals.
14 *Shaw v Gould* (1868) LR 3 HL 55.

The House of Lords, in upholding the ruling of Kindersley VC, held that, as the divorce was not recognised in England,[15] it followed that the marriage to John Shaw was, in fact, void and that the children of the marriage were therefore illegitimate and thus unable to come within the class of those 'lawfully begotten'. As Lord Chelmsford expressed the matter: 'Whether the appellants answer the description respectively of "sons lawfully begotten" and of "children" depends upon whether their parents were lawfully married; and this, again, depends on the effect of the divorce in Scotland.'

That legitimacy depended on the validity of the marriage was the approach followed by Bennett J, in *Re Paine*,[16] where the facts were as follows: a testatrix left property to the 'child or children' of her daughter Ada. In 1875, Ada had gone through a ceremony of marriage in Germany. The marriage was valid in Germany but void in England because Ada had married the husband of her deceased sister. Of the three children of the marriage, one survived the mother. The question arose as to whether that child could take under the will. Bennett J followed the approach in *Shaw v Gould* and reasoned that, because Ada lacked capacity under the law of her domicile, the marriage was void, the children were illegitimate and, thus, they were unable to take under the will. So, this case is consistent with the 19th century cases, in holding that legitimacy depends upon finding that there is a valid marriage.[17]

However, there is a second theory, which holds that the legitimacy of the child depends on his domicile of origin and there are some judicial observations that may be taken to favour this approach.[18] However, as John Westlake indicated, the difficulty with this theory is that it is circular. As the domicile of origin of a legitimate child is that of his father and that of an illegitimate child is that of the mother, then the legitimacy of the child cannot depend on the domicile of origin if the domicile of origin is itself contingent on legitimacy. In any event, there was no case prior to 1945 that endorsed the theory and there was no case in which a child not born or conceived in lawful wedlock had been held legitimate.

The validity of the second theory arose in the case of *Re Bischoffsheim*,[19] where the facts were as follows: a testator, probably domiciled in England, devised and bequeathed real and personal estate to the children of his granddaughter, Nesta. In 1917, Nesta married, in New York, the brother of her deceased first husband. The domicile of both parties was English. In 1917, the

---

15 This was because neither party was domiciled in Scotland and, in any event, Elizabeth had the domicile of her then husband.

16 *Re Paine* [1940] Ch 46.

17 The argument put by Herbert Hart (later, Professor Hart) was to the point: 'The marriage ... was invalid. It takes two to make a contract. If one is incapacitated, there can be no contract.'

18 *Re Goodman's Trusts* (1881) 17 Ch D 266; *Re Andros* (1883) 24 Ch D 637.

19 *Re Bischoffsheim* [1948] Ch 79 (Romer J).

marriage was void under English law, being within the prohibited degrees set out in the Marriage Act 1835. The marriage was valid under the law of New York. In 1920, a child, Richard, was born and a summons was taken out to determine whether this child could benefit under the will.

The questions for Romer J, therefore, were (a) was the child legitimate? and (b) could he take under the will? Romer J reasoned that the operative date was the date of the birth of the child and that, at that date, the parties had acquired a domicile in New York and that, by the law of New York, the marriage was valid and the child legitimate. In respect of the judgment, a number of points arise: (a) the attempt to distinguish *Shaw v Gould* as founded on title to real property is not convincing;[20] (b) the learned judge appeared to accept that *Re Goodman's Trusts*[21] had established a general proposition that a person's legitimacy is determined by the law of his domicile at the date of his birth; and (c) if a person is legitimate by the law of his domicile of origin, that legitimacy will be recognised in England. Although the case is out of line with *Shaw v Gould*, it is possible to view *Re Bischoffsheim* as establishing that a child is legitimate for the purposes of English law if he is legitimate by the domicile of each of his parents at the time of his birth.[22] If the parents have different domiciles, it would seem that the one to select is not the one to which the enquiry relates, that is, whether the child can succeed through the mother or father, but the law of the father's domicile alone.[23]

The liberal approach in *Re Bischoffsheim*[24] is supported by subsequent changes in domestic law in respect of the putative marriage. The doctrine of the putative marriage holds that a child born of a void marriage will be legitimate if his parents, at the time of insemination or conception, believed the marriage to be valid. The doctrine derives from canon law, which was anxious to preserve legitimacy, even though the grounds for nullity had been extended; from canon law, the doctrine was accepted into the legal systems of civil law countries but it was not introduced into English law until s 2 of the

---

20 It has been argued that this was based on a misreading of *Birtwhistle v Vardill* (1840) 7 Cl & F 895, which concerns the effect of a legitimation by foreign law upon intestate succession to realty; *Shaw v Gould* (1968) LR 3 HL 55 concerned the testate succession to both real and personal property.

21 *Re Goodman's Trusts* (1881) 17 Ch D 266 (Cotton LJ, James LJ, Lush LJ dissenting). The case concerned legitimation by foreign law. Cotton LJ observed 'the question as to legitimacy is one of status and, in my opinion, by the law of England, questions of status depend on the law of the domicile'. It is interesting to note that the Court of Appeal overruled the first instance judgment of Jessel MR ((1880) 14 Ch D 619), who had held that, for a child to be legitimate, he must be born in lawful wedlock. Jessel MR had acted as counsel in *Shaw v Gould* (1968) LR 3 HL 55.

22 It is noteworthy how the law on recognition of legitimacy was being influenced by judgments turning on legitimation by foreign law: see *Re Goodman's Trusts* (1881) 17 Ch D 266; *Re Andros* (1883) 24 Ch D 637.

23 *Re Grove* (1888) 40 Ch D 216.

24 *Re Bischoffsheim* [1948] Ch 79; followed by Brown P in *Motala v AG* [1990] 2 FLR 261; see, also, *Bamgbose v Daniel* [1955] AC 107.

Legitimacy Act 1959. The relevant provisions are now contained in s 1 of the Legitimacy Act 1976, as amended by s 28 of the Family Law Reform Act 1987. The child will be legitimate if his parents reasonably believed, at the time of insemination, that the marriage was valid and such a belief is presumed unless the contrary is demonstrated. This legislation indirectly supports the *Bischoffsheim* principle because there was no doubt that the parties in that case intended to establish a domicile of choice in New York and thus contract a valid marriage.

There is a third theory,[25] that holds that, where a question of legitimacy at birth arises in relation to a matter of succession, then it should be regarded as a question of construction to be governed by the *lex successionis*. There are a number of points that arise: (a) the theory does not properly distinguish between questions of status and entitlement to succeed; (b) there is no case law that supports the theory; (c) the case law is clear in regarding legitimacy as a matter of status;[26] and (d) the theory provides no guidance as to how to proceed when a question of legitimacy arises independent of any question of succession.

Thus, in respect of the narrow question of the rule to govern legitimacy at birth (as distinct from subsequent legitimation), it is probably not possible to reconcile all the case law within a single principle. However, the case law does indicate two principles: (a) that a child will be legitimate if, and only if, he is born in lawful wedlock;[27] and (b) that legitimacy is a question of status and is therefore to be governed by the child's domicile of origin.[28] It has to be acknowledged that the first theory finds it difficult to accommodate the doctrine of the putative marriage, while the second theory is circular if the father and mother are domiciled in different countries.[29]

The late Professor Cross[30] indicated that it was possible to reconcile most of the case law around the principle that a child would be legitimate if, at the date of his birth, he was legitimate by the law of the domicile of both of his parents. Thus, in *Brook v Brook*, the child was illegitimate because, at the date of his birth, both parents were domiciled in England; in *Shaw v Gould*, the children were illegitimate because the mother remained domiciled in England; in *Re Bethell*, the child was illegitimate because the father remained domiciled in England; in *Re Paine*, the children were illegitimate because the

---

25 See Welsh (1947) 63 LQR 65.

26 *Re Goodman's Trusts* (1881) 17 Ch D 266, p 291, *per* Cotton LJ.

27 The view held by Westlake and Dicey and supported by *Brook v Brook* (1861) 9 HLC 193; *Shaw v Gould* (1868) LR 3 HL 55; *Re Bethell* (1887) 38 Ch D 220; and *Re Paine* [1940] Ch 46.

28 The view held by Story, Cheshire, Wolf and Schmitthoff and supported by *Re Goodman's Trusts* (1881) 17 Ch D 266; *Re Andros* (1883) 24 Ch D 637; *Re Bischoffsheim* [1948] Ch 79.

29 Which was not a problem in *Re Bischoffsheim* [1948] Ch 79.

30 Although better known today as the dominant writer on the law of evidence, Rupert Cross did, in fact, act as an editor of Dicey, *The Conflict of Laws* (6th edn, 1949).

mother was, at the time of the marriage, domiciled in England; and, in *Re Bischoffsheim*, the child was legitimate because both his parents were domiciled in New York. The learned editor of Dicey, the late Dr Morris, made the point that, while this formula might reconcile the decisions, it did not reconcile the actual reasoning; to this it might be added that the earlier decisions of *Brook v Brook* and *Shaw v Gould* were handed down before the concept of domicile became the dominant element in the allocation of a personal law.

If the better view is that the issue of legitimacy or, rather, the removal of the legal status of illegitimacy, is a matter of status referable to the child's domiciliary law at the time of the birth, it follows that, if, by that law, no distinction is made between legitimate and illegitimate children and all children are treated equally, then no distinction should be taken by any other legal system with regard to them. In short, they should not be entered into another legal category by a different legal system on the basis, for example, that their parents were not married.

Succession by legitimate persons

A person who is recognised as legitimate in England can succeed to property by will or upon intestacy to the same extent as if he was regarded as legitimate under domestic law.

It has to be acknowledged that English law was slow to acknowledge the discriminatory nature of illegitimacy. At common law, a child born to unmarried parents was regarded as *filius nullius* and had no rights to succeed to their property. However, early in the 20th century, two trends began to emerge. First, the concept of legitimacy was widened to allow a child to be legitimated by the subsequent marriage of the parents[31] and legislation provided that the children of void marriages could be legitimate.[32] Secondly, legislation was passed to allow illegitimate children to obtain property rights in certain areas on virtually the same basis as the legitimate child, particularly in matters such as family provision[33] and in the law of tort.[34]

---

31 Introduced by the Legitimacy Act 1926, s 1 and extended by the Legitimacy Act 1959 to a child born of adultery; the provisions are now contained in the Legitimacy Act 1976, s 2. The Legitimacy Act 1976, s 8, provides that a legitimated person shall have all the rights as a legitimate one.

32 Introduced by the Legitimacy Act 1959, s 2; see, now, the Legitimacy Act 1976, s 1, as amended by the Family Law Reform Act 1987. The change had been recommended by the Morton Commission (Cmnd 9678, 1956), in order to bring English law into line with Scotland.

33 Family Law Reform Act 1969, s 18; Inheritance (Provision for Family and Dependants) Act 1975, ss 1, 25.

34 Fatal Accidents Act 1976, as amended by the Administration of Justice Act 1982.

A significant reform was effected by Part II of the Family Law Reform Act 1969. By s 14 of the legislation, it was provided that an illegitimate child should succeed on an equal basis to the legitimate child in respect of the intestacy of a parent. In the case of testate succession, s 15 of the Act provided for the reversal of the normal rule of interpretation, stipulating that, in the absence of contrary intention, any reference to a child or children of any person shall be construed as including a reference to an illegitimate child of that person.

The growth of cohabitation from the 1970s prompted the Law Commission to set up a working party to examine the entire law on illegitimacy. A working paper was produced in 1979[35] and a report appeared, together with a draft Bill, in 1982, which provided for the removal of some of the disadvantages of illegitimacy.[36] The Law Commission came down against removing the status of illegitimacy altogether. However, legislative action did not follow because the Scottish Law Commission produced a report on the same subject in 1984 and its proposals formed the basis of the Law Reform (Parent and Child) Act 1986.

The Law Commission considered that it would be desirable to avoid two different legislative schemes, so a further report[37] was produced, which formed the basis for the present law, now contained in the Family Law Reform Act 1987.[38]

Section 1(1) of the Family Law Reform Act 1987 provides that, unless a contrary intention appears, in all legislation and instruments made after 4 April 1988, 'references (however expressed) to any relationship between two persons shall be construed without regard to whether or not the father and mother of either of them, or the father and mother of any person through whom the relationship is deduced, have or had been married to each other at any time'. The legislation also provides that the rule of interpretation is to be applied to certain existing statutes.[39]

By s 18 of the Family Law Reform Act 1987, in the case of an intestacy arising on or after 4 April 1988,[40] references in the intestacy rules in Part IV of the Administration of Estates Act 1925 to any relationship between two persons are to be construed without regard to whether the parents of either of them, or of any person through whom the relationship is deduced, were at any time married to one another. By s 19 of the legislation, any reference in an *inter vivos* disposition or will executed after 4 April 1988 shall be construed in like fashion, unless the contrary appears.

---

35 Law Commission Working Paper No 74 (1979).
36 Law Commission Report No 118 (1982).
37 Law Commission Report No 157 (1986).
38 Most provisions were effective from 1 April 1989: see SI 1988/425; SI 1989/382.
39 Family Law Reform Act 1987, s 2.
40 The date of the coming into effect of ss 18 and 19.

There may, in the future, be problems as to relevant dates. The provisions of the Family Law Reform Act 1969 relate only to succession or dispositions of property arising after 1969, while the provisions of the Family Law Reform Act 1987 are operative only after April 4 1988, so that there may be litigation in the future where the operative date is of some importance.

Legitimation

In respect of the recognition of foreign legitimations, it is important to draw a distinction between the rules at common law and the statutory provisions introduced since the enactment of the Legitimacy Act 1926.

Recognition of foreign legitimations at common law

Legitimation is the name given to the legal doctrine whereby a child that is illegitimate at the date of its birth becomes legitimate upon the happening of a subsequent event, normally the subsequent marriage of the parents (that is, *legitimatio per subsequens matrimonium*). The doctrine of legitimation was introduced into English law as recently as 1926.[41] One of the reasons for this delay had been that, prior to the property reforms of 1925, it was important to establish the heir at law for the purpose of intestate succession to realty.[42]

Although English law had been slow to accept the concept of legitimation,[43] the doctrine had been recognised in both Roman law and canon law and was accepted by the legal systems of other European States. By the end of the 19th century, legitimation had been accepted in many States of the USA and in the common law jurisdictions of Australia and Canada. Therefore, even before 1926, the English courts had considerable experience in dealing with cases involving legitimation in other jurisdictions.

In the 19th century, it came to be accepted[44] that, at common law, a child might be recognised as legitimated if the father was domiciled, both at the time of the child's birth and at the time of the subsequent marriage, in a

---

41 Legitimacy Act 1926, s 1; extended in the Legitimacy Act 1959 to where the child was born in adultery; see, now, the Legitimacy Act 1976, s 2; *Re Lowe* [1929] 2 Ch 210.

42 See, now, the Administration of Estates Act 1925, s 33.

43 An attempt to introduce legitimation into English law was rejected in the Statute of Merton 1235; this may have been due to the peers, who are thought to have cried, *'nolumus leges Angliae mutare'*. For an historical survey, see the dissenting judgment of Lush LJ, in *Re Goodman's Trusts* (1881) 17 Ch D 266, p 269.

44 It has to be admitted that the case law is less than clear but it can be traced from *Re Wright's Trusts* (1856) 2 K & J 595 (Page Wood VC); *Goodman v Goodman* (1862) 3 Giff 643 (Stuart VC); *Boyes v Bedale* (1863) 1 H & M 798 (Page Wood VC); *Skottowe v Young* (1871) LR 11 Eq 474 (Stuart VC); *Re Goodman's Trusts* (1880) 14 Ch D 619 (Jessel MR); (1881) 17 Ch D 266, CA; *Re Andros* (1883) 24 Ch D 637 (Kay J); *Re Grove* (1887) 40 Ch D 216, CA; *Re Grey's Trusts* [1892] 3 Ch 88 (Sterling J); *Re Askew* [1930] 2 Ch 259 (Maugham J).

country where the law permitted legitimation. This two fold test was said to derive from the majority judgment of the Court of Appeal in *Re Goodman's Trusts*,[45] where the facts were as follows: Leon Goodman, domiciled and resident in Holland, had a daughter, Hannah, by an Englishwoman, whom he later married in 1822. This legitimated the daughter under the law of Holland but not under English law. At a later date, the sister of Leon Goodman died intestate and the question arose as to whether Hannah could succeed as a child under the Statute of Distribution.

At first instance, in an unreserved judgment, Jessel MR held that the child could only claim if she were legitimate under English law as a child born in lawful wedlock. This judgment was reversed by a majority of the Court of Appeal, who held (a) that legitimacy or legitimation were matters of status, which, in principle, were to be determined by the law of the domicile; and (b) that, under the relevant law of the domicile (the law of Holland), the child became legitimate through the process of legitimation and was therefore entitled to succeed to personal property on intestacy. The majority of the Court of Appeal appeared to indicate that, for a foreign legitimation to be recognised in England, then the father must be domiciled, both at the time of the birth and at the time of the subsequent marriage, in a country where legitimation is part of the domestic law. It has been argued that the authority for this two fold requirement was limited and the reasons for it were less than compelling.

The matter was not fully considered again by the Court of Appeal until judgment was given in *Re Luck's Settlement Trusts*,[46] where the facts were as follows: an Englishman, Charles Luck, left England and his wife and two children, in 1905, and went to live in California. From 1905 until 1918, he lived with one Martha Croft and had a son, David, in 1906. However, in 1922, he secured a dissolution of his marriage in California and married one Alma Hyam. In 1925, he signed a document publicly recognising David as his son. Under Californian law, this made David legitimate from the date of his birth. At a later date, a question arose as to whether David was legitimate and entitled to succeed under a marriage settlement and will. Farwell J held that David was entitled to be recognised as legitimate, notwithstanding that his father was not domiciled in California at the date of his birth. The majority of the Court of Appeal allowed the appeal.

The reasoning of the majority of the Court of Appeal was that, although this was a case of legitimation by public recognition, it was desirable to have a single rule in respect of foreign legitimations and that the existing rule required the two fold test to be met. Secondly, it was argued that the twofold

---

45 (1881) 17 Ch D 266 (Cotton, James, Lush LJJ dissenting); reversing (1880) 14 Ch D 619 (Jessel MR).
46 [1940] Ch 864 (Lord Greene MR, Luxmoore and Scott LJJ dissenting); reversing [1940] Ch 323 (Farwell J).

test was based on a relationship arising at birth and that, in any event, if recognition depended simply on domicile at the time of acknowledgment or subsequent marriage, this might lead to injustice in the cases where a man had more than one illegitimate child from different women but only married the mother of one of them. This was not particularly convincing and the force of the judgment was undermined by the dissenting opinion of Scott LJ, who argued that domicile was the determining factor and that status and recognition flowed from it, and that there was no good public policy reason to withhold recognition. The learned judge questioned whether it was sensible to confirm a common law rule that had already been modified by statute[47] and which had been developed in the case of legitimation by subsequent marriage rather than that of legitimation by public recognition. The dissenting opinion of Scott LJ has been broadly accepted by subsequent commentators.[48]

Legitimation by statute under domestic law

As indicated above, under the terms of s 1(1) of the Legitimacy Act 1926, it was provided that, where the parents of an illegitimate person had married one another, whether before or after 1 January 1927, the marriage would, if the father is or was at the date of the marriage domiciled in England or Wales, render that person, if living, legitimate from 1 January 1927 or from the date of the marriage, whichever was the later event. Legislation to like effect was passed in Northern Ireland.[49] The original provisions in the Legitimacy Act 1926 had adopted the Canon law position that legitimation would not operate if either party was married to another at the time of the child's birth. This restriction was removed by the Legitimacy Act 1959 and both provisions were repealed and replaced by the Legitimacy Act 1976, which requires that the father be domiciled in England or Wales at the time of the marriage and that legitimation would not be retrospective but from the date of the marriage.[50]

Recognition of foreign legitimations by statute

Section 8 of the Legitimacy Act 1926 (now re-enacted as s 3 of the Legitimacy Act 1976) introduced a new statutory rule providing for foreign legitimations. The section provides that, where the parents of an illegitimate person marry

---

47 Legitimacy Act 1926, s 8.
48 Mann, FA (1941) 57 LQR 112.
49 Legitimacy (Northern Ireland) Act 1928.
50 This could be important, as in cases such as *Re Luck's Settlement Trusts* [1940] Ch 864, where it had to be shown that the grandson was alive and legitimate on a certain date so as to avoid a perpetuity under the relevant trust instruments.

one another before or after 1 January 1927 and the father of the illegitimate person is not, at the time of the marriage, domiciled in England or Wales but is domiciled in a country by the law of which the illegitimate person becomes legitimated by virtue of such subsequent marriage, that person, if living, shall in England and Wales be recognised as having been so legitimated from the date of the marriage, notwithstanding that, at the time of his birth, his father was domiciled in a country, the law of which did not permit legitimation by subsequent marriage.

The new statutory rule may have been intended to abolish the common law rule but it has been held that it does not.[51] It is clearer than the common law rule, in that it looks at the domicile of the father at the time of the marriage. There are, however, certain advantages to the common law rule which may, in certain cases, be appropriate, and certain distinctions can be drawn: (a) the statutory regime effects legitimacy from the date of the marriage, while the common law rules operate from birth; (b) the statutory rules apply only in respect of *legitimatio per subsequens matrimonium*, while the common law rules extend to all forms of legitimation;[52] (c) if the law of the father's domicile does not recognise *legitimatio per subsequens matrimonium*, then there can be no reliance on the statutory rules;[53] (d) the common law rules would have to be relied upon in cases turning on whether a person was legitimate prior to 1 January 1927; (e) as the Legitimacy Act 1926 did not apply where either party was married to another and as this restriction was not removed until October 1959, by the Legitimacy Act 1959, then the common law rules might be invoked in cases prior to the coming into effect of the Legitimacy Act 1959; and (f) as a matter of construction, the statutory rules will not apply in cases where the individual was not living at the date of the subsequent marriage.

It has been remarked that the rules on the recognition of foreign legitimations are unnecessarily complex, particularly having regard to the limited number of circumstances in which legitimacy is crucial. However, at the risk of gross over simplification, it would appear that, if a question concerning foreign legitimation is before the court, then it is necessary (a) to determine the appropriate date when the question arises; (b) to determine the position at common law; and (c) to determine which of the relevant pieces of legislation are in force on the operative date.[54]

---

51 *Re Luck's Settlement Trusts* [1940] Ch 864.
52 *Ibid.*
53 *Motala v AG* [1990] 2 FLR 261 (Brown P); Indian law did not recognise legitimation by subsequent marriage.
54 Ie, Legitimacy Acts 1926, 1959 or 1976.

Succession by legitimated persons

Difficulties arose in the 19th century in respect of succession by legitimated persons. There were two reasons for this: first, the caution to be expected of the English courts in respect of a concept that had not, at that time, been accepted by domestic law and, secondly, because of the different rules that existed on intestacy in respect of real and personal property. Thus, in *Birtwhistle v Vardill*,[55] after some hesitation, the House of Lords ruled that a child legitimated under the law of Scotland could not succeed under intestate succession as heir to real estate in England, even though the father was domiciled in Scotland at the time both of the birth and the subsequent marriage. However, the case was confined to intestate succession of real estate by the majority of the Court of Appeal in *Re Goodman's Trusts*,[56] who allowed a child legitimated under Dutch law to succeed to personal property. This more liberal approach was continued in *Re Grey's Trusts*,[57] where Stirling J confined the rule in *Birtwhistle v Vardill* to cases of intestate succession to real estate and so allowed a child legitimated under the Roman Dutch law of the Cape of Good Hope to succeed to real property by will.

Thus, by the time of the property reforms of 1925, the rule in *Birtwhistle v Vardill* was confined to cases of intestate succession of real estate. Section 45 of the Administration of Estates Act 1925 abolished descent of the heir in the case of the fee simple absolute in possession and provided, instead, that it should be sold and distributed like personalty under the terms of ss 46 and 47.

Section 3 of the Legitimacy Act 1926 set out rules in respect of the succession to property by legitimated children; those rules were to apply whether the child was legitimated under s 1 or 8 of the Legitimacy Act 1926.[58] These rules made provision for the succession of legitimated persons, provided that legitimation was prior to the *inter vivos* deed or the death of the testator;[59] this restriction appears to contrast with the greater liberality allowed to those legitimated at common law, where the effect was normally fully retrospective.[60] The interpretation placed on the rules indicated that a child whose foreign legitimation was recognised at common law might have superior rights to the child whose legitimation arose under ss 1 or 8 of the Legitimacy Act 1925. An attempt was made to modify the position, in s 15(4) of the Family Law Reform Act 1969 but these provisions were replaced, as of 1

---

55 (1826) 5 B & C 438, Court of King's Bench; (1835) 2 Cl & F 571 (first hearing); (1840) 7 Cl & F 895 (second hearing, at the request of Lord Brougham).

56 *Re Goodman's Trusts* (1881) 17 Ch D 266.

57 *Re Grey's Trusts* [1892] 3 Ch 88.

58 Legitimacy Act 1926, s 1 (now, Legitimacy Act 1976, s 2); Legitimacy Act 1926, s 8 (now, Legitimacy Act 1976, s 3).

59 *Re Hepworth* [1936] Ch 750; *Re Hoff* [1942] Ch 298.

60 *Re Askew* [1930] 2 Ch 259; *Re Hurll* [1952] Ch 722.

January 1976, by the provisions set out in s 5 of the Legitimacy Act 1976. By virtue of s 10, the provisions apply to persons legitimated under the various possible methods.[61] By virtue of s 5(4) and (5), the will of a testator made after 1 January 1976, leaving property to X for life, remainder to the children of X, will include the legitimated children of X, regardless of whether legitimation took effect before or after the death, unless a contrary intention is indicated.[62]

As has been noted above, the statutory provisions in respect of domestic and foreign legitimations apply only if the person is living at the time of the subsequent marriage.[63] However, in respect of succession, the rule is modified so that, if X is born illegitimate and then dies and, subsequent to his death, the parents marry, then the provisions of s 5 will continue to apply.[64]

ADOPTION

Introduction

Adoption is the process whereby the child's links with his natural parents are legally severed and legal relations with his adoptive parents are established in their place.

In England, the domestic law begins with the Adoption of Children Act 1926.[65] However, the legislation was later considerably amended and then consolidated in the Adoption Act 1958.[66] In 1965, the UK signed the Hague Convention, relating to the adoption of children, and this was given effect to in the Adoption Act 1968. However, the dissatisfaction with the domestic law on adoption led to the establishment of a departmental committee to review adoption law and procedure, and the committee produced its report in 1972.[67] The recommendations of the committee reached the statute book in the form of the Children Act 1975 and then the entire legislation on adoption was consolidated in the Adoption Act 1976.[68] The Adoption Act 1976 came into

---

61 Ie, Legitimacy Act 1926, ss 1, 8; Legitimacy Act 1976, ss 2, 3; together with those legitimated at common law.

62 *Ibid*, s 5(1).

63 *Ibid*, ss 2, 3.

64 *Ibid*, s 5(6).

65 Based on the Hopkinson Report (Cmnd 1254, 1921) and the Tomlin Report (Cmnd 2401 and 2469, 1925). The concern had been raised by social changes, in particular, the rise in the number of *de facto* adoptions.

66 Following upon the Hurst Report (Cmnd 9240, 1954).

67 Houghton Report (Cmnd 5107).

68 The Adoption Act 1976 therefore consolidated provisions drawn from the Adoption Acts 1958, 1960, 1964 and 1968 and the Children Act 1975.

force on 1 January 1988 and has been subject to limited amendments made by the Children Act 1989.

From the outset, English law has emphasised the legal nature of adoption as being in the nature of a transfer, the social purpose being to establish ties between the child and the adoptive parents. In contrast, civil law systems draw upon the Roman law concepts of *adoptio* and *adrogatio*; under Roman law, one of the purposes of adoption was to prevent a family becoming extinguished and to create heirs. This legacy is to be found in civil law systems, where adoption may be used to provide heirs or to affect the inheritance of other relatives.[69]

It is worth noting that, in the last 30 years, there have been a number of social changes that have had a considerable impact on the law of adoption.[70] First, there have been fewer children to adopt in England and Wales; partly, this is caused by factors such as the availability of contraception and abortion but, also, by the fact that more women are keeping their children rather than offering them for adoption. In consequence, couples anxious to adopt are often minded to seek a child for adoption. Secondly, the impact of the mass media in drawing attention to child victims in poor countries or politically unstable regimes has led to attempts to adopt abroad. Thirdly, the development of civil aviation and the fall in the cost of air travel has made it possible for couples to travel abroad when seeking to adopt.[71] The net effect of these social changes has been to increase the foreign element in adoptions and questions arise as to the circumstances in which persons resident in England should be allowed to adopt abroad and problems naturally arise as to the criteria for the recognition of foreign adoptions.

Jurisdiction to make an adoption order in England

The Adoption Act 1976 regulates the making of adoption orders in England. The legislation provides that applicants must be aged at least 21[72] and the applicant[73] or, in the case of a joint application, one of the applicants must be

---

69 One of the best known cases was the attempt of the English writer, W Somerset Maugham (1874–1965), to a persuade a French court to allow him, in 1962, to adopt his secretary, who was then aged 56. The adoption order was quashed on appeal because it was ruled that the lower court should have applied British law. In the will of 1964, made shortly after the quashing of the adoption order, all royalties on the writer's works passed to the secretary. See Calder, *Willie: The Life of W Somerset Maugham* (1989).

70 In 1968, the number of adoption orders was just below 25,000; by 1987, the number had fallen to just over 7,000.

71 All these factors came together after the fall of the Ceausescu regime in Romania, in December 1989, when the reports of the media as to the poor conditions in orphanages lead to a large number of adoptions.

72 Adoption Act 1976, ss 14(1)(A), 15(1).

73 *Ibid*, s 15(2).

domiciled in a part of the UK, Channel Islands or the Isle of Man, unless the application is for a convention order.[74] An adoption order can only be sought in respect of a person under the age of 18 who has never been married.[75] The domicile of the child does not affect jurisdiction, partly because the domicile may be one of dependence and this would act as an obstacle to foreign adoptions.[76] The law that will be applied is English law and that law requires the agreement, in the case of married parents, of each parent and, if the parents are not married, that of the child's mother but not the father.[77] The agreement must be freely given and cannot be lawfully given until the child is six weeks old.[78] The legislation contains provision for the dispensing with agreement in appropriate cases.[79] In a contested case, the court is required to consider whether adoption is in the child's best interests[80] and then to consider whether parental agreement should be dispensed with.[81]

The effect of an English adoption order is to establish the legal relationship of parent and legitimate child between the adopter and the adopted child.[82] The rights and obligations of the natural parents are extinguished by the adoption order.[83] The adopted child and the adoptive parent come within the prohibited degrees for the purposes of marriage[84] and the adopted child continues to be within the prohibited degrees in relation to his natural parents and other relatives as if he had not been adopted. A child who was not entitled to British citizenship will acquire it if the adopted parent possesses it.[85]

One of the obvious problems with a national regime of adoption law is that it will have its own values and procedures and that any order made may not necessarily be recognised elsewhere. If an order is not recognised, then there is the danger of the 'limping child', whose status is recognised in one jurisdiction but not in another. Indeed, there is some reference in the authorities to the question of whether an English court, when deciding to make an adoption order, should first inquire as to to whether the order will be recognised in the domicile of the child. It has to be admitted that the tendency

---

74   Adoption Act 1976, s 14; for convention orders, see below.

75   *Ibid*, ss 12(5), 12(6), 72(1).

76   *Re B(S) (infant)* [1968] Ch 204; [1967] 3 All ER 629.

77   Adoption Act 1976, s 16.

78   *Ibid*, s 16(4).

79   *Ibid*, s 16(1)(b)(ii), (2); for the case law, see *O'Connor v A and B* [1971] 1 WLR 1227; 2 All ER 1230; *Re W (an infant)* [1971] AC 682; 2 All ER 49; *Re D (an infant) (adoption parental agreement)* [1977] AC 602.

80   *Ibid*, s 6.

81   *Re P* [1977] Fam 25.

82   Adoption Act 1976, s 39(1)(a).

83   *Ibid*, s 39(2).

84   Marriage Act 1949, Sched 1, as amended by Children Act 1975, Sched 3, para 8.

85   British Nationality Act 1981, s 1(5).

in each individual case is to concentrate upon what is in the best interests of the specific child; the wider question of securing uniformity of status in different countries is (as with other areas in private international law) to be achieved through the implementation in domestic law of international agreements that provide for uniform rules. Further, it has to be acknowledged that progress in the area of area of adoption law has been very limited.

Convention adoptions

In the year following the 10th session of the Hague Conference on Private International Law 1964, the UK signed the Hague Convention on Adoption. Legislation to give effect to the Convention was introduced in the Adoption Act 1968,[86] although the jurisdictional requirements were modified by s 24 of the Children Act 1975. The UK ratified the Convention in 1978 and the domestic legislation came into force thereafter. The relevant domestic legislation is now contained in the Adoption Act 1976. The guiding principle of the Convention is to provide uniformity of status by balancing the rules of the country of the adoptive parents with the legislative requirements of the country of the natural parents.The legislation does not apply to domestic adoptions, where the applicants and the child are UK nationals living in British territory.

The effect of the provisions is to extend the jurisdiction so as to enable an English court to make an order in favour of an applicant or applicants who are UK nationals or nationals of a Convention country and who must be habitually resident in British territory or a Convention country.[87] The child must also be a national of, and be habitually resident in, the UK or a Convention country. Although, in general, English law will apply, the national legislation reflects the Hague Convention in providing that, where the applicant or applicants are from a Convention country, then no order must be made if it conflicts with the internal law of that country.[88] In cases where the child is not a national of the UK, then an order will only be made if the rules in respect of consents and consultations arising under the internal law of the Convention country of which the child is a national have been complied with and those who consent do so with full understanding.[89] The legislation contains provision for quashing orders where there has not been compliance with these requirements.[90]

---

86 Adoption Act 1968, ss 1–3, replaced by the Children Act 1975, s 24; the relevant provisions are now contained in the Adoption Act 1976, s 17.

87 The jurisdiction requirements set out in the Adoption Act 1976, s 17(4), (5) reflect the provisions of the Hague Convention 1964, Art 3.

88 Adoption Act 1976, s 17(4), (5), as specified under s 17(8).

89 *Ibid*, s 17(6), (7).

90 *Ibid*, s 53.

It has to be acknowledged that these provisions have had only limited effect, since only two countries have ratified the relevant Hague Convention.[91]

Recognition of foreign adoptions

There are many circumstances in which a case may arise in which an English court is concerned with whether a foreign adoption order should be recognised and, if so, with the effect of any such order. The case law indicates that the question will often arise incidentally, for example, in property and succession cases as to whether a particular person can succeed under a will.[92] Questions of recognition also arise in cases in immigration law, social security law or rights on intestacy.[93]

There are three distinct aspects of recognition, namely, (a) recognition of adoptions made elsewhere in the British Isles; (b) recognition under the Adoption Act 1976; and (c) recognition at common law.

A number of statutory provisions are directed to the recognition in England and Wales of an adoption order made in another jurisdiction. An adoption order made in Scotland will be recognised in England and Wales[94] as will an adoption order made in Northern Ireland, the Channel Islands or the Isle of Man.[95]

The Adoption Act 1976 makes provision for both 'overseas adoptions' and 'regulated adoptions'. An overseas adoption[96] is an adoption effected under the law of a country outside Great Britain of such a description as is specified by the Secretary of State in a statutory instrument. The object of the provision was to permit the recognition of adoptions that were granted by legal systems that followed criteria broadly the same as those in England and Wales. By delegated legislation, the adoption must have been made under statutory provision and the person to be adopted must be under the age of 18 and unmarried.[97] The provisions of the Order in Council have been extended to in excess of 40 countries; these include most Commonwealth countries and the majority of States in Western Europe. The legislation also provides for the

---

91   In May 1993, the Hague Convention on the Protection of Children and Co-operation in Inter-Country Adoption was concluded.

92   *Re Marshall* [1957] Ch 507.

93   *Re Wilson* [1954] Ch 733; *Re Wilby* [1956] P 174.

94   Adoption Act 1976, ss 38(1)(c), 39.

95   *Ibid*, s 38(1)(c), previously, the Children Act 1975, Sched 1, Pt II. The provisions can be traced back to the Adoption Act 1964; the Adoption of Children Act 1926 made no provision in respect of the conflict of laws.

96   *Ibid*, ss 38(1)(d), 72(2); the provisions derive from the Adoption Act 1968, s 4.

97   SI 1973/19, para 3(3).

recognition of regulated adoptions, which are overseas adoptions which have been made by a country that is party to the Hague Convention 1965.[98]

The Adoption Act 1976 provides for the recognition of overseas adoptions (and, therefore, also regulated adoptions). The statute provides two circumstances in which recognition will be denied, namely, where the adoption is contrary to public policy or where the authority that made the order lacked jurisdiction,[99] save that the English court will be bound by any finding of fact pertaining to jurisdiction.[100]

There will still be countries to which the statutory rules do not extend and recognition will be dependent on the relevant common law rules. The early case law was inconclusive as to whether English courts would give any effect to an adoption effected in a foreign country.[101] In *Re Marshall*,[102] Harman J indicated that he was prepared to recognise a foreign adoption if the child and the adoptive parents were domiciled in the same country but, on the facts of the case, the learned judge found that the child did not enjoy full rights of succession. The Court of Appeal, in upholding the judgment, did not find it necessary to deal in detail with the circumstances in which a foreign order of adoption might be recognised.

The leading authority on the recognition of foreign adoptions at common law is *Re Valentine's Settlement*,[103] where the facts were as follows: a British subject domiciled in Southern Rhodesia created a settlement of funds for his son, Alastair, for life, remainder to his children. Alastair, who was domiciled and resident in Southern Rhodesia, married and had a child, Simon. At a later date, he and his wife adopted two children in South Africa; these adoption orders were not recognised in Southern Rhodesia. The question for the court was whether the two adopted children could benefit under the settlement.

The Court of Appeal, by a majority, upheld the judgment of Pennycuick J and refused to recognise the adoption. Lord Denning MR ruled that, at common law, for the adoption to be recognised, the adoptive parents must be domiciled, and the child resident, in the country where the order was made. This was in line with the *Travers v Holley* principle of the English court recognising a jurisdiction which, *mutatis mutandis*, it claimed for itself. Dankwerts LJ agreed, save that he was doubtful as to whether the child needed to be ordinarily resident in the country in which it was adopted. Salmon LJ, in a dissenting judgment, argued that adoption, provided there

---

98 Adoption Act 1976, s 72(1).

99 *Ibid*, s 53(2)(a).

100 *Ibid*, s 54(3).

101 See Dicey, *The Conflict of Laws* (6th edn, 1949), p 513, and the subsequent cases of *Re Wilson* [1954] Ch 733; *Re Wilby* [1956] P 174.

102 *Re Marshall* [1957] Ch 263, CA, p 507.

103 *Re Valentine's Settlement* [1965] Ch 226 (Pennycuick J); [1965] Ch 831 (Lord Denning MR, Dankwerts, Salmon LJJ).

were proper safeguards, was a social good and that, unlike divorce, there was a strong case for the application of liberal rules in respect of the recognition. In all the judgments, there appeared to be an acceptance that the adoption orders might have been recognised under the principle in *Armitage v AG*[104] if they had been recognised in Southern Rhodesia.

One other point that emerges from *Re Valentine's Settlement* is that the Court of Appeal agreed that a foreign adoption order would be refused recognition in England if it was contrary to public policy. This is a matter of some practical importance, given that, in some countries, adoption orders are applied for in respect of adults in order to achieve some advantage in respect of succession.

The effect of a foreign adoption order

As Lord Denning MR indicated, in *Re Valentine's Settlement*, there is an important distinction between (a) the recognition of a foreign adoption order; and (b) the effect of any such recognition. As a general principle, the Adoption Act 1976 provides that an adoption order recognised by statute or common law will have the same effect as an English adoption order.[105] English law regards the adopted child as the legitimate child of the adoptive parents.[106]

In respect of succession by adopted children, the law prior to 1 January 1976 was less than clear. The law on the matter had changed several times since 1926 and the relevant statutory rules applied to adoptions made in Great Britain.[107] However, the succession rules in respect of children adopted abroad were governed by common law and it was difficult to reconcile the case law.[108]

The provisions of s 38 of the Adoption Act 1976 provide that a child adopted abroad will have the same legal status as one adopted in England and Wales. Section 39 of the same legislation then provides that, in respect of any instrument taking effect after 1 January 1976, the adopted child will be treated as if he had been born in lawful wedlock.[109] So, if a testator dies after 1 January 1976, devising or bequeathing property to X for life, remainder to the children of X, then an adopted child may, in the absence of a contrary

---

104 [1906] P 135. It should be noted that, even if the adoptions had been recognised, then, because the settlement had been created prior to 1 January 1950, the children could not have taken having regard to the terms of the Adoption of Children Act 1926, s 5(2).

105 Adoption Act 1976, ss 38, 39.

106 *Ibid*, s 39.

107 Adoption Act 1958, ss 16, 17; Adoption Act 1976, s 1.

108 *Re Wilson* [1954] Ch 733; *Re Wilby* [1956] P 174; *Re Marshall* [1957] Ch 507; *Re Valentine's Settlement* [1965] Ch 831.

109 Adoption Act 1976, ss 39, 42, 46, 72(1).

intention, take under the will, regardless of whether the adoption was before or after the death of the testator. Although s 38 provides that 'adoption' includes both overseas adoptions and adoptions recognised at common law, it would seem that the provisions of s 39, in so far as they pertain to succession, will only apply when English law is *the lex successionis*. If the *lex successionis* provides for only limited rights for adopted children, then such limited provision will apply. Although there is no direct authority on the point, it is in line with the distinction drawn in *Re Valentine's Settlement* to the effect that recognition of the status of adoption is determined by the *lex domicilii* but rights of succession should be governed by the *lex successionis*.[110]

CUSTODY

Introduction

The jurisdiction of the English courts in respect of children can be traced back a very long way. Originally, the jurisdiction vested in the sovereign as *parens patriae* but this was then delegated to the Lord Chancellor and the Court of Chancery.[111] This was the natural venue at the time because many of the disputes concerned the property rights of those who were under age. The jurisdiction passed to the Chancery Division of the High Court in 1875 and was, in 1971, transferred to the Family Division.

The orders that might be made in court proceedings were very wide ranging. By 1971, jurisdiction existed to award orders of guardianship, wardship, custody and access. A guardianship order was an order made by the court appointing someone to take care of a parentless child,[112] while a custody order normally involved the right to determine questions of care, control and residence.

Domestic law in England was subject to fundamental change in the Children Act 1989. Section 1 of the legislation provided that, in any question with respect to the upbringing of a child, 'the child's welfare shall be the court's paramount consideration'. By s 8 of the Children Act 1989, the court may make a number of specific orders which have come to be known as s 8 orders; these include (a) a prohibited steps order (prohibiting a parent taking certain steps in relation to a child, for example, removing them from England); (b) a residence order (for example, stipulating where a child is to live); (c) a specific issue order (stipulating a specific requirement in relation to a child, for

---

110 *Re Valentine's Settlement* [1965] Ch 831.
111 After the abolition of the Court of Wards in 1660.
112 See Guardianship of Infants Act 1886; Guardianship of Infants Act 1925; Guardianship of Minors Act 1971; Guardianship Act 1973.

example, as to his education or holiday abroad); and (d) a contact order (allowing a child to stay with another person for a limited time).

The changes in domestic law have led to a modification of language. The concept of wardship has now been replaced by that of the 'inherent jurisdiction of the court' and, for the purpose of domestic law, the terminology of custody has been abandoned. However, the expression, custody, continues to be employed in everyday language and it remains the most useful term to describe the various orders made in a foreign court.

One of the most obvious changes in social life in England since 1945 has been the increase in foreign travel. The steady expansion in the number of English domiciled persons taking foreign holidays or working abroad has been made possible by the growth of affordable civil aviation. In consequence, there are many marriages or partnerships where the parents have contact with more than one jurisdiction. The steady increase in the divorce figures in the 1960s and 1970s led to a situation where a family court in England might find that the courts of more than one jurisdiction had an interest in the welfare of a child. Nothing could be more damaging to an orderly system of family law than if a parent, having received an unfavourable judgment in Country A, simply removed a child to Country B, in the hope of securing a different judgment. Such conduct is objectionable for four reasons: (a) in such disputes, there is a natural tendency for the courts of Country A to regard their legal system as superior; (b) abduction leads to a degree of instability and lack of continuity that is damaging to the proper development of the child; (c) if the court orders of Country A can be so easily flouted a rational system of family dispute resolution is frustrated and the rule of law is undermined; and (d) if abduction were allowed to flourish, then it is highly unlikely that any legal dispute would ever be satisfactorily concluded. For these reasons, considerable efforts have been made in the last two decades to secure international co-operation in matters concerning the custody of children.

In respect of matters concerning children in private international law, three areas require consideration: (a) the circumstances in which an English court is entitled to exercise jurisdiction; (b) the law to be applied; and (c) the recognition and enforcement of judgments and orders given by a foreign court. It is proposed to take each matter in turn.

Jurisdiction

By the late 1970s, the jurisdictional rules in respect of orders for custody, guardianship and wardship were far from clear. It was only by the good sense of judges that difficulties between the courts of Scotland and England did not arise.[113] This contrasted with the position at common law in respect of the recognition of judgments, which was relatively clear. The Law Commission was asked to investigate the matter and concluded that, if there was to be recognition in respect of judgments given in different parts of the UK, then it was desirable to reach agreement as to the circumstances in which each court might assume jurisdiction in family law matters. The Law Commissions of Scotland and England recommended, in the *Report on the Custody of Children – Jurisdiction and Enforcement within the UK*,[114] that an English court should have jurisdiction in respect of the custody of children in four circumstances: (a) in the course of proceedings for divorce, nullity or judicial separation; (b) where the child was habitually resident in the jurisdiction; (c) where the child was present in England but not habitually resident;[115] and (d) where the child was in England and the intervention of the court was necessary for the protection of the child (the 'emergency jurisdiction').

Matrimonial proceedings

Where an English court has jurisdiction under the Matrimonial Causes Act 1973 and the Domicile and Matrimonial Proceedings Act 1973 in respect of matters of divorce, nullity and legal separation, the court will also have jurisdiction to make an order under s 8 of the Children Act 1989 (that is, a contact order, residence order, prohibited steps order or specific issue order).[116] Thus, if a parent is domiciled in England and begins proceedings for divorce, then the court will have jurisdiction in respect of the child, even if such a child has only limited connections with England. The principle underlying the Family Law Act 1986 is to give priority to divorce proceedings, so a court in England dealing with an application for legal separation will not have jurisdiction in respect of the child if there are proceedings for divorce continuing in Scotland or Northern Ireland.[117] Such a restriction would not apply if the court in Scotland or Northern Ireland had declined jurisdiction in respect of custody.[118]

Where an English court has jurisdiction to make a s 8 order in matrimonial proceedings, it may decline to do so if it considers that it is more appropriate to be dealt with outside England.[119]

---

113 *Re H* [1966] 1 WLR 381; *Re L* [1974] 1 WLR 250.
114 Law Commission Report No 138 (1985).
115 The residual presence basis.
116 Family Law Act 1986, s 2A (inserted by the Children Act 1989).
117 *Ibid*, s 2A(1)(b), 2A(2) (inserted by the Children Act 1989).
118 *Ibid*, s 2A(4) (inserted by the Children Act 1989).
119 *Ibid*, s 2A(4) (inserted by the Children Act 1989).

Habitual residence

The court in England and Wales has jurisdiction to make a s 8 order in respect of a child habitually resident,[120] provided that there are no divorce proceedings continuing in Scotland or Northern Ireland, unless that court has made an order disclaiming jurisdiction in respect of the child.[121] These provisions indicate that the 'divorce basis' should have precedence over the 'habitual residence' basis; this is consistent with the principle that disputes concerning divorce should have priority but, also, with the equally important consideration that any allocation of jurisdiction should be concerned to prevent the proliferation of litigation about related matters.

A particular additional safeguard is provided by s 41 of the Family Law Act 1986, which stipulates that, if a child habitually resident in a part of the UK is removed from that part without the consent of those who have the authority to determine where he resides, then the court will have jurisdiction to determine custody for a period of one year after the abduction. So, if a child is habitually resident in Birmingham with his mother and is taken without consent by his father to Glasgow, then an English court will have jurisdiction for a period of one year after the unlawful abduction.

The residual presence basis

The English court has jurisdiction to make a s 8 order if the child is present in England and not habitually resident in any other part of the UK,[122] and there are no matrimonial proceedings continuing in Scotland or Northern Ireland.[123] The purpose of the provision is to confer jurisdiction on an English court if a child is wrongfully taken to England and the matter does not fall under any other relevant provision.

Emergency jurisdiction

The principal purpose of the above provisions is to harmonise jurisdiction within the UK. However, there may be circumstances in which a child is present in England or Wales and speedy court action is required. Section 2(3)(b) of the Family Law Act 1986 confers jurisdiction on an English court if a child is present in England or Wales and the court considers that immediate action is necessary for its protection.

---

120 Family Law Act 1986, s 3.
121 *Ibid*, s 3(2).
122 *Ibid*, ss 2(2), 3(1)(b).
123 *Ibid*, s 3(2).

Declining jurisdiction and stays of proceedings

By the terms of s 5(1) of the Family Law Act 1986, a court in England or Wales may decline jurisdiction if the matter in question has already been determined in proceedings outside England and Wales. The purpose of this provision was to put an end to the question of whether the court was entitled to decline jurisdiction in custody cases.[124]

By s 5(2), the court may stay proceedings where like proceedings are taking place outside England and Wales or it would be more appropriate for these matters to be determined outside England and Wales. This is an attempt to give effect to the doctrine *of forum non conveniens*, as set out in the commercial context in cases such as *Spiliada*[125] and extended in the family law environment in *De Dampierre*.[126] Clearly, in most cases, it will be necessary simply to weigh the evidence and apply the statutory words. However, a number of points can be made. First, it would seem that, where a choice of jurisdiction is in issue, the welfare of the child is an important consideration but not the paramount consideration, as set out in s 1 of the Children Act 1989.[127] Secondly, it would seem that any form of jurisdiction agreement will not have the same weight as would apply in a commercial case.[128] Thirdly, the wording of s 5(2) is widely drawn, so that the discretion might be exercised 'at any stage of the proceedings'. Fourthly, while the habitual residence of the child is important, the judge will be required to determine 'appropriateness', and the ability of parties to participate in proceedings may be a relevant factor.[129]

Guardianship and inherent jurisdiction

As indicated above, one of the earliest forms of jurisdiction over children was based on the inherent jurisdiction of the court.[130] Since this jurisdiction was founded on the position of the sovereign as *parens patriae*, the inherent jurisdiction could be invoked in respect of British subjects (resident in England or abroad)[131] or in respect of an alien domiciled abroad but ordinarily resident in England.[132] If the inherent jurisdiction is invoked in

---

124 *Re X's Settlement* [1945] Ch 44.

125 *Spiliada Maritime Corpn v Cansulex Ltd* [1987] AC 460.

126 *De Dampierre v De Dampierre* [1988] AC 92.

127 *Re S* [1993] 2 FLR 912.

128 *Hallam v Hallam (Nos 1 and 2)* [1993] 1 FLR 958.

129 *Re H* [1992] 2 FCR 205; Waite J was influenced by the inability of the mother to participate in litigation in Wisconsin.

130 Normally, in the form of wardship proceedings.

131 *Hope v Hope* (1854) 4 DM & G 328; *Re D* [1943] Ch 305; *J v C* [1970] AC 688; *Re A* [1970] Ch 665. Jurisdiction is often founded on presence within the allegiance; for the concept of allegiance, see *DPP v Joyce* [1946] AC 347.

132 *Re P* [1965] Ch 568.

respect of matters that pertain to care, control or education, then the jurisdictional rules of the Family Law Act 1986 have to be complied with.[133] If the object of the application is wardship, then the common law rules have to be complied with.

In the 19th century, many of the applications to the High Court for wardship were for the purpose of appointing a guardian. The domestic law on guardianship has been subject to recent review[134] and the law was restated in the Children Act 1989. The Children Act 1989 provides for the express selection of guardians and the appointment by court order.[135] The legislation is silent on the relevant jurisdictional rule and a guardianship order does not come within Part I of the Family Law Act 1986.[136] The powers may be exercised by the High Court, the county court or the magistrates' court.[137] It would seem, in the absence of specific statutory provision, that jurisdiction may be exercised in reliance on the prior common law principles if the child is a British subject.

A further related problem is that the Children Act 1989 permits an application for a parental responsibility order under ss 3 and 4; the legislation is silent on jurisdictional rules and the matter is outside s 1 of the Family Law Act 1986. However, the Court of Appeal appears to have assumed that jurisdiction existed hypothetically to enable a father in England to seek a parental responsibility order in respect of an illegitimate child born and living in India.[138]

Choice of law

In circumstances where an English court has jurisdiction to make a s 8 order or where the application is based on the inherent jurisdiction of the court, then there is no doubt that English law applies as the *lex fori*. The Children Act 1989 provides that, in any question with respect to the upbringing of the child, the child's welfare shall be the court's paramount consideration and that the decision to make a s 8 order shall pay regard to a number of statutory criteria.[139] To some extent, this reflects the prior law, where an English court would apply the welfare principle and regarded even a foreign custody order as simply a matter to be taken into account in determining what would be in the best interests of the child.[140]

---

133 Family Law Act 1986 ss 1(1)(d), 2(3).

134 Law Commission Working Paper No 91 (1985); Law Commission Report No 172 (1986).

135 Children Act 1989, s 5.

136 Family Law Act 1986, s 1.

137 Children Act 1989, s 92(7).

138 *In re S (parental responsibility: jurisdiction)* (1998) (unreported, 28 April), CA.

139 Children Act 1989, s 1(1), (3), (4).

140 *McKee v McKee* [1951] AC 352.

Recognition of foreign orders and the problem of abduction

Introduction

The approach of English courts at common law was to determine the best interests of the child. This precluded the automatic acceptance of a foreign custody order. The status of a foreign custody order and any subsequent abduction were matters simply to weigh in the balance in determining the best interests of the child. This was in contrast to the approach of other common law jurisdictions, where provision had been made for the automatic recognition of a foreign custody order. The authorities in the post War period derived from the leading case of *McKee v McKee*,[141] where the facts were straightforward: the Supreme Court of California had awarded custody to the mother. Without consent, the father took the child to the Province of Ontario. The mother began habeas corpus proceedings to have the child returned. The trial judge, with whom the Court of Appeal agreed, after investigating the merits, came to the conclusion that the child would be better with his father. This judgment was set aside by the Supreme Court of Canada. The Privy Council reversed the judgment of the Supreme Court of Canada and restored the ruling of the trial judge. In giving the judgment of the Privy Council, Lord Simmonds had no doubt that the central question was the welfare of the child and that the discretion of the trial judge should not be lightly set aside and he set out the position clearly:

> Once it is conceded that the court of Ontario had jurisdiction to entertain the question of custody and that it need not blindly follow the order made by a foreign court, the consequence cannot be escaped that it must form an independent judgment on the question, although, in doing so, it will give proper weight to the foreign judgment ... It is the law ... that the welfare and happiness of the infant is the paramount consideration in questions of custody ... To this paramount consideration all others yield. The order of a foreign court is no exception ...[142]

It was, therefore, the duty of the trial judge to act in the interests of the welfare of the child. If the foreign order had recently been given and there had been a flagrant breach, then immediate return might be ordered but, in other cases, the court might hold a full hearing with cross examination upon affidavits before reaching a determination as to what was in the best interests of the child. The case law in the 1960s and 1970s indicated that the trial judge was to act in the interests of the child and that the element of kidnapping was no more than one consideration to be weighed in the balance.[143] However, there

---

141 *McKee v McKee* [1951] AC 352.

142 *Ibid*, pp 364, 365.

143 For case law, see *Re P (GE)* [1965] Ch 568; *Re H (infants)* [1966] 1 WLR 381 (Cross J); 1 All ER 886 (Wilmer, Russell, Harman LJJ); *Re E (an infant)* [1967] Ch 287; Ch 761, CA; *Re T (infants)* [1968] Ch 704 (Pennycuick J), CA; *Re TA (infants)* (1972) 116 SJ 78 (Rees J).

was already concern at the position an English court might find itself in when the orders of a foreign court were flagrantly breached. The dilemma was well expressed by Cross J (as he then was) in *Re E (an infant)*, where the learned judge referred to the general problem:[144]

> This is one of those cases which have become all too frequent of late, in which a ward of a foreign court has been brought to this country without the consent and indeed contrary to the order of that court ... To my mind it is wrong to look at such a case solely from the point of view of the welfare of the particular child ... In modern conditions, it is often easy and tempting for a parent who has been deprived of custody by the court of country A to remove the child suddenly to country B and set up home there. The courts in all countries ought, as I see it, to be careful not to do anything to encourage this tendency. The substitution of self-help for due process of law can only harm the interests of wards generally, and a judge should, as I see it, pay regard to the orders of the proper foreign court unless he is satisfied beyond reasonable doubt that to do so would inflict serious harm on the child.

Determining what was in the best interest interests of the child might involve a summary hearing and a swift return or a more lengthy hearing. The courts were anxious to avoid entering into 'the last dregs of the dispute between the parties'.[145] What was required was 'a swift, realistic and unsentimental assessment of the best interests of the child, leading, in proper cases, to the prompt return of the child'.[146]

However, with the increase in incidents of abduction, three attempts were made to ensure recognition of the judgments of foreign courts; these were (a) by the introduction of the criminal law; (b) by legislation to provide for the recognition of judgments in custody matters made in other parts of the UK; and (c) by co-operation at the international level. It is necessary to say a little about the first two matters before turning to the new schemes of international co-operation.

The criminal law

One attempt to ensure respect for court orders in custody matters was the enactment of the Child Abduction Act 1984. Section 1 of the legislation provides that 'a person connected with a child under the age of 16 commits an offence if he takes or sends the child out of the UK without the appropriate consent of the child's mother or any other person having parental responsibility for him'. The principal purpose of the legislation is to ensure compliance with court orders made in the UK.

---

144 [1967] Ch 287, p 289; approved by Wilmer LJ in the Court of Appeal [1967] Ch 761, p 769.

145 *Re T* [1968] Ch 704.

146 *Re R* [1981] 2 FLR 416, *per* Ormrod LJ.

The maximum sentence is seven years imprisonment and it would seem that open defiance of a court order, by taking the child abroad, will normally attract a custodial sentence.[147] However, it is quite clear that the criminal law is an unsuitable vehicle in cases of child abduction and it is probably only appropriate to punish after the most serious cases. In normal circumstances, an aggrieved party will be seeking the immediate relief available in the civil courts, often *ex parte* and on affidavit.

UK orders

As indicated above, Part I of the Family Law Act 1986 introduced uniform jurisdictional rules in respect of custody disputes within the UK. This was not an end in itself but a first step to facilitate the recognition of court orders. Section 25 of the Family Law Act 1986 provides that a custody order made in one part of the UK shall be recognised in another part. Section 27[148] provides that the person in whose favour the order was made requests the court which made the order to send a certified copy of it to the appropriate court where the child has been taken. Under the terms of s 27(4), the order will be registered by an officer of the appropriate court and, under the terms of s 29(1), an application may be made to enforce it.

The international aspect

The main problem in respect of child abduction was when a parent resident in the UK took a child abroad without authority or where a child was brought to some part of the UK in flagrant defiance of a court order. Such a problem could only be solved by international co-operation between States. To this end, the UK signed and ratified the Hague Convention on the Civil Aspects of International Child Abduction 1980 and the European Convention on the Recognition and Enforcement of Decisions Concerning the Custody of Children 1980. Both these conventions were implemented by the Child Abduction and Custody Act 1985 and even a cursory glance at the law reports indicates that the legislation has led to a considerable volume of case law. It is necessary to take each in turn.

The Hague Convention on the Civil Aspects of Child Abduction 1980

The Hague Convention on the Civil Aspects of International Child Abduction 1980 was implemented by the Child Abduction and Custody Act 1985. There

---

147 Child Abduction Act 1984, s 4(1); see *R v Downes* (1994) 15 Cr App R (S) 435 (three years' imprisonment for taking a child abroad in defiance of a court order).
148 Family Law Act 1986, s 27(1), (2), (3).

are now nearly 50 Contracting States.[149] Section 1(2) of the 1985 Act provides that the Convention shall have the force of law and the text is set out in Sched 1 of the enactment. The broad objective of the Convention is to prevent the unlawful removal of children from their place of habitual residence. In consequence, the Convention applies whether or not a court order has been made.

The Convention operates where a child who is habitually resident in one Contracting State is wrongfully removed or retained in another contracting State.[150] The Convention requires each Contracting State to establish a Central Authority to enable that State to perform its obligations. By s 3 of the Child Abduction and Custody Act 1985, the function of the Central Authority is discharged in the UK by the Lord Chancellor's Department.

The Convention applies where a child is under the age of 16 and is habitually resident in a Contracting State.[151] The Convention protects the rights of custody attributed to a person or institution, whether exercised solely or jointly, provided those rights are being exercised at the time of the removal or retention.[152] The rights to custody may arise by operation of law or as a result of a judicial or administrative decision.[153] The right may be simply the right to consent to the child being taken abroad.[154] The approach of the courts has been to adopt a liberal interpretation to the concept of custody rights.[155] Custody rights may be vested in a court[156] or may simply have been acquired under an interim court order.[157] Custody rights may be acquired under a legally binding agreement.[158]

The broad scheme is that, where a child has been removed from Country A, a person with custody rights may apply with the appropriate documentation to the Central Authority of Country A, seeking the return of the child.[159] If the Central Authority of Country A has reason to believe that the child has been taken to Country B, then it will contact the Central Authority of Country B,[160] who will then be under a duty to take all appropriate measures to secure the return of the child. In the first instance,

149 See Child Abduction and Custody (Parties to Conventions) Order 1986 SI 1986/1159, as substituted by SI 1996/2565.
150 Hague Convention 1980, Art 3.
151 *Ibid*, Art 4.
152 *Ibid*, Art 3(a), (b).
153 *Ibid*, Art 3.
154 *C v C (abduction: rights of custody)* [1989] 1 WLR 6542.
155 *Re B (A Minor) (abduction)* [1994] 2 FLR 249.
156 *B v B* [1993] Fam 32.
157 *Re O (A Minor) (child abduction: custody rights)* (1997) (unreported, 24 June) (Cazalet J).
158 Hague Convention 1980, Art 3.
159 *Ibid*, Art 8.
160 *Ibid*, Art 9.

this will involve persuasion but, failing this, it will entail legal proceedings before the courts of Country B.[161] The structure of the Convention is therefore directed to ensuring that as many cases as possible can be resolved by intergovernmental co-operation at an administrative level. If the country to which the child has been taken is England, then the Lord Chancellor's Department, as the Central Authority, will be under a duty to take all appropriate steps to secure the voluntary return of the child and, if this proves impossible, to initiate the relevant legal proceedings to secure compliance.[162] If legal proceedings need to be initiated, then they will be in the Family Division of the High Court.[163] The Convention therefore seeks to use both administrative means to secure its objectives

While much can be achieved at an administrative level, there will, nevertheless, be many occasions when court action is required. If the removal or retention has taken place less then 12 months previously, then the general rule set out in Art 12 is that the court must order the return of the child. There are a limited number of situations when return need not be ordered. First, return need not be ordered if the person, institution or body having the care of the person of the child was not actually exercising custody rights at the time of the removal or retention.[164] Secondly, return need not be ordered if the person exercising custody rights consented or subsequently acquiesced in the removal or retention.[165] Thirdly, the court need not order the return of the child if 'there is a grave risk that his or her return would expose the child to physical or psychological harm or otherwise place the child in an intolerable situation'.[166] Fourthly, the court may refuse to order the return if the child objects and he has acquired an age and a level of maturity that it is appropriate to take account of his own views. As a matter of logic and common sense, the court is first required to determine whether the applicant has custody rights before considering the other three specific defences.

In litigation where a period of 12 months has not elapsed from the time of the wrongful removal or retention, then the contested cases indicate that the

---

161 Hague Convention 1980, Art 10.

162 *Ibid*, Arts 7, 11; see the 1985 Act, s 3. The 1985 Act enables the Lord Chancellor to acquire the relevant information as to whereabouts from the Social Services Departments of Local Authorities. See the 1985 Act, s 6.

163 This enables the specialist judges of the Family Division to acquire detailed knowledge of the working of the Convention. The cases therefore come before judges who are very familiar with the philosophy and objectives of the Convention. When cases have been appealed to the Court of Appeal, it is normal for the leading judgment to be given by a specialist family law judge.

164 Hague Convention 1980, Arts 3(a), 13(a).

165 *Ibid*, Art 13(a).

166 *Ibid*, Art 13(b).

defence will fall within one of the four grounds listed above.[167] The question arises as to what is the effect of adducing evidence of any of the defences. In respect of the first defence, if there is evidence that the applicant was not exercising custody rights, then this is probably fatal to an application under the Convention; however, it may well be that the court might still be minded to order the return of the child under its inherent jurisdiction if it was satisfied that this was in the best interests of the welfare of the child.[168] However, the main difficulty arises with the three substantive defences. One approach would be to say that return should be ordered to reflect the general objectives of the Convention, unless there is evidence of an exceptional nature. A second approach would be to argue that, once the discretion has arisen, then return should not be ordered unless the welfare of the child clearly indicates that this is desirable.

The case law indicates that, in general, English courts have interpreted the exceptions contained in Art 13 narrowly, in conformity with the principle that return should normally be ordered[169] and that the judicial discretion arising should be exercised in favour of returning the child, unless clearly outweighed by other considerations.[170] This is in conformity with the view in European law that, where a treaty sets out a general principle, then any exceptions to the general principle should be narrowly interpreted so as not to undermine the paramountcy of the general principle.

One defence that has given rise to difficulty in the case law is where the abducting parent argues that the wronged parent has consented or acquiesced. This raises questions about the meaning of 'acquiescence' and how evidence is to be interpreted. In a series of judgments, the Court of Appeal has held that, while evidence of consent needed to be 'clear and cogent',[171] cases of subsequent acquiesence could be divided into those of active acquiesence and passive acquiesence, the former being capable of objective determination. This distinction did not appear in the text of the Convention and relied upon analogies drawn from English domestic law.[172] The distinction between active and passive acquiescence had been introduced following the judgment of the Court of Appeal in *Re A (Minors) (abduction:*

---

167 Hague Convention 1980, Art 12 (which draws a distinction between applications made before and after a period of months).

168 *Re O (A Minor) (child abduction: custody rights)* (1997) (unreported, 24 June) (Cazalet J).

169 For the case law, see *Re A* [1988] 1 FLR 365; *Evans v Evans* [1989] 1 FLR 135; *C v C* [1989] 1 WLR 654; *Re G* [1989] 2 FLR 475; *V v B* [1991] 1 FLR 266; *Re N* [1991] 1 FLR 913; *Re S* [1991] 2 FLR 1; *W v W* [1993] 2 FLR 211.

170 See *Re A* [1992] Fam 106, *per* Donaldson MR, discussing the nature of the judicial discretion.

171 *Re C* [1996] 1 FLR 414, p 419 (consent probably has to be express).

172 The distinction was not accepted by all judges in the Court of Appeal: see *Re A (Minors) (abduction: custody rights)* [1992] Fam 106; *In re AZ (A Minor) (abduction: acquiescence)* [1993] 1 FLR 682; *In re S (Minors) (abduction: acquiesence)* [1994] 1 FLR 819; *Re R (child abduction: acquiesence)* [1995] 1 FLR 716.

custody rights); this majority judgment had attracted some criticism in giving a liberal interpretation to the expression 'acquiescence'.[173]

In any event, this stream of case law is probably now redundant, having regard to the guidance given by the House of Lords in *Re H (minors: abduction acquiesence)*,[174] where the facts were as follows: both parents were strict orthodox Jews. In November 1995, the British born mother removed the three children from Israel to England in breach of the father's rights under the law of Israel. The mother secured a county court order. The father pursued the matter before the Beth Din (religious court). The father was then authorised by the Beth Din to begin proceedings. The mother alleged the father had acquiesced under Art 13. The judge at first instance (Sumner J) held that there had been no acquiesence, as recourse to the Beth Din was not inconsistent with a later application under the Hague Convention. This was reversed by the Court of Appeal. The House of Lords allowed the appeal and restored the judgment of Sumner J.

In giving judgment for the House of Lords, Lord Browne Wilkinson emphasised that the object of the Hague Convention was to protect children from the harmful effects of abduction and that interpretation should, as far as possible, be in line with that in other contracting States. The learned judge held (a) that acquiesence was a question of fact to be determined on evidence and not a rule of law; (b) that distinctions between 'active' and 'passive' acquiesence were wrong; and (c) that the abducting party bore the *onus probandi* of demonstrating acquiesence. The overall effect of the judgment is that it indicates that the concept of acquiesence is to be given a narrow scope and a wronged parent is not to be held to have acquiesced merely because he engaged in civilised negotiation or sought some form of mediation. Further, Lord Browne Wilkinson indicated that, having regard to the traumatic effect of abduction on an innocent party, the court should be slow to find acquiesence. It is reasonable to assume that, in future, it will be much more difficult to demonstrate acquiesence.

The case law indicates that the ground of psychological harm provided for in Art 13(b) also needs to be narrowly interpreted. It is clear from the wording of the text that there must be grave risk that return would place the child in an intolerable position. Only the clearest evidence of 'substantial harm' will suffice and it is not enough to be able to point to the general unhappiness that is associated with a custody dispute.[175]

---

173 *Re A* [1992] Fam 106 (Thorpe J, Donaldson MR, Stuart Smith, Balcombe LJJ) (the authority of case being undermined by a forceful dissent by Balcombe LJ, who agreed with the judge at first instance); see, also, *Re A (No 2)* [1993] Fam 1 (Booth J, Brown P, Staughton and Scott LJJ).

174 *Re H* [1997] 2 WLR 653.

175 *Re A* [1988] 1 FLR 365; *Re N* [1991] 1 FLR 413.

The final ground arises when a child is of an age that the court is entitled to take account of his views.[176] This envisages a three stage process, namely: (a) is the child old enough and sufficiently developed intellectually to express a view? (b) if so, that view then needs to be considered; and (c) having considered the child's view, the judge must exercise his discretion in respect of the entire matter. It would seem that the views of a child below the age of seven will carry little weight and much will depend on the level of development of the child and his or her ability to express a rational preference.[177] Moreover, the judge must be vigilant to ensure that the children have not been coached or otherwise indoctrinated, since it is the view of the child that is to be received by the court.[178] Lastly, the judge must draw a distinction between the child who says 'I do not wish to return' and the child who says 'I do not wish to return because I wish to stay with X'.[179] As a matter of principle, where an experienced judge of the Family Division has heard and weighed all the relevant evidence and correctly applied the law, then an appellate court should be slow to substitute their view as to how any discretion should be exercised, unless it can be shown to be manifestly unreasonable.

In cases where the application is made after a period of 12 months, all the grounds stated above can be raised with the addition that Art 12(2) provides that the court 'shall order the return of the child, unless it is demonstrated that the child is now settled in its new environment'.

The Convention contains a number of subsidiary provisions in Arts 16–19. By Art 16, once a requested State has received notice of abduction, then no decision on the merits of custody can be taken until it has been determined that the child is not to be returned. Article 17 provides that the recognition rules of a contracting State are, of themselves, no reason for refusing to order the return of the child. Article 19 provides that any decision under the Convention shall not be considered as a decision on the merits, while Art 18 provides that the Convention does not derogate from other powers the court may have to order return.

The European Convention on the Recognition and Enforcement of Decisions Concerning the Custody of Children and on the Restoration of Custody 1980[180]

The European Convention on the Recognition and Enforcement of Decisions Concerning Custody of Children and on the Restoration of Custody was signed on 20 May 1980 and implemented by the UK in Part II of the Child

---

176 Hague Convention 1980, Art 13.
177 *B v K* [1993] Fam Law 17; *Re R* [1995] 1 FLR 716.
178 *B v K* [1993] Fam 17.
179 *S v S* [1993] 2 WLR 775.
180 See Jones (1980) 30 ICLQ 467.

Abduction and Custody Act 1985. With nearly 20 contracting States, the Convention operates within a narrower geographical scope than the Hague Convention. Unlike the Hague Convention, which operates to protect custody rights, the European Convention only applies where there has been a decision on custody by the courts of a contracting State. The Convention applies in respect of children aged under 16.[181] All the States who participate in the European Convention (save Belgium) are also contracting States to the Hague Convention. The Child Abduction and Custody Act 1985 provides that, in a case where both Conventions can be relied upon, a claim under the Hague Convention shall have priority.[182] The operation of the European Convention has many features in common with that of the Hague Convention, with each contracting State being required to establish a Central Authority to administer the Convention.[183]

Supposing a custody order has been made in Germany, then an application can be made to the Central Authority in Germany (for onward transmission) or directly to the Central Authority in England. The Central Authority in England will assist in ensuring that the order is registered with the appropriate court.[184] Once the order has been registered, it may be enforced in the same fashion as an order granted by that court.[185]

The European Convention contains, in Arts 9 and 10, a number of grounds on which recognition and enforcement may be refused. First, where the decision was given in the absence of the defendant because of a failure to serve documentation, then recognition may be refused.[186] This conforms to the basic principle of natural justice *audi alteram partem*. However, failure by a court to serve documents at the correct address will not be an obstacle if the defendant participates in subsequent proceedings.[187] Secondly, a decision may be refused recognition if it was given in the absence of the defendant or his legal representative and the jurisdiction of the court was not founded on the habitual residence of the defendant, the last common domicile of the parents or the habitual residence of the child.[188] Thirdly, a decision may be refused recognition if it was incompatible with a decision on custody given in England, unless the child was habitually resident in the territory of the requesting State for one year before his removal.[189] Fourthly, refusal may be

---

181 European Convention 1980, Art 1(a).

182 Child Abduction and Custody Act 1985, s 16(4)(c).

183 The Lord Chancellor's Department acts as the Central Authority for both the Hague Convention (s 3) and the European Convention (s 14) in respect of England and Wales. The Secretary of State for Scotland acts in respect of Scotland.

184 Child Abduction and Custody Act 1985, s 16(2).

185 *Ibid*, s 18.

186 European Convention 1980, Art 9(1)(a).

187 *Re G (A Minor) (child abduction: enforcement)* [1990] 2 FLR 325.

188 European Convention 1980, Art 9(1)(b).

justified if the effects of the foreign decision are manifestly incompatible with the principles of family law prevailing in England.[190] Fifthly, recognition may be refused on grounds of change of circumstances, including the passage of time,[191] although, where this ground is relied upon, then the court should ascertain the child's views, unless this is impractical.[192] Sixthly, recognition may be refused if, at the time of the institution of the foreign proceedings, the child was a national of the UK or habitually resident in England.[193]

The list of the exceptions is longer than in the Hague Convention and, although the European Convention expressly states that a decision shall not be reviewed as to its substance, there is a danger that the exceptions may be used to re-open matters already determined by the foreign court.[194] The approach of the courts in England has been to resist such arguments and children have been returned who have lived in England a long time.[195] Raising one of the grounds simply raises a judicial discretion to refuse enforcement; even if a ground has been raised, then the presumption is in favour of return, unless such return is demonstrably contrary to the interests of the child.[196]

As regards choice of the Conventions, there will be no choice unless a State is a party to each. The Hague Convention requires a wrongful abduction and has a narrower list of exceptions but does not require a foreign custody order. The European Convention requires a custody order, contains machinery for registration and enforcement and embraces a long list of exceptions, but does not require a wrongful abduction. Having regard to the wider geographical scope and the absence of the need for a court order, cases under the Hague Convention tend to come before the courts more frequently than those under the European Convention. Orders in respect of access can be registered and enforced under the European Convention, while the provision in Art 21 of the Hague Convention simply requires the Central Authority to act 'to promote the peaceful enjoyment of access rights'. Such a duty may arise in public law but has been interpreted as not creating rights enforceable in private law.[197]

---

189 European Convention 1980, Art 9(1)(c), (d); Child Abduction and Custody Act 1985, s 15(3).

190 *Ibid*, Art 10(1)(a).

191 *Ibid*, Art 10(1)(b); see *F v F* [1989] Fam 1.

192 *Ibid*, Art 15.

193 *Ibid*, Art 10(1)(c).

194 *Ibid*, Art 9(3); *F v F* [1989] Fam 1, p 189; see Hall [1989] CLJ 189.

195 *Re K* [1990] 1 FLR 387; *Re G* [1990] 2 FLR 525 (notwithstanding the expressed wish of child); *Re L* [1992] 2 FLR 178; *Re A* [1996] 3 FCR 165.

196 *F v F* [1989] Fam 1; *Re L* [1992] 2 FLR 178; *Re H* [1994] Fam 105.

197 *Re G* [1993] 1 FLR 669.

Non-convention countries

In respect of abduction, the question arises as to how an English court should respond in those cases where a State is not a party to either the Hague Convention or the European Convention. One approach would be to apply the general presumption in favour of return contained in the Conventions; the other possibility would be to continue with the common law emphasis on the welfare of the child. It as to be admitted that the courts have fluctuated between these two principles. At first, the courts tended to proceed by analogy with the provisions of the Convention.[198] However, the Court of Appeal has now ruled that the welfare principle should prevail. In *Re A*,[199] the Court of Appeal upheld the refusal of Singer J to order the return of a child to the United Arab Emirates. In giving judgment in the Court of Appeal, Ward LJ ruled that, where return is being sought to a non-convention country, then the English court would need to be satisfied that the child's welfare would be fully protected by the courts of a foreign country and that, in so far as doubt might have been cast upon this principle in *Re M*,[200] then those remarks required qualification.

DECLARATIONS

The courts had power both under the inherent jurisdiction and under s 45 of the Matrimonial Causes Act 1973 to grant declarations and these powers were used in respect of declarations as to the validity of marriage or legitimacy.[201] However, in 1984, the Law Commission[202] expressed reservations as to the state of the law in respect of declarations in family law matters. The Law Commission expressed the view that it was uncertain what declarations could be made under the inherent jurisdiction and categorised the state of the law as a 'hotchpotch of statutory and discretionary relief'. The Law Commission proposed that legislation should be introduced to establish a new code in respect of declarations in family law matters. The recommendations were given effect to in Part III of the Family Law Act 1986.[203] In that year, the Law Commission recommended that the court should be capable of granting

---

198 *Re F* [1991] Fam 25; *Re S* [1993] 1 FCR 789; *Re M* [1995] 1 FLR 89; *Re M* [1996] 1 FLR 478

199 *Re A (A Minor) (non-convention country)* (1997) (unreported, 3 July), CA (Lord Woolf MR, Ward, Mummery LJJ).

200 *Re M (Minors) (abduction: peremptory return order)* [1996] 1 FLR 478.

201 But not of illegitimacy (*Mansel v AG* (1877) 2 PD 265; (1879) 4 PD 232), nor of invalidity of marriage (*Kassim v Kassim* [1962] P 224), which required nullity proceedings.

202 Law Commission Report No 132 (1984).

203 Family Law Act 1986, ss 55–63.

declarations in respect of parentage and effect was given to this proposal in the Family Law Reform Act 1987.[204]

The effect of the reforms introduced in Part III of the Family Law Reform Act 1986 was to repeal s 45 of the Matrimonial Causes Act 1973 and to provide that the inherent jurisdiction would not operate where provision was made by statute.[205] Part III of the Family Law Act 1986 permits the court to make declarations in three broad areas.

Declarations as to marital status

Section 55 of the Family Law Act 1986 permits the court to make five forms of declaration under this heading, in particular:

(a) that the marriage was valid at its inception;

(b) that it subsisted on a date specified in the application;

(c) that it did not subsist on a date so specified;

(d) that the validity of a divorce, annulment or legal separation obtained outside England and Wales is entitled to recognition in England and Wales; and

(e) that such a divorce, annulment or legal separation is not entitled to recognition in England and Wales.

The legislation provides that jurisdiction will be established if either party was domiciled in England and Wales on the date of the application or habitually resident for the year prior to that date.[206] Although the legislation allows an application by any person, the section further provides that the court can dismiss an application as lacking *locus standi* if the applicant does not have a sufficient interest in the determination.[207]

Declarations of parentage, legitimacy and legitimation

Section 56 of the Family Law Act 1986, as substituted by s 22 of the Family Law Reform Act 1987, provides for four forms of declaration within this category:

(a) that a person was the parent of the applicant;

(b) that the applicant is the legitimate child of his parents;

204 Family Law Reform Act 1987, s 22.
205 Family Law Act 1986, s 58(4).
206 *Ibid*, s 55(2).
207 *Ibid*, s 55(3).

(c) that the applicant has become a legitimated person; and

(d) that the applicant has not become a legitimated person.

An application may be made by a person domiciled in England and Wales or who has been habitually resident for one year prior to the application.[208] In respect of legitimation, a declaration may be sought by a person claiming to have been legitimated by statute or under the common law rules pertaining to the recognition of foreign legitimations.[209] No declaration may be made that a person is illegitimate.[210] Only a person who alleges he is the child of a particular person may apply for a parentage declaration and only a person whose status is in issue may apply for a declaration of legitimacy or legitimation.

Declarations as to foreign adoptions

Having regard to the far reaching effects of an adoption order, it is not surprising that questions of the status of an adoption order have arisen incidentally in property litigation.[211] Statutory provisions exist in respect of the recognition of adoptions in other parts of the UK.[212] The Law Commission recommended, in 1984, that there should be statutory provisions in respect of declarations and Parliament implemented this proposal. Section 57 of the Family Law Act 1986 makes provision for the court to grant declarations in respect of adoptions effected overseas. Section 57(2) specifies that a declaration may be granted that a person is or is not the adopted child of another person.

Jurisdiction is founded on domicile in England and Wales or habitual residence for one year prior to the application. The court can grant a declaration both in respect of an overseas adoption recognised by statute and one that meets the common law requirements.[213]

Effect of declarations

A declaration granted in any of the three classes listed above will operate *in rem* and is intended, in the absence of fraud, to be binding and conclusive.[214] Because the effect of such a declaration of status may have consequences in

208 Family Law Act 1986, s 56(3).
209 *Ibid*, s 56(5).
210 *Ibid*, s 58(5).
211 *Re Wilson* [1954] Ch 733; *Re Marshall* [1957] Ch 507; *Re Valentine's Settlement* [1965] Ch 831.
212 Adoption Act 1976, s 38(1)(c).
213 Family Law Act 1986, s 57(1)(a), (b).
214 *Ibid*, s 58(2).

the area of public law, the legislation provides safeguards to ensure that the public interest is protected. Section 59 enables the court, of its own motion, at any stage in proceedings to serve all necessary papers on the Attorney General.[215] The legislation further provides that the Attorney General may, regardless of whether he has been sent papers, intervene in the proceedings and make any submissions to the court that he deems appropriate.

A declaration will be granted only if the truth of the proposition to be declared has been proved to the satisfaction of the court.[216] In the event of the *onus probandi* not being discharged, the court is obliged to dismiss the application; it is not entitled to make a declaration in negative form.[217] In addition, no declaration will be granted if to do so would be manifestly contrary to public policy; this continues the policy under s 45 of the Matrimonial Causes Act 1973, where the court had argued that no declaration binding the Crown could be made if it had been procured by a history of fraud and deception.[218]

---

215 Family Law Act 1986, s 59(1).

216 *Ibid*, s 58(1).

217 *Ibid*, s 58(3).

218 *Puttick v AG* [1980] Fam 1. An application for a declaration as to validity of marriage was made under s 45, the applicant seeking to establish a valid marriage and nationality as part of an attempt to avoid extradition to Germany to stand trial for serious offences arising from the activities of the Baader-Meinhof terrorist group. Baker P appeared to indicate that, where fraud was in issue, a declaration could be refused on the simple ground that 'no man can take advantage of his own wrong'.

CHAPTER 21

PROPERTY

As has been indicated earlier, many of the cases within the English conflict of laws concern some form of property dispute. The rules of English private international law in relation to property disputes require a number of distinctions to be drawn. First, there are those property cases that give rise to a problem of jurisdiction. In resolving problems as to jurisdiction, a distinction has to be drawn between movable and immovable property. Secondly, movable property is, itself, divided into tangible and intangible property. Thirdly, different rules apply in respect of transfers *inter vivos* and transfers upon death. Fourthly, particular problems arise in respect of matrimonial property, partly because of statutory regulation and partly because of social policy considerations.

There are a considerable number of cases in the area of property law and a number of points should be noted. Until 1914, property law was the principal area of civil law in England and many of the cases concern property rights that were modified by the 1925 property legislation. As with domestic law, a distinction has to be drawn between a pre-1925 property case and a post-1926 authority. A second matter that the reader will note is that many of the cases have (since 1875) been brought in the Chancery Division of the High Court and a considerable number concern family property; in these circumstances, many of the judgments are at first instance and have not been subject to appeal. Thirdly, if the litigation was by way of an originating summons in the Chancery Division, then, however wide the argument may range, the judge will be principally concerned to answer the specific questions posed by the parties in the originating summons.

JURISDICTION AND CHOICE OF LAW
IN THE LAW OF PROPERTY

Introduction

Property rights are at once the most concrete and the most abstract of legal interests. They are the most concrete, in that their origin is physical and territorial, and the most abstract, in that they can exist without the interpersonal nexus which characterises all other legal relations. At the same time, they can be the most simple rights, which every social system has to acknowledge – some protection for current use – and the most complex, as when rights are recognised in something which is currently neither possessed nor controlled by the owner and where the subject matter may not even have a physical existence.

Small wonder, then, that different legal systems have very different ideas about what can be owned, by whom it can be owned and on what terms and how ownership can be exercised, protected, transferred and extinguished. Equally unsurprising are the very different classifications of property interests which legal systems have, based on physical form, use, means of transfer, portability, value and social utility, and the possibilities which those systems acknowledge of shared ownership in sequence, in parallel, in extent and for purpose.

The courts of common law and equity established a complex system of rules based primarily on the distinction between real property and personal property, with real interests centering on land[1] and personal interests extending to everything else, and with very different rules relating to the transfer of these interests both in life and upon death.

In the 17th century, the emergence of a commercial sector within the general agricultural economy prompted the development of those property rights known collectively today as industrial and intellectual property rights.[2] In the 20th century, these property rights have been influenced by international conventions.

In every other area of the conflict of laws, English courts have taken as their starting point the concepts of domestic law and have been content to adapt them for conflict purposes, adopting a more (for example, in contract and family law) or less (for example, in the law of tort) international approach. For property, it was realised that the distinctions adopted by the domestic law could not be adapted to provide a workable basis for the adjudication of conflict cases and a universal distinction which made sense for all systems, whatever their domestic rules might be, was substituted. This division of property rights is between interests in things which can be moved and interests in those which cannot.

The distinction between movable and immovable property

It is conventional to begin any discussion on the English conflict of laws on property by expounding the distinction between movable and immovable

---

1   Although leaseholds, not being a creature of the feudal system, were regarded as operating *in personam* and, thus, are strictly classed as personal property in domestic law.

2   In strict terms, patents, copyright and trade marks. Patent law is traceable to the Statute of Monopolies 1623, while copyright law can be traced back, beyond the Copyright Act 1709, to the regulatory activities of the Stationers Company. By contrast, trade mark legislation is a 19th century phenomenon, originating with the Merchandising Marks Act 1862 and the Trade Marks Registration Act 1875.

property as a universal distinction transcending the divisions of property which different domestic systems may have and, particularly, English law's distinction between real and personal property.

The distinction between real and personal property was a product of historical evolution and one of the objects of the draftsmen of the 1925 legislation[3] was to assimilate, as far as possible, the law relating to real property with that pertaining to personal property. The clearest evidence of the division before 1926 related to the devolution of property on intestacy. Prior to 1926, all the real property vested in the heir but all the personalty devolved through the personal representatives upon the next of kin. This distinction was set aside by s 33(1) of the Administration Estates Act 1925, which provides for the ending of primogeniture and unified succession under a trust for sale in respect of deaths after 1926.

However, the English conflict of laws had already began to develop in the 18th century and the courts had, prior to 1925, adopted the distinction between movable and immovable property, rather than concerning themselves with the intricacies of the distinction between real and personal property. So, in cases of property concerning a foreign element, the important distinction was between movable and immovable property. The position was well expressed by Farwell LJ, in *Re Hoyles*,[4] where the learned judge observed:

> In order to arrive at a common basis on which to determine questions between the inhabitants of two countries living under different systems of jurisprudence, our courts recognise and act on a division, otherwise unknown to our law, into movable and immovable.

In general, the distinction between movable and immovable property is most important in cases of succession. Succession to movable property is, in general, governed by the law of the deceased's last domicile, while succession to immovable property is governed by the *lex situs*. It is, therefore, arguable that English conflict law has not caught up with the developments in domestic law, in which unified succession was introduced by the property legislation of 1925.[5]

An obvious problem arises as to whether the *lex fori* or the *lex situs* should determine whether the property is movable or immovable. There is a solid stream of authority that holds that classification is to be determined by the *lex situs*.[6]

---

3 By the 1925 legislation, one means the Law of Property Act 1925, the Land Charges Act 1925, the Settled Land Act 1925, the Land Registration Act 1925, the Trustee Act 1925 and the Administration of Estates Act 1925.

4 *Re Hoyles* [1911] 1 Ch 179.

5 Administration of Estates Act 1925, s 33(1).

6 *Re Hoyles* [1911] 1 Ch 179; *Re Berchtold* [1923] 1 Ch 192; *Re Cutliffe's Will Trusts* [1940] Ch 565.

Thus, if X dies intestate, having been domiciled in England but leaving a house and antiques in Arcadia, then, if the antiques are classified as movable property by the law of Arcadia, they will be inherited by whoever is entitled to them in English law, since intestate succession to movables is governed by the law of the last domicile of the deceased. But, if they are classified as immovables (for example, because they are affixed to the house), then they will descend to whoever is entitled by Arcadian law, since the *lex situs* governs the question of intestate succession to immovable property.[7]

The distinction between movable and immovable property is reflected in all cases in England on the conflict of laws since the middle of the 19th century. This has meant that leasehold property, which would be regarded as personalty by domestic law, is classified as immovable property for the purpose of the conflict of laws.[8]

The cases on property law do reveal a willingness to act flexibly in order to achieve sensible results. This is illustrated by the litigation in *Re Piercy*,[9] where the facts were as follows: a testator domiciled in England devised his Sardinian land to trustees on trust for sale to hold the same after conversion on certain trusts for his children and remainder to remoter issue. Italian law would have regarded the gift as one to the children absolutely, not recognising a gift in remainder.

North J ruled that, while Italian law, as the *lex situs*, would apply to the land until sale, it did not itself restrain sale of the land and, after the sale, the proceeds were to be held by the English trustees, subject to the full terms of the trust document. The reasoning may have been doubtful but the conclusion is certainly sensible.

That the general approach of the courts to property cases in the conflict of laws was still subject to development was illustrated by the subsequent case of *Re Hoyles*,[10] where the facts were as follows: a testator who died in 1888 left one third of his real and personal estate after the death of his wife to charity. The property included monies extended on the mortgage of freehold properties in Ontario. At the operative time, the Mortmain Act 1736 provided that such gifts should be void. The legislation applied in both Ontario and England.

It was argued by those seeking to uphold the gift that, for certain purposes of domestic law, mortgages were regarded as personalty, so that succession was governed by English law as the law of the testator's last domicile. In

---

7   *In re O'Neill (Deceased)* [1922] NZLR 468 (New Zealand court classifies mortgages as movable property); *Hague v Hague (No 2)* (1965) 114 CLR 98 (Australian court classifies mortgages as movable property).

8   *Freke v Lord Carbery* (1873) LR 16 Eq 461; *Duncan v Lawson* (1889) 41 Ch D 394; *Pepin v Bruyere* [1900] 2 Ch 504.

9   *Re Piercy* [1895] 1 Ch 83.

10   *Re Hoyles* [1911] 1 Ch 179.

rejecting these arguments and holding the gift to be invalid, Farwell LJ[11] made the following points: (a) the gift was invalid under both English law and Ontarian law, which were identical in substance; (b) as a matter of principle, whether the property rights were movable or immovable should be determined by Ontarian law as the *lex situs*; (c) classified under that law, mortgages were immovable property; and (d) a gift of immovable property was void under the law of Ontario.

Thus, after *Re Hoyles*, it was sensible to assume that the question as to whether property was movable or immovable would be determined in accordance with the *lex situs*. The judgment of the Court of Appeal also impliedly asserted that, on intestacy, movable property will devolve according to the *lex domicilii*, while immovable property will devolve according to the *lex situs*.

The distinction between movable and immovable property was subject to further consideration in *Re Berchtold*,[12] where the facts were as follows: Count Richard Berchtold, a domiciled Hungarian, left freehold property in Birmingham by will upon trust for sale for his son, Count Nicholas. Before the property could be sold, Count Nicholas died intestate. The question arose as to the nature of the property rights held on trust for sale. Those entitled under Hungarian law claimed that the interest was personalty,[13] while those entitled under English law claimed that the property was immovable property devolving under the *lex situs*.

Russell J, in holding in favour of the heirs under English law, asserted four propositions: (a) that the critical question in such a case was whether the property was classified as movable or immovable property; (b) that such a task was to be undertaken by *the lex situs*; (c) that, while a trust for sale might, by virtue of the doctrine of conversion, be regarded by domestic law as personalty,[14] such a classification had no relevance in matters of private international law, where such an interest constituted immovable property; and (d) that immovable property includes all rights over things which cannot be moved. In consequence, the learned judge held that the persons entitled to the freehold property were those entitled to succeed under English law as the *lex situs*.

While the courts may be prepared to modify doctrines of domestic law to conform to the demands of private international law, more difficult questions arise when the court is confronted with an express statutory provision. In these circumstances, the constitutional principle that English courts must

---

11 *Re Hoyles* [1911] 1 Ch 179 (Farwell, Fletcher Moulton LJJ, Cozens Hardy MR).

12 *Re Berchtold* [1923] 1 Ch 192 (Russell J).

13 Having regard to the equitable doctrine of conversion: *Fletcher v Ashburner* (1779) 1 Bro CC 497.

14 See, now, the Trusts of Land and Appointment of Trustees Act 1996.

interpret and apply primary legislation has to prevail over any other consideration.[15]

This was illustrated by the case of *Re Cutliffe's Will Trusts*,[16] where the facts were as follows: an intestate who died, domiciled in Ontario, in 1897, was entitled to the proceeds of the sale of land arising by the exercise of powers under the Settled Land Act 1882.[17] If the money was regarded as land, then the English heir would benefit but, if it were regarded as personalty, then the Ontario next of kin would benefit. The problem that arose was that the Settled Land Act 1882 expressly provided that:

> ... capital money arising under this Act, while remaining uninvested, and securities on which an investment of any such capital money shall be made shall, for all purposes of disposition, transition and devolution, be regarded as land.[18]

Morton J, in considering the argument as to whether the monies were to be regarded as land and, thus, immovable property, ruled that it was for the *lex situs* to determine how property was to be classified and that express statutory provisions would prevail over any judge made rules of private international law. The court felt bound by the clear words of the statute in a way in which it had not felt bound by the equitable doctrine of conversion. In the face of such express statutory provisions, the court held that the property was to be classified as land and, thus, immovable property. It followed that, under English domestic law, the property would pass to the heir, as realty, and not to the next of kin, as personalty.

As the object of the initial classification is to give effect to the interests of the *lex situs*, it must follow that the law of the *situs* has the say in how the distinction is to be applied to the property in its territory:

> The question in all these cases is not so much what are or ought to be deemed *ex sua natura*, movables or not, as what are deemed so by the law of the place where they are situated. If they are there deemed part of the land ... they must be so treated in every place in which any controversy shall arise respecting their nature and character.[19]

The fact that another country would classify the subject matter in dispute in a different way is irrelevant. Suppose we are dealing with a 'mobile' home situated in France; we know that, under English law, the degree of physical connection to the land will determine whether the subject is movable or

---

15 Unless it is argued that the legislation violates European Union law, where a reference under Art 177 will probably be made.
16 *Re Cutliffe's Will Trusts* [1940] Ch 565 (Morton J).
17 Later replaced by the Settled Land Act 1925.
18 Settled Land Act 1882, s 33(5); Settled Land Act 1925, s 75(5).
19 Story, *Commentaries on the Conflict of Laws* (8th edn, 1883), section 447.

immovable;[20] therefore, evidence of the French law of property would be needed to classify the subject matter definitively

Jurisdiction of the English courts in property cases

There are three elements that need to be discussed under this heading, namely: (a) the operative rules at common law; (b) the exceptions to those rules; and (c) the position under the Brussels Convention. It is proposed to examine each of these in turn.

The rules at common law

There has been, for over 100 years, a common law rule (now subject to a number of exceptions) that an English court has no jurisdiction to entertain an action for (a) the determination of title to, or the right to possession of, any immovable situated out of England; or (b) the recovery of damages for trespass to such an immovable. The rule derives from the case of *British South Africa Company v Companhia de Mocambique*[21] and is sometimes referred to as the *Mocambique* rule. The facts in the case were simple: the plaintiffs, a Portuguese company, brought an action against the defendants, alleging that the defendant company had wrongfully taken possession of certain of their land in South Africa. The plaintiffs claimed (a) a declaration as to title; (b) an injunction; and (c) damages for trespass. The Court of Appeal, by a majority, ruled that the damages action should proceed. This judgment was reversed by the House of Lords.

The House of Lords ruled that an English court did not have jurisdiction to determine disputes over foreign land or damages actions arising therefrom. Lord Herschell LC made clear that this was a rule of substantive law and did not depend on a distinction between local and transitory venues. The majority in the Court of Appeal, noting that such a distinction had been abolished by the Judicature Act 1873, considered that the action for damages should proceed. The House of Lords stressed that, while the general principle might be subject to limitations, the rule itself was founded upon substantive considerations and did not derive from procedure. The fundamental principle was that any judgment over foreign land would be ineffective, unless recognised by the authorities within the *lex situs*, and that there might be many social policies in the *lex situs*, such as the protection of tenants, which require the attention of the court there.

---

20 *D'Eyncourt v Gregory* (1866) LR 3 Eq 382; *Leigh v Taylor* [1902] AC 157.

21 *British South Africa Co v Companhia de Mocambique* [1893] AC 602, HL; reversing [1892] 2 QB 358 (Fry, Lopes LJJ, Lord Esher MR dissenting).

After 1893, questions arose as to how far the *Mocambique* rule extended and what was the scope of any exception. The matter was considered in *St Pierre v South American Stores (Gath and Chaves) Ltd*,[22] where the facts were as follows: the plaintiffs brought an action against the defendants, two English companies, to recover arrears of rent in respect of leasehold premises in Chile. The defendants applied to have the action stayed. Porter J refused to stay the action and this refusal was upheld by the Court of Appeal.

The Court of Appeal allowed the action to proceed, asserting that the *Mocambique* rule only applied to actions founded upon disputed title and did not extend to actions founded upon personal obligations where no question of title arose. While the case concerned the precise ambit of the rule, it came to be accepted that there were three exceptions to the rule. It was accepted that the English court would not refuse jurisdiction solely on the basis that the case involved rights to, or to the possession of, foreign immovable property when the court was acting to give effect to the equitable jurisdiction *in personam*, or the administration of estates and trusts or the Admiralty jurisdiction *in rem*.

The *Mocambique* rule fell to be considered again by the House of Lords in the case of *Hesperides Hotels Ltd v Muftizade*,[23] where the facts were as follows: the plaintiffs, who owned hotels in Northern Cyprus, were forced to vacate the properties after the Turkish invasion of 1974. At a later date, the plaintiffs brought an action against a London travel agent, arguing that the organising of holidays in the hotels constituted a conspiracy to trespass. They added a claim in respect of the contents of the hotels.

Although the judgment of Lord Denning MR, in the Court of Appeal, had devoted considerable attention to the legal effects of the acts of an unrecognised government, the House of Lords were content to apply the *Mocambique* rule and ordered that the claim in respect of conspiracy to trespass be struck out for want of jurisdiction. However, the plaintiffs were allowed to pursue the claim in respect of the contents of the hotels. The failure of the House of Lords to restrict the *Mocambique* rule to cases where questions of title were directly in issue was the subject of some comment.[24]

The effect of the judgment was reversed by s 30(1) of the Civil Jurisdiction and Judgments Act 1982, which reads:

> The jurisdiction of any court in England and Wales or Northern Ireland to entertain proceedings for trespass to, or any other tort affecting, immovable property shall extend to cases in which the property in question is situated outside that part of the United Kingdom, unless the proceedings are

---

22 [1936] 1 KB 382 (Porter J, Greer, Scott, Slesser LJJ).
23 [1979] AC 508, upholding *Hesperides Hotels Ltd v Aegean Turkish Holidays Ltd* [1978] QB 205.
24 For comment, see Lloyd Jones (1978) 37 CLJ 48; Merrills (1979) 28 ICLQ 523; Shaw (1978) 94 LQR 500; Carter (1978) 49 BYIL 286.

principally concerned with a question of title to, or the right to possession of, that property.

It should be noted that, by s 30(2) of the Civil Jurisdiction and Judgments Act 1982, the operation of s 30(1) is expressly subject to the terms of the Brussels Convention on Jurisdiction and the Enforcement of Judgments 1968.

In recent years, the *Mocambique* rule has received considerable attention in the area of industrial and intellectual property law, following the judgment of Vinelott J in *Tyburn Productions Ltd v Conan Doyle*.[25] The facts of the case were as follows: the defendant, the last surviving daughter of Sir Arthur Conan Doyle was in dispute with the plaintiff company as to the extent of copyright in the USA respect of the characters Sherlock Holmes and Dr Watson. The plaintiffs brought an action in the Chancery Division, seeking a declaration that no such rights arose under US law.

Vinelott J refused to make the declaration, holding that the *Mocambique* rule rendered any question of foreign intellectual property rights non-justiciable in an English court. The learned judge reasoned that jurisdiction could not be assumed because any order made by an English court would not be effective in the USA. Clearly, difficulties can arise if an English court were to rule on intellectual property rights arising by statute and subject to a registration scheme in a foreign country.

The matter has received more recent judicial attention in *Pearce v Ove Arup Partnership*,[25a] where Lloyd J, in considering a case under the Brussels Convention of the alleged infringement of a Dutch copyright, expressed the view that, in non-convention cases, the *Mocambique* rule, as extended in *Tyburn Productions*, would have prevented an English court from ruling on the validity of intellectual property rights arising under a foreign legal system. Under the Convention, where jurisdiction is founded on domicile, it is now the subject of some debate as to whether the courts of State A can adjudicate on the validity of intellectual property rights arising under the legal system of State B.

In cases arising outside the Convention, the *Mocambique* rule, as modified by s 30(1) of the Civil Jurisdiction and Judgments Act 1982, will prevent jurisdiction arising where title to foreign land is directly in issue.

The exceptions to the Mocambique rule

At common law, there were two well established exceptions to the *Mocambique* rule. The first exception held that a defendant within the jurisdiction could be proceeded against in respect of the breach of a personal

---

25 [1991] Ch 75 (Vinelott J).
25a [1997] Ch 293

obligation concerning foreign property or other inequitable conduct. The distinction was that, while the court could not make an order directly in respect of the foreign land, it could make an order affecting the defendant personally. The exception is normally said to derive from the judgment in *Penn v Lord Baltimore*,[26] although it is clear that the doctrine can be traced back further.[27] In *Penn v Lord Baltimore*, Lord Hardwicke LC was prepared to grant an order for specific performance of an agreement made in England as to the boundary line between Maryland and Pennsylvania.

The jurisdiction was most appropriate in the case of contracts concerning foreign land[28] but it was not restricted to such cases and it extended to any inequitable conduct committed by a defendant who was within the jurisdiction. This relief was sought in *Bank of Africa v Cohen*[29] and was granted in *Re Smith*.[30] An early example is afforded by *Ex p Pollard*,[31] where a mortgagor deposited the title deeds to land in Scotland with a mortgagee and undertook to take any further steps necessary to make good the security.

The deposit of title deeds created an equitable mortgage by English law but not by Scots law. When the mortgagor went bankrupt, the mortgagee petitioned the English court to have his debt secured on the Scottish land in preference to the general body of creditors. He succeeded, as Lord Cottenham LC took the view that there was nothing to prevent a valid mortgage being created over the Scottish land and there was a personal obligation on the mortgagor's part to do so. Therefore, the mortgagee, by deposit of title deeds, was entitled to priority over the mortgagor's unsecured creditors, even though, by the *lex situs*, the deposit gave him no lien or equitable mortgage over the land at all.

Thus, an attempt to employ inequitable conduct in respect of foreign land to enforce a judgment can be the subject of relief.[32] Difficulties can arise in situations where the plaintiff asserts that the defendant holds foreign land as a trustee; if the beneficiary can make out his claim without reference to any dispute as to title, then the claim can proceed[33] but the *Mocambique* rule will operate if the court is being asked to rule on competing claims to the foreign

---

26 (1750) 1 Ves Sen 444.

27 *Anglasse v Muschamp* (1682) 1 Vern 76, citing the undated earlier case of *Archer v Preston* (which had concerned the sale of land in Ireland).

28 *Re Smith* [1916] 2 Ch 206; *Richard West and Partners (Inverness) Ltd v Dick* [1969] 2 Ch 424 (a contract for the sale of land in Scotland, where Megarry J observed that 'any inability of the court to enforce the decree *in rem* is no reason for refusing the plaintiff such rights and means of enforcement as equity can afford him': [1969] 1 All ER 289, p 292).

29 [1909] 2 Ch 129.

30 [1916] 2 Ch 206.

31 *Re Courtney ex p Pollard* (1840) Mont & Ch 239 (Lord Cottenham LC); the case was cited but distinguished in *Bank of Africa v Cohen* [1909] 2 Ch 129.

32 *Cranstown v Johnstone* (1796) 3 Ves 170.

33 *Ewing v Orr Ewing* (1883) 9 App Cas 34.

land.[34] In those cases where the rule in *Penn v Lord Baltimore* has been successfully invoked, the court has been able to identify a contractual relationship or a recognised equity flowing between plaintiff and defendant. It is difficult to identify a principle that is in perfect harmony with all the cases but the position was well expressed by Parker J (as he then was) in *Deschamps v Miller*,[35] where the learned judge noted that the cases seemed to depend:

> ... upon the existence between the parties to the suit of some personal obligation arising out of contract or implied contract, fiduciary relationship or fraud, or other conduct which, in the view of the Court of Equity in this country, would be unconscionable, and do not depend for their existence on the law of the *locus* of the immovable property.

There are a number of qualifications that need to be added. First, in accordance with normal equitable principles, the court will not make an order if it cannot supervise the carrying out of the order. Secondly, there is some authority for the view that an order will not be made if to carry it out would be contrary to the law of the *lex situs*. Thirdly, while an order can be made against a party to the contract or the equity, there seems no reason in principle, in accordance with normal equitable doctrines, as to why a party subject to constructive notice should not also be bound.[36] However, the cases have not always been consistent; so, in *Norris v Chambres*,[37] the buyer's knowledge of a previous contract for the sale of the land did not mean that he took the land subject to a charge in favour of the disappointed purchaser, as Lord Romilly MR saw no personal obligation between them. However, in *Mercantile Investment and General Trust Co v River Plate Trust Co*,[38] buyers who had taken the land 'subject to the mortgage, lien or charge now existing' were not allowed to argue that no such charge existed under the *lex situs* – they knew of the equitable mortgage in favour of the plaintiffs and were bound by it.

The second exception to the *Mocambique* rule concerns the administration of trusts and the jurisdiction in relation to the estates of deceased persons. The exception is probably no wider than the rule that, where an English court has jurisdiction to administer the estate of a deceased person who has left property in England and immovable property abroad, then the English court will have jurisdiction to determine incidental questions in respect of the foreign immovable property. This exception founded on the incidental nature

---

34   *Tito v Waddell (No 2)* [1977] Ch 106.
35   [1908] 1 Ch 856, p 863.
36   *Mercantile Investment and General Trust Co v River Plate Trust Co* [1892] 2 Ch 303.
37   (1861) 29 Beav 246 (Lord Romilly MR).
38   *Co* [1892] 2 Ch 303 (North J).

of the question may well have been acknowledged as an exception[39] by Lord Herschell LC in the *Mocambique* case.[40] In any event, there is a respectable line of authority that testifies to the existence of such an exception.[41]

The relevance of the Brussels Convention

As has been indicated elsewhere, if the immovable property is situated in a Contracting State to the Brussels or Lugano Convention, then Art 16(1)(a) confers exclusive jurisdiction on the courts of that State. Thus, a UK court will not be able to assume jurisdiction in respect of immovable property (including leasehold interests) if such property is located in a Contracting State; in this instance, the common law rules have no application. Secondly, the determination of the scope of Art 16(1)(a) is a matter for the European Court of Justice and the tendency has been to interpret it broadly.[42] Thirdly, s 30(2) of the Civil Jurisdiction and Judgments Act 1982 makes it clear that, in such cases, the rules of the Brussels Convention 1968 are to prevail. The *Mocambique* rule has no application in such cases.

General principles of the English conflict of laws on property

As has been indicated above, it is clear, since the *Mocambique*[43] case, that the English courts generally refuse jurisdiction when the matter concerns title to, or rights to possession of, foreign immovable property. In broad terms, this concept is also reflected in the Brussels and Lugano Conventions, where it is provided that the courts of the *situs* of the immovable shall have exclusive jurisdiction over proceedings *in rem* brought in relation to it.[44]

While the courts of the *situs* will generally have jurisdiction over matters relating to immovables there, it should not be assumed that all disputes will be subject to the rules of the *lex situs*, though, as we shall see, many are. In any event, it is clear that, in respect of property cases, English private international law is influenced by the principle of restricted jurisdiction

---

39 In the Divisional Court in the *Mocambique* case, Wright J had observed 'Courts of Equity have, from the time of Lord Hardwicke's decision in *Penn v Lord Baltimore*, exercised jurisdiction *in personam* with regard to foreign land against persons locally within the jurisdiction of the English court in cases of contract, fraud and trust, enforcing their jurisdiction by writs of *ne exeat regno* during the hearing and by sequestration, commitment or other personal process after decree': [1892] 2 QB 385.

40 *British South Africa Co v Companhia de Mocambique* [1893] AC 602.

41 *Nelson v Bridport* (1846) 8 Beav 547; *Re Piercy* [1895] 1 Ch 83; *Re Hoyles* [1911] 1 Ch 179; *Re Ross* [1930] 1 Ch 377; *Re Duke of Wellington* [1948] Ch 118.

42 *Rosler v Rottwinkel* [1986] 1 QB 33.

43 *British South Africa Co v Companhia de Mocambique* [1893] AC 604.

44 Brussels Convention on Jurisdiction and Judgments 1968, Art 16 (1).

Secondly, the law of property is influenced by the demands of procedure. In succession cases, the starting point, as far as English law is concerned, is the authorisation of the persons who are responsible for the administration of the estate in England. Such persons can only act in England if they have a grant of representation (probate or letters of administration) from the court. The beneficial distribution of the assets of the estate in accordance with the will or the intestacy rules is the final task of the personal representatives and that task is under the supervision of the court. English law governs the administration of the estate, though, of course, in the vast majority of cases, the actual supervision is nominal. As administration includes distribution and as the estate may have assets abroad which are immovable interests, this produces an exception to the *Mocambique* rule.

One can identify a third guiding principle in property matters. Having regard to the pragmatic spirit of the common law, it is sometimes argued that, in private international law, there is evidence of the courts seeking to be guided by the principle of effectiveness. To describe effectiveness as a principle is to elevate it beyond its merits.

However, every rule of law and every court decision is intended to have effect and decisions or rules which cannot be effectively enforced help no one. But, the fact that immovable property is permanently, and movable property temporally, under the control of the courts and officials of the *situs* has produced not only the jurisdictional limitations but, also, the belief that the law of the *situs* cannot be disregarded. Indeed, it is usually seen as the appropriate law to apply, at least in those cases where the courts of the *situs* would apply their own domestic law to the case, and a concern for complying with the *lex situs* or, rather, of assimilating the English court's decision to that which a court of the situs would give has led to the English doctrine of *renvoi*.

A fourth matter that requires to be borne in mind when considering the cases in the conflict of laws that concern property matters is the distinction between matters of contract and matters of conveyance. English lawyers are familiar with the distinction between contract and conveyance in the context of the transfer of land but not in the area of the sale of goods yet, analytically, the same matters are in issue. There is the relationship between buyer and seller (or recipient and donor) which is a purely personal relationship concerning only themselves and which is governed by the law applicable to the contract or gift; and there is the property interest which the buyer or recipient holds against the world at large. Whatever the law governing the personal relationship, that law cannot thereby determine the property relations.

Suppose S sells property to B, in circumstances where S has no title, authority or power to make a valid transfer. B's remedy against S is clearly contractual but the remedy of O, the owner, against S or B or both does not depend on the law governing the S-B relationship but upon a right which he has under the law of property. The conflict of laws relating to property is concerned entirely with the proprietary aspects of disputes; all other aspects are governed by the law appropriate to the interpersonal relations.

A fifth principle that can be identified in property law matters is the principle in English law that parties should be free to organise their own affairs and that there should be few restraints on the alienation of property. Indeed, this principle holds that, on death, the testator should be free to dispose of the whole of his property as he wishes.[45] This last is in contrast with the position in many civil law systems, where the family interests are seen to exist in the estate before the death of the current owner. His testamentary wishes operate on what remains after his family, characteristically his surviving spouse and his children, have automatically inherited their 'legitimate portions'.

A final principle that can be noted in relation to property law, which is in keeping with the concept of restricted jurisdiction and the idea of effectiveness, is the attitude that English law adopts to the conduct of other States. In keeping with these principles, is the recognition that States have powers of appropriation and confiscation over property within their territory, as a fact of international life,[46] and one to be controlled, if it is to be controlled at all, by the requirements of public international law[47] and not by the decisions of individual courts trying private law matters. It might be argued that, as the rules of public international law have developed to enable claims to be made by governments at the international level, there is little case for extending the jurisdiction of the courts in this area. In broad terms, this approach is reflected in the principle that the acts of a foreign executive or legislature within its own territory will be recognised in respect of property within it, unless to do so would be contrary to public policy or to the international obligations of the UK.[48]

---

45 In strict terms, complete testamentary freedom ended in 1938, with the enactment of the Inheritance (Family Provision) Act 1938; the extended legislation is now to be found in the Inheritance (Provision for Family and Dependants) Act 1975. See *Re Coventry* [1980] Ch 461; *Re Besterman* [1984] Ch 458; *Re Leach* [1986] Ch 226; see Bryan (1980) 96 LQR 165; Miller (1986) 102 LQR 445; Martin (1989) Conv 445; Martin (1992) Conv 442.

46 This matter is discussed under the title of 'Recognition of foreign laws', Chapter 9; examples of the traditional attitude of English law are to be found in *Luther v Sagor* [1921] 3 KB 532, CA; *Princess Olga Paley v Weisz* [1929] 1 KB 718.

47 In respect of unlawful expropriation, the starting point for discussion is the demand for 'prompt, adequate and effective compensation' (the so called 'Hull formula', propounded by Cordell Hull, US Secretary of State, 1933–44).

48 *Luther v Sagor* [1921] 3 KB 532; *Princess Olga Paley v Weisz* [1929] 1 KB 718; *Re Russian Bank for Foreign Trade* [1933] Ch 475; *Bank voor Handel en Scheepvaart NV v Slatford* [1953] 1 QB 248.

IMMOVABLE PROPERTY

Jurisdiction

As indicated earlier, the *Mocambique* rule[49] precludes the English courts generally from assuming jurisdiction where the subject matter of the dispute is title to, or right to possession of, foreign immovable property.[50] It is subject to certain established exceptions in favour of the traditional maritime jurisdiction of the English courts, the administration of estates and trusts and the equitable jurisdiction *in personam*.[51] Secondly, in cases of proceedings which have as their object rights *in rem* in immovable property or tenancies of immovable property situated in a Contracting State to the Brussels Convention or the Lugano Convention,[52] jurisdiction is accorded to the courts of the country in which the property is situated. These matters have been dealt with elsewhere but it is worth noting that the deference shown to *lex situs* at common law is continued in the statutory scheme.

Choice of law

The general presumption in favour of the lex situs

In England, Europe and the USA, the general rule is that the *lex situs* constitutes the governing law in respect of all questions that concern immovable property. This is supported by a consistent stream of case law.[53] The matter was candidly stated by Lord Langdale MR, in *Nelson v Bridport*,[54] a case in which Viscount Nelson, in his capacity as Duke of Bronte, had attempted to devise his Sicilian estates in a manner contrary to the law of Sicily:

> The incidents to real estate, the right of alienating or limiting it, and the course
> of succession to it depend entirely on the law of the country where the estate is
> situated.

Although the influence of the *lex situs* has been subject to some scholarly criticism, there is little doubt that it represents the governing law for the vast majority of questions that arise in respect of immovable property. The

---

49 *British South Africa Co v Companhia de Mocambique* [1893] AC 602.

50 But not to a simple action for trespass; see Civil Jurisdiction and Judgments Act 1982, s 30.

51 *Penn v Lord Baltimore* (1750) 1 Ves Sen 444.

52 Given effect to by the Civil Jurisdiction and Judgments Acts 1982 and 1991.

53 *Coppin v Coppin* (1725) P Wms 291; *Birwhistle v Vardill* (1840) 7 Cl & Fin 895; *Nelson v Bridport* (1846) 8 Beav 547; *Re Duke if Wellington* [1947] Ch 506; [1948] Ch 118.

54 (1846) 8 Beav 547, p 570.

question that does arise is as to the meaning of the expression *lex situs*. Does it mean the domestic law of the *situs* or the law of the *situs* together with the appropriate rules of its own private international law? An examination of the case law indicates that the expression, *lex situs,* is normally interpreted as meaning the domestic law but that such an interpretation should be arrived at with proper regard for the policy behind any such law. The writer WW Cook[55] took, as an example, the case of *Proctor v Frost,*[56] where the facts were as follows: by a law in New Hampshire, a wife was incapable of acting as a surety for her husband but there was no such restriction under the law of Massachusetts. A married woman who was domiciled in Massachusetts entered into a surety agreement that involved her land in New Hampshire. At a later date, a court in New Hampshire was obliged to consider the validity of the transaction and the enforceability of a mortgage of her land in New Hampshire.

In giving judgment, the Supreme Court of New Hampshire considered the purpose of its own law. Was the law principally concerned with the regulation of conveyances within New Hampshire or was it designed to to protect married women domiciled in New Hampshire against pressure from their husbands? The court decided that the purpose of the legislation was to protect married women domiciled in New Hampshire from pressure from their husbands and that there was no reason why the legislation should be extended to protect married women elsewhere. Having come to this conclusion, the court was able to uphold the mortgage. Of course, if the New Hampshire court had felt that its protectionary policy was so fundamental a matter that it should be applied whatever the domicile of the woman and whatever the attitude of her personal law, the decision would have been the other way.

Proctor v Frost can be viewed in a different way – as an issue of classification – that is, that the New Hampshire law on a contract of suretyship by a wife was not a part of the real estate law of New Hampshire but part of its law of matrimonial relations and, therefore, irrelevant to a Massachusetts wife. Such an approach, while leading to the same result, would have consequences beyond the non-application of this particular New Hampshire law. It would involve a preparedness to investigate, in transactions involving New Hampshire real estate, the protectionary rules of the domiciliary law, with effect to be given to them unless offensive to the public policy of New Hampshire. In any event, the case affords an example of the need to consider the purpose of the *lex situs* within the context of the case before the court.

---

55   Cook, *Logical and Legal Bases of the Conflict of Laws* (1942), p 274.
56   *Proctor v Frost* (1938) 89 NH 309.

Capacity to take and transfer immovables.

The general rule is that a person must have capacity to take and transfer immovable property by the *lex situs*. This proposition is attested to by the cases *of Duncan v Lawson*[57] and *Bank of Africa v Cohen*,[58] although the reasoning in the latter case has not escaped without criticism. In the case of *Duncan v Lawson*, the facts were as follows: a domiciled Scotsman left freehold and leasehold property in England for charities registered in England. Under English law, such a gift would have been void under the Mortmain and Charitable Uses Act 1888. Two questions arose:

(a) whether English law, as the law of the *situs*, rendered the gift void; and

(b) whether English or Scottish law should govern in the event of intestacy.

In giving judgment upon a special case remitted by the Court of Session, Kay J accepted that both questions were governed by the *lex loci rei sitae*, so that both the capacity of the charities to take and the intestate succession to immovable property were governed by English law.

While the determination of proprietary rights in immovables, the transferability of the interest, the capacities of the transferor[59] and transferee, the formalities required to effect the transfer[60] and whether the proposed transfer falls foul of legislation against perpetuities or accumulations,[61] or conflicts with restrictions on gifts of real estate to charity[62] are exclusively under the control of the *lex situs* (or whatever system of law the *lex situs* would itself apply), the personal relations between the parties will, on the ordinary principles of conflict law, be treated as distinct. There is some evidence that the earlier authorities may not have sufficiently drawn a distinction between the capacity to contract and matters of conveyance. In principle, a contract to transfer immovable property which does not effect the transfer under the *lex situs* does not necessarily fail as a contract. In *In re Smith*,[63] the court ordered specific performance of the undertaking to create an effective mortgage over land in the West Indies.

However, the law as to capacity to make a contract in respect of foreign immovables, which might be logically thought to be subject to the proper law of the contract, has been held, instead, to be subject to the *lex situs*. This derives from the much criticised case of *Bank of Africa v Cohen*,[64] where the

---

57 (1889) 41 Ch D 394 (Kay J).
58 [1909] 2 Ch 129 (Eve J, Buckley and Kennedy LJJ, Cozens Hardy MR).
59 *Duncan v Lawson* (1889) 41 Ch D 394; *Bank of Africa v Cohen* [1909] 2 Ch 129.
60 *Adams v Clutterbuck* (1883) 10 QB 403.
61 *Freke v Lord Carbery* (1873) 16 Eq 461; *Re Grassi* [1905] 1 Ch 484.
62 *Re Hoyles* [1911] 1 Ch 179.
63 *Re Smith* [1916] 2 Ch 206.
64 [1909] 2 Ch 129.

salient facts were as follows: the defendant, a married woman domiciled in England, agreed, by deed executed in England, to mortgage to the plaintiff bank certain lands in the Transvaal, in order to secure the business debts of her husband. Under the law of the Transvaal, a married woman was subject to certain restrictions in entering into a contract of suretyship. In an action brought by the plaintiff bank in England to obtain specific performance of the agreement, Eve J gave judgment for the defendant and this was upheld by the Court of Appeal.

The judgment of the Court of Appeal has been subject to considerable criticism and a number points need to be made:

(a) the judgment is taken as authority for the proposition that capacity to make a contract in respect of foreign immovables and capacity to convey are governed by the *lex situs*;

(b) it is arguable that the case did not turn on capacity at all: the relevant law of the Transvaal did not create incapacity but simply stipulated certain formalities;

(c) the judgment was out of line with the prior case *of Re Courteney ex p Pollard*,[65] which was distinguished as turning on effectiveness and not incapacity;

(d) the case was one of contract, not conveyance, so that, in principle, the relevant law should have been the proper law of the contract (that is, English law), under which no incapacity arose;

(e) the judgment was based on statements in the then edition of Dicey, which had been drawn from Story and were contradicted by Westlake as failing to to draw the distinction between capacity to contract and capacity to convey;

(f) in so far as the law in the USA was relevant, the American authorities were moving towards the view that capacity to contract as to foreign land was governed by the law of the place where the contract was made. In the case of *Polson v Stewart*,[66] cited in argument, Holmes J had observed:

> It is true that the law of other States cannot render valid conveyances of property within our borders, which our laws say are void, for the plain reason that we have exclusive power over the *res*. But, the same reason inverted establishes that the *lex loci rei sitae* cannot control personal covenants not purporting to be conveyances between persons acting outside the jurisdiction although concerning a thing within it ...;

(g) it is doubtful whether the law of Transvaal had any interest in protecting a married woman not domiciled there;

---

65 (1840) Mont & Ch 239.

66 (1897) 167 Mass 211 (Holmes J) (a judgment of Holmes J when still on the bench in Massachusetts and before elevation to the Supreme Court).

(h) even if the law of Transvaal constituted an obstacle to a decree of specific performance, it is difficult to understand how it prevented an action for damages; and

(i) it would seem that the judgment of Kennedy LJ in the Court of Appeal did not draw a sufficient distinction between contractual rights and proprietary rights and that the learned judge was overly influenced by the fact that the instrument of suretyship was intended to operate on real estate. A better decision would have been that the contractual obligation should be enforced, as the steps necessary to make the transfer effective were within her power and she had, implicitly, agreed to take them.

Formalities of alienation

It is generally accepted that the formal validity of a transfer of immovables is governed by the *lex situs*. Thus, in *Adams v Clutterbuck*,[67] a written conveyance of shooting rights in Scotland by two domiciled Englishmen was held valid, even though not under seal, because it complied with the requirements of Scotland as the *lex situs*.

Contracts

It is clear that some of the 19th century cases did not draw a sufficient distinction between rights arising under the contract and proprietary rights; there is a danger in assuming that all questions relating to immovable property will be governed by the *lex situs*. Indeed, there are some English authorities where English law, as the proper law of the contract, has been employed to circumnavigate procedural failure in respect of proprietary rights abroad.[67a]

If the instrument in question is to take effect as a contract, then it will have to comply with the Rome Convention on the Law Applicable to Contractual Obligations as implemented in the Contracts (Applicable Law) Act 1990. By Art 9(1) of the Rome Convention, a contract will be valid as to form if it complies with law of the place it is concluded or the law which governs it under the Convention. This is broadly in line with the common law approach in *Re Smith*,[68] where a party was able to enforce an agreement relating to land abroad, even though there had been defects as to execution under the *lex situs*. However, by Art 9(6), a contract in respect of immovable property is subject to the mandatory requirements of form of the *lex situs* if those requirements are

---

67   (1883) 10 QBD 403.

67a   *Re Courtney ex p Pollard* (1840) Mont & Ch 239; *Mercantile Investment and General Trust Co v River Plate Trust Co* [1892] 2 Ch 303; *Re Smith* [1916] 2 Ch 206; *Re Anchor Line* [1937] 1 Ch 483.

68   [1916] 2 Ch 606.

imposed, irrespective of the country where the contract was concluded and irrespective of of the law governing the contract.

In respect of essential validity, Art 3(1) provides that the parties are free to choose their own law but that, in the absence of such choice, Art 4(1) provides that the law shall be that with which the contract is most closely connected. This is in line with the common law approach of *British South Africa Co v De Beers Consolidated Mines Ltd*,[69] where a contract concerning land in Northern and Southern Rhodesia was held to be governed by English law. Article 4(3) of the Rome Convention introduces a rebuttable presumption that 'the contract is most closely connected with the country where the immovable property is situated'.

THE TRANSFER OF TANGIBLE MOVABLES

Introduction

Sometimes rather archaically described as the transfer *inter vivos* of choses in possession, what we are concerned with here is the transfer of the property interests in physical objects (chattels). Most commonly, such transfers are brought about by contract and, where they are, the contractual relationship between the parties which between themselves, but only between themselves, will subsume the property relations will be governed by the contract's applicable law. So, all aspects of the contract will be determined by the applicable law of their contract.

While English lawyers are familiar with the distinction between contract and conveyance, which is such a familiar feature of our land law, there is a tendency to forget that the same distinction, though not, happily, its cumbrous operation, applies equally to the sale of goods. The failure to mark the distinction is because there is a peculiar rule in English law about the passing of property, in default of contrary agreement between the parties, when the subject is specific goods in a deliverable State – here, property passes when the contract is made whether delivery has been made or not.[70] This is not the place to discuss details of English domestic law but it is worth pointing out that this rule – an exception which applies in the most common cases – has not come without difficulties to the English law on the sale of goods. The Sale of Goods Act 1979 contains rules that are clearly contractual in nature (for example, the statutory imposition of implied contractual terms) but it also contains rules that are clearly proprietary, such as those providing for the passing of property or those concerning the acquisition of title from a non-owner.[71] The distinction between contract and conveyance must be kept

---

69 [1910] 2 Ch 502.
70 Sale of Goods Act 1979, s 18, r 1.
71 *Ibid*, ss 17–19, 21–25.

in mind for the purposes of the conflict of laws and it is to the conveyancing aspects of the contract, that is, to the proprietary interests in the contract's subject matter, that this is directed.

There will rarely, if ever, be any difficulty in distinguishing a property issue from a contractual or other relation, for example, a gift, which gives rise to the transfer. First, the parties will be different or at least operating in different categories from those engaged in the transfer relation. Typically, the case will involve either the transferee attempting to assert his interest in the thing against someone other than the transferor, or a third party asserting a property interest over the thing which is the subject of the transfer.

To take a simple illustration of the sort of conflict that might arise here: suppose a domiciled Englishman, by a contract made in England and expressed to be governed by English law, sells goods which he owns in Country X. Suppose that, before the buyer gets control of the goods, the seller is adjudicated bankrupt. Is the buyer protected? By English domestic law, which is the stipulated governing law for the contract, assuming that the goods are specific and in a deliverable state, and that the parties have not agreed otherwise, property will have passed to the buyer immediately on the conclusion of the contract. The buyer can rest content in his property rights and the seller's collapse is not his concern. However, the goods are situated in Country X and Country X may require some act to be done,[72] some real or symbolic handing over to take place, before the property is regarded as having been transferred to the buyer. In default of such action, the property remains with the seller, becomes part of the bankrupt's estate, and the buyer is left to take his chance among the unsecured creditors.

The law on the transfer of tangible movables has given rise to some of the most difficult problems in the conflict of laws. Partly, this is because, in some of the cases, the judge is being forced to choose between two innocent parties and, partly, because the distinction between matters of contract and proprietary matters has not always been maintained. Inherent in the case law is the problem of whether all problems should be governed by a single law or whether different laws should apply to different aspects of the problem. It is necessary first to say a little about the various theories that have been advanced as to the law that should govern the transfer of tangible movables.

The law of the domicile

Some of the earlier authorities[73] held that the applicable law should be that of the owner's domicile. This was normally expressed in the maxim, *mobilia*

---

72 *Inglis v Robertson* [1898] AC 616; where the question, according to Lord Watson, was whether the state of title in country X could be altered by a foreign contract of sale which did not, according to the law of country X, have the effect of vesting the title in the buyer (or pledgee) on the facts of the case.

73 *Still v Worswick* (1791) 1 H Bl 665; *Re Ewin* (1830) 1 Cr & J 151.

sequuntur personam (movables follow the person); however, this did raise the question of whether the court should adopt the law of the seller or the buyer's domicile. Indeed, if the case gave rise to problems of a sub-sale, then there might be three possible laws to consider. The maxim was a useful one in cases of death, where the deceased might have left property in more than one country, but to adopt the law of the domicile would introduce a degree of uncertainty incompatible with the needs of modern commerce. Secondly, the Privy Council, in *Alberta Provincial Treasurer v Kerr*,[74] held that the maxim was confined to cases of devolution of property on death and movable property could not be presumed to be located where the owner was domiciled.

The law of the place of the act (lex loci actus)

A second possibility is that the governing law should be that of the country in which the transaction is completed. There are a number of objections to this approach. First, the location may be accidental and have no connection with the substance of the dispute. Secondly, although there are two Court of Appeal authorities[75] that appear to lend support, they were both concerned with the technicalities of negotiable instruments. In the case of *Alcock v Smith*, Kay LJ did observe:

> As to personal chattels, it is settled that the validity of a transfer depends not upon the law of the domicile of the owner but upon the law of the country in which the transfer takes place.

However, it is clear that the learned judge was drawing a distinction with the law of domicile and he was speaking in the case of a negotiable instrument, where the *lex loci actus* and the *lex situs* will be the same, since a negotiable instrument cannot be delivered or a cheque signed without it being in the physical possession of a party. The general tone of Kay LJ's judgment indicates that he was thinking of situations in which the *lex loci actus* and the *lex situs* coincide.

Thirdly, any attempt to adopt the *lex loci actus* would be contrary to the limited role of the *lex loci contractus*, which has been a feature of English private international law since the middle of the 19th century.

The proper law of the transfer (lex actus)

A third possibility is that the governing law should be the law of the country with which the transfer has the closest and most real connection, in similar terms to the doctrine of the proper law of the contract. There are a number of possible difficulties with this approach.

---

74 *Alberta Provincial Treasurer v Kerr* [1933] AC 710.
75 *Alcock v Smith* [1892] 1 Ch 238, p 267, *per* Kay LJ; *Embricos v Anglo-Austrian Bank* [1905] 1 KB 677.

First, the case in question may involve not a transfer but some other action (for example, theft). Secondly, a case may involve contemporaneous dealings affecting more than one country; suppose, for example, a businessman domiciled in England travels to Germany, where he transfers to a businessman domiciled in Denmark title to goods lying in warehouses in Montreal, New York and Mexico City, as well as property in transit from South Africa. Finding a single proper law might well prove to be difficult. A third objection is where the case concerns independent transactions operating in two different jurisdictions, such as in *Inglis v Robertson*,[76] where the conflict was between the unpaid seller and the pledgee of the purchaser.

The law where the chattel is situated (the law of the situs)

The fourth possibility is that the governing law should be the law of the *situs*. This solution has a number of advantages and the least number of disadvantages. First, unlike the law of domicile, it avoids having to choose between the law of the domicile of more than one party. Secondly, it is broadly in line with the territorial principle in both private and public international law, in that an individual, X, situated in Country A would expect to be subject to the laws of Country A. Thirdly, Country A has power over the chattel and it is logical to select a legal system which meets the test of effectiveness. Fourthly, such a choice leads to confidence and certainty in international business transactions. Fifthly, there is a considerable weight of legal authority in both the USA and the UK that has favoured such a choice in the last 100 years. Sixthly, and in accordance with the pragmatic spirit of the common law, no other test has been shown to be demonstrably superior.

The operation of the general principle in favour of the *lex situs*

A review of the case law indicates that it is important to draw a distinction between contractual questions (for example, the nature of implied terms), which will be governed by the proper law of the contract, and proprietary questions, which will be governed by the law of the *situs*. There is now a considerable body of authority that supports the proposition that the governing law in respect of the transfer of corporeal movables is that of the *lex situs*.[77]

---

76 [1898] AC 616.

77 *Cammell v Sewell* (1858) 3 H & N 617; (1860) 5 H & N 728; *Liverpool Marine Credit Co v Hunter* (1867) LR 4 Eq 62; (1868) 3 Ch App 479; *Inglis v Robertson* [1898] AC 616; *Re Anzani* [1930] 1 Ch 407; *Bank voor Handel en Scheepvaart NV v Slatford* [1953] 1 QB 248; *Hardwick Game Farm v Suffolk Agricultural Poultry Producers Association* [1966] 1 WLR 287; *Winkworth v Christie, Manson and Woods Ltd* [1980] Ch 496.

There are a number of unambiguous judicial assertions on the subject. In *Re Anzani*,[78] Maugham J observed, *obiter*:

> I do not think that anybody can doubt that, with regard to the transfer of goods, the law applicable must be the law of the country where the movable is situated.

A generation later, Devlin J asserted: 'There is little doubt that it is the *lex situs* which, as a general rule, governs the transfer of movables when effected contractually.'[79] More recently, Diplock LJ drew a distinction between contractual and proprietary questions, when he observed that:[79a]

> The proper law governing the transfer of corporeal movable property is the *lex situs*. A contract made in England and governed by English law for the sale of specific goods situated in Germany, although it would be effective to pass the property in the goods at the moment the contract was made if the goods were situate in England, would not have that effect if under German law ... delivery of the goods was required in order to transfer the property in them.

Although there was old authority that could be interpreted as looking towards the proper law of the transfer,[80] there is now little dispute that the *lex situs* of the movable at the time of the transaction in question determines any proprietary effects of a transfer. This follows from the leading case of *Cammell v Sewell*,[81] where the facts were as follows: a cargo of Russian timber was en route from Russia to Hull when the vessel was wrecked off the Norwegian coast. The master of the ship had the timber sold by public auction in Norway; an action by the plaintiffs to restrain the sale failed in the Norwegian courts. The buyer, A, brought it to England, where he sold it to B. The plaintiffs, who were the insurers of the cargo, had indemnified the original owner for the loss and sought to recover the value of the timber from the defendant, B. The Court of Exchequer gave judgment for the defendant, holding that the effect of the Norwegian judgment was to confer good title on A, enforceable against the entire world. The plaintiffs appealed.

The Court of Exchequer Chamber, in dismissing the appeal, decided to address the broader question of the proprietary title and found for the defendant. Crompton J held that the Norwegian sale had overridden the title of the former owners and created a good title in the buyer at the auction. It is sometimes said that the judgment is authority for three propositions: (a) that title of an original owner can be lost by conduct within the *lex situs*; (b) that, if a valid title is subsequently acquired under the *lex situs*, then it will override

---

78 [1930] 1 Ch 407, p 420.
79 *Bank voor Handel en Scheepvaart NV v Slatford* [1953] 1 QB 248, p 257.
79a *Hardwick Game Farm v Suffolk Agricultural Poultry Producers Association* [1966] WLR 287.
80 *Inglis v Underwood* (1801) 1 East 515.
81 (1858) 3 H & N 617 (Pollock CB, Martin B, Channell B), Court of Exchequer; (1860) 5 H & N 728 (Cockburn CJ, Crompton, Wightman, Williams and Keating JJ; Byles J dissenting).

and prevail over a prior title; and (c) that the subsequently acquired title in the *lex situs* is not lost by removing the goods to England.

The judgment in *Cammell v Sewell* was followed by Slade J, in the case of *Winkworth v Christie, Manson and Woods*,[82] where the facts gave rise to the competing claims of innocent parties: works of art were stolen from the home of the plaintiff in England. They were taken to Italy, where they were sold to the second defendant, A, an Italian who then sent them back to England to be auctioned by the first defendants. Under domestic Italian law, it was accepted that A acquired good title but he probably did not under English law. The court was required to determine whether, at the time of the transfer to A, title was governed by English law or by Italian law, as the law of the *situs*.

Slade J recognised the position of the innocent party but followed *Cammell v Sewell* and held that Italian law, as the law of the *situs* at the time of the transaction, was to govern and, by that law, the buyer had obtained good title when he brought the pictures in Italy. Furthermore, the learned judge held that considerations of commercial convenience as well as precedent required him to hold that title acquired under the *lex situs* would be recognised. Secondly, Slade J ruled that, following *Cammell v Sewell*, title was not lost by sending the works of art to England.

On the basis of these two authorities, it would seem that the following propositions can be advanced with some confidence. Let the country of the first *situs* be A, the second, B, and the third, C:

(a) title to goods originating in A will continue to be recognised if the same goods are removed to B;

(b) the fact that goods were removed from A to B without the consent of the owner will not affect the analysis;

(c) if new title to the goods is validly acquired under the law of B, then that title will displace the title arising under the law of A;

(d) if the goods were removed from B to C and a new title acquired under the law of C, then that title would prevail; and

(e) if the goods were then taken from C and brought to England and sold to D, then D will acquire good title; the returning of the goods to England from either B or C does not extinguish rights acquired under the laws of B or C.

Where there has been a series of transactions relating to the same goods, the search is for the most recent transaction, which, according to the *lex situs* where it took place, had the effect of definitively altering the previously existing title to the property. So, for example, where the seller has sold the same object to two different buyers, the order of priority will depend on the

---

82 [1980] Ch 496 (Slade J); see Nott [1981] Conv 279; Carter (1981) 52 BYIL 329.

situs of the object at the time of each sale. If the first sale had, by the *lex situs* of the goods at the time, the effect of transferring title, with no residual power in the seller to confer title on anyone else, the first buyer will have priority because the seller has nothing to convey to the second buyer. If the seller retains a power to confer title on another, that is, can trigger one of the *nemo dat* exceptions, by the *lex situs* of the second sale, the second buyer's claim will be preferred.

It would seem, from the argument in *Winkworth*, that there are a number of exceptions to the rule favouring the *lex situs*. Although it was not necessary for the purpose of the ruling, it is arguable that the following might be exceptions: (a) in the case of goods in transit or where the situs is unknown;[83] (b) in cases where a purchaser has not acted in good faith;[84] (c) in cases where the law of the *situs* was contrary to public policy in England; and (d) where the case involves a matter of bankruptcy or succession and is governed by the law of the domicile.

The meaning of the expression, 'the law of the *situs*'

In saying that the English court is required to look at the law of the *situs*, it is necessary to examine the expression, 'the law of the *situs*'. The first question is does this include the relevant rules of private international law, that is, does the doctrine of *renvoi* apply? There does not appear to be a case in which the doctrine has been applied. In *Winkworth*,[85] it was not necessary for the judge to rule on the point but he did observe:

> It is theoretically possible that the evidence as to Italian law would show that the Italian court would, itself, apply English law. In this event, I suppose it would be open to the plaintiff to argue that English law should, in the final result, be applied by the English court, by virtue of the doctrine of *renvoi*.

The second matter that arises is the question of whether the law of the *situs* is simply the internal law that would be applied in a normal domestic case or whether the court of the *situs* applies the law after making allowance for the fact that the case concerns foreign parties; in other words, is the law of the *situs* the law that the court would apply to the specific facts and these particular parties? The best view, deriving from the USA, is that this modified law of the *situs* that will be applied. An example is provided by the well

---

83 This might be one way to explain the old case of *Inglis v Usherwood* (1801) 1 East 515, where it was held that a Russian seller under an fob contract was allowed to reclaim goods delivered on board a vessel, in accordance with Russian law but contrary to English law. In that case, the *lex situs* and *lex actus* might be said to coincide.

84 This would seem to be important if equitable remedies were being sought in English proceedings.

85 *Winkworth v Christie, Manson and Woods Ltd* [1980] QB 496.

known case of *Goetschius v Brightman*,[86] where the facts were as follows: A, a Californian company, sold a car to B under a conditional sale agreement, whereby (a) title would not pass until the price was fully paid; and (b) the car was not to be removed from California without consent. B removed the car to New York and sold it to C. By the law of California, the title of A was superior to any subsequent title but, by the law of New York, such a title was void unless the agreement was registered. When C, a *bona fide* purchaser, brought an action, the New York Court of Appeals found for A.

In such a case, the New York Court of Appeals applied New York law as the law of the *situs* but with reference to the specific facts of the unauthorised removal from another State. The requirements of the registration legislation were held to apply only to domestic sales entered into within New York. Thus, although the law of New York, as the law of the *situs*, was adopted, it was founded upon the modified application of the rules of the *situs*.

There is some evidence that an English court would adopt this approach, namely, that the law of the *situs* does not involve every jot and tittle of the domestic law. The case is, after all, a conflict case and the international aspects of the case should not be disregarded. It may be that the particular rules of the system are intended for purely local consumption and that to apply them to an international case would be inappropriate or officious. In each case, the rules of the *lex situs* should be examined to see whether they provide a rule of purely internal order or represent a policy stance applicable generally. Courts do not readily engage in such purposive analysis but there is some evidence that an English court will be mindful of the context in appropriate cases. An example is afforded by the case of *Dulaney v Merry and Sons*,[87] where the facts were as follows: two American citizens executed a deed of assignment in Maryland, whereby they assigned all their property, wherever situated, to another domiciled American, whose task it was to treat with their creditors. Some of the property to which the assignment related was in England and it was argued for the English creditors that the attempted assignment of the English property would fail as it had not been registered under the Deeds of Arrangement Act 1887.

Had the assignment been made in England between English traders and concerning goods in England, then there is no doubt it would have been void for non-compliance with the legislation. However, Channel J concluded that the Deeds of Arrangement Act 1887[88] was not intended to bring within its ambit foreign assignments, notwithstanding that some of the property happened to be situated in England. Thus, the Maryland assignment was valid as regards the English goods. It should be noted here that the English

---

86 (1927) 245 NY 186.
87 *Dulaney v Merry and Sons* [1901] 1 KB 536.
88 See, now, the Deeds of Arrangement Act 1914.

creditors were not disadvantaged vis à vis the American creditors by this decision, though they lost whatever advantage there would have been in the segregation of the English assets.

Change of *situs*

There would be no point in deferring to the *lex situs* if the legal position could be immediately changed by the removal of the property from that jurisdiction. The *lex situs* is not simply a window of law; it is the system which determines the legal status of the property transaction which takes place within its territory. If that transaction has the effect of altering property rights, the new rights acquired there will remain in force until a later transaction takes place, which, according to the *lex situs*, further alters the position. It thus follows that the rights acquired under the *lex situs* at the time will stand until they are overridden by a new transaction having that effect by the current *lex situs*. They will not be destroyed by the non-recognition elsewhere of what has been done previously, simply because the new situs has no analogous provision.[89]

In *Todd v Armour*,[90] the plaintiff sought recovery of his horse, which had been stolen in Ireland, from the defendant, who had bought it in Scotland. The stolen horse had been sold in Ireland to a buyer in market overt, who had taken it to Scotland and sold it to the defendant. By Irish law, the sale in market overt passed good title to the buyer; Scots law had no such exception to the *nemo dat* rule. The Court of Session held that the buyer, since he had acquired a good title under Irish law, could lawfully pass that title on to the defendant and the original owner's rights had been entirely superseded, leaving him with whatever personal action he could pursue against the actual thief.

To take a couple of examples from English law: a seller, having sold but not delivered goods to the buyer, retains the power to transfer the property in those goods to a second buyer who acts in good faith and without knowledge of the prior transaction.[91] Similarly, a buyer who has deceived the owner into transferring the property to him, who has, in short, a voidable title, can transfer title to a *bona fide* buyer who is ignorant of the defect in title.[92] If the *lex situs* throughout is English law, the second buyer, in each case, will be protected. If the second sale, in each case, takes place abroad, the effect of the sale will have to be determined by the new *lex situs*. How does the second *lex situs* relate to the English transaction? In each case, the authority of the seller should be determined by English law, as the *lex situs* of the first transaction,

---

89 *Winkworth v Christie, Manson and Woods* [1980] Ch 495.
90 *Todd v Armour* (1882) 9 Rettie 901.
91 Sale of Goods Act 1979, s 24.
92 *Ibid*, s 23.

and, therefore, subject to any rule of the new *situs*, the second buyer will be in the same position as if the sale had taken place in England. By the same reasoning, if the deceived owner in the voidable title case avoids the contract before the second sale, then the second buyer will not obtain good title unless the sale in the new *situs* would, independently, give a good title to the buyer, that is, would, in short, constitute an independent exception to the *nemo dat* rule.

Reservation of title

In the last 20 years, there have been a considerable number of cases coming before the English courts raising problems concerning reservation of title clauses in sale of goods transactions;[93] in addition, problems of reservation of title arise in the various forms of hire purchase and conditional sale agreements. Suppose A grants possession of goods to B, in *situs* X, while retaining title in the goods. B then removes the goods to *situs* Y and sells the goods to C, a *bona fide* purchaser. In some circumstances, the courts of *situs* Y have adapted the internal law to prevent a claim by C.[94] The events in *situs* Y are capable of two possible interpretations: (a) that the events in *situs* Y override the prior reservation of title by A; or (b) the reservation of title by A under the law of X is not recognised as having this effect under the law of *situs* Y.[95]

The problems thrown up by such transactions were illustrated by the Canadian case of *Century Credit Corporation v Richard*,[96] where the facts were as follows: X, a finance company, sold a motor car in Montreal, Quebec under a conditional sale agreement to Y, which provided that the vehicle would remain the property of X until fully paid for. Under the law of Quebec, such an agreement did not require to be registered. Y took the car to Ontario, where he sold it to H, who then sold it to Z. Both H and Z acted in good faith. X, the plaintiffs, then sued Z for possession of the vehicle. The trial judge gave judgment for the plaintiffs. The Ontario Court of Appeals allowed the appeal.

There was no doubt that, under the law of Quebec, where the original transaction had taken place, the rights of the finance company were protected, in other words, there was a valid reservation of title under that law. Under Ontarian law – the *lex situs* of the subsequent sale transaction – a reservation of title was only valid if it was registered and a *bona fide* purchaser from a

---

93   *Aluminium Industrie Vaasen BV v Romalpa Aluminium Ltd* [1976] 1 WLR 676; *Re Bond Worth* [1980] Ch 228; *Borden UK Ltd v Scottish Timber Products Ltd* [1981] Ch 25; *Re Peachdart Ltd* [1984] Ch 131; *Clough Mill Ltd v Martin* [1985] 1 WLR 111.

94   See *Goetshius v Brightman* (1927) 245 NY 186.

95   See Morris (1945) 22 BYIL 232.

96   (1962) 34 DLR (2d) 291.

buyer in possession could, in some circumstances, obtain a good title. As to the first of these points, one could hardly expect a Quebec finance company to register its Quebec transactions in Ontario[97] and, in any case, the fact that a similar unregistered transaction under the law of Ontario would not have reserved the title had nothing to do with the prior transaction in Quebec. In giving judgment, the Ontarian Court of Appeal drew a distinction between recognising the transaction in Quebec and the overriding effect of the later transaction in Ontario. The rights vested by the Quebec transaction were valid and remained effective when the car was taken to Ontario. However, the transaction took place in Ontario and the new *lex situs* had the effect, by Ontarian law, of overriding the prior title and creating a new title in the innocent buyer. As Kelly JA, in giving judgment for the court, expressed it:

> If the law of Ontario were to seek to invalidate the respondent's title by refusing to recognise that the transaction which took place in Quebec had the effect of continuing the title in the respondent, this attempt of Ontarian law to invalidate a transaction taking part in Quebec would be bad because the validity of a Quebec transaction must be decided according to the law of Quebec, the *lex situs* ... However, if the laws of Ontario provide that a later transaction which takes place wholly within Ontario has the effect of overriding prior titles, then, since Ontario does not seek to give its laws any extra-territorial effect, the laws of Ontario prevail and title vested under the law of Ontario displaces the title reserved in the Quebec transaction.[98]

Hire purchase and conditional sale agreements customarily take place in one country, so that there is no problem of identifying the original *situs*. Where, however, an international supplier seeks to retain property in the goods supplied until the customer pays for them or until existing accounts are settled, or seeks to create some right of security over the goods,[99] more difficult questions arise. Where the goods have to be delivered to the customer in his own country, and as delivery in most systems is necessary to pass the property, the *situs* will usually be the customer's country and the validity of the title retention clause will depend on that law. If the customer has to collect the goods from the supplier, or if the supplier delivers fob, the *situs* will be the supplier's country and, if that law recognises the title retention as a proprietary interest, the retention will be recognised by the new *lex situs*, the law of the customer's country, unless it is contrary to its public policy.

While the goods remain in their original condition, the supplier should have the benefit of the title retention if that interest was recognised by the *lex situs* of the original transfer. When, however, the goods are incorporated into

---

97 See *Goetschius v Brightman* (1927) 245 NY 186.

98 *Century Credit Corporation v Richard* (1962) 34 DLR (2d) 291, *per* Kelly JA.

99 *Armour v Thyssen Edelstahlwerke AG* [1991] 2 AC 339; [1990] 3 All ER 481 (Scots law).

the customer's product or processed by him in some way, the effect of that on their ownership must be determined by the law of the new *situs*.[100]

Gifts

The authorities on *inter vivos* gifts are limited but it would seem, as a matter of principle, that the governing law is that of the *lex situs*. It is usual to make reference to the unusual case of *Cochrane v Moore*,[101] where the facts were as follows: the owner of a horse purported to make a gift of a quarter of the horse to its jockey, Moore. The parties were domiciled in England and the horse was stabled near Paris. The owner then mortgaged the horse to Cochrane. Cochrane agreed to respect the agreement with the jockey. At a later date, Cochrane exercised his power of sale and Moore claimed a quarter of the proceeds of sale.

The Court of Appeal held that the gift, not being by way of deed or delivery, was ineffective; French law was not pleaded, so no firm conclusions can be drawn on the relevant law. In any event, the Court of Appeal considered that the subsequent declaration by Cochrane constituted a binding oral declaration of trust in respect of a quarter share of the proceeds.

The second area of gifts where problems of the governing law may arise are in the context of *donationes mortis causa*; the essence of a *donatio* is that it is an *inter vivos* gift which is conditional on and takes effect on death.[102] In cases where the intention is that property should pass, then the best view is that the matter is governed by the law of the *situs*,[103] although it is possible to read the judgment of Farwell J, in *Re Craven's Estate*,[104] as favouring also the law of the testatrix's domicile.

State seizure

This matter has already been alluded to under the topic of recognition of foreign laws. However, the principle of territorial authority, which is enshrined in the reference to the *lex situs* on property transfers, implies that, when State authorities in the *situs* transfer property by legislation or decree, even to themselves and without compensation, English courts will recognise

---

100 *Zahnrad Fabrik Passau GmbH v Terex Ltd* 1986 SLT 84 (retention of title clause in supply of vehicle components supplied to a Scottish buyer, who used them to construct earth moving equipment before becoming insolvent; the Scottish Court held the effect of such acts to be determined by Scottish law, as the law of the new *situs*).

101 (1890) 25 QB 57 (Lord Esher MR, Bowen and Fry LJJ), CA.

102 *Cain v Moon* [1896] 2 QB 283.

103 *Re Korvine's Trusts* [1921] 1 Ch 343.

104 [1937] Ch 423; but, see (1937) 53 TLR 694, for a fuller report.

the transfer. By the same token, however, attempts by foreign States to seize property situated outside their territories, even if it is owned by their nationals, will have no effect.[105]

The leading case on the topic remains *Luther v Sagor*,[106] where the facts were as follows: in 1920, the defendant company bought a quantity of wood from the new Soviet Government of the USSR. The plaintiff Russian company claimed title to the wood on the ground that it had come from a factory in the USSR owned by it until 1919, when it was nationalised by a decree issued by the Soviet Government. The plaintiff argued, *inter alia*, that the decree should not be recognised by an English court, as the Soviet Government had not been recognised by the UK.

At first instance, Roche J held that the plaintiffs were entitled to succeed, since the legislative acts of an unrecognised government were not entitled to recognition in an English court. However, after the hearing at first instance and before the hearing in the Court of Appeal, the Secretary of State for Foreign Affairs decided to accord *de facto* recognition to the Soviet Government. The Court of Appeal allowed the appeal, holding that, having regard to the retrospective effect of a grant of recognition, the decree of the Soviet Government within its own territory had to be recognised as capable of conferring title.[107]

The importance of the judgment in *Luther v Sagor* is not that foreign State authorities can deal with property in their own territories whoever it belongs to – that is a fact of political power – but that the change in ownership will be recognised when the property is brought within the jurisdiction of the English courts.[108] It should not matter whether the property belonged to a national or a resident of the expropriating State or to a foreigner.[109] However, a foreign law directed at the property of an individual or class of individual which the English court regarded as discriminatory would probably not be recognised.[110]

---

105 See *Banco de Vizcaya v Don Alfonso de Borbon* [1935] 1 KB 140; *AG of New Zealand v Ortiz* [1984] AC 1 (but, both these cases involved 'penal' legislation); *Bank voor Handel v Slatford* [1953] 1 QB 248 (Devlin J).

106 *AM Luther v James Sagor and Co* [1921] 1 KB 456 (Roche J), reversed in [1921] 3 KB 532 (Bankes, Scrutton, Warrington LJJ).

107 The procedure would be slightly different today, in that, since 1980, the UK does not formally recognise Governments; the court is left to draw its own inferences and will normally follow the approach in *Republic of Somalia v Woodhouse Drake and Carey Suisse SA* [1993] QB 54 (Hobhouse J).

108 See *Williams and Humbert Ltd v W & H Trade Marks (Jersey) Ltd* [1986] AC 368 (and, in particular, the judgment of Nourse J at first instance).

109 See, on this, the doubtful decision in *Anglo Iranian Oil Co v Jaffrate; The Rose Mary* [1953] 1 WLR 246.

110 But, see *Frankfurther v WL Exner Ltd* [1947] Ch 629.

THE ASSIGNMENT OF INTANGIBLE MOVABLES

Introduction

The transfer of intangible movables is one of the least satisfactory areas of the English conflict of laws, though the dearth of modern authority may indicate that problems are rare or that they are dealt with in alternative ways.

An initial problem is the diversity of interests which can be classified as intangible objects – everything which is not a direct interest in a physical object or in land may fall within the category. So, debts, whether the repayment of loans or sums due under contracts, shares, patents, copyrights and securities fall within this category, whether or not they are characteristically evidenced by official documents like share certificates.

As with physical objects, a distinction must be drawn between the personal relationship of the transferee and the transferor, on the one hand, and the proprietary effects of the transfer, on the other. But, there is an additional distinction. Here, the property relationship is not between the transferee and the rest of the world but between the transferee and the person under the original obligation. The obvious example would be a simple debt – there is the original relationship between the debtor and the creditor, the relation between the creditor and the person to whom he assigns the debt, and the new relation which that transfer creates between the debtor and the person to whom the original creditor has transferred his interest – which is our principal concern here.

As well as the diversity of interests which can be classified as intangible movables, another problem, or opportunity, in this area, is that the choice of law remains open. While there are few and uncertain authorities, there are several potential candidates for the governing law, all of which have some support.

The claims of the *lex domicilii* and the *lex loci actus* (the place where the assignment takes place) cannot be taken seriously nowadays. The weakness of the *lex domicilii* is that it does not identify a single system of law. Debtor, creditor and transferee may have different personal laws and, while it would be possible to select the personal law of the debtor, that has an archaic ring about it, hardly appropriate for modern commerce. The *lex loci actus* is unsuitable because, even if it is not fortuitous, it may have no connection with the property interest and can be fixed by the parties to the assignment without reference to the debtor, who may be harmed in the process. The claims of the *lex situs*, the *lex actus* and the proper law of the debt are more substantial.

The lex situs

One possible solution is to give the intangible a notional *situs* and then treat it as if it were a physical object. Quite apart from the metaphysics of attributing a location to something which has no corporeal existence, the attribution of a *situs* to an intangible, while it may have some utility in the case of involuntary assignments,[111] misses the point about the essential difference between a physical object, or a right over one, and an interest in an intangible. For a physical object has an existence independent of the judicial relations which legal systems may recognise with regard to it – it can be lost, found, accidentally destroyed, etc – whereas an intangible interest only exists in the milieu of juridical relations: it cannot have an independent existence outside of them. The interest in an intangible is one which represents an existing set of relations – a debt owed by A to B, A's shares in B's company, A's patent or copyright.

The *lex situs*, for a debt, is characteristically seen as the place where the debt is properly recoverable. A debt is, usually, properly recoverable in the country where the debtor resides.[112] The *lex situs* could be used for the issues which arise here – whether the interest is assignable at all, how the assignment is to be effected and the priority of competing assignments – but its weakness is that it does not provide any continuity – the casual removal of the debtor from one place to another should no more affect legal relations than should the casual removal of a physical object form one place to another. Moreover, while the transfer of the physical object is usually a single event, the transfer of an intangible substitutes one set of continuing interpersonal relations for another.

The lex actus

The *lex actus*, if that is seen in context as the law which governs the substance of the relationship between the assignor and assignee, is not a good candidate for the law to govern the proprietary aspects of the transfer, as it is the law which the parties to the transfer may choose and the protection of the debtor is not a consideration in that relationship. To apply this law is to confuse the contractual or other basis of the assignment, which regulates the relationship between the assignor and assignee, with the proprietary effects of the transfer, that is, the regulation of the relationship between the assignee and the original debtor.

---

111 *Swiss Bank Corporation v Boehmische Industrial Bank* [1923] 1 KB 673; *Jabbour v Custodian of Israeli Absentee Property* [1954] 1 WLR 139; 1 All ER 145.
112 *Kwok Chi Leung Karl v Estate Duty Commissioners* [1988] 1 WLR 1035, PC.

The proper law of the debt

The proper law of the debt is the law which governs the original relationship between the debtor and the creditor and, thereby, controls the creation of the interest which is the subject matter of the assignment. The original relation between debtor and creditor will be governed by whatever law applies to its creation, thus, if the debt is a contractual debt, it will be governed by the law of that contract. If the contract is an international one, it will be governed by the applicable law under the Rome Convention 1980. If the debt was created by the gratuitous handing over of the money, the governing law will be the *lex actus* – the law which governs the gift, usually the law of the place where the transaction took place. The proper law of a cause of action will be the *lex fori* of the action,[113] that of a renewable copyright, the law of the system under which the copyright was taken out.[114] The validity of the original relationship is obviously vital to the subject matter of the transfer.

The *lex situs* and the proper law of the debt will often be the same. So, for example, where a customer deposits money in a bank, the contract, in default of a choice of a different system, will be governed by the law of the country where the transaction takes place, as all the significant connections, including the characteristic performance, are likely to relate to that country. As the debt created by that contract will be properly recoverable where the account is held, the *lex situs* of the debt will also be the law of that country.

A coincidence of the proper law and the *lex situs*, while common, is by no means inevitable. Suppose an English supplier agrees to deliver goods to a foreign commercial customer. Without agreement to the contrary, the proper law of the debt (the law governing the contract) will be English law (the law of the place of business through which the characteristic performance of the contract is to be affected). However, the *lex situs* of the debt will be the law of the customer's country (the place where the contract debt is properly recoverable). These different laws could well have different provisions on the property aspects of any transfer of the debt by the English supplier to, say, an export factor.

Although it is not easy to reconcile all the cases cited on the subject of the assignment of intangible movables, some help is to be derived by keeping four matters in mind: (a) the precise question that is before the court;[115] (b) questions related to the nature of the right assigned; (c) questions as to the assignment itself; and (d) questions as to the distinction between proprietary and contractual issues.

---

113 *Trendtex Trading Corporation v Credit Suisse* [1982] AC 679.
114 *Campbell, Connelly and Co v Noble* [1963] 1 WLR 252.
115 In many cases, the court is simply seeking to establish the *situs* and has no concern with any actual assignment, eg, *Standard Chartered Bank Ltd v IRC* [1978] 1 WLR 1160 (Goulding J).

The situs *of an intangible movable*

Since intangible property has a legal existence, it is necessary to determine its precise *situs*. Many cases come before the English courts where is is necessary to determine the location of intangible movable property; location may be important in determining liability to taxation,[116] jurisdiction or the administration of estates. English private international law has developed a number of rules to determine where such property is located. This legal system will be important if questions later arise as to the nature of the right assigned.

In respect of intellectual property rights (patents, copyright, trade marks), such rights will be situated in the jurisdiction in which the monopoly right is issued and that law will determine whether the right is assignable.[117] In the case of company shares, such property rights will normally be evidenced by a share certificate and transferred by means of entry on the company share register. In these circumstances, the shares will be sited where the register is held but, if there are two company registers, then the shares will be situated where it is normal to anticipate the transfer would take place.[118] A simple contractual debt will be located where the debtor resides because it is there that payment may be enforced[119] and the same principle applies to monies under an insurance policy.[120] If the debtor (or company) has more than one place of business, then the debt is located where it is payable.[121]

In the law of trusts, the trust will be located by reference to the express or implied choice made by the settlor in the trust instrument and, in the absence of such choice, the trust will be subject to the legal system with which it is most closely connected.[122]

In many cases, it will be sufficient for the court to determine the *situs* of the intangible property. However, in those cases where there has been an assignment of an intangible movable, then more detailed consideration will be required. Suppose A is owed money by B and then decides to assign the debt to C; three possible questions arise, namely: (a) the law as to assignability – that is, is the debt assignable at all? (b) the law concerning the validity of the contractual relationship between A and C; and (c) the law concerning any proprietary question arising from the assignment. It is proposed to take these

---

116 *Standard Chartered Bank v IRC* [1978] 1 WLR 1160.

117 *Campbell, Connelly and Co v Noble* [1963] 1 WLR 252 (US copyright of popular song).

118 *Standard Chartered Bank v IRC* [1978] 1 WLR 1160.

119 *New York Life Insurance Co v Public Trustee* [1924] 2 Ch 101.

120 *Jabbour v Custodian of Israeli Absentee Property* [1954] 1 WLR 139.

121 *Kwok Chi Leung Karl v Estate Duty Commissioners* [1988] 1 WLR 1035, PC.

122 *Le Feuvre v Sullivan* (1855) 10 Moo PCC 1; *Kelly v Selwyn* [1905] 2 Ch 117.

three matters under the heading of voluntary assignments before turning to the question of involuntary assignment.

Voluntary assignments

A distinction has to be drawn between a voluntary assignment where, for example, the creditor, by his own free will, transfers his interest to another and an involuntary assignment, which takes effect by operation of law. As indicated above, there are three areas of concern in respect of voluntary assignments.

Assignability: is the interest assignable at all?

At common law, it was probably the case that the governing law as to whether the interest was assignable was the law which governed the creation of the interest. Whether the debt was capable of assignment was determined by the law governing its creation, so, in the case of a contractual debt, the law which governs the relationship between the original parties will determine whether the interest created by the contract can be assigned. In the case of a gratuitous loan, the governing law was probably the *lex actus*. The object of the reference to the law of the original transaction was to ensure that the debtor's liability should not be increased by the assignment, in order to protect the debtor against the consequences which might otherwise arise from the weakness of his interest.

Thus, whether an American copyright was assignable or not was to be determined by the law of the USA;[123] whether an English cause of action is capable of being assigned is a question to be governed by English law.[124]

The policy of looking at the law governing the creation of the interest is the policy adopted by the Rome Convention 1980. The Convention will only apply to contracts within its ambit but, subject to this reservation, Art 12(2) provides as follows:

> The law governing the right to which the assignment relates shall determine its assignability, the relationship between the assignee and the debtor, the conditions under which the assignment can be invoked against the debtor and any question of whether the debtor's obligations have been discharged.

The policy of looking at the law governing the creation of the interest is sometimes described as seeking the proper law of the debt; the policy is

---

123 *Campbell Connelly and Co Ltd v Noble* [1963] 1 WLR 252.
124 *Trendtex Trading Corporation v Credit Suisse* [1980] QB 629; [1982] AC 679.

justified partly on the principle that under some legal systems certain debts cannot be assigned (for example, pensions, future wages and contracts of insurance under certain systems of law) and partly on the basis of prior authority.[125]

The validity of the assignment: the contractual question

An assignment may be effected by means of contract or gift. It has to be acknowledged that the common law cases concerning the relationship between assignor and assignee were less than clear and the position in this regard has been clarified by Art 12(1) of the Rome Convention 1980, which reads:

> The mutual obligations of assignor and assignee under a voluntary assignment of a right against another person ('the debtor') shall be governed by the law which under this Convention applies to the contract between assignor and assignee.

Thus, to the extent that the assignment is by way of a contract within the Rome Convention 1980, then contractual issues will be determined by the law that governs the contract of assignment. However, because of exclusions from the Rome Convention 1980, it may be necessary to refer to the prior common law authorities which, while restricted in number and providing only limited guidance, do not clearly favour the proper law of the assignment.

The earlier of the two relevant cases is *Lee v Abdy*,[126] where the facts were as follows: an English company issued a policy of life assurance. This was assigned by a husband to his wife in Cape Colony. The assignment was valid by English law but invalid under the law of the Cape Colony. When the insurance company was sued by the wife, it argued the assignment was void.

The Divisional Court concluded that, as the assignment was invalid under law of the Cape Colony, then it was void; the judgment can be taken as favouring the governing law as being the *lex domicilii* or the *lex loci actus*, which were the same on the facts of the case.

The question of the governing law in respect of contractual matters was raised before a strong Court of Appeal in the unusual case of *Republica de Guatemala v Nunez*,[127] where the facts were as follows: in 1906, the President of Guatemala deposited £20,000 in a London Bank. In 1919, he purported to assign the sum to his illegitimate son, Nunez. In 1920, he was deposed and, in 1921, his political opponents compelled him to assign the sum to the State. The State, as plaintiff, began an action to recover the sum. The relevant issues

---

125 *Re Fry* [1946] Ch 312; *Campbell Connelly and Co Ltd v Noble* [1963] 1 WLR 252; *Trendtex Trading Corporation v Credit Suisse* [1980] QB 629.
126 (1886) 17 QB 309 (Day and Wills JJ).
127 [1927] 1 KB 669 (Greer J, Scrutton, Bankes and Lawrence LJJ).

were: (a) what law governed the assignments? (b) was the first assignment valid? and, if not, (c) was the second assignment valid? Greer J dismissed the action and this judgment was upheld by the Court of Appeal.

In the leading judgment, Scrutton LJ held Guatemalan law to be the governing law, as both the *lex loci actus* and the *lex domicilii*. The first assignment was held formally invalid under that law and, even had that not been the case, it was ruled that the defendant, as a minor, had no capacity. The second assignment was held void as tainted by duress and contrary to public policy. It is a matter of debate whether any clear *ratio* can be extracted from the three judgments, although some hold that the case is authority for the proposition that questions of form or lack of capacity in respect of an assignment are to be determined by the proper law of the assignment, as determined by the *lex loci actus*. The previous edition of this work expressed the view that 'The question of the capacities of the assignor and the assignee, which are outside the Convention, should be governed by the general principles applicable to contracts – preferably the putative applicable law – rather than the old authorities, which should now be regarded as obsolete'. This seems to be a sensible judgment.

The assignment: proprietary questions

As to the proprietary questions that may arise in respect of the assignment, the cases indicate that there are broadly two issues: (a) whether the assignor has title to assign; and (b) the effect of successive assignments (that is, the question of priorities).

Thus, if A, the owner of a Swedish patent, agreed, by a contract governed by English law, to assign it to B, the prevailing view at common law, now sustained by the Rome Convention 1980, is that entitlement to transfer would be governed by Swedish law as the legal system responsible for the creation of the right; such an approach has been followed in the case of copyrights[128] and causes of action.[129] This approach has been followed in other jurisdictions. In *Coleman v American Sheet and Tinplate Co*,[130] an employee sought to assign future wages. The law governing the employment contract was the law of Indiana, that governing the assignment, the law of Illinois. By the law of Illinois, assignments of future wages were permissible; by the law of Indiana, they were not. The Illinois court applied the law of Indiana as the law governing the contract of employment and refused to give effect to the assignment.

---

128 *Campbell Connelly and Co Ltd v Noble* [1963] 1 WLR 252.
129 *Trendtex Trading Corporation v Credit Suisse* [1982] AC 679.
130 *Coleman v American Sheet and Tinplate Co* (1936) 285 Ill App 542.

The principal proprietary difficulty is the problem of priority arising from successive assignments. The approach of Art 12(2) of the Rome Convention is to make this question depend on the law governing the interest. There are only a limited number of English authorities but they probably support the proposition that the law governing the creation of the original debt is the appropriate law to decide on the order of priorities of competing assignments of the same subject matter. The three possible laws are the proper law of the debt, the *lex situs* of the debt and the *lex fori*. In *Le Feuvre v Sullivan*,[131] the Privy Council considered that English law governed priorities in respect of successive assignment of a life insurance policy taken out with an English company, on the basis that English law was the proper law of the debt. In the subsequent case of *Kelly v Selwyn*,[132] all three possible laws coincided and the ratio was more difficult to determine. The salient facts were as follows: a trust fund was established by a testator with English trustees. The son of the testator went to New York and executed an assignment of his equitable interest; no notice was given to the trustees because it was not required by the law of New York. At a later date, he mortgaged his interest and the mortgagees gave notice to the trustees.

Warrington J held that English law applied and the mortgagees had priority as the first persons to give notice; however, whether English law was adopted as the *lex fori*, the *lex situs* or the proper law of the trust is unclear from the judgment. It would seem that, in this case, as with *Le Feuvre v Sullivan*, the judgment can be rationalised, assuming that, in both cases, all three laws coincided and the court adopted the law under which the interest was created.

In disputes concerning priorities, care must be taken in identifying the form of intangible property in issue; this is particularly so with company shares, where not only do the interests of the transferor and transferee have to be weighed but attention has to be given to the position of the company and its role in paying dividends to the established owner of such shares. In the case of *Macmillan Inc v Bishopsgate Investment Trust plc (No 3)*,[133] the Court of Appeal was concerned with a dispute involving conflicting claims to company shares. The plaintiffs, a public company, were seeking to recover

---

131 (1855) 10 Moo PC 1.
132 [1905] 2 Ch 117 (Warrington J).
133 [1995] 1 WLR 978 (Millett J); [1996] 1 WLR 387 (Auld, Staughton and Aldous LJJ). The case itself was but part of the litigation arising from the business dealings of the late Mr Robert Maxwell. The plaintiffs, seeking to rely on claims of restitution and constructive trust, wished to adopt English law because they considered its provisions relating to notice were more favourable to their claim than those of the law of New York. However, the dispute as to whether New York law or English law applied to the knowledge of the defendants was academic because Millett J, at first instance, found that there was no evidentiary basis with which to fix the banks with constructive notice of the plaintiffs' interest. See Stevens (1996) 112 LQR 198; Forsyth (1998) 114 LQR 141.

shares that had been misappropriated and used as security for advances by bankers. The company in which the shares were held was incorporated in New York and some of the transactions relating to the shares had taken place in New York and some in London. The question for the Court of Appeal was whether the law to determine the knowledge of the lending banks was that of New York or England In upholding the judgment of Millett J at first instance, the Court of Appeal ruled that disputes concerning priorities, as they affected shares, should be governed by the *lex situs,* while Auld LJ was prepared to accept that, in general, 'disputes about the ownership of land and of tangible and intangible movables are governed by the the the *lex situs'.*

Involuntary assignments

Although the view has been taken that the governing law for the property which affects the transfer of an intangible movable should be the proper law governing the creation of the original relationship rather than the *lex situs* of the debt, there is clear contrary authority in the case of involuntary assignment, where different considerations apply. An involuntary assignment arises when a right is transferred from A to B against the will of A and by operation of law. The commonest situation in England concerns the situation of garnishment.

Garnishment arises where a judgment creditor, A, is allowed to attach a sum of money owed by the judgment debtor, B, which is in the hands of a third party (the garnishee, C). If there is no foreign element, then the garnishee will be free from any further liability once he has met the demands of the judgment creditor.

An English court will be entitled to act if the garnishee is within the jurisdiction; the judgment debtor may be outside the jurisdiction.[134] In these circumstances, there is a danger that the garnishee may be liable a second time if he were subsequently sued outside the jurisdiction. To guard against such dangers, the making of an order is discretionary and will normally only be made if the debt is 'properly recoverable' in England and there is no appreciable risk of subsequent proceedings. Thus, in *Swiss Bank Corporation v Boehmische Industrial Bank,*[135] the Court of Appeal upheld a garnishee order where the debt was recoverable in England and there was no risk of subsequent proceedings in Czechoslovakia. As a garnishee order is not a matter of right but of discretion, such an order will not be granted if the defendant is able to demonstrate that there is a real risk of being proceeded

---

134 RSC Ord 49.
135 [1923] 1 KB 673.

against twice in respect of the same sum.[136] In like terms, a garnishee order will not be made absolute if to do so would violate some other rule of English private international law, such as allowing the indirect enforcement of a foreign revenue law.[137]

Problems of involuntary assignment arise in situations other than garnishment proceedings. Where the assignment is not voluntary, that is, where the interest is transferred by operation of law or by a court order, the governing law will be that of the *situs* of the interest at the time the contract takes place. This was illustrated by the case of *Jabbour v Custodian of Israeli Absentee Property*,[138] where the facts were as follows: the plaintiff, who lived in part of the then Palestinian Mandated Territory, insured his property against fire and riot with the Yorkshire Insurance Company through its agency in the Palestinian Mandate. The property was burned down in a riot, part of the civil disturbances which attended the formation of the State of Israel. The plaintiff fled to Egypt and the State of Israel appointed a Custodian of Absentee Property. The insurers, anxious to avoid paying the money to the wrong party, paid the money into court and issued interpleader proceedings.

Pearson J ruled that the Custodian was entitled to the insurance monies rather than the policy holder. First, the learned judge had to decide the nature of the subject matter in dispute. Although an amount had been quantified, and indeed paid into court, he concluded that the subject matter was a claim for unliquidated damage, in other words, a chose in action, an intangible movable. Secondly, he held that such claims can be given a notional *situs*, which is where they are properly recoverable, and that they are properly recoverable where the debtor resides. Thirdly, the *situs* of this debt was Haifa, where Jabbour could expect to be paid for a claim arising under the insurance contract. Finally, the debt being sited in Haifa, only Israeli law could alter the title to it. Effect would be given to the law of Israel unless there was some overriding principle of English public policy which would prevent its recognition, for example, that its purpose was the confiscation of an individual's private property – on the facts, he held the legislation not to be confiscatory.

---

136 *Deutsche Schachtbau unde Tiefbohrgesellschaft mbH v R'As al-Khaimah National Oil Co* [1990] 1 AC 295.

137 *Camdex International Ltd v Bank of Zambia (No 2)* (1997) (unreported, 28 January), CA (Simon Brown, Otton and Phillips LJJ).

138 [1954] 1 WLR 139; 1 All ER 145.

SUCCESSION

Introduction

Despite the fact that English domestic law was reformed in 1925, so that the traditional distinction between realty and personalty became irrelevant for most purposes of succession, the English conflict of laws continues to operate on the basis of separate systems for movable and immovable property. The justification, if one can be found, lies in the idea of effectiveness, that only courts and officials of the *situs* can effectively deal with immovable property. While it is true that the *lex situs* of the immovable will have the last word on the succession to it, and may reject the intended beneficiary as lacking the necessary capacity or disallow the intended gift as contrary to its rules against perpetuities and accumulations,[139] there is no reason to adopt a divided succession in order to deal with these possible problems. Taken to its logical conclusion, such an approach would preclude an English court from dealing with any case of succession, however strongly connected with England, which involved foreign land. This would, of course, be nonsense. An established exception to the *Mocambique* rule is where the English court is operating its jurisdiction in the administration of estates. It could be argued that movable property in a foreign country is equally without the control of English courts but this has never prevented them from making decisions about movable property situated abroad. One explanation of this apparent illogicality is that there is a widely accepted view that *mobilia sequuntur personam* – that movable property is governed by the personal law, at least for purposes of succession – which is shared both by common law and civil law jurisdictions.

The administration of estates

Jurisdiction

Under English law, no English estate can be administered without the authority of the court. The personal representatives, the executors appointed by the will or the administrators on intestacy, require formal authorisation before they can carry out their tasks of debt administration and beneficial distribution.

Until 1858, grants were made by the ecclesiastical courts in respect of property within the diocese. After 1858, this jurisdiction passed to the Court of Probate, which, in 1875, came within the jurisdiction of the High Court; today, the functions are split between the Family Division and the Chancery Division

---

139 See *Freke v Lord Carbery* (1873) LR 16 Eq 461.

of the High Court.[140] Until 1932, the jurisdiction of the court was limited to those situations where the deceased left property in England. The Administration of Justice Act 1932[141] extended the jurisdiction to enable grants to be made in respect of any deceased person. However, if the deceased left no property in England and died domiciled abroad, the court is hesitant before a grant is made.[142]

In those situations where a testator leaves two wills, one in respect of foreign property and the other in respect of property in England, then it is normal to make a grant only in respect of the latter.[143]

Obtaining an English grant

Where a deceased dies domiciled in England, then probate of the will is normally granted to the executors named therein. In respect of intestacy, letters of administration will normally be granted to a person taking a beneficial interest in the estate. A situation that sometimes arises is where a person dies domiciled abroad, leaving the bulk of his estate abroad; in this situation, a granted will be required for the English estate but it will be 'ancillary' to the 'principal' administration in the country of the deceased's domicile.

The English court will normally make a grant to a person who has been charged with the administration of the estate of the deceased abroad.[144] It is arguable that this course is justified by the practical consideration of having a unified administration and it is certainly consistent with the rule that succession to movable property is determined by the law of the deceased's domicile. In cases where no such application is made, the court may make a grant to a person beneficially entitled.[145] In other situations, such as where the administration abroad has been aborted, the court may make a grant to that person it deems fit.[146] In general, the court will not investigate the ground of a foreign appointment[147] but will decline to make a grant if the applicant is incompetent by English law, such as where the application is made by a

---

140 Non-contentious probate business is determined in the Family Division and all other probate business (eg, challenge to testamentary capacity) is determined within the Chancery Division.

141 Administration of Justice Act 1932, s 2(1); the essence of these provisions is continued under the Supreme Court Act 1981, s 25(1).

142 *Aldrich v AG* [1968] P 281.

143 *Re Wayland* [1951] 2 All ER 1041.

144 Non-Contentious Probate Rules 1987 SI 1987/2024, r 30(1)(a).

145 *Ibid*, r 30(1)(b).

146 *Ibid*, r 30(1)(c); *Re Kaufman's Goods* [1952] P 325.

147 *Re Hill's Goods* (1870) 2 P & D 89; *Re Humphries's Estate* [1934] P 78.

minor.[148] The inclination of the English court to follow the grant made in the foreign domicile will be followed even though the majority of the estate in England comprises immovable property.[149]

The effect of an English grant

The title of the administrator extends to all the property of the deceased in England[150] and probably to any property brought into England at a later date[151] but does not extend to property that is out of England and remains out of the jurisdiction.[152]

While it is the duty of the administrator to identify and recover assets in England, it must be doubtful whether that duty extends to assets abroad, since recovery will depend on being able to obtain a foreign grant of representation. There is some indication in the authorities that, if an administrator in England comes into possession of assets located abroad, then the court would be able to restrain any misconduct by invoking the equitable jurisdiction *in personam*.[153]

Where the deceased died domiciled in England and where, therefore, there is a coincidence in the law governing the administration and the succession to movable property, there will generally be no problems of a conflicting nature, even if some of the deceased's movable property is situated abroad. If the estate includes foreign immovable property, the administration will continue to be governed by English law, though the foreign *lex situs* will have the last word on its distribution.

Where the deceased is not domiciled in England at the time of his death but leaves assets in this country, the role of the ancillary administrators acting under the English grant will, as far as the administration itself is concerned, be subject exclusively to the control of English law, as the *lex fori*. So, for example, those administering the English estate must pay all those debts, but only those debts, whether English or foreign, according to the creditor's entitlement under English law. Any remaining assets can then be transferred to the principal administrator or distributed beneficially immediately. The alternatives were illustrated by the case of *Re Lorillard*,[154] where the facts were as follows: a testator died domiciled in New York, leaving assets and creditors in England and the USA. Administration proceedings took place in both

---

148 *Re the Goods of the Duchess d'Orleans* (1859) 1 Sw & Tr 253.
149 *Re Meatyard's Goods* [1903] P 125.
150 Administration of Estates Act 1925, s 1; *IRC v Stype Investments (Jersey) Ltd* [1982] Ch 456.
151 *Whyte v Rose* [1842] 3 QB 493; *In the Goods of Coode* (1867) LR 1 P & D 449.
152 *Blackwood v R* (1882) 8 App Cas 82.
153 *Ewing v Orr Ewing* (1883) 9 App Cas 34; (1885) 10 App Cas 453.
154 [1922] 2 Ch 638 (Eve J, Lord Sterndale MR, Warrington and Younger LJJ).

countries. The American debts exhausted the assets in the USA. The American debts were statute barred in England. The English administrator asked for the directions of the court as to whether the surplus English assets should be (a) paid to the American administrator to discharge the American debts; or (b) be paid to those beneficially entitled under the law of the deceased's domicile.

Eve J ruled that the surplus English assets should be distributed beneficially, notwithstanding the unpaid American creditors, as their debts, though enforceable under the law of New York were statute barred under English law; and this ruling was upheld by the Court of Appeal.

Choice of law

In every case, the administration of so much of the estate as is located in England will be subject to English law as the *lex fori*, whatever the general *lex successionis*, that is, whatever law governs the beneficial distribution of the estate. The distinction between administration and distribution is a crucial one, although it is sometimes not easy to apply in practice. It is clear that questions as to the admission of debts or the priority of those debts are matters of administration for the *lex fori*,[155] as, indeed, are decisions to postpone the sale of assets;[156] however, decisions as to the re-arranging of beneficial interests will be a matter of succession.[157]

In cases where the administration in England is ancillary to that abroad, then, at the end of the ancillary administration, the English court will have a discretion whether to remit those assets to the principal administrator for beneficial distribution or whether that distribution shall be effected from England.[158]

Foreign administrators

The rule is that the grant by a foreign court will not entitle an administrator to deal with property in England; in principle, the grant relates only to the territory over which the foreign court has jurisdiction. To initiate litigation in England to recover property, the prospective plaintiff will require a grant; failure to obtain a grant may render him liable as an executor *de son tort*.[159]

---

155 *Re Kloebe* (1884) 28 Ch D 175 (Pearson J) (foreign creditors to rank alongside English creditors); *Re Lorillard* [1922] 2 Ch 638 (foreign creditors, who would have been statute barred, given two months to demonstrate claims).

156 *Re Wilks* [1935] Ch 645 (decision to postpone the sale of shares).

157 *Re Hewit* [1891] 3 Ch 568.

158 *Re Achillopoulos* [1928] Ch 433; *Re Manifold* [1962] Ch 1; *In the Estate of Weiss* [1962] P 136

159 *New York Breweries Co v AG* [1899] AC 62; *IRC v Stype (Investments) Jersey Ltd* [1982] Ch 456.

While a foreign administrator is not permitted to act in England on behalf of the deceased without a grant, he will be entitled to act in a personal capacity, even if the matter is closely related to the administration of the estate.[160] Likewise, it would appear that a foreign administrator cannot be sued in this country in respect of the debts of the deceased; the individual is only answerable for those debts in his capacity as administrator and, as that capacity and status is not recognised in England, he cannot be successfully sued for the debts.[161]

Commonwealth and other UK grants

Where a grant of administration has been made by a country to which the Colonial Probates Act 1892 has been extended by Order in Council,[162] the court may allow an application in England to seal (that is, reseal) the grant, so that the original grant 'shall be of like force and effect, and have the same operation in the UK, as if granted by that court'.[163] The legislation works on the basis of reciprocity, so that an Order in Council is not normally made unless the other country has indicated its willingness to make provision for the recognition of an English grant. The legislation has been extended to many Commonwealth countries.

In respect of the UK, s 1 of the Administration of Estates Act 1971 provides that a grant made in Scotland or Northern Ireland will be directly effective in England without the need for resealing; the provisions operate retrospectively.[164] The legislation also provides that English grants may be recognised in Scotland[165] and in Northern Ireland.[166]

Once the debts have been paid, the personal representatives may proceed to the beneficial distribution of the property, according to the will or the intestacy rules of the *lex successionis*. This is subject to a limitation, which is included here as, while, on one view, it relates to succession, it can be seen as affecting the administration of the estate as governed by the *lex fori*. A valid foreign judgment concerning the distribution of the estate will be recognised in England and given full effect with regard to the assets of the deceased in England, even if the scheme of devolution is not the same as English law would apply, if the deceased died domiciled in the country where the judgment is given.[167] Additionally, a valid foreign judgment, determining the

---

160 *Vanquelin v Bouard* (1863) 15 CBNS 341.
161 *Beavan v Lord Hastings* (1856) 2 K & J 724.
162 Colonial Probates Act 1892, s 1.
163 *Ibid*, s 2.
164 Administration of Estates Act 1925, s 1(6).
165 *Ibid*, s 3(1).
166 *Ibid*, s 2(1).
167 *Re Trufort* (1889) 36 Ch D 600.

succession to property situated within the jurisdiction of that court, will be recognised in England, even if English law is the *lex successionis* and would order the distribution differently. The principle of effectiveness places the court of the *situs* in a specially privileged position not only with regard to real estate but also with regard to movables.

When the estate of a deceased person has been administered (that is, the relevant debts and duties have been paid), the question arises as to the law by which beneficial distribution is to be made. As a general principle, succession to immovables is governed by the *lex situs* and succession to movable property is governed by the law of the deceased's last domicile. It is to these questions that one must now turn.

Testate succession

Movable property

The formal validity of wills

The Wills Act 1963 gave effect to the Hague Convention on the Conflict of Laws Relating to the Form of Testamentary Dispositions 1961 and sets out the choice of laws rules in respect of the formal validity of wills. It was a significant piece of legislation, in that the 1961 Convention was the first international convention on the conflict of laws to find its way into English law; the 1963 Act introduces a simple mechanical system for the formal validity of wills. The principle behind the 1961 Convention was to promote uniformity of decisions in different countries and to uphold the formal validity of wills whenever this was possible. The technique adopted was not to select uniform rules from the various possibilities which individual legal systems had arrived at but to resort to rules of multiple reference, so that different systems could have their own preferred solutions but only at the expense of accepting everyone else's. The result is that, for every will, there are seven legal systems whose rules on formal validity can be employed to render the will formally valid. A will is formally valid if it complies with the requirements of the internal law[168] of any one of the following:

(a) the law of the country where the will was executed; or

(b) the law of the country where the deceased was domiciled, habitually resident or a a national at the time the will was executed or at the time of his death.[169]

Where the will contains gifts of immovable property, in addition to the above, the will is formally valid if it complies with the domestic law of the *lex*

---

168 Wills Act 1963, s 6(1).
169 *Ibid*, s 1.

situs.[170] The operative time in each case is the date of the execution of the will but retrospective changes which validate the will can be taken into account.[171]

These provisions are remarkably widely drawn and it is hardly surprising that, since 1 January 1964, there have been so few cases on formalities. In contrast, the prior common law position had been that a will of immovables had to comply with the formal requirements of the *lex situs* and a will of movables had to comply with the law of the deceased's last domicile. This could cause difficulty if the testator changed his domicile after executing his will; because of these strict common law requirements, the English courts, anxious to uphold wills, would admit to probate a will valid by the internal law of the deceased's last domicile or a will that was valid by a system of law referred to by that legal system. Thus, the doctrine of *renvoi* entered into English law.[172] The law was modified by the Wills Act 1861 (Lord Kingsdown's Act) but this piece of legislation was confined to British subjects and soon acquired a reputation for causing difficulties of interpretation.[173]

In contrast, today, very few wills fail the test as to formal validity and there have only been a limited number of cases on the legislation since 1964; these have turned on questions of fact rather than matters of interpretation.[174] The application of the legislation has not proved difficult. English law will make the connections, that is, will determine where the will was made, where the deceased was domiciled, etc. Section 3 of the legislation extends the scope of questions of formality. Requirements relating to the capacity of the witnesses or to special procedures to be adopted by testators falling within a particular category are defined by s 3 of the Wills Act 1963 as relating to formal validity.

Because of the increase in mobility in the 20th century, a will might be made in a country where an individual was not domiciled or habitually resident and not a national. Although the 1961 Hague Convention has been a considerable improvement, a further step has been taken by the Washington Convention on International Wills 1973. This treaty has been ratified by the UK and was implemented by s 27 and Sched 2 of the Administration of Justice Act 1982. The Annex to the Convention provides that an 'international will' shall be valid notwithstanding the nationality, domicile or residence of the testator, provided it meets certain formalities. These formalities are that the will is in writing and signed or acknowledged by the testator in the presence of two witnesses and an 'authorised person', who has then attest the will in

---

170 Wills Act 1963, s 2(1)(b).

171 *Ibid*, s 6(3).

172 *Collier v Rivaz* (1841) 2 Curt 855; *In bonis Lacroix* [1877] 2 PD 94.

173 See Morris (1946) 62 LQR 172; Morris (1964) 13 ICLQ 684; Kahn Freund (1964) 27 MLR 55.

174 *Re Kanani* (1978) 122 SJ 611; *Re Wynn* [1984] 1 WLR 237.

the presence of the testator. The essence of the Convention is that a will may be formally valid by this alternative method.

Capacity

Capacity to make a will is governed by the testator's personal law at the time the will was made. This, for English conflict law, will be the testator's domiciliary law.[175] If the testator had personal capacity at the time the will was made – and we are concerned here with testamentary capacity in general terms, not with the capacity to make any particular gift in the will – by the law of his domicile at the time, any subsequent loss of capacity, whether by reason of infirmity or by reason of change of domicile to a country with more stringent testamentary requirements, should not make any difference. There is, however, one exception to this, which will be familiar to English lawyers: the rule of law that a will, not being one made in contemplation of marriage, is revoked by the subsequent marriage of its maker.

Where the estate contains immovable property, the distinction between testamentary capacity in general and the power to make particular gifts becomes less sharply defined. In such cases, we need to have regard to the *lex situs* to determine both the capacity and the power.[176]

The significance of the control exercised by the English *lex fori* over the administration of estates is clearly demonstrated when the issue is the competence of the beneficiary to take a gift. The real question is not the status of the beneficiary as such but the security of the executors, who need to be protected against the consequences of an unauthorised distribution – unless the will so directs, a receipt from an infant legatee will not be a valid discharge of the personal representative's duty.

The question, of reduced importance with the assimilation of ages of majority, would be characteristically posed when the beneficiary is of full age and competence under one system of law but not under another. There are three possible legal systems to which an English court could refer – the *lex fori* which governs the administration of the will, the general *lex successionis* (the law of the the testator's last domicile for movables, the *lex situs* for immovables) or the personal law of the beneficiary.

English courts have played an advantage rule in such cases and have been prepared to allow the beneficiary to take the legacy into immediate possession if he is of full age either by English law or by his personal law.[177] Where the gift is of immovable property, no transfer of the property is effective unless the beneficiary is competent to take it according to the *lex situs*.

---

175 *Re Fuld's Estate (No 3)* [1968] P 675.

176 *Re Hernanado* (1884) 27 Ch D 284.

177 *Re Hellman's Will* (1866) LR 2 Eq (girl aged 18 had capacity by Hamburg law, the law of her domicile, even though not by English law); *Re Schnapper* [1928] Ch 420.

Interpretation

Under the English conflict of laws, the concept of a will as an autonomous product means that the testator is free, within very wide limits, to make what provision he wishes. As he can say what he wants, it follows that he can select whatever law he wishes for the interpretation of his will. In the usual absence of any such choice, the law to govern the interpretation is the law of his domicile at the time when the will was made.[178] Section 4 of the Wills Act 1963 provides as follows: 'The construction of a will shall not be altered by reason of any change in the testator's domicile after the execution of the will.' It should be emphasised here that the issue of construction is confined to the interpretation of the testator's wishes, not their effectiveness. The quest is for what the testator wanted to achieve and is distinct form the practicability, legality or implications of his desires.

Although sometimes the distinction is not easy to maintain, there is a division between construction and identification which needs to be maintained. Suppose the testator uses the terms 'wife', 'husband', 'spouse' or 'children'; now, it is obvious that this is merely an alternative for Mary, William or the twins – in other words, there can be absolutely no doubt about who was meant and no one would wish to challenge the distribution. In other circumstances, the matter may be more complex and, where there is possible ambiguity, there will be no shortage of persons who want to join the fray. Suppose the testator used the term 'wife' but had been married twice and the validity of the second marriage is in doubt, or he has used the word 'children' and there are a number of them, some legitimate and some not. Whether the word 'children' does or does not include illegitimate children and whether 'wife' includes a divorced spouse are matters of construction of the will. It will, therefore, be for the testator's chosen law, or the law of his domicile, to answer these questions.

Once this interpretation has been made, for example, that only legitimate children qualify for the inheritance, the issue shifts from the area of construction to the area of status if the next question is: 'Is this person a legitimate child?' This raises an incidental question, the law on which has been discussed elsewhere.

Essential validity

The expression, essential validity, comprises a wide number of questions, such as whether particular gifts are invalid on grounds of public policy or whether certain proportions of the estate should be left to specific relatives.

---

178 *Re Price* [1900] 1 Ch 442; *Re Ferguson's Will* [1902] 1 Ch 483; *Re Cunningham* [1924] 1 Ch 68.

It is a well established principle of the conflict of laws that *mobilia sequuntur personam* – movables follow the person. The effect to be given to the testator's wishes with regard to a will of movables will be governed by the domiciliary law at the time of death.[179] That law will determine whether the gifts in the will can lawfully be carried into effect and whether the intended beneficiaries can inherit.

Where the testator has changed his domicile after the will was made, the domiciliary change can have profound effects; this was illustrated by *Re Groos*,[180] where the facts were as follows: the testatrix, a Dutch woman, made a will in the Netherlands, leaving her estate to her husband, subject to the legitimate portions to which her children were entitled. She died domiciled in England, leaving a husband and five children. Under Dutch law, the children would have been entitled to three quarters of the estate but, at that time, English law made no stipulation. It was held that the will was subject to English law and the entire estate passed to the husband.[181]

The law of the last domicile, the general *lex successionis*, governs all matters relating to the substance of the testamentary dispositions concerning movables – whether, for example, the testator has a limited or complete power of testation, whether dependants can challenge the will[182] and whether particular gifts comply with the rules about charities, accumulations and perpetuities.

In the case of wills of immovables, or of gifts of immovable property in mixed wills, the *lex successionis* is the *lex situs*[183] and the validity of the dispositions will have to be tested by that law.[184] The reference to the *lex situs* may involve the doctrine of *renvoi*.

It remains an open question whether the *lex successionis* is crystallised at the date of the testator's death or whether subsequent changes in that law can be taken into account. As far as gifts of immovables are concerned, the whole concept of effectiveness must involve the application of the *lex situs* as it stands at the time of proceedings. For movables, it is said that *Lynch v The Provisional Government of Paraguay*[185] established that it is the *lex domicilii* at the time of death which is to be applied. The facts of the case were as follows:

---

179 *Thornton v Curling* (1824) 8 Sim 310.

180 [1915] 1 Ch 572.

181 The case was decided prior to the passing of the Inheritance (Family Provision) Act 1938 and during the period when being free of testation permitted a spouse to ignore the claims of family members; today, a claim might be made under the 1975 Act.

182 Under the Inheritance (Provision for Family and Dependants) Act 1975, s 1, a claim for financial provision from the deceased's estate can only be made in respect of a person who has died domiciled in England and Wales; see, also, the Law Reform (Succession) Act 1995.

183 *Freke v Carbery* (1873) LR 10 Eq 461.

184 But, see *Re Piercy* [1895] 1 Ch 83 (North J).

185 (1871) LR 2 P & D 268.

Francisco Lopez was the dictator of Paraguay and died on 1 March 1870, domiciled there. He left personal property in England. After death but before a grant was made in England, there was a revolution and the new government of Paraguay passed a decree on 4 May 1870 to confiscate all the property of the the deceased. The plaintiff moved for a grant of probate and the defendants entered a caveat.

Lord Penzance ruled for the plaintiff, holding that the law of the place of domicile as it existed at the time of death ought to regulate succession. However, the strength of this authority is open to question because, in the particular case, the decree was both retrospective and confiscatory.

As with all other applications of the *lex causae*, it is only the substantive rules of that law which apply; matters of procedure are governed by the *lex fori*. What is a substantive rule and what a procedural one is not as self-evident as may be supposed and a case in this area furnishes an excellent example: *In Re Cohn*,[186] where the facts were as follows: a mother and a daughter, both German nationals and domiciliaries who had taken refuge in England, were killed in an air raid on London. It was impossible to tell which one had died first. In such cases of *commorientes*, there was a difference between German law, the *lex successionis*, and English law, the *lex fori*. By German law, they would be regarded as having died simultaneously, with the result that neither could succeed under the other's will; under English law, the younger is deemed to have survived the elder[187] and may therefore succeed to the estate.

So, if the the issue was a procedural question, it would be governed by English law, if a substantive one, the rule of German law would apply. Uthwatt J held that both the English provision and the German provision were rules of substantive law and that German law governed testate succession to movables; in these circumstances, the daughter could not succeed to the mother's estate.

Revocation

Under English domestic law, a will is said to be ambulatory, that is, it speaks from death. During the lifetime of the testator, it has no legal significance; it is merely a statement of intention which the testator is free to change, literally at will. There are two exceptions to this which are pertinent here; the first is that a testator who loses testamentary capacity and never regains it is stuck with whatever will he has already made; the second is that, under English domestic law but not necessarily under other systems, a will is revoked by the marriage of the testator unless it was made in contemplation of marriage.

186 *Re Cohn* [1945] Ch 5 (Uthwatt J showing a remarkable sensitivity to German law, having regard to the time and the substance of the matter).

187 Law of Property Act 1925, s 184.

A testator with capacity may, therefore, revoke his will at any time – what law should determine whether the alleged act of revocation was effective to destroy the original will or replace it? There is little authority on revocation but it would seem that the law of the testator's domicile at the time of the act of revocation is the key, though it must be said that, for wills involving gifts of immovable interests, the role of the *lex situs* cannot be ignored.

Suppose the testator physically destroys the will. If such an act of destruction is a valid way of revoking his will by his domiciliary law at the time, then the English conflict of laws will accept that the will has been revoked, at least as far as gifts of movables are concerned. If the testator has not replaced the will by another, the distribution of his movables will depend on the intestacy rules of his domiciliary law at the time of his death. Similarly, if the act of revocation is alleged to be some other statement by the testator, less then the physical destruction of the will itself, for example, a formal statement of repudiation, then the same rules would appear to apply. There is a case for determining the issue by reference to the law of the place where the revocation was done but there is no authority to support that suggestion.

A new will which replaces an existing one or operates as a codicil to it will be subjected to the same tests as we have already seen for the establishment of a will, with two additions. The first relates to formal validity; the revoking will is regarded as formally valid if it satisfies the standard tests that we have already seen but, also, if it satisfied the requirements which were or could have been applied to the original will.[188] The second relates to codicils, additions to the original will; these, too, can have a self-standing validity or can satisfy the formal requirements of the original will. In addition, as English domestic law regards a codicil as the republication of the original will, the whole testamentary set can be validated by the codicil.

Revocation of a will by marriage can present problems in two ways: first, not every legal system takes the same view as English domestic law, that is, that the subsequent marriage does revoke the will; and, secondly, it raises an issue of classification. Is the rule that marriage revokes the will, and the provisions in other legal systems to the like or to the opposite effect, a rule of the law of succession or a rule of the law of marriage? If it is a rule of succession, the governing laws will be the last domiciliary law for movables and the *lex situs* for immovables; if, on the other hand, it is a matter of matrimonial law, the reference should be to the personal law at the time of marriage. There is no logical answer to this question but there is a practical case for the application of the matrimonial law. It would be harsh if a will, valid despite a supervening marriage because the testator was wholly connected with a legal system which did not regard marriage as a revoking event, were to be revoked by the acquisition of a domicile in, say, England

188 Wills Act 1963, s 2(1)(c).

shortly before the death. This would add an even more bitter twist to the situation, as was seen in *Re Groos*,[189] whereby a subsequent change of domicile had a profound effect on the testamentary dispositions.

The issue was illustrated by the case of *Re Martin*,[190] where the facts were as follows: a domiciled Frenchwoman resident in England made a will of movables and then married a French national who had acquired a domicile in England.The question arose as to the governing law as to whether the marriage revoked the will when the testatrix died domiciled in France.

The Court of Appeal held that the governing law in respect of revocation was the husband's *lex domicilii* at the time of marriage. English law would have regarded her will as revoked by her marriage; French law would not. If, therefore, the matter was governed by the general testamentary law, her will would have stood but the court took the view that it was a matter of matrimonial law. It applied the premarital domiciliary law of her husband, which was English, with the effect that the will was regarded as revoked by the subsequent marriage. We must not confuse the outcome with the methodology here. In 1900, a wife acquired her husband's domicile, as a domicile of dependency, by operation of law, upon her marriage. Since 1973, marriage does not impose the husband's domicile upon the wife[191] and whether a common matrimonial domicile is acquired is a question of fact in each particular case, irrespective of whether you take the the dual domicile test or the matrimonial home test.

If we put the case into a modern setting, the result would have been different, as the starting point (leaving aside the matrimonial home test for the moment) would be the testatrix's premarital domiciliary law, which was French, and French law did not view the subsequent marriage as a revoking event. It could be argued that the idea of a subsequent marriage revoking a will is not for the benefit of the testator but for the benefit of the spouse. Certainly, historically, the rule must have been for the benefit of wives, whose property would be acquired by the husband on marriage and who therefore would need protection from accidental disinheritance. Today, if the rule serves any purpose at all, it must be to reflect the new relationship to which the marriage gives rise and the claims of the new spouse for consideration in the distribution of the partner's property on death. As it cannot be assumed that there will be a common matrimonial law, then the choice has to be made between the testator's personal law and the spouse's personal law, and I see now no reason to adopt the latter. There is certainly no longer a case for preferring the husband's domiciliary law to that of the wife, although, as we shall see, this anachronism may remain in other areas of family property.

---

189 [1915] 1 Ch 572.
190 [1900] P 211.
191 Domicile and Matrimonial Proceedings Act 1973, s 1.

Immovable property

As indicated above, at common law, a will of immovables had to comply with the formalities stipulated by the *lex situs*. The general reason for the prominence of the *lex situs* was that land was subject to the control of the authorities in question and it was also often the case that public policy considerations arose. Secondly, until the middle of the 19th century, land was the principal source of personal wealth and English courts were very cautious about any question concerning land in England; in these circumstances, it was inevitable that they would expect foreign courts to exercise a similar restraint. Thirdly, under the *Mocambique* rule, English courts would not involve themselves in disputes about title to foreign land. Fourthly, by the end of the 19th century, many countries were moving towards some form of registration of title whereby disputes as to title would be dealt with by a public authority. The officials of that body would be the final arbiters of title disputes subject to a ruling of their own courts.[192] In considering testate succession to immovables, a sensible distinction can be drawn between (a) immovable property in England; and (b) foreign immovables. It is proposed to take each in turn.

Immovable property in England

In England, with the country subject to the scheme of registration of title under the Land Registration Act 1925, then disputes concerning land will, in most cases, be subject to the traditional principles of English real property law, though subject to the following qualifications.

(a) Formal validity: the Wills Act 1963 provides that the criteria stipulated for a will of movable property are the same as for a will of immovable property, save that s 2(1)(b) of the legislation provides the additional ground that a will of immovables is to be regarded as formally valid if it complies with the *lex situs*.

(b) Capacity: there would seem to be no direct authority on the narrow question of the capacity of a person domiciled abroad to dispose of immovable property in England. In principle, the safe view is probably that capacity to make a will and capacity to take under the will should be governed by the *lex situs*.

(c) Essential validity: on the basis of the authority of *Freke v Lord Carbery*,[193] it is reasonable to assume that questions of essential validity in relation to a

---

192 See, eg, the provisions of the Land Registration Act 1925, ss 138–43, stipulating the jurisdiction of the courts and the relationship between the High Court and the Chief Land Registrar; in the 19th century, company law, patent law and trade marks law all acquired registration systems whereby the Registry would operate the day to day system, subject to an appeal to the national courts.

193 (1873) LR 16 Eq 461 (Lord Selborne LC).

will of English immovables are governed by the *lex situs*. In *Freke v Lord Carbery*, Lord Selborne LC ruled that a gift by will of leasehold property situated in London was void under the Accumulations Act 1800, notwithstanding the fact that the gift was valid in Ireland.[194]

(d) Construction: a will made by a person domiciled abroad in respect of immovable property in England will be interpreted in the light of the law expressly chosen by him or by the testator's *lex domicilii* at the time of execution.[195] So, in *Studd v Cook*,[196] the will of a testator domiciled in England was to be interpreted according to English law, notwithstanding that it concerned immovable property in Scotland.

(e) Revocation: in principle, there seems to be no reason why the rules in respect of immovable property situated in England should not be the same as those that prevail for movable property. There is only limited authority on this point. In the case of revocation by subsequent marriage, an English court has held that the will of a testator domiciled in Scotland but devising land in England was to be regarded as revoked by his subsequent marriage under English law, notwithstanding the fact that the marriage did not have that effect under Scottish law.[197]

Foreign immovables

Clearly, the principle of effectiveness demands that, as foreign immovable property is under the control of the courts of the foreign *situs*, then English courts should respect that jurisdiction and that any decision should be in harmony with that of the *lex situs*.

(a) Formal validity: the position as to the formal validity of a will relating to foreign immovable property is governed by the Wills Act 1963 and is no different to that prevailing in respect of land in England.

(b) Capacity: as a matter of principle, questions of capacity should be governed by the *lex situs*. There would seem to be little point in the courts of State A holding that the testator had capacity in respect of land in Country B if the courts or Land Registry of Country B were to hold that there was no evidence of capacity.

(c) Essential validity: the judgment of Luxmore J, in *Re Ross*,[198] makes it clear that questions of essential validity in respect of foreign immovables are governed by the *lex situs*.

---

194 *Freke v Lord Carbery* (1873) LR 16 Eq 461 (the case is also authority for the proposition that, while leasehold property is personal property under domestic law, it is classed as immovable property for the purpose of private international law).

195 *Philipson Stow v IRC* (1961) AC 727.

196 (1883) 8 App Cas 577.

197 *Re Earl Caithness* (1891) 7 TLR 354.

198 *Re Ross* (1930) 1 Ch 377.

(d) Construction: in principle, the governing law will be that intended by the testator. A rebuttable presumption arises in favour of the *lex domicilii* but, if particular language is used, the court might be justified in concluding that the governing law should be that of the *lex situs*.[199]

(e) Revocation: in respect of revocation by subsequent will or revocation by marriage, then the position is probably the same as with English immovables. In cases of revocation by destruction, then there is authority in the United States for the view that the *lex situs* should apply.[200]

Intestate succession

Those items of the intestate's property which are regarded as movables, and, of course, it is the *lex situs* of the particular item which has the last word on its characterisation, will devolve according to the scheme of intestate succession established by the legal system of the country of the intestate's last domicile. This is one of the oldest established rules of the English conflict of laws.[201] and accords with the widely accepted principle, *mobilia sequuntur personam*. The presumption is sometimes said to be that, by not making a will, the deceased is impliedy consenting to the distribution of his property by the intestacy rules of the law of his final domicile.

Immovable property will devolve according to the scheme of devolution prescribed by the *lex situs*.[202] Effectiveness may, however, involve a reference to the conflict rules of the *lex situs*, according to the doctrine of total *renvoi*, which has been employed by the English courts from time to time in the resolution of cases of succession to foreign immovable property.

Fairly straightforwardly, then, the administrators need only inform themselves of the classes of persons entitled to succeed according to the *lex successionis* (the intestate's last domiciliary law or the *lex situs*, depending on the nature of the property) and distribute accordingly. However, as we have seen with testate succession, incidental questions may arise relating to the membership of the classes identified by the *lex successionis*. The 'surviving spouse' or 'children' may raise questions about the validity of marriages or divorces, or issues of legitimacy, and these incidental questions will have to be resolved either according to the *lex causa* or the *lex fori*, in the same way as they are resolved in cases of testate succession.

One peculiarity which follows from the persistence of the English conflict of laws in separating movables from immovables for the purpose of

---

199 *Philipson Stow v IRC* (1961) AC 727
200 *Re Barrie's Estate* (1949) 240 Iowa 431; 35 NW 2d 658.
201 *Pipon v Pipon* (1744) Amb 25.
202 *Duncan v Lawson* (1889) 41 Ch D 394.

succession is that the surviving spouse may be able to collect a number of statutory legacies. Suppose the intestate dies domiciled in England, leaving property of either type here and immovables in other countries. Despite the fact that English domestic law has had unitary succession since 1926, and let us suppose that the other countries concerned have it too, the surviving spouse of the intestate appears to be entitled to the statutory legacy under English law and to any statutory legacies that the other systems may have. Pretend there are three countries involved, all with the same rules – that, where there are children, the surviving spouse is entitled to £75,000 outright – and suppose that each estate is worth £150,000 and that the two foreign estates consist principally of immovables. The deceased dies domiciled in England. Had all the property been in England, or had all the property been movable and, therefore, subject to English law alone, the surviving spouse would have been entitled to a statutory legacy of £75,000. As things stand, he or she is entitled to £225,000.[203]

It sometimes happens that there are no qualifying persons under the intestacy rules – that the deceased left no heirs or next of kin. The solution here would be to look to the *lex successionis* to determine what is to happen in such cases, what provisions exist to deal with the ownerless estate. In the English domestic law, the English estate of an intestate without next of kin passes to the crown as *bona vacantia* – this means, in effect, that the Crown is seizing ownerless goods under the prerogative power. Suppose the *lex successionis* is a foreign law, with a similar response. Will the foreign State or sovereign be able to claim the property in England or will it pass to the Crown on the basis that, if there is any confiscation to be done, the *lex situs* of the property, whether the property is movable or immovable, should prevail over the *lex successionis*?

In *Re Barnett's Trusts*,[204] the deceased, who died domiciled in Austria, left property. There was no one to succeed him and the Austrian State claimed the property in England. Kekewich J classified the matter as one of administration of estates and not of succession and, as administration is a matter for the *lex fori*, the Austrian claim was rejected and the property went to the to the Crown as *bona vacantia*. A distinction between a claim made as *bona vacantia* and a claim made as *ultimus heres* was advanced in *Re Maldonado's Estate*.[205] where, though the *lex successionis* was Spanish, the State's claim to succeed as *ultimus heres* was accepted as a genuine claim of succession and the Court of Appeal allowed the property to be taken by the Spanish State. Both cases, of course, involved movables. Had the property been immovable, the *lex situs*,

---

203 *Re Collens* [1986] Ch 505 (where Lord Browne-Wilkinson VC acknowledged that the state of the law might be open to criticism but recognised that he was bound to give effect to the plain words of the Administration of Estates Act 1925, s 46).

204 [1902] 1 Ch 847.

205 [1954] P 222 (Barnard J; Evershed MR, Jenkins and Morris LJJ).

English law, would govern the succession and any claim of the foreign State would be in vain.

FAMILY PROPERTY

Introduction

There are several ways in which a legal system can treat family property. Since the Married Woman's Property Act 1882, English law has recognised the separation of the husband and wife's property; there is thus no concept of family property and individuals may deal with their property as they wish. If the marriage terminates in divorce, then the English courts have wide ranging powers to make financial orders in favour of one or other party under the terms of the Matrimonial Causes Act 1973 and subsequent legislation. Additionally, in the event of the death of a spouse, the other party has a statutory right to apply for reasonable financial provision under the Inheritance (Provision for Family and Dependants) Act 1975. For many married couples, the most significant financial asset is the family home and English law makes provision for joint ownership in the form of both the equitable joint tenancy and the equitable tenancy in common.

Private family arrangements can have a significance for the ordinary operation of the domestic law and, thereby, affect conflict rules. To take a simple example from English law, while there is no community of property between husband and wife, it is common for the matrimonial home to be legally vested in the joint names of the spouses. In cases where there is an equitable joint tenancy at the time of death, then the *ius accrescendi* will apply. The interest which a spouse has passes to the other on death and does not form part of the deceased's estate for purposes of succession.[206] Equally, where the parties are not married and disputes arise as to the ownership of the legal title, the law of equity will intervene in appropriate cases to protect the innocent party, in the form of the resulting or constructive trust and by the application of the increasingly important vehicle of the proprietary licence.[207]

Other countries adopt different systems of family property. Many States adopt some form of community of property. The expression, 'community of property', has a number of meanings and may embrace at least four different systems, namely, (a) the so called full community of property; (b) community

---

206 In accordance with the maxim, *jus accrescendi praefertur ultimae voluntati* Co Litt 185. The case law demonstrates the problems that can arise in determining whether or not the equitable joint tenancy has been severed; see *Re Draper's Conveyance* [1969] 1 Ch 486; *Burgess v Rawnsley* [1975] Ch 429; *Harris v Goddard* [1983] 1 WLR 1203; *Barton v Morris* [1985] 1 WLR 1257; *Goodman v Gallant* [1986] Fam 106.

207 A development that became more noticeable after the judgment in *Pascoe v Turner* [1979] 1 WLR 431, CA; Crane [1979] Conv 379; Sufrin (1979) 42 MLR 574.

of gains; (c) community of gains and chattels; and (d) deferred community. Each of these systems operates differently: under (a), full community embraces all movable and immovable property acquired during the marriage.[208]

System (b), community of gains, comprises property acquired during the marriage but not gifts or property resulting from inheritance.[209] The third form of community, (c), community of gains and chattels, embraces all chattels, whether owned at the time of the marriage or acquired thereafter, but only such land as is acquired by labour and not land held at the time of the marriage or subsequently acquired by gift or inheritance.[210] The fourth system, (d), deferred community, provides that property is not held jointly during the marriage but, when the union terminates by death or divorce, a spouse receives a specific proportion.[211]

As can be seen from this brief outline, such systems differ greatly and it will normally be necessary for an English court to be assisted by evidence of foreign law before reaching a conclusion.[212] Secondly, such systems are common in those countries where there is a Civil Law tradition or the influence of Roman Dutch law has been felt. Thirdly, most countries operating a system of community of property permit the prospective spouses to contract out of the standard arrangements. In those cases where a contract is not entered into, it may be reasonable to infer that the parties have impliedly agreed to accept the standard regime of the country in which they are domiciled and in which they intend to marry.[213] Fourthly, most Civil Law systems regard surviving spouses and children as having direct interests in the succession which vest on death and, therefore, those 'legitimate portions'[214] do not form part of the deceased's estate.

Whatever form the family property regime of a particular country takes, conflict problems most commonly arise on succession; for transfers *inter vivos* raise problems either between family members themselves, which are most likely to be determined by local courts, or in sale contracts, where the question might arise of the seller's power to transfer a jointly owned item. This would not, in regard to the buyer, raise an issue any different from the common problem of the seller exceeding his authority.

---

208 As under Roman Dutch systems: Holland, South Africa.

209 The system in Spain, some Eastern European States and some States within the USA.

210 The system under the French Civil Code 1804 but modified since, and the system that pertained for a time in Belgium

211 As pertains in Germany and Quebec, Canada.

212 As in *De Nicols v Curlier* [1900] AC 21.

213 *De Nicols v Curlier* [1900] AC 21; *Re Martin* [1900] P 211.

214 *Re Annesley* [1926] Ch 692; *Re Ross* [1930] 1 Ch 377.

Where the issue of family property arises because a legal system gives automatic inheritance rights to the surviving spouse or the children, where, in other words, the deceased had power to dispose of the property in life but not to leave all of it away from the family on death,[215] the question is properly characterised as one of succession and is covered by the succession rules we have already considered.

Where, however, the property regime gives rights to property in life, as with a regime of community of property between husband and wife, although the issue may well present itself as a conflict problem involving succession, it does not follow that its proper classification is succession. English conflict law has taken the question of community property, like the question of whether a subsequent marriage revokes a will, as a matter of matrimonial law.[216]

The cases coming before the English courts can be divided into those where the parties have entered into an ante-nuptial agreement (or marriage settlement) and those where no such agreement has been made. Some of the cases on matrimonial settlements reflect the social mores of an earlier age, while many of the cases concerning agreements arise from attempts by the parties to modify the application of the rules pertaining to community of property. It is sensible to look at the two broad areas separately.

Where there is no marriage contract or settlement

Where the parties have not made a contract to determine their matrimonial property rights, the conflict of laws has to address questions such as: which law is to determine the regime of matrimonial property? Is the initial determination definitive? Can it be altered by act of parties or operation of law?

If the questions are to be treated as matters of matrimonial law, it would be sensible to refer them to the law governing the substance of the marriage rather than its form but there is a problem determining what that law is. The old cases, and there are no modern ones, applied the law of the husband's premarital domicile, a test which used to be applied for the essential validity of the marriage. Traditionally, that law would become the matrimonial domiciliary law by operation of law and, in most cases, would represent the social and economic reality of the marriage. However, the abandonment of that test in favour of the dual domicile test for the essential validity of the marriage, coupled with the liberation of married women from domiciliary dependence on their husbands, must raise doubts about the suitability and, indeed, the acceptability of the law of the husband's domicile. Nevertheless,

---

215 *Re Groos* [1915] 1 Ch 572.
216 *Re Martin* [1900] P 211; *Re Egerton's Will Trusts* [1956] Ch 593.

the conventional view, propounded in Dicey, is that, where the parties have made no agreement as to property, then the matrimonial property will be subject to the legal rules stipulated in the law of the matrimonial domicile. In the absence of special circumstances, this will be the law of the husband's domicile at the time of the marriage.[217]

The alternative view, advanced by the late Professor Cheshire, was that the law of the intended matrimonial home should apply to questions of matrimonial property; this was in accord with his view that questions of capacity should be governed by that law. However, this view is beset with the same difficulties in this regard as it is as a test of the validity of the marriage – what happens if the parties do not immediately, within a reasonable time or, indeed, ever establish a matrimonial home? Suppose they continue to have separate domiciles: what is the fallback or interim position? The reserve position seems to be the established rule – the law of the husband's premarital domicile.

Where the husband and wife have common laws on matrimonial property, though they are domiciled in different countries, this common factor might be enough to establish community or to deny it. Where the parties come from different countries with different regimes, there is an increasingly weak case, both in moral and in socio-economic terms, for preferring the husband's law to that of the wife. It may, however, accord with the way that the community regimes themselves deal with such 'mixed' marriages.

The different approaches of the husband's domicile and that of the intended matrimonial home were analysed in *Re Egerton's Will Trusts*,[218] where the facts were as follows: the testator, a domiciled English soldier, married a Frenchwoman, in England in May 1932, shortly after returning from service in India. At or about that time, the parties agreed to settle in France but they did not do so until 1935 at the earliest. The testator died in France in 1951, leaving a will. The widow argued that the estate was subject to the French law as to community of property. The executors took out a summons to determine the question.

Counsel for the widow,[219] after outlining the competing theories, argued for the approach of Professor Cheshire, that the property was subject to French law, as the law of the intended matrimonial domicile. Roxburgh J rejected the argument for two reasons: (a) on the facts, the parties did not immediately leave for France; and (b) in principle, he preferred the view of Dicey, that, *prima facie*, the property rights of the spouses were to be determined by the law of the husband's domicile at the date of the marriage, unless displaced by an agreement arising expressly or by inference. Thus, the

217 *White v Tennant* [1891] AC 639; *Re Martin* [1900] P 211.
218 [1956] Ch 593 (Roxburgh J).
219 RO Wilberforce QC (as he then was) and EI Goulding (as he then was).

widow was not entitled to demand that the estate be distributed in accordance with French law. This preference for the law of the husband's premarital domicile was consistent with earlier English authority[220] and the approach in other jurisdictions.[221]

Assuming that an appropriate law can be found for this first question, that law will determine whether the community regime applies to all property brought to the marriage or only that, or how much of that, acquired after it. What it cannot determine is what is to happen when there is a change of domicile by either of the parties or both. Community property regimes are not consistent on the effect of a change of domicile but there is clearly a strong case for recognising the rights acquired under the original regime and not to allow, for example, the husband to destroy his wife's community claims by the simple, expedient of change of domicile. However, a change of domicile to a country which, like England, does not have community of property could well be seen as terminating the community arrangement regarding any property acquired after the change.

In considering the effect of a change of domicile, a distinction must be drawn between the doctrine of immutability and the related approach of mutability. The doctrine of immutability holds that the rights of the parties are fixed and regulated by the law of the domicile at the time of marriage,[222] while the principle of mutability provides that the rights of a spouse over acquired property are determined by the law of the domicile at the time of acquisition[223] It is probably the case that English law holds to the doctrine of immutability but this depends on the inferences to be drawn from the two House of Lords cases of *Lashley v Hog*[224] and *De Nicols v Curlier*.[225] The former case of *Lashley v Hog* is often claimed as an authority in favour of mutability but the judgments may yield more than one *ratio* and are by no means conclusive; the salient facts were: Hog, a Scotsman, married an Englishwoman when domiciled in England. At a later date, the parties acquired a domicile in Scotland, where Hog outlived his wife and died in 1789. After his death, his daughter, as representative of the estate of her mother, claimed one third of the property passing upon death. Such a claim was allowed under the law of Scotland but not that of England.

The House of Lords upheld the claim of the daughter. There are a number of difficulties in the way of determining the *ratio*: (a) was the case one of matrimonial property or succession? (b) were the property rights regulated by the *lex domicilii* at the time of marriage or those pertaining on death? (c) was

---

220 *Re Martin* [1900] P 211.
221 *Estate Frankel v The Master* (1950) 1 SA 220.
222 Adopted in the Civil Law systems of Europe.
223 Adopted in parts of the USA.
224 (1804) 4 Pat 581.
225 [1900] AC 21.

the case authority for the limited proposition that a woman marrying in England where there was no relevant marriage contract would have the property rights arising under the intestacy law of her husband's final domicile? or (d) was the case authority for a general proposition that a change of domicile enhanced the property rights of the wife or carried with it the application of Scottish law to the property relations of husband and wife? It seems obvious that it is difficult to extract a single ratio from the case and that it would be unwise to assert that the case is authority for the principle of mutability.

The subsequent case of *De Nicols v Curlier*[226] is more favourable to the doctrine of immutability; the facts of the case were: a domiciled Frenchman and Frenchwoman married in France without a marriage contract. At a later date, they came to England, where they developed a successful business and acquired an English domicile. On the death of the husband, the widow claimed that movable property was subject to the French law of community of goods.

The House of Lords reversed the Court of Appeal and held that the widow was entitled to claim under French law, notwithstanding the attempt of the husband to dispose of it by will. In the subsequent case of *Re De Nicols (No 2)*,[227] the same approach was extended to immovable property. The House of Lords reasoned that, by marrying in France without the benefit of an express marriage contract, the parties had impliedly accepted the system of *communaute de biens* and that was binding on them, notwithstanding the change of domicile. This was in contrast to the approach of Lord Lindley MR, in the Court of Appeal, who had held that *Lashley v Hog* had established that the wife's rights shifted with the domicile of her husband.[228] So, it would seem that *De Nicols v Curlier* establishes that a change of domicile does not alter the legal position of the parties to a marriage in respect of property. Thus, a change of domicile to a country which, like England, does not have community of property should not be seen as terminating the community arrangement regarding any property acquired after the change. The same reasoning would suggest that a change from a separate property country to a community regime, while not affecting existing property rights, should have the effect of making all subsequent property acquisitions subject to community. This, however, appears not to be the case as it seems that the question is to be asked only at the inception of the marriage.[229]

The cited cases all concern the governing law in respect of movable property; in respect of immovable property, there is some authority for the

226 [1900] AC 21.

227 [1900] 2 Ch 410.

228 *De Nicols v Curlier* [1898] 2 Ch 60, p 70; an approach he was urged to take by AV Dicey QC, who appeared for the daughter.

229 *Re Egerton's Will Trusts* [1956] Ch 593.

view that the *lex situs* constitute the governing law between the parties. Such an approach dates from the House of Lords judgment in *Welch v Tennant*,[230] where the facts were as follows: a husband and wife married in 1877 and were domiciled in Scotland (that is, prior to the Married Woman's Property Act 1882). The wife sold land she owned in England and paid the proceeds to her husband. The parties then separated and the wife claimed the money, arguing that she was so entitled under Scots law. The Court of Session found for the wife.

The House of Lords reversed the decision of the Scottish courts, holding that the governing law in respect of a spouse's immovable property was, in the absence of a contract, to be determined by the *lex situs*. This decision was departed from by Kekewich J, in *Re De Nicols (No 2)*,[231] which was a case on immovable property arising out of the same marriage as had been considered by the House of Lords in *De Nicols v Curlier*. In the later case, the court was concerned with the immovable property purchased by the French couple in England. Kekewich J, following the logic of the earlier House of Lords judgment, held that the immovable property purchased in England was subject to the same implied contract of *communaute de biens* arising when a couple domiciled in France married there. The learned judge dismissed an argument that the contract was unenforceable for non compliance with s 4 of the Statute of Frauds 1677. It is arguable that the wife could have succeeded on the equitable basis that the immovable property was itself acquired out of the movable property that was imposed with the community regime. It is arguable that the case is distinguishable from *Welch v Tennant*, in that, in the latter case, there was no implied contract imposing the community regime. To select the *lex situs* for immovable property and the law of the matrimonial domicile for that of movables can lead to difficulties. It is also possible to argue that the cases can be reconciled by asking whether, at the time of the marriage, it was clear that the regime of community extended beyond the jurisdiction to immovable property elsewhere.[232]

Where there is a marriage contract or settlement

Where a country has a regime of matrimonial property or not, the couple are free to agree one for themselves or to vary one which the law implies. It is sensible to distinguish between (a) an express agreement between the parties as to property rights on marriage; (b) where the parties make no agreement

---

230 [1891] AC 63.

231 [1900] 2 Ch 410.

232 *Welch v Tennant* [1891] AC 63 (unclear whether extended elsewhere); *Chiwell v Carlton* (1897) 14 SC 61 (South African community system extended elsewhere); *Re De Nicols (No 2)* [1900] 2 Ch 410; (French system extended elsewhere); *Callwood v Callwood* [1960] AC 659 (Danish system did not extend elsewhere).

but the law implies a contract of standard terms of community;[233] (c) where there is a marriage settlement involving parties other than the couple marrying and conferring rights on third parties; and (d) cohabitation contracts regulating property rights in the absence of marriage, which are allowed in some countries but are probably not legally enforceable in England and Wales.[234]

It is clear that the validity of an ante-nuptial (or premarital) contract is governed by the law applicable to the contract. An agreement between a prospective husband and wife for, say, joint ownership of all property will be tested by the ordinary law of contract. The applicable law will be determined on the basis of common law principles. The Rome Convention on the Law Applicable to Contractual Obligations 1980, implemented by the Contracts (Applicable Law) Act 1990, does not extend to matrimonial agreements because Art 1(2)(b) excludes contractual obligations relating to 'rights in property arising out of a matrimonial relationship'. Thus, the common law will apply and the contract will be governed by the law expressly or impliedly chosen[235] or, in default thereof, the governing law will be the one with which the contract is most closely connected.[236] In appropriate circumstances, the governing law will be implied;[237] the contract may apply to both movables and immovables.[238]

As with commercial contracts, there are a number of aspects that require consideration. The first point that needs to be made is that, if there is a contract, it will govern the rights of the husband and wife in respect of all property within its terms; whether a particular item of property is within its terms is a question of interpretation to be determined by the proper law.

Formalities

In respect of formalities, it is well established by the authorities that a contract will be valid if it complies with the governing law of the contract[239] or the law of the place where it was made.[240]

---

233 *De Nicols v Curlier* [1900] AC 21.

234 Pawlowski (1996) 146 NLJ 1125.

235 *Re Bankes* [1902] 2 Ch 333.

236 *Duke of Marlborough v AG* [1945] Ch 78.

237 *De Nicols v Curlier* [1900] AC 21.

238 *Re De Nicols* [1950] 2 Ch 410.

239 *Van Grutten v Digby* (1862) 31 Beav 561; 54 ER 1256 (marriage settlement concluded in France did not meet the requirements of French law but was valid under English law as the governing law).

240 *Guepratte v Young* (1851) 4 De G & Sm 217.

Capacity

Although the authorities are by no means conclusive, it can be stated with a reasonable degree of confidence that a person will have capacity to make a marriage contract if that party has capacity under the law of his domicile or by the law of the country with which the contract is most closely connected. This proposition emerges somewhat uncertainly from three cases decided at the turn of the century.[241] The first of these was the first instance judgment in *Re Cooke's Trusts*:[242] a domiciled English girl, aged under 21, entered into a contract in France prior to her marriage to a French nobleman. Subsequently, the couple parted and the woman died domiciled in New South Wales, leaving her property to B by will. Her children sought to set aside the will on the grounds that they had vested property rights under the contract.

Stirling J rejected the claim, holding that, as a minor, the woman had lacked capacity by the law of her ante-nuptial domicile (England) and, under its law, the settlement was void. The force of the decision itself is questionable because less than a decade later, in *Edwards v Carter*[243] (not a case on conflicts of law), the House of Lords ruled that a marriage settlement made by a minor was voidable, not void, in the sense that it is valid unless the minor repudiates it during infancy or within a reasonable period after the attainment of majority.

The second case involving capacity is that of *Cooper v Cooper*,[244] where the facts were as followed: a girl, under the age of 21 and domiciled in Ireland, married a Scotsman in Dublin. By an ante-nuptial agreement, she renounced all rights that a widow might have under Scottish law in return for an annuity. Thirty six years later, after her husband died domiciled in Scotland, she sought to set aside the agreement. The House of Lords, on appeal, held that she was entitled to do so at the age of 54.

Lord Halsbury expressed the view that the contract was void because the woman lacked capacity under Irish law, while Lord Macnaghten considered it to be voidable for the same reason. It seems clear that the woman lacked capacity under her *lex domicilii* at the time of contracting and, also, under the *lex loci contractus* (both being Irish law) but the decision to allow repudiation after 36 years is difficult to reconcile with the subsequent decision in *Edwards v Carter*. Perhaps the only rationalisation is that any subsequent ratification of the agreement by the wife would have been ineffective under Scottish law as a revocable donation between husband and wife. In any event, the tone of the

---

241 *Re Cooke's Trusts* (1887) 56 LT 737 (Stirling J); *Cooper v Cooper* (1888) 13 App Cas 88; *Viditz v O'Hagan* [1900] 2 Ch 87 (Cozens Hardy J, Lindley MR, Rigby and Collins LJJ).
242 (1887) 56 LT 737.
243 [1893] AC 360.
244 (1883) 13 App Cas 88.

judgment is consistent with the view that capacity is governed either by the ante-nuptial domicile or the proper law of the contract.

The earlier case law was considered by the Court of Appeal in *Viditz v O'Hagan*,[245] where the facts were as follows: a domiciled Irish girl, aged under 21, married a domiciled Austrian. She entered into a marriage settlement in English form. Twenty nine years later, when the parties were domiciled in Austria, they tried to revoke the settlement. Revocation was permitted under Austrian law and the plaintiffs sought a declaration that revocation had been effected. Cozens Hardy J refused a declaration and his judgment was reversed by the Court of Appeal.

In giving judgment, Lord Lindley MR asserted that capacity was governed by the proper law of the settlement (English law) and, under that law, the woman lacked capacity to enter into an irrevocable settlement either before or after her marriage and that, by her change of domicile, she lacked the capacity to ratify the earlier agreement; the position was the same as in *Cooper v Cooper*, where the ability to ratify was lost by the change of domicile.

It has to be conceded that the case law is far from categoric and a degree of caution is justified; the three cases, taken together, indicate that capacity to enter into an ante-nuptial agreement is governed either by the law of the ante-nuptial domicile or by the law of the proper law of the agreement.

Essential validity

The interpretation and essential validity of a contract relating to matrimonial property will be governed by its proper law. In cases where there has been no express or implied choice, the law will be that of the legal system with which the contract is most closely connected. It is sometimes said that there is a presumption in favour of the law of the matrimonial domicile, although the evidence may be such as to rebut the presumption. An instance of such a situation is afforded by the case of *Re Bankes*,[246] where the facts were as follows: an English domiciled widow married an Italian domiciled army officer in Italy, in 1878. Prior to the marriage, the woman travelled to Italy and entered into a marriage settlement, covenanting that, after acquired, property would be conveyed to the trustees. The parties separated in 1898 and the question arose as to whether certain legacies received by the widow were to be paid to the trustees. Under Italian law, the settlement was void for non-compliance with rules of formality and also because it attempted to vary mandatory rules as to succession. The trustees sought a declaration as to the validity of the settlement.

---

245 [1900] 2 Ch 87 (Cozens Hardy J, Lindley MR, Rigby and Collins LJJ).
246 [1902] 2 Ch 333 (Buckley J).

Buckley J, in holding that the settlement was valid, ruled that, although there was a presumption in favour of the law of the matrimonial domicile, it was rebutted in this case because the form, language and technical terms all made reference to English law; in addition, the settlor, at the time of execution, had an English ante-nuptial domicile. In these circumstances, Buckley J held that English law was the proper law of the settlement.

The appropriate law to govern an ante-nuptial settlement was considered by the Court of Appeal, in *Duke of Marlborough v AG*,[247] where the court was once again prepared to accept that there was a presumption in favour of the law of the matrimonial domicile; the facts of the case were as follows: in 1895, Charles, the ninth Duke of Marlborough,[248] entered into a marriage settlement prior to his marriage to Consuelo Vanderbilt (who was a minor and the daughter of the very wealthy WK Vanderbilt). The funds comprised entirely American shares: the trustees were both English and American and, in 1896, Chitty J, in the Chancery Division, approved the settlement under the Infant Settlement Act 1855. It was always intended that the parties would reside at Blenheim and thus be domiciled in England. In 1934, the Duke died and the question arose as to the proper law of the settlement. If the proper law were English, then full succession and estate duty would be payable. Vaisey J held that the proper law was English and this determination was upheld in the Court of Appeal.

In considering the case law, it would appear that the English courts are particularly ready to hold that an ante-nuptial marriage settlement is governed by English law; unlike with commercial contracts, the trust is a concept much more familiar to common law jurisdictions and the technical language may clearly indicate England. Notwithstanding this tendency, it has to be admitted that the factors in *Re Bankes* and *Duke of Marlborough v AG* pointing towards English law were particularly strong.

TRUSTS

Introduction

The English concept of the trust is a creation of the system of Equity and does not find its counterpart in the laws of countries outside the common law tradition. The administration of trusts, along with the administration of estates of deceased persons is, as we have seen, one of the exceptions to the refusal of

---

247 *Duke of Marlborough v AG* [1945] Ch 78; 1 All ER 165.

248 Perhaps better known as the cousin of Winston Churchill (1874–1965), himself the son of Jennie Jerome (1854–1921); having regard to the history of the family, there could be no room for doubt as to the intended matrimonial domicile.

jurisdiction in matters of real estate under the *Mocambique* rule. The trusts in these cases are trusts recognised under English law and the law governing their administration is English law as the *lex fori*.

This does not mean that these are not cases involving reference to foreign law; the interpretation of the settlor's intentions may fall to be determined by a foreign law chosen by him or by the law governing the interpretation of the will if the trust is a testamentary one; the status of beneficiaries may raise incidental questions which need to be referred to foreign law and, of course, trust property may be situated abroad.

Although the English trust is commonly used as an example of the problem of classification in the conflict of laws – how can a system classify an institution which does not have its counterpart in the domestic law – there was sufficient interest in the trust to attract the attention of the Hague Conference on Private International Law. At the 15th session of the Conference,[249] delegates adopted a draft Convention on the Law Applicable to Trusts and on their Recognition. It has to be admitted that the title of the Convention is unusual, in that much of the text is concerned with choice of law rules in respect of trusts and only a few provisions are concerned with recognition. The Convention was given effect to within the UK by the Recognition of Trusts Act 1987. From the perspective of the UK, the principal attraction of the Convention was that it would facilitate the recognition of English trusts by other countries' courts.

The Convention 'on the law applicable to trusts and their recognition' substantially gives codified form to the position reached in the English conflict of laws. It enables countries which do not have this particular concept of a trust to apply 'off the peg' choice of law rules and thereby avoid the problems and uncertainty which might otherwise arise when trust property is acquired in a 'non-trust' country and it allows the UK, which has adopted the Convention for internal conflicts, to retain its own internal rules. The Convention does not introduce the concept of the trust into the internal law of a State that does not have it; the Convention merely provides for the recognition of the trust in private international law. Secondly, the Convention does not affect the internal law of those States, like the UK, which have a developed law of trusts.

The Convention defines a trust, in Art 2, in the following terms:

> For the purposes of this Convention, the term 'trust' refers to the legal relationships created – *inter vivos* or on death – by a person, the settlor, when assets have been placed under the control of a trustee for the benefit of a beneficiary or for a specified purpose.

The Article then proceeds to list the characteristics of the trust – the trust assets, constituting a separate fund which is not part of the trustee's estate; the

---

249 October 1984.

title to the trust assets residing in the trustee or in another on his behalf; and the trustee being under an accountable duty to manage, employ or dispose of trust assets in accordance with the terms of the trust or the general law. Finally, the Convention makes it clear that neither the reservation of rights and powers by the settlor nor the fact that the trustee may have rights as a beneficiary are necessarily inconsistent with this concept. Such a definition is broadly in line with the Anglo American approach and 'non-trust' countries should be able to recognise a trust relationship without difficulty.

The Convention applies only to trusts created voluntarily and evidenced in writing[250] but the UK has extended its application to 'any other trusts of property arising under the law of any part of the UK or by virtue of a judicial decision, whether in the UK or elsewhere'.[251] So far as the UK is concerned, 'resulting', 'statutory' and 'constructive' trusts are covered.[252] But, for those countries which adopt the bare Convention, 'statutory' and 'constructive' trusts will not be included, as they are not voluntary, but 'resulting trusts' will if they are evidenced in writing. An 'automatic' resulting trust (one which arises on the failure of the original trust purpose) is included, in so far as the original trust was voluntary, and a 'presumed' resulting trust may fall within the Convention unless it is imposed by the court,[253] that is, is seen as a constructive trust.

Choice of Law

Where the trust is testamentary or has been created *inter vivos*, there is an important preliminary issue, namely, whether the instrument itself is valid. Article 4 of the Convention reads: 'The Convention does not apply to preliminary issues relating to the validity of wills or of other acts by virtue of which assets are transferred to the trustee.' The Convention therefore does not apply to the preliminary issues of of formality, validity or capacity which relate to the instrument of the will or the *inter vivos* settlement; the choice of law rules in respect of the document creating the trust are outside the Convention. In respect of a will, the choice of law rules will be those governing the formal or essential validity of the will. Thus, the settlor cannot use his power under the Convention to determine the validity of the instrument creating the trust. However, there may be issues (for example, the rule against perpetuities and accumulations) where it is unclear whether the

---

250 Hague Convention on the Law Applicable to Trusts and on their Recognition, Art 3.

251 Recognition of Trusts Act 1987, s 1 (2).

252 *Ibid*, s 1 (2).

253 See *Re Vanderwell's Trusts (No 2)* [1974] Ch 269 for classification by Megarry J of resulting trusts into three distinct categories.

rule relates to the instrument (for example, the will) or to the trust provisions arising thereunder.

A trust may be created by a settlor transferring property to trustees to hold for ascertained persons or by the same individual declaring himself to be a trustee in respect of identifiable assets.[254] The effect of Art 4 is to exclude such disputes from the ambit of the Convention. The Convention only applies to trusts which have been set up, whether or not they are valid; it does not relate to earlier acts or transactions, however closely related they are to the establishment of the trust.

The Convention provides that the applicable law shall be that chosen by the settlor, either expressly or by implication. This is stipulated by Art 6, which reads:

> A trust shall be governed by the law chosen by the settlor. The choice must be express or be implied in the terms of the instrument creating or the writing evidencing the trust, interpreted, if necessary, in the light of the circumstances of the case.

The settlor may choose different laws to govern different aspects of the trust. Article 9 provides that 'a severable aspect of the trust, particularly matters of administration, may be governed by a different law'. The settlor could, for example, select the legal system of the country where particular trust assets are situated to govern the operation of the trust with regard to those assets; or he could choose one law for the interpretation of the trust and another for its administration.[255]

Where the settlor has failed to select the applicable law, the Convention provides, in Art 7, that the applicable law shall be that of the country with which the trust is most closely connected and, in ascertaining that law:

> ... reference shall be made, in particular, to:
>
> (a) the place of administration of the trust designated by the settlor;
>
> (b) the *situs* of the assets of the trust;
>
> (c) the place of residence or business of the trustee; and
>
> (d) the objects of the trust and the places where they are to be fulfilled.

Where a settlor chooses an applicable law which does not have a domestic concept of the trust, Art 6 provides that, in such an event, the choice fails and the rules for determining the applicable law in default of choice apply. It is possible that a court considering the matter under Art 7 might still select the applicable law of Country X which has no domestic law of trusts. In such circumstances, Art 5 provides that the Convention ceases to operate and the court is left to whatever other rules that system probably does not have to determine the issue.

---

254 *Richards v Delbridge* (1874) LR 18 Eq 11, p 14, *per* Jessel MR.
255 Hague Convention on the Law Applicable to Trusts and on their Recognition, Art 9.

A legal system may, while not possessing a general law of trusts, recognise particular types of trust, for example, charitable trusts. In that case, the chosen or found applicable law will apply if the substance of the trust is in the recognised category.

Suppose the settlor were to choose the law of a composite State in conflict terms, for example, UK law or US law. The Convention expressly excludes the operation of the doctrine of *renvoi* in Art 17, so reference can be made only to the domestic law of the chosen system. It is arguable whether rules of internal reference within a composite State amount to renvoi anyway and efforts should surely be made to implement the settlor's wishes if at all possible. In the event that localising proves impossible, the choice would have to be disregarded and the rules for the objective discovery of the applicable law applied.

Scope of the applicable law

By the terms of Art 8, the law specified in Arts 6 or 7 shall govern the validity of the trust, its construction, its effects and the administration of the trust. In particular, the law governs:

(a) the appointment, resignation and removal of trustees, the capacity to act as a trustee, and the devolution of the office of trustee;

(b) the rights and duties of the trustees among themselves;

(c) the right of trustees to delegate in whole or in part the discharge of their duties or the exercise of their powers;

(d) the power of trustees to administer or to dispose of trust assets, to create security interests in the trust assets or to acquire new assets;

(e) the powers of investment of trustees;

(f) restrictions upon the duration of the trust and upon the power to accumulate the income of the trust;

(g) the relationship between the trustees and the beneficiaries, including the personal liability of the trustees to the beneficiaries;

(h) the variation or termination of the trust;

(i) the distribution of trust assets; and

(j) the duty of trustees to account for their administration.

The provisions of Art 8 have to be read with Art 10, which provides that the applicable law will also determine whether a change may be made in the law applicable to the whole or part of the trust where, for example, the settlor has empowered the trustees to alter the law governing the trust.

It is desirable that a single law should apply to trust property, regardless of whether it was movable or immovable, save and in so far as the issue is capable of severance. This was the approach at common law, as was illustrated by *Re Fitzgerald*,[256] where the Court of Appeal were prepared to accept that a small sum of money (£500) should be governed by the same proper law of the trust as governed the remaining and substantial immovable property.

The recognition of trusts

The general provisions

Besides the determination of the law applicable to trusts, the Convention's object is to regulate the recognition of trusts, particularly in those States which do not have a domestic law of trusts. With the increases in the mobility of both capital and labour, it is increasingly the case that trust assets and beneficiaries are to be found in civil law countries. It had become increasingly the case that the Anglo American trust might experience difficulty in countries where the concept was unknown; there might be problems with the status of the trustee, beneficiary or settlor and with the distinction between legal and equitable rights. To this end, Art 11 provides for the recognition of trusts and is thus of particular interest to the UK, which is anxious that English trusts secure recognition in other Contracting States. Article 11 provides as follows:

> Such recognition shall imply, as a minimum, that the trust property constitutes a separate fund, that the trustee may sue and be sued in his capacity as a trustee, and that he may appear or act in this capacity before a notary or any person acting in an official capacity;
>
> (a) that personal creditors of the trustee shall have no recourse against the trust assets;
>
> (b) that the trust assets shall not form part of the trustee's estate upon his insolvency or bankruptcy;
>
> (c) that the trust assets shall not form part of the matrimonial property of the trustee or his spouse nor part of the trustee's estate on his death; and
>
> (d) that the trust assets may be recovered when the trustee, in breach of trust, has mingled trust assets with his own property or has alienated trust assets. However, the rights and obligations of any third party holder of the assets shall remain subject to the law determined by the choice of law rules of the forum.

Article 11 therefore provides that a trust created in accordance with the applicable law shall be recognised with the minimum implications that the trust property shall be regarded as a separate fund, that the trustee may sue

---

256 [1904] 1 Ch 573, CA.

and be sued in that capacity, and act in that capacity before notaries and other officials. In addition, if the applicable law of the trust so provides, the recognition implies that personal creditors of the trustee shall not have recourse to the trust assets and that trust assets shall not form part of the trustee's estate on insolvency, bankruptcy or death nor of his or his spouse's matrimonial property.

Where the trustee has mixed trust assets with his own property or otherwise alienated them, the Convention provides that tracing of the trust assets shall not affect third parties beyond what is allowed by the rules of the system indicated by the choice of law rules of the forum. As we have seen, the general rule which English conflicts law shares with other systems is that the property effects of a transfer are governed by the *lex situs* of the property at the time the transfer takes place. The sale of trust assets by a trustee in breach of the terms of the trust will generally transfer title to a purchaser who has no actual or constructive notice of the breach of trust.[257] If the trustee's disposal is not by sale but by gift, there might be a difference between 'trust' and 'non-trust' countries; 'trust' countries, following English law, will not protect the innocent volunteer,[258] whereas 'non-trust' countries may well do so.

If the transferee is aware of the breach of trust, the transaction will not confer good title and both the trustee and the receiver of the trust property may be tortiously liable for fraud – though this would depend on the tort law of the *situs* of the transfer.[259]

Whatever the position regarding tracing, the trustee will remain personally liable for his breach of trust – this action is not dependant on any other law other than the applicable law of the trust itself.

A restriction on recognition is provided by Art 13, which reads:

No State shall be bound to recognise a trust, the significant elements of which, except for the choice of applicable law, the place of administration and and the habitual evidence of the trustee, are more closely connected with States which do not have the institution of the trust or the category of trust involved.

The effect of this provision is to confer a discretion to refuse to recognise a trust if its central elements are more closely connected with a 'non-trust' State. Parliament considered it unnecessary for the courts to have such a discretion;

---

257 See *Sinclair v Brougham* [1914] AC 398; *Re Diplock's Estate* [1948] Ch 465. The principle that emerges from these two cases is that, where there is an initial fiduciary relationship, a beneficiary can trace into the hands of anyone holding the property except a *bona fide* purchaser for value without notice.

258 Unless the remedy itself is inequitable, for example, where trust money has been used to extend a domestic residence – see *Re Diplock's Estate* [1948] Ch 465.

259 Whether a constructive trust is imposed will depend on the state of knowledge; for a discussion of the categories of knowledge, see *Baden, Delvaux and Lecuit v Societe Generale pour Favoriser le Development du Commerce et de l'Industrie en France SA* [1983] BCLC 325 (Peter Gibson J).

this provision is therefore omitted from the Schedule to the Recognition of Trusts Act 1987.

In order to safeguard trust funds and to facilitate the acquisition of trust property in 'non-trust' States, the Convention provides[260] for the trustee to register trust assets as such in the country where they are situated if this is allowed by the law of that country.

The Convention seeks to establish minimum standards, not to curtail the provisions of more generous and developed trust laws. Article 14 of the Convention provides that 'the Convention shall not prevent the application of rules of law more favourable to the recognition of trusts'. If the law of the country concerned, say, as *lex situs* of trust assets, has a more extensive law on trusts than that provided in the Convention, the recognition of the trust under the Convention rules allows access to those more favourable laws.

Exceptions

Where the choice of law rules of the forum indicate a system of law other than the law applicable to the trust (for example, the *lex fori* itself, the personal law or the *lex situs*) to govern certain matters and that law's provisions are mandatory, in the sense that they cannot be derogated from by voluntary act, the Convention does not seek to override these laws. This is provided for under Art 15, which reads:

> The Convention does not prevent the application of provisions of the law designated by the conflicts rules of the forum, in so far as those provisions cannot be derogated from by voluntary act, relating in particular to the following matters:
>
> (a) the protection of minors and incapable parties;
>
> (b) the personal and proprietary effects of marriage;
>
> (c) succession rights, testate and intestate, especially the indefeasible shares of spouses and relatives;
>
> (d) the transfer of title to property and security interests in property;
>
> (e) the protection of creditors in matters of insolvency; and
>
> (f) the protection, in other respects, of third parties acting in good faith.

Article 15 concludes by stating that, where the above exceptions lead to the application of a law which prevents the recognition of the trust, the Convention provides that 'the court shall try to give effect to the objects of the trust by other means'. The purpose of Art 15 is to stipulate that the Convention does not oust mandatory rules; it is designed to ensure the application of the mandatory rules applicable under the forum's conflict rules,

---

260 Hague Convention on the Law Applicable to Trusts and on their Recognition, Art 12.

regardless of what the applicable law of the trust may provide. Where the mandatory rule is of an international nature, then Art 16(1) provides for its application.[261] The article provides that the 'Convention does not prevent the application of those provisions of the law of the forum which must be applied even to international situations, irrespective of the rules of conflict of laws'. Thus, an English court could refuse relief in the case of a beneficiary suing a trustee in respect of failure to export property where such export was prohibited under the *lex fori*.

In common with many international conventions, the Convention provides, in Art 18, that the provisions may be disregarded when their application would be manifestly contrary to public policy.

The Convention applies to all trusts irrespective of the date on which they were created but the Recognition of Trusts Act 1987 makes it clear that the Convention shall not affect the law to be applied in relation to anything done or omitted to be done before the coming into force of the legislation.[262]

The variation of trusts

Section 1 of the Variation of Trusts Act 1958 provides that, where real or personal property is held on trust, the court may, if it thinks fit, approve any arrangement varying or revoking all or any of the trusts, or enlarging the powers of the trustees of managing or administering any of the property subject to the trust. The general purpose of the legislation was to extend the jurisdiction of the court following the restrictive nature of the House of Lords judgment in *Chapman v Chapman*.[263] Prior to 1958, the heads of jurisdiction under which an arrangement might be approved were limited indeed. After 1958, applications would be made to a judge of the Chancery Division to approve an arrangement; the motivation in nearly all cases was to minimise the incidence of capital taxation.

Shortly after the coming into force of the legislation, the question arose as to whether the court had jurisdiction to approve an arrangement where the proper law of the trust was not English. In *Re Ker's Settlement Trusts*,[264]

---

261 The UK has entered a reservation in respect of Art 16(2), so that these provisions do not appear in the Schedule to the Recognition of Trusts Act 1987. Article 16(2) reads: 'If another State has a sufficiently close connection with a case, then, in exceptional circumstances, effect may also be given to rules of that State which have the same character as mentioned in the preceding paragragh.' It was thought unnecessary to incorporate this provision, having regard to the fact that the Court of Equity will not make an order which required performing an act that is unlawful by the place of performance.
262 Recognition of Trusts Act 1987, s 1(5); the legislation came into effect on 1 August 1987.
263 [1954] AC 429.
264 [1963] Ch 553 (Ungoed Thomas J).

Ungoed Thomas J held that the jurisdiction was not restricted to settlements governed by English law. In a subsequent case, Cross J (as he then was) held, in *Re Paget's Settlement*,[265] that the jurisdiction was not confined to those settlements where the proper law was English. The learned judge reasoned that to accept such a restriction would mean that a trust established in Australia in 1920 could not be varied by an English court if the trustees and all the beneficiaries were resident in England.In an oft cited passage, the judge explained:

> Where there are substantial foreign elements in the case, the court must consider carefully whether it is proper for it to exercise the jurisdiction. If, for example, the court were asked to vary a settlement which was plainly a Scottish settlement, it might well hesitate to exercise its jurisdiction to vary the trusts simply because some, or even all, the trustees and beneficiaries were in this country. It may well be that the judge would say that the Court of Session was the appropriate tribunal to deal with the case.[266]

The question logically arises as to the effect of the Hague Convention on the Law Applicable to Trusts and their Recognition 1986; it is clear from Art 8(h) that a matter concerning 'the variation or termination of the trust' should be governed by the applicable law and not by the law of the forum. A number of points can be made. First, the object of the Variation of Trusts Act 1958 was to extend the jurisdiction of the English court, whereas Art 8 of the Hague Convention operates as a choice of law provision. Secondly, the English courts had already recognised that there might be circumstances where jurisdiction should be declined. Thirdly, as a matter of principle, it would seem that, when an application is made to approve an arrangement, the English court should apply the proper law; if, under that law, the arrangement would not be permitted, then the application should be rejected.

A second area of variation that has attracted attention since 1958 is when an application has been made to an English court to 'export a trust'. Normally, the application takes the form of an application to appoint foreign trustees subject to a like trust instrument and then for the transfer of assets by the English trustees. The English courts have long had power to appoint foreign trustees of an English settlement[267] and they have been prepared, in appropriate cases, to countenance such arrangements. In *In re Seale's Marriage Settlement*,[268] Buckley J approved the appointment of a Canadian corporation as trustee and the transfer of the trust assets by the English trustee. In this case, there was a clear financial benefit and the parties intended to live the remainder of their life in Canada, where there was a well developed system of

---

265 [1965] 1 WLR 1046 (Corss J).

266 [1965] 1 WLR 1046, p 1050.

267 *Meinertzhagen v Davis* (1844) 1 Coll 335; *In re Liddard* (1880) 14 Ch D 310; *In re Freeman's Settlement Trusts* (1888) 37 Ch D 148; *In re Simpson* [1897] 1 Ch 256, CA.

268 [1961] Ch 574.

equity. That the discretion will depend on the precise facts was evidenced by the judgment of the Court of Appeal in *In re Weston's Settlements*,[269] where the facts were as follows: a settlement was established in 1964. After the introduction of capital gains tax in 1965, the settlor removed to Jersey with his two sons. Shortly after, an application was made to appoint Jersey trustees and to reconstitute the trust under Jersey law. The application was refused by Stamp J and the Court of Appeal.

Although the reasons of the judges differed, a common theme in the judgments was that an English court should be slow to exercise its discretion where the parties had only a limited connection with the country of transfer. Lord Denning MR doubted[270] whether the arrangement could be shown to be for the benefit of the beneficiaries, while Harman LJ emphasised that the approval of foreign trustees is a matter of discretion not of right. That the connection with the country of transfer must be well established and normally irrevocable was stressed by Pennycuick J in *In re Windeatt's Will Trusts*,[271] where he approved a transfer of trust assets to Jersey to benefit a life tenant who had lived there for 19 years at the time of application.

The effect of such applications is that the governing law of the trust will be changed when a successful application is made to constitute a foreign trust; however, this is consistent with Art 10 of the Hague Convention, which provides that 'the law applicable to the validity of the trust shall determine whether that law or the law governing a severable aspect of the trust may be replaced by another law'.

---

269 [1969] 1 Ch 223 (Stamp J, Denning MR, Harman and Dankwerts LJJ).

270 Lord Denning also doubted whether the parties would remain in Jersey for long. In this case, the objective was to avoid capital gains tax on any disposal; in most applications, the object is to avoid income tax or inheritance tax/estate duty, where it is normally necessary to remain out of England on a permanent basis. The learned judge drew a distinction between removing to another country to start a fresh life and removing to a tax haven to avoid taxation. At p 245, he observed: 'There are many things in life more worthwhile than money ... I do not believe it is for the benefit of children to be uprooted from England and transported to another country simply to avoid tax.'

271 [1969] 1 WLR 692.

BIBLIOGRAPHY

Abbott, E, 'Is *renvoi* part of the common law?' (1908) 24 LQR 133

Albrecht, A, 'The enforcement of taxation under international law' (1950) 30 BYIL 454

Allen, CK, 'Status and capacity' (1930) 46 LQR 277

Anton, A, 'The introduction into English practice of continental theories as to the conflict of laws' (1956) 5 ICLQ 534

Annand, R, 'The Law of Property (Miscellaneous Provisions) Act 1989' (1989) 105 LQR 553

Atiyah, P, *The Rise and Fall of Freedom of Contract*, 1979, Oxford: OUP

Baker, PV and Langan, P, *Snell's Equity*, 29th edn, 1990, London: Sweet & Maxwell

Bartholomew, GW, 'Polygamous marriages' (1952) 15 MLR 35

Bartin, E, *'De l'imposibilité d'arriver à la suppression definitive des conflits de lois'* [1897] Clunet 225 ['On the impossibility of arriving at the definite suppression of the conflict of laws']; see, also, [1891] Clunet 1171

Bartlett, L, 'Full faith and credit comes to the Common Market' (1975) 25 ICLQ 44

Baxter, I, 'International business and choice of law' (1987) 36 ICLQ 92

Beale, JH, 'What law governs the validity of the contract?' (1909) 23 HLR 1

Beale, J, *The Conflict of Laws*, 1935, New York: Baker, Voorhis

Beck, A, 'A South African homeland appears in the English courts' (1987) 36 ICLQ 350

Beckett, WE, 'The recognition of polygamous marriages under English law' (1932) 48 LQR 341

Beckett, WE, 'International law in England' (1939) 55 LQR 270

Beckett, WE, 'The question of classification in private international law' (1939) 15 BYIL 46

Beckett, WE, 'Consular immunities' (1944) 21 BYIL 34

Bell, A, *Modern Law of Personal Property in England and Ireland*, 1989, London: Butterworths

Bennett, TJ, 'The Draft Convention on the Law Applicable to Contractual Obligations' (1980) 17 CMLR 269

Bentley, L and Coughlin, P, 'Informal dealings with land after s 2' (1990) 10 LS 325

Berkovits, B, 'Transnational divorces – the *Fatima* decision' (1988) 104 LQR 60

Blackstone, W, *Commentaries on the Laws of England*, 1765, Oxford: Clarendon

Bloch, M, *Feudal Society*, 1961, London: Routledge

Blythe, M, 'The extra-territorial impact of the anti-trust laws' (1983) 31 AJCL 99

Bowles, R and Phillips, J, 'Judgments in foreign currencies: an economist's view' (1976) 39 MLR 196

Bowles, R and Whelan, C, 'Judgments in foreign currencies: extension of the *Miliangos* rule' (1979) 42 MLR 452

Briggs, A, 'Forum non conveniens – now we are ten' (1983) 3 LS 74

Briggs, A, 'Polygamous marriages and English domiciliaries' (1983) 32 ICLQ 737

Briggs, A, 'Which foreign judgments should we recognise today?' (1987) 36 ICLQ 240

Briggs, A, 'Restraint of foreign proceedings' [1987] LMCLQ 391

Briggs, A, 'Forum non conveniens and the Brussels Convention again' (1991) 107 LQR 180

Briggs, A, 'Jurisdiction over restitutionary claims' [1992] LMCLQ 283

Briggs, A, 'The international dimension to claims for contribution' [1995] LMCLQ 437

Briggs, A, 'Choice of law in tort and delict' [1995] LMCLQ 519

Briggs, A, 'The Halley – holed but still afloat?' (1995) 111 LQR 18

Briggs, A, 'The unrestrained reach of an anti-suit injunction: a pause for thought' [1997] LMCLQ 90

Briggs, A, 'Two undesirable side effects of the Brussels Convention?' (1997) 113 LQR 364

Bromley, PM, Bromley's Family Law, 7th edn, 1987, London: Butterworths

Brownlie, I, 'Recognition in theory and practice' (1982) 53 BYIL 197

Brownlie, I, Principles of Public International Law, 4th edn, 1990, Oxford: OUP

Bryan, M, 'The mistress and the multiplier' (1980) 96 LQR 165

Calder, R, Willie: The Life of W Somerset Maugham, 1989, London: Heinemann

Carswell, R, 'The doctrine of vested rights in private international law' (1959) 8 ICLQ 268

Carter, PB, 'Foreign torts' (1970) 44 BYIL 222

Carter, PB, 'Note on Sayers v International Drilling Co NV' (1971) 45 BYIL 404

Carter, PB, 'Note on Black Clawson Ltd v Papierwerke AE (1975)' (1975) 47 BYIL 381

Carter, PB, 'Jurisdiction over foreign immovables' (1978) 49 BYIL 286

Carter, PB, 'Transfers inter vivos of movable property' (1981) 52 BYIL 329

Carter, PB, 'Rejection of foreign law: some private international law inhibitions' (1984) 55 BYIL 111

Carter, PB, 'Classification of a marriage: note on Hussain v Hussain' (1982) 53 BYIL 298

Carter, PB, 'The Foreign Limitation Periods Act 1984' (1985) 101 LQR 68

Carter, PB, 'Capacity to remarry after a foreign decree' (1985) 101 LQR 496

Carter, PB, 'Domicile: the case for radical reform in the United Kingdom' (1987) 36 ICLQ 71

Carter, PB, 'Jurisdiction to restrain foreign proceedings' (1988) 59 BYIL 342

Carter, PB, 'Transnational recognition and enforcement of foreign laws' [1989] CLJ 417

Carter, PB, 'Choice of law in tort and delict' (1991) 107 LQR 405

Carter, PB, 'The role of public policy in English private international law' (1993) 42 ICLQ 1

Carter, PB, 'Choice of law in tort: the role of the *lex fori*' [1995] CLJ 38

Carter, PB, 'The Private International Law (Miscellaneous Provisions) Act 1995' (1996) 112 LQR 190

Cavers, DF, *The Choice of Law Process*, 1965, Ann Arbor: Michigan UP

Cavers, DF, 'A critique of the choice of law process' (1933) 47 HLR 173

Cavers, DF, 'The two "local law" theories' (1950) 63 HLR 822

Cheatham, E, 'American theories of conflict of laws – their role and utility' (1945) 58 HLR 361

Cheshire, GC, *Private International Law*, 1st edn, 1935, Oxford: OUP

Cheshire, GC, North, P and Fawcett, J, *Cheshire and North's Private International Law*, 12th edn, 1992, London: Butterworths

Clarence Smith, J, 'Torts and the conflict of laws' (1957) 20 MLR 446

Clarkson C, 'Marriage in England: favouring the *lex fori*' (1990) 10 LS 80

Clarkson, C and Hill, J, *Jaffey on the Conflict of Laws*, 1997, London: Butterworths

Cohn, EJ, 'Submission to foreign jurisdiction' (1972) 21 ICLQ 157

Collier, JG, *Conflict of Laws*, 2nd edn, 1987, Cambridge: CUP

Collier, JG, 'Foreign court orders on status' [1962] CLJ 36

Collier, JG and Sealy, L, 'The European Communities Act 1972' [1973] CLJ 1

Collier, JG, 'Foreign judgments: enforcement at common law' [1975] CLJ 219

Collier, JG, 'Public policy and foreign judgments' [1984] CLJ 47

Collier, JG, 'Foreign divorces and capacity to marry' [1985] CLJ 378

Collier, JG, 'Conflict of laws and the enforcement of foreign public laws' [1989] CLJ 33

Collins, L, *The Civil Jurisdiction and Judgments Act 1982*, 1983, London: Butterworths

Collins, L, *Dicey and Morris: The Conflict of Laws*, 12th edn, 1993, London: Sweet & Maxwell

Collins, L, *Essays in International Litigation and the Conflict of Laws*, 1994, Oxford: Clarendon

Collins, L, 'Interaction between contract and tort in the conflict of laws' (1967) 16 ICLQ 103

Collins, L, 'Exemption clauses, employment contracts and the conflict of laws' (1972) 21 ICLQ 320

Collins, L, 'Some aspects of service out of the jurisdiction in English law' (1972) 21 ICLQ 656

Collins, L, '*Harris v Taylor* revived' (1976) 92 LQR 268

Collins, L, 'Contractual obligations – the EEC Draft Convention on Private International Law' (1976) 25 ICLQ 35

Collins, L, 'Note on *Re Harrods (Buenos Aires) Ltd*' (1990) 106 LQR 535

Cook, WW, 'The logical and legal bases of the conflict of laws' (1924) 33 YLJ 457

Cook, WW, *Logical and Legal Bases of the Conflict of Laws*, 2nd edn, 1942, Cambridge, Mass: Harvard UP

Cosgrove, R, *The Rule of Law: The life of Albert Venn Dicey*, 1980, London: Macmillan

Crane, FR, 'Casenote on *Pascoe v Turner* (1979)' [1979] Conv 379

Crawford, J, 'The effect of non-recognition; the effect of *Gur Corporation*' (1986) 57 BYIL 405

Cretney, S, 'Foreign divorces – the other side of the coin' (1972) 116 SJ 1121

Cretney, S, 'Immigrants' marriages' (1972) 116 SJ 654

Cretney, S, 'The Nullity of Marriage Act 1971' (1972) 35 MLR 57

Currie, B, *Selected Essays on the Conflict of Laws*, 1963, Durham, NC: Duke UP

Currie, B, 'Comments on *Babcock v Jackson*' (1963) 63 Col L Rev 1233

Dicey, AV, *An Introduction to the Study of the Law of the Constitution*, 10th edn, 1959, London: Macmillan

Dicey, AV, *The Conflict of Laws*, 1st edn, 1896, London: Stevens

Dicey, AV, *The Conflict of Laws*, 6th edn, 1949, Morris, JH *et al* (eds), London: Stevens

Dicey, AV and Morris, JH, *A Digest of the Laws of England with Reference to the Conflict of Laws*, 9th edn, 1973, London: Stevens

Dicey, AV and Morris, JH, *A Digest of the Laws of England with Reference to the Conflict of Laws*, 10th edn, 1980, London: Stevens

Dicey, AV and Morris, JH, *A Digest of the Laws of England with Reference to the Conflict of Laws*, 11th edn, 1987, Collins, L *et al* (eds), London: Stevens

Dicey, AV and Morris, JH, *A Digest of the Laws of England with Reference to the Conflict of Laws*, 12th edn, 1993, Collins, L *et al* (eds), London: Sweet & Maxwell

Dobrin, S, 'The English doctrine of the *renvoi*' (1934) 15 BYIL 36

D'Oliviera, M, 'Characteristic obligation in the Draft EEC Obligation Convention' (1977) 25 AJCL 303

Ehrenzweig, A, *Treatise on the Conflict of Laws*, 1962, St Pauls, Minn: West

Ehrenzweig, A, 'Beale's translation of Bartolus' (1963) 12 AJCL 384

Elphinstone, H, 'Notes on the English law of marriage' (1889) 5 LQR 44

Falconbridge,JD, 'Characterisation in the conflict of laws' (1937) 53 LQR 235

Falconbridge, JD, 'Conflicts rules and the characterisation of question' (1952) 30 Can Bar Rev 103

Falconbridge, JD, *Selected Essays in the Conflict of Laws*, 2nd edn, 1954, Toronto: Canada Law Book

Farrar, J and Powles, DG, 'The effect of s 9 of the European Communities Act 1972 on company law' (1973) 36 MLR 270

Fawcett, J, 'Result selection in domicile cases' (1985) 5 OJLS 378

Fawcett, J, 'Law Commission Working Paper No 88, *The Law of Domicile*' (1986) 49 MLR 224

Fawcett, J, 'A new approach to jurisdiction over companies in private international law' (1988) 37 ICLQ 645

Fawcett, J, 'Trial in England or abroad – the underlying policy considerations' (1989) 9 OJLS 205

Fawcett, J, 'Evasion of law and mandatory rules in private international law' [1990] CLJ 44

Fawcett, J, 'The interrelationship of jurisdiction and choice of law in private international law' (1991) 44 CLP 39

Fentiman, R, 'The validity of marriage and the proper law' [1985] CLJ 256

Fentiman, R, 'Activity in the law of status: domicile, marriage and the Law Commission' (1986) 6 OJLS 353

Fentiman, R, 'Tort – jurisdiction or choice of law' [1989] CLJ 191

Fentiman, R, ' Domicile revisited' [1991] CLJ 445

Fentiman, R, 'Foreign law in English courts' (1992) 108 LQR 142

Fentiman, R, 'Anti-suit injunctions and the appropriate forum' [1996] CLJ 46

Foster, N, *German Legal System and Laws*, 2nd edn,1996, London: Blackstone

Forsyth, C, 'Expropriatory legislation – recognition and enforcement' [1985] CLJ 376

Forsyth, C, 'Characterisation revisited' (1998) 114 LQR 141

Furmston, M, *Cheshire, Fifoot and Furmston's The Law of Contract*, 12th edn, 1991, London: Butterworths

Galliard, E and Trautman, D, 'Trusts in non-trust countries: conflict of laws and the Hague Convention on Trusts' (1987) 35 AJCL 307

Giuliano, M and Lagarde, P, *Report on the Rome Convention*, OJ C 282, 1980

Gotlieb, A, 'The incidental question in the Anglo American conflict of laws' (1955) 33 Can Bar Rev 523

Gotlieb, A, 'The incidental question revisited' (1977) 26 ICLQ 734

Graveson, RH, 'Reform of the law of domicile' (1954) 70 LQR 492

Graveson, RH, 'Domicile on the ending of dependence' (1957) 6 ICLQ 1

Graveson, RH, 'The 10th Session of the Hague Conference on Private International Law' (1965) 14 ICLQ 528

Graveson, RH, 'Towards a modern applicable law in tort' (1969) 85 LQR 505

Graveson, RH, *Conflict of Laws: Private International Law*, 7th edn, 1974, London: Sweet & Maxwell

Griswold, E, '*Renvoi* revisited' (1938) 51 HLR 1165

Grodecki, JK, 'Conflicts of law in time' (1959) 35 BYIL 58

Grodecki, JK, 'The status of incompetency' (1962) 11 ICLQ 578

Guest, AL, 'Public policy and contracts entailing a breach of law in a foreign country' (1957) 73 LQR 32

Gutteridge, H, 'Reciprocity in regard to foreign judgments' (1932) 13 BYIL 49

Gutteridge, H, 'A new approach to private international law' (1936) 6 CLJ 16

Hall, JC, 'The Nullity of Marriage Act 1971' [1971] CLJ 208

Hall, JC, 'Common law marriages' [1987] CLJ 106

Hall, JC, 'Defiance of a foreign custody order' [1989] CLJ 189

Harris, J, 'Restraint of foreign proceedings – the view from the other side of the fence' [1997] CJQ 283

Harris, J, 'Choice of law in tort – blending in with the landscape of the conflict of laws' (1998) 61 MLR 33

Hartley, T, 'Bigamy in the conflict of laws' 16 ICLQ 680

Hartley, T, 'Note on Case 166/80 *Klomps v Michel* [1983] ECR 1593' (1983) 7 EL Rev 419

Hartley, T, 'Polygamy and Social Policy' (1969) 32 MLR 155

Hartley, T, 'The Law Commission, *Report on Polygamous Marriages*' (1971) 34 MLR 305

Hartley, T, 'Policy basis of the English conflict of laws on marriage' (1972) 35 MLR 571

Hartley, T, 'Note on Case 42/76 *De Wolf v Cox*' (1977) 2 EL Rev 146

Hartley, T, *Civil Jurisdiction and Judgments*, 1984, London: Sweet & Maxwell

Hartley, T, 'Note on Case 145/86 *Hoffmann v Krieg*' (1991) 16 EL Rev 64

Hayton, D, 'The law applicable to trusts and on their recognition' (1987) 36 ICLQ 260

Hood Phillips, O, 'Dicey's *Law of the Constitution*' [1985] PL 587

Hopkins, N, 'The Trusts of Land and Appointment of Trustees Act 1996' [1996] Conv 411

Howard, A, *Crossman: The Pursuit of Power*, 1990, London: Cape

Howard, MN, *Phipson on Evidence*, 14th edn, 1990, London: Sweet & Maxwell

Huber, U, *Praelectiones Juris Romani et Hodierni*, 1689, Holland, '*De Conflictu Legum Diversarum in Diversis Imperiis*', Vol II, Bk I*

Hughes, AD, 'Redundancy payments and the conflict of laws' (1967) 83 LQR 180

Hunter, M, 'The Draft Bankruptcy Convention of the EEC' (1972) 21 ICLQ 682

Hunter, M, 'The Draft EEC Bankruptcy Convention: a further examination' (1976) 26 ICLQ 310

Huntley, A, 'The Protection of Trading Interests Act 1980' (1981) 30 ICLQ 213

---

* The text of '*De Conflictu Legum …*' was first translated into English by Alexander Dallas in 1797 for the purpose of *Emory v Greeenough* (1797) 3 Dallas 369, a case before the US Supreme Court. The work was then incorporated into the text of Story, *Commentaries on the Conflict of Laws*. The original Latin text was included in the second edition of William Guthrie's translation of Savigny (see below), which appeared in 1880.

Inglis, B, 'Judicial process in the conflict of laws' (1958) 74 LQR 493

Jaffey, A, 'Recognition of a defendant's foreign judgment' (1975) 38 MLR 385

Jaffey, A, 'The essential validity of marriage in the English conflict of laws' (1978) 41 MLR 38

Jaffey, A, 'Choice of law in tort: a justice based approach' (1982) 2 LS 98

Jaffey, A, 'The foundation of rules for the choice of law' (1982) 2 OJLS 368

Jaffey, A, 'Recognition of foreign nullity decrees' (1983) 32 ICLQ 500

Jaffey, A, 'The English proper law doctrine and the EEC Convention' (1984) 33 ICLQ 531

Jaffey, A, 'The incidental question and capacity to remarry' (1985) 48 MLR 465

Jaffey, A, *Introduction to the Conflict of Laws*, 1st edn, 1988, London: Butterworths

James RD, 'Polygamy and capacity to marry' (1979) 42 MLR 533

Jones, RL, 'The Council of Europe Convention' (1980) 30 ICLQ 467

Juenger, FK, 'Conflict of laws: a critique of interest analysis' (1984) 32 AJCL 1

Karsten, I, 'Child marriages' (1969) 32 MLR 212

Karsten, I, '*Chaplin v Boys*: another analysis' (1970) 19 ICLQ 35

Karsten, I, 'Capacity to contract a polygamous marriage' (1973) 36 MLR 291

Kaye, P, *Civil Jurisdiction and Enforcement of Foreign Judgments*, 1987, London: Dartmouth

Kaye, P, 'The *situs* of debts and jurisdiction to make orders of garnishee' [1989] JBL 449

Kaye, P, 'The EEC judgments convention and the outer world: goodbye to *forum non conveniens*' [1992] JBL 4

Keane, A, *The Modern Law of Evidence*, 4th edn, 1996, London, Butterworths

Khan, F, '*Gesetzkollisionen*' (1891) 30 Ihering's Jahrbucher 1

Khan Freund, O, '*Locus regit actum*' (1946) 7 MLR 238

Khan Freund, O, 'The Wills Act 1963' (1964) 27 MLR 55

Knott, JA, 'Foreign currency judgments in tort: an illustration of the wealth time continuum' (1980) 43 MLR 18

Kunzlik, PF, 'Staying and restraining actions: the application and limits of *forum non conveniens*' [1987] CLJ 406

Kunzlik, PF, 'Dual residence and domicile of choice' [1988] CLJ 187

Lando, O, 'The EEC Convention on the Law Applicable to Contractual Obligations' (1987) 24 CMLR 159

Lane, S, 'Free movement of judgments within the EEC' (1986) 35 ICLQ 629

Lasok, D and Bridge, J, *Law and Institutions of the European Community*, 5th edn, 1991, London: Butterworths

Lasok, D and Stone, P, *Conflict of Laws in the European Community*, 1987, London: Professional

Law Commission Report No 33, *Report on Nullity of Marriage*, 1970, London: HMSO

Law Commission Report No 34, *Report on the Recognition of Divorces and Legal Separations*, 1970, London: HMSO

Law Commission Report No 42, *Report on Polygamous Marriages*, 1971, London: HMSO

Law Commission Report No 48, *Report on Jurisdiction in Matrimonial Causes*, 1972, London: HMSO

Law Commission Report No 114, *Classification of Limitation in Private International Law*, 1982, London: HMSO

Law Commission Report No 124, *Report on Private International Law: Foreign Money Liabilities*, 1983, London: HMSO

Law Commission Report No 137, *Report on Recognition of Foreign Nullity Decrees and Related Matters*, 1984, London: HMSO

Law Commission Report No 146, *Report on Polygamous Marriages – Capacity to Contract a Polygamous Marriage and Related Issues*, 1985, London: HMSO

Law Commission Report No 165, *Report on Choice of Law Rules in Marriage*, 1987, London: HMSO

Law Commission Report No 168, *Report on Private International Law: the Law of Domicile*, 1987, London: HMSO

Law Commission Report No 170, *Facing the Future: a Discussion Paper on the Grounds for Divorce*, 1988, London: HMSO

Law Commission Report No 172, *Review of Child Law, Guardianship and Custody*, 1986, London: HMSO

Law Commission Report No 193, *Private International Law: Choice of Law in Tort and Delict*, 1990, London: HMSO

Law Commission Working Paper No 75, *Classification of Limitation in Private International Law*, 1980, London: HMSO

Law Commission Working Paper No 80, *Foreign Money Liabilities*, 1981, London: HMSO

Law Commission Working Paper No 87, *Private International Law: Choice of Law in Tort and Delict*, 1984, London: HMSO

Law Commission Working Paper No 88, *The Law of Domicile*, 1985, London: HMSO

Law Commission Working Paper No 89, *Choice of Law Rules in Marriage*, 1985, London: HMSO

Law Commission Working Paper No 91, *Guardianship*, 1985, London: HMSO

Law Reform Committee, *Evidence of Opinion and Expert Evidence*, Cmnd 4489, 1970, London: HMSO

Laws, J, 'Is the High Court the guardian of fundamental constitutional rights?' [1993] PL 59

Leflar, RA, *Cases and Materials on American Conflicts Law*, 1982, Charlottesville, Virginia: Michie

Lipstein, K, '*Bona vacantia* and *ultimus heres*' [1954] CLJ 22

Lipstein, K, 'The 10th Session of the Hague Conference on Private International Law' (1965) 14 ICLQ 528

Lipstein, K, 'The conflict of laws (1921–71) – the way ahead' [1972] CLJ 67

Lipstein, K, 'The Evidence (Proceedings in Other Jurisdictions) Act 1975: an introduction' (1990) 39 ICLQ 120

Lloyd Jones, D, 'Conflict of laws – trespass to foreign land' [1978] CLJ 48

Lloyd Jones, D, 'Protection of Trading Interests Act 1980' [1981] CLJ 41

Locke, J, *Two Treatises of Government* (1689), 1967, Laslett, P (ed), Cambridge: CUP

Lorenzen, E, 'The *renvoi* doctrine and the application of foreign law' (1910) 10 Col L Rev 190

Lorenzen, E, 'The *renvoi* doctrine in the conflict of laws – meaning of law of a country' (1918) 27 YLJ 509

Lorenzen, E, *Selected Articles on the Conflict of Laws*, 1947, New Haven: Yale UP

Lowe, AV, 'Blocking extra-territorial jurisdiction' (1981) 75 AJIL 257

Lucas, P, 'Common law marriage' [1990] CLJ 117

Lysyk, K, 'Unity of domicile' (1965) 43 Can Bar Rev 107

Mann, FA, 'Any civil or commercial matter' (1986) 102 LQR 505

Mann, FA, 'Contract conflicts: a review' (1983) 32 ICLQ 265

Mann, FA, 'Extra-territorial effects of confiscations and expropriations' (1950) 13 MLR 69

Mann, FA, 'Illegality and the conflict of laws' (1958) 21 MLR 130

Mann, FA, 'International delinquencies before municipal courts' (1954) 70 LQR 181

Mann, FA, 'Legitimation and adoption in private international law' (1941) 57 LQR 112

Mann, FA, 'Note on *Miliangos v George Frank (Textiles) Ltd*' (1976) 92 LQR 165

Mann, FA, 'Outlines of a history of expropriation' (1959) 75 LQR 188

Mann, FA, 'Proper law and illegality in private international law' (1939) 18 BYIL 97

Mann, FA, '*Spycatcher* in the High Court of Australia' (1988) 104 LQR 497

Mann, FA, *Studies in International Law*, 1973, Oxford: OUP

Mann, FA, 'The confiscation of corporations, corporate rights and corporate assets in the conflict of laws' (1962) 11 ICLQ 471

Mann, FA, 'The effect in England of the compulsory acquisition by a foreign State of shares in a foreign company' (1986) 102 LQR 191

Mann, FA, 'The effect in England of the compulsory acquisition by a foreign State of shares in a foreign company' (1987) 103 LQR 26

Mann, FA, 'The judicial recognition of an unrecognised State' (1987) 36 ICLQ 348

Mann, FA, 'The primary question of construction and the conflict of laws' (1963) 79 LQR 525

Mann, FA, 'The proper law in the conflict of laws' (1986) 36 ICLQ 437

Mann, FA, 'The proper law of the contract – an obituary' (1991) 107 LQR 353

Mann, FA, 'The Redundancy Payments Act 1965 and the conflict of laws' (1966) 82 LQR 316

Mann, FA, 'The sacrosanctity of the foreign act of State' (1943) 59 LQR 42

Mann, FA, 'The time element in the conflict of laws' (1954) 31 BYIL 217

Mann, M, 'Foreign revenue laws and the English conflict of laws' (1954) 3 ICLQ 465

Mann, M, 'The Seventh Report of the Private International Law Committee' (1963) 12 ICLQ 1326

Martin, J, 'Note on Inheritance (Provision for Family and Dependants) Act 1975' [1989] Conv 43

Martin, J, 'Note on Inheritance (Provision for Family and Dependants) Act 1975' [1992] Conv 438

McGregor, H, 'The international accident problem' (1970) 33 MLR 1

Mclachlan, C, 'Splitting the proper law in private international law' (1990) 51 BYIL 311

Merrills, J, 'Trespass to foreign land' (1979) 28 ICLQ 523

Mersinghe, L, 'The modern law of sovereign immunity' (1991) 54 MLR 664

Miller, JG, 'Provision for a surviving spouse' (1986) 102 LQR 445

Morris, JH, *The Conflict of Laws*, 4th edn, 1993, London: Butterworths

Morris, JH and North, P, *Cases and Materials on Private International Law*, 1984, London: Butterworths

Morris, JH, *The Conflict of Laws by Lawrence Collins and others*, 12th edn, 1993, London: Sweet & Maxwell

Morris, JH, 'The law of the domicile' (1937) 18 BYIL 32

Morris, JH, 'The transfer of chattels in the conflict of laws' (1945) 22 BYIL 232

Morris, JH, 'Note on *Re Priest*' (1945) 61 LQR 114

Morris, JH, 'Note on *Re Cohn*' (1945) 61 LQR 340

Morris, JH, 'The choice of law clause in statutes' (1946) 62 LQR 172

Morris, JH, 'Note on *Re Bischoffsheim*' (1948) 12 Conv (NS) 22

Morris, JH, 'Torts in the conflict of laws' (1949) 12 MLR 248

Morris, JH, 'The proper law of a tort' (1951) 64 HLR 881

Morris, JH, 'The Wills Act 1963' (1964) 13 ICLQ 684

Morse, C, 'Choice of law in tort: a comparative survey' (1983) 32 AJCL 51

Morse, C, 'Tort, employment contracts and the conflict of laws' (1984) 33 ICLQ 449

Morse, C, 'Products liability in the conflict of laws' (1989) 42 CLP 167

Morse, C, 'Consumer contracts, employment contracts and the Rome Convention' (1992) 41 ICLQ 1

Morse, C, 'Letters of credit and the Rome Convention' [1994] LMCLQ 560

Morse, C, 'Torts in private international law: a new statutory framework' (1996) 45 ICLQ 888

Morton Commission, *Morton Commission Report on Marriage and Divorce*, Cmnd 9678, 1956, London: HMSO

Nadelman, K, 'The outer world and the Common Market: experts' Draft of a Convention on the Recognition of Judgments' (1967) 5 CMLR 409

Nadelman, K, 'Jurisdictionally improper *fora* in treaties on the recognition of judgments' (1967) 64 Col L Rev 995

Nadelman, K, 'Nationality versus domicile' (1969) 17 AJCL 418

North, P, 'Recognition of foreign divorce decrees' (1968) 31 MLR 257

North, P and Webb, PH, 'Foreign torts and the English courts' (1970) 19 ICLQ 24

North, P, 'Contract as a tort defence in the conflict of laws' (1977) 26 ICLQ 914

North, P, 'The EEC Convention on the Law Applicable to Contractual Obligations' [1980] JBL 382

Nott, S, 'Title to movables acquired abroad' [1981] Conv 279

Nott, S, 'Title to illegally exported items of historic or artistic worth' (1983) 33 ICLQ 203

Oakley, AJ, 'The Trusts of Land and Appointment of Trustees Act 1996' [1996] Conv 401

O'Connell, DP, 'A critique of the *Iranian Oil* litigation' (1955) 4 ICLQ 267

Pawlowski, M, 'Cohabitation contracts – are they legal ?' (1996) 146 NLJ 1125

Pearl, D, 'Muslim marriage in English law' [1972] CLJ 120

Pearl, D, 'Capacity for polygamy' [1973] CLJ 43

Pearl, D, 'Family Law Act 1986, Pt II' [1983] CLJ 26

Pettit, PH, 'Farewell s 40' [1989] Conv 431

Pettit, PH, 'Demise of trusts for sale and the doctrine of conversion?' (1997) 113 LQR 207

Pilkington, M, 'Transnational divorces under the Family Law Act 1986' (1988) 37 ICLQ 131

Pollak, W, 'Domicile' (1933) 50 SALJ 449

Pollak, W, 'Domicile' (1934) 51 SALJ 1

Posnak, B, 'Choice of law: interest analysis and its "new crits"'(1988) 36 AJCL 681

Poulter, S, '*Hyde v Hyde* – a reappraisal' (1976) 25 ICLQ 475

Poulter, S, 'Ethnic minority customs, English law and human rights' (1987) 36 ICLQ 589

Prentice, D, 'Section 9 of the European Communities Act 1972' (1973) 89 LQR 518

Private International Law Committee, *First Report*, Cmnd 9068, 1954, London: HMSO

Private International Law Committee, *Seventh Report*, Cmnd 9068, 1954, London: HMSO

Rabel, E, 'The Statute of Frauds and comparative legal history' (1948) 63 LQR 174

Raphael, F, *Somerset Maugham*, 1989, London: Macdonald

Reed, A, 'The Private International Law (Miscellaneous Provisions) Act 1995 and the need for escape devices' (1996) 15 CJQ 305

Reed, A, 'Extra-judicial divorces since Berkovits' [1996] Fam Law 100

Reese, WL, 'Choice of law: rules or approach' (1972) 57 Cornell L Rev 315

Reese, WL, 'Choice of law in tort cases' (1970) 18 AJCL 189

Reese, WL, '*Depecage*: a common phenomenon in choice of law' (1973) 73 Col L Rev 58

Robertson, AH, 'The "preliminary question" in the conflict of laws' (1939) 55 LQR 565

Robertson, DW, '*Forum non conveniens* in America and England' (1987) 103 LQR 398

Rogerson, P, 'The *situs* of debts in the conflict of laws – illogical, unnecessary and misleading' [1990] CLJ 441

Ruff, A, 'The Immigration (Carriers' Liability) Act 1987' [1989] PL 222

Schiff, D, '*Astrid Proll's Case*' [1979] PL 353

Schmidt, TS, 'The preliminary question and the question of substitution in the conflict of laws' (1968) 17 SSL 91

Schreiber, EO, 'The doctrine of *renvoi* in Anglo-American law' (1917) 31 MLR 523

Seidl Hohenveldern, I, 'Extra-territorial effects of confiscations and expropriations' (1950) 13 MLR 69

Shapira, A, 'A transatlantic inspiration: the proper law of the tort doctrine' (1970) 33 MLR 27

Shaw, M, 'Legal acts of an unrecognised entity' (1978) 94 LQR 500

Shuz, R, 'Stays in matrimonial proceedings' (1983) 46 MLR 653

Sinclair, IM, 'Note on *Starkowski v AG*' (1952) 29 BYIL 479

Sinclair, IM, 'Further note on *Starkowski v AG*' (1953) 30 BYIL 523

Slater, AG, '*Forum non conveniens*: a view from the shop floor' (1988) 104 LQR 554

Smart, P, 'Corporate domicile and multiple incorporation in English private international law' [1990] JBL 126

Smart, P, 'Domicile of choice and multiple residence' (1990) 10 OJLS 572

Smart, P, 'Ordinarily resident: temporary presence and prolonged absence' (1989) 38 ICLQ 175

Smart, P, 'Public policy and the conflict of laws' (1983) 99 LQR 24

Smith, R, 'International employment contracts – contracting out' (1972) 21 ICLQ 164

Smith, R, *Conflict of Laws*, 1st edn, 1994, London: Cavendish Publishing

Smith, R and Cromack, V, 'International employment contracts: the applicable law' (1993) 22 ILJ 1

Spiro, E, 'Forum regit processum' (1969) 18 ICLQ 949

Stevens, R, 'The law applicable to priority in shares' (1996) 112 LQR 198

Stoel, T, 'The enforcement of foreign non-criminal, penal and revenue judgments in England and the United States' (1967) 16 ICLQ 663

Stone, PA, 'Capacity for polygamy – judicial rectification of legislative error' [1983] Fam Law 76

Stone, PA, The Conflict of Laws, 1st edn, 1995, Harlow: Longman

Story, J, Commentaries on the Conflict of Laws, 8th edn, 1883, Melville Bigelow, G (ed), Boston: Little, Brown

Sufrin, B, 'An equity richly satisfied' (1979) 42 MLR 574

Sykes, EI, 'The essential validity of a marriage' (1955) 4 ICLQ 159

Symons, C, 'United Kingdom abolition of the doctrine of the recognition of governments' [1981] PL 249

Szasy, S, 'The basic connecting factor in international cases in the domain of civil procedure' (1966) 15 ICLQ 436

Tapper, C, Cross and Tapper on Evidence, 8th edn, 1995, London: Butterworths

Thayer, J, A Preliminary Treatise on Evidence at Common Law, 1898, Boston: Little, Brown

Thomas, JA, 'Note on Starkowski v AG' (1954) 3 ICLQ 353

Thornby, J, 'Champertous assignments of causes in action' [1982] CLJ 29

Unger, J, 'Uses and abuses of statutes in the conflict of laws' (1967) 83 LQR 427

Von Mehren, AT and Trautman, DT, The Law of Multistate Problems: Cases and Materials on the Conflict of Laws, 1965

Von Mehren, AT, 'Recognition and enforcement of sister State judgments: reflections on general theory and current practice in the EEC and the United States' (1981) 81 Col L Rev 1044

von Savigny, FC, Das Recht des Besitzes [The Law of Possession], 1803, Berlin

von Savigny, FC, Vom Beruf unserer Zeit für Gesetzebung und Rechtswissenschaft [On the Vocation of our Age for Legislation and Jurisprudence], 1814, Berlin

von Savigny, FC, System des Heutigen Romischen Rechts, 1849, Berlin*

Wade, JA, 'Choice of law rules and polygamous marriages' (1973) 22 ICLQ 571

Wade, JA, 'Domicile: a re-examination of certain rules' (1983) 32 ICLQ 1

---

* The eighth and final volume of the work was translated by William Guthrie: von Savigny, FC, Private International Law: A Treatise on the Conflict of Laws, 1st edn, 1869 (2nd edn, 1880), Edinburgh: Clarke.

Warbrick, C, 'The new British policy on the recognition of governments' (1981) 30 ICLQ 568

Warbrick, C, 'Recognition of governments' (1993) 56 MLR 92

Webb, PH, 'Evidence of foreign law and the writing on the wall' (1960) 23 MLR 556

Webb, PH, 'Bigamy and capacity to marry' (1965) 14 ICLQ 659

Webb, PH, 'English conflict of laws and Italian social security legislation' (1965) 28 MLR 591

Webb, PH, 'Mutation of polygamous marriages' (1967) 16 ICLQ 1152

Welsh, RS, 'Legitimacy in the conflict of laws' (1947) 63 LQR 65

Wengler, W, 'Die Vorfrage im Kollisionenrecht' (1934) 8 Rabel's Zeitschrift 148

Westlake, J, A Treatise on Private International Law, 3rd edn, 1890, London: Sweet & Maxwell

Westlake, J, A Treatise on Private International Law, 7th edn, 1925, Bentwich, N (ed), London: Sweet & Maxwell

White, JD, 'Marriages at sea' (1901) 17 LQR 283

Williams, PR, 'The EEC Convention and the law applicable to contractual obligations' (1986) 35 ICLQ 1

Williamson, RM, 'Note on Re Priest' (1944) 60 LQR 114

Woodliffe, J, 'Consular marriages' (1969) 32 MLR 59

Wyatt, D, 'Choice of law in contract matters' (1974) 37 MLR 399

Yntema, H, 'Review of Falconbridge, Essays on the Conflict of Laws' (1949) 27 Can Bar Rev 116

Yntema, H, 'The historic bases of private international law' (1953) 2 AJCL 297

Yntema, H, 'Equity in civil and common law' (1967) 15 AJCL 60

Young, J, 'The recognition of extra-judicial divorces in the United Kingdom' (1987) 7 LS 78

Younger Committee, The Report of the Committee on Privacy, Cmnd 5012, 1972, London: HMSO

INDEX